Canadian Cities in Transition

Local Through Global Perspectives

THIRD EDITION

Edited by **Trudi Bunting and Pierre Filion**

OXFORD
UNIVERSITY PRESS

OXFORD

UNIVERSITY PRESS

70 Wynford Drive, Don Mills, Ontario M3C 1J9
www.oupcanada.com

Oxford University Press is a department of the University of Oxford.
It furthers the University's objective of excellence in research, scholarship,
and education by publishing worldwide in

Oxford   New York

Auckland   Cape Town   Dar es Salaam   Hong Kong   Karachi
Kuala Lumpur   Madrid   Melbourne   Mexico City   Nairobi
New Delhi   Shanghai   Taipei   Toronto

With offices in

Argentina   Austria   Brazil   Chile   Czech Republic   France   Greece
Guatemala   Hungary   Italy   Japan   Poland   Portugal   Singapore
South Korea   Switzerland   Thailand   Turkey   Ukraine   Vietnam

Oxford is a trade mark of Oxford University Press
in the UK and in certain other countries

Published in Canada
by Oxford University Press

Library and Archives Canada Cataloguing in Publication

Canadian cities in transition : local through global perspectives/edited by
Trudi Bunting and Pierre Filion.—
3rd ed.
Includes bibliographical references and index.
ISBN-13: 978-0-19-542219-1
ISBN-10: 0-19-542219-8

1. Cities and towns—Canada—Textbooks.
2. Urbanization—Canada—Textbooks.   I. Bunting, Trudi E., 1944–   II. Filion, Pierre, 1952–   .

HT127.C32 2006   307.76'0971   C2005-907389-6

Cover Design: Brett J. Miller

Cover Image: © stockbyte/Metropolis

4–09 08
This book is printed on permanent (acid-free) paper ∞.
Printed in Canada

Contents

Preface: A Guide to the Text

Canadian Cities in Transition exposes readers to the state of the art on the study of Canadian cities; the contributors to this third edition are experts on different aspects of the Canadian urban phenomenon. The book strives to achieve regional balance in order to reflect the unique characteristics that distinguish Canadian cities from each other. A central objective of the text is to be as comprehensive as possible in its approach to cities. While it gives considerable weight to the land-use concerns of its two foremost targeted readerships—geographers and planners—it links these concerns to a constellation of urban-related issues of an economic, social, political, engineering, environmental, design, and historical nature, which makes the book inherently multidisciplinary. In this sense, chapters in the book explore how different societal issues impact cities and their land-use and development patterns, but also their economic well-being, political dynamic, social structure, quality of life, and environmental condition. As further discussed in Chapter 1, the text is intended to provide information that will both help readers understand cities and assist them in making judicious urban-related personal and collective decisions. It aspires to help the next generation of citizens, consumers, experts, business people, and politicians in their efforts to solve the urban problems (traffic congestion, different forms of environmental damage, crime, social segregation . . .) they will inherit.

Chapter 1, by Pierre Filion and Trudi Bunting, provides general information on the urban phenomenon and the Canadian city, which serves as a background for the remainder of the book. After describing properties that distinguish the urban phenomenon, the chapter narrates the evolution of the urban structure of Canadian cities. It closes with an exploration of options for the future. The remainder of the book is divided in eight sections.

Part 1, 'Contextual Background: From Mercantilism to Globalism', is about 'mega trends' affecting Canadian cities: what has caused them to become different from their US counterparts; major forces behind the evolution of the Canadian urban system; and the impact of globalization on Canadian cities. Chapter 2, by Kim England and John Mercer, concentrates on the distinctions between Canadian and US cities. It considers Canada's historically greater intervention in public affairs and a somewhat divergent choice of municipal policy options to be major factors distinguishing Canadian urban development from what has been witnessed in the United States. In Chapter 3, Jim Simmons and Larry McCann provide an overview of the history of the Canadian urban system, examining uneven urban growth levels over different periods of time. The chapter uses this information to forecast demographic and economic trends across the country. Finally, Chapter 4 identifies international trends that have an impact on the Canadian urban system and on the inner structure of cities. The authors, Trudi Bunting and Tod Rutherford, take a broad view on globalization, including intensified international competition, immigration, and multiculturalism.

Part 2, 'The Structure of Canadian Urban Development', introduces features and parameters that contribute to the urban form and structure of Canadian cities as well as to their dynamics. In Chapter 5, Andrejs Skaburskis and Diana Mok concentrate on the impact of land economics on urban form. They demonstrate how land values, which adjust to accessibility patterns as well as to consumer preferences and economic cycles, determine the location and density of different urban activities. Chapter 6 charts the urban transportation planning process and relates it to present features of transportation systems. The author, Eric Miller, identifies transportation problems, in particular an overreliance on the automobile, and proposes approaches to deal with these problems. Chapter 7, by Igor Vojnovic, draws attention to the importance of urban infrastructure—power transmission, sewers, water treatment and distribution—as a dimension of cities that is too often overlooked. It describes the evolution of infrastructure development in Canadian cities and the problems associated with both an undersupply and oversupply of infrastructures. Demography and lifestyles, the subject matter of Damaris Rose and Paul Villeneuve in Chapter 8, may appear to be less tangible than the subjects of earlier chapters, but these social parameters have a strong influence on urban patterns. Among other things, Chapter 8 considers the impacts of an aging population; it also relates how different places within cities change in response to new lifestyle trajectories. The final chapter of this section (Chapter 9), by Robert Murdie and Carlos Teixeira, maps out transitions in social structure that contribute to a changing geographic mosaic. Not unlike transportation or infrastructure, divisions in urban social space represent constraints and opportunities influencing households' decisions about where to live and where and how to carry out everyday activities. This chapter emphasizes how present-day patterns diverge from mid-twentieth-century urban social geographies. In particular, Chapter 9 highlights the impact of immigration on Canadian urban social structure.

In Part 3, 'The Zonal Geography of the Canadian City', each chapter concentrates on one zone defined both geographically (from the downtown to the urban fringe) and historically (from the oldest to the most recently developed areas). In Chapter 10, Pierre Filion and Gunter Gad describe the evolution of large-city downtowns and the present trend for massive high-rise residential development therein. The chapter also considers issues specific to middle-size city and suburban downtowns. Chapter 11, by David Ley and Heather Frost, focuses on the next zone: the inner city. After an account of the history of the inner city, which describes its formerly predominant working-class status and the intense poverty of some of its neighbourhoods, the chapter moves to recent changes, including gentrification and growing ethnic diversity. In Chapter 12, Peter Smith dispels the impression that suburbs are socially homogeneous. He underscores the growing income, life-cycle, and ethnic diversity of suburban areas. He also depicts

emerging forms of development found in suburban portions of metropolitan regions, such as neo-traditional communities. Finally, Chapter 13, by Christopher Bryant and Clare Mitchell, documents the transformations and environmental concerns that affect the nearby countryside as it is increasingly occupied by urban-related activities. Bryant and Mitchell consider the different functions of the urban fringe and contrast these functions with the traditional agricultural role of the countryside.

Part 4, 'Functions in the City: Patterns of Employment, Housing, and Commercial Services', introduces three key activities and land uses (related to production, shelter, and consumption) that are essential to the very existence of the urban phenomenon. The urban dynamics described in this book, that is, relations between transportation and land use, real estate trends and distributions of social groups, largely stem from the interactions among these three functions. Chapter 14, by William Coffey and Richard Shearmur, raises employment-related issues. The fate of cities is intimately tied to the evolution of their employment base, for without the presence of jobs there is little reason to live in a particular city and there would be insufficient resources to consume housing and other goods and services. The chapter concentrates on present employment trends, especially the redistribution of jobs between the downtown and the suburbs. Chapter 15 begins with a history of housing form and provision in Canadian cities. Its author, Richard Harris, then takes a critical approach to recent housing trends, particularly rising costs and the decrease in government support for affordable housing. In Chapter 16, Ken Jones and Tony Hernandez chart the progression of retail forms developed over the twentieth century, culminating with present-day power malls and big-box stores. By way of explanation, they cite economic transition and the evolution of consumer preference, as well as changes in urban structure and transportation patterns.

Part 5, 'Governance and Planning: The Urban Control Function', deals with public-sector decision-making in urban areas. It investigates institutional structures that have an impact on cities and the planning system. Chapter 17, by Andrew Sancton, describes government processes that affect cities, stressing the fact that both senior and municipal governments control cities. Sancton also considers how different municipal government agencies operate, and discusses present claims that municipalities are underfunded by senior governments. The next two chapters deal with the planning system. Jill Grant in Chapter 18 presents a history of Canadian planning, concentrating on the turning points that have shaped the present system and on the models that have found their way into our contemporary land-use patterns. The focus of Chapter 19, by Raphaël Fischler and Jeanne Wolfe, is on the contemporary planning process and the issues that the planning system has to confront. Fischler and Wolfe emphasize the goals and achievements of planning and the significance of the growing gap between planning policy formulation and implementation.

Part 6, 'The Urban Natural Environment: The Grassroots of Sustainability', focuses on what we believe to be the fundamental problem facing our world today—the increasing compromises placed on the natural environment by human activities. Here, the contributors examine the numerous environmental issues generated by cities. The chapters are ordered according to the scope of their perspectives: from a wide view that looks at the broad environmental impacts of urbanization to a consideration of neighbourhood effects and local grassroots interventions. Chapter 20, by Kevin Hanna, highlights the environmental impacts of urbanization in general and evaluates the measures taken to mitigate the environmental consequences of cities. In Chapter 21, Hugh Millward addresses the environmental theme from the perspective of the metropolitan region, investigating damages caused at that scale as well as possible remediation. It uses the Halifax experience to illustrate the form a metropolitan-wide environmental protection strategy can take. Finally, in Chapter 22, Stephen Murphy concentrates on the local level and describes environmentally driven measures that can

be initiated at the neighbourhood level. These involve actions meant to protect the environment and repair damages done in the past.

Part 7, 'Pressing Issues', picks up on the call to address problems associated with change and transition in Canadian cities, an important theme that represents a fundamental subtext for most of the chapters in this volume. While it was not possible to provide comprehensive or exhaustive coverage of the huge array of concerns that might be addressed on this topic, each of the four chapters introduces a serious issue presently faced by virtually all Canadian cities. In Chapter 23, Christopher Leo and Kathryn Anderson address the problem of the growing inequality between fast- and slow-growth metropolitan regions. By emphasizing the positive and adverse sides of both slow growth and fast growth for municipal administrations and residents, Leo and Anderson depart from the view that only growth can bring advantages to an urban area. The chapter compares situations faced by Vancouver and Winnipeg. Chapter 24 deals with immigration, a phenomenon presently transforming Canada's large metropolitan regions. The authors, Heidi Hoernig and Margaret Walton-Roberts, describe the Canadian immigration policy as well as municipal responses and land-use consequences. The urban issue related to this theme is how to integrate immigrants in a fashion that allows them to participate fully in civic society. In Chapter 25, Alan Walks examines issues associated with housing inaffordability and homelessness in Canadian cities, the ultimate expression of urban poverty. He presents the circumstances associated with homelessness, discusses its extent, and evaluates possible solutions. The presence of homeless people on the sidewalk grates of large-city downtowns or in inner-city public parks is but one of many factors that define and redefine 'place' for those who live in and visit Canada's cities. In Chapter 26, Ute Lehrer assesses the image-making process associated with the growing or declining appeal of urban areas. This chapter raises concerns about how to design good urban form by examining four distinct changes of 'place' in Toronto.

The final part, 'Future Transitions of Urban Canada', consists of Chapter 27, written by urban geographer/planner Larry Bourne. In this concluding chapter Bourne synthesizes material discussed in depth in previous chapters and relates what we have learned to a series of contemporary issues affecting Canadian cities.

There are two appendices in this volume. Appendix A outlines sources of information on urban Canada and Appendix B presents a series of major statistical indicators on Canada's census metropolitan areas.

Contributors

Kathryn Anderson
Politics Department
University of Winnipeg

Larry S. Bourne
Department of Geography
University of Toronto

Christopher R. Bryant
Département de géographie
Université de Montréal

Trudi Bunting
Department of Geography and School of Planning
University of Waterloo

William J. Coffey
Département de géographie
Université de Montréal

Kim England
Department of Geography
University of Washington

Pierre Filion
School of Planning
University of Waterloo

Raphaël Fischler
School of Urban Planning
McGill University

Heather Frost
Department of Geography
University of British Columbia

Gunter Gad
Department of Geography
University of Toronto

Jill Grant
School of Planning
Dalhousie University

Kevin S. Hanna
Department of Geography and
Environmental Studies
Wilfrid Laurier University

Richard S. Harris
School of Geography and Geology
McMaster University

Tony Hernandez
Centre for the Study of Commercial Activity
Ryerson University

Heidi Hoernig
School of Planning
University of Waterloo

Ken Jones
Centre for the Study of Commercial Activity
Ryerson University

Paul Langlois
School of Planning
University of Waterloo

Ute Lehrer
Department of Geography
York University

Christopher Leo
Politics Department
University of Winnipeg

David Ley
Department of Geography
University of British Columbia

Larry McCann
Department of Geography
University of Victoria

John Mercer
Department of Geography
Syracuse University

Eric J. Miller
Department of Civil Engineering
University of Toronto

Hugh Millward
Department of Geography
St Mary's University

Clare J.A. Mitchell
Department of Geography
University of Waterloo

Diana Mok
Department of Geography
University of Western Ontario

Robert A. Murdie
Department of Geography
York University

Stephen D. Murphy
Department of Environment and Resource Studies
University of Waterloo

Damaris Rose
INRS–Urbanisation, culture et société
Montréal

Tod Rutherford
Department of Geography
Syracuse University

Andrew Sancton
Department of Political Science
University of Western Ontario

Richard G. Shearmur
INRS–Urbanisation, culture et société
Montréal

Jim Simmons
Centre for the Study of Commercial Activity
Ryerson University

Andrejs Skaburskis
School of Urban and Regional Planning
Queen's University

Peter J. Smith
Department of Earth and Atmospheric Science
University of Alberta

Carlos Teixeira
Department of Geography
University of British Columbia-Okanagan

Paul Villeneuve
Aménagement du territoire et développement régional (ATDR)
Université Laval

Igor Vojnovic
Department of Geography
Michigan State University

R. Alan Walks
Department of Geography
University of Toronto

Jeanne M. Wolfe
School of Urban Planning
McGill University

Margaret Walton-Roberts
Department of Geography and Environmental Studies
Wilfrid Laurier University

Chapter 1

Understanding Twenty-First-Century Urban Structure: Sustainability, Unevenness, and Uncertainty

Pierre Filion and Trudi Bunting

This third edition of *Canadian Cities in Transition* is about urban Canada in the early twenty-first century. It identifies the major issues confronting contemporary urbanization and tries to understand the factors that account for present circumstances. The book attempts to cast as broad a perspective as possible on Canadian cities, looking at their different dimensions. To achieve this objective it draws on different fields of knowledge. The purpose of this first chapter is to provide general knowledge on the city that will facilitate understanding the chapters to follow. It addresses a number of questions: What is a city and what differentiates urban places from other settlement types? What sets the present period apart from previous periods of urban development? What were the major stages in the evolution of cities that brought us to this point? And what is the likely trajectory of Canadian urbanization?

Three themes run throughout this chapter and the rest of the volume. The first theme relates to *sustainability*; the second to *unevenness*; and the third to *uncertainty*. These themes are closely related in that they impact on each other. The three themes are not specific to the contemporary city; cities have always faced sustainability and unevenness issues, and uncertainty about the future is hardly a new experience. But the themes raise more concern at present than in the past—especially in regard to environmental sustainability. They have also become more manifest as differences between people and places have been accentuated over the last decades, and as globalization has eroded local control over the economy and thus raised uncertainty levels.

Policies driven by deepening concern about *sustainability* have resulted in a reduction of some

pollutants—a trend driven, as well, by deindustrialization, which has caused the removal of many sources of pollution. Improvements have been most evident in the case of water quality. Still, many forms of pollution remain unacceptably high, including the presence of toxic substances in water. Especially when summers are hot, residents of large metropolitan regions are reminded by successive smog alerts of the environmental consequences of industrialization, power generation, and transportation. The scope of environmental consciousness has broadened over the last decades. We are no longer preoccupied only by the local and metropolitan effects of air pollution, but equally by global warming caused by the burning of fossil fuels. We have also become less tolerant of the environmental impacts of our lifestyle, as evidenced by reactions against landfills and negative sentiments about the loss of rural and natural areas to urban sprawl. Yet, despite not-in-my-backyard (NIMBY) reactions to localized issues, little has been done to alleviate the consequences of consumption and urban development: households have not changed their travel or purchasing habits; business seems complacent; and governments have yet to take a strong leadership role.

The second theme, *unevenness*, pertains to rising inequality both within and between cities. Economic globalization and the attendant massive loss of relatively well-paid manufacturing employment, the shrinkage of the public sector, and attrition of the trade union movement have resulted in a smaller middle class. As a result, a growing number of households now live in poverty. At the other extreme are the very rich, who have enjoyed a disproportional rise in their income. Of course, such polarization finds expression in the urban landscape, in the stark contrast between impoverished neighbourhoods and luxury condominiums and upscale suburban communities. Inter-urban unevenness, the outcome of economic and demographic trends, will position a few growing centres—large metropolitan regions that may be very extensive and include a metropolitan core and many smaller outlying metropolitan and non-metropolitan places plus a sprinkling of other smaller centres—against the majority of cities that will experience stagnation or decline. Economically driven inter-urban unevenness will be exacerbated by demographic trends. Given several decades of below-replacement birth rate, only urban regions with the capacity to attract immigrants will be able to maintain or expand their population. These will be the regions with dynamic economies. All other urban areas (apart from retirement communities) will face demographic decline. Opposition between growing and declining regions is not a new phenomenon. The difference, however, is that in the past virtually all metropolitan regions were gaining population at the expense of rural areas. In the near future many large cities will be losing population.

Uncertainty, the third theme, refers to the instability generated by intensification of economic competition, which, propelled by globalization, is a source of increased risk for the numerous economic sectors facing international competition. Uncertainty for large numbers of people will mean frequent changes of employment. Urban areas will have much less confidence that the economic sectors presently driving municipal economies will continue to maintain their performance. Uncertainty can also be associated with the future availability of the economic conditions and natural resources underlying auto-dependent suburban lifestyles. Rising fuel prices and falling wages may mean, for example, that it will be difficult for many to maintain current consumerist lifestyles. Worse, some even predict that we are about to engage in a downward trend in terms of oil production, with dire consequences for suburbia, the type of development that has dominated urban growth over the past 60 years and where the large majority of

Canadians reside and much of the country's economic activity takes place.[1]

One cannot address issues such as the ones mentioned here without sound knowledge of how cities operate and how they relate to broader societal trends. More often than not, past mistakes can be seen in hindsight to be the result of deficient understanding of the urban dynamic. Yet cities resist understanding because they are such very complex systems. It can be argued that, along with language, the large city is the most intricate of human creations. In both cases, complexity stems from the presence of a relatively stable structure upon which interchangeable elements can be affixed. In the case of language the structure is syntax, which supports nearly unlimited combinations of words; cities, on the other hand, owe their structure to major infrastructure networks that provide connections between different assemblages of buildings and other land uses. The degree of complexity further increases when we consider economic and value systems that underpin the urban built environment, the multiple ways people use this environment, and the perceptions and interpretations of this environment and the activities that take place therein.

The present chapter is divided into three parts. The first part introduces universal properties that define the city. The second part is more empirically focused. It elucidates the interplay of change and continuity in a historical overview of the evolution of land-use patterns over the twentieth and early twenty-first centuries. The last part draws from the information of the two previous ones to examine future problems and possible solutions.

1:   Properties of the City

Six properties are fundamental to understanding the urban phenomenon: *production*; *reproduction*; *proximity*; *capitalization*; *place*; and *municipal/urban governance*. These have been inherent in the city from its very beginnings some 4,000 years ago in China and Mesopotamia, and are present in cities across the world today (Morris, 1972). As expected, their manifestations vary from period to period, as we will see in Part 2 of this chapter, which describes transitions over the last century. The six properties we discuss below explain why cities exist and how they function, while providing a framework to discuss problems confronting the contemporary Canadian city.

Production

The fundamental raison d'être for urban settlement has been to accommodate specialized economic production activities that could not survive in rural settings—e.g., markets, labour- and capital-intensive manufacturing, centralized governance. Economic production creates jobs and is thus the main reason for urban growth (see Chapter 14). Many economic activities are, of course, aimed at the consumption needs of a city's own residents. Catering to local demand does not in itself differentiate the city from other forms of settlement, however. In a self-reliant farming situation, for example, the land a family occupies fulfills virtually all its needs. What most sets urban settlements apart from traditional self-reliant rural economies is the historic inability of the city to satisfy all its consumption requirements and the resulting imperative to export goods and services for profit in order to be able to acquire and pay for required products from outside. At the most fundamental level, the need for specialized activities to be close to one another to survive and also to be close to workers (the proximity property discussed below) rules out the presence within cities of the large surfaces needed to feed their population. A city must also reach beyond its territory to secure other products and resources essential to sustain its population and economic activity. This includes different forms of staples and energy and, often, water. Research records cities' dependence for their natural resources on a territory (or 'ecological footprint') that far exceeds the urbanized perimeter (Rees and Wackernagel, 1994; Wackernagel and Rees, 1996).

For a city to exist, it must be in a position to export sufficient goods and services to counterbalance its imports. But exports need not be tied to products. Capital cities, for example, export deci-

sions and derive their monetary returns from tax revenues; in medieval times, it was not unusual for cities to draw taxes, often in kind, from a hinterland to which they extended military protection. Cities that fail to export decline and may disappear altogether, as has been amply illustrated throughout the Canadian periphery by the fate of resource ghost towns whose staple has run out (see Chapter 3).

Over recent decades, goods and resources (including labour) that cities draw from outside their territory have increasingly originated from foreign countries and continents. Canadian producers have also moved towards new international markets. This change in the reach of economic exchange is loosely referred to as globalization. In the global period, the interdependence between the city and a well-defined hinterland has lost much of its importance (Derudder and Witlox, 2004; Friedman, 2005; Taylor, 2001). The tendency today is for cities to transform and consume goods from around the world and sell their products on international markets.

With the decline of routine production, developed countries such as Canada must rely on innovation and knowledge-intensive activities to compete on the world stage. This explains the key role in propelling the economy that Florida (2002, 2005) attributes to a 'creative class' and the stress he gives to measures cities can take to attract this class. He readily acknowledges that some cities are much better endowed than others to appeal to members of this class.

Above all, the growing importance of the service sector relative to the manufacturing sector has marked the last decades (Daniels and Bryson, 2002). The transition is highly visible in the urban landscape. On the one hand, we see abandoned industrial premises (occasionally transformed into lofts in certain cities), and on the other, an explosion of restaurants, business and personal services, places of entertainment and cultural activities (Jones et al., 2005). The shift towards the service economy is also felt, albeit with less intensity, within cities' export sphere. Among services Canadian cities export are engineering and development expertise, culture, and tourism.

Reproduction

As properties of the urban phenomenon, production and reproduction are intimately related.
Reproduction, in the Marxian sense, centres on the
conditions essential to the presence of a labour
force. These conditions include, of course, birth and
child-rearing, but equally, other processes are necessary for the provision of the labour force input to
production: health care, education, social services,
family and community support, etc. (Castells, 1977;
Jessop, 2002: 47, 77). At the most fundamental level,
Canada's current inability to reproduce its own
population is the reason why rates of foreign immigration have soared over recent decades. Examples
of reproduction-related urban facilities include
homes, schools, hospitals, water treatment and distribution systems, as well as parks and other recreational facilities that promote health and reduce
stress. A smooth operation of the reproduction system allows employers to find an abundant workforce that is healthy, qualified for the available tasks,
and possesses a work ethic compatible with types of
employment present in a given city.

Reproductive activities are often centred in the
home but are increasingly supplemented with services provided by outside agencies in the public and
private sectors. Today, in fact, reproduction-related
consumption of both services (e.g., fast food, child
care) and goods (e.g., dishwashers, microwave ovens,
health and hygiene and home maintenance products) also represents an important outlet for the
production sector. Meanwhile, resources needed for
reproduction-related goods and services are derived
from the production sector in the form of household income and tax revenues.

Feminist thinking provides an important perspective on present reproduction circumstances.
Feminism has also been an influential force that has
contributed to the movement away from the
traditional role of women with respect to the nur-
turing aspects of reproduction. In the past and still
to a large degree, women have assumed the major
burden of reproductive work without payment.
While 'equal pay for equal work' has yet to be
achieved in most sectors of the economy, the

majority of Canadian women today who are of age
are in the labour force. Women's roles in both the
productive and reproductive spheres have considerable impact on the way we live (see Chapter 8) and
on how essential services such as health, education,
and child care are delivered. Increased participation
of women in productive sectors of the economy
also appears to be an important factor driving consumerist lifestyles, while also contributing to demographic stagnation.

An important policy issue pertains to growing
public-sector difficulties in providing essential conditions for reproduction. From the Great Depression
until roughly the early 1980s, governments
expanded their role in the reproduction sphere. In
recent decades, however, the opening of international markets has allowed producers to seek
lowtax jurisdictions offshore, thereby cutting
corporate-based fiscal revenues; at the same time,
public resentment about high tax levels has made
increasing income tax an unrealistic political option.
The result has been that governments have faced
reduced spending capacity (see Chapter 4).
Paradoxically, resulting cutbacks in public reproduction services have coincided with a time of rising expectations and demand for such services. For
example, the knowledge-intensive economy places
a growing burden on the post-secondary education
system. The response has been a gradual shift from
public to private funding, evidenced by inflating
college and university fees. Overall, the persistent
shift towards private funding is a major source of
social inequality (see Chapter 25). And underfund-
ing of reproduction-related public infrastructures
and services can cause tragedies whose costs, in
terms of suffering and monetary expense, far exceed
initial savings. Two examples come to mind. In
Ontario, attempts to economize on water quality
inspection have been associated with the 2000
Walkerton E. coli outbreak, causing seven deaths
and making 2,000 residents ill. More recently, in
2005, insufficient maintenance of levees and
destruction of coastal swamplands by developers
have caused hundreds of billions of dollars in damages in New Orleans (as well as numerous casualties) in the wake of Hurricane Katrina. The same

logic pertains, albeit in a less dramatic fashion, to the consequences of reduced services in sectors such as social services, education, and health care.

Proximity

Historically, individuals and activities congregate in cities to be close to each other in order to facilitate communication and minimize the cost (in time, effort, and monetary expense) of interaction. If we probed reasons why people live in cities, most would place the need to be close to work at, or near, the top of their list of answers. Other explanations would include proximity to educational establishments, shopping opportunities, cultural activities, entertainment, family and friends, medical facilities, etc. People opt for urban living because of their need for frequent and repeated interaction outside the home. Likewise, businesses and institutions locate in cities so they can be close to their market, labour force, and the establishments with which they maintain linkages. By concentrating activities and people and thus creating proximity, the city makes frequent interactions affordable in terms of both cost and time. In a rural setting, in contrast, many recurring contacts that are routine in the city would involve prohibitive transportation times and/or costs due to long distances. A by-product of interaction is innovation (Hall, 1999); ease of interaction is why cities have been catalysts for change in social, economic, technological, and cultural realms. The concept of 'creative' cities is based on the assumption that the urban fabric can be designed, developed, and spatially structured to promote and welcome all kinds of interaction (Florida, 2005).

The city can be perceived as comprised of numerous overlapping markets of frequently repeated exchanges. The fact that cities are fundamentally places of economic enterprise makes daily commuting between residences and workplaces of unparalleled importance in explaining urban structure. Examples of other markets of frequent exchanges that affect the size and spatial organization of cities include the ones that tie retail facilities to their market and public services to their clients. Also worth mentioning are the markets that

connect cultural and recreational activities to their public—the archetypal attraction of the city's 'bright lights'.

The inherent importance of proximity has a number of highly visible consequences on urbanization. One obvious repercussion is the high cost of land in the city relative to the country (see Chapter 5). The appeal of proximity raises demand for space in the city, which, in turn, elevates land values. In this same vein, high land cost compels establishments to make judicious use of their urban land and to build intensively rather than extensively.

Proximity is a relative condition largely determined by prevailing transportation systems and activity distribution patterns (see Chapter 6). In the pre-industrial city, which depended on non-mechanized forms of transportation (primarily walking and horse-powered) and where activities were centralized, this principle severely confined the expanse of urbanized territory. Things are different in the contemporary car- and truck-oriented city, and consequently the city takes on a highly decentralized form. In the decentralized or dispersed metropolis, adequate accessibility levels can be maintained over large territories so that residents and activities can consume far more land than in the past (Bottles, 1987) (see Chapters 12 and 13). But the proximity principle remains influential even in these more dispersed circumstances as evidenced by the enduring existence of higher densities in cities than in the countryside and by accessibility peaks within the city itself (at rail transit stations and junctions of major arterials and/or expressways). Part 2 of this chapter will demonstrate the role accessibility has played since the early twentieth century in promoting, first, centralization and high density, second, dispersion and low density, and recently, a return to high residential density in the inner city of large metropolitan regions.

Today, debate rages as to whether our ability to substitute telecommunications for actual movement holds the potential for an even more dispersed urban form. As rush-hour gridlock across an extensive section of Highway 401 attests, the effective early twenty-first-century boundaries of the Greater Toronto Area run from Kitchener–Waterloo–

Cambridge in the west to beyond Clarington in the east. Similarly, high levels of commuting exist between the City of Toronto and points south towards Niagara Falls and north towards Orillia. But forecasts predicting the death of the city as we know it have proven to be greatly off-base because they did not anticipate the impact of a changing mode of production on urban form. The 'new' urban economy has considerably elevated the importance of face-to-face contact and centralized provision of advanced services.

Capitalization

The fourth property of cities derives from their compact spatial form. Because urban land is a scarce resource, it becomes the object of substantial capital investment so its use can be maximized. Capitalization refers to the vast resources invested to accommodate agglomerations of residents, businesses, and services. The nature of capitalization and, hence, the form cities take are largely influenced by the engineering possibilities of the time. Over the centuries, improving technologies have promoted larger city size and, until the relatively recent predilection for suburban forms, higher densities. Density models have been used to chart the transition of urban form throughout the twentieth century from centralized (Clark, 1951) to decentralized (Bunting et al., 2002). Most recently, polycentricity has been captured with cubic polynomial versions of the distance-decay statistical model of urban density profiles (Anderson, 1985; Richardson, 1988). These statistically calibrated models of intra-urban density thus serve to corroborate more nuanced historical interpretations of the engineered forms of capitalizing growth and development, from the days of the pedestrian-based city to the contemporary period focused on expressways and vehicle traffic.

Once capitalized and populated, built-up urban environments become highly durable. Durability obviously contributes a considerable degree of continuity to the urban landscape. However, as technology and lifestyles tend to change faster than urban form, capitalization of urban land also engenders obsolescence. Change, especially concerning modes of production or transportation technologies, demands adjustments of the built environment to new conditions. But a city is not easily retrofitted. Everywhere, the costs of redevelopment (on brownfield or greyfield sites) are much higher than development costs on greenfield sites at the urban edge. While financial constraints can play a critical role, they are not the only impediment to altering the urban environment. One obstacle to urban environment adaptability is the symbiosis that binds patterns of behaviour to built environments. For example, the presence of high-capacity road systems encourages reliance on the automobile and the truck, and high rates of car and truck use generate a continued demand for improved and expanded roads (Noland, 2000; Parthasarathi et al., 2003).

Another obstacle to changing the way the built environment is capitalized comes in the form of citizen resistance that occurs when proposals for redevelopment of previously built-up areas clash with residents' strong emotional attachment to their homes and neighbourhood. An important challenge facing planners and politicians today is how to reconcile citizens' attachment to their home 'places', where they desire to maintain the status quo (NIMBY), with the need for change—particularly in the face of looming environmental crisis.

Place

Sense of place is the least tangible of the urban properties discussed in this chapter. The noted geographer, Yi Fu Tuan (1974), coined the term 'topophilia' to denote the personal identity with, and love of, a place. More recently, scholars such as Relph (1976, 1987) used the term 'sense of place' in a related fashion to speak about subjective and emotional feelings associated with different parts of the environment. Thus, whereas space relations in cities are mostly about objective attributes of proximity and access, 'place' is all about subjective attachment. It is increasingly argued, however, that the perpetuation of monotonous landscapes and the lack of concern about imaging and good urban design have left a vacuum in the urban entity. There is widespread belief that most people who live in big cities are missing out by virtue of being 'detached' from their surroundings, and that both quality of individual and collective life and quality of the physical environment are reduced as a result (e.g., Kunstler, 1993, 1996).

Over time, as spatial factors have become less important in determining what happens where within the metropolitan realm, those of 'place' have been elevated. Today, for example, households are more apt to choose a dwelling unit for its place properties—how it looks, feels, accommodates lifestyles, expresses personas—rather than for spatial attributes such as access to place of work. Sense of place is also fluid. This, for example, is the case with former industrial areas, which were avoided by most until their rebirth as loft developments (Zukin, 1982). Finally, as Chapter 26 demonstrates, people's previous experience and socio-economic and cultural status greatly influence what appears to be attractive in the urban landscape as opposed to what is feared or distained.

Design-oriented professionals—such as Jane Jacobs (1961), Jon Lang (1994), planner Kevin Lynch (1964, 1984), and architect Christopher Alexander (1979; see also Alexander et al., 1977)—believe that there are fundamental principles of good urban form. They argue that, applied to urban development, such principles will lead to higher-quality life (the topophilia factor) as well as more efficient use of urban space. Coming out of this tradition are a cohort of proactive advocates for urban community design such as the New Urbanists (see Chapters 12 and 26) or those committed to a 'greening' of the urban domain.

Place is the intangible something that makes some locales feel good while others do not, and that invites or repels visitors. Place interfaces with all the other properties discussed here. Under conditions of the 'new' economy, the manipulation of place properties has become a marketing device used to attract global interest and bring in outside investment to cities (Zukin, 1991; see also Chapter 4). Place

features can further be seen as a lure for the creative class, and thus can be associated with the economic benefits stemming from a strong presence of members of this class (Florida, 2002, 2005).

Urban/Municipal Governance

As understood here, governance denotes the intrinsic need for administrative structures and political processes that can generate policies suited to the specific circumstances confronting cities. The proximity and capitalization properties that are central to urban as compared to non-urban settlement structure demand that distinct management measures be an intrinsic property of the urban community. Proximity requires collective control and co-operation between nearby neighbours over communal space. The smooth functioning of cities relies on shared infrastructures (transportation, communication, electricity, water mains, and sewers) and services (policing and garbage collection) and on a battery of legal measures (property rights, payment for shared facilities, bylaws) intended to assure the orderly cohabitation of a wide variety of land uses. Haphazard development decisions can plunge a city into a state of chaos. For example, without planning controls incompatible land uses such as noisy and polluting industry and high traffic generators could locate in residential areas. Likewise, new developments could proceed without heeding infrastructural capacity, thus provoking all sorts of bottlenecks. A pure laissez-faire approach is clearly not suited to the city. The origins of urban planning can in fact be traced back to nineteenth-century public health interventions intended to reduce the risk of epidemics in densely built environments (Hodge, 1998; see Chapter 18).

Various types of administrative arrangements have developed over time in response to the need to provide urban infrastructures, services, and controls within built-up urban realms. These administrations have been local or regional or have been lodged in senior governments, as is the case with provincial ministries of municipal affairs or federal housing programs (see Chapter 17). Issues of governance generally belong to the public sector, but some urban management responsibilities can be vested in community-based or private-sector organizations. Over historic time, as cities grew, as buildings became bigger and required more infrastructure (roads, water, sewage), as reliance on mechanized forms of transportation (particularly the automobile) increased, and as the public demanded more and better services, administrations responded by becoming larger and more complex—so complex and so costly to maintain that the recent trend has been to 'downsize' governments (municipal or otherwise) and to engage in the privatization of public facilities and services (Donald, 2002; Lightman and Irving, 1991).

Today, coincidentally with growing realization of the importance of local governance in matters such as environmental protection, economic development, the equitable provision of services, and the promotion of health and quality of life, comes the harsh reality that municipal administrations are facing severe financial restrictions. Even more than higher levels of government, local municipalities have been dealt huge budget cuts. In the absence of a reliable funding stream from these higher levels, municipalities presently rely primarily on limited property tax revenues. Yet, at the same time, municipalities have incurred increased costs associated with the added responsibilities they have assumed. In Ontario, for example, the responsibility for social housing has been downloaded to cities. As we progress into the twenty-first century, the local governance issue will largely be centred on municipal financial capacity. Depending on the nature of the solution ultimately arrived at, it is quite possible that emancipation from senior government jurisdictional domination will strengthen the hand of local administrations in matters related to urban governance.

2:   Urban Transitions: The Land-Use Dimension

The 'horizontal' view of cities presented above, which distinguishes the urban phenomenon by identifying and describing its distinctive properties,

provides only a partial understanding of cities because it neglects the historical, 'vertical' perspective on how and why cities evolved to their present form. To understand the contemporary city and how its problems might effectively be addressed, it is important to know about historical circumstances that have given rise to present land-use arrangements. In this part, we discuss twentieth-century transitions at the intra-urban scale, focusing on land use. We identify three periods: *city development* that runs roughly until the end of World War II; *metropolitan development* that covers the period from the war to the mid-1970s; and *suburban domination* that takes us to the present and possibly beyond. In the simplest sense each of these periods is characterized by a new layer of urban development added to the pre-existing built-up area. But urban growth dynamics are not so simple because direct and indirect impacts of each new wave of development on older forms generate additional land-use change, most often in the form of retrofitting and redevelopment.

Given the land-use orientation of the discussion to follow, *proximity* and *capitalization* are the properties that will be most emphasized, but all properties will serve in Part 3 to structure a final discussion on the emergence of a new urban vision and its implementation potential. Table 1.1 provides a summary outlining how the six urban properties evolved through the three different periods discussed here.

City Development before 1945

The period from a city's founding to the end of World War II, when what we today call the 'inner city' was developed, comprises the era we refer to as one of 'city development'. In many older metropolitan areas, the inner city coincides roughly with the boundaries of the central city (a metropolitan region's oldest municipal administrative unit, which occupies its centre). A generic outline of land-use patterns characteristic of city development is provided in Figure 1.1. Spatially, the city development area includes: the central business district (CBD); a 'zone of transition' with a mixed and changing

Table 1.1   **Evolution of Canadian Urban Form**

Urban Properties	Pre-1945	1945–75	1975–21st Century
Production	Manufacturing is a major source of employment in many cities. Reliance on waterways and railways for freight transportation. Larger metropolitan areas house high-density office concentrations downtown.	Manufacturing relocates in suburban industrial parks. Heavy dependence on trucks. Increasing importance of the service sector translates into service centres in suburbs and office development in both the CBD and suburbs.	More flexible forms of production, intense truck-based linkage patterns. Added importance of service sector leads to more and larger suburban concentrations than over the previous period. Concentrations of corporate head offices and of advanced services persist in the core parts of the largest metropolitan areas.
Reproduction	Importance of the family unit as a provider of services. High residential occupancy levels; frequent overcrowding.	Baby boom takes place in the early part of the period. Development of the welfare state.	As the period progresses, difficulties in maintaining welfare state due to unstable economic performance, intensified international competition, and health services required by aging population. Below replacement birth rate, high immigration levels.
Proximity	Proximity determined by walking and public transportation, which results in a strong CBD, steep accessibility and land value gradients, and tight urban texture.	The accessibility range is vastly expanded by the car and new road networks. This causes flatter accessibility and land value gradients and a decentralization of activities.	The suburban land-use pattern becomes dominant. Ongoing flattening of accessibility and land value gradients and reduced constraints on location. Greatly augmented automotive travel leads to congestion and responses to congestion result in further dispersion of activities.
Capitalization	Until 1945 capitalization is a result of a gradual development of different sectors. Infrastructures consist in basic facilities: water, sewage, roads, and streetcars.	Generalization of a new, costly, suburban-style form of urban development and adaptation/retrofitting of some older 'city' parts. This urban form is consistent with the economic climate of the time.	The high cost of the suburban form of urbanization causes tensions for households and governments in a more constrained economic climate.

(continued)

Table 1.1   **(continued)**

Urban Properties	Pre-1945	1945–75	1975–21st Century
Place	Strong identification with the neighbourhood and downtown, which represent major hubs of activities and social relations.	Little attachment to suburban areas with the exception of local residential areas.	Same as for the previous period; but pressures for redevelopment give rise to NIMBY objections partly based on preservation of character of residential areas.
Urban/Municipal Management	Provision of basic infrastructures but little land-use control. The central city controls most of the built-up area.	Intense infrastructure development and land-use control; urban renewal. In spite of metropolitan government reform, co-ordination problems at the metropolitan scale emerge.	Same approach as over previous period, but less publicly sponsored urban renewal and greatly increased difficulty to maintain required levels of expenditure on urban infrastructures and services. Also severe ongoing co-ordination problems at the metropolitan scale.

land-use pattern (Preston and Griffin, 1966); factory belts along waterways and railways; and relatively high-density, though not high-rise, residential neighbourhoods, most of them segregated along lines of income and ethnicity. Industrial production was the main force pushing urban growth over this period, though administrative activities played an important role in larger service centres and resource extraction supported the economies of many communities outside the Canadian heartland.

On the demand side of the 'city development' equation, modest incomes accounted for relatively low rates of home ownership. Despite households' large size, domestic space consumption was limited by affordability constraints. Women generally worked unwaged in the home and this, along with limited incomes, attenuated demand for household goods and purchased services. Workers put in long hours. Available time (the workweek included Saturday), monetary constraints, and a general reliance on transit and walking (in a period when the car remained the preserve of the rich) limited regular journeys to nearby places. Accordingly,

buildings were closely packed together, residential density was high, distance between home and work was short (except for a small contingent of well-heeled suburban commuters), and shopping facilities were found throughout the city, at walking distance from virtually every house (Adams, 1970; Colby, 1933; Jacobs, 1961). Commercial streets catered to most retail needs with the exception of high-order goods found in the CBD. The high density of the built environment also made it easy to walk to schools, medical services, churches, and other facilities. Transit was then composed primarily of fixed-line rail services (streetcars and, in larger cities, commuter trains). Its linearity left a profound mark on the inner city's urban structure and skewed growth outward along its lines (Adams, 1970; Hoyt, 1939; Warner, 1962). The CBD enjoyed unchallenged accessibility potential with virtually all transit lines radiating from this point.

As seen in Figure 1.2, the pre-1945 city was characterized by a steep accessibility gradient that peaked at the CBD, the central activity focus, and dropped off rapidly towards transit's outer limit at

Figure 1.1   **City Development Land-Use Patterns (before 1945)**

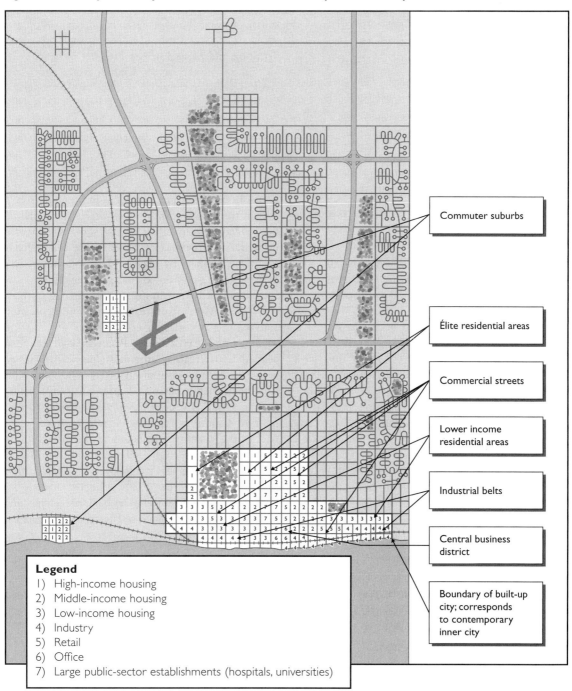

Commuter suburbs

Élite residential areas

Commercial streets

Lower income
residential areas

Industrial belts

Central business
district

Boundary of built-up
city; corresponds
to contemporary
inner city

Legend
1) High-income housing
2) Middle-income housing
3) Low-income housing
4) Industry
5) Retail
6) Office
7) Large public-sector establishments (hospitals, universities)

Figure 1.2   **Pre–1945 Density Gradient**

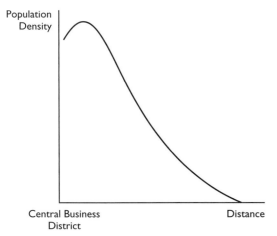

Population Density

Central Business District   Distance

the edge of the city. Accessibility gradients were mirrored by land values, a consequence of demand levels that varied primarily according to transportation costs. The expression 'distance decay' is used to describe this basic parameter of early twentieth-century urban form. Accessibility, land and real estate values, as well as population and building density, all dropped off rapidly as a function of increased space friction or interaction costs that were largely dictated by distance from the centre of the city. Accordingly, the CBD concentrated activities that could afford the most expensive land—office buildings, major institutions, and high-order retail and service outlets. These relationships are detailed in Chapter 10.

Like industry, elite residential areas stretched out along radial sectors usually defined by the best roads and transit routes and also by proximity to amenities such as major institutions and large parks or attractive landscape features (e.g., water, valleys, scenic views). The neighbourhoods of North Toronto and West Montreal are good examples. Most of these high-income sectors grew from wealthy neighbourhoods built near the edge of the city in the late nineteenth century and the first decades of the twentieth century, when pollution and other negative externalities associated with heavy industrial growth made living in the core area

less desirable (see Beaudet, 1988; Goheen, 1970; Hoyt, 1939). Today many of these neighbourhoods remain among the most established elite residential locations, e.g., Westmount in Montreal, Rosedale in Toronto, and Shaughnessey Heights in Vancouver. In direct contrast to high-income housing, working-class residential districts were generally located within walking distance from factories and thus were in close proximity to heavy manufacturing and other less appealing features like railways. Meanwhile, increasingly between the two world wars, some middle-class households took advantage of streetcar and commuter train lines, seeking out a better home environment in commuter suburbs.

In the pre-1945 period, neither environmental nor social sustainability was a serious concern. Growth trends were largely predictable and unevenness was defined by well-understood differences between rich and poor or old and new. In the policy domain, urban planning was not the major force it is today. Most institutionalized planning-related activity was devoted to concerns about reducing squalor and threat of disease. Planners were also concerned with creating amenities (particularly large parks) under the inspiration of the City Beautiful Movement that grew in the early years of the twentieth century (Boyer, 1983: 43–56; Hodge, 1998: 58–63). Zoning was timidly introduced in the early part of the century but its application was limited to areas such as high-income neighbourhoods. Master and official plans were pretty much unknown before the 1950s. The occurrence of mixed-use districts in the older parts of today's contemporary city can be traced back to this relative absence of planning. This is not to say that pre-war city development was spatially disorganized. Quite the contrary, as shown in Figures 1.1 and 1.2, steep transit-induced accessibility gradients worked in association with market-driven competition for prime real estate sites to produce clear land-use zoning.

Metropolitan Development, 1945–75

The immediate post–World War II period, 1945–75, has become known as a distinctive 'boom' era of brisk economic and demographic growth. This period of economic prosperity was achieved through a balancing of the forces of big business, big government, and big unions and heavy reliance on Keynesian policies to regulate national political economies (Amin, 1994). Under what has been called the 'Fordist' economic growth regime, rapid productivity gains were directly linked to consumption growth. In terms of urban form, this period marks the time when the term 'metropolitan' was first used in reference to Canadian cities. In its geographic meaning, the term connotes a balance between city and suburban styles of urbanization, between a densified and still powerful central city and rapidly growing, expansive suburban municipalities (Blumenfeld, 1967; Hitchcock and McMaster, 1985; Hoover and Vernon, 1962). These two different forms manifest very different distance-decay density gradients, as seen in Figure 1.3.

Suburban areas developed over this 30-year period are now generally referred to as 'mature' or 'inner' suburbs. It is easy to distinguish areas built after 1945 from earlier, 'city' ones because, as a result of the Great Depression and World War II, the 1929–45 period experienced little urban development. However, the 16-year lull witnessed considerable technological advancements and value changes, which were directly reflected in the composition and

style of newly developed suburbs in the post-World War II period. The new suburbs spread rapidly because, across all of urban Canada, growth occurred at an unprecedented rate, driven by pent-up demand and spiralling population expansion (the baby boom), in a period of sustained prosperity.

Widespread home ownership and increased indoor and outdoor per capita residential space consumption distinguished the new suburbs from the inner city (Miron, 1988; Spurr, 1976). Over this era, well-paid blue-collar and public-sector workers swelled the ranks of the middle class so that a much higher proportion of families could afford to own their homes. Meanwhile, the production of relatively large homes on relatively large lots (by comparison to earlier residential consumption standards) generated an unprecedented demand for mass-produced goods (cars, furniture, appliances). Lifestyles, characterized as 'modern', were conformist: they were consumer-oriented and centred on the nuclear family and the single-family home (Clark, 1966; Dobriner, 1958; Florida and Feldman, 1988; Hamel, 1993; Harvey, 1989a; Hayden, 2003; Muller, 1981; Popenoe, 1977). Increased car ownership and use were inextricably linked to the rise in residential space and single-family home ownership. With prosperous times and a proliferation of low-density environments that made automobile travel a necessity rather than a matter of choice or indulgence, auto ownership became commonplace. In turn, this abrupt change in travel mode profoundly transformed spatial arrangements as greatly increased accessibility translated into heightened land consumption needed to house low-density buildings and accommodate automobiles as well as to conform to new standards regarding the provision of green space.

At this time, too, enhanced government intervention marked a profound change in how cities were managed. In the 1950s, professionally trained planners were hired in cities throughout Canada to aid, manage, and guide urban growth (Carver, 1962; Chapin, 1965; Cullingworth, 1987; Hodge, 1998; Sewell, 1993). Comprehensive urban planning with its main tools—zoning and master planning—configured the new suburb into a car-oriented

Figure 1.3   **1945–75 Density Gradient**

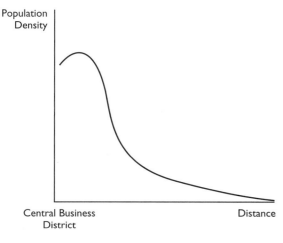

Population Density

Central Business District   Distance

environment where land use was highly segregated to assure the livability of residential areas. The territory and jurisdiction of municipal governments were reformed so as to marry the 'city' with newer outlying suburban jurisdictions. Governments intervened directly in the urban landscape by building educational establishments, hospitals, subsidized housing, and, most notably, roads and expressways (on the development of suburbs over this period, see Fishman, 1987; Harris, 2004; Rowe, 1991). The federal government played a prominent role in stimulating suburban development through a mortgage subsidy and guarantee program for new single-family homes (Dennis and Fish, 1972).

It needs to be emphasized that the predominant land use in early suburbs was residential. In fact, suburbs in their first period of development were often spoken of as 'bedroom communities' (Mackenzie and Rose, 1983; Mazy and Lee, 1983; Reisman, 1958). But with previously centralized functions relocating to newly developed areas, suburbs soon came to host a wide range of functions. Figure 1.4 identifies some of the more salient properties of suburban areas developed in the immediate post-war metropolitan period. The construction of highways and high-capacity arterials, combined with rising car and truck use, greatly altered accessibility. As suggested earlier in Figure 1.3, land value and density gradients became flatter and more even throughout suburban space, creating numerous nodes of equivalent importance.

High-accessibility nodes located at major expressway interchanges and arterial intersections became sites for regional malls. Able to secure large catchment areas from such strategic locations, these malls accommodated the largest concentrations of retail establishments, with the exception of CBDs in very large metropolitan regions (Jones, 1991; Jones and Simmons, 1990). Other locations offering good accessibility along, off, or close to high-capacity roads attracted industrial and business parks, small retail malls, and self-standing retail and service establishments (fast-food outlets, car dealerships, gas stations, and so on). Chapters 14 and 16 examine how this decentralization process was played out on

the employment and retail scene. Also attracted to the periphery were space-hungry activities such as university campuses. The list of universities that opted for suburban sites in the 1950s and 1960s includes: Université Laval in Quebec City, Carleton University in Ottawa, York University in Toronto, University of Waterloo in Waterloo, University of Calgary in Calgary, Simon Fraser University in Vancouver.

In yet another fashion, suburbs distinguished themselves from the central city by adopting an inwardly focused system of curvilinear streets. Ties with older parts of the city and, for that matter, with other suburban areas were maintained via a limited number of high-capacity expressways and arterial roads (see Figure 1.4). A generalization of car use and the construction of arterial road and expressway networks made it possible for households to reach activities within a greatly enhanced perimeter, thus broadening available choice. However, the combination of a dispersion of activities and lower density was damaging to public transit (Bottles, 1987; Cervero, 1986, 1989; Miller and Shalaby, 2003; Perl and Pucher, 1995). When public transit was extended to the suburb, deficits soared because densities were insufficient and origins and destinations too scattered to generate the level of patronage required to support effective services (see, e.g., Pushkarev and Zupan, 1977).

Quality of life in inner-city neighbourhoods suffered considerably from efforts to improve suburban commuters' accessibility to the CBD. Most dramatic was the impact of expressway construction through pre-existing older neighbourhoods (Nowlan and Nowlan, 1970). Another consequence of suburban development was a dramatic fall in the CBD's share of metropolitan sales once regional malls became well established. The exodus of much of the middle class towards the suburbs triggered a 'filtering down' of inner-city housing (that is, a decline in households' socio-economic status, conversions of single-family units into multi-family accommodation, and subsequent physical deterioration of an aging housing stock) (see Figure 1.4 and Chapter 15). Perceived decline in older housing

Figure 1.4   **Metropolitan Development Land-Use Patterns (1945–75)**

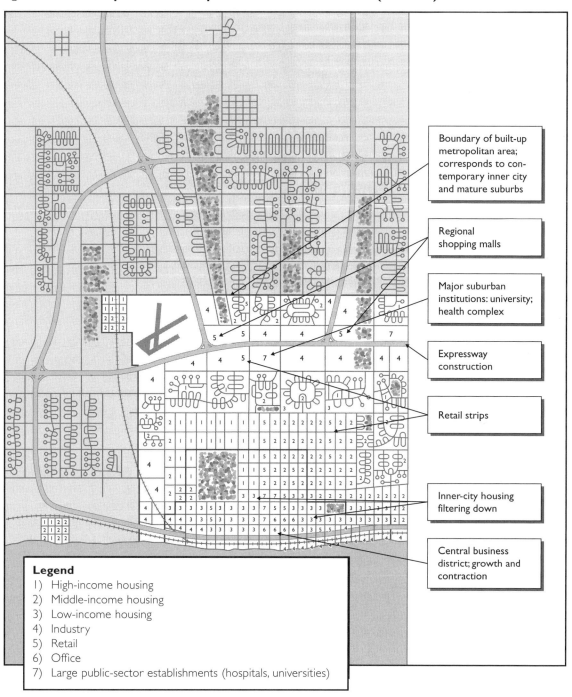

Boundary of built-up metropolitan area; corresponds to contemporary inner city and mature suburbs

Regional shopping malls

Major suburban institutions: university; health complex

Expressway construction

Retail strips

Inner-city housing filtering down

Central business district; growth and contraction

Legend
1) High-income housing
2) Middle-income housing
3) Low-income housing
4) Industry
5) Retail
6) Office
7) Large public-sector establishments (hospitals, universities)

stocks was a major incentive for urban renewal schemes that demolished existing structures to make way for public housing based on growing concern for social sustainability. More frequently, though, 'slum clearance' was directed at private redevelopment (Birch, 1971; Bourne, 1967; Dennis and Fish, 1972; Hoover and Vernon, 1962; Miron, 1993a; Smith, 1964; see also Chapter 26). It must be stressed that proverbial inner-city blight was more characteristic of American than Canadian cities (Chapter 2 elaborates on this point). Many Canadian inner cities were fortunate in that the period of rapid suburbanization coincided with a huge wave of post-World War II immigration. This initiated a cycle of do-it-yourself, private home improvement/renovation in older inner-city neighbourhoods that would subsequently find fuller expression in the process of gentrification (see Chapter 12 on inner-city change). Indeed, towards the end of this period in the late 1960s, early gentrification of select inner-city neighbourhoods marked a small but significant reversal of overwhelming attraction to the suburbs (Ley, 1996a).

Over the 1945–75 period, downtown redevelopment was encouraged by massive public-sector investment in widening roads and, in larger agglomerations, in public transit. The erection of highly symbolic public buildings such as the new City Hall in Toronto and Place des Arts in Montreal was intended to improve the image of the core. Redevelopment was also promoted by liberal zoning regulations authorizing high-rise structures over much of the inner city (Bourne, 1967; Leo, 1994; Sewell, 1993). In larger agglomerations, 1960–75 was a time of feverish office employment growth in the CBD that produced much altered cityscapes profiled by new towers (see Chapter 10; also Code, 1983; Gad, 1991a; Lortie, 2004a). Core area retailing was also transformed. In virtually every Canadian downtown, malls reproducing conditions offered by their suburban counterparts were erected (Curtis, 1994; Frieden and Sagalyn, 1989; Paumier, 1988; Redstone, 1976). Thanks to such developments, many CBDs were able to maintain, or even increase, their absolute retail activity level, at least

for a time. Everywhere, however, massive suburban retail developments caused a serious drop in downtowns' relative importance within the metropolitan-wide retail marketplace.

On the whole, the period of 'metropolitan' development favoured the less environmentally sustainable suburb over the central city and there was distinct unevenness/difference between the two coterminous urban forms. Increasingly over the 1945–75 years, a growing dependence on the car, a taste for modernism, and a drive to accumulate durable goods placed the higher-density inner city at a disadvantage relative to the space-profligate suburb. It is not surprising that so many middle-class households, businesses, and even major public institutions opted for suburban locations.

Suburban Domination, 1975–Present

In the contemporary, post-1975 period the suburbs surpassed the central city in terms of sheer population size, but equally in regard to retail activity, manufacturing, and, more recently, office and public institution employment. Despite the enduring symbolic pre-eminence of the CBD in the largest agglomerations, Canadian metropolitan areas have followed the trend set earlier in the US so that most economic activity is now situated in the suburbs (Baldassare, 1986; Bourne, 1989; Bunting and Filion, 1999; Knox, 1994; Muller, 1981). Moreover, over this period, dispersed styles of suburbanization have resulted in a rate of outward physical expansion that far exceeds demographic growth. Even cities that saw little population increase over this period experienced considerable peripheral suburban development. The dense inner-city environment with its heavy reliance on walking and transit use has become a subsidiary urban form within an agglomeration dominated by suburban, car-oriented land uses. In these circumstances, the implication that *sub*urban territory is dependent on, or in any way lesser than, the central city is inappropriate (Evenden and Walker, 1993; Kling et al., 1991; Knox, 1994). This said, it must also be noted that recently, some cities, such as Vancouver and Toronto, have enjoyed substantial residential development in their central parts. At this point in time, however, it is difficult to assess the extent to which this form of residential redevelopment represents a significant counter-tendency to suburban growth.

By 1975, metropolitan-wide accessibility hubs had multiplied throughout the suburbs. The suburban-style transportation/land-use pattern inherited from the previous period had become the norm, enhanced in most large metropolitan areas by an expanded expressway system. As a result, densities in the inner zones dropped and became markedly lower than in earlier periods, although this drop largely stabilized after 1981; indeed, as suggested above, a few large-city neighbourhoods have actually enjoyed substantial density increments. A more widespread response to continued suburban expansion has been infilling in select suburban parts reflecting, among other things, the attraction of expressway-induced accessibility. Overall, the low population densities in the outermost suburbs perpetuate the transportation/land-use pattern set in the early post-war period. Importantly, however, net residential densities have risen in the outermost suburban zones in most CMAs over the last decade, though because of smaller households and even more expansive space consumption by other land uses—employment, commercial, institutional, open space—this does not generally translate into gross density gains.

Today, any expressway exit constitutes a high-accessibility site, and any location within a 15-minute drive from such an exit offers adequate accessibility for housing (a situation that has been characterized as the 'exit ramp economy'). The slackening of accessibility constraints on location produces the complex land-use patchwork quilt that characterizes contemporary suburban areas. Specialized suburban zones come in different sizes and are juxtaposed in apparent random fashion, which makes it more difficult to grasp the structural parameters of the contemporary metropolis than of earlier urban forms (Filion and Bunting, 1990; Filion et al., 1996). Postmodern urban theorists have

characterized the apparently random patterning of different land uses and communities of different socio-economic and ethnic status as the product of the roll of dice on a game board (Dear and Flusty, 1998). Another outcome of this transportation/land-use dynamic is a further extension of access to rural hinterlands surrounding metropolitan regions. The movement of activities like employment and shopping to the outer edge of the built perimeter encourages residential relocation to rural areas that are within commuting range from the urban periphery (Coppack et al., 1988; Joseph et al., 1988). As discussed in Chapter 13, this growth in 'urban' rural living in turn transforms the retail and service landscape of those villages that cater to the tastes of former city dwellers as well as to those of visitors from nearby larger places (Bourne et al., 2003; Coppack, 1988; Mitchell, 1992).

As suggested in Figure 1.5, land-use arrangements changed with the transition from 'metropolitan balance' to 'suburban domination'. A number of innovations distinguish the current period from the preceding period of suburbanization. With the decentralization of offices, the post-1975 period witnesses the creation of suburban business (or office) parks, and more recently, the emergence of so-called suburban downtowns that combine office and retail concentrations with civic centres, generally smaller in scale but comparable in many respects to so-called US edge cities (Cervero, 1989; Garreau, 1991; Kling et al., 1991; Stanback, 1991). As in the case of inner suburban infill, higher-density nodes in the outer suburbs produce a poly-centric, metropolitan density gradient that can no longer be captured by a simple curvilinear relationship (Figure 1.6). On the retail scene, the appearance of factory outlets, 'big-box' stores, and 'power malls' transforms the shopping centre hierarchy (local, community, regional) inherited from the previous period (Berry, 1963; Brown, 1992; Dawson and Lord, 1985; Guy, 1994; Howe and Rabiega, 1992; Jones and Doucet, 2000; Jones and Simmons, 1990). These establishments achieve unprecedented size for specialized outlets and thus enjoy substantial economies of scale. They opt for

Figure 1.5   **Suburban Domination Land-Use Patterns (1975–21st Century)**

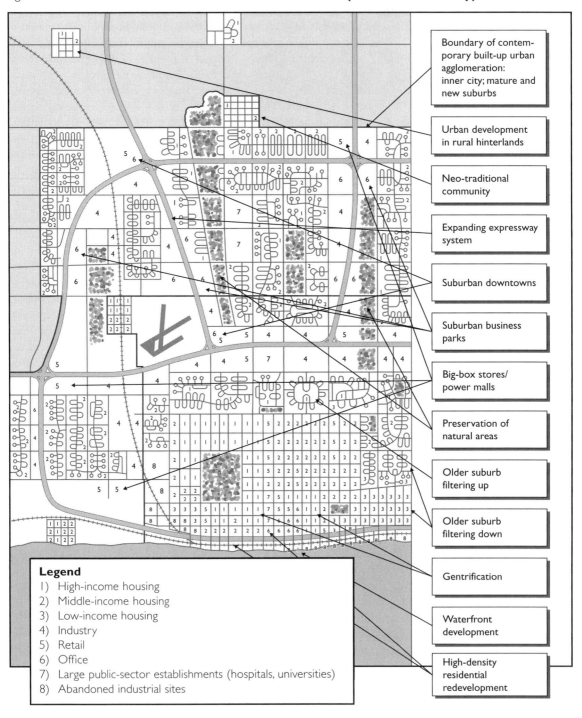

Boundary of contemporary built-up urban agglomeration: inner city; mature and new suburbs

Urban development in rural hinterlands

Neo-traditional community

Expanding expressway system

Suburban downtowns

Suburban business parks

Big-box stores/power malls

Preservation of natural areas

Older suburb filtering up

Older suburb filtering down

Gentrification

Waterfront development

High-density residential redevelopment

Legend

1) High-income housing
2) Middle-income housing
3) Low-income housing
4) Industry
5) Retail
6) Office
7) Large public-sector establishments (hospitals, universities)
8) Abandoned industrial sites

Figure 1.6   **Post–1975 Density Gradient**

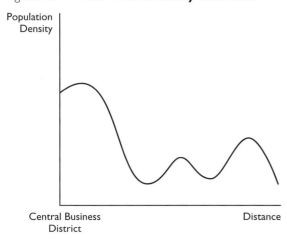

relatively inexpensive but highly accessible sites, usually near one or more expressways. This locational advantage, along with their strong appeal in terms of price and merchandise variety, allows the new big-box stores and power malls to capture catchment areas that vastly exceed those of regional malls.

In contrast to substantial retailing transformations, residential communities built over the last 25 years conform generally to the pattern set over the previous period, notwithstanding above-mentioned density increments. The general conformity of new housing tracts with earlier suburban patterns does not mean that there have been no innovations. For one thing, as implied earlier, new houses, though generally larger, usually sit on smaller lots. From the sustainability perspective, most significant is a heightened environmental awareness, which translates in some subdivisions into measures to protect water quality involving the preservation of natural settings along marshes, streams, ponds, lakes, and rivers (see Chapter 22). There is also a tendency to safeguard other environmentally significant areas such as woods and habitats for unusual botanical and animal species. The outcome is more and different forms of green space than in earlier, more standard forms of subdivisions. Another new trend

is seen in the appearance of 'neo-traditional' communities. The neo-traditional movement promotes the creation of neighbourhoods that replicate positive features of late nineteenth- and early twentieth-century forms of urbanization: a main street, less visual intrusion of the car, vernacular architectural styles, picket fences, etc. Presently, though numerous new developments borrow some elements of neo-traditionalism, there have been few attempts in Canada to create full-fledged neo-traditional neighbourhoods (examples of such projects include Mackenzietown in Calgary and, in the Greater Toronto Area, Cornell in Markham, River Oaks in Oakville, and Montgomery Village in Orangeville) (Gordon and Vipond, 2005; Grant, 2003). Moreover, despite all the media hype, there is no evidence to support the contention that this new form of development is able to induce, as intended, a marked increase in walking and transit use. In this fundamental respect, all new residential subdivisions in the outer suburbs perpetuate, even escalate, unsustainable patterns set by the first postwar suburbs—rates of car ownership and distances travelled are significantly greater today than they were in the past.

The suburbs, as a whole, have become more socially heterogeneous (Miron, 1988; Poulton, 1995). For one thing, as pointed out in Chapters 9 and 12, there is now a great amount of ethnic and racial diversity in the suburbs. The drift of social housing towards greenfield sites in the 1960s and 1970s has also created distinct pockets of poverty in some suburban parts. Much of the older suburban landscape has also undergone filtering down as the original occupants have been replaced over time (Conrad, 1996; Gutowski and Field, 1979; Vischer, 1987). Other suburban communities have, in contrast, experienced a new kind of filtering up as 'mega-homes' replace the original stock in some more desirable locales. Overall, however, the near-homogeneous, upper-middle-class composition of the outer suburbs is generally believed to have substantially augmented the geography of social polarization. Research further suggests that the new affluent suburbs tend to be ideologically more conservative and supportive of right-of-centre political agendas (Walks, 2004a).

The impact of suburban domination on the inner city has been more varied than in the immediate post-war period when decline and government-sponsored renewal were in evidence. Over the post-1975 period, a stark discrepancy and unevenness exist between the ascending trajectory of attractive inner-city sites located in large, prosperous metropolitan areas with well-developed public transit systems, and the decline characteristic of many smaller and/or slow-growth places. Where circumstances are favourable, full-fledged gentrification and condominium infill predominate and make housing inaffordability a feature of inner cities, which in the pre-World War II era and subsequent decades were home to the poorest of residents. Likewise, public–private-sector partnerships lead to large-scale redevelopment of select sites such as waterfronts and well-placed 'brownfields' (i.e., former industrial properties). But there is stark unevenness among Canadian cities, with the central parts of most medium-size cities experiencing stagnation and decline (see Chapter 10).

In the post-1975 period, uncertainty prevails, not just in the inner city but throughout the metropolitan realm in part because the retrenched public sector can no longer be counted on to 'fix things up'. Across the board, the planning of cities tends to have been fragmented, at a time when co-ordination was more than ever needed. Within the contemporary Canadian agglomeration, the attentive planning of individual subdivisions contrasts with poorly co-ordinated growth and infrastructure development at a metropolitan scale. This situation is largely due to the absence in all large Canadian metropolitan regions of agencies capable of formulating and implementing plans at an agglomeration-wide scale. The problem is that few municipal administrations are willing to relinquish power to a metropolitan-wide agency. Suburban administrations, which are concerned about possible limitations on their expansion and a sharing of their tax base with fiscally ailing central cities, are especially averse to any form of politically powerful metropolitan agency.

3:   Towards a New Urban Vision?

The second and third periods in the chronology of urban development demonstrate a generalization over the last 60 years of the automobile-oriented, suburban formula. The vast majority of Canadian urbanized territory has been developed in suburban, dispersed style (auto orientation, land-use segmentation, generalized low density, augmented green space), and most of the population now lives in this type of environment. Interventions intended to accommodate ever larger volumes of cars and trucks and the ongoing replication of suburban-type settings have dominated the past six decades. Most planning innovations over this period have further advanced the suburban style of development. They have involved, for example, increases in road capacity, more rigid suburban land-use segregation, and a succession of innovative land uses suited to this system: shopping malls, industrial and business parks, power centres, parking garages. Even ecologically driven adaptations, such as the protection of environmentally sensitive areas or 'greening' of cityscapes, have in most respects further promoted dispersion.

Yet, from its very beginning, automobile-dependent suburbanization was the target of harsh criticism (e.g., Mumford, 1961). And as time progressed, attitudes towards this form of development further soured. Calls for developments that are more transit- and walking-hospitable, less environmentally damaging, more conducive to a sense of community and quality of life, and that make reduced demand on the public purse have become ever louder as we advance into the twenty-first century. Many of these requests are presently subsumed under the 'smart growth' label (Bolbier, 1998; Daniels, 2001). Growing problems related to sustainability, unevenness, and uncertainty, as discussed throughout this volume, all point to the need for alternative styles of managing urban growth. Yet, the entrenched dynamic that binds low-density land-use arrangements to auto-based transportation and people to consumerist lifestyles and suburban landscapes as their preferred 'place' would seem to be almost impossible to break.

Transition to an Alternative Growth Style?

Disenchantment with the dominant suburban form of growth has its roots in four different contingencies. The first downside of suburban dispersion is its high development costs in a context of fiscal restrictions. A second major concern stems from growing and profound awareness of adverse environmental and health effects. A third relates to the quality-of-life implications and overall costs to households that arise as a result of difficulties experienced in accessing essential activities alongside frustrations over time lost due to traffic congestion. A fourth, long-lamented downside of suburban form is the lack of appeal of many land uses associated with this urban form. Given these growing disenchantments, we should at least briefly consider the feasibility of change and transition to alternative forms of urban development, considering both factors conducive to change and those that are likely to hinder major transformation.

As a conclusion to this introductory chapter about urban transition in Canada we make the deliberate assumption that an alternative model of urban development is now past due. However, instead of making predictive statements about what form a new urban development pattern might assume, we refer, once again, to the urban properties described at the opening of the chapter in order to articulate the nuanced frame of reference that will surround decisions made about future urban transition. Table 1.2 provides a synoptic outline of the most salient circumstances that have engendered a rethinking of urban growth formulas. It sets these within the six different property domains discussed earlier in order to identify contextual factors that will facilitate or impede the kinds of transition that are being called for.

Starting with *proximity*, worsening congestion, often referred to as 'gridlock', underscores the need for profound transformations in the way we develop cities. But the dynamic of land use and transportation has resulted in reliance on the car and the truck, on one hand, and, on the other, low-densities and specialized land uses designed to accommodate these vehicles. These characteristics of urban life are deeply entrenched. Episodic and localized interventions are destined to fail because they are unable to alter this overriding metro-wide dynamic. For example, creating a pedestrian-conducive environment involves de-emphasizing the presence of the car, which generally raises objections in a context where stores, services, workplaces, institutions, and residential units all depend on automobile accessibility. Moreover, even residents who live in the few higher-density communities designed to New Urbanism standards have the majority of their daily and weekly activities located outside their immediate environs. Access of residents of neo-traditional communities to metro-wide activities and services generates just as many auto-based trips as are found in communities of more conventional suburban design. The fact that cars are parked in back lanes in New Urbanism neighbourhoods has not reduced their use.

One possible way to initiate change at an intra-metropolitan scale would involve the creation of walking and transit-conducive nodes and/or corridors, along which people who choose to reduce their car reliance could live, work, shop, etc. (Filion, 2003). It would represent a small-scale change at first but one that would offer a new, alternative manner of living in the contemporary Canadian city.

Ideally, breaking with present forms of development would entail the creation of extensive high-quality public transit networks, which would reach deep into peripheral zones of growth where new developments, from the start, would be compatible with transit use. Such efforts to reorganize land use around public transit would need to be of a scale comparable to that of the massive urban highway programs of the post-war decades, which fully adapted the city to the car. In essence, such investments would involve a *capitalization* in the built environment equal to that of the 1950s, 1960s, and early 1970s. The rub is that *production*-related circumstances limit resources available to the public sector (slower growth and intense international competition) and *reproduction*-related spending priorities (increasingly driven by health-care demands, in part a consequence of an aging population) have first call on those limited resources. Thus, funds available for such an ambitious public transit

Table 1.2   **Towards a New Urban Vision?**

Urban Properties	Circumstances Causing a Rethinking of Urban Trends	Context for Transition
Production	Changes in production, in part the outcome of international competition, cause uneven growth (winner and loser cities) and limit government revenues.	Economic trends are responsible for reduced funding for infrastructures and greater demands for social services. Insufficient funding for current-style infrastructures may have a role in bringing about transition to alternative development styles.
Reproduction	Aging is partly responsible for strain on public-sector resources. Immigration concentrates in large metropolitan regions, thus accentuating a development gap between cities.	Reinforces the trends associated with production: uneven urban development and insufficient funding for contemporary infrastructure forms or for infrastructures supporting alternative development patterns.
Proximity	Loss of metro-wide accessibility due to congestion, thus loss of advantages of living in large metropolitan regions. Also loss of local access, due to car-based markets for retail and services.	Congestion raises awareness of need for transition. But auto/truck-based land-use dynamic is deeply entrenched and many activities seek car-based economies of scale.
Capitalization	Massive infrastructure systems laid down over the 1950s, 1960s, and early 1970s, a period of rapid economic growth and plentiful public-sector funding. These systems were a prerequisite for auto-oriented urbanization.	Difficult to deviate markedly from present urban structure because it is reinforced by land use and behaviour. Absence of funding of a scale comparable to the 1950s, 1960s, and early 1970s is another obstacle to urban transition. But there is room for localized interventions, which are most likely to be successful if they adopt a corridor pattern.
Place	Reaction against lack of meaning and appeal of auto-oriented suburban environment, but continued strong attachment to prevailing character of suburban residential areas.	Support for some meaningful and better-designed environments results in new downtown projects and neo-traditional communities in the suburbs. But sense of place also fosters NIMBY sentiments, which hamper change.
Urban/ Municipal Governance	Discourse and some interventions (e.g., higher residential density, core area housing) promote urban transition. But overall, inaptitude to deal with problems generated by present forms of urban development: congestion, pollution, and high cost.	Apparent rise in government support for urban transition. But persistent gap between vision and reality of urban development. Governments have to decide between going along with interests and behavioural patterns that reinforce present urban forms, or attempting to alter the course of development originally set in the 1950s.

strategy are unlikely to materialize in the foreseeable future. This bleak forecast will be compounded in increasing numbers of metropolitan regions that will experience stagnation or decline. In declining places we can anticipate that there will be minimal resources for retrofitting auto-oriented land-use and transportation systems.

Sense of place can both encourage and forestall change. In the first instance, *sense of place* themes have been instrumental in marshalling forces supportive of well-designed pedestrian-friendly projects, such as waterfronts, new downtown squares, and neo-traditional communities. However, sense of place can also fan NIMBY sentiments, especially when the character of existing residential areas is perceived as threatened by new projects. Such reactions can cripple efforts at channelling as much new development as possible within the existing urban perimeter. For example, the intent of the City of Toronto to transform low-density, strip-like arterials into mid-rise residential/commercial corridors has faced nearly insurmountable opposition from nearby neighbourhood organizations committed to the preservation of the low-density character of their residential areas (Toronto, 2002).

Within *urban/municipal governance*, tensions between factors that are favourable to the status quo and those that call for a transition are most tangible. Aware of long-term consequences of present urban development patterns, many administrations have subscribed to 'smart growth' principles. For example, in 2005 the Ontario government adopted 'Places to Grow' legislation aimed at containing sprawl within the Toronto region (Ontario, 2005a). At the same time, however, public administrations are compelled to come up with short-term responses to needs and demands, the cumulative effect of which is generally to reinforce present development tendencies. This is notably the case of the provision of additional road space to alleviate congestion. The aggregate outcome of incremental expansion of auto-based facilities is to increase vehicular use and accentuate the car orientation of a city. It is also important to remember that the public sector is subject to electoral and fiscal

imperatives that constrain the range of policy options. To stay in power, public administrations must heed preferences of the electorate, and to maintain or expand their tax base, they must assure that the needs and interests of their important taxpayers (and job creators) are met. One can easily understand why, in constituencies composed primarily of car users, governments shy away from restrictions on car use. In the same vein, major assembly plants that depend on highway accessibility will weigh heavily in debates about whether to give priority to road or light-rail transit investment.

Change or Status Quo?

The picture drawn here suggests tensions between forces of change and those of continuity or status quo. In the end, the resolution of resulting conflicts mostly favours the status quo. Such an interpretation is hardly surprising given the tendency over the last decades for urban outcomes to frustrate partisans of alternative models of development. Still, we may yet be at the cusp of major urban transformations. In large metropolitan regions, the downsides of car-oriented suburban development are felt with growing acuity, and reduced energy availability and resulting escalating prices may challenge the premises on which this model is based. Moreover, in some of our cities—Vancouver, Toronto, Montreal, Halifax, and Victoria are among places that stand out—counter, re-urbanizing trends have already begun to gain momentum.

The exact form future urban transitions will take is a source of uncertainty. The models on which coming transitions will rest have yet to be worked out. This is a major task for the coming generation. The challenge, then, is to provide future urban scholars and practitioners with prerequisite knowledge of how cities operate so that the best possible interventions can be implemented successfully.

Note

1. This is the message of the 2004 documentary entitled *The End of Suburbia* produced by the Post Carbon Institute.

Chapter 2

Canadian Cities in Continental Context: Global and Continental Perspectives on Canadian Urban Development

Kim England and John Mercer

Contemporary cities are the product of the inter-action of large-scale processes with local urban forms, mediated through a variety of institutions. Canadian cities can be differentiated from those in Europe, Latin America, East Asia, and the like in terms of prevailing urban forms, political geographies, and socio-economic characteristics. However, from a global perspective Canadian cities are commonly seen as being more similar to US cities, giving rise to the concept of 'the North American City'. And, from an international per-spective, this concept has real utility and some coherence for both teaching and research. Indeed, given the global prominence of American social sci-ence and theorizing about the city, it is not sur-prising that 'the North American city' has considerable intellectual purchase and appeal. Yet, there is great value in geographers' claim that place matters, that local and regional contexts do make a difference—a difference not merely evident on urban landscapes but also important in the every-day lives of Canadians.

In this chapter we challenge the singular con-cept of 'the North American city' by highlighting Canada–US differences and the variation among the cities within each country. We reflect on differ-ences and similarities between Canadian and US cities and how they have persisted or changed over approximately the last 30 years.[1] At the outset we should be clear that during this period cities on both sides of the border have become more vari-able and complex at both the intra-urban and inter-urban scale, making it increasingly difficult to make broad generalizations about differences between 'the' US city and 'the' Canadian city (hence the plural 'cities' in our title). We draw out several Canadian–US differences with respect to the nature of the urban form, including housing and trans-portation, and the urban processes that shape cities in both countries. We also draw attention to global processes that directly produce change in cities, but note that as lives and landscapes are increasingly globalized, it is important to remember that these changes are not necessarily experienced in a simi-lar way in different places. Of course, some urban areas are relatively untouched by certain global processes (international immigration, for example). But our point is that cities are open systems in an era marked by increasing economic and cultural globalization, rapid digital and wireless changes in telecommunications, massive increases in interna-tional travel for business, administration, and tourism, and new dynamics in international migra-tion and settlement. A wide range of such large-scale processes markedly affects cities in Canada. Other chapters in this volume provide more detail on specific features of Canada's urban regions with respect to the interplay between these processes and local structures.

Urban Canada in Context

In common with other Global North countries, including the US, a high proportion of Canadians live in urban places. Of greater importance is that the vast majority of Canadians live in metropolitan areas, defined by Statistics Canada as census metro-politan areas—CMAs (see Appendix B for a full list-ing). Just under two-thirds of Canadians (and four-fifths of Americans) reside in these major locations. In terms of metropolitanization, the last century witnessed vast transformations. In 1900, just over 1 million Canadians lived in the principal metropolitan regions, but by its close, more than 19 million did so (2001 figure). The scale of these metropolitan areas has also increased such that by the end of the twentieth century there were four 'million plus' metropolitan areas in Canada (and 47 in the US, a roughly equivalent number keeping in mind that the US population is larger than Canada's by a factor of approximately 10). However, there are two particularly notable cross-national differences in the two contemporary metropolitan systems. First, the Canadian urban system (that is, including urban places smaller than CMAs) grew more slowly than the US urban system in the 1990s (14 per cent versus 19 per cent in the US), whereas in the 1980s Canada's growth (13 per cent) was slightly ahead of the US (12 per cent). Second, geographic concentration is more marked in the smaller Canadian urban system, with one-third of the national population living in the three largest CMAs, whereas only about 17 per cent of Americans live in the three largest metropolitan statistical areas (MSAs)—New York, Los Angeles, and Chicago (although, of course, in absolute terms this amounts to more people). Thus, Toronto, Montreal, and Vancouver continue to dominate the Canadian urban system, and now that the national capital region (Ottawa–Hull–Gatineau) has joined the 'million plus' club, the principal cultural, economic, and political Canadian players are well represented at the top of its urban hierarchy. Globally (see Chapter 4), Canada's largest cities are increasingly important anchors in the global cities network.

As the absolute size of the metropolitan population grew over the twentieth century there has been an important geographical redistribution throughout North America. First, a strong relationship exists between metropolitan growth and economic performance of the regional hinterland, and increasingly (at least for certain favoured metropolitan areas) growth is linked to performance in the international economic system. Thus, we find in both the Canadian and US urban systems considerable variation in terms of population and household change depending on their location within their respective national space economies. In general terms, metropolitan areas in western Canada and those in southern Ontario have prospered and grown, while CMAs in Atlantic Canada, Quebec, and parts of the Prairie provinces have done less well. Characterizing the US situation is more challenging because there is much greater variation within that system. However, particularly dramatic growth is evident in the metropolitan areas in the Pacific states and in Arizona, Texas, Florida, Nevada, and Utah, while the places of slower growth, stagnation, or decline are concentrated in the old industrial heartland states.

Major redistribution has also occurred within the metropolitan regions themselves. As a consequence of continued suburban growth and decentralization of economic activity, some argue that demonstrably different urban forms have been created, such as urban sprawl and edge cities. Today, half of all Americans live in suburbs, and within MSAs those residing in the outer city now outnumber those in the central city by roughly two to one. In Canada, metropolitan suburbanites account for 38 per cent of the national population and the ratio of outer to central-city population is 1.5 to 1. Thus, while suburbanization is common in both countries, suburban populations remain more dominant in the US than Canada. This is more than a geographical curiosity. For example, (predominantly white) American suburbanites are a major political force whose allegiance is eagerly sought in national and state elections. While Canadian suburbanites are of less demographic significance, their voting patterns, especially in Toronto and Montreal, are pivotal in provincial and national elections (Walks, 2004b).

Canadian and US Cities: Differences and Similarities in Urban Form

Conventionally, Canadian cities are characterized as having more vital central cities and as being more compact and less dispersed than their US counterparts. In this section we compare the urban form of

Canadian and US cities along several dimensions identified in previous research as significant in cross-national comparisons.

Population and Household Change

The dynamics of population and household shifts within metropolitan areas are useful indicators of structural changes in urban form. To capture population shifts in the two urban systems we developed a five-type classification based on population change in metropolitan areas and their central cities. We define 'central/original city' as the incorporated political unit around which outlying units have grown; it is usually the largest and oldest municipality. The results of our classification are presented in Figures 2.1 and 2.2, which provide a visual and immediate way of making cross-national comparisons.

For the 1981–91 decade (see Figure 2.1), there are no Canadian cases where both the central city and the overall metropolitan region lost population (Type 1), and hence there were no places that faced the difficulties associated with urban decline. There are not even many CMAs (less than a fifth, examples being Windsor and Saint John) that fall into Type 2, what we call the 'classic type' of urban population change: central-city decline despite overall metropolitan growth (indicating high suburban population growth). The majority of the CMAs (76 per cent) are in the two classes that capture either a stagnating central city with metropolitan growth (Type 3), or a solidly growing central city alongside metropolitan growth (Type 4)—examples from Type 3 are Montreal, Hamilton, and Halifax, and from Type 4, London, Calgary, and Vancouver. So, although during the 1980s only two CMAs (Kitchener–Waterloo and Saskatoon) exhibit what we term 'booming' central-city and metropolitan growth (Type 5), only a few of Canada's CMAs suffered central-city population decline (Types 1 and 2). In stark contrast, the US system had 39 cases (out of 230—almost one-fifth) where the metropolitan area and its central city lost population (Type 1) and another 54 cases (23 per cent of all MSAs) experienced the 'classic' urban population change (Type 2). Examples of

Type 1 MSAs are Buffalo, Detroit, New Orleans, Flint, and Akron, and Type 2 examples include Philadelphia, Denver, Memphis, Syracuse, and Mobile. Indeed, the most striking aspect of the US evidence is its diversity, echoing the 1970s results of Goldberg and Mercer (1986). So while there are 93 MSAs with central-city population decline (Types 1 and 2), Figure 2.1 also indicates that there are 37 MSAs classified as 'booming' (Type 5), with high central-city growth combined with overall metropolitan growth.

Central cities lose population because of absolute loss due to out-migration, or because households in the central city, where smaller households are typical, are becoming even smaller. While politicians and journalists lament population loss, a more profound loss for a local jurisdiction is that of households. The loss of households' effective demand for goods and services, including housing, has a cumulatively negative effect on a city's quality of life. The US experience is more threatening in this regard, as some 60 central cities experienced a loss in households (over 20 per cent of the nation's cities with populations larger than 50,000) in the 1980–90 period. Such a loss is common in Type 1 and 2 cities: 28 of the 39 grouped into Type 1 and 25 of the 54 in Type 2 also suffered this potentially devastating reduction. The occurrence of household loss was most pronounced in the inner parts of the larger metropolitan areas and poses a longer-term problem if this decline cannot be reversed. Furthermore, the most affected central cities are spatially clustered in America's manufacturing core, which includes Pennsylvania, New York, New Jersey, Ohio, Indiana, and Illinois. In Canada, by contrast, only four CMAs are in Type 2 (there are no Type 1 CMAs), and none of them experienced household loss. The Canadian–US difference points to the continued overall vitality of Canadian central cities compared to US cities. In addition, households in the central cities of both countries are generally more varied than suburban households in terms of household and family structure and marital status. But an important difference between Canada and the US (and one that explains some of the patterns described here) is that households in

Figure 2.1   **Metropolitan Population Change: Distribution of Metropolitan Areas by Type of Change, Canada and the US, 1980/1–1990/1**

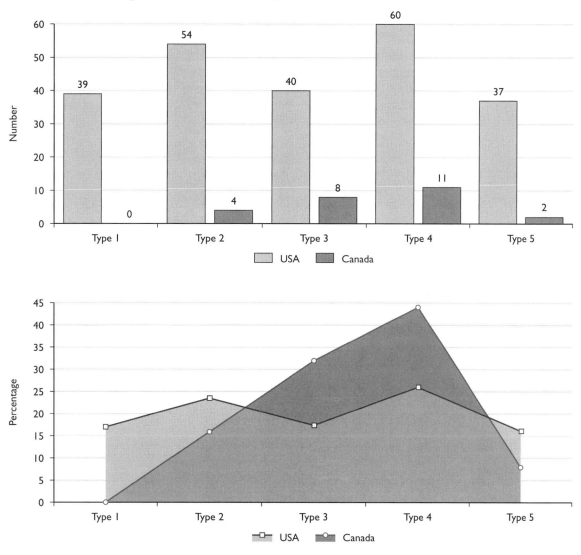

Legend
Type 1: central city decline allied to metropolitan decline
Type 2: central city decline and metropolitan growth
Type 3: central city stagnation (equal to or less than 1% over five years) and metropolitan growth
Type 4: solid central city growth (in the 1.1 to 3.9% range) and metropolitan growth
Type 5: booming central city growth (4% and over) and metropolitan growth

Canadian central cities are much more likely to house families with children.[2]

We applied the same classification procedure to population change data for the 1990s, using the 1991–6 and 1996–2001 inter-censal periods for Canada (Figure 2.2).[3] Unlike the 1980s statistics, these data do indicate some convergence between Canadian and US metropolitan regions. The most notable contrast in the 1990s is in Type 2, the 'classic' pattern. This likely reflects a much improved economic performance in many parts of Canada in the latter part of the past decade that enabled greater central-city growth to occur, creating more Type 3 than Type 2 patterns of population change. For the past decade, the greatest similarity again occurs in Types 3 and 4. In Canada, most metropolitan areas fall into these two categories (60 per cent in 1991–6 and 70 per cent in 1996–2001); in the US, 72 per cent of all metropolitan areas fall into these two types. There is also some convergence at the two extremes—booming (Type 5) and declining (Type 1) central cities/metropolitan areas. There are no Canadian areas in the most rapidly growing group (Type 5), but there are also only a few US cases in this 'booming' category, the most notable being Las Vegas. The higher proportion of cases in the Canadian system now in Type 1 indicates a significant number of metropolitan areas in distress. This demonstrates that economic growth is not even. Cities such as Regina and Greater Sudbury are within regions facing severe economic decline; almost all of these Type 1 places are located in Atlantic Canada (excluding Halifax), parts of Quebec, and northern Ontario. This shift (especially compared with the patterns of the 1980s, shown in Figure 2.1) may suggest a need for concern (see also Chapter 3). However, it may also reflect the depth of recession in Canada in the early 1990s compared with the strength of the US economy in the Clinton years.

Within the US, the regional pattern of metropolitan and central-city decline has persisted. Type 1 places include Pittsburgh, Buffalo, Dayton, and Syracuse and Type 2 examples include Cleveland, Detroit, Hartford, Milwaukee, and Philadelphia. The recovery of a number of America's principal metropolitan regions in the 1990s is demonstrated by Atlanta, Chicago, Denver, and Salt Lake City, all of which saw a reversal of previous central-city decline in the 1980s analysis and are now classified in Type 3. Sustained central-city growth contributes to substantial metropolitan growth (Type 4) in, for example, Austin, Charlotte, Dallas, Houston, Phoenix, and San Diego, as well as many smaller urban areas.

Urban Transportation

In a global context, North American cities are enormously dependent on autos and trucks for the movement of goods and people. While this allows great individual mobility and flexibility for road users, massive environmental and infrastructure costs must be borne collectively (see Part 6 of this book). Nevertheless, the commitment to the car is particularly strong. While Canadians have long been greater users of public transportation than Americans, negotiating the low-density outer city makes the automobile particularly attractive and mass transit particularly costly (and hence in need of substantial subsidy) in both countries.

The size, density, and form of an urban area likely dictate the forms of urban transportation that can be effectively provided, but, once provided, transportation systems have an important effect on private, speculative development that characterizes capitalist cities like those in North America (for more detail on urban transportation in Canada, see Chapter 6). Previous research shows that Canadian commuters were significantly less likely to use automobiles in their daily commute (about two-thirds compared to 85 per cent for Americans). Although the gap has narrowed, that cross-border difference still exists; in 2000–1, 77 per cent of Canadians drove autos or carpooled compared to almost 90 per cent for US metropolitan commuters (see Table 2.1). The rates of auto use in both countries are lower for some groups of women and certain racialized groups, who rely more heavily on public transit. Canadians are also far less reliant on expressway

Figure 2.2   **Metropolitan Population Change: Distribution of Metropolitan Areas by Type of Change, Canada: 1991–6, 1996–2001 and the US, 1990–2000**

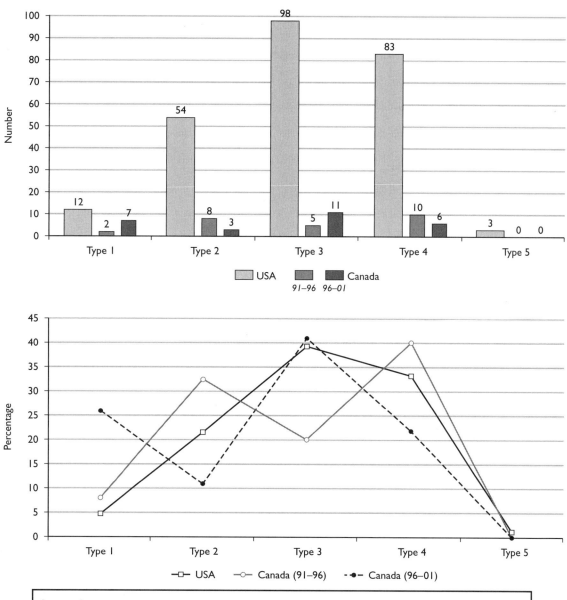

Legend

Type 1: central city decline allied to metropolitan decline
Type 2: central city decline and metropolitan growth
Type 3: central city stagnation (equal to or less than 1% over five years) and metropolitan growth
Type 4: solid central city growth (in the 1.1 to 3.9% range) and metropolitan growth
Type 5: booming central city growth (4% and over) and metropolitan growth

systems as there is less expressway capacity in metropolitan Canada than in metropolitan America (for more details, see Goldberg and Mercer, 1986). The difference can be traced back to the two countries' different transportation policies of 1940s and 1950s. In the US there was enormous federal funding for the interstate system and other highways, whereas in Canada the federal contribution was comparatively small. And the US developed the 'Highway Trust Fund' based on gas and fuel taxes to finance highways; in Canada those funds went into general revenue budgets.

There is a striking difference in public transit. Table 2.1 shows that the proportion of transit users among commuters in metropolitan America is a low 6.1 per cent. However, some places exceed this considerably (such as New York, Chicago, San Francisco, and Washington) by factors ranging roughly from 8 to 2. Given the costs of mass transit provision in lower-density suburban settings, it follows that transit use would be higher in central cities. It is, but for US central cities alone, the proportion reached only 12 per cent. Transit use in metropolitan Canada is almost 2.5 times greater

than in the US, and Canadians are more than twice as likely to walk to work, both suggestive of a denser urban environment.

Clearly, notable cross-national differences persist in urban public transportation. There were, however, some worrying signs for Canadian transit. Perl and Pucher (1995) compared ridership trends from 1950 to 1990 and found that following massive post-World War II declines in both countries, ridership on Canadian transit systems recovered strongly in the 1970s and 1980s, but US ridership had only modest gains (yet another indication of the greater importance of transit in Canadian cities). However, they also reported that ridership had steadily declined and at a faster rate in Canada than in the US (1990–4). Increased employment opportunities in dispersed locations, growing numbers of women combining paid employment with family responsibilities (child-care centres are often in different locations from workplaces, both of which often are located away from retail nodes), fewer transit-dependent youth, auto price competition, and fiscal austerity in the public sector are all factors challenging the effectiveness of Canadian transit systems. However, the steady decline noted by Perl and Pucher bottomed out in 1996; then ridership increased almost every year to 2003 at an annual rate of 1.9 per cent. In the US, transit ridership declined until 1995, then rose each year to 2001, dropping again in 2002 and 2003. The overall annual rate of increase (1995–2003) is 2.4 per cent (APTA, 2005). APTA attributes improved US ridership to the strong economy, better service, and higher levels of public and private investment in public transportation following from 1991 federal legislation and subsequent funding bills.

Table 2.1	**Modal Choice and the Journey to Work: Metropolitan Areas in Canada and the US**	
	United States (2002–3)	Canada (2001)
	(%)	(%)
Driving self	80.4	70.8
Carpool	9.2	6.6
Mass transit	6.1	14.8
Walking	2.6	5.7
All other	1.7	2.1

Note: Mass transit refers to bus, streetcar, subway, elevated railroad, and railroad; carpool includes those who are passengers in cars, trucks, or vans driven by others. These are the modes used by workers in the week prior to the survey or census.
Sources: Statistics Canada, 2001 census; Supplement to the American Housing Survey for the US, 2002 and 2003.

Housing

The housing stock of a city is one of its most durable features. Of course, until recently many suburbs have been the domain of the single-family detached dwelling unit (mostly in an owner-occupied tenure). Indeed, a common and accurate enough perception of North American cities is that their stock is dominated by owner-occupied, single-detached housing units, although in a number of large cities in both countries other forms of housing, such as row housing or apartment structures, predominate—a partial listing includes Montreal, Quebec City, St John's, and Toronto; and Baltimore, Philadelphia, San Francisco, and New York. In both countries, the level of home ownership remains broadly similar, typically in the 60–5 per cent range of all units (levels of home ownership in both countries vary across social groups such as 'race'/ethnicity, age, and gender). However, Canadians do not have the tax advantages provided to Americans to promote home ownership, widely seen as an essential underpinning of capitalist democracy and another example of US individualism and commitment to private property.

Although single-detached units are the majority of all units in both sets of metropolitan areas, a clear cross-national difference exists. For 2000–1, they account for 62 per cent of all housing in metropolitan America and 55 per cent in Canadian areas. The typically higher average percentages for the US are also found for central cities—52 per cent in the US and 46 per cent in Canada. The generally lower proportion of single-family units in Canadian metropolitan housing stocks, together with urban transportation differences, suggest a more compact and less dispersed form in Canadian cities—a goal sought by their historically more effective local planning and regulatory systems compared to land-use controls in the US. Also, in the US, the strong demand for housing in the outer suburbs, compared to soft demand in central cities, has driven up land values in recent decades. Land costs, changing household structures in the suburbs, and environmental regulations reducing land supply have all contributed to a greater production of multiple forms of housing. These factors are likely also at work in the outer parts of Canadian metropolitan areas but their aggregate impact seems reduced, probably because Canadian inner cities remain a mainstay of higher-density multiple-family dwelling, especially high-rise condominiums. In the US, vacant housing, abandonment, and eventually clearance have reduced the aging single-family housing stock in many central cities.

In the US, gated communities, some of which have created local governments, are clear expressions of the American ideology of individualism and represent a withdrawal from the larger metropolitan community (including an abdication of any responsibility for its social condition) (McKenzie, 1996; Low, 2003). Gated communities also reflect the extraordinary concern of Americans over violent crime, especially in the central city. Of course, relatively few folk live in gated communities compared to the millions of ordinary suburbanites who live in non-gated communities; nevertheless, many suburbanites will feel they too have achieved an acceptable level of security in their homes, schools, and parks by moving to outer-city locations and investing in personal security systems. While there has been increased concern about crime in Canadian metropolitan regions, even in their suburban parts, defended or gated communities are far less common, though this does not mean there are not exclusive suburbs and personal estates (Grant, 2005).

The suburbs of US and Canadian cities are infinitely more diverse than ever before and are shedding the image of being residential 'bedroom' communities, with visual uniformity associated with the mass production of so-called 'little boxes' and social uniformity based on their generally middle-class appeal and affordability (see Chapter 12). Historically, suburbs have been associated with women engaged in (unpaid) domestic labour and the reproduction of the family unit in the home. Strong-Boag and her collaborators argue that in Australia and especially in the US, suburban life stands close to the core of the national vision but that in Canada and Britain, suburbs do not embody the nation in the same way (Strong-Boag et al., 1999). The small town of America's republican heritage has been recreated in the sprawling realms of the suburbs. Indeed, while US and Canadian suburban forms may be similar, their meanings can differ. For example, both countries now have suburbs developed around neo-traditional planning. However in the US, their popularity coalesces around safety issues and nostalgia for nineteenth-century small-town living. In Canada neo-traditional communities are more likely to be prized for their affordability and environmental advantages (Grant, 2003).

Planning and Local Government Fragmentation

Evidence on population and household change, urban transportation, and housing structure has often been used to argue that Canadian cities are more compact. But newer evidence is mixed; decentralization may now be more common in dynamic metropolitan areas, such as Toronto, Vancouver, Kitchener, Oshawa, and Ottawa–Gatineau, but less common elsewhere in Canada where pressures for growth, development, and space are less (for examples, see Bunting et al., 2002). In addition, an important factor contributing to the compactness and livability of Canadian cities is government regulation. Almost 20 years ago, Barry Cullingworth, the scholar of comparative planning policy, observed that 'Canadian urban and regional planning has a more wide-ranging and acceptable role than is the case in the United States' (1987: 462). Research comparing Canadian and American metropolitan systems reveals that in Canada planning is more developed and possesses more fiscal power and authority than in the US. But processes of decentralization are undermining historically stronger Canadian metropolitan systems because so much growth (and associated tax bases) is outside metropolitan jurisdictions (e.g., Rothblatt, 1998). Despite the expectation of increased provincial/state involvement to shape more effective institutions to address metropolitan development, some believe that cross-national convergence is occurring and will accelerate.

One striking difference between Canadian and US cities that remains, however, is local government fragmentation. In the US, where local governments have a greater degree of local autonomy, weaker planning systems are exacerbated by highly fragmented local government systems. While metropolitan fragmentation does occur in Canada, it is not at the US level. Metropolitan fragmentation means that among the different governments of the metropolis, central cities are often the losers in the struggle for investment, taxable property, affluent residents, and higher government fiscal transfers. Such a portrayal seems less appropriate for Canadian cities, but it is clear that in Canada's few largest metropolitan areas this scenario is becoming increasingly fitting (Razin and Rosentraub, 2000).

Some 20 years ago, one measure of metropolitan fragmentation was approximately 2.5 times higher in metropolitan US than in Canada (Goldberg and Mercer, 1986: 214). Little has changed since. In fact, the number of local governments per US metropolitan area increased, contributing to even greater fragmentation (Rothblatt, 1998; Razin and Rosentraub, 2000). In contrast, there is a Canadian predilection for unilateral local government reform through provincial action and legislation, completely disregarding local autonomy in a way that is almost unthinkable in the US. In the last several years significant reductions have occurred in the numbers of Canadian municipal governments, the intent being to achieve greater efficiencies and reduce expenditures. For example, in the Halifax urban region, the Nova Scotia government created a new metropolitan-wide municipal government, dissolving the cities of Halifax and Dartmouth, as well as smaller suburbs, and amalgamating this urbanized core with a huge rural territory. Other examples include Ottawa, Hamilton, Kingston, and most recently Montreal and Quebec City. The creation of the Toronto 'mega-city' in 1998 is particularly significant given this region's pre-eminence and size (see Chapter 17). Prior commentary suggests that US and Canadian cities are most alike in the outer city (Goldberg and Mercer, 1986; Harris, 1996), though even here Goldberg and Mercer found important differences. Two other features of the contemporary outer city are 'edge cities' with regional and super-regional malls. Edge cities, popularized by Joel Garreau's 1991 book of the same name, are characterized by several million square feet of office and retailing floor space (usually in malls), adjacent residential developments at higher than typical density, and an almost total reliance on automobiles (Garreau, 1991). These massive complexes have been produced across the US by private-sector initiatives. Such new forms are rarer in Canadian cities but suburban downtowns, or town centres, have been actively promoted in Toronto and Vancouver (see Chapter 10; see also Filion, 2001, for discussion of Toronto's suburban mixed-use centres). The major cross-national difference is that public planning ideology generated high-density suburban centres in the Canadian context, although their actual development remained in private hands. In Canada these planned centres were intended to reduce pressures on core central business districts (CBDs) and related inner districts, and at the same time to contribute towards the 'intensification' of suburbs.

Canadian and US Cities: Differences and Similarities in Urban Processes

A whole host of large-scale or global processes influence Canadian and US cities; those of particular importance to Canadian cities include economic restructuring and the changing trends in immigration. These processes also affect US cities, but how they are worked out both locally and cross-nationally suggests some distinctiveness that challenges 'the North American city' concept, and highlights the significance of comparative research to uncover and understand similarities and differences between Canadian and US cities. In this section, we address a series of large-scale processes—economic restructuring; immigration, 'race', and ethnicity; and inequality and poverty—to investigate how the Canadian or US context makes a difference.

Economic Restructuring and Urban Economic Geographies

Given the economic transformation of the last three decades or so, the manufacturing basis for previous waves of metropolitan growth has been severely eroded and replaced by a knowledge-based econ-omy (see Chapter 14). The magnitude of this transformation is marked by the increasing use of terms like 'the informational city' and 'the post-industrial city'. This rapid economic change is evident in the spatial organization of Canadian and US cities because both economies are increasingly globalized and integrated under free trade agreements, suggesting that there may be reduced cross-national differentiation. However, the mediating role of the government (federal, provincial/state, and municipal) is important. In Canada, the historically greater role of the public sector in economic development and the stronger commitment to social support systems continue to make a meaningful difference, even with increasingly neo-liberal policies of deregulation and reduced public expenditures.

Given recent rhetoric, one might expect the landscapes of American and Canadian cities to be littered with signs of industrial decay. Many are, but industrial growth and even boom must not be overlooked. Manufacturing industries, though reshaped, have not vanished and remain important in numerous metropolitan areas in both countries. Nonetheless, industrially based metropolitan areas generally have done poorly in terms of growth in recent decades; examples include Detroit, Youngstown–Warren, Flint, Erie, and in Canada, Chicoutimi–Jonquière and Montreal. Conversely, metropolitan areas with diverse economies and growing populations have prospered, with new kinds of industries emerging; for example, Calgary and Vancouver, and Los Angeles, Phoenix, Raleigh–Durham, San Jose, and Atlanta. However, one striking difference is that Canada's core region has retained manufacturing employment more than the US manufacturing belt. As of 2001, three-quarters of manufacturing jobs were still located in Ontario and Quebec, chiefly in the Windsor–Quebec corridor where the Toronto and Montreal CMAs alone contain 32 per cent of national manufacturing employment. The Toronto CMA is the dominant manufacturing region, a position now occupied by the Los Angeles agglomeration in the US, far from the traditional manufacturing heartland of the Northeast. And there are other important national differences. While Canadian manufacturing employment declined both absolutely and proportionately in the 1985–95 decade and plant closures increased steadily from 1986 onward (MacLachlan, 1996), since the mid-1990s manufacturing employment has actually grown in absolute terms (a growth of 6.6 per cent from 1996 to 2001) and the proportional decline within overall employment evident since the mid-1980s levelled off by 2001. In contrast, the US economy has not seen a similar reversal—manufacturing employment declined by 7.2 per cent between 1995 and 2001.

A pattern of manufacturing decline in the central city and inner suburbs alongside expansion in outer city and beyond is evident on both sides of the border. In medium-sized American metropolitan areas where manufacturing employment has steadily declined, the recent geographic pattern is suburban closure and job loss—central-city locations were abandoned decades ago when alternative suburban sites opened up (for example, Akron and Syracuse). Moreover, the loss of manufacturing employment in US central cities combines with racialized residential patterns to create spatial mismatch whereby inner-city minority (especially male) workers are spatially disconnected from growing job opportunities in the outer city. With industrial decline comes rising poverty (half of the cities with poverty rates over 20 per cent are located in the 'manufacturing belt' and the burden continues to fall disproportionately on African Americans). Although the 'race' dimension is much less salient, similar industrial decline in the city of Montreal has exacerbated poverty in this particular Canadian city.

The economic landscapes of American and Canadian cities have also changed with the explosive growth of service-related employment. The downtown high-rise and suburban office parks have replaced the factory as emblematic of the age. Moreover, the rise of the service sector has been in tandem with the increase in Canadian and American women's paid employment since the 1970s. As a result, the widely observed sense of decline in US CBDs has been arrested in certain instances, such as Philadelphia, Cleveland, and St Louis. In the cities

that house key command-and-control functions in the continental and global economy, massive reinvestment has occurred in the CBD producing new office towers (and dramatic skylines) that not only house information-rich activities, but create architectural reputations and lucrative commissions. Core-area workers seeking inner-city residences (especially two-income couples) have stimulated demand for housing that has been met by condominium redevelopment and gentrification. But (as detailed in Chapter 10) even when there have been absolute increases in central area office floor space, the rapid growth of office space in outer-city locations often means that the core is less important proportionately in the overall metropolis.

In both countries, the transformation of the largest cities means that they are becoming somewhat more similar as participants in a global, knowledge-based economy, while less well situated or connected places further down the hierarchy are passed by. In a new study, Courchene (2005: 13) identifies several global city-regions in Canada, describing them as 'the principal repositories of human capital and, therefore, [knowledge-based economy] competitiveness'. Research comparing Toronto, Vancouver, and Calgary, for example, with Hamilton, Kitchener, and Sudbury would be instructive and might reveal similar outcomes to comparing Boston, Atlanta, and Denver with Buffalo, Milwaukee, and Omaha.

Immigration, 'Race', and Ethnicity[4]

Both countries have similar histories of immigration and, indigenous peoples aside, are nations of immigrants—a social, historical, and geographic fact of profound importance. Bearing in mind the factor of 10 regarding population size, Canada has admitted immigrants at three times the rate of the US since 1960: 7.4 million entering Canada (2.3 million between 1991–2001 alone) and 24.3 million entering the US. Both countries have experienced significant shifts in the source countries of their recent immigrants, and the proportion of 'traditional immigrant stock' of European origin has declined. This is particularly important in Canada where this shift has reduced the significance of the cultural links to Britain. However, while immigration from non-European sources has increased, there are key cross-national differences demographically, culturally, and politically. Broadly, the Americas, especially Mexico, and other Central American countries, as well as various Caribbean countries, are the most important source for the US, followed by countries in Asia and Africa. In Canada, the countries in East, Southeast, and South Asia alone accounted for 50 per cent of all immigrants in the 1996–2001 period, with the countries in the Caribbean and Africa also contributing notable flows (around 12 per cent combined). Even within the broad category 'Asian', there are differences reflecting Canada's membership in the Commonwealth and the US geopolitical involvement in Pacific Asia. Thus, peoples from India and Hong Kong are proportionately greater in Canada, whereas people from Korea, the Philippines, Taiwan, and Vietnam are more significant in the US (for Canada, see Schellenberg, 2004, and Abu-Laban and Garber, 2005; for the US, see Singer, 2004). The impact, culturally and in ethnicized/racialized terms, on the cities where the immigrants migrated has been major, in terms of not only social relations but also labour and housing markets, as well as service provision, with education being particularly emotionally charged (see Ley, 2004, for a discussion of transnationalism and everyday life).

Canadian and US cities both share the 'gateway' model of immigrant settlement. Over the course of the twentieth century, new immigrants settled disproportionately in just a few urban regions. In Canada, the leading destinations are Toronto and Vancouver, which attracted a remarkable 61 per cent of all immigrants who arrived in the 1990s. Montreal, attracted proportionately fewer (12 per cent), a product of the joint effects of perceived language barriers and more limited economic growth prospects (Mercer, 1995). The 'traditional' gateways also continue to dominate in the US, although the concentration is in a larger set of cities than in Canada. The vast metropolitan complexes centred on Los Angeles and New York remain the principal US destinations, followed at

some distance by Chicago, Houston, and Miami; these remain the five pre-eminent places for immigrant settlement. However, an array of cities have become or are emerging as new 'gateways', including Atlanta, Dallas, and Las Vegas, which had few foreign-born residents until the last decade or two (Singer, 2004).

Outward population shifts in US cities are not new and have long been associated with racial relations (e.g., 'white flight'). Although racialized minorities have increased significantly in numerous Canadian cities, there is absolutely no counterpart to the way that 'race' marks the US city. As of 2001, only seven CMAs have proportional shares of visible minorities greater than the national proportion of 13.4 per cent (Table 2.2). Only in the Toronto and Vancouver CMAs does the proportion of visible minorities exceed one-third. For the central cities of Vancouver and Toronto the visible minority proportion is 49 per cent and 43 per cent respectively,

Table 2.2   **Leading Metropolitan Areas for Visible Minorities, 2001**

CMA	% Visible Minority
Vancouver	36.9
Toronto	36.8
Abbotsford	17.8
Calgary	17.5
Edmonton	14.6
Ottawa–Hull	14.1
Montreal	13.6
Windsor	12.9
Winnipeg	12.5
Kitchener	10.7
Canada	13.4

Note: 'Visible minority' does not include Aboriginal Canadians.
Source: Statistics Canada, 2001 census.

indicating that visible minorities are somewhat more concentrated in the city, but also that there is not much difference from the overall CMA proportion. In fact, of the other 10 municipalities with more than one-third visible minorities, all but two are suburbs of Vancouver and Toronto. These suburbs are examples of 'ethnoburbs', a settlement pattern noted by Wei Li among the Chinese in Los Angeles (Li, 1998).

The seven leading CMAs (all above the national average) account for the vast majority (85 per cent) of all the visible minorities in Canada. Again, there are marked concentrations in the largest cities; 72 per cent of all visible minorities reside in the Toronto (43 per cent), Vancouver, (18 per cent), and Montreal (11 per cent) CMAs alone. Not surprisingly, then, racialized issues are most prominent on the public agenda in the local governments and neighbourhoods of these CMAs. At the same time, this also means that many Canadians living in smaller cities do not experience 'lived-in diversity' first-hand, or the social and cultural issues around immigration and racialization—especially controversial and divisive issues—except through the media. This places considerable moral responsibility on media owners and workers, and there is continued debate about representations of racialized groups and immigrants in the media (Abu-Laban and Garber, 2005; Henry and Tator, 2002).

In the US, 'race', often reduced to a black–white dualism, has been enormously important in most cities. This is made more complex by the incredible growth of Asian and Latino populations in the last two decades, especially significant in the rapidly growing metropolitan areas of the Southwest and Florida, as well as in New York City, Washington, DC, and Chicago. However, distinctive geographical patterns associated with the arrival of new groups overlay those resulting from the concentration of blacks in America's central cities. In 2000, 20 US central cities had majority black (mostly African-American) populations (Gary, at 85 per cent, Detroit, 82 per cent, and Birmingham, 74 per cent, had the largest proportions), and fully one-fifth of all central cities had

proportions above one-third, including Atlanta, St Louis, Cleveland, Chicago, and Philadelphia (in Canada only two central cities, Toronto and Vancouver, have visible minority populations greater than one-third). Increasingly, African Americans participate in suburbanization, but there is still segregation and they experience mortgage discrimination (Wyly and Hammel, 2004). There is nothing comparable in scale in Canada. The central city of Vancouver attracts many Asian immigrants and second-generation Asian Canadians, but only in a few small areas, such as Chinatown, does the concentration begin even to approach US levels of racial segregation. And Toronto is the only Canadian city with a substantial Afro-Caribbean population and their segregation from whites is not only low by American standards, it is lower than for other racialized groups (Myles and Hou, 2004). This suggests that while weaker than in the past in the US, the persistence of African-American segregation will continue to be an important cross-national difference. Similarly, while there is greater diversity than ever before in Canadian cities, nothing compares to the rapidly expanding Latino population in the US; Latinos are now a majority in 12 US central cities and represent 20 per cent or more in 36 others. Although their residential segregation from whites is not as pronounced as it is for African Americans, it is significant and points to the avoidance behaviour of whites, housing market discrimination, and a large poverty gap (see Pulido, 2000, for a Los Angeles example).

Inequality and Poverty

Socio-spatial polarization has been well-documented, especially in relation to extensive economic restructuring and its geographic outcomes. The debate over the extent of increasing inequality in industrial countries is complex. Economic inequality has increased in both countries in recent decades, although poverty rates in the US are higher. Over the most recent decade, attempts to balance public budgets have placed increased fiscal pressure on the welfare systems in each country, eroding or eliminating long-established support programs. One might thus expect more convergence in inequality. But the work of social economists Gottschalk and Smeeding (1997) indicates that whereas income inequality in the US rose significantly from the mid-1970s to the mid-1990s, there was actually a modest decrease in Canada from the mid-1970s to the mid-1980s, and no change through to the mid-1990s (their study is based on a summary of numerous national studies of 24 countries).

Using 1970s data, Goldberg and Mercer (1986: Table 7–12) created a ratio showing income disparity between the central city and the whole metropolitan area for both metropolitan systems; a ratio value of 100 means that central-city income equals that of the entire urban area (no disparity). The overall ratio value for the US was lower than in Canada, indicating greater internal disparity for US metropolitan areas. One-quarter of all the US cases showed acute disparity (they had ratios of 79 or lower), whereas no Canadian cases had such low ratios.

We repeated this analysis for 2000–1 and the cross national difference persists. Higher overall ratio values for median family income distinguished Canadian central cities (mean = 97; median = 99) from US cases (mean = 87; median = 90). Again, there is a clear distributional difference. Almost two-thirds (63 per cent) of the Canadian central cities have ratio values in the 90–9 range, with only 7 per cent below 80 and none under 70. In contrast, over 30 per cent of US central cities have values under 80, with 15 per cent under 70. As expected, proportionally more Canadian (8) than US (57) central cities had ratios exceeding 100. Economic segregation in Canadian cities is on the rise. A recent study found high levels of residential segregation based on income in prairie cities (Winnipeg, Saskatoon, and Regina), and among the three largest cities Montreal was the most economically segregated (Ross et al., 2004). Bourne (1993a) argues that the intra-geography of income goes beyond the rather arbitrary central city–suburban distinction in urban studies. Canadian central cities reveal continued, even deepening impoverishment, pronounced accumulation of wealth and expansion

of elite districts, and a remarkable persistence in both the location and composition of well-established high- and middle-income districts. This characterization does not fit the inner parts of most US urban areas (although undoubtedly some individual cities are a better fit—Seattle, Houston, Dallas, and Minneapolis–St Paul). An important factor in producing this complexity is the widespread construction of luxury as well as more modestly priced condominiums in Canada's central cities. Such construction means demolishing cheaper, often rental, housing and displacing its residents. And with a declining or static social housing sector without capacity to house such folk, homelessness and living in shelters is increasing, intensifying the view that Canadian cities are becoming more like US ones.

The simplistic city-versus-suburbs dichotomy distorts underlying urban realities that do not respect local government boundaries and homogenizes the suburbs at great analytical cost. Yet it is hard to see it disappearing from public discourse. It frames debates over fiscal health and equity issues concerning taxation and the financing of services. In the US context in particular, 'city' is too often an emotional signifier of a heavily racialized 'other' that white suburbanites avoid by distancing themselves in outer residential communities. Despite increasing urban 'revival', a steady diet of nightly local TV news paints a depressing picture of the city as a racially marked 'place left behind', replete with arson, violent crime, complaints over inadequate public services, and mounting fiscal problems (see Beauregard, 2003, on 'voices of decline').

Conclusion

Students of North American cities have to grapple with increasing variability and complexity within the metropolitan areas, which are principally the result of enormous economic transformations and social changes that are global in nature and impinge directly on open metropolitan systems. Some of the most fundamental changes are the shift away from manufacturing to a knowledge-based economy as the principal economic foundation for urban growth, and dramatic shifts in immigration source leading to complex social changes in both inner cities and suburban districts. Given the large scale of these transformations, the changes they produce are felt more or less equally in the metropolitan areas of Canada and the United States. This could result in greater similarities or convergence between the two sets of cities, a direction supported by some of the empirical evidence reviewed here.

Persistent cross-national differences have arisen over time as one society made different choices from the other. The United States experienced colonialism and then gained nationhood via revolutionary independence, whereas Canada experienced a gradual and still contested nationhood after a much longer colonial dependence. Canada became a resource-based economy tied to the prosperity of external markets, initially in Britain and then the US itself, while the United States grew into a significant industrial power and eventually a global power. Both countries expanded their territories—sometimes in conflict with each other—and both experienced massive inward population movements, but with different social consequences in subsequent social histories and geographies (French and English, as against black and white). These strategic choices—and the distinctive urban places those choices produced—occurred in the context of common and widely experienced processes. Canadians continue to desire to differentiate themselves from their huge neighbour despite increased and closer economic integration. But inherited urban forms, the social mores that shape interpersonal and inter-group relations, and the political culture and institutional structures all demonstrate effective resistance to continental homogenization. Thus, significant cross-national urban differences persist.

So while some assert that Canadians and Americans are becoming more alike under the imperatives of globalization and continental trade integration, an important contrary view is expressed by others, including Michael Adams (2003: 140). Based chiefly on cross-national surveys for 1992, 1996, and 2000, Adams provides strong evidence to

Figure 2.3   **The Public-Private Continuum**

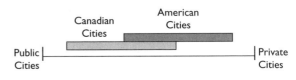

support his claim 'that the social values of the two countries are once again becoming more distinct, not melding as conventional wisdom would have it.'

We propose that the distinctiveness of Canadian cities continues—Canadian cities are more public in their nature and US ones are more private. But rather than these being sharply drawn polarities, there are both range and overlap along a public–private continuum anchored by ideal types (Figure 2.3). In proposing this continuum, we attempt to capture a series of characteristics that differentiate the American and Canadian contexts, including (1) the strong national commitment in the US to individualism and individual freedoms; (2) the protection of private property rights under the US Constitution; (3) the US reliance on private mechanisms and individual user fees in the provision of infrastructures, as well as certain public goods and services; (4) the emphasis on home ownership, especially of the single detached residence as the ideal type; and (5) the power of local autonomy in government, reflected in the still increasing profusion of special-purpose districts and small municipalities as extensions and expressions of relatively homogeneous social groupings. In a privatized society, problems are solved in a highly individualized manner. The conditions of daily life in many US central cities and certain metropolitan areas have led to withdrawal of certain groups to suburban and ex-urban places. This listing is partial but does convey the essence of the privatized city.

The public city is more attuned to Canadian values, ideologies, and practices. It expresses a strong commitment to a greater emphasis on collectivities over individuals (though perhaps this has weakened with the emphasis on individual rights and freedoms of the Canadian Charter of Rights and Freedoms); to the maintenance of social order and effective public practices over individual pursuits; to a greater trust and belief in the competence of governments and their bureaucracies (though this has clearly diminished in recent decades as the effectiveness of the public sector has been widely and relentlessly attacked by ideologues in Canada and elsewhere); and to the idea of active intervention in the chiefly private process of city making by city and suburban planners, some working for innovative forms of metropolitan government. Public cities are also places with a higher quality of urban development consistent with high servicing standards set by local authorities; they have extensive networks of high-quality public transportation systems, publicly funded schools, community centres, and quality parks and open spaces.

This key distinction owes much to the nature of state intervention rather than to the degree of intervention. Governments in the US have been extremely active in supporting private consumption and facilitating private (corporate) gain (although the latter is not uncommon in Canada). This is well illustrated by the vast expenditures on urban freeways that encourage private auto and truck use. By contrast, governments in Canada have adopted a more balanced approach to urban transportation, although this, too, may now be tilting away from the public transit sector in an effort to reduce public expenditures. The willingness of provincial governments to reorganize municipal governments to achieve regionally integrated forms means a more uniform distribution of municipal services and planning. With US state governments being more sensitive to 'home rule' arguments voiced by those opposed to metropolitan ('big, inefficient, remote') government and being unwilling in most cases to take the lead, sharp variations persist in service standards and property tax levels within metropolitan regions.

Over 25 years ago, the question was put: 'Is there a distinctive Canadian city?' (Kerr, 1977). While we avoid the singularity of the Canadian city, as it does not allow sufficiently for the inherent variability in Canadian cities, we answer confidently 'Yes, but . . .', for there is an important qualifier. While distinctive within their continental context, the North American character of Canadian cities

needs also to be acknowledged as they are inevitably and always open to continental and global interaction and influences.

Notes

1. We revisit certain findings of Goldberg and Mercer (1986) regarding North American comparisons. A fuller analysis than we can provide here is desirable (but see Zolnik, 2004).

2. A large literature develops the idea of family- and women-friendly cities. The argument is that multi-purpose, mixed-use, compact neighbourhoods mean greater proximity to services (and perhaps less reliance on cars), while higher densities provide sufficient concentrations of users to support a greater diversity and choice of services within a smaller geographic area (see Miranne and Young, 2000, for Canadian and US examples).

3. We calculated the types based on central-city boundaries that existed before the amalgamations of the late 1990s; for example, for Toronto we used the boundary for the city that existed before 1998.

4. Throughout this chapter we use 'race' in a fashion that is consistent with the position that the division of people into separate, distinct 'races' is a social construction, not a biological truism. Racialized and ethnicized identities are highly contested and socially significant (for example, inclusion within named categories has important effects in counting for national censuses), and consequently becomes important electorally and fiscally. Furthermore, the social construction of 'race' (and also ethnicity) means the naming of particular groups changes over time and space (for example, 'black' and 'African American' in American discourse, and 'Aboriginal', 'First Nations', 'Native', and 'Indian' in Canadian discourse). On the 1996 and 2001 long form Statistics Canada census survey on ethnic origins, a question asks: 'Is this person: White; Chinese; South Asian (e.g., East Indian, Pakistani, Punjabi, Sri Lankan, etc.); Black; Filipino; Latin American; Southeast Asian (e.g., Cambodian, Indonesian, Laotian, Vietnamese, etc.); Arab; West Asian (e.g., Armenian, Egyptian, Iranian, Lebanese, Moroccan); Japanese; Korean; or other (specify).' Debate continues over the appropriateness of descriptive categories (e.g., West Asian) to capture ethnicized identities and the political implications of collecting information about certain groups (e.g., 'Arabs').

Chapter 3

The Canadian Urban System: Growth and Transition

Jim Simmons and Larry McCann

From the first urban settlements of early seventeenth-century New France, to the present when nearly 80 per cent of Canadians live in a variety of urban places, urbanization has left an indelible mark on the social and economic development of Canada. Spatial processes such as inter-city trade and migration have transformed the urban makeup of the country. In fact, over the course of four centuries, Canada's towns, cities, and metropolitan centres—in short, its urban system—have served as bellwethers of colonial and national well-being. But at no time in Canada's development have urban places functioned independently. All are linked through an intricate geography, that is, by a space economy of core and periphery with regional, national, and global connections. Globally, Canada's urban centres are swayed by the changing world system that has evolved through various phases of mercantile, industrial, and post-industrial growth. Trade in staple commodities, manufactured goods, or producer services is enormously vital to the demographic and economic growth of individual centres. So, too, is the political economy of federal and provincial government spending, immigration policy, and other forms of public intervention (Savitch and Kantor, 2002). The net result is a Canadian urban system that is marked today by wide variations in the age, size, function, well-being, and livability of its component settlements (Simmons and Bourne, 2003).

Most prominently, Canada's space economy is now directed by a few large and rapidly growing metropolitan centres, in particular by Toronto, Montreal, and Vancouver (McCann, 1998). These centres continue to surge ahead of competitors, their central-city and suburban landscapes burgeoning in complexity, while most other urban places grow slowly or even suffer decline. For students of city structure, the urban system forms the context—the essential backdrop—against which any interpretation of the changing landscape of Canadian cities must be made. During the rise of the modern industrial city, for example, the landscapes of heartland manufacturing centres differed substantially from hinterland resource towns (consider an integrated steel complex as opposed to a solitary pulp mill). In the current era of post-industrial growth and transition, the central business districts and suburban downtowns of national and regional centres like Toronto, Vancouver, Montreal, Ottawa, and Calgary support—at disproportionate and higher levels—more producer-service functions than do the small and flagging business cores of peripheral places. As the economic and social structures of cities change, so do their landscapes (Ley, 1996a).

This chapter examines the geography of Canada's urban system. We first consider the basic conceptual, geographical, and structural properties of Canada's core-periphery urban system by addressing some fundamental questions: How is an urban system defined? What is the current level of urbanization in the major Canadian regions? What are the functions and sizes of cities found in today's core and periphery regions? What location factors influence these patterns? We then explore economic, demographic, and political or institutional aspects of the urbanization process, emphasizing selected examples of Canada's urban past. Subsequently, we describe newly gathered and comprehensive data that measure current features of growth and transition in Canada's urban system: the unevenness of its patterns of change; the spatial bias of demographic and economic trends; and the critically important role of the public economy in mediating urban well-being (Simmons and Bourne, 2004). The chapter closes with a discussion of projected and future growth possibilities.

The Core-Periphery Structure of Canada's Urban System

The all-embracing term 'urban system'—called 'system of cities' by some—includes many relationships and forces that affect the geography of urban centres. When an urban system is described in aggregate, the resulting structural characteristics are more or less the same for any developed country like Canada, including uneven patterns of growth and well-being within the context of a national space economy. Whatever pairing of terms is used to describe an urban system's space economy—core and periphery, heartland and hinterland, metropolis and hinterland, centre and margin, or developed and underdeveloped—geographers and other social scientists usually agree with Fernand Braudel's assertion that 'geographical space as a source of explanation affects all historical realities, all spatially-defined phenomena' (Braudel, 1984: 21).

Within countries distinguished by a core-periphery space economy, core regions are, of course, the more dominant spaces. They are characterized by a highly urbanized and concentrated population that forms a well-integrated regional system of urban places. Although overshadowed by global cities, most notably by New York and London, cities in Canada's heartland (in southern Ontario and Quebec) display a diversified profile of secondary, tertiary, and quaternary industries, as well as a complete division of labour (Coffey, 1994). Thanks to its large cities, core areas are well-advanced along the development path and possess the capacity for innovative change. Core regions are

also able to influence and control economic, social, and political decisions of national importance. They do so through the power of large corporations, which are usually headquartered in metropolitan centres, and by holding more legislative ridings in provincial legislatures and the federal Parliament. There is no guarantee of well-being for all heartland residents, but opportunities for personal advancement are more available in core areas than elsewhere. The least developed of peripheral regions are distinguished by opposite qualities: fewer economic opportunities; an emphasis on primary resource production; a more dispersed population; restricted innovative capacity; limited political power; specialized (and vulnerable) urban economies; and sometimes—particularly on Canada's east coast—weakly integrated urban systems. Although still peripheral, some Canadian regions, especially in central Alberta and southwestern British Columbia, have achieved attributes of core area status, distinguishing them from less developed regions (McCann, 1998).

The growth and well-being of any particular city, whether located in a heartland or hinterland region, depends on its relationships with other cities in other parts of its regional or national urban system, and increasingly with competitors and markets in the global system at large. Despite some unpredictability, growth impulses within the Canadian space economy are mostly felt in predictable ways. Big cities attract more growth than small ones. Nearby cities have greater impact than more distant ones. Some economic sectors are more localized than others, in the sense that inputs and outputs affect places located nearby. In most cases, though, the key linkages affecting growth and competition in a core-periphery system like Canada's accrue to national metropolitan centres, to regional commercial centres, and to provincial capitals. And like the regions to which they belong, the continued growth and well-being of any city is highly dependent on existing cumulative advantages associated with its size, its range of economic functions, and its place within the national space economy.

The Size and Function of Canadian Cities

At the opening of the twenty-first century, 79.4 per cent of Canada's 30 million people resided in urban places—defined here as cities with a population greater than 10,000.[1] In the latest census year, 2001, Statistics Canada identified 140 such places. Although these centres occupy very little space, they house most of the country's economic, socio-cultural, and political strength. The census metropolitan areas (CMAs) and census agglomeration areas (CAs) that comprise Canada's urban system are shown in Figure 3.1. The map reveals clear core-periphery differences within the Canadian ecumene of settlement and production. The term 'ecumene' refers to areas settled and exploited (or worked) by a country's labour force. The nation-wide distribution pattern shows a dominant core area in the Great Lakes–St Lawrence Lowlands region (also referred to as the industrial heartland, or the Windsor–Quebec City corridor or axis); the resource ecumene (the Canadian Shield and eastern and most of western Canada); and the largely uninhabited zones or non-ecumene of the North.

The urban features of these generalized zones are summarized in Table 3.1. The most intense concentration is found in the Windsor–Quebec City corridor that envelops the country's two largest urban nodes: Toronto and Montreal. Most of the country's manufacturing and post-industrial activity occurs in this zone, yielding a population density exceeding 100 people per square km. The

Figure 3.1   **Urban Places in the Canadian Urban System, 2001**

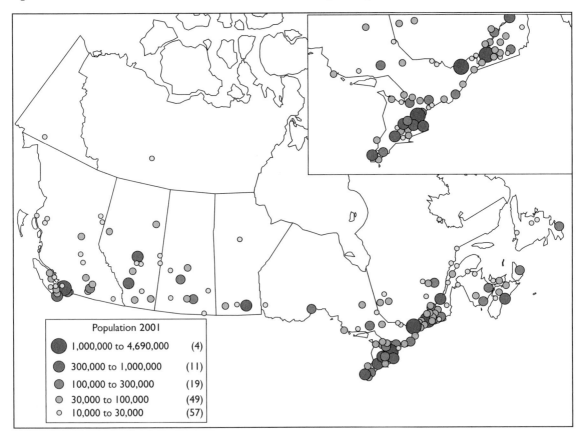

Population 2001
- 1,000,000 to 4,690,000   (4)
- 300,000 to 1,000,000   (11)
- 100,000 to 300,000   (19)
- 30,000 to 100,000   (49)
- 10,000 to 30,000   (57)

Table 3.1   **Regions of Urbanization, Canada, 2001**

Region	Area (sq. km)	Population (000s)	Population Density (sq. km)	Number of Cities	Urban Population (000s)	Percentage Urban
Windsor–Quebec City Corridor	166,500	16,665	100.1	51	14,655	87.9
Remainder of Ecumene	920,000	9,756	10.6	45	7,650	78.4
Total Ecumene	1,086,500	26,421	24.3	96	22,305	84.4
Non-Ecumene	7,925,700	3,586	0.452	44	1,534	42.8
Total Canada	9,012,100	30,007	3.33	140	23,839	79.4
United States Context*	3,086,200	131,250	42.5	101	101,814	77.6

*The United States context is defined as those states located within 500 km of Canada: Washington, Oregon, Idaho, Montana, Wyoming, North Dakota, South Dakota, Minnesota, Wisconsin, Illinois, Indiana, Michigan, Ohio, Pennsylvania, New York, New Jersey, Maryland, West Virginia, Virginia, Connecticut, Massachusetts, Rhode Island, Vermont, New Hampshire, and Maine (but not Alaska). Note that only those cities over 100,000 population are included.

Sources: Statistics Canada, 2001 *census;* US Bureau of the Census, *Census of Population, 2000* (Washington: Government Printing Office).

51 cities found in this national core region house almost half of Canada's total population. Producing both manufactured goods and financial and producer services, they compete fiercely for investment capital that creates new jobs (Yeates, 1998a). By contrast, in the resource ecumene population density is roughly one-tenth that of the industrial heartland. Smaller core areas, including the Georgia Basin region in southwestern British Columbia and the Edmonton–Calgary corridor in Alberta, organize the population and economic activities of surrounding resource hinterlands. During the late twentieth century, these peripheral core areas garnered increasing strength and well-being, but their prominence in economic activity and metropolitan power still ranks below the central Canadian heartland. Many cities in the resource ecumene remain focused on basic service functions or the processing of primary commodities. But the post-industrial economies of some—especially Vancouver, Calgary, and Edmonton—have matured to the point where

they market financial and producer services to expanding global markets. The area beyond the resource ecumene—the non-ecumene—includes some urban places but very little urbanization. Settlements are small and widely dispersed in northern Canada. Functionally, they serve mainly the local community and some remote and distant customers.

The core-periphery distinctiveness of Canada's urban system is further illustrated by differentiating cities that serve the primary sector from those that produce manufactured goods. Also noteworthy are those places supported by the public sector (Figure 3.2). Urban-centred regions in the Windsor–Quebec City corridor have traditionally produced goods and services for the entire Canadian market, taking advantage of external (urbanization and localization) economies and the savings associated with transfer economies and relative market accessibility. The manufacture of producer and consumer goods for the domestic market was aided historically

Figure 3.2   **Economic Specialization of Canadian Cities in 2001**

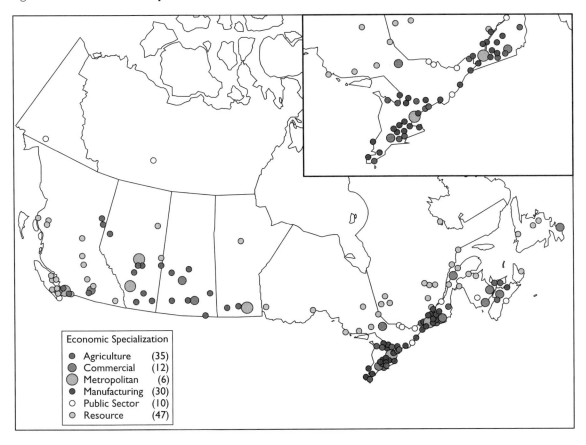

Economic Specialization
- ● Agriculture   (35)
- ● Commercial   (12)
- ● Metropolitan   (6)
- ● Manufacturing (30)
- ○ Public Sector   (10)
- ● Resource   (47)

by protective tariffs, but this situation has changed. Following the free trade agreements of the late 1980s and early 1990s (e.g., the North American Free Trade Agreement), central Canadian cities are becoming increasingly linked to manufacturing centres in adjacent parts of the United States, jointly serving North American customers. Globalization is also a new reality for these core manufacturing places. In their search for world markets, they increasingly share attributes with manufacturing towns and cities across the periphery, which continue to emphasize the export of primary and secondary resource products to the United States, Europe, or Asia (e.g., natural gas, lumber, and pulp and paper).

Networks of Connection

Interdependence among places is a central feature of any urban system, shaping the geographic patterns of core and periphery. The size of cities and their location in the space economy generate uneven flows of information, migrants, and capital among cities; and economic diversification requires adjusting flows of goods and services to satisfy consumers. In fact, the patterns of interactions and integration reveal the essential geographic features of the Canadian urban system. Consider, for instance, the movement among cities by means of air travel (Figure 3.3). Most moves happen between a few centres that are very large and located nearby. Thus,

Figure 3.3   **Air Passenger Flows within Canada, 1999**

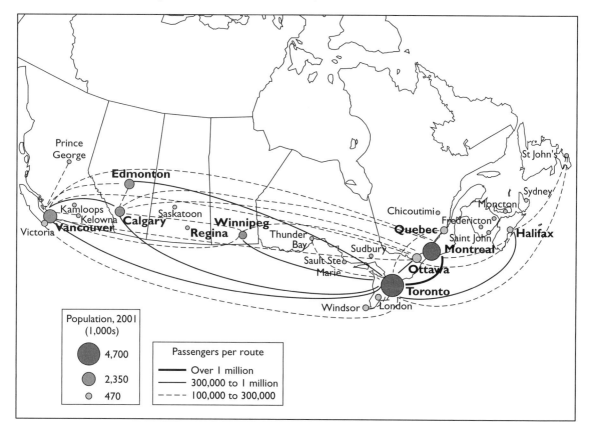

Victoria connects with Vancouver, Edmonton with Calgary, Ottawa with Toronto, and Quebec City with Montreal. But the pull of the metropolis is even stronger. St John's, Halifax, Saint John, Winnipeg, and other leading provincial centres are linked most strongly with Toronto, no longer Montreal. This hierarchical pattern of inter-city interaction is widely observed in most industrial societies, with minor variations shaped by the relative importance of city size and distance.[2]

Simmons (1986) argues that three subsystems or networks of connections—economic, demographic, and political—capture most of the linkages that shape Canada's core-periphery structure and

growth patterns in the urban system (Table 3.2). Interaction within the *economic subsystem* measures production and consumption processes, such as the movement of raw materials to global markets or the flow of manufactured goods and producer services to consumers. As a system, change in one place is transmitted to other cities, whether located nearby or far away, according to the strength of their linkages with that place. For Canada, this subsystem is the one most open to external influences and the one most rapidly changing. It is also the most vulnerable to cyclical business fluctuations, yielding highly variable economic growth rates through time and across space.

Table 3.2   **Types of Inter-City Linkages**

Type of Subsystem	Examples	Characteristic Patterns
Cultural/demographic	Migration, information flows, telephone calls, airline passengers	Proportional to city size and distance Reduced flows across national and linguistic boundaries Depending on content, larger centres attract more flows (migration) or generate more flows (information)
Economic activity	Commodities, manufacturing products, consumer goods, financial products	High volume of continuing flows reflect overall activity Roughly symmetrical Specialized flows (commodities, automobiles, other production systems)
Public sector	Taxes, provincial and municipal transfers, pensions, welfare, employment insurance, health and education, government wages	Roughly 50 per cent of GNP Spatial variability shaped by the different responsibilities of each level of government Net flows from larger, richer places to smaller and poorer regions

The *demographic subsystem* measures flows of people and information. Though sensitive to economic impulses, the demographic network usually responds slowly to economic change. In fact, local demographic structures are always struggling to keep up with shifts in the economy. While changes in economic conditions—especially jobs—determine the location of urban population growth, there is usually a fairly long response time to the restructuring of the urban system. True, in resource-based regions there might be a sudden exodus of workers from a declining town, especially a single-enterprise resource community that abruptly closes its only mill or mine. But this is the exception, not the rule (Bradbury, 1984). The slow population reaction to economic descent is exemplified by the perseverance of long-declining manufacturing towns in the Maritimes—places like Sydney (steel), Amherst (railway cars), and New Glasgow–Trenton (metal products). Here, the gritty landscapes of

abandoned factories emphasize the fact that urban places mirror the larger urban system (Wynn, 1998). Likewise, as pointed out in subsequent discussion, fast-growing areas must rely on migration or immigration to sustain immediate employment growth impulses.

The *political subsystem* as a network of city connections refers to the movement of political influence and the exchange of money both within and among political jurisdictions. Movement and exchange are illustrated by tax revenues that flow to governments from firms and individuals and by transfer payments and services that flow in other directions (Davis, 1996; Simmons, 1984). This subsystem is more closed than open, with connections moving through the urban hierarchy from Ottawa or the provincial capitals to other places in the national urban system: connections are seldom international. Different levels of government (especially federal and provincial) redistribute funds in an attempt to mediate tensions between economic change and the resistant, more immobile demographic structure. Traditionally, this has been accomplished largely through federal policies that support declining regions by taxing areas of growth—i.e., a kind of subsidization of geography. From one point of view (Courchene, with Telmer, 1998), these fiscal measures actually slow down the response to economic innovation and prevent the national economy from achieving its full potential. From another, more liberal, viewpoint (Savoie, 1992), these programs are the necessary relief systems for people suffering the effects of unpredictable economic changes through no fault of their own. They represent counter shifts in financial support that ultimately, according to Kent (1997), should benefit both regional and national economies.

Within the context of the political subsystem, it is important to remember that Canada's provinces are also important units of spatial variation. Comparison of British Columbia to Ontario, or of Alberta to Newfoundland, reveals considerable differences in urban system features such as population size, growth rates, and urbanization levels (Table 3.3). Different, too, are the sources of revenues that provinces generate from various taxes and from federal transfer payments. Clearly, provinces in Atlantic Canada are much more dependent on transfer payments than more prosperous provinces like Alberta, Ontario, and British Columbia, whose economies (measured by gross domestic product, or GDP) are among the largest in the country. It is no coincidence that Canada's largest urban places are found in the provinces

Table 3.3   **The Provinces**

Measure	BC	Alta	Sask.	Man.	Ont.	Que.	NB	NS	PEI	Nfld-Lab.	Canada
Size Variation											
Population, 2001 (000s)	3,908	2,975	979	1,120	11,410	7,238	730	908	135	513	30,007
Percentage growth 1991–2001	19.1	16.9	−1.0	2.5	13.1	5.0	0.8	0.9	4.2	−9.8	9.9
Per cent urban	86.2	75.7	56.9	66.6	87.0	78.4	52.7	63.3	55.0	46.5	79.4
Largest city	Vancouver	Calgary	Saskatoon	Winnipeg	Toronto	Montreal	Saint John	Halifax	Charlottetown	St John's	Toronto
Population of largest city (000s)	1,987	951	225	671	4,683	3,426	123	359	58	173	4,683
GDP, 2001 ($billions)	126.2	123.1	30.7	33.1	437.6	217.8	19.2	26.6	3.1	12.5	1,038.8
GDP per capita ($000s)	32.3	41.4	31.4	29.6	38.4	30.1	26.3	29.3	22.9	24.3	34.6
Provincial Revenues (per cent)											
Income tax	20.7	17.8	16.8	19.3	28.1	31.8	16.4	20.2	14.1	15.6	25.1
Corporate tax	4.0	9.3	3.4	3.6	9.1	4.4	3.0	3.3	2.8	2.1	6.3
Sales tax	33.7	17.5	33.3	28.9	40.6	35.0	27.7	26.6	30.0	26.7	33.4
Resources	19.6	40.8	19.1	17.4	4.2	6.2	13.5	6.8	6.4	7.6	12.4
Federal transfers	12.3	8.7	23.1	27.4	11.4	16.3	36.2	37.9	42.5	43.1	16.4

Source: Statistics Canada, *Census of Canada,* 2001.

with the strongest economies and the most advanced levels of urbanization.

Urban Interaction and Integration

The amount and degree of interaction among cities are important features of an urban system. Regional differences in the Canadian space economy shape complex flows of capital, labour, and goods between cities. Within the Windsor–Quebec City corridor, many cities are closely interconnected, more so than in other parts of Canada. Here, manufacturing inputs and semi-finished producer goods move frequently and readily from one place to another, or to nearby American factories, but seldom to peripheral places. Shipments within the core are facilitated by a dense network of highways, railroads, and water routes (Yeates, 1998a). Despite recent setbacks wrought by changes in the global production system, the manufacture of automobiles and their parts still exemplifies the basic integrative features of central Canada's urban system. Steel and plastics from Hamilton and Sarnia are fabricated into various car parts—e.g., bodies, axles, engines, dashboards, bumpers, distributor caps—in a number of Ontario and Quebec cities. They are then shipped to assembly plants in Alliston, Cambridge, Oakville, Oshawa, and Windsor, or across the border into Michigan or Ohio. In other manufacturing sectors, after a period of uncertainty and adjustment fostered by recent free trade agreements and corporate restructuring, growth and expansion continue, led by both new and renewed industrial sectors such as telecommunication products and pharmaceuticals (Britton, 1996). Beyond this resurgence, the most significant economic upswing has been fuelled by specialized post-industrial activities. Producer-service industries like bio-medical research, global financial services, and cultural and educational activities are very important. Job creation associated with the post-industrial economy is concentrated in southern Ontario's largest cities, notably in Toronto.

Across the periphery, staple products continue to support regional specialization, but with mixed results. Most successful is Alberta, thanks to income flowing from its reserves of oil, natural gas, and tar sands (Pratt and Richards, 1979). Less important are offshore oil and gas in Newfoundland and Nova Scotia, minerals and pulp and paper in the Maritimes and the Canadian Shield, and lumber and pulp and paper in coastal and interior British Columbia. Early in the twenty-first century, mad cow disease and weather-plagued wheat yields have depressed agricultural production in Saskatchewan, Manitoba, and Alberta. The output of resource industries in the periphery remains targeted for American and other international markets. Because bulky products move out of Canada by the most direct route to minimize transportation costs, urban integration within the resource hinterland is quite limited. Peripheral networks are therefore connected externally, seldom internally. Conversely, the control and management of resource production remain highly centralized in a few core centres. Within Canada, these include Toronto, Montreal, Calgary, and Vancouver. Externally, global cities like New York, London, and Tokyo are the all-important control points (Sassen, 1991; Semple, 1996).

Boundaries and the Urban System

Discussion of networks of connection and the degree of network openness suggests that boundaries are an integral part of Canada's urban system. But the significance of boundaries has changed over time. To understand the historical dimensions of urbanization, at least before the early twentieth century, it made sense to study cities within a regional context (McCann and Smith, 1991). At mid-century, a national system was clearly in place (Davies and Donoghue, 1993). Today, if current changes in the world economy persist, it might be necessary to take a continental or even global—rather than a national—approach. To be sure, the economy operates at an international scale, with corporate, financial, and production systems connecting many countries. But the demographic (e.g., migration) and political (e.g., fiscal transfers and taxation) components of the Canadian urban system are still national in scope. Consider, for example, the fact that linkages associated with air travel between Canada and the United States are only one-tenth the magnitude of flights within Canada for cities of comparable size and distance apart. International migration is still less frequent than the interprovincial movement of Canadians. And almost all activities of the political subsystem stop at the border. Indeed, the properties of the national border—that is, its permeability to various flows of information, money, people, and goods—are of enormous importance to the functioning of the urban system. Maintaining a boundary is one of the most important actions carried out by the federal government. Without the national border, the Canadian urban system would likely disappear as a distinct entity and blend into a larger North American system. For now, a national urban system prevails.

Despite this reality, in spite of international security issues, or regardless of nationalist sentiments about continental integration, the United States is an immense presence that simply cannot be ignored. Figure 3.4 emphasizes this contextual relationship by drawing attention to the population distribution within the United States. The United States includes over 280 million people and at least 250 cities with populations of more than 100,000 people. The American presence is almost 10 times the size of the Canadian population and economy. These American cities provide markets for industrial goods and act as sources of finance, recreation,

Figure 3.4   **Urban Places in Canada and the United States**

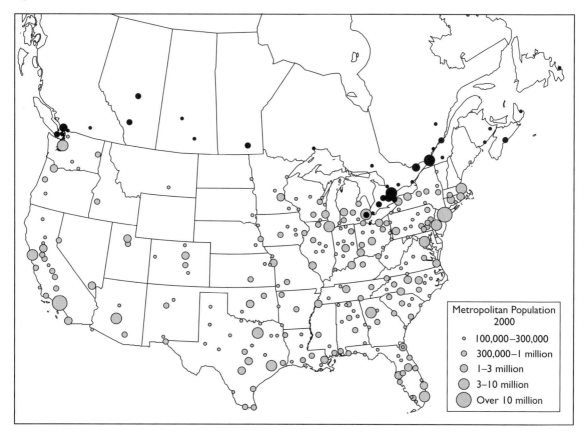

Metropolitan Population
2000

∘   100,000–300,000
◦   300,000–1 million
◯   1–3 million
◯   3–10 million
◯   Over 10 million

and information (via TV, radio, magazines, and newspapers) for the people and businesses of the Canadian urban system. Without these connections, the Canadian urban system would be profoundly different. As it is, the landscapes of Canadian cities are heavy with American branch businesses and franchises of all types, including department stores, fast-food outlets, auto dealerships, gas stations, movie chains, factories, banks, and brokerage houses.

Urbanization and the Canadian Urban System

Urbanization in all its dimensions has shaped the evolving geography of Canada's urban pattern. The process itself can be defined from several perspectives (Stelter, 1990): structurally or economically, demographically, and behaviourally.

Structurally or economically. Urbanization is expressed by the growth of cities, the emerging settlement hierarchy, and the changing economic relationships between urban places. For example, in Canada, the regional sequence of settlement and urban system development—hence the founding of towns and cities—has proceeded roughly in an east-to-west direction beginning in Quebec (seventeenth century), followed by the Maritimes (mid-eighteenth century), southern Ontario (early nineteenth century), and more recently western Canada (late nineteenth century). A scattering of mining and pulp and paper towns emerged across the southern edge of the Canadian Shield in the late nineteenth and early twentieth centuries. Concurrently, industrialization intensified the urban pattern of central Canada and parts of the Maritimes.

Demographically. Urbanization occurs when a region becomes more urban, that is, by increasing its proportion of people residing in urban places relative to the total population of the region. At Confederation, the urbanization level had not quite reached 20 per cent. The 50 per cent threshold was achieved just after World War I, as industrialization

made its mark. By the early twenty-first century the urbanization level was holding constant at nearly 80 per cent.

Behaviourally. Urbanism represents a growing way of life. Seemingly a paradox, 'counter-urbanization' (Chapter 13) illustrates the behavioural perspective and explains why Canada's urbanization level has recently stabilized at the threshold point of 80 per cent while urbanism continues to increase. Counter-urbanization is the tendency for people to escape cities and take up residence in nearby rural areas or small towns, even though they will usually commute daily to workplaces in a large, nearby city. In advanced economies, large cities tend to experience certain diseconomies, sometimes encouraging people to seek residence elsewhere. The strength of the metropolitan economy is not diminished by counter-urbanization, but it does change the spatial patterns of social integration around large cities and it has huge impacts on the environment (see Part 6 in this book).

Although a country's system of urban places maintains fundamental properties during the course of urbanization—e.g., core and periphery, a hierarchical structure, the power of metropolitan centres—the spatial pattern of the Canadian urban system has been marked by critical historic events or junctures that have given new shape and direction to this system. Three very powerful examples can be considered: the basic economic and system-defining impact of staple production; the demographic force of immigration on turn-of-the-century settlement and urban growth in the Prairie provinces; and the political effect of Canada's National Policy of incentives and tariff protection on the nineteenth-century industrialization of central Canada and the subsequent deindustrialization of the Maritimes. Together with the contemporary period of globalization and post-industrial growth, which we consider in the last section of this chapter (see also Chapter 4), each of these events or junctures was responsible for bringing about spatial transformation within the Canadian urban system.

Staples and Economic Networks

The sequence of discovering and developing various staple commodities over long periods of time—the early cod fishery, timber, coal and hard-rock mining, wheat, pulp and paper, natural gas, and oil—has indelibly and forever shaped the geographic character of Canadian urbanization (Harris, 1974). Strongly affected, for example, are distinctive settlement patterns, the size and specialized functions of urban places, the necessity of export-oriented transportation systems, and the degree of regional well-being.[3] Take the case of Atlantic Canada's cod fishery, which for the past four centuries has been geared to export markets located mainly and successively in the West Indies, Southern Europe, and the United States. The nature of the staple is such that it creates some backward linkages but few forward linkages or ones of a final-demand nature. As a result, fishing settlements across Atlantic Canada are scattered along the coast in relation to inshore and offshore fishing grounds. Moreover, these settlements have remained quite small and poorly integrated within the local urban system. Their viability has always been subject to fluctuating incomes as the catch rises or falls and markets for fish expand or contract. But the recent collapse of the cod stocks has brought a virtual halt to a certain kind of commercial fishing that threatens the foundation of many communities (Muise et al., 1993).

In contrast to fishing, coal and base-metal production gained momentum through the nineteenth century in response to changing mining technologies, increased accessibility aided by railroad construction, and, of course, rising national and even continental and world demand. Similar forces pushed the lumber, pulp and paper, oil, and natural gas industries to the forefront of Canadian economic development in early twentieth-century British Columbia and the Canadian Shield. Coal-mining settlements in the Maritimes, Alberta, and British Columbia and their hard-rock counterparts across the Canadian Shield were necessarily fixed in space. Clusters of specialized company towns developed at pit head, served by railroads built across coalfields or mineral deposits. Unfortunately, the depletion of the mineral base could mean the collapse of the resource-town economy. This has been much less likely to happen in lumber and pulp and paper towns because forests are a renewable resource, although the efficiencies achieved from technological change have led to a smaller workforce or even to the shutting down of obsolete plants. Forest communities are also small in size—few have more than 10,000 people—but are much more scattered across Canada, whether fronting British Columbia tidewater sites on the Pacific Ocean, stretching across the boreal forest in the Prairie provinces and Ontario and Quebec, or seeking Atlantic Canada's fall zone (for hydroelectric power). They continue functioning today wherever forests provide wood for saw and pulp mills, their location determined as well by rivers supplying access and power, and further by the size of allotments for wood harvesting (Marchak, 1995). Even the natural gas and oil towns of Alberta, Saskatchewan, and British Columbia share the standard settlement features of staples production: orientation to mineral deposits (that is, oil and gas fields), a specialized economic base, an export focus, small population size, and, frequently, transience in the town's social order (Pratt and Richards, 1979).

Each staple network shapes its own distinctive settlement pattern within Canada's 'hinterland'. As part of the larger urban system, staple-based towns and cities share common ground: control by external and often foreign corporations; low position in the urban hierarchy; volatile growth through periods of boom and bust; and dependency on export markets. The planned landscapes of many resource towns have been engineered by multinational corporations to ensure a stable labour force (McCann, 1980). When functioning at full production, staple-based industries yield good wages that ensure family well-being. But resource towns are among the least stable of Canada's urban communities. Abandoned settlements record the difficulties faced by these communities—e.g., resource depletion, shifts in consumer preferences, and falling commodity prices. Nonetheless, even today they remain as one of the most distinctive features of the Canadian urban system. Collectively, they affect the growth patterns of the regional centres that supply them with goods and services; in turn, they are shaped by the decision-making power of metropolitan-based corporations.

Demographic Networks and Western Settlement

The mobility of labour, such as the movement of immigrants or migrants to a newly opened resource frontier or to industrializing cities, is a powerful demographic agent of urbanization. Depending on the resources or industries that initially attract settlement, immigration will shape the demographic network in particular and significant ways. Canada's urban development was profoundly influenced historically by the movement of hundreds of thousands of Western and Eastern European immigrants to the Prairie region at the opening of the twentieth century (c. 1896–1913). Shaped by the federal government's decision to encourage agricultural settlement, this burst of immigration spurred the so-called 'wheat boom', triggering the highest rate of urbanization in Canadian history (Artibise, 1981; Voisey, 1975). Moreover, the 'boom' significantly affected a number of central and western Canadian cities, tying sectors of their economies to the development of western agriculture—e.g., Hamilton and Ottawa (farm machinery and government) and Saskatoon and Calgary (wholesaling).

Winnipeg was the 'gateway city' for western Canada's expanding agricultural hinterland. Through it passed most of the immigrants, capital, and goods and materials destined for the developing West, as well as many of the agricultural products bound for eastern Canadian and European markets. Winnipeg's heritage-designated wholesaling district and its remaining examples of early twentieth-century Edwardian bank and office buildings record this period of rapid development. The movement of immigrants through the city and onto prairie homesteads was formulated by government policy-makers in Ottawa but directed by local federal officials in Winnipeg. The city's banking, wholesaling, and transportation sectors were connected primarily through branch businesses of financial, distribution, and industrial corporations based in Montreal and Toronto (McCann and Smith, 1991).

The size and spacing of urban places that emerged in the West were influenced by the federal government's township survey system, by the space-extensive form of agriculture (e.g., grains, cattle), and by the location of railway depots serving export-oriented agricultural production. In the small towns and larger cities that quickly grew across the Prairie region, the services of central places prevailed over manufacturing activities, even flour milling and meat-packing (Kerr et al., 1991; MacLachlan, 2001).

The opening of the West stands as one of the more remarkable historical examples of how the urban system was shaped by political and demographic processes. Major cities of the West experienced phenomenal growth. Between 1901 and the 1931, for instance, Winnipeg climbed from 42,000 to 219,000 people; Edmonton and Calgary from 4,000 each to 79,000 and 84,000, respectively; and Vancouver—which shared in the growth of the Prairie region chiefly by supplying it lumber and exporting its grain—rose from 26,000 to nearly 300,000 (Table 3.4). In the process, Canada's urban system was extended from coast to coast, and its spatial form became indelibly structured during this country-wide transformation. A host of factors—external demand for staple products, immigration, technological change, transportation innovations, government policies—shaped the growth of the early twentieth-century urban system.

Heartland Growth and Hinterland Decline: The National Policy, Industrialization, and Deindustrialization

The political subsystem, it will be recalled, primarily involves the spatial impact of government policies and financial flows (e.g., transfer payments). In

Table 3.4   **Changing Population of Canada's Largest Urban Places, 1901–2001**

	Population (000s)				
	1901	1931	1961	1996	2001
Toronto	208	631	1,824	4,264	4,684
Montreal	268	819	2,110	2,921	3,426
Vancouver	26	297	790	1,832	1,987
Ottawa	60	127	930	1,010	1,064
Edmonton	4	79	338	863	938
Calgary	4	84	250	822	951
Quebec City	69	131	358	672	683
Winnipeg	42	219	265	667	671
Hamilton	53	156	395	557	662
London	38	71	181	399	432
Kitchener	10	31	155	383	414
St Catharines	10	25	84	372	371
Halifax	41	59	93	333	359
Victoria	21	39	154	304	312
Windsor	12	63	193	378	308
Oshawa	4	23	62	269	296
Saskatoon	—	43	96	219	226
Regina	2	53	112	194	193
St John's	29	39	91	174	173
Sudbury	2	19	111	160	155
Chicoutimi–Jonquière	4	12	32	160	154
Sherbrooke	12	29	67	147	154
Trois-Rivières	10	35	53	140	138
Saint John	41	98	64	126	123

Source: Statistics Canada, *Census of Canada,* various years.

the interest of the 'public good', the federal government has, at crucial stages in Canada's urban-industrial development, established policies that have directly shaped the spatial character of growth in the urban system. A number of these actions were implemented in the years immediately after Confederation, including policies that encouraged

province-building, established the Canadian Pacific Railway, set the regulations for the Canadian branch banking system, and specified the National Policy of industrial incentives and tariffs to foster and protect Canadian manufacturing. The National Policy had long-standing impacts, affecting the organization of the urban system for over a century until the recent North American Free Trade Agreement (Williams, 1994). The tariffs created a metaphorical wall around the country, designed to encourage domestic production and discourage reliance on imports. By defining a captive domestic market (particularly in the periphery), these measures supported a Canadian manufacturing region, the industrial heartland, and a transportation and distribution system to serve it. To be sure, investment in infrastructure, such as railways and urban utilities, generated economic development in the periphery, but in doing so it also increased the demand for high-value-added goods, further spurring the growth of central Canadian manufacturers, wholesalers, and transportation companies. By adopting the policies of a free-market system but within a closed market supported by generous subsidies, these government actions favoured the continued concentration of urban growth at the core of the space economy.

Industrialization lay at the heart of late nineteenth-century and subsequent twentieth-century urbanization in the central provinces. Towns and cities began to specialize in certain products. Steel came from Hamilton; automobiles from Windsor, Oshawa, and Oakville; rubber from Kitchener; plastics from Sarnia; textiles from Sherbrooke. Urban industrial development was aided and abetted by many other economic and geographic factors operating within the context of the National Policy. These include: agglomeration economies that encouraged linked activities; a skilled labour force; access to regional markets that reduced production costs and in turn made long-distance shipping across Canada more bearable; proximity to the United States manufacturing belt, which encouraged the proliferation of American branch plants; the availability of raw materials and producer goods; and cheap hydroelectric power and later natural gas. By the close of World War II, the consolidation of urban-industrial strength in the Windsor–Quebec City corridor was an unmistakable and established reality (Kerr, 1998).

But consolidation and concentration in the industrial heartland carried a price: the deindustrialization and subsequent prolonged indigence of the Maritimes, now Canada's least urbanized region. Yet, the Maritimes had shown strong promise for urban development through the late nineteenth century when various National Policy incentives fostered considerable growth (Acheson, 1972). From the mid-nineteenth century, coal from Cape Breton and Pictou County fuelled factories and dwellings in the St Lawrence region; and by 1882, Canada's first steel enterprise emerged in Nova Scotia's Pictou County. Small towns like New Glasgow, Amherst, and Moncton made the transition from mercantile to industrial capitalism. For a brief span, their steel mills, railway car plants, and textile factories were prominent on the national stage. But the urban system was fragmented, poorly integrated, and weakly led by its regional centres. Halifax and Saint John battled strenuously with each other, not as major industrial or financial centres, but as potential national ports competing for products of distant markets.

The region's urban-industrial base collapsed with devastating effects in the 1920s. The cumulative disadvantages of earlier business takeovers by Montreal corporations, the new Toronto outreach of branch businesses, a peripheral location and marginal resource base, regressive government policies (e.g., severe cuts in rail and industrial incentives), and hesitant investors, among other factors, caused industries to close and many towns to lose population. Rather than move into towns and cities, many Maritimers chose to retain a small farm and work a seasonal round of rural (and sometimes urban) activities to earn a livelihood. Such pluralistic patterns of work and residence help to explain the limited urbanization of the region even today (McCann, 1994). Bucking this trend, Halifax, Saint John, Moncton, and a few other cities attracted the region's young and footloose, but few immigrants. No urban centre controlled the regional economy.

Only in the 1970s and 1980s (and continuing today) did Halifax emerge as a place of singular importance, although dependent still on external metropolitan centres.

The Metropolitan Factor: Montreal vs Toronto

Within the emerging urban system, a few cities—particularly Montreal and Toronto—grew as power centres in the late nineteenth and early twentieth centuries to control hinterland markets, to attract the majority of urban-bound immigrants, and to use the political process to their definite advantage. Montreal occupied the top position in the urban hierarchy well into the twentieth century, growing rapidly from 268,000 in 1901 to over 819,000 in 1931 (Table 3.4). As Canada's metropolis, it dominated the transportation, manufacturing, trade, and financial sectors of the country. Its entrepreneurs organized these sectors through branch businesses to control much of the Maritimes, the West, Quebec of course, and even parts of Ontario (McCann and Smith, 1991). Montreal possessed many locational advantages, including an initial advantage and accessibility to markets and materials offered by the Great Lakes–St Lawrence system, an efficient and low-wage labour force, access to capital markets, and strong personal and business connections to the political complex of subsidies and industrial incentives.

The competition to topple Montreal's supremacy came mainly from Toronto, particularly after World War I, when the Ontario city reorganized its stock market to tackle the need to finance industrial development in many new manufacturing sectors (e.g., industrial machinery, home appliances, and chemicals). Toronto also took advantage of new business strategies associated with the rise of managerial capitalism. For example, access to the American manufacturing belt, facilitated by proximity and a common language, helped Toronto attract American branch manufacturing plants. As the twentieth century progressed, Toronto's Canadian-controlled corporations reached deep into the hinterland, becoming leading agents in the wholesale and retail sectors, organizing resource development across the Canadian Shield, and expanding financial, insurance, and banking networks to compete successfully against Montreal (McCann and Smith, 1991).

Toronto and Montreal are Canada's largest metropolitan centres. They have long set the pace for many features of the metropolitan lifestyle that give character to the social and cultural fabric of the country. While local traits are important, giving regional distinctiveness to peripheral cities, there can be little doubt that Toronto and Montreal have affected patterns of consumption in fields such as publishing, architecture, and radio and television programming. The features they promote have been widely adopted throughout the country—albeit sometimes begrudgingly, because that is the nature of Canadian regionalism. It must be remembered, of course, that even Toronto and Montreal fall under the larger orbit of economic and cultural influences stemming from such first-order global cities as New York and London, and even those of a second order: Paris, Los Angeles, and Chicago. But internally, just as Toronto surpassed Montreal to earn first rank in the Canadian urban hierarchy, other Canadian cities are stepping to the fore. Increasingly, Vancouver, Calgary, Edmonton, and other regional centres are joining in the organization of vast resource hinterlands, formulating distinctive cultures, and tapping more and more directly into the new global economy. In Canada, as in any urban system, power centres at the top of the hierarchy have been dealt the controlling national economic, cultural, and political development cards.

Recent Growth Trends in the Canadian Urban System

Even as Canada embraces post-industrialism, processes that have shaped Canada's urbanization since Confederation continue to influence the urban system, but with rather different consequences. This section begins with an overview of recent population growth trends in Canada. The pattern demonstrates that urban growth can no longer be taken for granted, because many smaller industrial towns and traditional service centres are losing population. An examination of various growth processes—demographic, economic, and public-sector driven—reveals trends that will determine the amount and location of future urban growth. Underlying many of the potential changes is the relentless advance of globalization (Chapter 4), especially as it accelerates the immigration component of population growth (Chapter 24) and reshapes economic specialization in the Canadian space economy.

Before examining recent changes in urban growth, it is essential to consider several measures of spatial linkage that confirm the globalization process. Over the 20-year period 1981–2000, there was a relatively modest increase (27 per cent) in the level of air travel within Canada, even with deregulation at the beginning of the 1990s and the resultant reductions in airfares. The most rapid increases in air travel during this period occurred along international flight routes—not just to and from the United States (a 106 per cent increase), but especially to and from other countries (251 per cent). The same is true of migration: inter-city moves within Canada have actually declined as the population continues to age and to concentrate in large cities. But immigration flows more than doubled during this period. Similarly, the flow of goods among the provinces has remained roughly proportional to the growth of the economy, while imports and exports have increased by nearly 50 per cent. Clearly, in a variety of ways—hastened by rapid advances in the use of the Internet and the World Wide Web—Canadians are now integrated more closely than ever before within a continental and global economy.

Recent Growth Patterns

Within this context, Figure 3.5 shows the growth pattern of the urban system over the last census decade. We use the term 'growth' loosely, because 49 of the 140 cities (more than one-third) actually lost

Figure 3.5   **Urban Growth, 1991–2001**

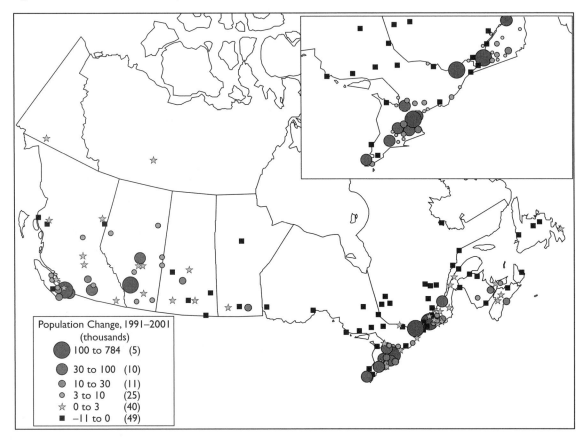

population during the 1991–2001 census interval; and it seems very likely that this trend will continue, or even accelerate, in the future. The loss of population is especially evident in an east–west zone of towns and cities running across the northern edge of the resource ecumene, in places like Kitimat, British Columbia, Sudbury, Ontario, and Corner Brook, Newfoundland. The decline of these centres has been offset by rapid population growth in the southern parts of central Canada, in the Calgary–Edmonton corridor, and in the Georgia Basin and Okanagan regions of British Columbia. Growth in these core regions is concentrated in the largest cities. Between 1991 and 2001, Toronto added 784,000 people; Vancouver, 384,000; and

Montreal and Calgary, close to 200,000 each. For business firms and newly arriving immigrants, these large cities are the main points of contact that join Canada with the rest of the world. Clearly, the map shows striking variations in urban growth across the country (Simmons and Bourne, 2003).

Spatial variations in urban growth are underscored when growth rates are aggregated according to region and city size (Table 3.5). Regionally, rates in Ontario and western Canada are more than twice as high as those of Quebec and the Atlantic provinces. The variation by city size group is even more dramatic. Growth rates for the smallest cities were only 3.4 per cent over the 1991–2001 census decade, while the largest metropolitan regions grew

Table 3.5   **Urban Growth (%) by Region and City Size, 1991–2001**

City Size	British Columbia	Prairie Provinces	Ontario	Quebec	Atlantic Provinces	Canada
>1,000,000	24.0	—	20.1	6.8	—	15.9
300,000–1,000,000	—	13.5	11.1	7.8	8.6	11.4
100,000–299,999	18.3	4.0	8.7	1.4	−0.5	7.0
30,000–99,999	17.2	9.0	7.7	1.5	4.7	7.7
10,000–29,999	7.7	8.0	3.0	0.0	−4.5	3.4
Total urban	20.3	11.5	14.2	5.6	2.2	11.8
Total rural	11.0	5.6	6.2	2.7	−6.0	2.9
Total region	18.8	9.7	13.1	5.0	−1.6	9.9

Note: Territorial cities are grouped with British Columbia. Ottawa CMA is divided into Quebec and Ontario portions.
Source: Statistics Canada, *Census of Canada,* various years.

by 15.9 per cent. The city size variations are also consistent within each of the major regions, whether in a core or periphery situation. These consistent variations imply that many smaller centres will likely continue to lose population.

City size differences require further analysis. While east-to-west variation in regional population growth rates has been a feature of the Canadian urban system for a long time, differences by city size have only emerged—and dramatically so—since the early 1990s. Two key processes have contributed to the concentration of growth in the largest cities. The first is the extraordinary demographic transition that occurred during the 1990s. Figure 3.6 graphs the two principal types of population growth: by *natural increase* (births minus deaths) and through *net immigration* (immigrants less emigrants). As the natural rate of population increase declined dramatically during the 'baby bust' that followed the post-war 'baby boom', the federal government opened the immigration door further, welcoming people from around the globe, contributing to Canada's current status as the most multicultural

society in the world (Foot and Stoffman, 1996). As a result, Canada's population total has increased steadily by 250,000 to 300,000 people per year, but the geography of this growth has changed significantly. Unlike immigration, natural increase is a spatially dispersed growth process—it occurs roughly in proportion to the existing population distribution. Recent immigrants, in contrast, tend to concentrate spatially. They prefer those big cities where many people speak the same language and share the same cultural organizations, and where they can benefit from family and ethnic employment networks that help newcomers adjust to a new urban reality. Toronto typically absorbs almost half of recently arrived immigrants; Vancouver also attracts a high proportion, generally more than Montreal. Other cities pale by comparison to the three largest CMAs.

Sectoral Changes in the Economy

Recent shifts among the growth sectors in Canada's economy have encouraged job creation in the

Figure 3.6   **Sources of Population Growth, 1961–99**

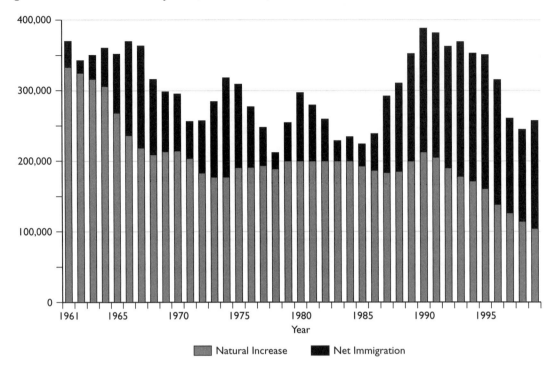

largest cities, attracting newcomers alongside Canadian-born households from smaller places. Table 3.6 shows employment growth rates by economic sector between 1991 and 2003. During this period, employment growth in the primary activities, including agriculture, has been negative, thus helping to explain the decline of communities across much of the resource ecumene. Some of the most dramatic sectoral growth has taken place in retail and wholesale activities and in business and other commercial services. These activities typically favour big cities. Not all jobs in these sectors are well-paying, however, meaning that many newly arrived immigrants and even inter-city migrants can experience economic hardship. Nonetheless, if the processes of demographic growth continue as discussed above, almost all of Canada's future population growth will

eventually concentrate in perhaps a dozen or so of the country's largest cities. It is difficult to foresee a change in this scenario. Manufacturing and public-sector employment, which traditionally favoured smaller cities in central Canada, have grown more slowly. So, too, have the economies of most peripheral urban places. Thus, the question can fairly be asked: Will recently arrived immigrants ever take up residence in large numbers, either freely or at the behest of government policies, in towns and cities that are small in size and that offer few job opportunities? The gulf between the largest metropolitan regions—Toronto, Vancouver, and Montreal, centres that some people are beginning to call 'city states'—and other places in the urban system and rural hinterlands is an essential fact of Canada's changing geography and identity.

Table 3.6   **Employment Growth by Sector: Canada, 1991–2003**

	Employment (000s) 2003	1991–2003 Change (000s)	Percentage Change	Share of GDP (%)
Agriculture, fishing, forestry	440	−161	−26.8	2.3
Mining	150	−2	−1.5	3.6
Manufacturing	2,047	203	14.4	17.3
Construction	643	146	29.5	5.4
Transportation and utilities	725	37	5.4	7.2
Trade	2,349	416	21.5	11.8
Finance and real estate	803	51	6.8	20.1
Business services and communication	1,689	617	57.6	10.7
Commercial services	1,680	361	27.4	5.5
Community services (education and health)	2,314	244	11.8	10.5
Public administration	766	−4	−0.5	5.7
Total	**13,606**	**2,268**	**20.0**	**100.0**

Sources: Statistics Canada, *Employment, Earnings and Hours: Annual Estimates, 1991–2003* (uncatalogued); *The Labour Force: Historical Statistics,* Catalogue no. 71–201; *Canadian Economic Observer: Historical Statistics,* Catalogue no. 11–210. Gross domestic product in 2003 was $1,219 billion.

Sectoral shifts in urban-based employment cannot be explained simply in terms of globalization. Most changes have resulted from innovations in production technology (see also Chapter 14). As well, the slow growth in manufacturing employment is due to the opening of the Canadian border that reversed the defensive measures of the one-time National Policy of protective tariffs. The impact of globalization is at once pervasive and subtle, occurring primarily in the form of increased economic specialization. The Canada–US Free Trade Agreement of 1989, followed five years later by the North America Free Trade Agreement, signalled a heightened integration of Canada within the continental and international economies. Within this context, the core-periphery division of labour that once characterized Canada's space economy is being replaced by a labour force that is becoming more specialized, city-based, and driven by the global economy. For example, Ontario's auto industry is now more embedded within a continental market, competing with American and Mexican cities to capture American markets. By weakening the boundaries around the Canadian domestic market, globalization has compelled the manufacturing cities of Canada's core region to compete with other manufacturing regions worldwide, especially in the United States, Japan, and increasingly China. The growth rates of central Canadian cities—once tied strongly to consumer demand in Canada—now depend increasingly on the ability of manufacturers to capture export markets. As a result, urban growth rates of manufacturing centres in the core have become almost as variable as those of urban places across the Canadian periphery.

Governments and Globalization

All levels of government, but especially the federal system, play a central role in negotiating the impacts of globalization through trade agreements, immigration procedures, and other urban-related policies. Governments also support complex patterns of financial transfers that attempt to reduce the spatial effects of uneven urban growth rates. In recent years, the expansion of services provided by governments—notably health care, education and a variety of infrastructure investments such as roads and utilities—gives government a direct role in locating facilities and defining the accessibility that affects urban growth. This expanded role of public expenditures is falling increasingly to the provinces, since they provide most of the funding for health care and education. Provinces, in aggregate, now spend the equivalent of 22 per cent of Canada's national income (that is, the country's GDP), so that the amounts provinces spend, on what services, and in which locations significantly affect urban growth and the well-being of Canadians. Unfortunately, because some provinces are richer than others, it seems inevitable that urban places in rich provinces will prosper and enjoy greater benefits than their counterparts in relatively poorer provinces. In Alberta, for example, royalties from oil and natural gas production have enhanced employment growth in a variety of sectors providing government services (see Table 3.3). Those provinces not endowed with abundant resources, and hence public wealth, argue that—in name of national parity, if not unity—revenues should continue to be transferred from rich to poorer provinces, thus providing all Canadians with equal access to essential health and educational services, and perhaps even to new jobs.

Globalization, however, weakens the pressure to redistribute income among governments. One can interpret the financial flows of the transfer system as the mirror image of the spending that once supported Canada's core-periphery space economy. A generation or so ago, cities in the industrial heartland profited immensely from the sale of goods and services to customers in the periphery. In order to maintain a national market based on tariff protection and other restrictions, core provinces redistributed income to the provinces that initiated the wealth, that is, the places that controlled raw material resources and also provided significant markets for final demand. For example, Toronto corporations made money from serving the Atlantic Canada market, and then returned (via taxes paid to the federal government in Ottawa) money to the east coast provinces. Globalization has disturbed this relationship, however. The industrial cities of central Canada now produce goods mainly for export within a continental or the wider global economy, and are less dependent on Canadian markets. As calls for separation by some political groups indicate, Alberta and British Columbia, wealthy from the sale of resources to international markets, are becoming impatient with equalization payments that provide them with no direct or obvious benefits. Increasingly, the same can be said of the largest cities, which view themselves as the income-generating magnets of the new economy (Chapter 17). If the system of transfer payments is diminished by globalization, the variations in income levels and in growth rates among cities will surely increase in the future. More than ever before, each region and urban centre will grow or decline independently of other regions and urban places in the Canadian space economy.

Canada's Urban System in the Future

Knowledge of specific economic and demographic features of Canada's existing urban system, combined with information about growth trends, encourages speculation about the system in the future, or at least invites making some simple projections about which cities will or will not grow, and by how much. The projected growth rates vary substantially, which raises another question: What does a high rate of growth—or conversely, of decline—imply for a particular city? We can propose two basic scenarios: a landscape of growth, and a landscape of decline. Finally, we draw attention to the degree of spatial concentration emerging within the Canadian urban system. Of the 140 urban centres Statistics Canada identified in the 2001 census, 48—including almost two-thirds of the Canadian population—can be grouped into nine metropolitan regions (the Toronto region, the Montreal region, etc.). These urban complexes encompass contiguous urban areas that share facilities (e.g., airports), services (e.g., shopping centres, hospitals, universities), and workplaces. These clusters of cities are gradually coalescing into single entities that are very large indeed.

Population Projections

Estimates of future urban growth patterns are provided in Table 3.7. The results are based on Statistics Canada's projections of population growth by provinces from 2001 until 2026. Note that Statistics Canada expects, as the population everywhere ages, that the country as a whole will grow quite slowly in the future. Based on trends in the rate of natural population increase and expected levels of immigration, the projections call for a total of about 36 million people in 2026, up from 30 million in 2001, for an increase of 20 per cent over 25 years. The

Table 3.7	**Projected Population Growth within the Canadian Urban System, 2001–26**					
	Percentage Change					
City Size	British Columbia	Prairie Provinces	Ontario*	Quebec*	Atlantic Provinces	Canada
>1,000,000	52.1		54.3	5.9		33.8
300,000–1,000,000	23.5	22.9	20.6	10.6	27.4	21.0
100,000–299,999	109.6	21.3	36.2	2.2	3.2	30.3
30,000–99,999	45.1	29.7	4.2	4.3	22.8	17.9
10,000–29,999	22.0	10.8	8.9	−7.0	1.7	7.8
Total urban	50.9	22.9	34.7	5.5	13.2	27.2
Total rural	−15.0	−6.3	4.2	−4.6	−10.1	−4.8
Total region	41.1	14.2	30.8	3.3	2.8	20.6

Projected Population (000s) of Regional Cities in 2026

British Columbia		Prairie Provinces		Ontario*		Quebec*		Atlantic Provinces	
Vancouver	3,022	Calgary	1,355	Toronto	6,925	Montreal	3,557	Halifax	458
Victoria	385	Edmonton	1,055	Ottawa	1,426	Quebec City	755	St John's	226
Abbotsford	346	Winnipeg	739	Hamilton	785	Sherbrooke	174	Moncton	134
Kelowna	272	Saskatoon	282	Kitchener	597	Chicoutimi	141	Saint John	116
Nanaimo	139	Regina	226	London	521	Trois-Rivières	141		

*The projection splits the growth of Ottawa between Ontario and Quebec.

Source: Projections by the authors, based on provincial projections by Statistics Canada.

If P_t and $Prov_t$ represent the populations at time t of the city and the province, respectively, then

$$P_{26} = Prov_{26} \times (P_{01}/Prov_{01}) \times ((P_{01}/Prov_{01})/(P_{76}/Prov_{76}))$$

population estimates for each city are based on a city's share of its provincial total in 2001; they also assume that this share will change over the 25-year period in the same way that it did in the previous 25 years. If we aggregate the 2026 projections for 140 cities by region and city size, we obtain the results shown in Table 3.7. The growth rates for cities are proportional to city size, since the rates extrapolate changes that have occurred since 1976. On average, the largest cities will be almost one-third larger than they are at present, but the smaller places will grow by only 7.8 per cent—limited gains, indeed. Regional variations are even more substantial, ranging from a lowly 5.5 per cent in Quebec to more than 50 per cent in both British Columbia and Ontario. Keep in mind that these estimates are based on assumptions made by Statistics Canada about future immigration and domestic migration.

Table 3.7 also records the projected size of the largest cities in these regions. Not unexpectedly, it is anticipated that Toronto will continue to grow as Canada's largest city, reaching close to seven million people by 2026, when it will be almost twice the size of Montreal. Vancouver, Ottawa, Calgary, and Edmonton will follow in order, each housing a million or more people. There are few surprises among the smaller regional centres, where growth is projected to occur at lower rates. An exception is Kelowna. At 272,000 people in 2026, it will house almost twice the number of its 2001 population (148,000). Other cities are projected to become substantially smaller over the next 25 years. Of the 140 cities comprising the urban system, 46 (about one-third) are actually forecast to decline, and several might lose as much as 20 per cent of their population. The largest centres of the declining group are located in the Cape Breton industrial region, the Sudbury Nickel Belt, and along the Saguenay River, particularly Chicoutimi. Also expected to decline are small northern resource towns where technological advances will continue to reduce the need for industrial workers.

It is possible to broaden the inquiry of urban futures to consider a city's prospective social and economic character, uncovering in the process land-scapes of either growth or decline. Cities that lost population over the period 1971–2001 were resource towns or service centres located mainly in Quebec and the Atlantic region. Their landscape of decline is distinguished by several features. First, languishing places are generally small in size. Second, there are more old people and fewer immigrants, hence these places are home to small numbers of people born outside of Canada—the demographic group that accounts for most of the recent urban growth. Third, the economic performance of declining places has been weak. This is indicated by a variety of measures, including a gloomy employment rate, low per capita income, and a minimal participation level in the labour force. Fourth, where urban places have suffered a loss of population, investment in new housing or commercial activity is low. Fifth, decline means more jobs in the public sector compared to privately funded commercial services. Finally, the dollar value of housing in slow-growth cities is half that of housing in the large and rapidly growing places. By comparison, the landscape of growth is marked by twice as many people born outside the country, incomes higher than those of slow-growth places, and a housing stock that is large, newer, and more expensive.

Most of Canada's largest cities will continue to prosper by pursuing post-industrial growth strategies that emphasize specialized producer services (Savitch and Kantor, 2002). Beyond this economic perspective, support for recently arrived immigrants will be provided by long-standing immigrant communities. And these newcomers, in turn, will generate jobs and have children, further enhancing and favouring big-city growth. Although environmental sustainability is becoming the mantra of post-industrial growth, and despite the buildup of multi-family housing and encouragement of public transit, huge automobile-oriented and multicultural suburbs are under construction in these larger centres. Some are marked by themes of material consumption presently in vogue—neo-traditional architecture and New Urbanist subdivision design, as practised at Cornell in Markham and MacKenzie Town in Calgary.

Metropolitan Regions

Some of Canada's largest urban areas are beginning to coalesce by absorbing nearby small communities or growing together (Table 3.8). The list is topped by four metropolitan regions that will continue to form the strategic growth points in Canada's future urban system: Toronto, Montreal, the Georgia Basin (Vancouver–Victoria), and the Calgary–Edmonton corridor; and by five other regions determined on the basis of size or interdependence. The members of this elite group currently range in size from the Toronto region that houses seven million people (in an area stretching from Peterborough through Kitchener–Waterloo to Niagara Falls), down to Halifax, with less than 500,000 people. In 2001 they held 64 per cent of Canada's population; but by 2026 this share will increase to almost 70 per cent. The Toronto area alone will surge to 10 million people. Collectively, the nine regions are projected to grow at a rate of 30 per cent, compared to 12.3 per cent for other cities and losses of 4.8 per cent for rural areas. These metropolitan regions will be the dynamic elements of the future urban system, attracting capital and in-migrants from within Canada and abroad. They are projected to generate 95 per cent of Canada's future population growth. At the same time, not all of them will sustain vigorous growth. The projections suggest that

Table 3.8   **The Size and Growth of Metropolitan Regions, 2001–26**

	Urban Components	Population 2001 (000s)	Population Share (%)	Percentage Growth 1991–2001	Population 2026 (000s)	Percentage Growth 2001–26
Toronto region	11	6,972	23.1	17.90	9,975	43.1
Montreal region	7	3,683	12.3	6.40	3,821	3.7
Georgia Basin (Vancouver)	8	2,679	8.9	22.20	4,128	54.1
Alberta corridor (Calgary/Edmonton)	5	1,983	6.6	18.22	2,545	28.3
Ottawa–Gatineau	1	1,064	3.5	14.27	1,426	34.1
Southwestern Ontario (London/Windsor)	8	1,060	3.4	8.29	1,212	14.3
Quebec City	2	711	2.4	5.98	793	11.6
Winnipeg	2	692	2.3	1.54	759	9.7
Halifax region	4	465	1.5	6.49	576	23.9
Total metro regions	48	19,309	64.2	13.96	25,234	30.7
Other urban centres	92	4,530	15.1	3.26	5,086	12.3
Rural areas	0	6,168	20.6	3.39	5,871	−4.8
Canada	140	30,007	100.0	9.93	36,191	20.6

Source: Statistics Canada, *Census of Canada*, 1971–2001.

Montreal, Quebec City, Winnipeg, and southwestern Ontario will grow rather slowly. Thus, even within this group of metropolitan regions, there will be landscapes of growth and slow growth, because competition for immigrants and markets in a capitalist system always produces winners and losers.

Conclusion

Urban systems are dynamic and always susceptible to change and transition, even unpredictable alteration. In the process, the urban system has become by far the most important context for interpreting the development, characteristics, and landscapes of individual cities. It affects the amount and timing of growth, and especially the economic, demographic, and political processes that—separately or intertwined—shape and reshape the landscape of cities. But the sheer weight of the existing urban system suggests that future change can be reasonably predicted. A particular location in the core-periphery space economy remains important in the prediction equation: space *does* matter. Whatever the topic in urban studies, whether poverty (Chapter 25) or immigration (Chapter 24), politics (Chapter 17) or power shopping centres (Chapter 16), the characteristics and the process of change in Prince Albert, Saskatchewan, will be different from those of Sydney, Nova Scotia, or of Ottawa. Cities have different histories, different present conditions, and will have different futures, as we have tried to point out in this chapter. As a result, in the future, there will certainly be even greater inter-city variations and intra-urban landscape differences characterizing the Canadian urban system.

Notes

1. The various maps and graphs that accompany this chapter are based on analysis of CMAs and CAs only. At other times, when we discuss in a descriptive way the overall urban pattern of Canada, we include settlements of 1,000 or more people, which Statistics Canada defines as the minimum population threshold of any urban place in Canada. Over 700 such places meet this population criterion.

2. Readers who would like to examine the map of migration patterns in the urban system are encouraged to refer to the most recent (5th) edition of *The National Atlas of Canada* (Ottawa: Geographical Services Division, Energy, Mines and Resources, Surveys and Mapping Branch, n.d.). Many maps in this atlas are very relevant for understanding the geography of Canada's urban system.

3. Each of Canada's major staples-based industries, as well as all varieties of economic, demographic, and political processes, are well-illustrated by maps in the three volumes of *The Historical Atlas of Canada*.

Chapter 4

Transitions in an Era of Globalization and World City Growth

Trudi Bunting and Tod Rutherford

By the early 1980s, key 'global' cities had emerged as sites of capital accumulation and creation, headquarters of transnational corporations, and homes to concentrations of professional, producer, and other advanced services. This emergence brought recognition that global city regions had taken over as the motor driving national and global economies. Since then, concern over the city and its role in globalization has emerged as a point of critical scholarly and policy debate. In Canada today globalization has brought major transition in growth trajectories, in economic and social structure, and in urban form and function. The policy environment, too, is very different from a generation ago. However, in Canada—a relatively small country in terms of population whose export base remains heavily resource-dependent and whose industrial and corporate operations are mainly controlled by US-owned enterprise—the experience of globalization remains especially enigmatic.

This chapter begins by reviewing the meaning of globalization, world cities, and more general critical global discourse. At the inter-city level, we briefly describe where Canadian cities are positioned in the new order—briefly, because there is not much to say; Canada's global window is small, although impacts on the ground have been profound. Discussion of new, macro-level national imbalances constitutes the third section. In the fourth, we focus on change within key Canadian cities and, finally, consider transformations in Vancouver, the Canadian city believed to have experienced the greatest globally induced transformation—from 'urban village to world city, 1966–91' (Ley et al.,

1992). We conclude with a question about the essential meaning of globalization—in Vancouver and across Canada as a whole.

Scope, Terminology, and Discourse of Globalism

Today, we are accustomed to hearing Toronto described as Canada's 'world city', Vancouver as 'gateway to Pacific Asia', and fast-growing metropolitan areas like Calgary characterized as 'world-class'. Our language is replete with references to the new order—'going global', 'wannabe', 'global competitiveness', etc. However, globalization itself remains hard to define. In fact, there has not been much empirical research on the topic because internationally comparable data sources are limited and tend not to be urban-based, a problem that has been referred to as globalization's 'dirty little secret' (Short et al., 1999: 8).

We have clear understanding of processes abetting globalization. The post-industrial economy with its emphasis on advanced services, knowledge, and innovation (Chapter 14) is inextricably tied to globalization. Other important, interrelated factors include: the 'death of distance' by revolutionary advances in transportation and telecommunications; the growth of multinational/transnational corporations (TNCs); increased portability of traded products (including knowledge); huge growth of markets in newly industrializing countries; increased mobility of capital; and greater foreign direct investment (Castells, 1996; Dunning, 1993; King, 1990; Robertson, 1992). Ordinary Canadians are familiar with more mundane circumstances that lead to and/or accompany globalization—instant hookup with the World Wide Web; international travel; soaring consumer lifestyles that depend on massive flows of inexpensive products from around the globe; foreign in-migration. Canadian business and ordinary Canadians alike are privileged by the fact that English is the 'lingua franca' of globalization.

None of this brings us closer to clear definitions. Held et al. (1999: 16) speak of:

> a process or set of processes which embodies a transformation in the spatial organization of social relations and transactions—assessed in terms of their extensity, intensity, velocity and impact—generating transcontinental or interregional flows and networks of activity, interaction, and the exercise of power.

Though debate continues (see Saul, 2005), the world economy,[1] if not fully globalized, is unquestionably a globalizing one (Dicken et al., 1997), articulated by 'world' cities that play the role of hub points of concentration and connectivity in the global network and 'command' and 'control' points for global capitalism.

The Global Cities Model

In the mid-1980s, urban planner John Friedmann (1986; Friedmann and Wolff, 1982) wrote about transformed growth and interaction between large metropolitan areas. Friedmann argued that shifting patterns in inter-city interconnectedness had produced a new hierarchical system redefining urban geographic primacy under conditions reflective of the new global economy.

From a North American perspective, globalization as we know it today began in the mid-twentieth century with the entry of an increasing variety of consumer items (generally of low value and light in weight—e.g., toys, clothing, footwear) from offshore, low-wage manufacturing centres. Over time, as consumption rates soared and transportation costs declined, heavier products (e.g., automobiles and

electronics) joined the flow. In response, producers in developed countries themselves began to play the global relocation game by moving production facilities to more cost-efficient locales beyond national boundaries and thus depleting manufacturing jobs onshore. Concomitant restructuring and expansion within and between firms shifted the scale of economic dominance from the national to the transnational corporate sphere.

More recently, offshore movement has included exodus of some producer and consumer services that entail routine information-processing (e.g., insurance claims, call centres). Meanwhile, the new economy has concentrated management and professional services in major urban centres. The simultaneous explosive demand for low-wage services to support both business enterprise and growing numbers of increasingly affluent, professional-class, dual-wage households has polarized employment. In Canada, high volumes of immigrants have joined either the low-wage or management/professional classes of workers.

At the inter-city level, different cities have attracted control functions of different magnitude and rank. This has produced a new set of hierarchical arrangements between cities across the globe, as outlined in Table 4.1 and illustrated in Figure 4.1. Friedmann (1986: 70) argued that some metropolitan economies 'carry out headquarter functions, others serve primarily as a financial centre, and still others have as their main function the articulation of regional and/or national economies with the global system. The most important cities, however, such as New York, may carry out all of these functions simultaneously.' While Friedmann was very clear about the way primary world cities functioned, he had considerably less to say about lower-order places such as Toronto, Montreal, and Vancouver.

Sassen (1991, 2001a) offered a more encompassing view of global cities. For her, global cities are not principally centres of corporate control, but centres of commercial services and financial markets and the producers of financial innovations. She recognizes that global cities are command points for the global economy, but gives more emphasis to

Table 4.1	**Hierarchy of World Cities**		
Core Countries		Semi-Periphery Countries	
Primary	Secondary	Primary	Secondary
Europe			
London	Brussels		
Paris	Milan		
Rotterdam	Vienna		
Frankfurt	Madrid		
Zurich			
Americas			
New York	Toronto	São Paulo	Buenos Aires
Chicago	Miami		Rio de Janeiro
Los Angeles	Houston		Caracas
	San Francisco		Mexico City
Asia and Oceania			
Tokyo	Sydney	Singapore	Hong Kong
		Manila	
			Bangkok
			Seoul
Africa			
			Johannesburg

Source: From J. Friedman, 'The World city hypothesis', *Development and Change* 17 (1986): 72. Reprinted with permission of Blackwell Publishing.

financial/commercial service production and innovation through which large corporate networks are controlled and managed. Sassen (2001a: 83) further emphasized that global cities, because they employ large and growing numbers of high-level and well-paid professionals while also relying on relatively low-paid service workers, are characterized by significant social inequality. Other scholars (e.g., Camagni, 2001; Zukin, 1995) add re-'placing' (as in the sense of reconstructing to create distinctly different ambience or 'sense of place') the symbolic 'heart' of the city as a fundamental characteristic of world cities' new 'look'. William Coffey (1994) points out that culture and leisure have also become an intrinsic part of the newly expanded, global urban economic base. Others emphasize world cities' significance as nodes of flows of information and knowledge (Castells, 1996; Storper, 1997). An emphasis on knowledge leads Storper to conclude that what makes cities (global and otherwise) unique is the manner in which dense, untraded external economies serve as knowledge-based interdependencies to produce strong clustering effects for economic activities (Storper, 1997: 238).

Given that Canadian cities cannot lay claim to being headquarters of many large TNCs, Sassen's and others' refinement of Friedmann's original thinking probably applies best to Canadian CMAs—and to

Figure 4.1   **The Hierarchy of World Cities**

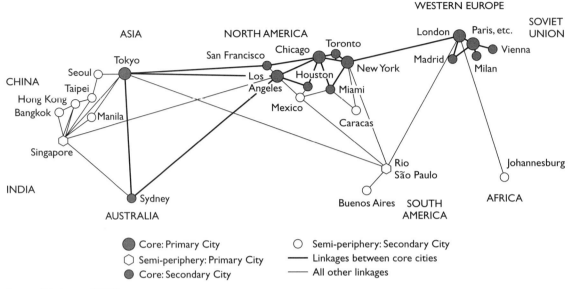

Source: Friedmann (1986).

most other 'secondary'-level world cities around the globe.

Global Discourse

While a body of (mostly business and neo-liberal) literature views globalization as both a necessary and rational process (see Ohmae, 1990), most observers perceive globalization as contradictory and crisis-ridden (Brenner, 2001; Dicken, 2003; Webber and Rigby, 1996). For example, financial deregulation and flows of highly speculative 'hot money' have made it more difficult for nation-states to control their macro-economies and have also been inclined to accelerate and deepen existing crisis tendencies—as during the East Asian crisis in 1997–8. Likewise, the emergence of a truly global labour market by the late 1990s has contributed to competitive pressures on wages and standards not only in lower-skilled occupations in developed nations but also in some higher-skilled work (Freeman, 2004; Kaplinsky, 1999). These pressures have accentuated impoverishment in the face of increased material well-being overall.

Growing evidence of globalization's intrinsic paradox has invited critical scholarly response. Within Canada, as elsewhere, the largest and most critical response to globalization concerns its innumerable negative impacts.[2] All sorts of issues of fairness and justice have been raised, ranging from the demise of small, locally based business (Jacobs, 1969, 2000) and even the 'hollowing out' (Arthurs, 2000) of larger, more mature Canadian establishments (e.g., the auto industry—see Holmes, 1991—or iron and steel—see Masi, 1991), to a greatly increased need to protect national culture and heritage. The real concern is that social and environmental needs have been overshadowed because the political economy is heavily focused on cost-cutting and maintaining a 'competitive edge'. Thus, despite being wealthier today than ever, we seem unable to afford the essential social and environmental conditions to ensure quality of life. Highways are pushed through highly sensitive ecological areas to keep the Toronto-centred region 'competitive' (McKay, 2002). Likewise, funds are allocated to monumental public buildings designed to attract the eye of the world at the expense, many argue, of a growing 'underclass'. Vancouver's new public library, designed by world-renowned architect Moshe Safdie, juxtaposed against the city's infamous Downtown Eastside (Lees, 1987, 1998, 1999) is but one prime example.

On the environmental front, urban economist Wilbur Thompson (1995) has argued that environmental conditions, like social ones, will also polarize—improving in 'wannabe' places seeking to attract global business while deteriorating elsewhere. The elevation of environmental issues in the Greater Vancouver area (Artibise and Hill, 1993), taken against the continued practice of unsustainable forestry management in BC's interior, serves as a classic example.

Understanding the full impact of globalism on non-economic concerns requires that we understand changing balance in the relative power of major players in the Canadian economy. While Canada has always had a relatively high level of economic openness (especially continentally), during the Fordist period (c. 1920–80) there was unique balance within the national power structure among big government, big labour, and big business (Jenson, 1989). As a result of this balance an affluent society, made up primarily of middle-class urban homeowners, developed. This society was supported by strong, government-led social welfare programs that encompassed major domains of social reproduction—health, education, and social assistance (welfare, unemployment benefits, and a variety of other supports ranging across child care and job retraining) (see Chapter 1). The Great Depression and World War II saw the federal state take the lead role in funding social welfare and unemployment insurance, and with the advent of the Canada Assistance Plan (CAP) in the 1960s the government set national standards that provinces were required to meet. Globalism, in contrast, has made transnational global corporations (TNCs) all-powerful brokers of the new economy, greatly diminishing the authority of labour unions and national-level governments. The crisis of Fordism after 1975 has meant a reversal of these trends as state fiscal problems intensified, in part due to increasing unemployment and contingent work

arrangements (Rutherford, 1996). National governments have become increasingly preoccupied with bringing down debt and mounting an agenda to retain and attract TNCs or other important international sources of economic growth and connection.

Many scholars hold Canada's current neo-liberal political economy directly responsible for attrition of the social welfare net. Among other things, this has been witnessed in erosion of welfare and family benefits, the near-elimination of government-supported housing starts (Dreier and Hulchanski, 1993; Wolfe, 2003), increasing fees for higher education, and privatization of some medical services. Cutbacks have been accompanied by transfer of responsibilities from provincial and federal levels of government to the private sector, municipalities ('downloading'—see Chapter 17; also Andrew, 2003), and to family units that are today smaller and more engaged in full-time work in the paid economy than ever before. During the 1990s, for example, CAP was abolished, and federal and provincial governments moved from passive income support towards more active labour market measures and mounted a drastically reduced federal Employment Insurance (EI) program. Meanwhile, provincial governments cut social assistance programs and redefined their eligibility criteria. Simultaneously, the 1990s witnessed a significant rescaling of labour market governance as the federal government sought to offload many of its responsibilities to the provinces through a series of labour market development agreements (LMDAs) (McIntosh, 2000). This has contributed to the erosion of Fordist welfare arrangements 'from below' at provincial and local scales through the adoption of workfare and other regressive welfare work (Peck, 2002). Courchene (2001: 163–71) describes how this kind of process unfolded in Ontario in the mid-1990s during the transition from NDP to Conservative governance. So while the GDP escalates, social spending has plummeted. Chapter 25 discusses how these contingencies have given rise to 'new' poverty, to unaffordable housing, and even to homelessness.

Scholars who position themselves more to the ideological middle acknowledge the relative absence of support for social and environmental problems but attribute this to corporate and especially government policy rather than to globalism per se. This group of scholars tends to advocate 'broadening globalization' (see Chodos et al., 1993: 178), calling for other sectors of society such as environmentalists, human rights activists, political parties (centre and left-of-centre), NGOs, and even corporations ('green' business) to develop and market an alternative global vision.

At the other end of the spectrum is promotional literature about global cities or wannabe places, some of which passes as scholarly.[3] Much of this work ignores negative impacts altogether or dismisses the downsides out of hand as a cost of doing global business. Some of the recent, Vancouver-based research reviewed later in this chapter has been criticized as falling into the genre of 'boosterism'. Web-based sources are particularly notorious as platforms designed to create competitive advantage, mixing fact with fiction to market metropolitan regions attempting to position themselves within the new global hierarchy.

Canada's Position and Role in Global City Ratings

A major body of statistically based research (e.g., Beaverstock et al., 1999) uses numeric indicators of either functions (e.g., TNCs, major NGOs, major banks, stock exchanges) or linkages (airline travel, immigrants, foreign direct investment) to refine the global hierarchy and further explore urban connectivity.[4] Many different metrics have produced somewhat variable results. Canadian cities fare relatively well when bank head offices are enumerated, due to our centralized, federal banking system, but less well on other metrics. Either way, findings continue to place London, New York, and Tokyo as global cities (see Hall, 2001a; Short and Kim, 1999).

Toronto was the only Canadian city to figure in Friedmann's original global model, though a later, updated version of the work (Friedmann, 1995) included all three of Canada's largest metropolitan area—at the fourth (lowest) tier of

'subnational/regional articulations' where all North American 'world' cities other than New York registered. Most recent research continues to put Toronto at the top of the Canadian hierarchy. Using international air passenger volume as one indicator of 'world city' status, Toronto ranks nineteenth (London is first and Paris second). Head-office locations of the world's largest banks registered Toronto tenth, with three such banks, and Montreal ranked fifteenth with two major bank head offices (Short and Kim, 1999). A compendium of places identified in 'world cities' research over the period 1986–99 cites Toronto in 11 of 16 major studies; Montreal was enumerated in seven and Vancouver in only three (Taylor, 2004: 40–1).[5]

Imbalances across the Country

Everywhere, globalism has produced new unevenness between the old and the new economy, between places favoured versus ones disconnected from or exploited by globalism, and, as in the discourse of globalism, between economic versus social and environmental issues (Smith, 1990). In Canada imbalance is accentuated because of the considerable regional disparities that have always been part of this country's geography and, in turn, because resources that might otherwise be targeted towards the downsides of world city growth (e.g., homelessness) are already tied up in equalization payments between 'have' and 'have-not' provinces and other long-standing support systems such as health care and seasonal employment benefits.

Concentrated Urban Growth

The impact of globalization on cities was at first confusing to researchers.[6] Technological change was originally seen as making business and industry more footloose, gravitating away from central parts of large metropolitan areas (Nelson and Dueker, 1994; Toffler, 1980). Among other things, the fact that workforces in these areas were viewed as less organized than in central cities and older metropolitan areas (Bluestone and Harrison, 1982; Massey and Meegan, 1978) appeared to put the central city and especially older urban regions at a distinct disadvantage. However, by the 1990s, growing internationalization of economic activity was pronounced (see Dicken, 2003) and it quickly became clear that global business preferred and depended on big-city locales as described in early formative writing about global cities.

From the new global perspective, cities, especially those in the second and third tiers of the global hierarchy, are viewed as a critical social nexus for many 'new economy' and cultural industries, from biotech to multimedia and software. The composition of urban advantage has shifted from one emphasizing physical infrastructure, linkages between activities, and other traditional agglomeration economies (see Lloyd and Dicken, 1990) to one stressing human and social capital (such as trust stemming from face-to-face contact) and knowledge overflows between related activities (Amin and Graham, 1997; Malmberg and Maskell, 2002). Special emphasis has been placed on the role of cities in attracting young educated and skilled 'talent', which in turn fosters creativity and innovation (Florida, 2002; Gertler et al., 2002). In this view the cultural amenities and diversity of the city become a prime source of competitive advantage.

Creativity has replaced raw materials or natural harbours as the crucial wellspring of economic growth. Such talented people are not spread equally across nations or places, but tend to concentrate within particular city-regions. The most successful city-regions are ones that have a social environment that is open to creativity and diversity of all sorts. The ability to attract creative people in the arts and culture fields and to be open to diverse groups of different ethnic, racial and lifestyle groups provides distinct advantages to regions in generating innovations, growing and attracting high technology industries, and spurring economic growth. (Gertler et al., 2002)

Territorial perspectives have also shifted—from global cities to city regions (see Gertler et al., 2002;

Sassen, 2001a; Scott, 2001; Scott et al., 2001)—because global city regions 'include a cross section of a country's economic activities [including] . . . manufacturing and basic infrastructure' (Sassen, 2001a: 80). In Canada, the 'Greater Golden Horseshoe Area' (GGHA) (Ontario, 2005b), bounded past Oshawa in the east, Barrie in the north, Kitchener–Waterloo in the west, and Niagara Falls in the south, seems to be a reasonably good approximation of the Toronto-based world city region, though what role it might take in political and policy initiatives remains to be seen.[7] Future administration of the GGHA will be important because global cities like Toronto are integrated socio-spatial entities whose economic performance and socio-spatial equity are seen as threatened by fragmented government structures that can pit wealthier suburbs against the urban core (see Courchene, 2001; Gertler, 1999).

Although regionally based statistical accounts are not available for major Canadian cities at this point in time, even conventional CMA-based trends clearly reveal marked re-concentration of urban growth around Canada's three largest CMAs. Table 4.2 outlines growth rates across larger Canadian CMAs over the period 1971–86 as compared to 1986–2001. While overall growth rates are higher and more even for the earlier period, during the more recent globalizing period the cities of Toronto and Vancouver, and to a lesser extent Montreal, recorded soaring growth, considerably above the 1971–86 trends. In contrast, other Canadian CMAs registered 1986–2001 growth rates that fell below the previous period (except for CMAs located within the greater Toronto region or places like London whose boundaries were expanded by annexation or amalgamation). Along with similar observations made in Chapter 3, trends seen here serve as sure evidence that the global period has been marked by increased unevenness or, as Bourne and Simmons (2003) put it, 'new fault lines'. It is notable that unevenness is further recognized as a factor elevating economic development goals over traditional municipal concerns such as transportation, land-use planning, and social equity, as

Table 4. 2   **Growth Level in 15 CMAs, 1971–2001**

City	CMA Population, 1971	CMA Population, 1986	CMA Population, 2001	Total Growth, 1971–86	Total Growth, 1986–2001	Percentage of Growth, 1971–86	Percentage of Growth, 1986–2001
Toronto	2,604,661	3,384,950	4,661,351	780,289	1,276,401	30.0	37.7
Montreal	2,737,110	2,921,425	3,413,821	184,315	492,396	6.7	16.9
Vancouver	1,082,335	1,362,445	1,986,965	280,110	624,520	25.9	45.8
Ottawa–Hull	602,685	811,260	1,063,644	208,575	252,384	34.6	31.1
Edmonton	495,670	777,770	937,650	282,100	159,880	56.9	20.6
Calgary	403,320	665,805	951,395	262,485	285,590	65.1	42.9
Quebec City	479,870	595,920	682,757	116,050	86,837	24.2	14.6
Winnipeg	534,550	617,800	671,274	83,250	53,474	15.6	8.7
Hamilton	494,740	551,530	662,285	56,790	110,755	11.5	20.1
London	286,930	337,605	432,451	50,675	94,846	17.7	28.1
Kitchener	226,850	308,290	414,279	81,440	105,989	35.9	34.4
St Catharines–Niagara	303,430	339,455	377,009	36,025	37,554	11.9	11.1
Halifax	222,340	293,085	359,168	70,745	66,083	31.8	22.5
Victoria	195,800	250,835	311,902	55,035	61,067	28.1	24.3
Windsor	265,160	251,070	307,877	−14,090	56,807	−5.3	22.6

Sources: Statistics Canada, 1971, 1986, and 2001 censuses.

discussed below, or giving rise to calls for a 'new deal' between higher levels of government and local municipal ones (see Chapter 17). There is also the very costly need to manage issues associated with the exaggerated, if different, kinds of problems that accrue to very fast-growing places (e.g., traffic gridlock, affordable housing) as well as to very slow-growing ones (e.g., employment support, welfare) (Bunting and Filion, 2001).

The Nation-State

As early as a decade ago, Jessop (1994) spoke about diminution of the nation-state through increased decentralization (regionalism and, in Canada, provincialism), on the one hand, and growing supra-national enterprise and institutional alignment, on the other. Speaking directly to the Canadian situation, Kincaid (1995: 73) raised the possibility of the 'breakup of Canada . . . national disintegration in the face of global integration', while Helleiner (2003) speculated about a common North American currency. These scholars side with those who believe that globalization and the use of advanced telecommunication technology have meant the 'end of geography', or others who explain the growth of TNCs as leading to the end of the nation-state and its replacement by a series of globally connected region-states (Ohmae, 1990). Such positions have been heavily criticized. Many researchers argue that geographic unevenness and its importance to economic activity have actually intensified national import (Scott, 2001). Furthermore, while some nation-state powers have declined, others are being reconstituted and the nation-state itself can be seen to have a major role in defining and negotiating globalization (see Dicken, 2003; Glassman, 1999; Hirst and Thompson, 1999).

Debate continues about the impact of globalization on Canada as a nation. Over a decade ago Drache and Gertler (1991) perceived 'new dangers and challenges' that globalization brought to Canadian nationhood: greatly increasing regional disparities; the Quebec separatist agenda; and erosion of the Canadian social welfare net. Today, another challenge has surfaced, as witnessed in strident demands for federal support of urban-based need. In Canada, the particular challenge will be providing programs aimed at balancing out emerging urban inequities while maintaining traditional, territorially based programs and transfer payments (Wolfe, 2003). Focusing on the Ontario/GTA-based global economy, Courchene, for example, sees major 'challenges' in the need for the federal government to provide pan-Canadian leadership while responding to the very real needs of the Toronto-based, income-generating node. He speculates that there may be grounds for the GTA region to demand becoming a 'city-province along the lines of the German city-länder' (Courchene, 2001: 185). Certainly globalization means that Keynesian-rooted federal spending (e.g., infrastructure development programs in economically depressed regions) is significantly less effective today than in the past simply because 'multipliers' are less easily contained within the country and are increasingly prone to 'leak' offshore.

In part, any alleged breakup of the Canadian nation-state or, as Courchene and Telmer (1998) argue, its breakdown into region-states (see also, Rodriguez-Pose and Gill, 2004; Ward and Jonas, 2004) is driven by increasing north–south trade and investment flows replacing the predominantly east–west flows of earlier periods. The growing openness of a post-NAFTA Canadian economy makes the already permeable nature of Canadian Fordism even less amenable to Keynesian stimulation measures

than in the past. Thus researchers such as Clarkson (2001) argue that the Canadian state is increasingly a nested, multi-tiered set of institutions whose links are being restructured and reconstituted. Like Jessop (1994), Clarkson argues that formal government is being reconstituted as a more fluid and negotiated form of governance. The nation-state remains a central institution, not only in economic terms but in establishing broader 'citizenship regimes' that give way to a more diverse and individualized regime.

Globalization: The Perspective within Global Cities

There is a reflexive relationship between the global and the local, aptly referred to by some as 'glocalization', wherein forces and establishments of globalization are embedded locally within global cities. A substantial body of knowledge addresses the internal linkages and changes that occur on the ground in direct response to global imperatives. Foreign migration, unquestionably the most tangible impact of globalism in Canada today, is discussed more fully in Chapters 9 and 24. The more salient of the other internal linkages and changes are discussed below.

Polycentricity

Peter Hall (2001a: 73–4), one of the few scholars to consider the new geography of 'nodes' and 'networks' that globalism has wrought on the internal structure of the city, believes that need for face-to-face contact has been distributed across a 'quintessentially polycentric', metropolitan field. He points out that the intra-urban nodes that have grown in response to globalism are not limited to traditional ones, i.e., downtown cores, but are also found in newer forms such as 'internal' and 'external' edge cities. Table 4.3 outlines nodes identified by Hall alongside some examples we add from Canada's three global cities. The relative paucity of these examples suggests to us that Canadian cities continue to concentrate most of the new activity generated by or for global business, at the core, in the form of re-urbanization.

Table 4.3   **Nodes within the Largest CMAs**

Nodal Type	Description	Canadian Example(s)
The traditional downtown centre	Based on walking distances and served by a radial public transportation centre. This serves the oldest informational services (banking, insurance, government) and is found in the cores of old cities: the City of London, Châtelet-Les Halles, Downtown Manhattan, Maronouchi/Otemachi.	Traditional downtowns in Vancouver, Toronto, and Montreal.
A newer business centre	Often developing in an old prestige residential quarter, and serving as the location of newer services that have expanded in the twentieth century, such as corporate headquarters, the media, new business services (advertising, public relations, design): London's West End, the 16e arrondissment, Midtown Manhattan, Akasaki/Roppongi.	Bay/Bloor; Yonge and Eglinton, Toronto.
An internal edge city	Resulting from pressure of space in traditional centres and speculative development in old industrial or transport land, now redundant, near to them: London Docklands, La Défense, World Financial Center, Shinjuku.	Distillery District, Toronto; False Creek, Vancouver; Canal Lachine, Montreal.
An external edge city	Often located on the axis of the main airport, more rarely a high-speed train station: London Heathrow, Paris Charles de Gaulle, Amsterdam Schiphol, Stockholm Arlanda, Washington Reagan/Dulles corridor.	Suburban downtowns in Toronto (Square One, North York, Scarborough Town Centre); Fairview area in Pointe Claire, in Montreal; regional town centres in Greater Vancouver.
Outermost edge city complexes	For back offices and R&D, typically at major train stations 20–40 miles distant from the main core: Reading, St Quentin-en-Yvelines, Greenwich (Connecticut), Omiya, Shin-Yokohama.	
Specialized sub-centres	Usually for education, entertainment and sporting complexes, exhibition and convention centres: Royal Docks (London), Milton Keynes (Open University), Tokyo Waterfront. These take a great variety of forms and locations: some are on reclaimed or recycled land close to the traditional core; some are older centres, formerly separate and independent, that have become progressively embedded in the wider metropolitan area (Oxford, Cambridge, Uppsala, New Haven). Some of these may take on new functions: witness the emergence of the Cambridge region as a major high-technology centre ('Silicon Fen') since 1970.	Old Port, Montreal; Waterfront, Toronto; Pacific Place, Vancouver

Source: Modified from Hall (2001a: 73–4).

Re-urbanization

In the 1970s marked attraction of the inner city to the middle class was first witnessed as gentrification in some neighbourhoods (see Chapter 11), though population loss continued in these neighbourhoods. We use the term 're-urbanization' to capture accelerated development in the inner city that produces substantial increase not only in social status, as in the case of gentrification, but also in population and new housing production. This trend, found in all three of Canada's largest cities, can be seen in Table 4.4 which outlines zonal growth in Canada's 15 largest CMAs. Vancouver has enjoyed the greatest gain in the inner-city and core area; Toronto has had substantial growth while Montreal's trends are more muted.

Among other things, Ley (1996a) attributes the attraction of inner-city living to increased centrally located employment for the 'new middle class', believed to possess more intellectual than financial capital and prone to take advantage of the somewhat deflated cost of central-city real estate. Florida (2002), in turn, speaks in terms of a 'creative' class drawn by the amenity of cosmopolitan living. Either way, these newcomers to the central city are attracted to diversity, ambience, and service-rich amenities that have exploded in inner parts of some cities over the last couple of decades—galleries, theatres, concert halls, restaurants, new waterfront activities (Hutton, 2004a). Some refer to this trend as 'commodification'; Ley (1996a) writes about the 'convivial city' where, metaphorically speaking, there is 'pasta to die for'. The relative availability of former industrial or 'brownfield' sites assures space for the new growth, whether residential, commercial, or mixed, as in the case of Toronto's Distillery District.

Planning the Competitive City

Re-urbanization is, in part, produced by deliberate policy designed to 'package' cities for global customers, among others. The drive to compete, whether national or international in origin, has become a central issue dominating municipal policy, sometimes referred to as an 'entrepreneurial' agenda (Begg, 1999, Harvey, 1989b). Immense public spending has been committed to 're-placing' the obsolescent landscape of the modern, Fordist city, primarily in the most visible symbolic 'heart' of the city. Quality-of-life amenities, such as arts and culture, expensive urban design projects, monumental architecture, and greater concern for the environment, are features deemed essential to attracting new business and residents.

The range of initiatives undertaken to drum up business and maintain a 'cutting-edge' profile emphasize fiscal austerity and new ways of marketing urban places and creating new amenities (see, e.g., Clark and Cosgrove, 1991; Gregory, 1995; Hall and Hubbard, 1998; Heilbrun, 1992; Keating, 1997; Kresl, 1995; McCann, 2002; Todd, 1995). Mega-events such as trade symposiums, world fairs, and Olympic Games and other international sporting events 'showcase' competitive cities to the world as 'open for business' (Olds, 1995, 2001; Short and Kim, 1999). In some instances, entrepreneurial economic initiatives—e.g., new improved public transit to relieve unacceptable traffic congestion—may actually complement non-economic goals. Other practices, including international business missions or setting up 'sister city' or other promotional programs (Fry, 1995) with offshore places, stretch the limits of jurisdictional responsibilities via 'municipal para-diplomacy' (Smith and Cohn, 1994).

In a recent study, 'Toronto Inc.?', Kipfer and Keil (2002: 243) describe a city devoted to 'proactive pursuit of real estate investments through financial incentives, "deal-making" and mega-projects'. They uncover three separate strands—entrepreneurialism, difference, and revanchism—witnessed in the competitive politics of Canada's primary global city. Entrepreneurial policies promote fiscal austerity and corporate management principles to market Toronto as business-friendly platform for globally connected investment and industry. The 'city of difference' agenda (Fincher and Jacobs, 1998) advances 'place'-based initiatives and cultural projects. 'Difference' is achieved through encouraging luxury

Table 4.4   **CMA Population, Inner City and Suburbs, 1971–2001**

Canadian Metropolitan Area	Core Area/Inner City					Suburbs				
	Population			Change (%)		Population			Change (%)	
	1971	1986	2001	1971–86	1986–2001	1971	1986	2001	1971–86	1986–2001
Toronto	834,555	709,775	784,470	−14.95	10.52	1,523,570	2,334,855	5,492,108	53.25	135.22
Montreal	668,030	447,875	460,471	−32.96	2.81	1,741,850	2,064,735	2,358,249	18.54	14.22
Vancouver	284,020	276,035	355,214	−2.81	28.68	619,740	812,535	1,244,867	31.11	53.21
Ottawa–Hull	143,085	110,770	119,748	−22.58	8.11	354,525	537,890	712,144	51.72	32.40
Edmonton	42,365	31,630	32,509	−25.34	2.78	384,100	547,640	645,787	42.58	17.92
Calgary	61,005	52,585	57,716	−13.80	9.76	312,410	538,560	778,100	72.39	44.48
Quebec	120,825	89,655	84,399	−25.80	−5.86	279,455	376,170	472,842	34.61	25.70
Winnipeg	182,325	191,900	182,325	5.25	−4.99	234,890	337,330	419,801	43.61	24.45
Hamilton	147,320	118,350	118,479	−19.66	0.11	257,600	357,585	460,936	38.81	28.90
London	74,950	56,000	56,092	−25.28	0.16	144,965	209,790	268,953	44.72	28.20
Kitchener	44,080	33,315	35,109	−24.42	5.38	157,565	227,790	327,388	44.57	43.72
St Catharines–Niagara	56,700	45,390	42,059	−19.95	−7.34	152,005	199,050	226,809	30.95	13.95
Halifax	51,085	41,350	39,549	−19.06	−4.36	129,705	173,465	204,692	33.74	18.00
Victoria	48,370	48,795	56,203	0.88	15.18	100,025	148,165	189,205	48.13	27.70
Windsor	87,355	74,830	69,706	−14.34	−6.85	125,155	130,975	176,487	4.65	34.75

Sources: Statistics Canada, 1971, 1986, 2001 censuses.

condominium projects (Chapter 26), up-market loft conversions, unique annual festivals, distinctive historic and waterfront districts, and, in Toronto especially, multiculturalism as devices to 'brand' the city. Revanchist policies (Smith, 1996a), on the other hand, are designed to produce good places to live, work, and invest by targeting crime and safety. Toronto's escalating police budget, juxtaposed against cutbacks in most other services, such as garbage collection and public transit, has been cited as a case in point.

Social Polarization

Sassen's (1991) observations about occupationally induced polarization have today been confirmed in all ranks of world cities. Spatial as well as social polarization has also been documented in Toronto, where, comparing Fordist (1971) versus post-Fordist global (1991) regimes, Walks (2001) established that the greatest difference was dramatic increase in the numbers of professional-class households with above-average incomes, alongside growth, though less substantial, in the numbers of low-order service employees.[8] Walks further showed how global trends had changed Toronto's spatial structure. Dominant Fordist patterns—more homogeneously middle-class suburbs and a more variable but overall lower-ranking central city, alongside sectoral alignment of both high- and low-status neighbourhoods—had become more complicated. Change was greatest in the inner city, where some tracts declined in status while gentrification had also produced many new, higher-income neighbourhoods. The broad band of mature suburbs, built between 1946 and 1970, notwithstanding some established wealthy neighbourhoods, seemed to have taken over the stereotypical role of the central city as home to the poor. Newer suburbs were more homogeneously above-average in household income. The emergence of 'ethnoburbs', also polarized in status, was another distinctive feature of Toronto's new geography.

Unfortunately, there has not been a study of Toronto's socio-spatial structure over the most recent period. Evidence suggests, however, that the inner city has gained increased numbers of middle- and upper-middle-income households, just as poverty has become more entrenched in older or mature suburbs (Bunting et al., 2004; Ley, 1996a; Ley and Smith, 2000).

Citizenship, Equity, Protest

Issues of representation and tolerance are critical to global cities (Florida, 2002; Scott et al., 2001) because they typically attract significant shares of new immigrants and also engender social polarization. Early on, scholars such as Castells (1983) postulated that globalization produced middle-class collective consumption. Juxtaposed against these consumerist trends, however, was increasing grassroots unrest that exposed globalization's darker sides and rearticulated concerns about social justice (Harvey, 1973, 1996). Massive protests in Seattle (1999, World Trade Organization meeting) and Quebec City (2001, Organization of American States Summit of the Americas) brought resistance to globalization to the forefront across North America. Like global economics, global protest movements are rooted in urban places where similar conditions—a built environment that sustains elevated volumes of intra- and inter-urban flows—support and maintain high levels of interconnectedness.

Social action revolves around a perceived absence of attention given to ordinary people's views regarding social and employment equity, the rights, privileges, and responsibilities of citizenship, and the deteriorating condition of the environment. Issues and forums that have gained the attention of social activists include: the G-8; the war in Iraq; health-care reform; global diseases such as mad cow disease, AIDS, and SARS; women's issues; racism and discrimination; genetically modified crops; and poverty and homelessness. While protests continue to grow, recent history suggests that protest remains largely ignored in the policy realm. Thus, while there has been immediate scholarly response decrying issues of escalating injustice, effective alternative strategies have been slow to materialize.

Problems articulated by protest focus on a global paradox: accentuated social polarization and mounting need alongside a decrease, at the policy level, in traditional concerns with equity (Ward, 2000). The power shift within cities has favoured politically conservative and middle-class agendas over local bread-and-butter issues such as maintaining equitable standards of living for growing cohorts of low-income households and minority groups. Although a guise of participatory decision-making is maintained in cities like Vancouver and Toronto where 'embourgeoisement' (Ley, 1996a) of the central city marries well-heeled citizens to municipal administrators (Boschken, 2003), civic life in Canada's largest cities is today fraught with contradiction—well-established trends to social empowerment and participatory decision-making stand against an increasingly right-of-centre corpo-

rate municipal strategy (Boudreau, 2000; Conway, 2004; Isin, 2000; Kholer and Wissen, 2003; Pickvance, 2003).[9] In Canada today, one concern that affects all Canadians, rich or poor, is environmental deterioration. Interestingly, Greenpeace and Canada's Green Party were established in Canada's fledgling global city, Vancouver.

Vancouver as a World City?

Access to Pacific Asia (Figure 4.2) is the salient feature that links Vancouver to the offshore world. Since 1970, Asia has replaced Europe as Vancouver's foremost source of immigration.[10] However, immigration and access are not the only factors accounting for Vancouver's new-found global attractiveness. Often described as having one of the world's

Figure 4.2   **Vancouver-based National and International Connectivity**

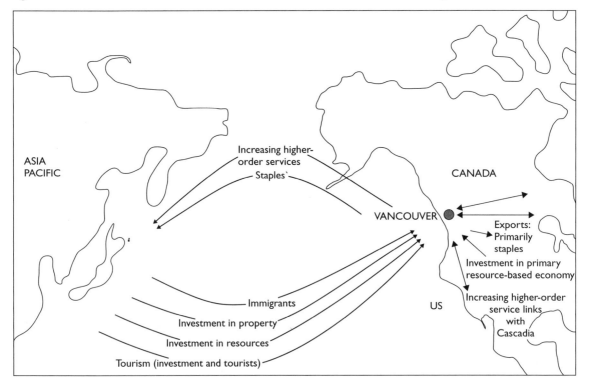

outstanding natural settings, Vancouver has intrinsic attributes sought out by international business, immigrants, and tourists alike (Berelowitz, 2005). Punter (2003: 3) claims that 'Vancouver has achieved an urban renaissance, more comprehensive than any other city in North America', and argues that strategic emphasis on massive new housing development has served to significantly reverse inner-city population decline, intensify the urban fabric, and bring new vitality to the core in a carefully orchestrated landscape that mixes new economic enterprise with all sorts of residential, cultural, and recreational venues.

Throughout the 1980s Vancouver enjoyed dramatic growth in its downtown office core, first established to house head offices of staple-producing giants in the 1920s. By 1990 Vancouver's office district was proportionally one of the largest in all of North America. Office and 'new' industry (motion pictures, marine technologies, software) growth has been stimulated by Vancouver's expanded management and service role within Canada and internationally (Davis and Hutton, 1991)—e.g., engineering consultants, boutique law and accounting services, financial services, language schools/translation facilities, and real estate. Japan has replaced the UK as the province's main source of tourists and tourism itself has become a major staple in the provincial economy. Japanese trading companies have also set up Vancouver subsidiaries representing some of the largest private companies in British Columbia. However, head offices, even of Japanese subsidiaries, do not locate in Vancouver but remain offshore or drift eastward to Toronto.

Over the last 25 years Vancouver's central area has developed a new look that has been socially and politically constructed by a competitive planning regime partnered with development and investment interests, often offshore (Hutton, 2004b). The tone, which is consciously place-based, has shifted planners' attention from public intervention to public regulation of private development (see also Chapter 23). In comparison to Toronto (Kipfer and Keil, 2002), Vancouver has been primarily preoccupied with creating a 'city of difference' (Fincher and

Jacobs, 1998) achieved through middle-class support for urban design and for municipal platforms that stop freeways and promote neighbourhoods. (Paradoxically, the catalyst for Vancouver's unique system of design guidelines was protest against the influx of 'monster' homes built by affluent Hong Kong immigrants in established middle-class neighbourhoods in the 1980s—see Chapter 24.) The 1991 *Central Area Plan,* illustrated in Figure 4.3, and subsequent *City Plan* (1995) and *Livable City Region Plan* (GVRD, 1994; Vancouver, 1991, 1995) have given Vancouver the reputation as being one of the world's best-planned cities (Punter, 2003).

Much of the new development in Vancouver's central area has taken the form of urban megaprojects: massive, high-end developments, often luxury condominiums, located on large tracts of deindustrialized land (former rail and port terminal lands and related industrial properties), as seen in Figure 4.4.[11] Olds (2001: 6) characterizes such projects as being developed with a myriad of capital resources, planned by teams of internationally experienced architects, developers, and financiers, and often marketed overseas. He likens the development corporations that put these projects together to a new kind of TNC specializing in amassing land, capital, and technical resources for mega-scale development.[12] Vancouver politicians have actively encouraged this kind of investment by mounting overseas trade missions and establishing investment offices to bond international ties. The Vancouver-based International Finance Centre put in place by all three levels of government—local, provincial, and federal—is, for example, able to exempt urban megaprojects from some provincial and federal taxes.

Critics postulate that Vancouver has taken on a 'sanitized aesthetic' driven by 'conspicuous consumption' (Ley, 1996a: 365–6) to become a 'highly contrived, ideologically controlled and economically commodified reality' (Berelowitz, 1998: 6). Others raise the issue of affordable housing, while still others (McCann, 2002) are concerned that Vancouver's established record of participatory policy-making is jeopardized by development models that pay little attention to local context. The

Figure 4.3   **Vancouver's 1991 Central Area Plan**

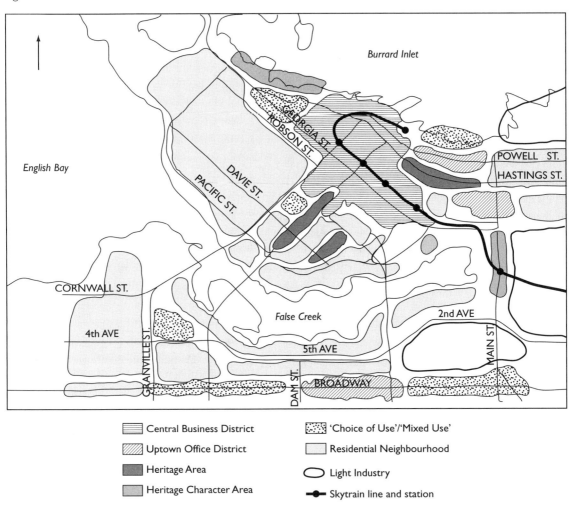

▤	Central Business District	▦	'Choice of Use'/'Mixed Use'
▨	Uptown Office District	▨	Residential Neighbourhood
■	Heritage Area	⬭	Light Industry
▦	Heritage Character Area	●━●	Skytrain line and station

main concerns, however, are the neglect of social welfare needs and the notable absence of social housing starts. Deteriorating conditions in Vancouver's Downtown Eastside, the most impoverished community in all of Canada outside of First Nations reserves, are directly blamed on the city's neo-liberal urban agenda. Today there is concern that encroaching gentrification will further disenfranchise the Eastside's most needy citizens (Lees, 1998, 1999).

There can be no question that Vancouver has enjoyed unprecedented affluence and new economic growth over the last quarter-century. Questions remain, however, regarding the extent of globalization. Vancouver has, in the past, been characterized as a 'village on the edge of the rain forest'. Today, Vancouver undoubtedly qualifies as 'global village' but whether it qualifies as 'world city' remains a question. The city's continued, if lessened,

Figure 4.4   **Urban Megaprojects in Central Vancouver**

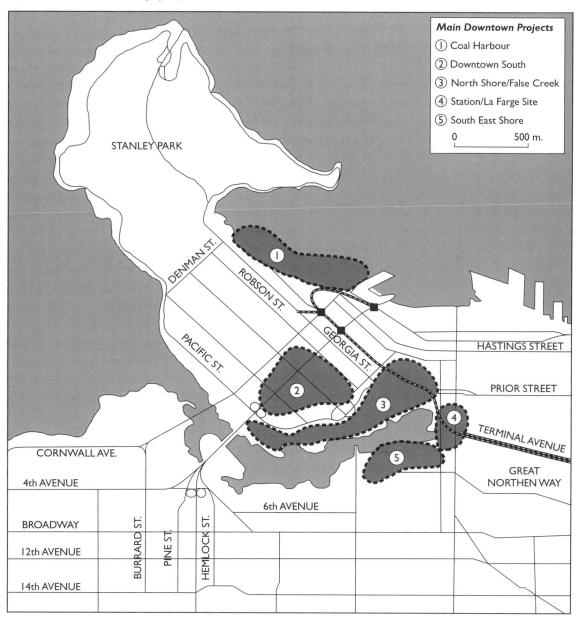

Source: From *Globalization and Urban Change: Capital, Culture and Pacific Rim Mega-projects*, by K. Olds (Oxford: OUP, 2001), 109.
Reprinted by permission of the publisher.

dependence on resource-based exports juxtaposed against distinct absence of national, much less international, corporate strength raises doubts for some about Vancouver's claim to fully global status. Notably, the city's economy was not sufficiently strong to prevent severe downturn when the staple economy crashed in 2002. Subsequently, the entire province suffered. Either way, the question, 'Is Vancouver a world city?', may well be moot because evidence presented briefly here attests to strong international connectedness and also to 'world-class' styles of growth.

Conclusion

The literature on global cities and global city regions has created new understanding about changing scales of inter-city relationships and about restructuring of contemporary urban form alongside socio-economic and political paradox. Table 4.5 summarizes some of the more salient trends that feature in Canada's response to globalization. Yet, it remains questionable as to just how salient the trends and processes identified in the global cities research really are, or whether global cities and global city regions conflate description with explanation. Questions surrounding the essential realness of the global city are compounded in Canada by our weak hold on command-and-control functions of the global economy, a characteristic deemed most central to the world cities model. Thus, we conclude by asking if Vancouver's narrative, writ large, might not well be applied to the entire country? After all, most Canadian cities remain relatively disconnected from the global economy. Even the three that have some claim to global status—Toronto, Vancouver, and Montreal—are, at best, tenuously connected to the sources of global power and decision-making.

Notes

1. Hirst and Thompson (1999) argue that international capital flows and export/import shares of gross domestic product (GDP) were higher in the pre-1914

world economy than in the 1990s; similarly, there are few truly global TNCs because so-called TNCs remain largely based in their domestic economies; and further, they suggest that the nation-state's continued central role in economic management suggests an international rather than a global system. Considerable Canadian rhetoric echoes this sentiment while emphasizing this country's historic interconnectedness. For an interesting take on this theme, see, for example, Norcliffe (2001). In rebuttal, critics (see Dicken, 2003, 2004; Perraton, 2001) argue that by focusing narrowly on quantitative measures of global integration, Hirst and Thompson miss significant qualitative changes such as the emergence of global production chains and flows of foreign direct investment and currency speculation, which increasingly cut across national boundaries. Thus, whereas the pre-1914 world economy represented a shallow form of integration, the contemporary global economy is increasingly characterized by deep integration (Dicken, 2004).

2. Representative Canadian research in this critically discursive genre includes work by: Adkin (2003); Boudreau (2000); Carroll (1989); Caulfield and Peake (1996); Clement and Vosko (2003); Conway (2004); Desfor and Keil (1999); Kholer and Wissen (2003); Kipfer and Keil (2002); Myles and Pierson (1997); Porteous and Smith (2001).

3. See, in this regard, Beauregard's (2003) chiding comments about city 'boosterism' in recent academic writing.

4. This sub-area is best exemplified by the work of Peter Taylor (2004; Taylor et al., 2002) and others at the Global and World Cities Study Group and Network at Loborough University in Britain <www.lboro.ac.uk/gawc/index.html>.

5. New York, London, Paris, and Tokyo are cited in all 16 sources; Los Angeles gets 15 out of 16 citations; San Francisco gets 10; Miami gets 8; Houston gets 6; Detroit gets one.

6. From the mid-1960s to the mid-1980s, policymakers regarded the city as increasingly vestigial or archaic (Amin and Graham, 1997); in other words, the restructuring of advanced economies from the late 1960s onward adversely impacted the fortunes of many urban economies, which suffered from deindustrialization, misguided urban renewal projects, population decline, suburbanization, and rising crime levels (see Harvey 1989b; Tabb and Sawyer, 1978).

Table 4.5   **Salient Transitions Associated with Globalization: Inter- to Intra-Urban Scales**

Global Process	New Structural Features within Metropolitan Regions	Other Interrelationships
Deindustrialization as a Product of offshore industrialization	• Social polarization; erosion of 'blue-collar' middle class. • 'Brownfields' available for new development, 're-placing'/re-urbanization in the inner city.	Leads to 'professionalization' of onshore workforce—'new middle class'; advanced service sector; women play greater role in the new economy; growth of dual-income households exaggerates trends towards polarization, high price of new housing, and consumerism.
Transnational corporations (TNCs) gain economic control	• Location preference for core parts of large, internationally connected metropolitan areas. • Attracts new economic activity e.g., producer services, low-order business services, culture, entertainment. • Impetus for re-urbanization and 're-placing'.	TNCs grow out of national corporate giants as a result of internationalization of business activity that starts with offshore industrialization; TNCs are also the product of advanced business services that serve to streamline corporate growth. National governments court TNCs and other 'global' connections; socio-political swing to the right of centre.
'World' cities become sites of capital accumulation, investment, and production	• Bank head offices and agglomeration of advanced financial services provide capital sources for innovation and expansion. • Sited in core in traditional or reconstructed financial district.	Provides for all sorts of niched and partnered investment opportunities that support innovative business enterprise; probably also a major factor behind the new urban 'creativity', whether arts and cultural, technological, design, or business. Substantial investment funds available to 're-place' obsolescent core landscapes from the Fordist period.
Knowledge-based, 'new' economic enterprise; advanced service sector	• As above, favours the core. • 'Creative' class of workers grows out of previous generation's blue-collar cohort. • Upside of social polarization. • Re-urbanization and 're-placing'—gentrification, luxury condominiums, etc.	Consumerist lifestyles of enriched middle class depend on high-volume import of inexpensive consumer goods and ready availability of recreational, personal, and household services. Meeting places for face-to-face interaction become an important fixture of the urban landscape.
Low-order service sector expands	• Increasing impoverishment of some neighbourhoods, especially in aging tracts of rental, high-rise housing in the inner suburbs. • Downside of social polarization. • Housing inaffordability crisis; homelessness.	Polarization exacerbated by demise of the social welfare net and competitive municipal agenda and by new household forms. *(Continued)*

Table 4.5   *(continued)*

Global Process	New Structural Features within Metropolitan Regions	Other Interrelationships
High volumes of international and domestic immigration focused on world cities	• New 'ethnoburbs' in suburbs and enclaves in the central city. • Nature of immigrant intake accentuates both sides of social polarization. • Over-heated housing markets.	Ethnic and cultural diversity believed to be a major contributor to 'creative city' growth. Huge costs of very fast growth—e.g., housing inaffordability. Exacerbates problem of balancing municipal budgets—service provision for new Canadians is costly and generally not adequately provided by higher levels of government. Accentuates problems of social justice, equity, citizenship.
Transportation/ telecommunications hub	• Large international airport complex. • Centre for IT and related enterprise. • Emergence of polycentric nodes.	Business enterprise is more footloose than ever before in history; cities work hard/compete to attract and retain major employers and innovative enterprises.
Accelerated intercity competition	• Cities mount expensive marketing campaigns that might entail reconstructing the symbolic heart of the city, hosting world events and other 'showcasing' venues while curtailing municipal spending in order to balance budgets and retain/attract more footloose enterprise.	Neo-liberal agenda at higher levels of government leaves cities 'strapped' financially. Municipal cutbacks further erode social welfare support and deepen impoverishment.
Erosion of social welfare net	• High levels of social spending are deemed unacceptable to the global imperative. • Socio-political shift to the right of centre.	Polarization exacerbated. Paradoxical growth of wealth alongside poverty. Some properties of world city growth—e.g., diversity, tolerance, efficiency—threatened by lack of public support.

7. The political jurisdiction of the Greater Vancouver Regional Authority is, on the other hand, not sufficiently extensive to capture Vancouver's functional metropolitan region, which would have to include White Rocks, Abbotsford, and maybe even Victoria on Vancouver Island.

8. Diminished growth in low-order workers was believed dampened by the relative availability of social support in Canada as suggested by Fainstein (1997) and Levine (1995). Note, however, that the major impact of the 1990s dismantling of Canada's social service net, which produces increased ranks of low-income households, occurred after the end-date of the Walks research.

9. An example of this schism at the grassroots level could be seen in the oppositional politics of the citizen-based protest group, Bread Not Circuses Coalition (2000), that rallied (unsuccessfully) against massive public spending in support of Toronto's (subsequently also unsuccessful) bid for the 2008 Olympic Games.

10. It is notable that while Toronto and Vancouver together gained the lion's share of new immigrants over the last 15 years, Vancouver has enjoyed far greater numbers of business- and investment-class entrants.

11. These developments sell themselves on qualities of classic elegance and sophistication, fine crafting, outstanding views and exclusivity, and, of course, careful surveillance.

12. On the ground, development is often run out of branch-plant operations set up by offshore property magnates (often from Hong Kong or China); sometimes these branch plants are headed by relatives or close friends.

Chapter 5

Cities as Land Markets

Andrejs Skaburskis and Diana Mok

Why do we find parking lots on very expensive downtown land? Why is suburban development discontiguous in places? Why is the selling price of agricultural land at the edge of the city so high in comparison to the capitalized agricultural rents? Why are farmers at the outskirts of Toronto so upset with the greenbelt plan that would preserve their farmland?

We develop our knowledge of cities in many ways. We can gain a sense of the city by walking its streets and talking to its people. Novels provide views of the kind of neighbourhoods we seldom visit. Newspapers tell us about the forces that change cities and conversations with friends and colleagues may help us form images of the kind of city we want. For most purposes, the knowledge developed through these informal ways is enough. However, when trying to predict the effects of demographic or economic changes, when having to assess the efficacy of plans, or when analyzing problems or assigning blame for current conditions, we can often benefit by relying on more formal explanations of the factors that shape cities. We can focus on some aspects of cities by building models that can be made progressively more exact by increasing the number and severity of their underlying assumptions. Economists tend to build very precise mathematical models at the cost of having to accept unrealistic assumptions.

This chapter introduces some of the models of land value and land use that economists use to predict the spatial effects of changes in demography, economy, and preferences. It describes some of the factors that affect land markets in ways that change cities. It defines land rent, relates rent to price, and then presents some of the classical and neo-classical models showing the relationship between land rent and land use. It discusses density and price gradients and the factors that determine their profiles. The effects of changing expectations regarding city growth rates and the basic concepts behind the 'new urban economics' are presented. The economic factors encouraging the expansion and polynucleation of cities are discussed, as are the trends that gentrify inner-city neighbourhoods. Some of the demographic and social trends that have been observed over the last few decades are related to land markets and to the changing structure of cities. The role of land markets in shaping cities concludes the chapter.

The Classic Model of Land Rent

Adam Smith (1970 [1776]), founder of modern economic theory, defined 'rent' as the amount paid for the use of the land for a period of time while the 'selling price' is paid for the transfer of ownership. Land rents are 'the highest amount a tenant can pay . . . considering the actual circumstances of the land' (p. 139). David Ricardo, founder of rent theory, defines land rent as 'that portion of the produce of the earth, which is paid to the landlord for the use of the original and indestructible powers of the soil' (Ricardo, 1969 [1817]: 33). Economists use the concept of 'rent' to describe the value of the flow of services rendered by an asset over time and 'price' as a payment for the transfer of the ownership of the asset. The price is usually set by the 'capitalization' of the future stream of rents; this process will be described later.

Sir Peter Hall credits von Thünen (1996 [1826]) with developing the world's first land value model. Von Thünen places his hypothetical city on an undifferentiated plain with equally fertile land to answer questions about the patterns and intensity of agricultural land use. We are given the market prices for the produce and the cost of production and transportation per hectare of produce. To simplify, the quantity of produce is measured in units defined by the amount that can be grown on a one-square-kilometre plot of land. Figure 5.1a shows the cost and price as functions of distance from the market and Figure 5.1b shows the resulting land rent gradient. In this example, agricultural land surrounds the town up to a distance of five kilometres. The land rent is created by transportation costs, by the friction of space, and by the resulting gap between revenues and costs at different locations. The furthest extent of agriculture is set by the point at which no rents can be generated.

A reduction in transportation costs expands the radius of agricultural production and rotates the rent schedule counter-clockwise, as in Figure 5.1c. The increase in supply, however, lowers the market price of produce and the area needed for cultivation contracts, shifting the rent gradient downward. Landowners at the periphery gain rents while the owners closer to the centre lose rents.[1] Distinct land uses form concentric circles around the centre, as illustrated in Figure 5.2. The use with the highest

Figure 5.1. The Von Thünen Model of Agricultural Land Rent
The figures assume that it costs $1 per square kilometre to grow agricultural produce and $2 per kilometre to transport the produce to the market, and that the produce can sell for $11. In Figure 5.1a, the selling price of the produce is represented by the horizontal line at $11, regardless of distance, while transportation costs increase linearly with distance. Figure 5.1b shows the corresponding land rent as residual. For example, at 2 kilometres away from the market, the selling price is $11, while the total cost is $5, giving a land rent of $6. At 5 kilometres, land rent becomes zero so that the town has a boundary of 5 kilometres. Figure 5.1c illustrates the impact of a reduction in transportation costs and selling prices. 'Rent 1' shows the land rent when transportation cost per unit distance decreases to $1 per kilometre, while selling price stays unchanged. The boundary of the town increases from 5 to 10 kilometres. 'Rent 2' illustrates the impact of a drop in selling price from $11 to $8 due to an increase in supply.

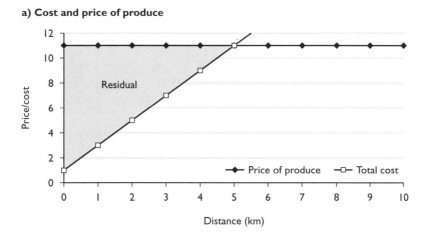

a) Cost and price of produce

(continued)

Figure 5.1.   **(continued)**

b) Land rent

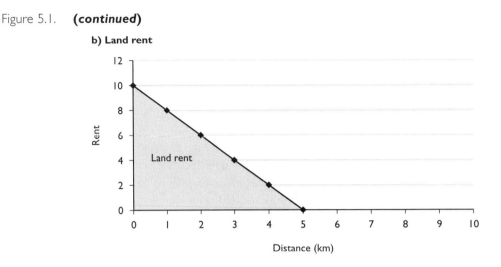

c) The effect of a reduction in commute costs

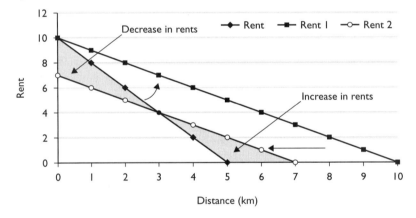

transportation cost per hectare of produce will locate next to the centre, provided it can generate a rent greater than that offered by any other land-use. Within any type of land use, the higher density or intensity of use generates higher transportation costs per hectare of land and, therefore, will be located closer to the centre than the less dense or more extensive use. Although von Thünen models explained agricultural land-use patterns, his concepts are applied to cities. Commercial and office uses most highly value proximity to the centre and therefore form the inner circle. Higher-density housing is then followed by lower-density housing, with increasing distance from the centre.

Neo-Classical Urban Land Rent

Richard Hurd (1903), founder of urban land economics, could have coined the realtors' mantra, 'location, location, location'.

> Since value depends on economic rent, and rent on location, and location on convenience, and convenience on nearness, we may eliminate the intermediate steps and say that value depends on nearness. (Hurd, 1903: 13)

Cities are shaped and reshaped by the competing centrifugal force of cheap land at the periphery and

Figure 5.2   **Boundaries between Land Uses**

'Rent 1' refers to the land rent of produce 1, which costs $2 per kilometre to transport to the market; 'Rent 2' is the land rent of produce 2, which has a transportation cost of $1 per kilometre. Produce 1 will be grown within 2 kilometres of the market, whereas produce 2 will be in the outer part of the town.

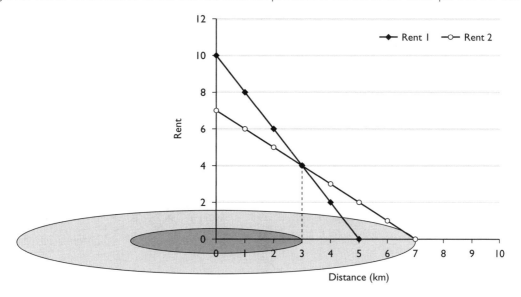

the centripetal attraction of the city centre with its agglomeration of businesses and access to the region's households and employees. Land, Hurd points out, goes to the higher bidder, to the one who can make the land earn the most. The classical economists define this amount as the 'residual' value, the difference between the cost of production at a site and the revenue generated. The neo-classical economists explain factor prices in terms of the value produced by adding one more unit of the factor. To maximize profits, firms continue to hire factors (labour, capital, land) until the amount they pay for an extra unit (marginal cost) equals the revenue generated by that unit (marginal revenue). In short, land rents are set by the land's contribution to our overall well-being. A developer proposing a project that would increase the value of a parcel of land would be making the land more productive and would be contributing to the well-being of society, provided that third parties are not adversely affected (a condition rarely met in practice).

The neo-classical models also place the city on an undifferentiated plain and assume that all employment is in the centre. The Haig (1926), Ratcliffe (1949, 1955), and Lowdon Wingo Jr (1961) models have land rents decreasing with distance from the centre by an amount equal to the households' savings in commute costs, as illustrated in Figure 5.1. The land rent at each point is equal to the agricultural rent at the periphery plus the commute costs that households save by not living at the periphery. The rents gained by the land just outside the city form the base for the rents inside the city.

William Alonso (1964), founder of neo-classical location theory, recognized that land rent and the consumption of land, housing, and other goods and services are related: the higher the rent, the less land is used; the less people spend on housing, the more they can spend on other goods and services. Households, in these models, maximize their utility by considering all of these factors. Since higher-income households tend to occupy larger lots, they are drawn towards the periphery by the lower land costs. Lower-income and/or smaller households occupy the more expensive inner-city land at higher densities to reduce their commute costs. Since they buy less housing, they would not save as much as higher-income households by moving further out. Alonso's model explains the growth of the suburbs and the spread of the urban region as a function of increasing incomes and the preference for housing and other goods and services. The model explains the curvature in the density gradients that were observed earlier by Colin Clark (1951) and Newling (1969). Richard Muth (1969) and Edwin Mills (1979) expand the theory and explicitly introduce housing markets.

Alonso invents the concept of a household's 'bid-rent' map, which has contours tracing the rents at each location that would keep their level of well-being constant. The bid-rent curves in Figure 5.3 show the rent/distance trade-off that would make the household indifferent as to its location with regard to the city centre. Households maximize their utility by trying to locate on the lowest bid-rent curve possible because this leaves them with the most money for other goods and services. Landowners try to select the households that are willing to pay the most for their land, but they have to compete with each other. The base price of urban land is set at the periphery where landowners would convert their land to housing if the land rents offered by this use were just higher than the rents they were gaining from agricultural uses. In Figure 5.3, household A would have to pay a rent of at least R(a) to bid land away from agricultural acres at the periphery, but it would be willing to pay more for closer locations up to the point on the bid-rent curve going through R(e) at the city's periphery. Household B may have steeper bid-rent curves to reflect its greater valuation of proximity to the centre.

The urban land-rent profile is described by Alonso as the outcome of a game played by the households seeking the lowest rent and landowners the highest rents. The equilibrium is attained when the household most valuing the central location has it at a rent that differs from the rent charged at the

Figure 5.3   Alonso's Bid-Rent Map
The figure assumes that there are two households, A and B, each trying to bid for one of the two sites from agriculture for its own use. The solid lines are the bid rents of household B, and the broken lines are those of household A. Higher bid-rent curves, as indicated in grey, give lower welfare to a household because the household pays more rent for the site. Lines in black represent the highest household welfare, but are the minimum rent to landowners. Land rent from agriculture is denoted by the dotted line.

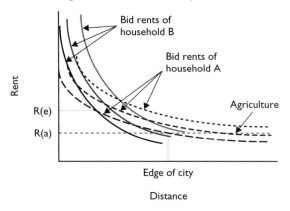

next further out location by no more than its valuation of the difference in the access attributes. The rent at locations further from the city centre is set by that household's valuation of its location relative to the next best option, and so on. The rent at the periphery is set by the agricultural uses.

Explanations of changes in city form often use the bid-rent concept. For example: increasing income flattens bid-rent curves because it lets people buy larger lots and, therefore, makes them less willing to pay the higher rents close to the city centre. All other things being equal, rising incomes are therefore expected to increase the spread of the city should all other factors remain constant. Increasing commute costs make the bid-rent curves steeper due to the increasing tendency of households to move closer to their place of work. The decrease in average household size may increase the slope of the bid-rent curves as the smaller households buy less housing and, thus, are more willing to pay to be close to the downtown. The increase in the proportion of dual-income families increases both the household's commute costs and income, and the effect on the city's spatial structure depends on which factor is more important.

The 'New' Urban Economics

Why does the cost of agricultural land at the urban edge skyrocket in value? The price of land at the urban periphery is set by the opportunity cost of the land in its agricultural use and the present value of the expected future growth in rents.[2] In a growing city, the boundary is continuously being pushed further from the centre, making the land within the built-up part of the city relatively more attractive. Since buyers recognize that the agricultural or raw land at the current edge will command higher rents in the future after the city has expanded, they are willing to pay a premium now to benefit from the future rent increases.[3]

Anticipated future changes in land use affect its current price. The announcement of a transportation improvement, for example, increases the value of the affected land as people anticipate the future increase in rents due to the improved accessibility. Regulations that affect the use of land change its prices at the time they are announced. When the Ontario government announced plans to form a greenbelt around Toronto, the price of the farmland that was ready for development dropped because the restriction would eliminate the potential to gain the future growth in urban rents. The *Globe and Mail* reported a farmer complaining that he could sell an acre of land for $250,000 for development but for only $10,000 if it was restricted to agricultural uses. The value of new amenities that will affect future residents is also capitalized into current prices.

Another interesting complication is introduced by the changing development options over time. If a vacant lot was trapped for a long time within an expanding city, it is likely that its development would be different from the development that would have taken place much earlier when the land was at the edge of the city. A lot developed 20 years

ago might have supported a townhouse complex, but in a larger city the land may now be developed as a high-rise condominium creating larger profits for the landowner. The intensity with which land inside a growing city can be developed increases over time and this, in turn, elevates the residual value of the land. It can pay an owner to wait with vacant or underdeveloped land before developing or converting it to more intense use.[4]

How long will profit-maximizing landowners hold the land off the market before developing or redeveloping it? Hotelling (1931) starts by recognizing that equilibrium in investment markets requires that assets appreciate in value at a rate equal to the relevant interest rate. If the rate at which the asset's price increases were lower than the rate available in other equally risky investments, then its price would drop as investors shift to the more profitable assets. The reduction in the price of an asset increases the *rate* of return when the absolute increase in price remains the same. Wicksell (1935) explains the profit-maximizing timing decision with the example of a landowner waiting for trees to grow before cutting them down to sell their lumber. Waiting allows the trees to grow larger and yield more lumber when they are cut, but waiting precludes the use of the funds that would be gained by the sale of the lumber. The most profitable time to harvest the trees is when the rate of growth in their value drops to equal the rate of return on alternative investments. As the price of an asset increases by the same amount, the rate of return decreases because the denominator keeps getting larger.

Donald Shoup (1970: 40) applied the profit-maximizing timing model to urban land use and dispelled the notion that 'development or redevelopment would or should occur as soon as the development value of a site, net of clearance cost, exceeds the value of the existing improved property, as is sometimes stated.' The most profitable development time is when the rate of change in the value of the development that can take place on a site is equal to the interest rate on equally risky alternative investments. Holding land vacant, or using it as a parking lot, is worthwhile when the rate of increase in the present value of the most profitable project that can be placed on the land exceeds the rate of return on alternative investments. The change in the profitability of development is due to the change in what would be built on the land and due to the fact that development freezes that use for a long time. If the development potential is not changing over time, then a site will be developed now or never and the conditions described by von Thünen and the neo-classical economists would hold.

Arnott and Lewis (1979) show that waiting for development changes the density of development. As owners hold vacant land and the suburbs grow around them, land prices increase and less is used in developing real estate: higher land prices encourage higher-density development. Keeping some land vacant can make cities more compact in the long run by leaving room for new waves of high-density development (Peiser, 1989). Had room for infill development not been left, the new development would be at the periphery of the urban region and the total time and effort spent on commuting to the centre would be higher. Property taxation also affects development timing and density (Skaburskis, 1995). Taxing the land portion of real estate at much higher rates than the building portion would increase the cost of holding vacant or underused land and would tend to speed up development. While the timing effect would tend to reduce density, the 'substitution' effect increases density. The lower tax on the building reduces building costs and thereby increases the amount of built form placed on the land. The shift to land value taxation in Pittsburgh was intended to stimulate inner-city growth after the decline of the steel industry. Portland, Oregon, is considering a higher tax on land and a lower one on the building to encourage more intense development. Melbourne, Australia, has been using land value taxation for over a century.

The capitalized growth premium is not the only factor explaining the gap between urban and agricultural land prices. The development of land fixes its use for a long period and, thereby, prevents the property owner from taking advantage of possible future changes. The presence of uncertainty increases the value of having options, and owners will delay development until their expected returns rise to cover their perceived cost of the uncertainty. Since the development decision is not reversible, owners will wait until prices rise to cover their perceived cost of the irreversibility of the development decision (Capozza and Helsley, 1989). The resulting land price gradient is illustrated in Figure 5.4a. The growth, uncertainty, and irreversibility premiums are added to the opportunity cost of the land in non-urban use. The cost of infrastructure is also added when determining the market price of buildable lots. The capitalized differential rent, described by the neo-classical models, is added and increases with proximity to the centre. Constraints on development at the periphery or increases in development cost charges at the edge of the city will increase the price of all land and housing inside the city. The city is also formed by neighbourhoods of different quality generating rent differences, as described by Ricardo. Zoning bylaws also create discontinuities in the rent and price profiles, resulting in a broken price gradient as illustrated in Figure 5.4b (Evans, 2004: 25).

The new urban economics models explain why some suburban development skips over unused land. Owners have many different reasons for holding land, as pointed out by Brown, Phillips, and Roberts (1981). Some are keeping the land for their children and have no interest in making a profit. Some may place intrinsic value on the ownership itself regardless of the returns they can get for its sale or development. Others may have different discount rates or expectations of growth rates that affect their timing of the sale or development. The variety of reasons for owning land means that owners will sell or develop their land at different times. The result is the discontiguous pattern of suburban development that most city planners deplore.

The Spread and Polynucleation of Low-Density Urban Regions

The classical and neo-classical models help us relate changes in land value, use, and density to changes in the accessibility and amenity value of different locations. To expand our understanding of land markets we have to give up some of the assumptions that make the models tractable and consider cities that are more realistic. We start by recognizing that our cities have been evolving multiple centres and that employment has been decentralizing. Even at the beginning of the twentieth century, firms were moving out into the countryside. New assembly line processes created the need for large continuous floors and firms were attracted by the cheap land outside the built-up city. As the firms moved, their workers followed. Richard Harris (1996, 2004) shows that the draw of low-priced land brought all income groups to the city's edge, not just the rich as in the models of the economists and early social ecologists. The corporate suburb developed in the post-war era after the Central Mortgage and Housing Corporation (now known as Canada Mortgage and Housing Corporation) helped create the financial markets that made mortgages available to middle-income Canadians.

The spreading out of our cities is partly the result of increases in income levels and our standard of living. Increasing income lets people buy the larger houses they prefer and this brings them to the suburbs. However, income growth would cause cities to spread only when the increase in housing demand exceeds the contracting effect of the increase in the perceived cost of commuting. The net effect is expected to vary across demographic groups: families with children may move outward while the affluent young households seek inner-city locations (Ley, 1996a; Meligrana and Skaburskis, 2005). Suburban expansion is also encouraged by technological innovations that lower commute costs. The earliest nineteenth-century suburbs were the result of new streetcar lines. The general availability of automobiles and the development of intra-urban highways turned us into a 'suburban nation', in Richard Harris's words. Smart highways that eliminate congestion by charging variable tolls will expand the city further by reducing commute costs for the households that value most and can best afford large semi-rural estates. Advancements in telecommunication technology encourage the spread of cities by letting people maintain close contact with their work from large distances (Mok et al., 2005).

Figure 5.4   **Land Price Gradients**
The price of an inner-city lot is set by the present value of the agricultural rents at the periphery plus the growth, uncertainty, and irreversibility premiums. It is set by the developers' cost of providing the on-site infrastructure plus the development cost charges for the public facilities and off-site infrastructure. Prices inside the city are also determined by the capitalized differential rents due to the relative increase in the attractiveness of locations closer to the centre.

a) Hypothetical Land Price Gradient

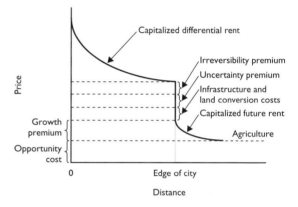

Neighbourhood quality varies across the city and zoning restricts land uses. The price gradient in reality, which is expected to be a broken profile reflecting differences in neighbourhood quality, may generate rent and price differences much the same way as fertility differences created rent differences in Ricardo's model.

b) A More Realistic Price Gradient

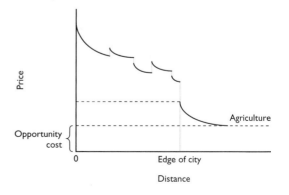

Contemporary building technology lowers costs by mass-producing dwelling units on site within large, low-density tracts. The quest for scale economies through large-tract low-density development helps spread cities. The reduced cost of the houses helps lower-income households to become suburban homeowners. The combination of increased demand for floor space, the reduced size of lots, the monotony of mass-produced dwellings, and the need for several automobiles per household brings garage-snouted streetscapes into the greenfields at the edge of the city (Figure 5.5). Monotonous streetscapes also cause housing units to be seen as equal substitutes to each other. The conformity implies that all the housing units are sensitive to a price change in their suburban neighbourhood and that housing as an asset would, therefore, become much more risky than it was while the dwellings were differentiated (Hernandez et al., 2003; Mok, 2005a).

Planners and local politicians encourage the low-density suburban development with exclusionary zoning policies that maintain their tax revenues and pacify their detached house occupants' quest for the status quo. The demand for more land at the periphery is also fuelled by rising crime rates and deteriorating neighbourhoods in the inner city. More recently, a feedback loop may have evolved as people move further from the main city centre to live closer to their suburbanizing workplaces and big-box shopping centres. Income change, technology, planning, crime, and the relocation of employment conspire to push away the countryside. 'Solitude', Huxley (1960: 21) observes, 'is receding at the rate of four and a half kilometres per annum.' Most Canadian cities have developed new centres in their suburbs. Some have been planned, as in the Greater Vancouver Regional District and in Mississauga, while others evolve through the operation of the land market. Why would firms move to

Figure 5.5   Conventional Suburb in Kingston, Ontario, with Garage Front Streetscape

form new centres away from the traditional central business district? A simple model can help answer this question: assume that the city rests on a line and consists of firms that use land for production and households that use land for housing. Firms and residents occupy space in this linear city. Firms produce intermediate outputs and incur transportation costs to move outputs among other firms; hence, proximity to other firms lowers their transportation costs—this drives firms to agglomerate to move closer together. At the same time, firms hire workers who have to commute to work and pay wages that cover their commute and other costs. As firms cluster in one location, they have to pay higher wages to compensate for the longer commute. To be closer to the employees and, thereby, reduce their payrolls, some firms move to the suburbs. The city is an outcome of competing forces: the quest for agglomeration economies brings firms together in one part of the city; and the diseconomies created by congestion and increasing distance to their employees encourage their dispersion.

Suburban densities are also affected by planners adopting the principles endorsed by the New Urbanists (Gordon and Vipond, 2005). Markham, a northeast suburb of Toronto, has the highest concentration of New Urbanist-inspired subdivisions in North America with Cornell being its flagship (Figure 5.6). New Urbanism encourages households to embrace higher-density living for the charm and community spirit that can only be created through well-designed higher-density development (Duany et al., 2000). However, the extent to which New Urbanism will reduce the demand for raw land at the city's periphery will depend on the future cost of commuting and on households' willingness, throughout their housing careers, to accept higher densities in exchange for the attractive attributes of New Urbanist neighbourhoods (Skaburskis, 2005).

The increases in land costs and the city planner's growing concern with the costs of city spread have been changing suburban development and influencing density gradients (Bunting et al., 2002;

Figure 5.6   **Residential Street in Cornell, a New Urbanist Community in Markham, Ontario**

Figure 5.7   **Population Density Gradients, Toronto, 1971 and 2001**

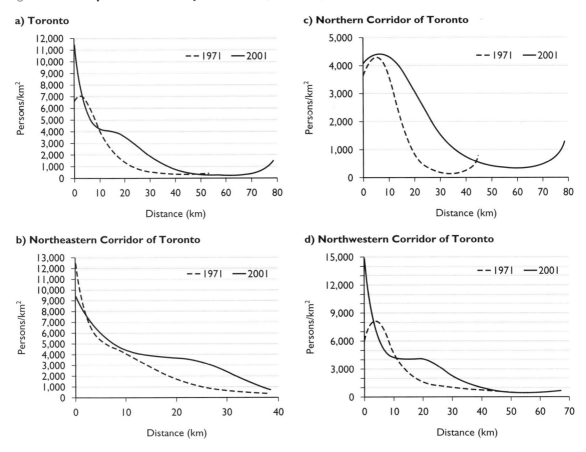

the CBD, a sub-centre that did not exist in 1971. Figures 5.7b, c, and d separate the Toronto density gradient into three corridors: northeast, north, and northwest. They show that the sub-centres are emerging mostly towards the northeast and northwest. These sub-centres in Scarborough, North York, and Mississauga provide population with access to local employment centres, municipal government offices, expressway interchanges, and, to some extent, space for high-order services such as theatres and recreational complexes. The figures illustrate the increasing density in the suburbs as well as the rising interest in the inner city.

Skaburskis, 1989). Figures 5.7a, b, and c show how the density gradient in the Toronto census metropolitan area (CMA) changed between 1971 and 2001. Population density is almost everywhere higher in 2001 than in 1971. In the city centre, density increased by more than 50 per cent, from 7,000 persons per km² in 1971 to about 11,000 persons per km² in 2001. The 2001 gradient is steeper than the 1971 gradient within the first 10 kilometres from the central business district (CBD) but rapidly flattens beyond 10 kilometres. The most intriguing difference, however, is due to the 2001 gradient showing a second peak at 20 to 25 kilometres from

The Gentrifying Inner City

Condominium towers have been helping households trade away lot size for maintenance-free living, security, and proximity to downtown amenities (Skaburskis, 1988). The combination of changing lifestyles and increasing income levels is drawing people back to the inner cities and changing the character of their neighbourhoods as well as their political influence (Filion, 1991). Changes in rent between 1981 and 1996 for dwellings of different vintage or age (i.e., built in different periods) in our major cities are illustrated in Figure 5.8a. In all metropolitan areas, the rent of the older dwellings increased more than the rents in buildings built in the early 1980s. In the 1950 and 1960s, the rapid expansion of the suburbs left much of the older stock to be occupied by lower-income households, as can be seen in Figure 5.8b by the steep 1971 rent/age gradients for standardized dwellings in Toronto and Montreal (Skaburskis, 2005). Figure 5.8b also shows how much the rent structure has changed since 1981. Rather than depreciating, the older stock increased in value due to the increasing demand for inner-city locations. By 1996, no difference in rent could be found across cohorts in the Toronto or Montreal markets. Since the oldest stock is in the inner city, the changes in the relative value of housing built during different periods points to the resurgence of market demand for inner-city land.

Changes in demography, income, and tastes are bringing higher-income households back to the inner city. Since these households have higher incomes, they buy or rent larger dwellings than the previous lower-income occupants and, thereby, lower the residential density of the inner-city neighbourhoods (Meligrana and Skaburskis, 2005). While the number of dwelling units in these neighbourhoods increased in the 1980s and 1990s, their population decreased. With growing affluence, delayed family formation, and reduced fertility, the 'upgrading' of the older inner-city neighbourhoods will continue along with the spreading out of the city.

The Changing Factors

Land markets are driven by changes in demand for housing, commercial, and industrial floor space, and they are affected by infrastructure development and planning regulations. Some of the changes can be predicted with the help of the models presented earlier in this chapter. We know that our population is aging. Incomes are rising, yet income disparity is increasing as higher-income groups get richer and lower-income households get poorer. We have observed a steady decrease in the average household size for more than a century and this will have a direct effect on the bid-rent curves described by Alonso. Women have greater employment opportunities than they had decades ago, resulting in increasing household incomes and changing demographic patterns. The following paragraphs draw on the models presented earlier to describe the expected effects of these changes on the relative demand for inner-city and suburban land.

The Aging of the Population

With population aging, we might expect the bid-rent curves of the older households to become steeper as access to the centrally located services becomes more important and as their mobility decreases. The aging of the population might reduce the rate at which cities expand into the countryside. However, cities are complex and a change in a factor can have a number of consequences. A study by Skaburskis (1999, 2000) showed that aging is associated with wealth accumulation, which tends to increase the household's propensity to buy and to stay in a single-family detached house to maintain their shallow bid-rent schedules. Of course, a larger proportion of the population will move to condominiums and to adult-oriented enclaves, but we do not expect an aging population to change demand enough to alleviate the concerns raised by the continuing expansion of our large cities into the countryside.

Figure 5.8   **Rent/Age Gradients for Dwelling in Selected Canadian Cities**

a) Proportional Change in Rents for a Standardized Dwelling between 1981 and 1996

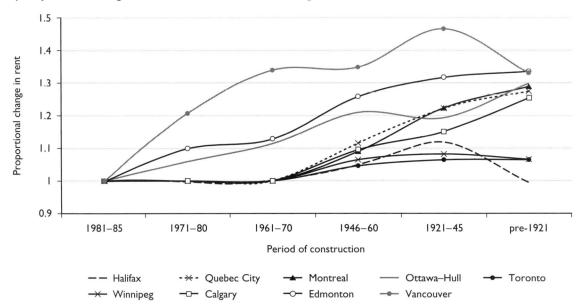

b) Comparison of the 1971 and 1996 Rent/Age Profiles for a Standardized Dwelling in Toronto and Montreal

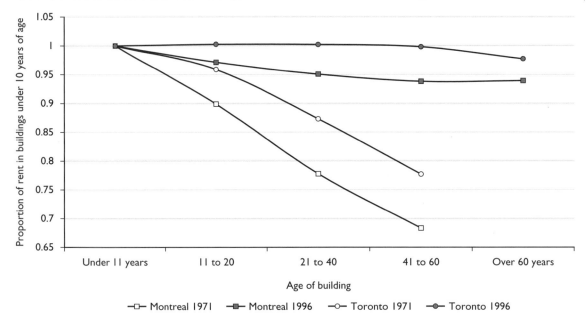

Decreasing Household Size

Urban and housing economists often associate household characteristics with specific preferences for location and housing consumption (Mok, 2005b). Particularly, larger households require more space to satisfy their housing needs. The neo-classical models posit that, all else being equal, increasing housing consumption is associated with increasing demand for lower-density suburban housing. However, the average household size has been consistently declining in Canadian cities. According to the 1981 census, average household size was 3.9 persons among primary households. By 2001, the average household size had dropped to 3.6 persons. This trend has two implications for land markets. First, smaller households may demand smaller housing units, thereby increasing their demand for locations closer to the CBD. Second, because of the smaller dwellings, the amount of land they occupy decreases, making the city more compact. Both instances imply that Canadian cities are likely to observe a movement of smaller households back towards the CBD.

Increasing Household Income

Individuals and households in Canadian cities have been receiving higher incomes in the last two decades. Average personal incomes increased by more than 15 per cent from $25,320 in 1981 to $29,111 in 2001. Median household incomes also rose from between $50,000–$60,000 in 1981 to $60,000–$65,000 in 2001 (all values are measured in 2001 dollars). The increase in personal and household income has an ambiguous location outcome. If changes in income do not affect the marginal value that individuals place on time spent (i.e., lost) commuting, then the neo-classical models predict that households would consume more housing space and live in locations that are further away from the CBD. However, increases in income also increase the perceived time cost of commuting, which makes central locations more attractive. The income effect on location hinges upon the relative size of housing demand and marginal transportation cost-income elasticities.

Increasing Income Disparity

Accompanying the general increase in personal and household income in Canadian cities is the widening of the spread of income across households and individuals. In 1981, the lower and upper quartiles for personal income were $12,450 and $39,525; by 2001 these figures had grown to $14,780 and $45,000, and the difference between the lower and upper quartiles had increased by more than $3,000. Income disparity is even more prominent at the household level: the classes of lower and upper quartiles for household income were $45,000–$50,000 and $60,000–$80,000 in 1981, which widened to reach $35,000–$40,000 and $85,000–$100,000 in 2001. The neo-classical models show that households with higher incomes outbid the lower-income households for the desirable locations and push them into the crowded and less desirable neighbourhoods that are often less accessible to job sites.

The classic models of land rent explain how the land uses gaining the most value from proximity to the city centre are located next to the centre, *provided* that the residual value they generate is higher than can be produced by any other use. The bipolarization of income is associated with housing tenure, and the increasing wealth of homeowners has stimulated condominium demand that has raised land value in the central cities of Vancouver and Toronto to a level that makes it impossible for developers to build unsubsidized rental housing for most families. The income bipolarization plays out in the land market in ways that are detrimental to the lower-income renters. Alan Walks (2001) relates the changes to post-Fordist economic restructuring and illustrates the effects on the social ecology of Toronto, where there are more low-income earners than in the past competing for a supply of low-cost housing that has decreased over time.

Reduction in Gender Inequality

Perhaps the most dramatic change since the 1960s that affects our cities is due to the increasing labour force participation of women. The most obvious change is in the household income of couples and the resulting increase in housing demand. Higher household income has been considered a primary reason for the very large increases in land prices during the 1970s, and studies of the increasing proportion of households that have to pay over half of their income for housing point to the importance of the number of wage earners in a household (Moore and Skaburskis, 2004; Skaburskis, 2004). Equalizing the earnings prospects of women will increase the rates of women as heads of households and reduce fertility rates. Women with higher income are less likely to marry or form couples (Skaburskis, 1997); among those who do have a partner, women with higher income are also less likely to bear children (Mok, 2005b), and those who have children tend have fewer of them than do the women with lower incomes.

The application of neo-classical models would suggest that the trend will make the bid-rent schedules steeper for many of the women heads of households and would, therefore, reduce sprawl. In addition, Rose and Villeneuve (1998) showed that the increase in the number of households with women professionals increases the demand for inner-city locations, in part because professional women's job locations are more often in downtowns as opposed to the suburban locations of the male-oriented professions. Skaburskis (1997) also showed that increasing women's income prospects raises the proportion of women demanding inner-city locations. However, the increase in the number of households due to reduced rates of family formation rates, combined with growth in women's income, also raises the aggregate demand for suburban houses. The structure of inner cities will change as a result of the dramatic shifts in women's opportunities, but market pressures will continue to push the suburbs outward.

The Role of the Market

The process of competition within a perfect market would allocate resources and distribute goods and services in a way that lets people maximize their well-being as they themselves see it. Land markets help ensure that the potential users of a parcel of land who most value its attributes, and are most able to pay, gain the use of the land. The market process yields an efficient plan should the conditions defining a perfect market hold true. The markets respond to the broad demographic, economic, and technological forces interacting and help reassign land uses with the help of the pricing mechanism that decentralizes the decision-making. Land markets, however, do not build cities. When we think of a city sector developed through the market alone, we might think of the *favelas* in Brazil and the squatter settlements in other developing countries. Look at the classical and neo-classical models: the horses draw wagonloads of produce in straight lines across adjacent fields; there are no roads here. We need to know more about rents created by human endeavour, by the decisions to build bridges and concert halls, by their effect on the spatial structure of cities.

The role of land markets can be viewed from at least two very different platforms. The conventional view that economists tend to adopt in North America accepts the dominance of the marketplace. Policy analysis starts by accepting the desirable outcomes produced by perfect markets, adjusted for equity, then examines how real markets deviate from this ideal. The analysis looks for market failures, institutional shortcomings, and equity issues. The easiest questions may ask:

- Are the participants in the land market atomistic, or are there monopolies that curtail land supply?
- Is information perfect and available to all?
- Are transaction costs zero?
- Are the production processes and household utility maps independent, or do the actions of some affect others?
- Is everyone free when making his or her choice or is there coercion?

Since all answers are 'no', further analysis of the nature of land markets and the relevant institutional failures can form the basis for developing corrective policies. The largest deviations today are due to the external costs imposed by a number of factors, including continuously expanding suburbs, the loss of access to the countryside, increasing congestion, extra infrastructure costs not covered by development charges, and increased CO_2 emissions. The fact that these consequences are not traded in land markets leads to inefficient patterns of suburban expansion. The inner-city trends discussed here may be moving towards a more efficient city, but one that treats lower-income people unfairly through economic evictions.

The other platform might be raised on Charles Schultze's (1977: 30) bold assertion that 'the free enterprise system carries the label "made by government"'.[5] Land ownership and its transactions are possible only within the protected environment formed by government. The basic structure of cities is a planned one, for better or worse. Until the last two centuries, most cities were surrounded by defensive walls that were built, maintained, and guarded at considerable public expense. Church and state created the central square and in conjunction with commerce laid out the first streets. Atomistic producers or consumers do not initiate highway or transit systems. Self-centred, but blameless, consumers will not volunteer contributions to building parks when they expect that their neighbours will pay for them. The free-rider problems, externalities, and equity issues limit the role that land markets can and should play in shaping cities.

The difficulty with this view stems from its audience committing itself to a particular play: property ownership is a right not to be tampered with. Just fly over Britain and see the neat boundaries between town and country, not much leapfrogging here, nor any loose incursions into the countryside. Developers gain permission to build their projects only after their contributions (planning gain) are deemed to be in the public interest. Differences in culture create differences in the role of land markets. Of course, the differences in culture may be wrought by differences in land markets. We can fly over Canada for hours and hardly see any development. We have plenty of land and when the supply of a resource appears boundless, not only is it freely used, but also the public's attitude towards its conservation is lax. We have a lot of land—it is only location that is scarce.

Notes

1. Whether the total amount of rents collected by all landowners in the region increases or decreases depends on the size of the price decrease, on the price elasticity of demand for the produce. If produce prices drop by a large amount, then the total rents collected in the region decrease.

2. The 'opportunity cost' is the value of the highest alternative forgone. The opportunity cost of land refers to the cost of using it for a certain purpose, measured by the benefit given up by not using it in its best alternative use. Land used for farming vs land used for fully developed subdivisions has a huge 'opportunity cost' from the point of view of the farmers'/pre-development owners' immediate monetary gain. The opportunity cost is quite different when environmental costs and benefits are factored into an equation that considers the 'public good' over a longer period.

3. If the land rents were expected to grow forever at a constant and compounding rate, then the formula for determining the preset value of the land is as follows:

$$\text{Present Value} = \text{Current Rent}/(\text{Discount rate} - \text{Growth rate in rents})$$

For example, if the current rent was $12,000 a year and the discount rate was 6 per cent, then in the absence of growth the present value of the property would be $12,000/.06 = $200,000. However, if the rents were expected to grow forever, with certainty, at a compounding 2 per cent a year, then the present value would be $12,000/(.06–.02) = $300,000. The extra $100,000 is the 'growth premium' due to the anticipated future growth in rents. Land prices at the edge of the city will be set by the value of the land in its agricultural use plus the growth premium due to the expected future growth in value.

4. Karl Marx's 'absolute rent' theory might appear to apply:

> The mere legal ownership of land does not create any ground rent for the owner. But it does, indeed, give him the power to withdraw his land from exploitation until economic conditions permit him to utilize it in such a manner as to yield him a surplus. (Marx, 1962 [1887]: 739)

5. Director, US Bureau of the Budget (1965–7), and Chair of the US President's Council of Economic Advisors (1977–80).

Chapter 6

Transportation and Communication

Eric J. Miller

Perhaps no component of physical infrastructure is more fundamental to the economic, social, and environmental sustainability of the twenty-first-century city than its transportation system. Over the past 50 years urban planning has given priority to accommodating the car. We are increasingly confronted with problems resulting from this strategy: traffic congestion; high urban development expenses; and, most seriously, pollution. Transportation planning, along with land-use planning, has contributed to low urban density and high levels of land-use segregation, that is, to the post-war urban form that is still replicated today.

This chapter discusses the urban transportation system and the planning process associated with the design and evolution of this system. A primary focus is on the interaction between transportation and urban form. Key transportation policy issues are discussed, as are the range of alternatives available for addressing these issues. Important attributes of both the demand and the supply sides of the transportation system are described, as well as the analytical methods used to forecast travel behaviour.

Transportation and Urban Form

The role of the urban transportation system is to provide access to land and activities, to provide the means by which people and goods can move from point to point within an urban area in order to participate in the broad range of activities (economic, social, recreational, etc.) that define urban life. In so doing, the transportation system provides 'operational spatial definition' to an urban area. That is, the distance between two points, per se, is not of primary importance in the determination of the level of interaction between these points. Rather, the relative ease of travel (as defined by travel time and cost, frequency and reliability of service, etc.) affects where, when, and how often people will travel for various purposes.

Figure 6.1a provides a simplified representation of the interaction between the transportation system and the *urban activity system*. The urban activity system consists of:

- the spatial distribution of *land uses* (buildings of different types, purposes, and densities), which is determined through the land development and redevelopment process;
- the spatial distribution of the *location* of people (i.e., where they live) and activities (jobs, stores, schools, etc.), which is determined through the location choices of households, firms, etc.;
- the spatial and temporal distribution of the daily *activity patterns* in which people engage.

The transportation system, in turn, consists of:

- the *network* (streets, expressways, rail lines, etc.), other physical infrastructure (stations, control systems, etc.), and *services* (transit, taxi, etc.), which collectively provide the potential for travel within the urban area (that is, the *supply* of transportation services);
- the extent to which people have *access to automobiles* for their personal use;
- the spatial and temporal distributions of *flows* of people and vehicles over the transportation network resulting from people's participation in activities that are distributed in both time and space.[1]

Figure 6.1   **Transportation-Activity System Interactions**

a) The Urban Activity and Transportation Systems

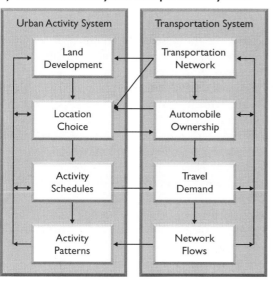

b) System Interactions

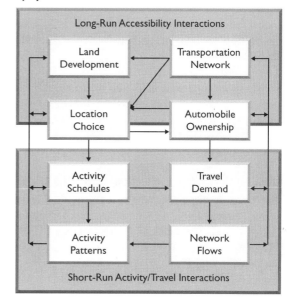

Source: Adapted from Meyer and Miller (2001).

As highlighted in Figure 6.1a, both the activity and transportation systems can be viewed as semi-independent systems, each of which is evolutionary and dynamic in nature. The activity system evolves over time (new land is developed and old land uses redeveloped; households and firms move in and out of the urban area as well as relocate within this area; activity schedules and patterns change) in response to a wide variety of stimuli, some of which are endogenous to the system (e.g., new land-use patterns may emerge in response to changing activity patterns) and some of which are exogenous to the system per se (e.g., interest rates, macroeconomic trends). The transportation system similarly has its own 'internal logic' by which both the supply of and demand for transportation services will respond over time to endogenous factors such as roadway congestion levels and exogenous factors such as government subsidies, gasoline prices, and the like.

As depicted in Figure 6.1b, however, the two systems are also interconnected in several significant ways, with these interconnections running in both

directions and occurring in both the short and long runs. As already discussed, the transportation system defines the *accessibility* of each point in space to every other point in space, and thereby influences long-run (year by year, decade by decade) decisions concerning both land development and location choice. In the short run (daily, weekly), the activity participation and travel demand processes are inextricably linked, given that the participation in out-of-home activities requires travel and that the location, timing, and duration of these out-of-home activities may well all be influenced by the availability, cost, etc. of the travel options available to the participant.

Auto ownership decisions can be denoted as 'medium-run' in that they occur more frequently than most location choices but much less frequently than most activity/travel decisions. Auto ownership, however, interacts with both the longer-run location decisions—residential and employment location choices may affect auto ownership level and/or may be constrained in turn by feasible ownership levels—and the short-run activity/travel decisions. These short-run decisions, of course, depend on whether the household can afford a car, or another car, but over time such decisions influence changes in the household's auto ownership level so as to better match individual travel needs.

Over the very long run, the historical influence of transportation on urban form has been profound and readily apparent. Prior to the mid-nineteenth century, walking and horse-drawn vehicles were the primary means of transportation, resulting in small, dense cities that were often circular or semicircular in shape to maximize accessibility. The inner cores of many Maritime cities display characteristics of the 'horse-cart–pedestrian city' (Yeates and Garner, 1980), while the old town portion of Quebec City provides a classic example of this urban form.

The Industrial Revolution and associated technological innovations in transportation generated dramatic changes in urban form in the second half of the nineteenth century and early twentieth century. Industries depended heavily on rail transportation for the movement of both raw materials into and finished products out of their factories.[2] The result was high-density industrial areas, stretching along the rail lines passing through the city. Given that the railway was the primary means of inter-city travel for people as well, these lines invariably penetrated directly to the centre of the city (the point of maximum access to the resident population and business community) (see Chapter 10).

Industrialization created considerable new demand for labour, attracting many workers and their families to the city. The poorer among these workers settled in high-density housing located within walking distance of the factories in which they were employed, both because they could not afford to live elsewhere and because higher-income households avoided these areas due to the high pollution levels typical of nineteenth-century industrial areas (see Chapter 11).

Given the need for face-to-face contact, direct access to clients, and the still relatively rudimentary state of communications and transportation, retail and commercial activity remained concentrated in the city centre (the central business district or CBD). This concentration was further encouraged by advances in building technology (i.e., the emergence of high-rise buildings) that permitted significant increases in the density of commercial activities. Unlike factory workers, however, the white-collar employees of CBD businesses were not tied to housing within walking distance of their places of employment. Rather, new modes of transit—principally street railways (first horse-drawn but then much more effective electric-powered streetcars) and longer-distance commuter railways (first steam, later electric or diesel)[3]—permitted middle and upper-middle-class households to move out of the city centre to new homes located on larger lots in lower-density 'streetcar suburbs' (Warner, 1962).

Although densities along these rail lines were lower than in the CBD, the need to be within convenient walking distance of the streetcar line or commuter rail station ensured that densities in most cases remained at least moderately high. Further, amenities such as local stores and restaurants serving the streetcar suburb tended to concentrate with relatively high density along the streetcar line (or at the commuter rail station) so as to be within either walking distance or a short streetcar ride of the resident population.

The result of these various trends was, by the beginning of the twentieth century, much larger cities (in terms of space, population, and economic activity) than could possibly have existed a century before. While the detailed arrangements of these cities were dictated by local geography and historical evolution, their overall structure tended to be quite similar: a dense central area containing most major commercial activities; well-defined industrial areas with associated low-income worker housing stretching along inter-city rail corridors penetrating the city; and middle and upper-middle-class white-collar residential neighbourhoods of moderate to high density stretching along streetcar and commuter rail lines radiating from the CBD. All major Canadian cities of the time (Montreal, Toronto, Vancouver, Winnipeg) displayed this general structure, which survives to this day in these metropolitan regions' older portions.

The automobile first emerged as a cost-effective means of transportation for many people with Henry Ford's mass-produced Model T in 1908. Although the impact of the auto on travel patterns (e.g., declining transit ridership per capita) could be discerned in the United States as early as the mid-1920s (Jones, 1985), it was not until after World War II that the full impacts of the automobile on lifestyles, travel, and urban form were felt. The post-war period was one of considerable economic and demographic growth throughout Canada, creating an unprecedented demand for new housing. Most of this new housing was provided on newly developed land on the urban fringe in low-density suburban housing tracts. The near-ubiquitous availability of the automobile both facilitated and encouraged this low-density, dispersed suburban design. Indeed, the post-war low-density suburb requires universal access to the automobile, since almost no 'trip ends' (stores, jobs, etc.) are within walking distance of the suburban home and conventional transit cannot cost-effectively serve the dispersed travel patterns generated by such low-density developments (see Chapter 12).

Retail and other population-serving activities quickly followed their markets to the suburbs. Generally, they first located in unplanned strip developments along major arterials. Calgary's Ventura Boulevard is a classic example of this type of location, although similar examples can be found in all Canadian urban areas. But it is now more typical for such activities to opt for large, planned shopping malls located at points of transportation advantage such as expressway intersections. In the last 20 years or so manufacturing and office activities have also suburbanized to a considerable extent, reflecting changes in transportation (shifts from rail to trucking for shipping goods), communications (advanced communications systems reduce the need to be tied to CBD locations), production methods, land values, and taxes, among other factors.

Associated with the suburbanization of people and activities is the trend to segregate land uses. In both the pre-industrial and the nineteenth-century cities land uses generally were mixed (i.e., stores, houses, offices, etc. were intermingled) so as to maximize pedestrian accessibility and maximize the use of scarce land within a dense urban structure. Partially as a result of the automobile, which eliminates the perceived need for diverse activities to be in close proximity (let alone walking distance) of one another, and partially as a result of modernist planning principles, traditional suburban land uses are almost invariably segregated into planned single-use areas: industrial parks, shopping centres, and residential developments differentiated by type and cost of housing. This leads to a considerable increase in the amount of travel required to accomplish a given set of tasks and to a total dependence on the automobile as the mode of travel.

The net result of these trends in the second half of the twentieth century was, again, a dramatic increase in urban area size (with respect to population, economic activity, and, most dramatically, spatial area) and a radically different aggregate urban form. This new form involves dispersed, low-density distributions of residential, commercial, industrial, and retail areas, often in planned, segregated developments. Travel patterns are no longer concentrated within a few radial corridors. Rather, they consist of dispersed flows from many origins to many destinations. Although this dispersion results in a tremendous amount of daily travel and often considerable congestion at various points in the road network, the 'many-to-many' nature of the flows does not generate sufficient density of travel along any one corridor or route to make public transit cost-effective. In addition, distance between trip ends has become too long for walking to be an option for the vast majority of trips. As a result, the automobile represents the only viable means of transportation for most people.

Garreau (1991) has described such post-war suburban/urban forms as 'edge cities'. Many US metropolitan regions are almost completely dominated by the edge city form, with the traditional central city downtown being virtually irrelevant for most purposes. Most large Canadian agglomerations display a more complex pattern in that they have maintained a strong (and usually still growing), relatively dense central city, combined with considerable dispersed, low-density growth of both population and economic activity on the urban fringe. The transportation system and associated travel flows for Canadian metropolitan regions are similarly complex, involving both heavy radial flows into/out of central cities (which are generally well served by a competitive transit system) and more dispersed many-to-many flows throughout the suburban periphery (which is fully auto-oriented).

This thumbnail sketch of the historical evolution of Canadian urban form illustrates the two-way nature of the transportation interaction described in Figure 6.1. We have seen that major shifts in transportation technology fundamentally redefined accessibility within urban areas, giving rise to new urban forms. In particular, technological advances have tended to extend the 'reach' of travellers, allowing them to travel at higher speeds and so travel further within a given amount of time. This has resulted in an expansion in the amount of land covered by urban areas (with associated reductions in average densities) as people take advantage of this extended reach to consume more land for their activities (residential or commercial). The trend towards using increased transportation speed to consume more land, which has been at work for the better part of two centuries, is a worldwide phenomenon as global levels of automobile ownership and usage continue to increase. This trend shows little sign of abating.

At the same time, once a given land-use pattern is in place it reinforces the need for, or suitability of, a given type of transportation system. High-density, mixed-use, radial development patterns encourage and support cost-effective rail transit systems. Walking is also a viable alternative in such high-density, mixed-use areas. Low-density, segregated use, edge city patterns can only support auto-based travel: trip distances are too long to walk and flow densities too low to support cost-effective transit. Thus a positive feedback loop connects a given transportation technology to a given form of urban development, and vice versa.

This observation underscores the importance of an integrated approach to transportation and land use (that is, urban) planning if we are to achieve integrated urban planning goals. Unfortunately, this rarely occurs effectively in practice. As is implied in Figure 6.1a, the two 'systems' are typically dealt with in virtual isolation from each other. This largely reflects institutional and professional divisions. Different government agencies are typically responsible for transportation and land-use planning, and they tend to be staffed with people possessing different professional backgrounds and world views. The result of this division is myopic decision-making, in which transportation planners take land-use plans as given and plan the transportation system around these, while land-use planners do the reverse (if they consider the transportation system at all). Such an approach severs the dynamic feedbacks of Figure 6.1, replacing them with static inputs from the other side of the flowchart (an example of this approach is provided in the conventional travel demand modelling process shown in Figure 6.6 and discussed below). Loss of the dynamic interaction between transportation and land use is responsible for serious flaws in the planning process.

Separating transportation from land use may well cause us to look in fundamentally wrong ways at our urban problems and their possible solutions. Congestion is generally viewed as a chronic and worsening transportation problem in most Canadian cities. Since it is defined as a 'transportation problem' we seek 'transportation solutions': increases in roadway capacity, real-time traffic control, congestion pricing, etc. A more comprehensive, integrated view of the 'problem', however, might well generate quite a different diagnosis: perhaps much of our congestion arises from a land-use pattern that places too heavy a burden on the road system. An alternative land use, which could make better use of higher-capacity transit lines and encourage shorter and/or fewer trips, might well provide a more lasting solution to the problem.

The Greater Vancouver Regional District (GVRD) developed both medium-range and long-range transportation plans that intentionally adopted an integrated approach to land-use and transportation planning. The plans take the view that current land-use and transportation trends (increasing sprawl and auto orientation) are inconsistent with Vancouver's planning objectives, and recommend alternative forms of development. A number of designs combining land use and transportation are investigated. The result is a plan that calls for a departure from current development patterns, with inner suburbs designated to receive more growth, and outer areas less, than projected by current trends, and for central areas to generally maintain current trends. Combined with these land-use controls is a range of medium- and long-range transportation proposals (involving both demand management and infrastructure investment) designed to support and promote the desired land-use structure. The Vancouver plan is also of interest in that it deals both with 'macro' urban form issues (that is, the overall distribution of population and employment within the urban region) and with the role that 'micro' neighbourhood design plays in influencing travel behaviour (Transport 2021, 1993a, 1993b).[4]

Transportation Impacts: The Policy Challenge

Virtually every resident is directly affected on a daily basis by the transportation system, as is virtually every economic activity. Ideally, we would all like to travel wherever we want, when we want, at modest cost, with minimal delay. In reality, travel is obtained at significant cost (especially if the full personal cost of auto ownership is factored in), varying degrees of schedule convenience, and, depending on the time of day and the urban area in question, considerable delay and frustration due to roadway congestion.

In addition to the direct impacts that the transportation system has on the daily activities of people and firms (that is, the *users* of the system) and its longer-run impacts on urban form, this system generates significant indirect social and environmental impacts on urban residents, users and non-users

alike. These impacts are labelled 'indirect' because they are unintended consequences of transportation system operations. They include:

- *Consumption of land.* The transportation network—in particular the road network—is a significant land use in its own right. Construction of roads and other physical transportation facilities obviously displaces previous land uses, natural or human.
- *Neighbourhood intrusion.* Over and above the physical displacement of other land uses, the physical presence of a major transportation facility can have adverse impacts on adjoining neighbourhoods. Depending on the facility, these can include physical unsightliness, physical barriers within neighbourhoods, noise, and reduced safety on local streets.
- *Safety.* The road system is a major cause of death, personal injury, and property damage. Despite a consistent decline in accidents per capita over an extended period of time, 2,778 Canadians were killed in 2001 in traffic-related accidents, while 222,260 were injured in 156,721 collisions involving casualties (Transport Canada, 2004).
- *Security.* In transportation 'safety' usually refers to the level of risk due to accidents. 'Security', in turn, generally refers to the risk people feel when interacting with others within the transportation system. Growing concerns within many cities about issues such as crime on the transit system, 'road rage' on crowded highways, and the potential for terrorist attacks on major transportation facilities exemplify potential security impacts.
- *Atmospheric pollution.* Fossil fuel-based vehicles are a source of many damaging atmospheric pollutants. Of particular concern are the various precursors of low-level ozone—carbon monoxide (CO), various nitrogen oxide compounds (generically referred to as NOx), different uncombusted hydrocarbons (also referred to as volatile organic compounds—VOCs), as well as particulate matter of varying size. In the United States, federal law (particularly the Clean Air Act amendments of 1990) mandates maximum acceptable levels for

most of these pollutants. Urban areas that are neither in compliance with these mandates nor actively moving towards compliance are subject to serious financial penalties (e.g., loss of federal funds) and risk lawsuits from environmental groups. In Canada, comparable legislation does not exist at the federal or provincial level despite concern over high air pollution levels in many Canadian metropolitan regions.

- *Other pollutants.* Other pollutants can be generated by transportation operations. Perhaps most notable is the pollution of soils and groundwater due to runoff from roadways that carries contaminants such as salt and oil.
- *Greenhouse gas emissions.* Carbon dioxide (CO_2) is one of the primary emissions from fossil fuel combustion in road vehicles. While not a pollutant per se (because not directly harmful to human health), it is the dominant greenhouse gas contributing to global warming and climate change (TTNCCP, 1998). The Kyoto Protocol commits Canada to a 6 per cent reduction in CO_2 emissions relative to 1990 levels by 2012 at the latest. If this very ambitious objective is to be met, significant reductions in CO_2 emissions from the transportation sector will have to be achieved.
- *Energy consumption.* Urban transportation systems are very dependent on fossil fuels (gasoline and diesel fuel). Over and above the pollution and greenhouse gas emissions associated with burning fossil fuels, the price and supply of fossil fuels are of growing concern. Experts in the field agree that world petroleum production will peak and then begin to decline irreversibly sometime in the early twenty-first century, while world demand for oil for transportation and other purposes will continue to grow. Inevitably, this demand–supply imbalance will have significant impacts on the availability and price of fossil fuels in Canada, with commensurate ramifications for auto-based mobility within Canadian cities.

The policy challenge facing transportation planners and decision-makers is how best to provide the level and mix of transportation services that maximize the direct benefits derived from these services, at the same time minimizing/mitigating their adverse impacts. Central to responding to this challenge are a number of key questions (Kennedy et al., 2005) related to the following issues:

- How can we best maintain and improve the transportation system given the fiscal constraints facing all levels of government? Associated with this issue are questions concerning who pays for transportation services, the extent/nature of subsidies, how to properly price transportation services, etc.
- What is the appropriate balance between public and private provision of services, construction of infrastructure, etc.? The opening in 1997 of the privately built and operated electronic toll road, Highway 407, running east–west just north of Toronto, provided a new model for highway construction and operation. Similarly, transit industry deregulation and/or privatization has occurred in recent years in many countries, most notably the United Kingdom.
- What is or should be the role of transit? It is almost routinely assumed by planners that transit represents a significant part of the solution with respect to increasing urban transportation sustainability. How this can occur in the face of the urban form trends discussed above (which are driven by and promote auto usage) is not entirely clear.
- What is or should be the role of the automobile in the twenty-first-century city? To what extent should we build more roads to meet demand? To what extent should we curtail auto usage in the name of urban sustainability?

Dimensions of Travel Behaviour

The key dimensions characterizing travel demand include space (from where to where are trips made?), time (when is the trip made, and how long does it take?), mode (what combination of technology/service is used to undertake the trip?), and purpose. The spatial, two-dimensional nature of travel demand complicates the analysis due to the difficulty involved in visualizing travel flows over space and in dealing with the very large and complex data sets required to describe these flows. Modern Geographic Information Systems (GIS) are of considerable assistance in this task. Still, the data and computational requirements associated with the analysis of travel demand in medium and large cities are formidable, even given modern computing capabilities.

Typical trip purposes used in travel demand analyses include: work, school, shopping, socio-recreational, personal business, work-related (trips to visit clients, etc.), and the ubiquitous catch-all 'other'. Trips are often further categorized as being *home-based,* if either the origin or the destination of the trip is the home, or *non-home-based* if neither 'trip end' is the home.

It is clear that the choice of travel mode is of central concern to transportation planners. Modes usually considered in planning analyses are: auto driver; auto passenger; transit; walk; and (when numbers warrant) bicycle. Auto passengers are typically separated from drivers, since their characteristics and behaviour tend to be quite different (auto passengers are more similar in their attributes to transit riders than to auto drivers), as is their impact on the transportation system. An auto driver, by definition, generates a vehicle trip with its attendant pollution and contribution to roadway congestion, while an auto passenger, per se, does not. Alternatively, auto drivers and passengers can be 'repackaged' into a drive-alone mode (often referred to as a 'single-occupant vehicle' or SOV trip) and a shared-ride mode (carpool, 'high-occupancy vehicle' or HOV trip). In addition, in larger metropolitan regions with complex multi-modal transit systems, such as Montreal and Toronto, the transit mode might be further divided by sub-mode (e.g., local transit versus commuter rail). In such cases, mixed modes of travel, such as trips involving the use of the car to access a commuter rail or subway line, may also be of interest.

Table 6.1 tabulates daily person trips for Edmonton in 1994, categorized by trip purpose and mode. As shown in the table, nearly three-quarters (74.4 per cent) of all trips in Edmonton are home-based, with 30.5 per cent of all trips being home-based work or school-related. Auto travel dominates, with nearly 80 per cent of all trips being made in a car, either as driver or passenger. Seventy-eight per cent of all workers drive, while 60 per cent or more of trips for almost all purposes except school are accomplished by driving a car. Although only 8.6 per cent of home-based work trips are made by transit, these represent a significant proportion of transit ridership (21.3 per cent), second only to school-related travel (35.9 per cent in total).

Figure 6.2 presents work trip mode splits in Canadian CMAs, as reported in the 2001 census. As shown in this figure, auto-drive is the dominant work trip mode throughout the country, with the variation in auto-drive mode split correlating roughly with city size (that is, the larger the CMA, the lower the proportion of people who drive to work), with a Canada-wide mean value of 70.7 per cent. Transit usage is roughly the mirror image of auto-drive, with transit ridership increasing with city size. The Canada-wide transit use mean is 14.9 per cent. Although scattering exists among the smaller urban areas, in general auto-passenger and other mode (walk, bicycle, etc.) usage is relatively constant across city sizes. Collectively, non-drive/transit modes account for 14.4 per cent of work trips nationwide—virtually as many trips as are made by transit. This result, however, is heavily skewed by transit usage in the larger urban regions. Figure 6.3 shows work trip mode shares for non-drive modes for CMAs under half a million population. As can be seen, auto-passenger and walk-plus-other modes each attract more usage than transit in virtually all cases and cumulatively exceed transit in every case.

Table 6.2 provides work trip mode choice for the largest CMAs. Many factors influence transit usage in addition to city size. These include: socio-economic factors such as auto ownership levels, income, age, and occupational mix of the labour force; urban factors such as population density, density and concentration of employment centres,

Table 6.1	**Daily Person Trips by Trip Purpose and Mode, Edmonton CMA, 1994**					
Trip Purpose	Auto Drive	Auto Pass.	Transit	Walk	Other	Total
a) Modal Split by Trip Purpose (%)						
Home-based work	78.1	7.7	8.6	4.4	1.3	100
Home-based post-secondary	37.4	8.8	38.1	13.2	2.5	100
Home-based school	2.7	34.3	12.3	32.5	18.2	100
Home-based shopping	64.3	21.6	6.2	7.2	0.6	100
Home-based social/recreation	50.0	37.1	2.5	9.2	1.3	100
Home-based other	61.0	28.5	3.3	6.1	1.1	100
Home-based subtotal	54.1	24.2	7.4	10.6	3.8	100
Non-home-based work	71.5	8.6	5.8	12.8	1.2	100
Non-home-based other	58.4	26.8	4.4	8.8	1.6	100
Non-home-based subtotal	60.1	24.4	4.6	9.3	1.5	100
Total trips	55.6	24.3	6.7	10.2	3.2	100
b) Distribution of Trip Purposes by Mode (%)						
Home-based work	23.2	5.3	21.3	7.1	6.7	16.5
Home-based post-secondary	1.7	0.9	14.9	3.3	2.1	2.6
Home-based school	0.6	16.1	21.0	36.1	64.7	11.4
Home-based shopping	11.7	9.0	9.4	7.1	2.0	10.1
Home-based social/recreation	8.6	14.6	3.6	8.6	3.9	9.6
Home-based other	26.5	28.4	12.1	14.5	8.2	24.2
Home-based subtotal	72.3	74.3	82.2	76.7	87.7	74.4
Non-home-based work	4.3	1.2	2.9	4.2	1.3	3.4
Non-home-based other	23.3	24.5	14.8	19.1	11.0	22.2
Non-home-based subtotal	27.7	25.7	17.8	23.3	12.3	25.6
Total trips	100	100	100	100	100	100

Source: AMCL (1995).

mixture of activities within neighbourhoods, and the extent to which neighbourhoods and activity centres have been designed in a 'transit–oriented' manner; and both road and transit network service characteristics such as the extent of the freeway system, transit frequencies, fares, travel times, and parking costs, among others. As shown in Table 6.2, these factors combine in Winnipeg to generate a work trip transit mode share that is the same as that for Calgary, an urban region that is 43 per cent

Figure 6.2   **2001 Work Trip Mode Shares, Canadian CMAs**

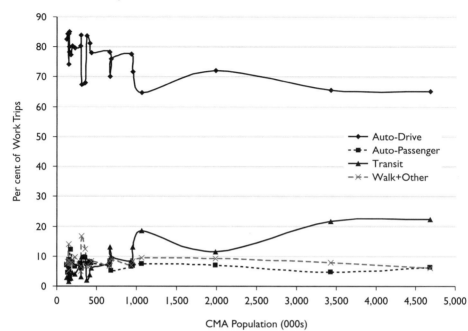

Source: Statistics Canada, 2001 census.

Figure 6.3   **Non-Auto-Drive Work Trip Mode Shares, CMAs under Half-Million Population**

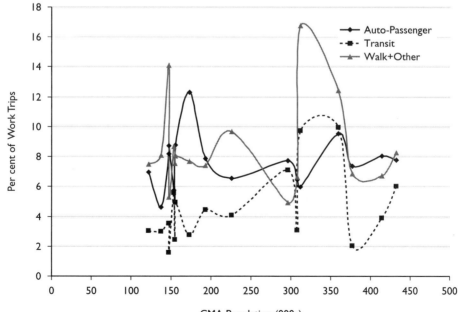

Source: Statistics Canada, 2001 census.

Table 6.2   **2001 Work Trip Mode Shares, Large Canadian CMAs**

Census Metropolitan Area	Population (000s)	Auto Driver	Auto Passenger	Public Transit	Walk	Other
Hamilton	662	78.2%	7.1%	8.0%	5.1%	1.6%
Winnipeg	667	70.0%	8.4%	13.2%	6.1%	2.3%
Quebec City	683	76.0%	5.2%	9.8%	7.0%	2.0%
Edmonton	938	77.7%	6.6%	8.6%	4.7%	2.4%
Calgary	951	71.8%	6.8%	13.2%	5.9%	2.4%
Ottawa–Hull	1,064	64.6%	7.4%	18.5%	6.8%	2.7%
Vancouver	1,987	72.2%	7.0%	11.5%	6.5%	2.8%
Montreal	3,426	65.6%	4.8%	21.7%	5.9%	2.0%
Toronto	4,683	65.2%	6.3%	22.4%	4.6%	1.6%
All CMAs	19,170	70.7%	6.5%	14.9%	5.7%	2.1%

Source: Statistics Canada, 2001 census.

larger in population than Winnipeg. At the same time, Calgary has a higher transit mode share than Vancouver, a region over twice as large as Calgary.

Given the importance of work and school trips in urban travel, combined with the relatively fixed schedules associated with these activities, typical urban weekday travel will exhibit strong morning and afternoon peaks. Figure 6.4 illustrates this phenomenon, showing 2001 trip start times, broken down by trip purpose, generated by residents of Hamilton for a typical weekday. Work and school trips display very pronounced morning and afternoon peaks (particularly school trips), reflecting work/school start and end times. Other purpose trips grow gradually from the mid-morning onward, maintaining a relatively steady level throughout the remainder of the day. Superimposing these trip purposes, the total trip pattern shows a relatively sharp morning peak period, a much broader afternoon peak (reflecting the greater importance of non-work/school travel in the afternoon/evening period, as well as the fact that the school day ends before the workday), and lesser but still signifi-

cant travel throughout the midday and evening periods. This general pattern of travel occurs in all Canadian cities.

Mode choice also varies dramatically by location within a given urban area. Figure 6.5 presents travel information for three major employment centres within the Greater Toronto Area GTA): the Toronto central area (the largest employment centre in the GTA), Mississauga Square One (Mississauga's 'downtown' area), and the Pearson International Airport employment district (the second largest employment area in the GTA). The 24-hour weekday trip origins during 1996 for all trip purposes for each of these three centres are shown in the three maps in this figure. As can be seen, the central-most part of Toronto attracts very large flows in a concentrated, radial pattern fanning out from the downtown core. The Mississauga Square One pattern is similar, but smaller in magnitude and spatial extent, reflecting the much smaller size of this centre. The pattern for Pearson Airport, however, is much different from the other two. Its range is almost as great as the Toronto

Figure 6.4   **Trip Start Time by Trip Purpose, Hamilton, 2001**

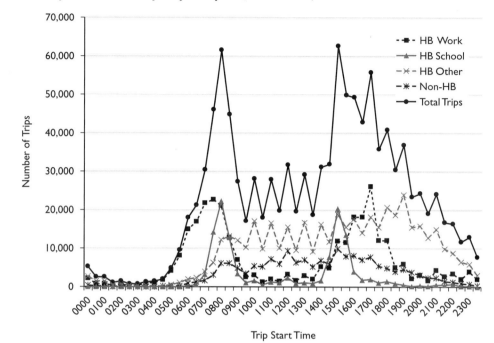

Note: HB = home-based, i.e., trips from or to home.
Source: 2001 Transportation Tomorrow Survey.

downtown's: it attracts trips from throughout the GTA. But the trip origins are much more dispersed in nature. Given the nature of transit services, the Toronto downtown travel pattern can be (and is) cost-effectively serviceable by transit in a manner that is competitive to the automobile and attractive to trip-makers. The Pearson Airport travel pattern, at the other extreme, is almost impossible to serve by transit in any cost-effective, competitive manner. The Mississauga Square One case obviously lies in between these two extremes. These assertions are borne out by the transit mode shares experienced for trips to the three centres. The chart in Figure 6.5 shows 2001 morning peak and all-day transit mode shares for the three centres, disaggregated by trip origin (the Toronto central area is labelled 'PD1' in this chart). Regardless of trip origin, transit attracts a very high percentage of the travel market to the Toronto downtown (both during the peak

periods and over the entire day), while transit usage for trips to the Pearson airport area is almost negligible.

It is well-known that travel behaviour (and, in particular, mode choice) varies with several key socio-economic variables such as auto ownership, age, gender, occupation and income. Table 6.3 offers a profile of transit riders in Quebec City by gender, age, and employment status. As is typical of Canadian transit properties, a majority of Quebec City transit riders are female, young, and workers or students. Students are disproportionately represented among transit users. A somewhat more detailed breakdown of transit work trip mode splits for Hamilton by household auto ownership level, possession of a driver's licence, occupation, and gender shows that the likelihood of using transit declines with levels of auto ownership and driver's licence possession. Men are generally somewhat less

Figure 6.5

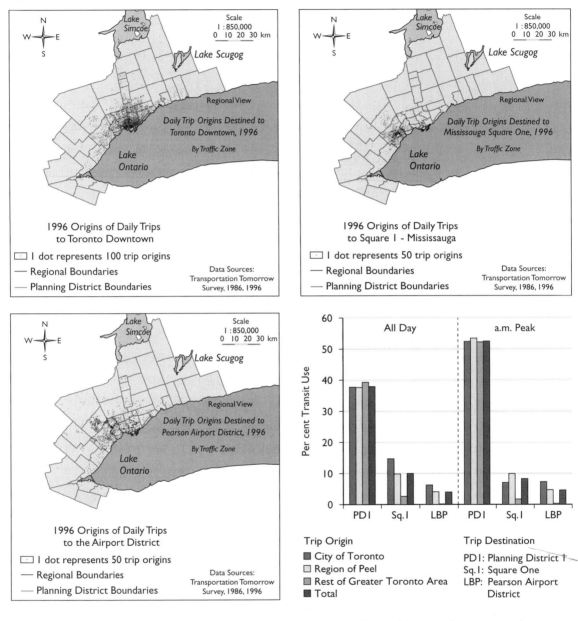

likely to take transit, even when occupation and possession of a driver's licence are accounted for. The effect of occupation is somewhat mixed, but in general white-collar workers are more likely than blue-collar workers to take transit.

Conventional Travel Demand Modelling System

Mathematical, computer-based models are used by transportation planners as one means of assessing

Table 6.3   **Transit User Profile, Quebec City, 2001**

Employment Status	%	Gender	%	Age	%
Worker	39.9	Female	58.1	0–19	30.3
Student	48.8	Male	41.9	20–34	32.7
Homemaker	2.0			35–49	18.7
Retired	7.7			50–64	11.9
Other	1.6			65+	6.4

Source: Quebec Ministry of Transport and Réseau de transport de la Capitale, 2001 Origin-Destination Survey, Quebec City, Summary of results, p. 156.

the likely impacts of alternative transportation (and land-use) policies on the demand for travel (by mode, purpose, and time of day), the performance of the transportation system (congestion levels, level of service, etc.), and the various environmental and social impacts associated with urban transportation systems. Given the complex nature of travel behaviour, it is not surprising that these models are themselves complex, as well as costly and difficult to construct and use.

A standard approach to urban travel demand modelling employed throughout the world, wherever resources permit and need dictates its use, was first developed in pioneering comprehensive transportation planning studies in Detroit and Chicago in the mid- to late 1950s.[5] It quickly spread to other US and Canadian cities, as well as outside North America, through the 1960s, during which time the process and procedures that we use to this day were developed. Since the 1960s, improvements have been made in individual sub-models, in the data sets used in the models, and in the computer hardware and software used to run the models. But the overall model paradigm has changed surprisingly little over the last 40 years.

Figure 6.6 presents the basic urban travel demand modelling system, which is most often simply referred to as the four-stage or four-step process. Primary inputs to this model are estimates of population and employment for each zone in the urban area for the forecast year, as well as a detailed computerized representation of the road and transit networks. Primary outputs from the process are person and vehicle flows by mode, both on an origin-destination (O-D) and network link basis, as well as travel times and costs (again at both O-D and link levels). From these primary outputs additional measures of system performance (volume-to-capacity ratios, transit boardings by station, etc.) and impacts (emissions, energy use, accidents, etc.) can subsequently be estimated. As shown in Figure 6.6, travel demand is estimated in four sequential steps, consisting of:

- *trip generation*, in which the total number of trips that originate from each zone and that are destined to each zone are estimated;
- *trip distribution*, in which the 'trip ends' estimated by the trip generation model are linked together to provide estimates of the total 'O-D flow' of trips between origins and destinations for all O-D pairs in the urban area;
- *modal split*, in which the total O-D flows are 'split' or allocated among the various modes (auto, transit, walk, etc.) available for use between any given O-D pair;
- *trip assignment*, in which the paths or routes taken by auto users on the road network and transit users on the transit network are determined, and the road and transit O-D flows are assigned to these paths.

Trip generation actually involves two models for each trip purpose: one to predict trip origins by zone and one to predict trip destinations by zone. As shown in Figure 6.6, the fundamental inputs to these models are population and employment totals for each zone in the urban area, as well as, perhaps, additional information concerning these people and jobs (auto ownership, household size, type of employment, etc.).

Figure 6.6   **The Urban Transportation Modelling System**

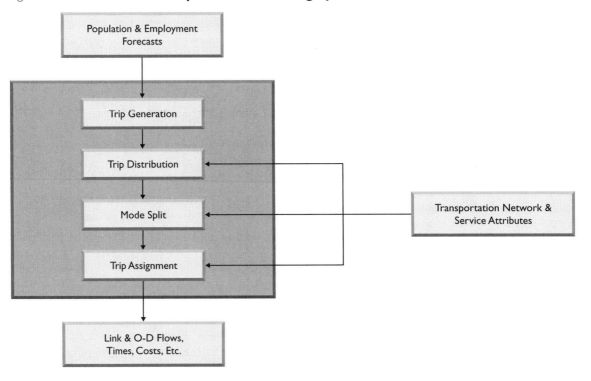

As is also indicated in this figure, it is usually assumed that the transportation system does *not* affect trip generation. That is, the total number of trips made in an urban area is assumed to be independent of the transportation level of service provided. This greatly simplifies the analysis, but, as has been discussed above, can potentially introduce significant bias into the analysis.

The methods used to perform trip generation analysis are typically quite simple, and primarily fall into two categories: linear regression models and cross-classification analysis. Linear regression assumes that a linear relationship exists between the number of trips generated (e.g., the number of morning peak-period home-to-work trips originating in a given zone) and one or more explanatory variables. Advantages of the linear regression approach include: ease of development and use; modest data requirements; ability to handle many

explanatory variables; and transparency of the model procedure and results to users.

The assumption of a linear relationship between the number of trips made and the explanatory variables is easy to make but can be misleading. To avoid this assumption, cross-classification analysis is often used. In this approach persons or households are gathered into homogeneous groups based on a small number of variables or attributes, and average trip rates are computed from observed data for each group. Table 6.4 provides an example of this approach for Edmonton. In this model, households have been grouped based on their number of vehicles and the number of people in the household, and average trip rates for each group have been computed. Thus, for example, the average number of daily person trips generated by three-person households owning one car is 9.46. Note the non-linear relationship exhibited in this

Table 6.4	**Cross-Classification Trip Generation Model, Edmonton**					
Daily Person Trips per Household						
No. of Vehicles	Household Size					
	1	2	3	4	5+	Total
0	2.82	6.17	9.73	n/a	n/a	4.19
1	4.03	6.55	9.46	13.47	17.39	6.81
2	4.61	7.59	11.24	15.13	20.17	11.69
3	4.93	7.86	11.12	15.03	19.95	12.71
4	n/a	n/a	12.42	17.38	17.08	14.11
5+	n/a	n/a	n/a	n/a	n/a	12.01
Total	3.77	7.12	10.69	14.83	19.3	9.17

Source: AMCL (1995).

table between trip rates and both explanatory variables, as well as the existence of interactions between the two variables. For example, moving from one to two vehicles in the household increases daily person trips by 1.04 trips per day for two-person households (from 6.55 to 7.59 trips per day), while it only results in a 0.58 trip per day increase for one-person households—a sensible result, since two people can clearly take better advantage of a second car than a single person can. Cross-classification models, however, generally require more data for their development and application than linear regression models do.

While alternative methods exist, by far the most common approach to trip distribution modelling is to use a doubly constrained *gravity* or *entropy* model. Such a model provides the most likely estimates of the O-D flow pattern, given the known information concerning these flows (e.g., trip origins and destinations by zone, zone-to-zone travel times, etc.). Gravity models are discussed in detail in many geography and travel demand modelling texts (see, for example, Ortuzar and Willumsen, 2001; Meyer and Miller, 2001).

The O-D flows predicted by the trip distribution model are next 'split' among the various modes available for travel between each O-D pair. This is usually done using some form of *logit* model, derived from *random utility theory*.[6] A logit model expresses the probability P_{mt} that a person 't' will choose mode 'm' from a set of feasible alternatives as a function of the 'utility' of mode 'm' for person 't', relative to the utilities of all competing modes. The 'utility' of mode 'm' for person 't' is, in turn, usually assumed to be a linear function of a set of attributes of mode 'm' (travel time, travel cost, etc.) and person 't' (age, income, sex, etc.).

Once the number of auto-drive (and hence vehicle) trips and the number of transit trips have been computed for all O-D pairs, these trips can be *assigned* to specific paths through the road and transit networks, respectively. Various transit assignment algorithms exist that determine likely paths used as a function of transit service headways, in-vehicle travel times, number of transfers required, etc.

Road network assignment is usually performed using the concept of *deterministic user equilibrium*. The user equilibrium assumption is that drivers individually choose routes to minimize their own personal travel times. Equilibrium is achieved when no one driver can unilaterally change routes and improve his/her travel time. Figure 6.7 illustrates the user equilibrium concept for a single O-D pair that only has two feasible routes, each of which consists of a single link. If V_{ab} is the flow between origin A and destination B, then the flows on links (routes) 1 and 2, V_1 and V_2, must satisfy the constraint:

$$V_{ab} = V_1 + V_2$$

Each link in a road network will have a *volume-delay* curve that determines the travel time along the link as a function of the volume of traffic using the link (Figure 6.7a). Drivers are free to choose either link (route) to minimize their individual travel times. As shown in Figure 6.7b, equilibrium occurs when the travel times are the same on the two routes (that is, $t_1 = t_2 = t^*$, which occurs when the volume flow on link 1 is V_1^* and the flow on link

Figure 6.7   **Deterministic User Equilibrium Example**

a) Volume-Delay Curves for the Two Routes

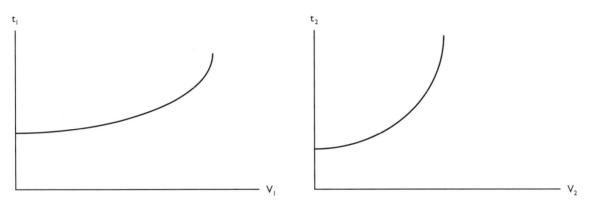

b) User Equilibrium Solution, Two-Route Case

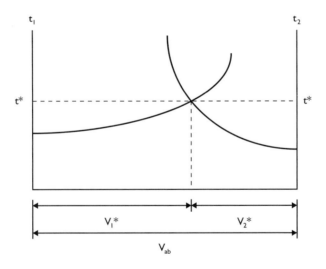

2 is V_2^*), since otherwise some of the drivers on the slower link can and will switch to the faster link.

Although Figure 6.7 is extremely simplified, its results can be shown to generalize to networks of any size and complexity. For example, the network model for the Greater Toronto Area has over 1,700 traffic zones (close to three million O-D pairs), over 40,000 links, and thousands of feasible paths for any given O-D pair. User equilibrium assignments are routinely made to this network using commercially available software.[7]

Emerging Modelling Methods

The research state of the art has progressed considerably beyond the conventional modelling state of practice described above, to the point that we are on the verge of a 'paradigm shift' to a fundamentally different approach to urban transportation demand and network performance modelling (Pas, 1990). The need for such a paradigm shift is driven by the long-standing recognition that the conventional methods described above simply are not adequate for addressing the complex range of transportation issues and policies facing contemporary urban areas. The capability to undertake this paradigm shift is provided by a combination of a significant improvement over the past 30 years of travel behaviour and transportation system performance theory, considerably improved databases and data collection methods to support improved model development, and vastly enhanced computational capabilities.

While a detailed discussion of these emerging modelling methods is well beyond the scope of this chapter, key elements of the 'next generation models' include the following (Spear, 1994):

- The new travel demand models are explicitly *activity-based* in nature; that is, they take seriously the notion (shown in Figure 6.1) of travel as a demand derived from the need to participate in activities, many of which are dispersed in time and space and hence require travel. Thus, the first three stages of the four-stage process—generation, distribution, and mode choice—are replaced with a modelling system in which people schedule their activities over the course of a day (in terms of what activities they are going to engage in, when, for how long, at what location). Travel (including mode choice decisions) arises out of the execution of this activity schedule. Region-wide, comprehensive activity-based models that can fully replace the regional four-stage models are emerging as operational tools (Arentze and Timmermans, 2005; Bowman and Ben-Akiva, 2001; Miller and Roorda, 2003; Vovsha, Petersen and Donnelly, 2002).

- Static user-equilibrium network assignment models are being replaced by dynamic (often probabilistic) models of network performance and route choice. These dynamic network assignment models provide much more realistic representations of vehicle performance and traveller route choices within the road network (e.g., effects of queuing, more realistic vehicle speeds and acceleration/deceleration profiles, more realistic assumptions concerning driver decision-making), and so provide a much better basis for estimating vehicular emissions and energy use, the impact of real-time control and other strategies related to Intelligent Transportation Systems (ITS), etc. (Golledge, 1997).

- Both the activity/travel models and the network performance/assignment models require a much more detailed, disaggregated representation of trip-makers and the transportation network. That is, the aggregate, zone-based representations of the conventional four-stage model simply cannot support the new models. *Microsimulation* is an emerging method for implementing disaggregate behavioural models in which individual actors (households, trip-makers, vehicles, etc.) are explicitly modelled within a dynamic simulation framework (Miller, 2003a).

- Integrated models that simultaneously model land use and transportation processes (that is, all of Figure 6.1) have existed for 40 years, but have not received widespread application due in large part to their complexity (Lee, 1973). In recent years, interest in developing and applying integrated urban system models has increased considerably, as have the operational capabilities of these models. Given the growing recognition that the land use-transportation interaction must be taken seriously if sustainable urban systems are to be achieved, it is expected that integrated models will play an increasingly important role in the planning process (Miller, 2003b).

Transportation and Communications

Communication—by phone, fax, e-mail, the Internet, mobile phone, text messaging, and other interactive media—represents the second major way we relate to one another across space; as such it is potentially a substitute for travel. Historically, however, communications and transportation have had strong complementary effects: improved communication stimulates interactions among more people over greater distances, which in turn stimulates the demand for more travel. The net result is that increased usage of both transportation and communications has tended to go hand-in-hand with economic and demographic growth.

In addition to direct substitution and complementary impacts, communications can have indirect effects, either through secondary and tertiary impacts on people's activity/travel schedules or by altering household and firm location choices, which, in turn, will alter activity/travel patterns. The key question of interest to urban transportation planners is which of these effects will dominate the impact on travel behaviour as current and emerging information systems continue to play increasingly important roles in homes and businesses.

Three communications-based activities of particular interest are: (1) *telecommuting,* in which a person works at home rather than travels to the office; (2) *teleshopping,* in which a person orders goods to be delivered to the home, either over the telephone or via computer; and (3) *teleconferencing,* in which groups of people 'meet' via conference telephone calls or video-conferencing without having to travel to a common site.

Empirical evidence concerning the impact of telecommunications on travel is far from definitive, but, on balance, the evidence suggests that it is much smaller than forecast (Mokhtarian and Salomon, 1997). Substitution and complementary effects typically are both at play, so that the net effect can vary from one type of activity to another, but may, on balance, result in net complementary effects (Mokhtarian, 2003). To understand the effect of communications on travel, one must take a complete sociological view of the problem (Salomon, 1986), but there are at least three reasons why communications may not have strong net substitution effects for travel.

First, work possesses social as well as utilitarian dimensions; shopping is a form of recreation/entertainment for many people; etc. It is far from certain that most people want to stay home, interacting with the world only via telephone and computer. People enjoy the stimulation of location change and social encounter. Thus, to date, market penetration of tele-activities has been less than expected due to these factors. Figure 6.8 shows the trend in the percentage of full-time workers in the

Greater Toronto Area (GTA) who worked at home during the period 1986–2001. With the exception of the increase from 1986 to 1991 (which may at least be partially the result of changes in the survey procedure between the two years), very little trend can be perceived in the proportion of employed persons who work at home. This category of workers includes both telecommuters (that is, people whose place of employment is not their home) and people whose workplace is their home and so is at best a proxy for the trend in telecommuting. Nevertheless, the data strongly suggest that telecommuting has not changed radically, at least since 1991.

Second, new travel can be induced, which at least partially offsets trips forgone. For example, more home-based non-work travel may replace work trip commuting; or more delivery van trips replace home-based shopping trips. Third, in addition to this direct induced travel, indirect latent demand can materialize in response to system capacity that has been freed by telecommunications-related travel reductions. For example, the non-worker in the household mentioned above now has access to a car. Similarly, if large numbers of commuters work at home each day, this will reduce congestion on roadways, thereby encouraging other people to take advantage of this extra supply, either by switching from transit to auto-drive or by making additional trips. Table 6.5 shows the effect of in-home workers on auto usage and total trip-making for GTA households having at least one full-time worker. As shown in this table, households with in-home workers (again taken as a proxy for telecommuters) appear very similar to other households in terms of average auto usage, trip distances, and total trip-making.

Even less clear is the long-run effect that modern telecommunications may have on urban form (and, hence, travel). To the extent that telecommuting means that one can live anywhere and dial into work, and that teleshopping means that physical access to stores loses importance, telecommuting is further loosening bonds between the home (and, for that matter, the firm) and activity locations, and so further encourages the dispersed, low-density urban form discussed above. While anecdotal

Figure 6.8   **Fraction of Full-Time Workers Working at Home, Greater Toronto Area**

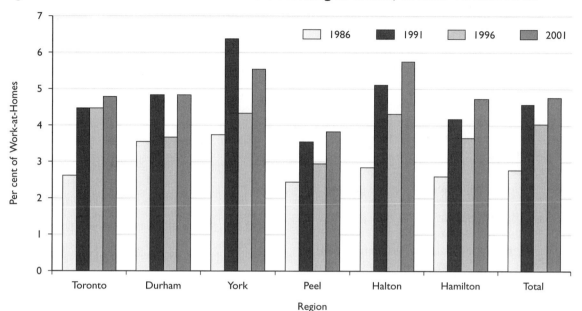

Source: 2001 Transportation Tomorrow Survey.

evidence supports this hypothesis, again, few hard data exist to indicate the extent of this impact. The travel implications of such a trend are similarly murky, although it is reasonable to speculate that while they might imply fewer traditional trips to work, shopping, etc., the trips that will be made will almost certainly be completely auto-based, and may well be significantly longer on average.

Canadian Urban Transportation in the Twenty-First Century

The long-run sustainability (in economic, social, and environmental terms) of our urban transportation systems is almost certainly the key issue facing planners in the twenty-first century. As documented above, current land-use trends and travel behaviour preferences are not conducive to improving sustainability, since these universally encourage automobile usage at the expense of transit and non-motorized modes of travel such as walking and bicycling. Many policy-makers implicitly

Table 6.5   **Summary Statistics for Households with One or More Full-Time Workers with and without In-Home Workers, Greater Toronto Area, 2001**

Variable	No. In-Home Workers	
	0	1 or More
Auto-drive mode share	64.6%	68.2%
Trips per person	2.21	2.25
Average trip length (straightline; km)	10.5	10.8

Source: 2001 Transportation Tomorrow Survey.

assume that 'technological fixes', such as ITS, cleaner cars, and advanced telecommunications, will solve this problem. While these technologies can and will have a positive impact, they will not, in and of themselves, ensure sustainability. This is particularly the case for greenhouse gas emissions, which will continue to be generated in considerable amounts by road vehicles as long as they burn carbon-based fuels, no matter how 'clean' these vehicles are otherwise.

Of the many policy questions that pertain to urban transportation planning, none is more central to 'the urban transportation problem' than that concerning the role of the automobile. For at least 40 years, planners, economists, engineers, and social scientists (among others) have wrestled with this issue.[8] Far from resolving the debate, this rich literature simply serves to illustrate the fundamental nature of the question for urban areas, as well as its endurance. We are no closer as a society to answering this question than we were 20, 30, or even 40 years ago. One can plausibly argue that no other single piece of technology affected twentieth-century life more than the automobile, computers and nuclear weapons notwithstanding. It provides us with levels of mobility unprecedented in human history. It is central to our personal lifestyles. It is fundamental to the modern economy (both as a medium through which the economy operates and a major industry in its own right). But at the same time these enormous benefits come at a very high cost. The automobile kills and maims thousands of people every year. It consumes enormous amounts of land, both directly for roads and indirectly in terms of the urban forms that it facilitates and promotes. It pollutes our air and is a significant contributor to global climate change. How we as a society deal with these huge trade-offs in benefits and disbenefits will go a long way towards determining the nature of our twenty-first century cities.

Notes

1. Figure 6.1 and its associated discussion focus on the activity system and transportation supply and demand

from the point of view of people and their personal participation in activity and travel. With only minor reworking, this discussion applies equally to the economic activity processes of firms and the associated issues of transportation supply and demand for the movement of goods within (and into/out of) the urban area. Similar comments apply to the role the truck has had on the location and nature of economic activities and their interactions, largely displacing rail as the primary mover of goods, except in specialized markets (e.g., long-distance haul of bulk goods). For simplicity of discussion, this chapter focuses on the personal activity system and personal travel. Goods movement, however, is clearly an equally important role for the transportation system, complete with its own behavioural relationships, policy issues, etc.

2. Although in many cases water transportation still played a major role, such as in the location of the steel industry in Hamilton and in the export of grain from ports such as Thunder Bay.

3. In the United States and many European cities, subways (underground heavy rail lines) were added to the mix of transit technologies available in the early twentieth century. These subways further accentuated the land-use trends generated by the street railways. No subway, however, was operated in Canada until the Yonge Street line opened in Toronto in 1954, replacing a very successful surface streetcar line. This was followed by the opening of the first Montreal Metro lines in 1966.

4. For reviews of the role of 'micro' urban design on travel behaviour, see, for example, Badoe and Miller (1997).

5. For a complete discussion of urban travel demand modelling methods see, among other works, Ortuzar and Willumsen (2001).

6. For a detailed, rigorous, but accessible presentation of random utility choice models and their application to travel demand modelling, see Ben-Akiva and Lerman (1985). Also see Meyer and Miller (2001) and Train (2003).

7. For a detailed discussion of user equilibrium assignment methods, see Sheffi (1985).

8. Classics in this literature not cited elsewhere in this chapter include Buchanan (1963), Meyer et al. (1965), Mumford (1960), and Owen (1966, 1972). Also of relevance is Pucher and Lefèvre (1996).

Chapter 7

Urban Infrastructures

Igor Vojnovic

Urban infrastructure investment is very much the 'hidden hand' of urban development. We generally take infrastructure networks for granted, but inadequate infrastructure provision (or any breakdown in facility—transportation, communications, water and sewage, and energy) carries the threat of economic stress, social disorder, and a greatly reduced quality of life. Not surprisingly, then, decisions regarding the provision and management of urban infrastructures have become central to modern city building. As well, as Aibar and Bijker (1997: 23) put it, 'the size and distribution of its streets, sidewalks, buildings, squares, parks, sewers and so on can be interpreted as remarkable physical records of the socio-technical world in which the city was developed and conceived.' This raises another important dimension of infrastructure—its relative permanence in the face of an ever-changing urban dynamic.

The intensification of cities, the transportation of goods and services, the movement of people, the distribution of energy, the filtering of urban wastes, and flow of information all depend on reliable and effective infrastructure. The critical importance of infrastructure networks has led Thissen and Herder (2003: 1) to argue that 'failure of these infrastructures . . . is one of the most important vulnerabilities of modern society.' In Canada, the scale of these vulnerabilities was evident during the January 1998 ice storm. At its peak, the storm disabled power to 1.4 million customers in Quebec and to over 230,000 in Ontario (Statistics Canada, 2005a). Some 100,000 people were forced to take refuge in shelters and 28 died. More recently, reported statistics regarding life and property loss in the New Orleans area in the wake of Hurricane Katrina, in

2005, have revealed a scale of devastation previously unparalleled in North America. Unpredictable disasters such as these storms serve as a reminder of the extent to which the proper functioning of infrastructures has become the sustenance of urban life.

People take urban infrastructure for granted partly because of its invisibility, a central feature of contemporary infrastructure management. As observed by Perry (1995: 2), when urban infrastructures 'work best, they are noticed least of all'. However, despite increasing infrastructure invisibility, in the current political climate of government cutbacks, there have been new concerns regarding urban infrastructures: the looming threat of gridlock on highways, contaminated water supplies, and power failures.

In the second half of the twentieth century, the decentralization of Canadian cities added another problem for infrastructure providers. Costs in areas characterized by dispersed growth began to place municipalities under increasing financial strain. The higher costs resulted from elevated capital expenditures (on, for example, roads, water, and sewage lines) and operating expenditures (on services such as street lights, snow removal, and garbage pickup) associated with low-density and scattered growth. Ironically, it was premature infrastructure investment on undeveloped lands that initially facilitated decentralization. In addition, considerable environmental stress followed, evidenced in increased pollution emissions, waste production, energy consumption, and negative impacts on biodiversity.

This chapter introduces various issues related to urban infrastructure development: the economics of infrastructure financing, resulting impacts on the urban built environment, and environmental and social implications of infrastructure investment. Different types of urban infrastructures are explored, as are the demands and constraints that guide their development. Special attention will be given to the financial dimension of urban infrastructures, whereby sufficient infrastructures are needed to support economic growth, but over-building results in excessive socio-economic and environmental costs.

Canada's Urban Infrastructure

The concept of urban infrastructure comprises both public and private support systems of modern society—including water and sewer networks, treatment plants, transportation systems, health, education, communication and computer networks, power systems, sport stadiums, and arts centres. Urban and economic development in Canada has been greatly influenced by advances and investment in urban infrastructure. Two distinct infrastructure types are apparent in this review. *Inter*-urban infrastructure connects cities into the national network, while *intra*-urban infrastructure connects homes and businesses to a city, enabling the functioning of a city as a system.

Urban Infrastructure to 1850

Canada's early settlements were extensively shaped by waterways, particularly the St Lawrence River. The St Lawrence guided the path of the fur trade, agriculture, and military expansion into the continent. Investment in canals began with the St Lawrence military canals near Montreal (Kendall, 1971). In 1815, increased investments in canals began across the St Lawrence and the Great Lakes, stimulating urbanization and economic development in Upper and Lower Canada.

While waterways were the cheapest form of travel and transport, roads were built for three main reasons (Glazebrook, 1964; Guillet, 1966; Miller, 1978). First, roads were used as alternative transport routes along stretches of rough waterways or as links

between bodies of water. Examples of waterway connectors include Yonge Street, which connected Lake Ontario and Lake Simcoe, and the route between St Jean and Laprairie (Quebec) that linked the Richelieu River with the St Lawrence. Second, roads were built in Nova Scotia and Upper and Lower Canada for defensive purposes, enabling the movement of troops. Finally, the building of roads was used for colonization, such as the Talbot roads, encouraging settlement in Upper Canada. These transportation networks not only tied the British colonies to Europe, but with more relevance to the development of Canada, they connected the colonies to a national urban network, establishing the early foundation of Canada's system of cities.

During the first half of the nineteenth century, very little intra-urban infrastructure investment was directed at Canadian cities. Only a few wealthy neighbourhoods had sewers, generally in the form of open drains, and there were only three fully completed water supply systems in British North America—in Saint John, NB (1837), Toronto (1841), and Halifax (1848) (Anderson, 1988). While urban and environmental pressures did exist because of the absence of what today would be considered basic urban infrastructures, these stresses were mitigated by the size of the cities. In 1815, for instance, Toronto had a population of slightly over 1,000 people, Montreal approximately 15,000, and Kingston about 6,000 (Hodge, 1991). As the cities grew, however, so did the need for intra-urban infrastructure provision.

Urban Infrastructure, 1850–1900

In 1850, water transport maintained its dominance, particularly when it came to bulk freight. With westward expansion, the Nelson, Winnipeg, Red, and Saskatchewan rivers emerged as important transportation routes. However, transport by ships was slow and seasonally limited. Montreal, for instance, was ice-bound five months of the year. Within this context, railways emerged as a solution for economical year-round transport. By 1850, railways in British North America were confined to the

Champlain and St Lawrence Railway near Montreal and local lines in Nova Scotia (Andreae, 1988). In total, there were 106.2 kilometres of rail line in 1850, but by 1900 about 27,000 kilometres of track existed in Canada. In fact, the completion of the Canadian Pacific Railway (1885), linking Ontario to the Pacific Ocean, was one of the great infrastructure achievements of the nineteenth century (Vance, 1995). By 1900, railways offered reliable year-round travel, increased speeds, and reduced land transportation costs, but waterways remained the lowest-cost option for freight.

The later nineteenth century also saw the diffusion of a number of intra-municipal infrastructure networks. After Dr John Snow demonstrated the relationship between cholera and water sources in London's 1854 epidemic, attention was directed at improving Canada's water supply (Anderson, 1984). By 1900, there were 235 water supply systems throughout Canada (Anderson, 1988).

As urban population increased, pressures were also placed on the disposal of human wastes. In the second half of the nineteenth century, after successive waves of cholera and typhus, the demand for sewer lines became louder (Bilson, 1980). However, the issue of costs and of who would pay for the connections limited sewer construction.

Major changes were also affecting roads over this era. On the one hand, railways made roads less relevant as inter-urban networks. However, as cities grew, the movement of people and goods within cities became a concern. The 1861 introduction of horse-drawn rail trolleys in Toronto and Montreal also placed a new emphasis on road surfaces, since horse hooves were degrading the traditional wooden and brick roads (McIlwraith, 1983). With the discovery of electricity, urban roads experienced another transformation. In 1886, Windsor, Ontario, introduced Canada's first electric streetcar system, followed by St Catharines, Ontario (1887), Victoria and Vancouver (1890), Ottawa (1891), and Toronto and Montreal (1892) (Linteau, 1988).

Around 1850, Canadian cities began to introduce another important infrastructural asset—public parks. The purpose of parks was to use the landscape to improve public health and the well-being of the urban population (Bresnan and Bresnan, 1990). The opening of Toronto's Exhibition Park (1848) was followed by Kingston's City Park (1852), Hamilton's Gore Park (1852), Halifax's Point Pleasant Park (1866), Toronto Islands (1867), London's Victoria Park (1869), Montreal's Île St-Hélène (1874), and Vancouver's Stanley Park (1886) (Hodge, 1991).

Urban Infrastructure, 1900–1950

Into the twentieth century, waterways continued to dominate freight transport. Andreae (1988: 98) notes that the cost differential of freight transport in 1914 'is illustrated by the distance one ton of freight could travel for one dollar: by ship, 828.8 km, by railway, 209.2 km., by horse and wagon, 6.4 km.' Because of their year-round transport capabilities and speed, investments in railways continued to remain strong into World War I, particularly in western Canada. Total railway track in Canada more than doubled between 1897 and 1917, increasing from 26,854 kilometres to 61,747 kilometres. New construction of rail lines stalled after 1917, however, largely due to the automobile and the truck.

During the 1930s, it was also recognized that the spatial importance of rail lines was not just limited to their capacity as inter-urban infrastructure networks. After completing a study of rental values in 142 American cities, Homer Hoyt (1939) concluded that the organization of cities was more appropriately characterized by sectors rather than by concentric zones, as suggested by Ernest Burgess (1925). Hoyt recognized that lower-income groups extended out in linear sectors from the inner city following industries, which themselves followed railroad lines. Richard Harris's (1996) research on suburbanization in Toronto during the first half of the twentieth century illustrates similar development patterns.

In the twentieth century, however, roads would have the most significant impact on travel and the spatial organization of Canadian cities. By 1918, 157,079 passenger cars were registered and

Figure 7.1   **Annual Private Automobile and Commercial Vehicle Registration in Canada, 1903–98**

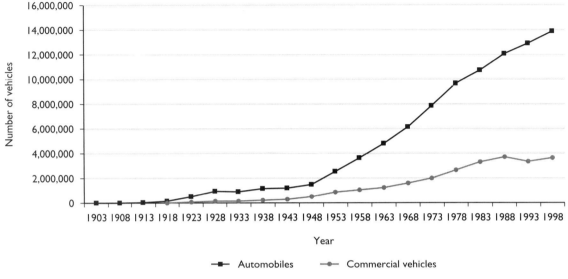

Sources: Urquhart et al. (1983); Statistics Canada (2005b).

increased pressure was placed on improving Canada's roadways (see Figure 7.1). Gravel, asphalt, and concrete roads in Canada grew from 78,000 kilometres in 1922 to 131,960 kilometres in 1930 (Canadian Tax Foundation, 1955). With access to more affordable automobiles and improved roads and highways, Canadians experienced a new level of mobility that shaped both travel behaviour and cities (Figure 7.2).

Canadian cities also made considerable improvements to water and sewage systems. Water supply systems in Canada increased from 235 in 1900 to 1,274 in 1940, with 664 new waterworks built during the 1930s (Berry, 1940). This was still the era when urban infrastructures were celebrated, as illustrated by Toronto's art deco R.C. Harris Filtration Plant—known locally as the 'Palace of Purification' (Keating, 1994: 18). With regard to sewage, considerable advancements were made in treatment. The first activated sludge plant in North America was constructed in 1915 in Brantford, Ontario, and by 1933 Ontario had built 32 more

treatment facilities. However, sewage plants were expensive and by 1950 Canada had only 334 treatment facilities (Baldwin, 1988). In the second half of the twentieth century, with new federal and provincial assistance and the introduction of new treatment techniques, the number and size of sewage treatment facilities expanded rapidly.

Hospitals were another urban infrastructure that received notable attention during this period, particularly with universal health insurance being proposed in 1919. While the 1867 British North America Act gave authority over health care to provinces, the provinces delegated health responsibilities to municipalities. In fact, into the mid-1900s, hospitals and hospital care were 'financed by municipal governments, religious groups, voluntary insurance programs, and patient payments' (Vayda and Deber, 1992: 127). It was with the Hospital Insurance and Diagnostic Services Act (1961) and the Medical Care Act (1968) that federal-provincial cost-sharing emerged, and hospitals and medical care expanded to take their present form.

Figure 7.2   **Urban Densities before and after the Introduction of the Car**

a) Urban densities in a city shaped by walking
   (Urban population: 500,000)

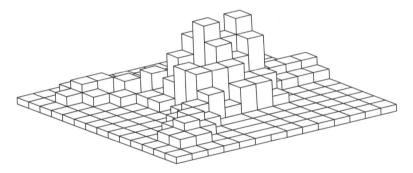

b) Urban densities in a city shaped by walking and rail. Development
   propensity towards star-shaped patterns following rail lines, leading
   to the development of streetcar suburbs.
   (Urban population: 500,000)

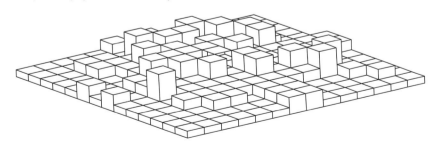

c) Urban densities in a city shaped by the car. Development propensity
   towards a general dispersion of the population facilitated by road and
   highway networks.
   (Urban population: 500,000)

Urban Infrastructure, 1950–Present

In the post-World War II period, roads and highways continued to establish their dominance as the transportation networks that shaped travel and cities. By 1970, approximately 90 per cent of all travel by Canadians was on roads (Transportation Development Agency, 1976). Access by businesses and households alike to affordable automobiles and trucks, along with post-war prosperity, public subsidies to suburban infrastructures, and preference for single-family detached housing, propelled urban decentralization to an unprecedented scale.

The combustion engine and development of extensive road networks favoured the bus at the expense of the streetcar. By 1954 Winnipeg had removed its streetcar lines, followed by Vancouver in 1955 and Montreal and Ottawa in 1959 (Linteau, 1988). However, the rapid growth of large Canadian centres, and the requirement to quickly move large numbers of people in a city, gave rise to a new type of rail transport, rapid transit. The first two lines that opened were subways—Toronto's line opening in 1954 and Montreal's in 1966—followed by light rapid transit lines in Edmonton (1978), Calgary (1982), and Vancouver (1986). While the car facilitated decentralization, the rapid transit lines strengthened inner-cities. By enabling the efficient movement of large populations within cities, rapid transit promoted higher inner-city densities. Downtowns were also main beneficiaries of rapid transit lines, since they were the focus of these networks (see Chapter 10).

Similar to health care, public education was a local initiative that became increasingly a provincial responsibility, with indirect federal influence largely through transfers.[1] Even in the first quarter of the twentieth century, the majority of the provincial-municipal expenditures on education were municipal, whereas by 1980 only 10 per cent of this share was local (Kitchen and McMillan, 1985). Dramatic changes occurred in education in the second half of the twentieth century, in terms of both expenditures and the importance of educational infrastructure in an economy increasingly dominated by high-tech and service industries. A significant expansion in educational infrastructure occurred in the 1950s and 1960s, fed by baby boomers and government expansion under the welfare-state model. After some three decades, this expansion was followed by deep cuts in education, particularly during the 1990s.

The location of educational investment is another important dimension of school provisioning. With regard to urban development, the US illustrates how spatial inequities in educational infrastructure influence urban form (Ghosh, 2004). The poorer fiscal base and lower quality of education in US cities encourages homebuyers to move into wealthier suburbs that offer higher-quality education, since educational infrastructure is one of the most important variables affecting housing demand among families with school-age children (Orfield, 2002). By pursuing greater equity in educational infrastructure, Canadian provinces minimize such decentralization pressures and ensuing inner-city decline.

The ability of educational and research infrastructure to facilitate the development of the high-technology sector has received notable recent attention (Castells and Hall, 1994; Hall and Markusen, 1985). In the UK and the US, examples of university–industry linkages include Cambridge University/Cambridge Tech-Corridor, MIT/Route 128, and Stanford University/Silicon Valley. In Canada, a recent study shows that the Greater Toronto Area (GTA) has the third largest concentration of private information and communication technologies (ICT) facilities among major North American metropolitan centres, behind San Francisco and New York. The study observes that 'educational institutions may play a key role in the fabric of industries since in addition to training the workforce, they are also frequently involved in research and development' (E&B Data, 2004: 28).

The growth of the service and high-tech sectors of the economy, and their reliance on telecommunications, also gave rise to new urban infrastructures. The 'network society' has produced a significant reorganization of market economies, which now extensively rely on the flow of information through data and video networks, wireless and radio systems, phone and cable networks, and satellites (Castells, 2000). The importance of fibre optics, first introduced in 1988, is illustrated by the fact that 'in the year 2000, more than 400,000 miles of fibre-optic cable will lie on the ocean floors, enough to circle the earth sixteen times' (Wheeler et al., 2000: 6).

The federal government's Information Highway Advisory Council (1997: 15) reflects on the importance of e-infrastructure to Canada:

> The Information Highway has become the major enabling infrastructure for the knowledge-based economy. The future competitiveness of Canadian industry at home and overseas will increasingly depend on the availability of high-quality information networks in all parts of Canada. Investments in network modernization, research and development, and technology deployment throughout the Canadian economy are therefore essential if Canadians are to prosper in the global marketplace.

The rise of the service economy initially raised concerns over how the digital revolution would impact cities. During the 1980s, a common perception was that e-shopping, telecommuting, and teleconferencing would lead to the dispersal of urban populations, diluting the importance of cities and intra-urban infrastructure—particularly transportation infrastructure (Graham and Marvin, 1996). However, as recognized by Canada's National Broadband Task Force (2001), the population, business, and service employment concentrations in metropolitan centres have made them the focus for complex telecommunication networks. The current concern, in fact, is with the 'digital divide', the lack of e-infrastructure in rural and Aboriginal communities, which further contributes to their economic and spatial marginalization.

In the later twentieth century, the 'infrastructure of play'—sports stadiums, convention centres, performing arts centres, and other tourism and entertainment complexes—also became a central element of urban life, further reinforcing the importance of urban economies (Judd, 2003). As with other urban infrastructures, government investment in tourism has been significant, and has generated considerable controversy in regard to the subsidization of professional sports and entertainment centres. In Montreal, for instance, Levine (2003) notes that conservative estimates have placed government subsidization of tourism infrastructure at approximately $7 billion since the 1960s—with Expo 67 and the 1976 Summer Olympic Games requiring considerable public support.

The Economics of Urban Infrastructures

Critical issues with urban infrastructures are the spatial dimension of investment, the distribution of costs, and the role of government in infrastructure provision. In response to the disorder of nineteenth-century industrial centres, economists began to recognize the need for government interventions to alleviate market failures (such as externalities and public goods), which were sources of inefficiencies and inequities (Pigou, 1948).

Public Goods and Externalities

Some goods (public goods) will either not be provided by the market or will not be provided at sufficient levels. Public goods have two properties that differentiate them from private goods and cause suboptimal provision (Bird and Slack, 1993; Stiglitz, 2000). First, public goods are non-rivalrous in consumption. Second, they are non-excludable. The lack of competition for public goods means that the benefits to the people who use a public good do not diminish as others use it, until congestion occurs. The case of traffic lights provides an example. Once introduced, traffic lights offer a service to many users at no, or little, extra cost. This is very different from private goods that can be consumed by one or few people, for example, an apple, where the benefits of that good are attributed exclusively to the person eating the apple.

Non-excludability means that once the public good is provided, it is either impossible or cost-ineffective to exclude non-payers from receiving the benefits. For instance, it would be very costly to restrict people from using traffic lights once they are introduced. A toll might be instituted, but the cost of initiating charges to use traffic lights is high. Because of non-rivalry and non-excludability, private companies have little interest in providing public goods, and unless governments intervene, public goods will be provided at suboptimal levels.

Externalities also justified government provision of urban infrastructures (Muth, 1975; Tindal and Tindal, 2004). One case of externalities occurs in instances where individuals may not fully recognize the social benefits of activities they engage in, thus causing a less than optimal involvement in these activities. For instance, while education and health care carry individual rewards, there are also extensive social benefits from an educated and healthy population. Government intervention is thus considered acceptable to encourage levels of goods or services that are socially optimal—for example, justifying public subsidies to encourage higher levels of education to improve national efficiency and equity. The importance of externalities was also evident with the provision of sewage. Subsidizing sewage connections for the poor was considered acceptable when it was recognized in the late nineteenth century that considerable cost advantages would result from such initiatives, stemming from fewer epidemics and productivity losses. Both examples above illustrate that improvements in efficiency and equity can be achieved simultaneously through appropriate infrastructure subsidization.

Infrastructure Financing, Urban Distortions, and Resource Use

As government intervention in the economy expanded in the post-World War II period, attention was directed to the relationship between inefficient public subsidies on urban infrastructures and distortions in urban form. As mentioned at the outset, greater than optimal subsidies on urban infrastructures generated premature infrastructure investment on undeveloped lands, precipitating suburbanization and the consumption of energy and land, with attendant environmental damages (British Columbia Round Table on the Environment and the Economy, 1994; CMHC, 1995; Fowler, 1992).

Table 7.1 provides an international urban comparison, showing how lower-density cities, in large part due to the increased separation of land uses, generate higher levels of energy-intensive transportation (greater automobile dependence), emissions, land consumption, and infrastructure provision. In a comparison of Canadian and US cities, higher densities in Canadian metro areas and inner cities result in lower per capita gasoline consumption, lower transportation CO_2 emissions, fewer private automobile passenger kilometres, fewer urban infrastructure requirements, as well as greater per capita public transit passenger kilometres (see Chapter 2). The higher densities of European cities lead to even lower resource and energy consumption and pollutant emissions. The connection between density, infrastructure, and transportation patterns is thus central to energy consumption, environmental degradation, and, to a large extent, the economic efficiency of urban areas.

Infrastructure Subsidies and Urban Decentralization

The subsidization of urban infrastructure reduces serviced land prices since the full infrastructure costs are not borne by land purchasers, thus encouraging increased land consumption. However, if the subsidy is higher than optimal, there will be an inefficient use of land in the construction of built space, resulting in lower than optimal densities. The fact that municipalities try to attract grants for infrastructures from upper-tier governments leads to further complications. In general, cities with the greatest success in obtaining infrastructure grants have been wealthier municipalities with a professional bureaucracy. For instance, from the early 1950s to the early 1980s, by manipulating its legal status former Metro Toronto received higher than

Table 7.1   International Comparison of Metropolitan and Inner-area Densities and Travel Behaviour, Gasoline Consumption, Emissions, Road Supply, and Parking

City	Population Density (Pop./ha)		Gasoline Use per Capita Private Transportation (MJ)	CO_2 Emissions Per Capita Total Transportation (kg)	Annual Travel in Private Cars (passenger km per capita)	Annual Travel in Public Transit (passenger km per capita)	Road Supply (meters per person)	CBD Parking Spaces (per 1,000 CBD jobs)
	Metropolitan Density	Inner-area Density*						
Calgary	20.8	22.7	35,684	3,393	11,078	775	4.9	522
Winnipeg	21.3	41.2	32,018	2,834	9,620	635	4.2	546
Edmonton	29.9	26.8	31,848	3,172	10,028	728	4.8	593
Vancouver	20.8	41.5	31,544	2,673	12,541	871	5.1	443
Toronto	41.5	60.0	30,746	2,434	7,027	2,173	2.6	176
Montreal	33.8	64.1	27,706	2,418	6,502	952	4.5	347
Ottawa	31.3	49.2	26,705	2,423	8,236	850	7.1	230
Canadian average	**28.5**	**43.6**	**30,893**	**2,764**	**9,290**	**998**	**4.7**	**408**
Sacramento	12.7	19.4	65,351	5,524	19,239	117	8.8	777
Houston	9.5	18.4	63,800	5,193	19,004	215	11.7	612
San Diego	13.1	32.1	61,004	4,846	18,757	259	5.5	688
Phoenix	10.5	16.4	59,832	4,654	15,903	124	9.6	906
San Francisco	16.0	59.8	58,493	5,122	16,229	899	4.6	137
Portland	11.7	23.7	57,699	5,094	14,665	286	10.6	403
Denver	12.8	16.3	56,132	4,961	13,515	199	7.6	606
Los Angeles	23.9	28.7	55,246	4,476	16,686	352	3.8	520
Detroit	12.8	28.6	54,817	4,518	15,846	171	6.0	706
Boston	12.0	43.1	50,617	4,238	17,373	627	6.7	285
Washington	13.7	38.1	49,593	4,403	16,214	774	5.2	253
Chicago	16.6	47.3	46,498	4,069	14,096	805	5.2	128
New York	19.2	91.5	46,409	3,779	11,062	1,334	4.6	60
American average	**14.2**	**35.6**	**55,807**	**4,683**	**16,045**	**474**	**6.9**	**468**

(continued)

Table 7.1 (continued)

City	Population Density (Pop./ha)		Gasoline Use per Capita Private Transportation (MJ)	CO$_2$ Emissions per Capita Total Transportation (kg)	Annual Travel in Private Cars (passenger km per capita)	Annual Travel in Public Transit (passenger km per capita)	Road Supply (meters per person)	CBD Parking Spaces (per 1,000 CBD jobs)
	Metropolitan Density	Inner-area Density*						
Canberra	9.5	8.6	40,699	3,240	11,195	660	8.8	842
Perth	10.6	16.3	34,579	2,980	12,029	544	10.7	631
Brisbane	9.8	20.3	31,290	2,899	11,188	900	8.2	322
Melbourne	14.9	27.2	33,527	2,916	9,782	844	7.7	337
Adelaide	11.8	18.7	31,784	2,672	11,173	572	8.0	580
Sydney	16.8	39.2	29,491	2,588	9,417	1,769	6.2	222
Australian average	**12.2**	**21.7**	**33,562**	**2,883**	**10,797**	**882**	**8.3**	**489**
Frankfurt	46.6	61.0	24,779	2,813	8,309	1,149	2.0	246
Brussels	74.9	91.0	21,080	2,114	6,809	1,428	2.1	314
Hamburg	39.8	85.7	20,344	2,680	7,592	1,375	2.6	177
Zurich	47.1	73.5	19,947	1,764	7,692	2,459	4.0	137
Stockholm	53.1	91.7	18,362	1,994	6,261	2,351	2.2	193
Vienna	68.3	128.6	14,990	1,505	5,272	2,430	1.8	186
Copenhagen	28.6	53.9	14,609	1,544	7,749	1,607	4.6	223
Paris	46.1	96.7	14,269	1,723	4,842	2,121	0.9	199
Munich	53.6	106.9	14,224	1,441	5,925	2,463	1.8	266
Amsterdam	48.8	89.3	13,915	1,475	6,522	1,061	2.6	354
London	42.3	78.1	12,884	1,704	5,644	2,405	2.0	?
European average	**49.9**	**86.9**	**17,218**	**1,887**	**6,601**	**1,895**	**2.4**	**230**

*The inner-area density refers to the pre-World War II city area developed mostly before the emergence of automobile-dependent lifestyles.

Source: Kenworthy and Laube (1999).

average subsidy rates on infrastructure from the province of Ontario (Vojnovic, 2000a). While all other cities qualified for provincial grants of up to one-third on public works expenditures, Metro Toronto and its municipalities were receiving recovery rates that ranged from 50 to 100 per cent. This enabled Metro's rapid growth, but also fostered inefficient development patterns.

Toronto provides a revealing case study of infrastructure underpricing and resulting distortions in urban form. The period under study covers the years 1954–66, when the current City of Toronto consisted of 13 individual municipalities—which were restructured into six municipalities in 1966 and consolidated into the City of Toronto in 1998. Figure 7.3 shows that low-density Metro suburbs, with less than 2,500 ppkm² (persons per square kilometre), benefited from per capita road subsidies that were over 300 per cent more than subsidies granted to municipalities with densities greater than 5,000 ppkm². In addition, Metro municipalities

occupied largely by middle- and upper-income groups were receiving subsidies as much as 800 per cent greater than subsidies to the fiscally weakest municipalities. Figure 7.4 illustrates the relationship between provincial grants and municipal expenditures for Weston (a former municipality in Metro Toronto that is now a neighbourhood in the City of Toronto). By reducing the price of roads, the grant itself was the incentive for higher road expenditures.

Besides inequities, discriminatory subsidies have also encouraged inefficient, low-density developments in the Metro suburbs. By 1990, when Metro Toronto had matured, the area density of the City of Toronto was 6,119 ppkm², York was 5,645 ppkm², and East York was 4,488 ppkm², while municipalities that received the special subsidies—North York, Scarborough, and Etobicoke—registered densities of 3,385, 2,595, and 2,411, respectively. Many neighbourhoods within these suburbs are now being torn down and rebuilt at higher intensities,

Figure 7.3   **Area Densities and Average Lower-Tier per Capita Road Subsidies, Metropolitan Toronto, 1954–66**

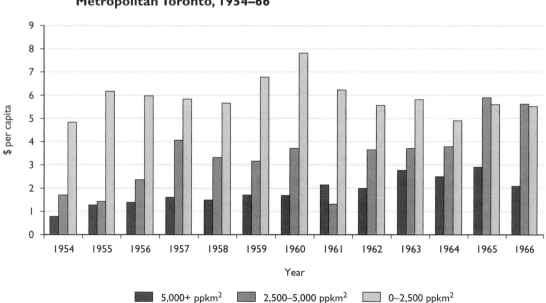

Source: Vojnovic (2000a). From 'Shaping Metropolitan Toronto: A Study of Linear Infrastructure Subsides, 1954–66', *Environment and Planning B: Planning and Design* 27 (2000). Reprinted by permission of Pion Limited London.

Figure 7.4   **Relationship between Road Subsidies and Road Expenditures, Weston, 1954–66**

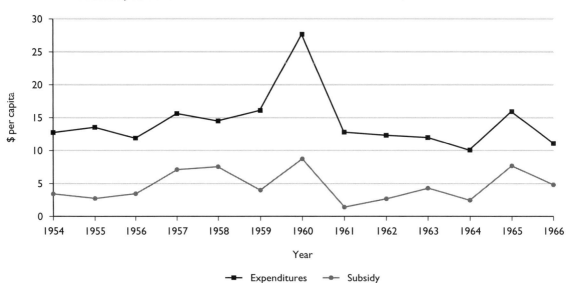

Source: Vojnovic (2000a). From 'Shaping Metropolitan Toronto: A Study of Linear Infrastructure Subsides, 1954–66', *Environment and Planning B: Planning and Design* 27 (2000). Reprinted by permission of Pion Limited London.

only a few decades after their original development, because of their suboptimal density.

It can be argued that the discriminatory grants to the Metro suburbs were strategic public initiatives intended to generate social welfare improvements. But a more likely interpretation is that these municipalities have benefited from a special treatment by virtue of their superior political skills and their abundant resources, which placed them in an advantageous position when attempting to manipulate the grant allocation process (Vojnovic, 2000a) As argued by Bailey (1994: 755), with public services 'there is an incentive for sub-groups to seek to increase their share of public service provision which is paid by the generality of local and national taxpayers.' Numerous examples in Canada illustrate how effective lobbying by the well-organized and wealthy has enabled them to shift the costs of customized services provided exclusively in their communities to the public at large, including the underprivileged (Vojnovic, 1998, 1999a, 1999b, 2000b).

Choice of Transportation Investment and Implications for the Built Environment

Historically, it is clear that the higher subsidization of roads and highways over other transportation infrastructures in Metro Toronto in large part encouraged a bias towards investment in this infrastructure type. Harold Kaplan (1967: 71) notes, '[w]ith the province willing to pay about half the costs of expressway construction but unwilling to contribute to subways, proceeding with expressways would impose less of a strain on Metro's early capital budgets.' In a similar tone, Stephen Clarkson (1972: 23) argues that '[p]rovincial subsidies for highway construction, far higher than those for rapid transit, had naturally pushed municipal politicians into biasing their transportation decisions in favour of expressways rather than subways.'

However, while the Toronto case illustrates that the generous subsidization of roads and highways encouraged   premature   suburbanization,   an alternative policy option, such as subsidization schemes in favour of public transit, would have shifted the direction of market incentives. Such initiatives would have encouraged higher inner-city densities by enabling the more efficient movement of people in the city itself—facilitating upward as opposed to outward urban growth. The high densities of cities such as New York, London, and Tokyo are supported by extensive subway networks for the quick movement of large populations. Without these networks, congestion would make the movement of people and goods in these cities unmanageable and the existing densities in these cities impossible to maintain. Thus, through the control of the subsidization of particular transportation infrastructures, policy-makers can use market mechanisms to induce expenditures on particular infrastructures and shape urban form.

Infrastructure Expenditures: Building versus Maintenance

Expenditures on urban infrastructures can be separated into two types—expenditures on the designing and building of infrastructure networks, and expenditures on the maintenance of these networks. Historically, emphasis has generally been placed on the former rather than the latter expenditure (Felbinger, 1995; Levy, 1985; Neutze, 1997).

A number of explanations have been advanced for the deferral of infrastructure repairs. Political rewards stemming from new projects far outweigh those associated with the maintenance of infrastructures, especially when these infrastructures are largely invisible. New infrastructure projects become particularly appealing if grants from upper tiers of government are available for the capital outlay, allowing for concrete results at a relatively low cost. Second, not only are many urban infrastructures buried and generally unnoticed, but the deterioration of these networks occurs slowly, over years of deferred maintenance, making it politically and administratively easier to delay necessary repairs. Finally, since infrastructures last significantly longer than terms of office, replacement and repair are

obvious places to cut budgets. The deteriorated urban infrastructure networks are then passed on to the next administration. An example of potential outcomes of deferred infrastructure maintenance occurred in the US in the early 1970s, when a truck fell through Manhattan's elevated West Side Highway onto the street below. The deterioration of the elevated highway due to maintenance neglect was so advanced that the whole structure needed to be torn down.

Neo-Liberalization and New Public Management

The opposition to the rising scale of government intervention in the Canadian economy, including in the provision of urban infrastructures, emerged on the Canadian political scene with the 1984 election of the Brian Mulroney Progressive Conservative government. The rise of neo-liberalism, however, was not limited to Canada. The minimal government ideology was felt throughout the English-speaking world—as evidenced by the governments of Margaret Thatcher in the UK and Ronald Reagan in the US—as well as in countries throughout continental Europe and Asia, including China. In the late twentieth century, government intervention as a response to market failures began to slowly decline, and a new emphasis was placed on market incentives and the adoption of private market values and practices in the public realm (Osborne and Gaebler, 1992). The interest in various forms of privatization (of Air Canada, the Gas Division of BC Hydro, Highway 407 in the Greater Toronto Area) is a reflection of this new political environment (Tassonyi, 1997). The economic downturn of the 1970s, the public perception of being 'overgoverned', increasing public opposition to taxes, and the loss of fiscal accountability in an environment characterized by increased public subsidies all facilitated the political emergence of the minimal government perspective. The importance of public goods and externalities in generating market efficiency and equity began to be increasingly dismissed under this new public management approach—with resulting impacts on Canada's urban infrastructures, public services, and lower-income groups (Filion, 1998; Fischler and Wolfe, 2000; Jenson and Phillips, 1996).

Instead of rationalizing the financial system to ensure that subsidies towards urban infrastructure were limited only to cases that generated improvements in equity and efficiency—a movement towards optimal market conditions—the overall use of public subsidies to address market failures and ensure optimal levels of urban infrastructure provision was largely abandoned. There was a reduction in intergovernmental grants and financial arrangements as the federal government downloaded fiscal responsibility to provinces and municipalities, and provinces downloaded the financial responsibilities of service delivery, and what were perceived as 'local government functions', to municipalities. In this fiscal reorganization, it was increasingly accepted politically that, as with private goods, consumers should pay for exactly what they receive in benefits from public goods, regardless of equity and efficiency conditions. The new public management approach was advocating simple cost-recovery charges, without any recognition of market failures or the uniqueness of public goods, including urban infrastructures.

A complementary neo-liberal advocacy that further strengthened the call for reduced local government accentuated the need for cities to become entrepreneurial. Within this framework, cities are encouraged to engage in inter-municipal competition with an important element of the strategy focused on maintaining low taxes in order to attract investment and ensure the economic success of the region. According to this stand, cities that maintain high public service expenditures (particularly on social services) also require high local taxes, making the city unattractive to investors (Peterson, 1981). This has become a justification for dispensing with many of the public roles and responsibilities of the twentieth-century welfare state, including the maintenance and provision of urban infrastructures. However, research completed on major US cities illustrates that the argument that high-taxing and high-expenditure cities cannot attract investment is simply not supported (Vojnovic, 2003a, 2003b).

In a financial profile of the largest US cities, the cities that maintain (and have historically maintained) the highest taxes and the highest local expenditures, including high expenditures on social services—cities such as New York, Washington, San Francisco, Los Angeles, and Boston—continue to be successful in attracting investment. For instance, three high-taxing/high-expenditure cities (New York, San Francisco, and Boston) maintain average per capita local taxes and expenditures at approximately $5,200 annually, with local per capita expenditures on social welfare at over $560 annually. In contrast, Houston, Dallas, and Phoenix maintain local per capita taxes and expenditures at around $2,000 annually and per capita expenditures on welfare at approximately $85 annually.[2]

Some Canadian municipalities have reacted innovatively to urban infrastructure financing in the face of recent political changes. In attempting to make public finances transparent and to limit the shift of costs between subgroup populations, the Halifax Regional Municipality (HRM) has established area rates reflecting urban expenditures—including urban infrastructures—to reveal the levels of public services and service costs in the different areas of the municipality. The initiative was introduced in recognition that rural HRM taxpayers who did not have services such as sidewalks, streetlights, and public transit should not be contributing to the provision of these services in the urban areas of HRM. By the 1998–9 fiscal year, approximately 60 different area rates existed in HRM. At the same time, however, Halifax recognized that infrastructure subsidies were critical to ensuring equity and efficiency within the municipality (Vojnovic, 2000c).

Recognizing the importance of infrastructure subsidies began with schools, but soon expanded to other services (Vojnovic, 2000c). Because of the wealth and tax base in urban Halifax, urban schools provided customized educational services. Many rural residents who lived in proximity sent their children to urban schools, generating overcrowded urban classrooms while many rural classrooms remained empty. Instead of expanding programs and building new schools in urban areas, it was recognized that a more cost-effective solution was to subsidize schools in rural HRM—standardizing education throughout the region, ensuring the full use of rural educational infrastructure, and eliminating crowding in urban schools. The subsidization of rural schools, while saving the municipality money, also improved regional equity, again illustrating that greater efficiency and equity can be achieved simultaneously through the appropriate subsidization of urban infrastructures.

Conclusion

Urban infrastructures have been vital in creating Canada's system of cities, in shaping cities, and in driving Canada's economic development. While the importance of various infrastructure types has changed over time, a consistent theme throughout Canada's history has been the scale and scope of government involvement in urban infrastructure provision. The current perspective on the role of government is most affected by neo-liberalism. This perspective questioned many of the fundamental principles in the public role of urban infrastructure investment developed throughout the twentieth century—principles that enabled Canadian cities to resolve the disorder of early capitalism. Since the 1980s, the federal and provincial governments have reduced their involvement in urban infrastructure provision, generating concerns over the quality of Canada's urban infrastructures. As noted by Andrew and Morrison (2002), the deteriorated condition of infrastructures by the early 1990s is what led to the

1994–8 Canada's Infrastructure Works Program. In the twenty-first century, the New Deal for Canadian Cities is yet another illustration of the necessity of public involvement, and particularly upper-tier government intervention, in infrastructure provision. However, the piecemeal nature of infrastructure investment without a systematic rationale for ensuring equity and efficiency continues to allow infrastructure financing to be distorted by effective political lobbying. Many of the fiscal distortions that have plagued past practices will likely continue, with resulting implications on urban form, environmental quality, and equity. Equity continues to be of particular concern, since the extent to which urban infrastructure has a capacity to include populations and ensure economic development and prosperity parallels its capacity to exclude populations and marginalize.

Notes

1. Federal and provincial transfers to municipalities are a form of financial assistance to local governments. These payments substantially expanded during the three decades following World War II, as the role and responsibilities of government in Canada increased under the welfare state model. Transfer payments were introduced for a number of reasons: to compensate for the limited capacity of cities to raise revenue; to allow municipalities to conform to provincial and federal policies; and to equalize revenues between rich and poor municipalities.
2. For a detailed financial profile and assessment of major US cities, see Vojnovic (2003a, 2003b).

Chapter 8

Life Stages, Living Arrangements, and Lifestyles

Damaris Rose and Paul Villeneuve

The residential location and patterning of different social groups within the city have long been concerns of urban social geography. Research has typically focused on differentiation and disparities between social groups in terms of the types of urban goods and services (public and private) to which they have access, on how divisions of urban space reflect different 'structures of consumption', and on the material and symbolic values that different groups attach to these various 'consumption landscapes'. A generation ago—when North American and European urban studies was much influenced by the mass mobilizations for social justice of the 1960s (Soja, 2000: 116; Topalov, 1989)—neo-Marxist scholars focused on how social class differences were mapped onto urban residential space. This residential differentiation (at worst, segregation) would in turn lead to increasing inequity in access to good-quality commercial consumption facilities, such as supermarkets, whose location is market-driven. At the same time, state policies regarding collectively consumed goods and services (e.g., social housing, public schools, transit) were critiqued for not living up to the redistributive promises of the welfare state in that the quality of goods and services was worse in poor neighbourhoods, which could in some cases lead to the reproduction of pervasive inequalities from one generation to the next.

In the 1980s and 1990s, urban social researchers paid increasing attention to other lines of demarcation and spatial differentiation. Gender relations and identities were shown to complicate the geometry and geography of class relations and modes of consumption, and attention was increasingly drawn to inequalities and exclusions based on sexuality, ethnicity, 'race', life stage, and ability status (Bondi and Rose, 2003; Jacobs and Fincher, 1998; Ray and Rose, 2000). It has even been suggested that '[t]o some degree, household income has become a function of demographics rather than occupation or social class' (Jones and Simmons, 1993: 428). Social movements such as feminism and identity- and rights-based claims by minority groups have made these other dimensions of inequality much more visible to urban researchers and policy-makers and have in some cases improved access to resources needed for individual self-actualization and collective empowerment.

In this chapter we aim to show that over the past few decades major demographic shifts—especially increased life expectancy and declining fertility, leading to smaller household sizes and an aging population—have intersected with other sets of transformations in the economy and society to generate an increasingly varied array of household types, living arrangements, and patterns of consumption in Canadian cities, as well as more fluidity in living arrangements over people's lifetimes. Without going as far as Foot and Stoffman's (1996) proposition that demographics explains 'almost everything', we suggest that this adds yet another layer of complexity to urban socio-spatial differentiation, along the lines of what is commonly referred to as 'lifestyle'.

'Lifestyle' is a broad concept as likely to be used by journalists and those in marketing as by academics. The 'postmodern' turn in sociology and related fields has paid increasing attention to how 'cultural styles' are playing an increasing role in identity construction. In fact, the concept of lifestyle is not inherently postmodern. It has older roots in analyses of the modern city. According to the Chicago School of urban sociology, important aspects of people's behaviour in everyday life were shaped by the size, density, and heterogeneity of human settlements—hence the emergence of concepts of 'urban' as opposed to 'rural' and 'suburban' lifestyles. But in a classic essay published over 40 years ago, Herbert Gans (1962a) argued that this perspective wrongly ignored the roles of social class and life cycle. Gans's critique seems highly prescient to us today. It is not for nothing that private-sector marketing researchers are the main clients of Statistics Canada's data products providing sociodemographic and economic profiles of urban residents at the geographical scale of the postal code, to which measures of values and attitudes are added in order to segment consumer markets in appropriate ways (Jones and Simmons, 1993: 113). The mass consumption of the Fordist economy and society has given way to a post-Fordist, postmodern fragmentation of consumption styles and fashions targeting different 'market segments' (Harvey, 1987). Individuals are said to have considerable freedom to construct their own identities (and project these to others) by means of the particular pattern of consumption they opt for—including how they look, what they buy, the kind of city and neighbourhood they live in, and where they engage in leisure activities. This is sometimes referred to as the 'niched society'. Critics, however, point out to a danger in this analysis, it being too easy to equate 'lifestyles' with 'fashions', implicitly assuming they are the product of a set of freely chosen tastes and preferences as though there were no constraints on choice (Campbell, 1995).

In urban studies there is also a growing interest in 'cultural style' and new consumption patterns. Some scholars suggest that shopping may now be more significant as a social activity than in terms of the acquisition of goods (Jones and Simmons, 1993: 53) (see Chapter 16). Central-area economies of post-industrial cities are indeed increasingly focused on consumption-based industries—including cultural facilities, specialized boutiques and eateries, retailing and leisure complexes—whose success depends on harnessing the 'lifestyles' of various groups with disposable income to particular kinds of consumption practices (Hannigan, 1998; Zukin, 1998). City governments engage in 'branding' based on 'lifestyle appeal' to the new urban elites and up-and-coming professionals (Kipfer and Keil, 2002). They see 'non-traditional' households with some disposable income as key to re-establishing a residential presence in city centres and as a means of reinforcing the clustering of 'new economy' jobs (artistic, cultural, and high-tech 'niche' sectors) at the fringes of the central business district (CBD) (Heath, 2001; Hutton, 2004b) (see Chapter 10).

Our own position is that 'lifestyle' is indeed an increasingly important dimension of social differentiation and identity construction in the postmodern, post-industrial city (Zukin, 1998). However, the literature has paid little attention to how living arrangements, 'lifestyle choices', and capacities to practise certain modes of consumption are shaped not just by income but also by prevailing social mores concerning gender, sexuality, 'race', or ethnicity, as well as the often neglected dimension of stage in the life course (Fincher, 1998; Monk and Katz, 1993). Each life stage can be seen as a constellation of education, employment and income situation, family-based commitments, and living arrangements. Life stages do not determine lifestyles in a mechanistic way but they do set some of the parameters or limits within which lifestyles are chosen.

All of this means that Canadian urban society now comprises a much-increased diversity of household types and living arrangements: 'traditional' nuclear families, dual-income couples (including dual-*career* couples), lone-parent families, 'blended families', same-sex couples, and one-person households. In the remainder of this chapter, we first sketch out the economic and social transformations that have led to this increased diversity of household types and living arrangements as well as to increasingly fluid life transitions. We then illustrate how a number of social dimensions, including gender, ethnicity, sexual orientation, occupational class, and life stage, intersect to nourish the present diversity. And finally, we discuss two emerging issues associated with these changes: the impact of dual-earner families and the diversification of the elderly population. Both issues raise policy challenges in that they have the potential to produce new forms of social inequality.

Periodizing Social, Demographic, and Lifestyle Change: A Century of Transition

Understanding the life stages that people go through, the transitions they make between stages, and their lifestyle at any particular life stage requires placing these in the broader historical and structural context of the times they live in. The twentieth century brought momentous changes in Canadian demographics and society—in life expectancy, in living environments, in the kinds of households and families Canadians lived in over their life course, in their living standards, and in their opportunities for educational, economic, and social advancement and emancipation as individuals. The transformations wrought in women's lives were especially dramatic. These various dimensions of change are not historically independent of one another. We have attempted to divide the century into periods characterized in economic, socio-cultural, and demographic terms. It is important, however, to avoid 'myths of total rupture', since much that seems new has a lineage in the past. We assembled the values (or reasonable estimates) of 13 such indicators for every census year from 1901 to 2001. The values of 10 of these indicators are graphed in Figures 8.1, 8.2, and 8.6 (the other three values are per capita disposable income and the percentages of managers in the female and male workforces). Using correlational techniques (not presented here due to space limitations) to examine the pace of change in the overall profile of Canadian society (in terms of all these indicators taken together) from one decennial

census year to the next, we find that the century divides into three broad periods (1901–31; 1941–61; 1971–2001), separated by decades of transition or even rupture in which social and demographic changes seemed to be accelerated. Table 8.1 summarizes the results of this exercise.

The Early Twentieth Century

The first period (1901–31) was characterized by rapid urbanization, especially the growth of metropolitan cities, fuelled by international immigration and domestic migration from agricultural areas (Figure 8.2). As can be seen from Figure 8.1, the long-term and dramatic decline in the fertility rate of Canadian women, known as the 'demographic transition', was already well underway in the early decades of the twentieth century. It had begun around 1870 and was closely linked to the urbanization process: couples were marrying later, large families were less necessary in a non-agricultural economy, sanitation and health care decreased childhood mortality, and women could increasingly gain access to birth control (Beaujot, 2000; Henripin, 1968). Consequently, overall household size also decreased. Marriage was almost always a lifetime commitment, but many women still became widows while raising their children (Lemieux and Mercier, 1992: 339–43). Children lived at home until marriage unless they went into the military or domestic service.

As to employment opportunities, in eastern and central Canada manufacturing predominated although white-collar employment grew rapidly in major urban centres after World War I. Working-class families needed the additional income from women's work in manufacturing and domestic service. Unmarried middle-class women (including nuns in Quebec) greatly increased their presence in professions such as teaching, but the mores of the times and officially sanctioned discrimination kept married women out of 'career'-track employment (Dumont et al., 1987: 209–24; Laflamme, 2001; Strong-Boag, 1988: 41–80). Nevertheless, urbanization, and especially the growth of diversified metropolitan areas, was already changing the horizons

Table 8.1	**Demographic and Lifestyle Changes in Canada in Broader Societal Context**	
	Urban Economy, Education, Labour Force	Demography, Lifestyles
1901–31	Rapid increase in metropolitan urbanization; growth of white-collar employment, including more openings for women	Demographic transition well underway; bohemia, 'freedom of city' for some young single women; marriage still lifetime commitment
1930s	Depression, Keynesianism, and nation-building institutions, e.g., Bank of Canada; capital-intensive production; automobile; slow-down in urbanization rate	Continued decline in fertility; rising age of marriage
1941–61	Post-war boom and Fordism; married women displaced from 'men's jobs'; rapidly increasing male university enrolment rates; tertiarization; gradual increase in female labour force participation	Baby boom; emerging home-ownership-based consumer society; suburban nuclear family; conformity
1960s	Welfare state; increasing female university enrolment rates	'Cultural revolution', with experimentation in living arrangements by middle-class youth, feminism, divorce law reform, legalization of homosexuality, more reliable contraception
1971–2001	Growth of advanced tertiary employment and professional occupations; acceleration of female university enrolment rates and labour force participation; post-Fordism, neo-liberalism, economic uncertainty	Population aging; more fluid life course, diversification of conjugal arrangements and household types; individualization; decentring of traditional family; dual-earner families become norm, household consumer patterns differentiated by number of earners

of some groups of women. Back in the early twentieth century, urban sociologists pointed to the modern metropolis as an arena for relatively anonymous social experimentation, where the strong and homogeneous social bonds of rural life and the obligations of family were at least partly displaced by more diverse social networks, with more fluidity and less commitment (Park, 1969; Simmel, 1950). Both feminist academics and novelists are increasingly showing us how, as early as the 1920s, moving to the 'big city' could be an emancipating step for young unattached middle-class women, opening horizons both economically and in terms of escaping the cultural mores of rural and small town

life—although such a move could also entail great personal risks and the loss of social support (Bondi and Rose, 2003; Garber, 2000; see also Richard Wright's 2001 novel, *Clara Callan*).

From the Great Depression to the Post-War Boom

The Great Depression of the 1930s was a moment of profound rupture in Canadian society. It led to interventionist state policies (Keynesianism) to help develop an economy based on mass production and laid the foundations for the society based on mass consumption that would flourish in the years after

Figure 8.1   **Fertility and Household Size in Canada, 1901–2001**

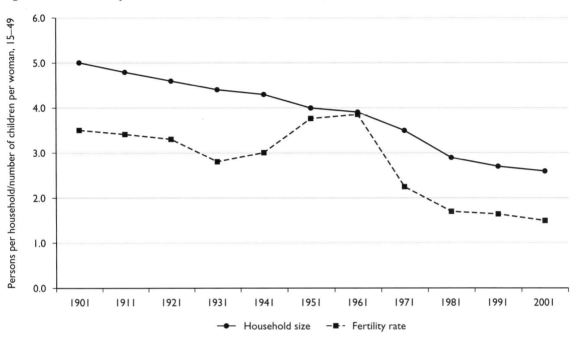

Sources: Statistics Canada, CANSIM Series A248–253 and Canadian censuses of 1981, 1991, 2001 (Catalogue nos. 91–535F, 84–210–XPB, and 11–001–XPF); Henripin (1968).

World War II. Consumer goods, housing, and sub-urban environments were increasingly characterized by a modernist aesthetic entailing standardization and homogeneity (Harvey, 1989a: 125–40). Capital-intensive industries expanded in central Canada, epitomized by the automobile industry, which paid high wages to its (mostly male) unionized workers. In this way 'Fordism' (named after Henry Ford) nourished the growth of automobile-dependent suburbs dominated by single-family housing, and in so doing it reinforced the ideal of the 'traditional' nuclear family and discouraged married women's paid employment once they were no longer needed for wartime production (Séguin, 1989).

The aftermath of World War II brought the 'baby boom' (much larger in Canada than in most other Western countries, relative to its population); this significantly interrupted the long-term downward trend in the fertility rate. The 1950s are generally characterized as a socially conformist era, the 'golden age' of the traditional nuclear family living in suburban homogeneity (Beaujot, 2000; see also CBC Radio, 1963). Nevertheless, social and gender discontents were not far below the surface, and women's labour force participation rates were beginning to accelerate as the growth of the service economy increased the demand for their labour (Figure 8.2). However, this was much more the case in large cities than in the small single-industry communities where a large proportion of Canadians still lived at mid-century and where a more traditional 'gender order' prevailed until destabilized by recent waves of economic restructuring (Preston et al., 2000).

In spite of the higher birth rate during the baby boom years, average household size continued to fall (Figure 8.1). This was because increasing numbers of people were living alone. Interestingly, as Miron (1993b) has noted, living alone changed from being a feature of rural non-farming areas (men working in seasonal occupations in the natural resource sector or as migrant labour in single-industry communities) to a phenomenon linked to growing urban prosperity and a change in socio-cultural values. The economic boom of the 1945–75 period brought rapid rises in disposable incomes. 'Boarding and lodging' by people who did not have families of their own went out of favour. For more and more young unmarried women and men in Canada's larger cities, it was becoming affordable, socially acceptable, and symbolically important to establish residential autonomy before marriage by moving out of their parents' home once they obtained employment—typically in the burgeoning tertiary sector. Such moves were made possible as private rental apartment buildings became an increasingly common feature of Canadian inner-city landscapes in the 1960s and 1970s.

From the 1960s to the New Millennium

The 1960s saw massive expansion of public-sector employment, education, and welfare state institutions (Moscovitch and Drover, 1987), including the secularization of health care and education in Quebec—a trend that continued into the mid-1970s and greatly increased women's labour market access. This was a time of major social experimentation and cultural upheaval across the country, as elsewhere in the Western world, with a broad questioning of the 'blandness of the quality of life under a regime of standardized mass consumption' (Harvey, 1989a: 139) and of established institutions such as marriage, the patriarchal family, and—especially in Quebec—the Church. Efficient contraception enabled much greater control over child-bearing (Beaujot, 2000: 92). Divorce laws were liberalized, leading to more people living alone in older age and paving the way for people to change their living arrangements more frequently over their life course. Presaging the 'gentrification' movement that would gain strength in the 1970s and 1980s, some elements of the young,

university-educated middle class 'rediscovered' the role that inner-city neighbourhoods had played much earlier in the century as a locale for bohemianism and countercultural lifestyles where unconventional living arrangements, gender identities, and sexualities could be explored openly (Appleton, 1995; Caulfield, 1994; Ley, 1996a; Séguin and Villeneuve, 1993).

The period formed by the last three decades of the twentieth century saw fertility rates resuming their earlier pattern of decline. This added momentum to the overall decline in household size (Péron, 1999). In other respects, the last third of the century saw a deepening of trends established in mid-century—tertiarization of the economy and rapid growth in women's higher educational opportunities and labour force participation (Cooke-Reynolds and Zukewich, 2004). The increase in university enrolment rates accelerated in the immediate post-war period for both men and women, but by 1991 women's enrolment rates had overtaken those of men (see Figure 8.2). The improvement in labour market opportunities for women was a major contributing factor to smaller family sizes. As well as being able to stay in employment after marriage, they also gained growing access to career-track employment in professional fields and, more recently, even in managerial fields previously the exclusive preserve of men (Fortin and Huberman, 2002; Rose and Villeneuve, 1993). This has led to spectacular growth in the number of 'dual-career' couples, that is, those couples where both partners are highly educated and hold professional or managerial jobs (Rose and Villeneuve, 1998). This phenomenon is most pronounced in Canada's major post-industrial cities, which have seen a strong 'professionalization' of their workforces with the growth in business services as well as in high-level government services (Rose and Villeneuve, 1993; see Chapter 14). Indeed, these cities act as magnets for highly educated workers from more peripheral parts of Canada's urban system (Heisz et al., 2005).

Increasingly, then, women have alternative sources of fulfilment to a life focused entirely on marriage and child-rearing. The age of first

Figure 8.2   **Urbanization, Education, Labour Force Participation in Canada, 1901–2001**

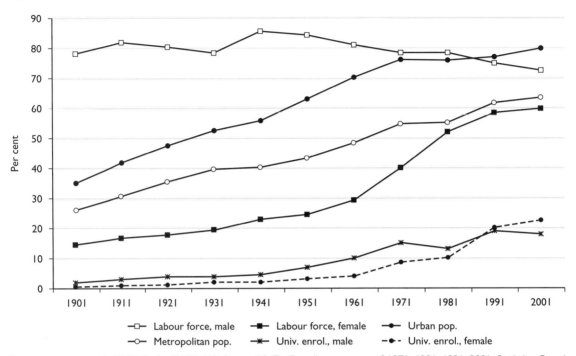

Sources: CANSIM matrix 3451, Series D107–122; Stone (1967); Canadian censuses of 1971, 1981, 1991, 2001; Statistics Canada, *Canadian Social Trends* 59 (Winter 2000): 6, 13, 14 (Catalogue no. 11–008).

marriage rose again in the last decades of the twentieth century—by 2001 it was 28 for women and 30 for men (Crompton, 2005). Not surprisingly, this trend is more pronounced in large metropolitan areas than in small-town and rural Canada. Childbirth is postponed or even, for a growing number, forgone entirely (Beaujot, 2004). In seven out of 10 two-parent families with children under six, both parents are in paid work, which also depresses fertility rates because of Canada's chronic shortage of adequate and affordable child-care arrangements (Cleveland and Krashinsky, 2003).

Women's economic advancement is not, however, the only reason for the drastic fall in birth rates. Employment prospects became more uncertain and the 'lifetime job' increasingly rare in the wake of the mid-1970s oil shocks, the growing globalization of

the economy since 1980, and government deficit-cutting strategies in the 1990s. Real earnings fell from 1980 to 2000, although those of university-educated women significantly bucked this trend (Morissette and Johnson, 2004). It has thus become risky to rely on a sole, male breadwinner in order to attain and maintain middle-class living standards (Rose and Villeneuve, 1998). In 2002, almost three out of five husband-wife families with employment income had two earners (ranging from 53 per cent in the Saguenay, Quebec, CMA to 64 per cent in Calgary and Saskatoon; calculated from Statistics Canada, 2004a). Also, young people are prolonging their studies and taking longer to launch themselves into full-time work, which largely explains why the cohorts reaching early adulthood in the 1980s and 1990s massively reverted to remaining in the parental home until their mid- or even late twenties, as well as set a new trend—'boomeranging' back home again (Beaujot, 2004; Beaupré and Le Bourdais, 2001). Although this may not necessarily compromise the acquisition of personal autonomy associated with the transition to adulthood (Rose et al., 1999), it is likely to delay the age of first marriage and childbirth and thereby reduce the number of children a couple will have over their lifespan.

Finally, the combined effects of increased life expectancy (see Figure 8.5), declining fertility, and the baby boom mean that the Canadian population is now aging rapidly, in spite of Canada's high immigration rates (see Chapter 9). A hundred years ago only 6 per cent of Canadians were over 65; by the mid-1990s their share reached 17 per cent, and this could reach 25 per cent within the next three to four decades. The share of the population aged over 80—and thus at high risk of being frail and alone—is increasing even faster (Martin-Matthews, 2001; Moore and Rosenberg, 2001).

Diversification of Living Arrangements

By the late twentieth century the hegemony of the 'traditional' nuclear family was being challenged from many directions. We turn now to a brief and necessarily incomplete look at some of the new household types and living arrangements that have become more prevalent and/or more socially acceptable over the past two decades.

Among families with children, easier divorce proceedings led to rates of lone parenthood returning to the high levels seen much earlier in the century when widowhood had been the main cause of this type of family (Péron, 1999). In 2001 over 21 per cent of all Canadian families with children were headed by a lone parent—a female in almost 90 per cent of cases since until recently custody decisions almost invariably favoured mothers. Although female lone parents are found in all socio-economic brackets (Rose and Le Bourdais, 1986), poverty rates are high, a major factor being the difficulty of finding decently paid work compatible with raising a child alone. In 2000, almost one-quarter

of employed lone mothers were in low-paid jobs compared to only 11 per cent of their male counterparts (Morissette and Picot, 2005). Since the mid-1990s the growth of 'step'- and 'blended' families resulting from remarriage or cohabitation with a new partner has outpaced that of lone parents (Statistics Canada, 2002a)—a telling indicator of the growing fluidity of living arrangements and life transitions.

Rates of living alone have also increased significantly. This has indeed been one of the most dramatic demographic shifts of the past half-century, from 2.6 per cent of Canadians in 1951 to 12.3 per cent in 2001 (Clark, 2002). Overall, population aging is the largest single contributor to the rise of living alone, because living longer (Figure 8.6) increases the likelihood of a spell of widowhood. However, living alone is also becoming more prevalent for both sexes in mid-life; in these age groups living alone by choice has become much more socially acceptable and is no longer necessarily associated with personal and economic instability.

Figure 8.3 presents changes in the frequency of living alone between 1981 and 2001 for the Montreal and Toronto census metropolitan areas (CMAs) as well as for the aggregate of five 'second-tier' CMAs (combined to minimize sampling error effects), while Figure 8.4 breaks down the 2001 data by gender. Toronto's lower rates are likely due to a combination of its high housing costs and greater cultural diversity: in some ethnocultural groups, young adults generally remain in the family home until marriage (Boyd, 2000) and widowed elderly persons are more likely to move in with their children (Pacey, 2002). The 2001 census also reveals that the frequency of those over 25 years old living with their parents, as well as those aged 75 and over living with relatives, increases with CMA or census agglomeration (CA) size (Statistics Canada, 2002b); again, this may reflect the greater ethnocultural diversity of (most of) Canada's largest urban areas. As regards variations across the entire Canadian urban system, the same data source reveals that the highest rates of living alone (in each age group, and for both sexes) are in the Montreal and Vancouver CMAs. Otherwise, there is little difference by size of

Figure 8.3   **Frequency of Living Alone, by Age, Both Sexes, Selected CMAs, 1981 and 2001**

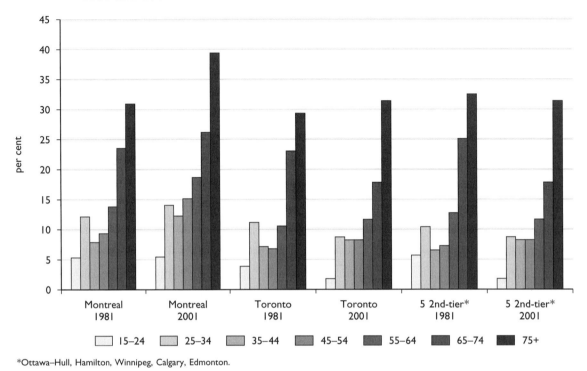

*Ottawa–Hull, Hamilton, Winnipeg, Calgary, Edmonton.

Source: Statistics Canada, 2001 census, Public use microdata files.

CMA or CA. In resource-based single-industry communities, however—where the traditional nuclear family still predominates (Preston et al., 2000)—only 3 to 8 per cent of women aged 25–44 live alone (Statistics Canada, 2002b); the higher figure for their male counterparts (12 to 19 per cent) no doubt reflects patterns of short-term migration in search of work (Halseth, 1999).

The rise of living alone is having important impacts on the housing market. Especially in advanced tertiary cities with widespread professional and managerial employment opportunities, one-person households, both female and male, form a rapidly growing segment of the home-buying market (CMHC, 2004a; Rose, 2004). The majority purchase condominiums because of their lower purchase price and also because maintenance

responsibilities are less onerous than in the case of a single-family home, which frees up time for a less 'home-oriented' lifestyle. For some single people, this type of home-buying symbolizes personal and economic autonomy and creates an anchor point in their lives. For others, it is an entry point to a housing career that may later take a more traditional, family-oriented suburban pathway.

Condominiums aimed at non-elderly singles tend to be centrally located. Developers pitch condos in 'brownfield' redevelopment districts—such as Montreal's Lachine Canal sector and Toronto's Liberty Village—using 'lifestyle marketing' to promote the urban 'experience', hedonism, and active leisure pursuits (Allen and Blandy, 2004; Fincher and Costello, 2005). Although these housing developments, as well as the commercial services they

Figure 8.4   **Frequency of Living Alone, by Age and Sex, Selected CMAs, 2001**

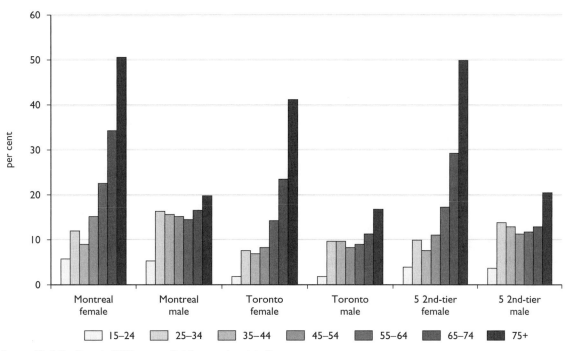

Source: Statistics Canada, 2001 census, Public use microdata files.

generate, are not targeting a 'luxury' segment of the market, they are a social world away from how people at the low-income end of the spectrum of singles live. This end of the spectrum is populated by divorced or never-married individuals out of work or on the margins of the labour market, migrants from deindustrialized regions, and others experiencing long-term economic and social exclusion for various reasons. Gentrification and urban redevelopment schemes are increasingly leading to their displacement from the low-rent inner-city rooming houses that were their traditional housing market niche, putting them at high risk of homelessness (see Chapter 25).

Another type of living arrangement that has gained increasing visibility is that of the same-sex couple. The 2001 census marked the first time that same-sex couples living together were able to identify themselves as such on the questionnaire *if they so wished*. While the responses to this new census question do not necessarily measure the actual numbers of same-sex couples, they do reflect the comfort levels of gay and lesbian couples in making a formal written, albeit confidential, affirmation of their status. There remains an unevenness within Canada—by region, religion, and ethnocultural background—in whether living as a same-sex couple is considered 'normal'. In the early twentieth century, as we saw earlier, the central areas of large metropolitan cities were bohemian places, a mecca—or refuge—for 'alternative' lifestyles including 'transgressive' social and sexual practices. Almost a century later, charting the reported frequency of same-sex couples compared to all couples for Canada's CMAs in 2001 (Figure 8.5) shows that three out of four of the largest CMAs ranked at the top. Montreal and Vancouver have a 'gay-friendly' reputation. Toronto, however (with Canada's largest immigrant population and a fairly high proportion of churchgoers), ranks lower in

Figure 8.5   **Prevalence of Same-Sex Common-Law Couples, by CMA Size, 2001**

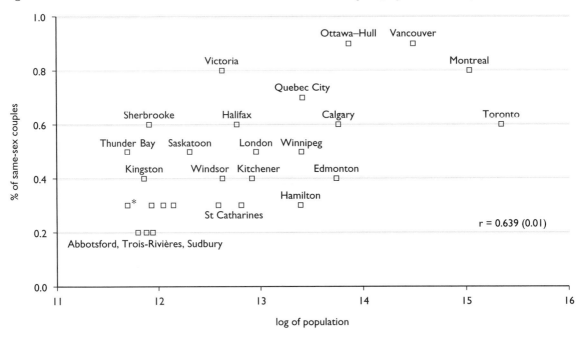

*From left to right, the first five cities at 0.3% are: Saint John, Chicoutimi, St John's, Regina, Oshawa.

Source: Statistics Canada, 2001 census, Same-sex common-law couples, by Census Metropolitan Area (CMA), 2001; at: <www12. statcan.ca/english/census01/products/analytic/companion/fam/sscma.cfm#ftnt1>, and Table OMN5794, Population of CMAs in 2001.

reported same-sex couples while Victoria (with a much smaller population but a 'west coast' ambience) ranked with Montreal and Vancouver. Perhaps tellingly, the lowest percentages are found for three of Canada's smallest CMAs: Abbotsford, BC, Sudbury, Ontario, and Trois-Rivières, Quebec.

Increasingly Fluid Life Transitions

Overall, the social and cultural shifts of the 1960s spurred both a major diversification of family forms and an increased 'fluidity' in living arrangements over the life course (Beaujot, 2000). By fluidity we mean the increased possibility and social acceptability of moving in and out of different living arrangements as emotional connections and economic necessities change. For large segments of the

population, certain major life transitions—those associated with forming and ending relationships and founding a family—have become much more a matter of choices made by individuals and couples and less a matter of following tradition or respecting an established institution. The couple and the family no longer have procreation, legally sanctioned by marriage, as their primary purpose (Beaujot, 2004), and are tending more to be ways of pursuing reciprocal relations of companionship and mutual aid between people who also have 'lives of their own' (Jones et al., 1990). The growing popularity of common-law unions—especially in Quebec but increasingly so elsewhere in Canada— is a clear example of such fluidity because such unions do not last as long as legal marriages, even when they produce children (Le Bourdais et al., 2000). For some demographers, the increased fluidity and flexibility in entering into and exiting from family and parenting relationships and household living arrangements represent such a major societal change that they now refer to it as the 'second demographic transition' (Ogden and Hall, 2004).

Some analysts interpret these fluidities in relationships and living arrangements as reflecting a secular rise in individualism and a decline in strong social bonds. But 'individualization' in the sense of identifying and trying to achieve personal life goals is not the same thing as individualism, which implies a devaluing of social relationships and a loss of a sense of common purpose with others (Bellah et al., 1985). Other authors argue that people's strong social ties and long-lasting commitments can no longer be read off from their living arrangements. To take some examples, living alone does not necessarily mean an abandonment of close family ties, and close friends may become 'surrogate kin' (Roseneil and Budgeon, 2004). Non-custodial parents may nevertheless maintain intense relationships with their children. And also, for reasons of choice or necessity, increasing numbers of couples with long-term commitments may maintain separate households or only live together on a part-time basis (Levin, 2004; Milan and Peters, 2003).

Some Emerging Issues and Challenges

Disparities in Urban Lifestyles: The Impact of Dual-Earner Families

The diversification of household types is also affecting changes in income distribution. There is a potential for rising income disparity and polarization of lifestyles between households with two earners and households with only one earner or without employment income (Bourne and Rose, 2001). The top family income quintile is increasingly populated by two-earner couples (Mongeau, 1999), while low wages remain a stubborn problem with the hourly wage of about one in six adults being less than $10 in 2004, unchanged from 1981. If a low-wage earner lives alone or heads a lone-

parent family, living in poverty is inevitable given the high cost of shelter and other essentials. But since the household is essentially an income pooling unit, if it has two earners it is less vulnerable to poverty (unless there are several dependent children) even if individual earnings are low (Morissette and Picot, 2005).

On the whole, household income polarization is more marked in the largest CMAs, which, as we have seen, are magnets for 'dual-career' couples with high incomes who pursue high-consumption lifestyles in gentrifying neighbourhoods, old elite suburbs, and 'new urbanism' developments (Grant, 2002). According to 2002 income tax-filers' data (Statistics Canada, 2004a), Canadian couples (with and without children) with both spouses employed have employment incomes well over double those of the 'traditional' single-male-earner couple. The size of this gap no doubt reflects the tendency for highly educated professionals and managers to seek partners of similar status (this is called educational and occupational 'homogamy') (Rose and Villeneuve, 1998). The highest differentials are found not only in Canada's three largest CMAs, as expected, but also in a few mid-size CMAs (Victoria, Kingston, London, and Gatineau), which could be explained by the presence of major universities and/or government service industries providing professional employment opportunities to both women and men. The same data set shows that in most CMAs the employment income contrasts between dual-earner families and unattached individuals are even greater. Here, we must remember that, while internally diverse, this 'unattached' category includes those eking out a marginal existence, sometimes at the fringes of the very neighbourhoods undergoing gentrification by dual-career families (Slater, 2004).

At the neighbourhood scale, the spatial concentration of high-income two-earner families who can afford to substitute privately purchased goods and services for domestic labour traditionally done within the household can significantly alter the local landscape of consumption. For example, high-income households eat out much more often than low-income households and purchase more

cleaning services (Williams, 2001). The 'boutiquiza-
tion' of supermarkets—catering both to the busy
couple's predilection for gourmet prepared food
and to the growth in one-person households disin-
clined to cook for themselves (Robbins, 1989)—
diminishes the accessibility of inexpensive food for
low-income residents of the neighbourhood.
Rather than helping to lobby for improvements to
the supply and quality of publicly supported daycare in their neighbourhood, dual-career couples
with children may opt to have both housework and
child care done by a live-in foreign domestic
worker (a special category of temporary migrants
created by the federal government) working for low
pay and receiving very little time off for leisure or
skills development (Pratt, 1999).

The growth of dual-career couples also
increases the demand for new housing requiring less
maintenance than the older housing stock. Those
without children at home may opt for condominium living. Large urban redevelopment schemes
catering to wealthy 'empty-nester' couples are often
de facto 'landscapes of exclusion' where public
spaces (waterfronts, for example) are privatized and
where shops and services integrated into the developments cater only to the rich. Municipalities may
even seek to disperse concentrations of low-income
singles in order to make a neighbourhood more
appealing to potential 'gentrifier' families (Slater,
2004). In general, household income disparities
seem to be increasing between census tracts due to
the diversification of household types combined
with variations in the number of earners per household (Bourne, 2005; Myles et al., 2000). All in all, the
lifestyles of dual-career couples raise uncomfortable
questions about how the 'choices of the affluent' can
shape urban inequalities (Bondi and Christie, 2000:
302) and pose complex policy challenges.

Diversification of the Elderly Population

We turn finally to a topic that draws together a
number of the issues raised in this chapter. We
explore briefly how the economic and social transformations of urban Canada over the past century
have affected the living arrangements and lifestyle

options of the fastest-growing segment of the
Canadian population—the elderly. While most
urban centres have lower proportions of elderly
than in rural Canada, population aging generates a
variety of wants and needs and poses a range of
challenges for cities and other regional and local
governance structures (such as community-based
health networks) in regard to service delivery and
urban and regional planning. The elderly population
is becoming more internally diverse: 'seniors' can no
longer be associated with a single life stage and are
differentiated by gender and ability or health status
as well as by socio-economic status.

Both biological and social factors make aging
a highly gendered phenomenon. Differences in life
expectancy (Figure 8.6) explain why 57 per cent of
people over 65 were female, rising to 70 per cent
among the very old (85 and over), and why elderly
women are much more likely to live alone than elderly men; for example, in the 75–84 group, an age
when health status declines rapidly and people start
to lose their autonomy, 61 per cent of women but
only 28 per cent of men live alone (Statistics
Canada, 2002b). The current cohort of elderly has
benefited from improving health care during their
lifetime, increasing their life expectancy and their
probability of remaining in good health until an
advanced age. Many (61 per cent of men, 35 per
cent of women) still live with spouses because fewer
are experiencing widowhood than in the past and
divorce is still rare among this generation (Statistics
Canada, 2002c). If their children are alive usually at
least one child is within an hour's drive (Martin-
Matthews, 2001). However, the formative years of
women in this cohort predated the feminist movement and the opening-up of employment opportunities for women. Consequently, few gained
economic autonomy and most have only modest
incomes combining state benefits and a share of
their husband's pension. Poverty has greatly diminished: in 2002 only 10 per cent of households with
an elderly head of household had low incomes,
down from 29 per cent among the generation that
was elderly in 1980 (Sauvé and People Patterns
Consulting, 2005), largely due to improvements in
state benefits. Nevertheless, the gender gap in

Figure 8.6   **Life Expectancy, Men and Women, Canada, 1901–2001**

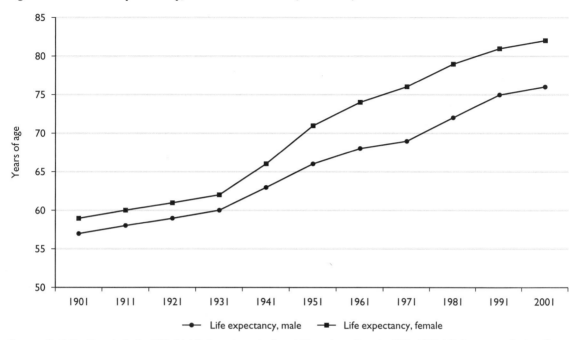

Sources: Statistics Canada, Series B65–74, Life Expectancy by Sex at Given Ages, Canada, 1871–1971; Life Expectancy by Age Group and Sex, Canada and Provinces, 1920–22 to 1990–92; Health Status Indicators: Disability-free Life Expectancy, by Provinces and Territories, 2001, at: <www.statcan.ca/francais/Pgdb/ health26f.htm>.

incomes persists into old age and worsens among those over 80 (Brotman, 1999; Moore and Rosenberg, 2001).

In contrast, the next cohort of elderly will be the baby boom generation, who will have been through more varied life course pathways and experienced more fluidities in personal relationships. Although the narrowing gender gap in life expectancy may mean that fewer elderly women will live alone as widows, many will have experienced divorce and only some will have new partners. Female baby boomers will be more economically autonomous and thus more able to choose their living arrangements, including moving closer to children or friends who become 'fictive kin' (Martin-Matthews, 2001). Baby boomers' extended families may also be more geographically dispersed than those of the present-day elderly. Consequently,

they may be more inclined to opt for congregate housing for its potential for sociability and for its on-site services, even if they do not have high physical care needs. In addition, because of the societal changes this generation has lived through, they are more educated, more assertive as health-care consumers, and overall more militant concerning their rights as equal citizens. As Canadians age, education and income have an increasingly important effect on health status (Prus, 2003).

Aging has important implications for mobility and migration at various geographical scales. Active seniors of middle and upper-middle income are fuelling migration flows to 'retirement communities' such as Victoria, as well as to less expensive cities with mild climates (see Chapter 3), or, more generally to municipalities with a strong enough tax base to offer good-quality public-sector services. Lower-income elderly have less freedom to move, however, and may be especially service-disadvantaged if they live in economically declining urban areas or communities located at the resource frontier, where they may also face reduced access to social support from children, because young families are migrating elsewhere in search of better job opportunities (Hanlon and Halseth, 2005; Moore and Rosenberg, 2001).

At the intra-urban scale, affluent empty nesters are contributing to the boom in condominium construction—in 2001 one-third of condominium residents were over 65 (CMHC, 2004a: 23). They are drawn to 'lifestyle-based' gated communities and all-inclusive private retirement complexes in the suburbs in which access to neighbourhood amenities is privatized (Grant et al., 2004), as well as to upscale leisure-oriented downtown redevelopments. However, many aging couples choose not to 'downsize' their housing, so much so that 'aging in place' has become one of the most important demographic trends shaping the face of Canadian urban areas (Moore et al., 1997). This trend is based on attachment to one's home and rootedness in a particular place (Després and Lord, 2002), and speaks to the importance of a different kind of rationale from that stressed by the traditional 'family life cycle' model of residential mobility, which postulated that households' preferences for dwelling size and neighbourhood type changed in predictable ways as they passed through a standardized sequence of life-cycle stages (Dieleman, 2001; Gober, 1990).

Aging in place, combined with the increasing share of elderly in the total population, is leading to a 'greying' of many suburban neighbourhoods (see Chapter 12). In Quebec, whose population is aging even faster than elsewhere in Canada, researchers argue that relatively autonomous elderly people who opt to remain in the familiar suburban neighbourhood would benefit from the 'retrofitting' of automobile-oriented subdivisions, commercial zones, and recreational space to create greater functional mix and higher-density environments better served by public transportation (Séguin and Apparicio, 2004). These recommendations are highly reminiscent of feminist urbanists' blueprints for inclusive urban planning (Hayden, 1981;

Mackenzie and Wekerle, 1985). Séguin and Apparicio (2004) also point to a growing socio-spatial polarization within metropolitan areas between the consumption landscapes of affluent seniors and those of low to modest incomes who must make do with the aging private rental stock in inner suburbs, where resources are often lacking both for housing maintenance and public or community-provided supports to independent living.

As people begin to lose their autonomy and their physical abilities, they become more dependent on services provided by others. Home care is still not assured by right in the Canadian health and social services system and tends to be provided by spouses (if still living), and children—sometimes complemented by a patchwork of supports from public social service agencies and voluntary organizations (Williams, 2001). Children who care for elderly parents and relatives face severe time stresses because, unlike earlier generations, most are in full-time employment (Frederick and Fast, 1999; Williams, 2004). Women put in more caregiving hours than men even when they have full-time jobs. Society needs to find more equitable ways of sharing elder care between men and women, within the family, in the community, and through the state (Joseph and Hallman, 1998).

Finally, if and when home care is no longer feasible, institutional care (a patchwork of public and private provision) comes into the picture. Rates of institutionalization have fallen in the past two decades, but the likelihood of such a move still rises dramatically past age 85 (Statistics Canada, 2002c). Long-term care residences need to be easily accessible to seniors' children and grandchildren but are not always conveniently located. Canada's immigrant and ethnocultural minority populations also make up an increasing share of the elderly, especially in major cities where immigration is increasingly concentrated (see Chapters 9 and 24), and almost 25 per cent of the immigrant elderly do not speak either official language. Since a long-term care institution is supposed to become an elderly person's final *home* in a psychological sense (Hallman, 1999) this raises the challenge of adapting the running of these 'collective households' to the diversity of cultural norms that now exist in Canadian society about aging and caregiving (Moore and Rosenberg, 2001).

Conclusion

For long, students of large cities have noted their social heterogeneity. During the twentieth century, the locus of Canadian society moved from the resource frontier to metropolitan places and spaces. This trajectory was accompanied by profound demographic, economic, and social shifts. Through complex processes that we have evoked in this chapter, this combination of social tendencies and individual liberation from traditional norms has produced an unprecedented diversification of lifestyles and living arrangements. This new diversity is first and foremost visible in the largest cities but is by no means restricted to these.

In *The Vertical Mosaic,* a classic of Canadian social science, John Porter (1965) argued that Canada could be as ethnically diverse as one could imagine (the mosaic), as long as ethnic affiliation was not an impediment to equality of opportunity in the society at large, which was itself strongly class-based (the verticality). To be sure, he also noted that ethnicity was not the only identity-based form of affiliation that counted. Forty years after Porter, other powerful forms of differentiation, including the ones explored in this chapter centred on gender, sexuality, and life stages, and conducive to new forms of living arrangements and lifestyles, interact with class and ethnicity to produce new layers of social complexity in Canadian cities. Yet this new complexity could also be bringing new impediments to equality of opportunity in the society at large. For example, we have shown that an income gap is forming between dual-career (professional/managerial) couples and other dual- or, even more so, single-income households. We have also suggested that, although poverty among the elderly has been greatly reduced during the last 20 years, a number of factors, including living alone, housing affordability, and access to health care, may produce new forms of polarization among the elderly population. Processes producing disparities in the access to resources and rights may change from one decade to the next but resulting unequal distribution patterns, in too many respects, seem to endure.

Chapter 9

Urban Social Space

Robert A. Murdie and Carlos Teixeira

This chapter concerns the city as social space, particularly the social mosaic of Canadian cities, the changing patterns of residential differentiation, and the processes that have created these patterns. We are concerned with social landscapes within Canadian cities and the variations between cities. Many of the empirical examples are drawn from Canada's three largest metropolitan centres—Toronto, Montreal, and Vancouver—because most research concerning the social mosaic of Canadian cities has focused on these centres.

Two spatial scales of analysis are considered—national and urban. First, at the national level, we view the social mosaic of the city as a reflection of the society within which it is located. Trends in economic restructuring, age structure and family and household formation, immigration, and declining support for the welfare state are particularly significant in understanding the changing social geography of Canadian cities. In some cases, these trends are the outcome of globalization processes that impact at the national level but over which city-level governments have relatively little control.

The second, or urban, level of analysis considers the general patterns of social differentiation within cities. Much of our understanding of the Canadian urban mosaic is based on delimiting the spatial distribution of social groups and the segregation between groups. These spatial patterns are the outcome of decisions made by numerous individual households seeking a residence within the constraints of household income, the existing built form of the city, and various gatekeepers who filter housing opportunities. The underlying theme of the chapter is transitional shifts in the social geography of Canadian metropolitan areas and the processes responsible for these newly emerging patterns of social space. These shifts in social geography reflect more general changes from a modern to a postmodern society, including increased societal fragmentation and the creation of an increasingly complex urban social mosaic.

The remainder of the chapter is divided into four sections. A brief overview of important societal trends is followed by a discussion of the emerging socio-spatial mosaic. The third section offers a more detailed examination of the changing geography of ethnicity, arguably the most visible post-World War II transformation of the social space of Canada's major cities. This section is followed by a brief conclusion, evaluating the implication of these trends for further transformation of Canada's urban social space.

Post-World War II Societal Trends and Their Impacts

Since the end of World War II, Canadian metropolitan areas have been impacted by four important societal trends. The first three—economic restructuring, changes in age structure and living arrangements, and immigration—relate closely to the three major divisions of society identified in the 1950s as a primary basis for the residential differentiation and spatial organization of modern North American cities. The fourth, declining support for the welfare state, cuts across societal divisions and affects the life chances of the most vulnerable groups in society, including the unemployed, female-headed single-parent families, and refugees.

Economic Restructuring

The first trend, economic restructuring (see Chapter 14), concerns the relative decline in manufacturing and increase in service jobs (e.g., Sassen, 2001b; Walks, 2001). In Canada these trends have been accentuated by trade liberalization (NAFTA) and the recession of the early 1990s, resulting in plant closures and layoffs throughout the country. While many new service-sector jobs are well paid, others are not. Of the latter, many are part-time and increasingly held by women and young people under the age of 25, so the potential for enhanced social and spatial inequalities within cities has increased. There has also been an increased spatial redistribution of employment within cities, especially a decentralization of manufacturing and routine office functions to the outer suburbs and a concentration of financial firms and business services in the core (Baldwin et al., 2001; Filion and Rutherford, 2000). In Toronto many lower-paid jobs are increasingly found in the inner and outer suburbs while lower-income households are still concentrated in parts of the central city and the inner suburbs (Frisken et al., 2000: 91).

Changes in Age Structure and Family and Household Formation

The second major societal trend concerns changes in age structure and family and household formation. Canada's age structure has been characterized by a decline in the number and proportion of children and youth and a rapid increase in the elderly. The proportion of Canada's population under 15 years of age declined from a post-war peak of 33.5 per cent in 1961 to 19.1 per cent in 2001 while the proportion of the population aged 65 and over increased from 7.6 per cent to 13.0 per cent during the same period.[1] City-specific differences, on the other hand, relate to variations in the age structure of migration streams—for example, elderly persons

moving to retirement centres such as Kelowna and Victoria and younger persons in the child-bearing years seeking employment opportunities in Calgary or relatively less expensive housing in cities within daily commuting distance of Vancouver (e.g., Abbotsford) or Toronto (e.g., Barrie, Oshawa).

This post-war demographic transition is also reflected in the emerging social geography of the city. For example, the aging of older central-city neighbourhoods and the rapid growth of suburban bedroom communities in the 1950s and 1960s were dampened in the 1970s and 1980s by the move by baby boomers to the gentrifying inner-city areas of Toronto, Montreal, Vancouver, Ottawa–Hull, Edmonton, and Halifax, and the reduced demand by the baby-bust generation for family dwellings in the suburbs (Harris, 2004; Ley, 1996b). Canada's family and household structure also changed dramatically during the post-war period. A major trend has been decline in household size. The number of one-person households, for example, increased from 7.4 per cent in 1951 to 25.7 per cent in 2001. At the same time, family structure has become increasingly diversified. The proportion of single-parent families increased dramatically from 2.3 per cent in 1951 to 15.7 per cent in 2001 (see Chapter 8). Of the latter, 81 per cent are headed by women, often with low incomes. Another major trend, especially beginning in the 1970s, has been the tendency for a larger proportion of young adults to move out of the family home, although in high-priced housing markets such as Toronto and Vancouver the trend of living at home may be increasing again. The outcome of these trends has been a fragmentation of living arrangements that has important implications at the individual level for the intersection of life-cycle stage and housing careers and in the aggregate for the city's social geography.

Increased 'Internationalization'

The third major trend is the increased 'internationalization' of Canada's population during the post-war period (e.g., Justis, 2004; Li, 2003; see Chapter 24).

From 1945 until the early 1970s immigrants were needed to provide labour for the rapidly developing Canadian economy. Preference was given to 'white' immigrants from other Commonwealth countries, continental Europe, and the United States. Beginning in the early 1970s, economic restructuring reduced the need for manual workers in manufacturing and increased the demand for both high- and low-skilled employees in the newly emerging service industries. Canada's immigration policies also changed during this period and a point system was introduced allowing people from other parts of the world to apply for entry into Canada. The objective was to remove the discriminatory policies of earlier immigration legislation. The result was a sharp decline in European immigration and a substantial increase in immigration from Asia, Africa, the Middle East, the Caribbean, and Latin America. This trend has continued and by 2001 almost 80 per cent of Canada's recent immigrants were from non-European countries. These newcomers represent a wide spectrum of immigrant categories, including refugees who are admitted on humanitarian grounds, those joining family members already in Canada, business people with money to invest, and independent immigrants who are admitted on the basis of educational achievement, labour market skills, and language proficiency. These shifts in source countries and the diversity of immigrant categories have meant a dramatic change in the ethnocultural mosaic and social geography of Canadian metropolitan areas, especially Toronto and Vancouver, the cities that have received the largest and most diverse group of recent immigrants.

Retrenchment of the Welfare State

The fourth major change, especially in the last decade, has been the retrenchment of the welfare state and the potential impact of these cutbacks for the development of a Canadian underclass. The life chances of low-income immigrants and refugees, as well as the Canadian-born, are determined to a considerable degree by various policies of the welfare state. Although Canada's social welfare policy has traditionally been closer to the United States than Western Europe, Canada, unlike the US, has a universal health-care system and somewhat more generous social service programs, such as employment insurance. Until the 1980s, Canada's two major political parties generally followed a pragmatic and centrist approach to social welfare provision. More recently, however, governments at both the federal and provincial levels have implemented changes in social welfare provision in order to control the deficit. Low-income people in Canada's largest cities have been particularly affected by cutbacks in new social housing construction, reduction in welfare payments, and cancellation of employment training programs and job creation initiatives.

The Emerging Social Mosaic: The Nature and Distribution of Social Groups in Canadian Cities

Traditional Models of the Social Mosaic

In the early 1950s, sociologists such as Shevky and Bell (1955) hypothesized that the social mosaic of the modern (industrial) city could be summarized by three major divisions of society: economic status, family status, and ethnic status (Figure 9.1). It was assumed that each of these summarized a separate dimension or component of social variation and that all three were needed to capture the social complexity of modern cities. Subsequently, the empirical validity of Shevky and Bell's social area model was tested using factorial ecology, a statistical method designed to tease out the interrelationships between census variables. When evaluated using a limited number of variables, Shevky and Bell's hypothesis of three major social dimensions was confirmed. But as additional variables were added to the analysis the factor structures became more complex. For example, analyses of Toronto and Montreal between the early 1960s and the early 1980s resulted in six major dimensions of social variation reflecting a more complex social mosaic (Foggin and Polèse, 1977; LeBourdais and Beaudry,

Figure 9.1   **Societal Divisions and the Social Mosaic of the City: From the Modern (Industrial) City to the Postmodern (Post-Industrial) City**

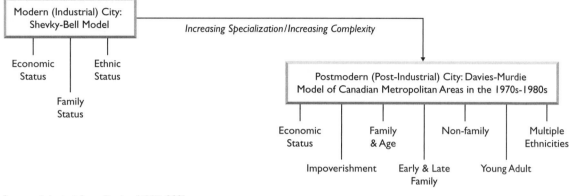

Source: Adapted from Davies (1984: 309).

1988; Murdie, 1969). Rather than denying the validity of the Shevky and Bell hypothesis, the inclusion of more variables in the analysis tended to add reality to the model by revealing additional societal and city-specific details of the three major social dimensions.

In addition to evaluating the validity of the Shevky and Bell hypothesis, factorial ecology researchers calculated scores for each census tract on each major dimension of social variation and mapped these scores to determine the spatial form of the social mosaic and to identify possible links with the classic spatial models of urban form: Burgess's concentric zones, Hoyt's sectors, and Harris and Ullman's multiple nuclei (Burgess, 1925; Hoyt, 1939; Harris and Ullman, 1945). These three models were developed primarily as summaries of the residential change taking place in North American industrial cities during the interwar period (Figure 9.2). Using Chicago as a laboratory, Burgess and his colleagues argued that immigrants first settled in older housing near the central business district, and upon improving their economic position moved outwards through a series of increasingly higher-status concentric zones towards the periphery. The process is best described as invasion and succession, with one group invading and

succeeding the residential space occupied by another. In contrast, Hoyt based his sectoral model on preferences by higher-income groups for amenity-rich locations such as elevated areas with a view and proximity to commuter transport lines and the homes of community leaders. Although the basic geometry of the model was characterized by alternating sectors of high- and low-income groups, Hoyt also allowed for variations within sectors. The underlying process was identified as filtering, with older houses being passed down to lower-income households as new housing was built at the periphery. Harris and Ullman's multiple nuclei model is the most recent of the three and takes into account the increased spatial complexity of the North American metropolis in the early 1940s. In particular, it was hypothesized that individual land uses, including various types of residential areas, tend to be organized around relatively discrete nuclei.

When scores from the factorial ecology studies were mapped, the results confirmed that the three spatial models were complementary. For example, using census data from the 1950s and 1960s for Toronto, Murdie (1969) determined that economic status was linked to alternating sectors of high and low economic status, family status to the concentric model, and ethnic status to various clusters or nuclei

Figure 9.2   **Traditional Spatial Models of Urban Form: Burgess (Concentric Zone), Hoyt (Sectoral), Harris and Ullman (Multiple Nuclei)**

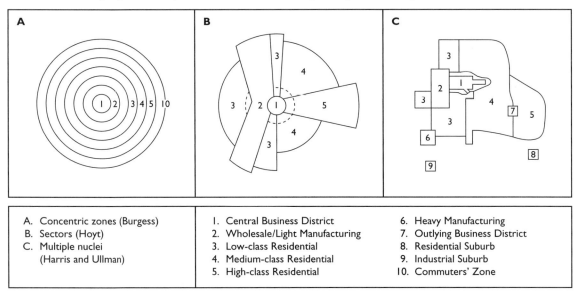

A. Concentric zones (Burgess)	1. Central Business District	6. Heavy Manufacturing
B. Sectors (Hoyt)	2. Wholesale/Light Manufacturing	7. Outlying Business District
C. Multiple nuclei	3. Low-class Residential	8. Residential Suburb
(Harris and Ullman)	4. Medium-class Residential	9. Industrial Suburb
	5. High-class Residential	10. Commuters' Zone

Source: Herbert and Thomas (1997: 199).

(Figure 9.3). These results have been generally con-firmed for other Canadian metropolitan areas such as Winnipeg (Nicholson and Yeates, 1969), Hamilton (Taylor, 1987), Kitchener (Filion and Bunting, 1996), and Montreal (Charron, 2002) but with variations based on the physiography, land-use structure, and historical development of each city (the physical space of the city in Figure 9.3).

Economic status takes on a sectoral form because high-status residents are attracted to desir-able features such as lakefronts or ravine lands and, given a choice, stay clear of noxious uses such as railroads and industries, as well as persons who are considered socially undesirable. Family status tends to be concentric because of the presumed prefer-ence of families with young children for a subur-ban environment, the attraction of households without children to the amenities of the central city, and the tendency of those aging in place to be located in the inner suburbs. This spatial form is based on locational decisions made by households during various stages of the life cycle, or life course, and links closely to models of urban residential mobility and housing careers (Clark and Dieleman, 1996). Ethnic status tends to be nucleated because of the tendency for many ethnic groups to cluster for mutual support and cultural preservation, or, in some cases, to avoid discrimination by members of the receiving society.

The Social Complexity of Canadian Metropolitan Areas in the 1970s and 1980s

Most studies of the social mosaic of Canadian metropolitan areas have been carried out for a single city. A series of studies undertaken by Davies and Murdie (1991, 1994a) for various census years from 1971 to 1991 extended these single-city analyses by identifying the social dimensionality of all Canadian metropolitan areas and the differences

Figure 9.3   **Idealized Spatial Model of the Modern (Industrial) City Based on Shevky-Bell and Murdie**

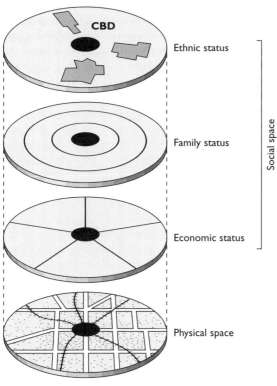

Source: Murdie (1969: 8).

included in the analysis. Individual ethnic origins were not incorporated because of the increased complexity and city-specific nature of ethnicity in many Canadian census metropolitan areas.

The results from the Davies and Murdie analyses indicate that the social dimensionality of Canadian metropolitan areas in the 1970s and 1980s was much more complex than the three-factor model hypothesized by Shevky and Bell. This complexity was characterized by two notable distinctions (Figure 9.1). The first was the presence of two separate economic status factors, one providing the familiar contrast between areas occupied by high-income managerial workers and lower-income blue-collar workers, and the other identifying areas of impoverishment originating outside the formal employment sector and characterized by low-income female lone-parent families and high levels of unemployment. This additional economic factor links closely to changes taking place at the national level, especially the increased number of low-paid employees in the rapidly expanding service sector. It also corresponds with general evidence that income inequality in major Canadian urban areas increased in the 1980s and 1990s, resulting in a substantially greater gap between richer and poorer neighbourhoods (e.g., Heisz and McLeod, 2004; United Way of Greater Toronto, 2004).

The second departure from the classic three-fold social area model was the emergence of four separate family status dimensions (Figure 9.1). These were identified as family and age, early and late family, non-family, and young adult. This increased fragmentation of the family status factor relates closely to changes in family and household structure noted earlier at the national level. The family and age factor most closely approximates the unidimensional family status concept hypothesized by Shevky and Bell. Areas containing relatively large two-parent families contrasted with those dominated by the elderly and an absence of children. The early-and-late family factor clearly contrasts areas characterized by adults in the early child-bearing years with those occupied by older children and

between centres using a common set of variables. The variables were selected to reflect the hypothesized Shevky and Bell dimensions, the results from previous factorial ecology studies of individual Canadian cities, and speculation about recent changes in the structure of post-industrial society. Each of the 15 hypothesized sources of variation was indexed by two to four census variables. Particular importance was given to family variables, in recognition of the increased importance of changes in the living arrangements of Canadian households, as noted above. In contrast, ethnicity was measured as a more general source of variation and only French ethnic origin, ethnic origins other than British or French, and immigrants were middle-aged adults. The non-family and young adult factors identify individual areas in the city characterized by non-family and divorced people, on the one hand, and single young adults, on the other. These two factors reflect the splintering of the family status dimension based on societal trends such as increased divorce rates and young adults leaving home at an earlier age. The opportunity for these groups to occupy separate areas of the city has been facilitated by the construction of new private rental apartments in the central core areas of many Canadian metropolitan areas, especially in the 1960s and 1970s.

Because ethnicity was measured as a general source of variation (British, French, and immigrant) only one ethnic status dimension emerged from the analysis. If individual origins of the various immigrant groups that have come to Canada in the post-war period had been included the result would have likely been a multiplicity of ethnic dimensions, reflecting the continued spatial segregation of many of these groups in Canadian metropolitan areas. This point is considered further later in this chapter. In the meantime, multiple ethnicities have been added to Figure 9.1 to capture the reality of ethnic differentiation in many of Canada's largest post-modern (post-industrial) cities.

It is impossible to show all the maps for the entire set of Canadian metropolitan areas. Therefore, a composite illustration of the general spatial form of each major economic and family status factor has been developed and discussed below with reference to specific cities where appropriate (Figure 9.4).

The traditional economic status factor revealed the continued presence of Hoyt-like sectors with high-status sectors connected to amenity-rich areas of the city, such as environmentally attractive shorelines and ravine lands, and low-status sectors juxtaposed with long-established industrial areas and rail corridors. Three major types of high-status areas can be recognized: older inner-city areas that have retained their traditional status (e.g., Rosedale and Forest Hill in Toronto, Westmount in Montreal, Shaughnessy in Vancouver); new suburbs that have often developed around a recreation complex such

as a golf course; and newly gentrified and redeveloped neighbourhoods (e.g., Don Vale and Harbour Square in Toronto, Fairview Slopes and Kitsilano in Vancouver).

The spatial distribution of high-impoverishment areas revealed the concentrated areas of poverty in cities such as Quebec City, Vancouver, and Winnipeg—'Le croissant de pauvreté' in Quebec City, the Downtown Eastside in Vancouver, and the North Main Street area in Winnipeg—that have existed since the beginning of the last century. Elsewhere, isolated examples of highly impoverished tracts are associated with large public housing estates (e.g., Regent Park in downtown Toronto, the Jane–Finch corridor in Toronto's inner suburbs, and Habitations Jeanne-Mance in Montreal) that were built in the early post-war era. For Toronto, in particular, poverty has become as much a phenomenon of the inner suburbs as the central city (United Way of Greater Toronto, 2004). The increased concentration of children, lone-parent families, and immigrants (especially recent immigrants and visible minorities) in these areas and the relative lack of community services have important implications for the life chances of these groups.

The family status dimensions revealed less consistent spatial patterns than the economic status factors. Nevertheless, using Calgary as an example, the family and age scores showed the hypothesized concentric ring pattern with middle-aged persons and completed families in the older central area of the city (developed prior to 1960) and younger families in the suburban periphery. The early-and-late family factor was also distributed concentrically but in a more complicated fashion than the family and age dimension—the youngest families in particular parts of the new suburbs, older families in the mature suburbs developed in the 1960s, and some younger families in the central city. The mapped pattern of the non-family dimension shows a tightly defined cluster of extreme scores in the central city and nearby areas of apartment complexes. Finally, tracts scoring high on the young adult factor were located close to downtown but also in the vicinity of major educational and

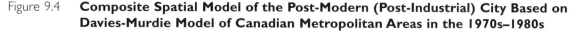

Figure 9.4   **Composite Spatial Model of the Post-Modern (Post-Industrial) City Based on Davies-Murdie Model of Canadian Metropolitan Areas in the 1970s–1980s**

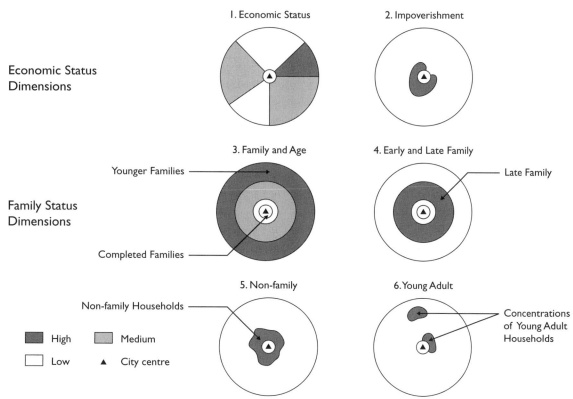

Source: Adapted from Davies (1984: 323) and Davies and Murdie (1993).

medical institutions in the northwestern part of Calgary.

The Postmodern Metropolis: A New Spatial Order or a Changed Spatial Order?

Beginning in the mid-1980s, a debate emerged concerning the continued relevance of the classical spatial models of urban social structure. These spatial forms, especially concentric zones and sectors, are based on the traditional monocentric city in which the central business district predominates over all other areas of the city. Members of the so-called Los Angeles 'school', who had begun to critically evaluate urban development in the Los Angeles region,

were at the forefront of the debate.[2] In particular, Los Angeles was viewed as an archetypal postmodern, polycentric metropolis that has developed under quite different circumstances and resulted in a much more spatially complicated urban form than envisioned by Burgess for Chicago in the 1920s (Dear, 2002). The basic premise of the Los Angeles 'school' is that urban form has been changed profoundly by many of the societal trends mentioned earlier in this chapter, including economic restructuring, demographic changes, and increasingly diverse immigration. Spatially, members of the Los Angeles 'school' argue that the postmodern polycentric city consists of a new spatial order, a collage of landscapes that have pre-empted the historical importance of the city core.

The Los Angeles 'school' has been heavily crit-icized and other authors have presented more nuanced views of contemporary urbanization and its socio-spatial outcomes (e.g., Gottdiener, 2002; Lake, 1999; Marcuse and van Kempen, 2000; Shearmur and Charron, 2004). In particular, these authors argue that many of the trends noted by the Los Angeles 'school' are not new and not limited to Los Angeles. Indeed, there seems to be considerable consensus that a sub-stantial but gradual shift in the spatial order of glob-alizing cities has been underway since the 1970s (Marcuse and van Kempen, 2000). Although most critics agree that the central city no longer dominates metropolitan regions, they argue that central cities have become more specialized, losing much of their manufacturing base but gaining employment in the relatively high-paying financial and business service sectors. In selected central cities, employment is also increasing in cultural sectors such as entertainment, film, and design, part of what Florida (2002) refers to as the 'creative class'. Increasingly, housing for these relatively affluent employees is available in downtown areas of the city, primarily through the revitalization of older housing stock and the construction of new condominium townhouses and apartments.

Marcuse and van Kempen (2000) identify two broad themes summarizing changes in the spatial order of postmodern cities: strengthened structural-spatial divisions, with increased inequality among them, and a greater prevalence and magnitude of specific spatial formations within these divisions. Strengthened structural-spatial divisions, along eco-nomic status and ethno-racial lines, have important implications for social exclusion and racism. Specific spatial formations include: (a) 'citadels' (high-tech, high-rise megaprojects for the global elite, often incorporating luxury condominium residences); (b) gentrified neighbourhoods (located in older inner-city areas, usually resulting in the displacement of working-class families); (c) exclu-sionary enclaves (including upper-class areas and retirement communities, often enclosed by fences and gates with strong security systems); (d) excluded ghettos (a new form of entrenched urban poverty, often associated with 'racial' exclusion); (e) ethnic enclaves (clusters of specific ethnic groups with associated retail, cultural, and institutional func-tions); and (f) edge cities (clusters of residence, business, and recreation on an urban scale, inde-pendent in daily life but linked to the central city—in this respect they differ from suburban bedroom communities). Edge cities illustrate an emerging characteristic of these spatial formations, the increased 'totalization of life' within each.

What about Canadian cities? Filion and Bunting (1996) have argued that in Canada's increasingly dispersed urban agglomerations more localized place-based features are likely to take on increased significance in structuring social space as the traditional monocentric city becomes less pre-dominant. While this is undoubtedly true, the core areas of most large Canadian cities are still major hubs of business and cultural activities for the entire region. At the same time, Canada's three largest cities (Toronto, Montreal, and Vancouver) exhibit many of the socio-spatial formations noted above, although often in a more nuanced form. For exam-ple, 'citadels', in their extreme form, do not exist in Canadian cities, but increasing numbers of global head offices and high-rise luxury condominiums do, particularly in the downtown areas of Toronto and Vancouver.

'Gentrified neighbourhoods' have been part of the urban landscape in Montreal, Toronto, and Vancouver since the 1970s and have continued to expand outward from the central city, especially into working-class immigrant communities (Ley, 1996b). The impact on low-income households that have been displaced is not well known, partially due to the difficulty tracing their subsequent moves. The high-income 'exclusionary neighbourhoods' identified earlier for Canadian metropolitan areas in the 1970s and 1980s remain, as do the concentra-tions of poverty referred to above as 'excluded ghettos'. In contrast to the US, however, these areas of entrenched poverty do not have the same 'racial' connotation, although it is likely that the economic gap between 'exclusionary neighbourhoods' and 'excluded ghettos' has widened. Also, gated com-munities are not as prevalent in Canada as in the US

(Grant, 2005). Most often, they have been designed as retirement communities and do not share the same fortress mentality as their US counterparts.

Given the increased 'internationalization' of Canada's population, it is not surprising that 'ethnic enclaves' have become increasingly important elements of the urban landscape in Canada's three major immigrant gateways: Toronto, Vancouver, and Montreal. These often incorporate ethnic malls and religious institutions for specific immigrant groups. Questions have also been raised about the concentration of ethnic poverty in Canadian metropolitan areas. For the period between 1991 and 2001, Smith (2004) found that the relationship between measures of deprivation and immigrant settlement in Toronto, Montreal, and Vancouver had generally increased and become more complex. In part, this relates to the diversity of immigrant arrivals in Canada's three major immigrant-receiving cities. This raises important questions about the residential location, housing careers, and economic mobility of immigrant groups, which we consider in the following section. Finally, although 'edge cities' are an important phenomenon at the periphery of many US metropolitan areas, they have not developed with the same intensity in Canadian cities (Germain and Rose, 2000: 127–8; Mercer and England, 2000: 66), where they are more accurately described as suburban downtowns.

The Changing Geography of Ethnicity

As noted earlier, one of the most important changes in Canadian society during the post-war period has been a shift in the origins of immigrants from Europe to various countries in Asia, Africa, the Middle East, Latin America, and the Caribbean. This shift has had a dramatic impact on the social space of Canada's largest metropolitan areas, where most recent immigrants reside. The settlement experiences and residential patterns of ethnic groups in most Canadian metropolitan areas are so varied that they cannot be easily captured by the more generalized dimensions and spatial models introduced in

the previous section. Some groups concentrate spatially and form ethnic enclaves, initially in immigrant reception areas close to downtown and more recently by either re-segregating in the suburbs or immigrating directly to suburban concentrations. Others tend to disperse after acquiring a working knowledge of English or French and improving their socio-economic position. Still others assimilate from the outset and do not experience spatial segregation. Varied and complex factors are responsible for different patterns. They include factors internal to the group, such as the retention of cultural traditions and the use of culturally biased information sources, and external factors, such as discriminatory practices by the receiving society that impose significant locational constraint.

The Spatial Segregation of Ethnic Groups

One way of illustrating differences in the spatial segregation of ethnic groups is by means of a segregation index. Segregation indexes for the Toronto, Montreal, and Vancouver CMAs for eight ethnic groups in 2001 are given in Table 9.1. The segregation index can take on values ranging from zero to 100 with an index value of 100 indicating complete spatial separation between a specific ethnic group and the rest of the population, and a value of zero indicating no spatial separation between the two groups. Of the three metropolitan areas, seven of the eight ethnic groups show their highest levels of segregation in the Montreal CMA. Bauder and Sharpe (2002) also found larger index values for a variety of visible minority groups in Montreal. Historically, this is due primarily to the relatively sharp spatial division between French (francophone) and English (anglophone) Montreal and the tendency for some non-English or non-French speaking ethnic groups (allophones) to reside in English Montreal, mainly for cultural and language reasons, or in ethnic enclaves apart from the majority French population (Figure 9.5). This pattern is changing, however, as a result of the increased migration of French-speaking immigrants to Montreal and the imposition of stricter French

Table 9.1   **Segregation Indexes for Selected Ethnic Groups in Montreal, Toronto, and Vancouver, 2001**

Ethnic Group	Montreal	Toronto	Vancouver	Group Average
Jewish	78	70	43	63
South Asian	64	44	52	53
Chinese	52	51	49	51
Caribbean black	46	36	33	38
African black	43	36	33	36
Italian	43	40	26	36
Central and Eastern European	41	30	14	29
Western European (excluding Italian)	28	29	22	26
CMA Average	49	42	34	N/A

Source: Balakrishnan and Gyimah (2003: 122). Based on total responses (single and multiple).

language laws (Germain and Rose, 2000: Chapter 7). As a result, more immigrants are settling in French-speaking areas of the city.

Among ethnic minority groups, Jews are the most segregated. Their concentration is more likely due to voluntary factors, such as the retention of cultural and religious traditions, than to discriminatory practices by the receiving population (Diamond, 2000; Hiebert, 1993a; Olson and Kobayashi, 1993). More generally, the growing cultural diversity of Canada's urban areas has been accompanied by increased religious diversity. This diversity is clearly evident in the multiplicity of churches, temples, mosques, and other religious institutions that have emerged in Canada's urban landscape. South Asians and Chinese also show high average levels of segregation. Both groups tend to live in owner-occupied dwellings in the suburbs and retention of cultural traditions is a more likely explanation for their continued segregation. Despite their visible minority status and generally lower incomes, African and Caribbean blacks are more spatially dispersed than

South Asians and Chinese. In Toronto this results from the over-representation of blacks in high-rise rental apartments that are scattered throughout the city (Bauder and Sharpe, 2002; Mensah, 2002: 84–5). In many instances these groups face affordability problems and inferior housing conditions. White European groups (Italians, other Western Europeans, and Central and Eastern Europeans) generally display lower segregation indexes than the Jews and visible minorities, reflecting their early arrival in the post-war period and lack of visible minority status. Compared to visible minorities, Europeans do not face the same constraints, based on discriminatory practices, of where to live in major Canadian CMAs. When viewed by generation, the European groups tended to show a decline in segregation with successive generations; in contrast, the visible minority groups showed little change, except for a modest decline by South Asians and Chinese in Toronto and Vancouver (Balakrishnan and Gyimah, 2003). Finally, the Aboriginal population, despite its status as native-born Canadians, is also highly segregated

Figure 9.5   **The Geography of Language, Island of Montreal, 2001**

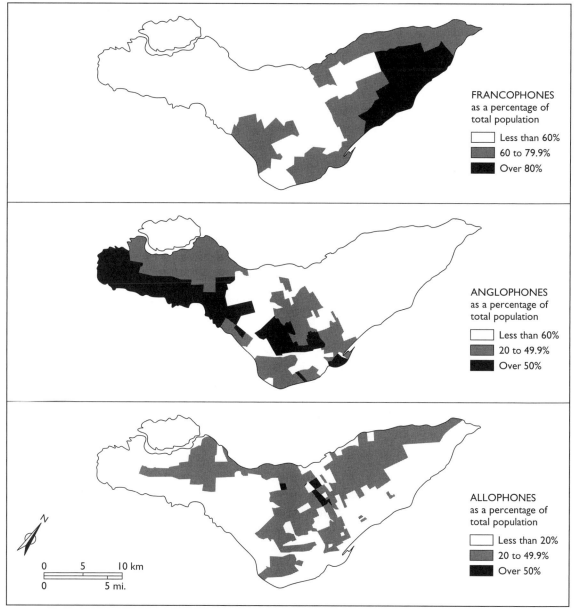

FRANCOPHONES
as a percentage of
total population

☐ Less than 60%
▨ 60 to 79.9%
■ Over 80%

ANGLOPHONES
as a percentage of
total population

☐ Less than 60%
▨ 20 to 49.9%
■ Over 50%

ALLOPHONES
as a percentage of
total population

☐ Less than 20%
▨ 20 to 49.9%
■ Over 50%

Sources: Lo and Teixeira (1998: 487), updated with Statistics Canada, 2001 census data.

(Bauder and Sharpe, 2002). The continued spatial segregation of this group, often in the poorest areas of the city, is indicative of their struggle with poverty and with discrimination in both housing and labour markets.

Although the index of dissimilarity is an effective measure of the spatial separation between immigrant groups and the receiving population, the variety of immigrant experiences can be best illustrated by more detailed analysis of a sample of groups who settled in metropolitan Canada under different circumstances in the post-war period. We do so by considering two separate periods or 'transitions' in Canada's immigrant history: the post-war European immigrant experience and the increased 'internationalization' of immigration following the 1960s.[3]

Post-War European Immigration

In contrast to the first half of the twentieth century when a majority of immigrants to Canada settled initially in rural areas in the West, immigrants in post-World War II Canada went primarily to metropolitan centres. During the 1960s and 1970s, Southern Europeans were among the largest immigrant groups to arrive in Toronto and Montreal. The arrival of entire families by means of chain migration encouraged the establishment of distinctive residential neighbourhoods with ethnic businesses and cultural and religious institutions (Germain and Rose, 2000: ch. 7; Murdie and Teixeira, 2003). These groups also tended to attach considerable importance to home ownership and home improvements.

The Portuguese are typical of the Southern Europeans (Lavigne, 1987; Teixeira, 1996: 186). In the 1950s and 1960s, Portuguese immigrants bought relatively inexpensive houses in the downtown immigrant reception areas of Toronto (Kensington Market) and Montreal (St Louis neighbourhood). Private sources of finance (particularly second mortgages) facilitated undercapitalized purchases (Lavigne, 1987; Murdie, 1991). As well, many families occupied part of the house and rented the

other part for extra income. During the post-war economic boom, many new immigrants achieved upward economic mobility through employment in the construction industry and reliance on their construction skills to renovate their own homes. By investing in housing (both home ownership and housing renovation), Southern European groups such as the Portuguese have contributed substantially to maintaining the vitality of older inner-city neighbourhoods in Montreal and Toronto (Germain and Rose, 2000: ch. 7; Murdie and Teixeira, 2003).

Home ownership also became a vehicle for economic mobility and provided capital through resale of the house for a move to a larger and more modern home in the suburbs. In both Montreal and Toronto many Portuguese moved from the immigrant reception area and relocated in suburban Mississauga in Toronto and Laval in Montreal (Teixeira and Murdie, 1997). This relocation is illustrated for Toronto in Figure 9.6. Some of these families live within, or in close proximity to, existing nuclei of Portuguese concentration, while others are more dispersed. In part, relocation occurs because of obstacles to corridor expansion (that is, decentralization along an axis) resulting from the presence of earlier immigrant groups, such as the Italians. Relocation is also made possible because relatively efficient transportation networks allow suburbanized minorities such as the Portuguese to return to their original ethnic neighbourhood to shop for special ethnic goods and participate in the institutional life of their community.

Recent Changes in Immigration: Towards a Multicultural Canada?

By 2001, visible minorities represented 37 per cent of the population in Toronto and Vancouver and 13 per cent in Montreal. These three cities are characterized, more than ever, by a rich mix of cultures distributed in a diverse array of ethno-racial communities. Newcomers to Canada also reflect a wide spectrum of economic groups. Here, we contrast immigrants and refugees at two ends of the

Figure 9.6   **Portuguese Population by Mother Tongue, Toronto and Mississauga, 1971 and 2001**

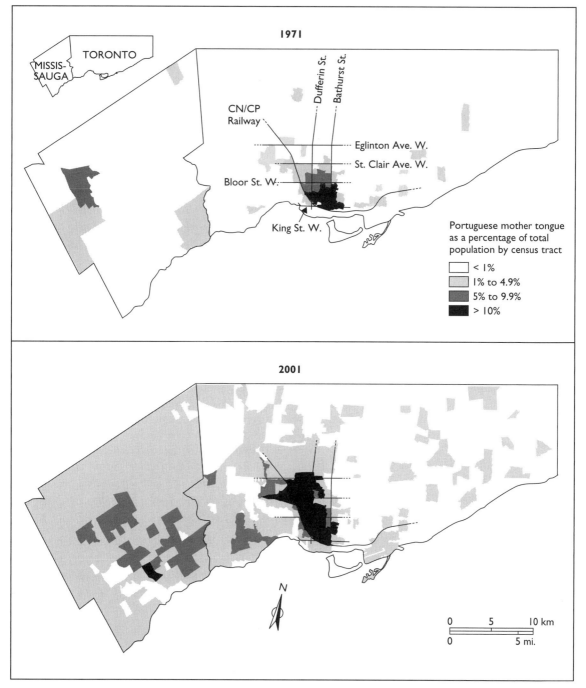

Sources: Statistics Canada, 1971 and 2001 census data.

spectrum—relatively wealthy Chinese business immigrants and lower-income immigrants and refugees from the Caribbean and Africa.

While the pre-war Chinese community was ghettoized and mistrusted, recent Chinese business immigrants have been welcomed for their financial resources, education, and occupational skills. These immigrants are often professionals and business people who have the economic resources to start small businesses and buy expensive housing in the suburbs of Vancouver (e.g., Shaughnessy Heights, Richmond, Kerrisdale, Oakridge) and Toronto (e.g., Scarborough, Markham, Richmond Hill). Their direct movement to these suburbs and the physical changes they have brought to existing neighbourhoods by building so-called 'monster homes' and Asian theme malls have sometimes led to racial tensions with longer-established residents (Ray et al., 1997; Smart and Smart, 1996).

Pockets of concentration of Afro-Caribbean migrants (often in public housing) have been identified in both the inner city and the suburbs of Montreal and Toronto (Germain and Rose, 2000: 221; Murdie, 1994a, 1996). In part, the increased number of Caribbeans in public housing is due to low household income, compounded by supply, cost, and discriminatory constraints in Toronto's private rental market (Murdie, 1996). It is important to reiterate, however, that none of these areas of concentration can be described as a ghetto, since they do not resemble the large-scale ghettos that characterize many US cities (Ley and Smith, 1997).

More recently arrived African immigrants from countries such as Somalia and Ghana live in high-rise apartments in the inner suburbs (Figure 9.7).[4] The suburban emphasis and residential concentration of the Ghanaians results from the relative affordability of these large-scale apartment areas, the highly structured social networks within the group, and opportunities for employment in manufacturing firms that are increasingly located in Toronto's suburbs (Owusu, 1999). In contrast, recent immigrants and refugees from Angola and Mozambique (former Portuguese colonies in Africa) have settled in established Portuguese neighbourhoods in the inner city, areas where they can communicate in Portuguese, their mother tongue.

Conclusion

In the second half of the twentieth century, Canada's cities have been transformed by a number of societal forces, including economic restructuring, an aging population and new approaches to family organization, changes in immigration patterns, and a rethinking of the traditional welfare state. Of these, immigration has most visibly transformed large Canadian cities. The settlement experiences of these immigrant groups have taken different forms—from pockets of ethnic concentration marked by a rich and distinctive cultural identity to dispersed populations lacking any defining features that distinguish them within the metropolis. Some immigrant communities, particularly recently arrived refugee groups, are highly marginalized with respect to the quality of housing and kinds of neighbourhoods where they live. Improvement of the life chances of these groups is a major challenge for Canadian policy-makers, especially in the context of a sharp retrenchment of the welfare state.

Finally, what about the future? In general terms, the social structure of Canadian metropolitan areas will likely be impacted by continued changes in the four major societal forces mentioned earlier (economic change, age and family structure, immigration, and the curtailment of the welfare state). The general sectoral pattern of economic status that has been in place for several decades will remain for many cities, but the potential for increased social and spatial inequalities will continue apace. As for age structure, cities will be forced to adapt to the aging of the baby-boom generation and the smaller numbers in younger generations. This will have a major impact on the housing stock of Canadian urban areas, particularly those where younger generations are not supplemented with newcomers. In these circumstances, the demand for diverse forms of retirement dwellings will increase, while the demand for other forms of housing will stagnate.

Figure 9.7   **The Ghanaian Population in the City of Toronto and Region of Peel (by Census Tract), 1994**

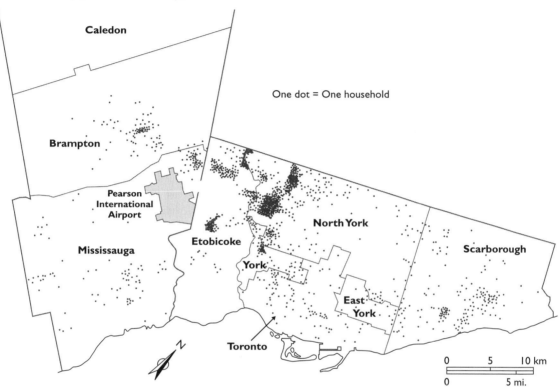

Source: Owusu (1999). Used by permission of Carfax Publishing, Taylor & Francis Ltd, P.O. Box 25, Abington, Oxfordshire, OX14 3UE, UK.

The flow of immigrants into major Canadian cities and the makeup of the immigrant population depend on policies established by the Canadian and Quebec governments as well as global economic and political circumstances.[5] The latter have become even more important since the events of 11 September 2001 and their aftermath. Regardless, it is likely that the annual volume of immigrants will remain at about 225,000, that a large majority of this population will settle in Toronto, Vancouver, and Montreal, and that the visible minority population will increase dramatically.[6] By 2017 it is estimated that about half of the population of the Toronto and Vancouver CMAs will belong to a visible minority group (Bélanger and Caron Malenfant, 2005). More

generally, it is likely that immigrant groups will continue to suburbanize, either resegregating in the suburbs following initial settlement near the downtown core, or, as is increasingly likely, immigrating directly to the inner suburbs of major metropolitan centres. The segregation levels between some immigrant groups and the rest of the population will remain high and the spatial outcome will be an increasingly fragmented and economically differentiated pattern of ethnic enclaves in many parts of the city.

Finally, the status of the Canadian welfare state remains uncertain as governments continue to emphasize the reduction of public debt and political uncertainty prevails. Although social housing programs and other social services may be expanded in the short run and welfare rates increased, it is unlikely that public funding for agencies serving immigrants and refugees will be increased to previous levels. Consequently, a deepening and widening of underclass areas, especially in those cities that attract disproportionate numbers of society's most vulnerable groups—the chronically unemployed, single-parent families, marginalized immigrants and refugees, and psychiatric out-patients—is a strong likelihood.

This is the general outline. The social dimensions will be more complex than portrayed here and the spatial patterns will depend on the physical space of individual cities, expressed as both the natural and built environment. The patterns will also depend on how social structures interact with physical space. The fortunes of disadvantaged groups and their integration with the broader society will depend to a considerable extent on the attitudes and generosity of individual Canadians as well as the willingness of politicians at the national, provincial, and local levels of government to place higher priority on the needs of the most vulnerable.

Notes

1. When not cited, Statistics Canada census data originate from the Statistics Canada Web page <www.statcan.ca>, or other forms of electronic dissemination.

2. Following Shearmur and Carron (2004), we put 'school' in quotations because not all of the contributors to the Los Angeles 'school' agree that it is a unified set of theories and methods.

3. More extensive discussions for Toronto are provided by Murdie and Teixeira (2003), for Montreal by Germain and Rose (2000: ch. 7), and for Vancouver by Hiebert (1999). See also Chapter 24.

4. A map from the 2001 census showing recent immigrants from Ghana (arrived 1996–2001) indicates a very similar pattern to Figure 9.7.

5. Quebec has had the right to select its own independent-class immigrants since 1978 and has had jurisdiction over integration and settlement programs for immigrants and refugees since 1991.

6. The Canadian government's objective is to increase the annual flow of immigrants to 1 per cent of the Canadian population, or 300,000, and disperse the immigrant population more evenly across the country. In the short run these objectives will be difficult to attain.

Chapter 10

Urban and Suburban Downtowns: Trajectories of Growth and Decline

Pierre Filion and Gunter Gad

There was a time, in all metropolitan regions, when the downtown was unchallenged as the foremost concentration of high-order activities. It contained the vast majority of office space, all department stores, and most specialty shops, as well as the best theatres and cinemas and sophisticated restaurants and nightclubs (e.g., Moore, 2004). What is more, it was generally in or close to downtown that prestigious institutions—universities and large specialized hospitals, for example—were found. The capacity to attract high-order activities was tied to downtowns' status as unchallenged points of maximum accessibility within their metropolitan region (Murphy and Vance, 1954a).

Over the past 50 years, the evolution of downtowns has taken different trajectories. If they have everywhere lost ground in relative terms (that is, in their proportion of metropolitan area employment, retailing, services, and cultural activities), the downtowns of large metropolitan regions have fared much better than those of medium and small urban areas. In large metros, downtowns have remained vital and still constitute the foremost concentration of activities, whereas in smaller centres they have become but a pale shadow of their former self.

In this chapter, we narrate the history of downtowns and describe their inner dynamics. We stress the features that distinguish them from the remainder of their region, such as high densities, the clustering of a broad mixture of activities and people, the street orientation of buildings, good public transit, and lively streets. We feel it important to declare our partiality towards downtowns; we plead for their continuing vitality or revitalization, depending on their circumstances, and for planning interventions that respect their specificity. In our view, downtowns can be foremost contributors to the economy and quality of life of a metropolitan region while abating some of its environmental impacts.

Traditionally, the notion of 'downtown' overlapped with that of central business district (CBD) (Howard and Boyce, 1959). The CBD essentially contained commercial office and retail areas. At the heart of the concept was the exclusion of housing, due to its incapacity to compete with commercial establishments for downtown space (Murphy, 1972; Murphy and Vance, 1954a, 1954b; Murphy et al., 1955). At the other end of the definitional range is the concept of 'central' or 'core' area adopted by some planning agencies in Canada, which includes not only the classical CBD land uses, but also public offices, cultural, educational, and health-care institutions, high-density industrial areas, and some residential pockets. Attempts at defining downtowns are further complicated by the collapse of CBD-type activities in the downtowns of some cities. Such circumstances rule out reliance on office and retail concentrations to define downtown areas. Our solution to these definitional problems is to follow definitions used in some large Canadian cities that de facto delimit downtowns as areas surrounded by traditional residential inner-city neighbourhoods or industrial districts (for example, Montreal, 2004: Section 2.3). There is the further issue of suburban downtowns, involving greenfield developments or, more rarely, redevelopments, which are at different stages of evolution. Here we rely on definitions based on density and multi-functionality adopted by municipal planning agencies (e.g., Mississauga, 2003: Section 4.06).

The Evolution of Downtowns

The Emergence and Growth of Downtowns, 1850–1950

Downtowns in the larger urban areas of Canada emerged slowly during the first half of the nineteenth century. By the 1850s they were recognizable as concentrations of stores, wholesale warehouses, artisanal 'manufactures', bank buildings, lawyers' offices, courthouses, and city halls. Between mid-century and the 1890s, these kinds of establishments shed their residential components. In the next decades, the formation of corporate capitalism spawned large business organizations, which controlled far-flung manufacturing, mining, transportation, or financial empires from downtown head offices. From these circumstances equity markets with stock exchanges and the offices of stockbrokers appeared, and accountants' offices became necessary to keep an eye on the dealings. And growing consumer markets with standardized goods meant the advent of advertising agencies. By 1914, noticeable office districts were firmly established.

Three factors assured the clustering of offices in a central location (Gad and Holdsworth, 1984: 294–8). There was first the wish for firms to be at the point of maximum accessibility in order to draw from a vast and diversified labour force (Hoover and Vernon, 1959: 98; Scott, 1982). Next, agglomeration economies generated in downtown areas favoured a central location. The downtown concentration of complementary firms facilitated face-to-face contacts between, for example, head offices and law firms or publicity agencies (Gad, 1979; Goddard, 1973; Haig, 1926; Weber, 1929 [1909]). Finally, we should not overlook the effect the prestige of a downtown address could have on location decisions.

The late 1800s also underwent profound retailing transformations. Specialized stores catering to a city-wide market were clustered in the central area, thus benefiting from the accessibility advantages of this location and the presence of droves of shoppers lured by the largest concentration of stores in a metropolitan area (Isenberg, 2004). But the advent of department stores most transformed retailing over this period. Their strong appeal to consumers combined with their predilection for downtowns assured the retail primacy of this district. In Toronto, for example, from 1883 onward the rapidly expanding Yonge Street Eaton's department store, equipped with innovations such as electric lighting and elevators, was a major draw for an emerging middle class (see Santink, 1990). After 1900, cinemas appeared and distinct entertainment clusters formed in close proximity to the retail hubs (Moore, 2004).[1]

Expanding Canadian cities supplied ever larger pools of workers and shoppers for downtown areas. The introduction of rail transit—commuter trains and streetcars—secured for decades to come the prominence of downtowns in terms of metropolitan accessibility. Successive periods of prosperity left their imprint on downtown areas in the form of extensive developments, involving ever increasing building size. By adding to the scale and number of downtown activities, and by prompting further extensions of largely downtown-focused public transport systems, each wave of growth reaffirmed the position of the downtown at the summit of the urban space hierarchy. A boom in the 1920s was apparent in a new generation of large-scale office buildings such as the 26-floor Sun Life Building in Montreal, the 34-floor Bank of Commerce Building in Toronto, and the 21-floor Marine Building in Vancouver (Gournay, 1998). These buildings, whose height can be attributed to the high cost of land in the emerging office clusters, but perhaps more to corporate pride and the influence of US models of downtown development, were to dominate the skyline of their cities until the 1960s (Gad and Holdsworth, 1984). More large office buildings and department stores were started or planned, but the Depression of the 1930s and World War II forced a pause on downtown development. Many of today's historical downtown buildings date from this early period of development, hence the prevalence of late nineteenth-century Victorian, early twentieth-century Edwardian, and art deco architecture.

Downtown development from the late 1880s to the early 1930s resulted in the formation of three specialized sectors. First was the office district, often referred to as the financial district because of the prominence of banks, tightly clustered along St James Street in Montreal, King and Bay Streets in Toronto, and West Hastings in Vancouver—which took the form of urban canyons hemmed in by the richly ornamented masonry of office buildings (Beauregard, 1981; Gad, 1991b). Second, retailing congregated on one or two streets where department stores served as anchors. Third, a band of public institutions, comprising universities, hospitals, museums, and, occasionally, legislatures and public-sector offices, edged many downtowns.

Modern Developments and Diversification, 1950–1990

Downtowns in Canadian cities began rising from their post-1930 development interruption in the 1950s with major projects such as the Yonge Street subway line in Toronto and the widening of Dorchester (now René Lévesque) Boulevard in Montreal (Nader, 1976: 149). Then, in the 1960s, downtown development really took off with the appearance of private projects of an unprecedented scale, featuring office buildings reaching hitherto unseen heights in Canada (43 floors in the 1963 Place Ville Marie complex in Montreal and 56 floors in the 1967 Bank Tower of the Toronto-Dominion Centre in Toronto) (see Figure 10.1 for an illustration of types of buildings associated with different phases of downtown development). Organized around open plazas and thus departing radically from the street orientation of previous-generation developments, these projects heralded a new downtown morphology (Collier, 1974; Lortie, 2004b). They also included underground shopping concourses, which, once linked to each other, formed extensive underground networks connected to train and subway stations. These 'winter city' downtown adaptations have been celebrated worldwide as a distinctive feature of Montreal and Toronto (Beauregard, 1972: 174–5). Underground networks were further extended with the opening of multi-storey shopping malls, the largest being

Toronto's Eaton Centre. The Montreal underground city comprises 30 kilometres of corridors, tunnels, and other publicly accessible spaces, and is accessed by 500,000 persons on a weekday (Montreal, n.d.). Variations on this theme include the 16-kilometre Calgary 'Plus 15' network of elevated walkways (about five metres or 15 feet above ground) connecting major downtown buildings, and the tri-level downtown Edmonton 'Pedway' system (see Byers, 1998; Robertson, 1993a).

Downtown growth in the 1960s, 1970s, and 1980s was fuelled by periods of economic prosperity, with important variations in intensity and timing between metropolitan regions (Gad, 1999: 157). Another factor of downtown expansion was the creation or expansion over these decades of rail transit systems that secured favourable downtown accessibility and thus placed this district in an advantageous position when competing with suburban locations (see Chapter 6). The first stretch of the Toronto subway opened in 1954 and the system underwent considerable expansion in the 1960s and 1970s. In the same vein, the Ontario government took over Toronto region commuter trains in 1967 (thus creating the GO system) and extended services over subsequent decades. The Montreal Metro was inaugurated in 1966, with major extensions opening from the mid-1970s to the late 1980s. Western Canadian metropolitan regions were later in adopting modern forms of rail transit. The Edmonton light rail transit was opened in 1978 and the Calgary system (called the CTrain) began operation in 1981. The Calgary network has been the object of ongoing extensions. Finally, the first line of the Vancouver SkyTrain opened in 1986. Ottawa took a different approach. Instead of developing a rail system it has created a network of roads dedicated exclusively to buses (the Transitway) and bus lanes. The first sections of the Transitway opened in 1983. The level of service in terms of speed and frequency is comparable to that of light rail. Either way, these public transit systems have made it possible for downtowns to grasp a substantial share of prosperity-induced office, retail, and hospitality service expansion.[2]

Figure 10.1   **Development/Redevelopment Sequence at King and Bay, Toronto**

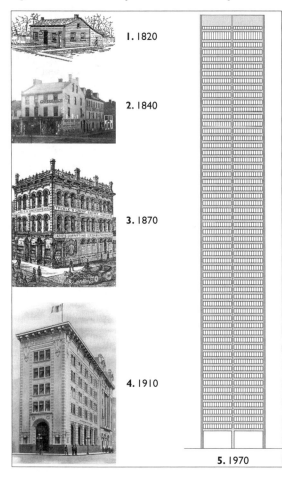

1. Wooden frame building, built 1820. Jordon Post house, clockmaker's shop and residence. From J.R. Robertson, *Robertson's Landmarks of Toronto*, vol. 2 (Toronto, 1896), 673, and vol. 5 (Toronto, 1908), 394.

2. 'Red brick warehouse', built 1840. Initially occupied by furniture company. Showrooms and warehouse. From J.R. Robertson, *Robertson's Landmarks of Toronto*, vol. 5 (Toronto, 1908), 394. Photo of c. 1870: Metropolitan Toronto Library.

3. Stone and brick (?) commercial building, Built c. 1877–8. Retail, manufacturing, billiard parlour. From *Canadian Illustrated News*, Supplement, 28 May 1881. National Archives of Canada.

4. Steel frame, stone and terra cotta, built 1910–11. Union Bank chambers, banking hall on ground and mezzanine floors; also bank offices on one of the upper four floors, several other occupants. Height of building: 95 feet. From *Construction* 5, 2 (1912): 62–3. Photo: Royal Bank of Canada, Archives.

5. Steel and glass skyscraper, built c. 1970–2. Commerce Court, multi-building complex developed by Canadian Imperial Bank of Commerce. Houses head office of bank and many other occupants. Height: 784 feet, 57 floors. Based on architect's drawing. Canadian Imperial Bank of Commerce, Development Corporation.

Meanwhile, as downtowns were losing much of their manufacturing and warehousing in the 1960s and 1970s, they were enhancing their educational, cultural, and recreational orientation, thereby raising their appeal to their metropolitan region population and tourists alike. Sectors once marginal to their downtowns, such as Old Montreal, Toronto's Yorkville, Winnipeg's Warehouse District, and Vancouver's Gastown, were taken over by exclusive restaurants and boutiques. Clearly, visitors preferred the atmosphere of traditional street-oriented settings to the brash modernity of sleek towers and underground shopping concourses.

Recent Transformations: Post-1990

With the 1990s, the downtowns of the large metropolitan areas may have entered a new phase. In the 1990s and in the early 2000s very little large-scale office or retail development occurred, resulting in employment and retail activity stagnation (Coffey et al., 1996). In downtown Toronto no large office tower has been erected since the early 1990s, and, at 400,000, downtown employment in 2001 was at roughly the same level as in 1991. Meanwhile, as the overall number of jobs grew in the census metropolitan area, the weight of the downtown declined.

In 1991, Toronto's central area accounted for 21.7 per cent of CMA employment. Ten years later, this proportion had dropped to 19.6 per cent.[3]

Yet as indicated by Table 10.1, there has been some office development in downtown Toronto between 1991 and 2005, albeit at a slower rate than in suburban areas. The location of downtown office growth along the east–west axis, and thus not in the traditional north–south Yonge and Bay Street corridors, suggests that much of this development resulted from the post-1996 rezoning and reuse of industrial loft space. These new facilities with their

Table 10.1   **Changes in Office Floor Space: Selected Toronto Districts, 1991–2005**

| | Floor Space in Square Feet | | | | | |
| | 1991 | | 2005 | | Change 1991–2005 | |
	Million Square feet	% of CMA	Million Square feet	% of CMA	Million Square feet	% Increase
Central Area, Yonge Street Axis (1)	56.9	40.0	57.2	35.6	+0.3	+0.5
Central Area, East–West Axis (2)	8.5	6.0	16.0	9.9	+7.5	+88.2
Central Area Total	*65.4*	*46.0*	*73.2*	*45.5*	*+7.8*	*+11.9*
North Central City (3)	8.6	6.1	7.8	4.8	−0.8	−9.3
Central Districts	*74.0*	*52.1*	*81.1*	*50.4*	*+7.0*	*+9.5*
North York City Centre (4)	7.2	5.1	9.0	5.6	+1.8	+24.3
Mississauga City Centre (5)	3.5	2.5	3.5	2.2	0.0	0.0
Don Valley North York (6)	11.5	8.1	11.8	7.3	+0.3	+2.6
Don Valley Markham (7)	10.9	7.7	14.6	9.1	+3.7	+33.9
Mississauga Business Parks (8)	11.8	8.3	19.3	12.0	+7.5	+63.6
Other Suburban	23.2	16.3	21.7	13.5	−1.5	−6.5
Suburban Districts	*68.1*	*47.9*	*79.9*	*49.6*	*+11.8*	*+17.3*
CMA Total	142.1	100	160.9	100	+18.8	+13.2

Notes on Royal LePage district aggregations:
(1) Central Area, Yonge Street Axis: Financial Core, Downtown North, Bloor.
(2) Central Area, East–West Axis: Downtown East, Downtown South, Downtown West, King West.
(3) North Central City: St Clair, Eglinton.
(4) North York City Centre: North Yonge Corridor.
(5) Mississauga City Centre: Mississauga City Centre.
(6) Don Valley North York: Don Mills and Eglinton, Duncan Mill, Consumers Road.
(7) Don Valley Markham: Woodbine & Steeles, Woodbine & 7.
(8) Mississauga Business Parks: Airport, Hurontario Corridor, Cooksville, Sheridan, Meadowvale.
Source: Royal LePage Commercial Inc., Toronto Office Space Market, Statistical Summary Table, Q1, 2005.

exposed brick walls and wood beams are particularly popular with art and design workers.

The evolution of downtown retailing paints a picture similar to that of employment. Between 1990 and 1998, total downtown sales as a proportion of metropolitan region retail activity for 16 surveyed metropolitan regions fell from 10.8 to 9.5 per cent (Lea et al., 2003). If in the downtowns of the three largest metropolitan regions the proportion of retailing either remained stable or regressed slightly, the situation was different in other regions. Decline was steep in Winnipeg, Edmonton, Regina, London, and Saint John (see Chapter 16).

Overall, large-city downtowns are not in a slump. On the contrary, it could be argued that that they are on a trajectory of qualitative change. New forms of 'creative' office employment are accompanied by the expansion of high-level cultural and educational activities—opera instead of run-of-the-mill cinemas; graduate instead of undergraduate programs; medical research centres instead of ordinary hospital beds; and a variety of specialized retail clusters rather than department stores or malls (on the role of art and culture as instruments of revitalization, see Strom, 2002; Wynne, 1992: ch. 2). Overall, the number of visitors, students, patients seeking specialized medical care, theatre-goers, business visitors, conference attendees, and tourists is growing as that of daily downtown workers remains stable.

Downtown features appealing to visitors have similarly lured residential development. Indeed, living within walking distance of theatres, cinemas, a vast choice of restaurants, and diversified shopping, let alone the metropolitan region's largest employment concentration, has become attractive to many individuals, in particular those who belong to a so-called 'new middle class' involved in occupations related to the arts and social sciences (Gouldner, 1979; Ley, 1996a).[4] This is not the first time downtowns stimulate nearby housing development (Bourne, 1967). From the late 1950s, high-rise residential redevelopment took place at the extremities and beyond the edge of large-city downtowns—most prominently in Vancouver's West End, in St James Town and the Annex in Toronto,

and in the Guy/de Maisonneuve district in Montreal. What differentiates the 1990s onward is the increasing mixture of new housing with traditional CBD features. This is particularly the case in downtown Vancouver (see Chapter 4) and Toronto, where high-rise housing invades the CBD, and thus makes it increasingly difficult to differentiate functionally the downtown from surrounding inner-city neighbourhoods. New condominium towers now rival office buildings on the skylines of these cities (Figure 10.2). Table 10.2 portrays residential growth in the downtowns of Canada's three largest metropolitan regions. Of all three, Vancouver is the one that experienced the highest expansion, followed by Toronto. In Montreal, where high-rise condominium development has been more modest, the central area population growth has been much lower.

It would be wrong to attribute all downtown residential growth to the condominium development boom. A closer look at Toronto's downtown illustrates the complex changes in the residential component of downtown. Table 10.3 shows that in the older CBD section along the Yonge Street corridor the residential population doubled between 1981 and 2001. As in the case of office space and employment, the greatest increase in population occurred in the former transportation and industrial areas along the southern east–west axis. Here the residential population surged by a staggering 242 per cent. Trends in other, older, residential areas are also interesting: in the older high-rise apartment and public housing sectors the population increased substantially without new development, a likely consequence of the replacement of small households by larger immigrant ones. In the gentrifying or older low-rise ethnic residential areas population was largely stable, while in the fully gentrified areas, such as Cabbagetown or the area west of the University of Toronto campus, population actually fell between 1981 and 2001.

Medium-size City Downtowns

The trajectory of the downtowns of medium-size metropolitan regions (100,000–500,000 population)

Figure 10.2   **Condominium Towers, Vancouver**

Massive condominium tower developments are responsible for a population surge in and around downtown Vancouver.

Table 10.2   **Population within Two Kilometres of Major Downtown Intersection***

	1991	1996	2001	Per cent Change 1991–2001
Montreal	66,615	69,402	70,650	6.1
Toronto	108,290	117,720	126,421	16.7
Vancouver	68,385	74,353	87,640	28.2

*Major intersections are Ste Catherine and Peel in Montreal, Yonge and Dundas in Toronto, and Robson and Granville in Vancouver.
Source: Statistics Canada, 1991, 1996, and 2001 censuses.

Table 10.3   **Changes in Residential Population in Downtown Toronto, 1981–2001**

	Population			
			1981–2001	
Area	1981	2001	Change	%
New residential areas south of Queen Street (1)	9,300	31,800	+22,500	+241.9
Infill in CBD area along Yonge Street (including financial district) (2)	30,400	52,200	+21,800	+73.5
High-rise and public housing residential areas (3)	38,000	47,400	+9,400	+25.7
Low-rise 'ethnic'/gentrifying areas (4)	14,500	17,100	+2,600	+17.9
Low-rise gentrified areas (5)	30,000	23,500	−6,500	−21.7
Central Area	122,200	172,000	+49,800	+40.8

Notes on census tract aggregations for population areas:
(1) CTs 8–13, 16, 17.
(2) CTs 14, 15, 34, 35, 62, 63, 88, 89–91.
(3) CTs 30–3, 64–6.
(4) CTs 36–9.
(5) CTs 59–61, 67, 68, 86, 87, 92.
Source: Statistics Canada, 1981 and 2001 censuses.

paralleled that of large urban areas until the 1960s. As in larger urban areas, transit was critical to the dominance of medium-size city downtowns, and both categories of downtowns contained virtually all their metropolitan region high-order retailing and services. Yet there were also differences between large and medium-size city downtowns. In large cities, downtown office employment was much more important than it was in medium-size city downtowns, which were by comparison more specialized in retailing.

From the 1960s, medium-size city downtowns fell victim to a profound land-use and transportation transformation of their urban areas, which involved near-universal automobile use and an attendant decentralization of activities (Bunting and Filion, 1999; Filion et al., 1999). Large metropolitan regions were experiencing similar trends but were able to maintain high levels of transit use and

a centralized configuration, even if attenuated by suburbanization. In medium-size urban areas where large suburban retail concentrations are easily accessible from everywhere, including the inner city, suburban competition proved fatal to downtowns (on suburbanization and its adverse impact on downtowns, see Berry, 1976; Bottles, 1987; Erickson, 1986; Fujii and Hartshorn, 1995; Hise, 1993; Lewis, 1983). Bereft of the economies of scale and agglomeration found in suburban malls and power centres, and of the car accessibility of locations along suburban arterials, downtowns in these urban areas have literally emptied out (Robertson, 1999, 2001; Yeates et al., 1996). First chain stores left, followed by department stores, and most recently cinemas. And the more they were depleted of activities and people, the fewer were the reasons to visit these downtowns; the shoddy appearance and absence of stimulation associated

Figure 10.3 **Colborne Street, Brantford, Ontario**

With the steep decline of retailing, many stores in medium-size city downtowns are vacant.

with boarded-up premises and empty sidewalks deterred visitors (Bunting and Millward, 1999; Millward and Bunting, 1999) (see Figure 10.3).

It would be unfair to attribute the decline of these downtowns to an absence of public-sector revitalization efforts. To the contrary, governments readily funded efforts at making these downtowns competitive with suburban locations (Filion and Bunting, 1993). Early interventions consisted in assuring the accommodation of growing volumes of automobiles through the widening of roads, one-way streets, and the creation of surface, underground, and structure parking spaces (Robertson,

1993b). Another popular strategy has been the erection of downtown indoor malls (Gillette, 1985; Lorch and Smith, 1993). The most recent efforts consist in locating cultural and public-sector institutions in downtowns and encouraging housing development so as to provide a market for existing and potential downtown stores and services. Also, lessons have been learned from successful medium-size city downtowns, such as those of Kingston and Halifax, which benefit from the animation generated by the large student population of nearby universities (Filion et al., 2004). In Waterloo Region, the City of Cambridge has successfully lured the University of Waterloo School of Architecture to its downtown, and downtown Kitchener will host the new University of Waterloo–University of Toronto School of Pharmacy as well as the Wilfrid Laurier University School of Social Work. In nearby Brantford, Wilfrid Laurier University has opened a new downtown campus. The downtown location of these institutions is facilitated by an abundance of available land and buildings. It remains to be seen, however, if the number of students these initiatives will bring downtown (from a few hundred in Cambridge to an eventual 2,500 in Brantford) will be sufficient to prompt a substantial revitalization process.

Suburban Downtowns

Planned subcentres first appeared in Ottawa. The 1950 *General Report on the Plan for the National Capital* prepared by the French architect and planner, Jacques Gréber, proposed subcentres to prevent too high a concentration of government employment in the downtown area and make better use of transportation facilities (Nader, 1976: 175, 180–1). Existing subcentres, such as Tunney's Pasture, are a legacy of this plan. It is noteworthy that this first generation of subcentres has remained exclusively government employment clusters, failing to acquire retailing and hospitality uses. It is thus difficult to label these districts as 'suburban downtowns'.

Subsequent interest for subcentres arose in the Toronto context. In the late 1950s and early 1960s planners proposed intensified development containing high-rise residential and office buildings around certain subway stations to encourage reliance on public transportation (Lemon, 1985: 143). Such development materialized around two Yonge line subway stations—St Clair and Eglinton. The concept resurfaced in the 1980 Metro Toronto plan in the form of multi-use suburban centres intended to capture some of the office development that would be diverted from downtown Toronto, which was then experiencing accelerated employment growth. It was believed that subcentres would also provide an alternative to mushrooming

automobile-oriented suburban office parks (Metro Toronto, 1980). These centres were to group offices, retailing, and housing in a high-density transit- and walking-conducive environment (Gad, 1979). The combination of different functions warrants their labelling as 'suburban downtowns'. Indeed, the proposed centres were to replicate at a reduced scale the dynamics of traditional downtowns. Two major suburban centres were designated on rail transit lines: Scarborough Town Centre and North York Centre, both of which are now mature suburban downtowns. The concept was soon adopted by out-of-Metro suburban municipalities. The largest to materialize was Mississauga City Centre; others include the Bramalea and Pickering centres (see Figure 10.4).

In the early 1990s, at a time of intense preoccupation with urban sprawl in the Toronto metropolitan region, suburban multi-use centres, by then rebranded as 'nodes', were heralded as a foremost instrument to intensify the suburb and thus contain outlying development. The purpose of nodes was also to provide concentrated destinations favourable to the operation of suburban transit services. Suburban regional and municipal governments enthusiastically adhered to the concept, which led to the designation, but far less frequent development, of an abundance of suburban nodes (IBI Group, 1990; OGTA, n.d.). At present, two major nodes—the Vaughan and Markham city centres—are at the point of being developed in suburban Toronto. Perhaps more than any other suburban downtown plan, the Markham centre proposal adheres to the principles of new urbanism and smart growth. This suburban downtown will cover 400 hectares and eventually contain 25,000 residents and 17,000 jobs. Its retailing will be street-oriented, and apart from a few buildings that will reach between 13 and 16 storeys, structures will be restricted to six to eight storeys. There will be a town square and an abundance of natural areas. The downtown will be served by a GO commuter train station and local rapid transit routes will connect it to Markham neighbourhoods. Strict measures will be taken to prevent a domination of the landscape by parking (Markham, n.d.).

Figure 10.4 **Location of Toronto Suburban Downtowns**

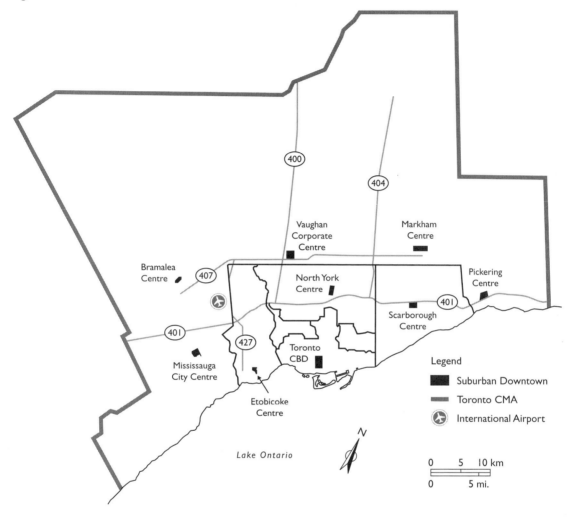

Other Canadian metropolitan regions have also used variants of the nodal concept to organize their suburban development. This is notably the case of Vancouver, which has designated eight such centres, called regional town centres, three of which are on a SkyTrain and two on a commuter train line (GVRD, 1975, 1999) (see Figure 10.5).

It is important to note that the Canadian understanding of suburban downtowns departs from the 'edge city' concept as advanced for the US by Joel Garreau. Edge cities connote large multi-use

developments that have sprouted within outer suburban areas of large US metropolitan regions. According to Garreau's definition, a full-blown 'edge city' contains a minimum of 5 million square feet of office space and at least 600,000 square feet of retailing and occupies a location that was recently predominantly rural or residential (Garreau, 1991: ch. 1). What differentiates edge cities from Canadian suburban downtowns is their occasional challenge of the metropolitan dominance of the traditional downtown, as in the case of Southfield and Troy,

Figure 10.5 **Location of Vancouver Suburban Downtowns**

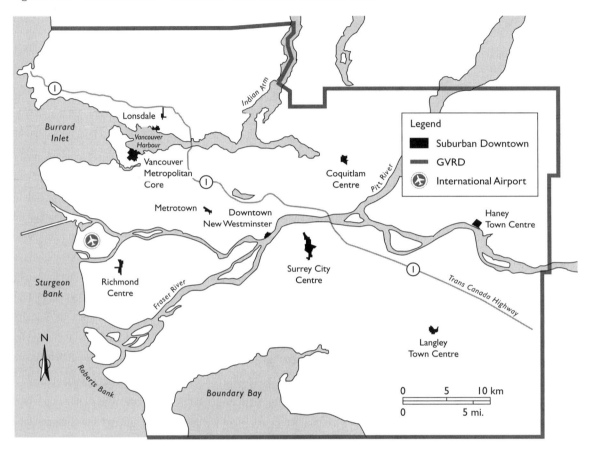

two large Detroit edge cities (Matthew, 2001). Nowhere does this happen in Canada. Other distinctions pertain to the unplanned (that is, developer- rather than government-induced) nature of edge cities and their near total dependence on the automobile, mirrored in their layout, which is dominated by arterials, access ramps, and various forms of parking (underground, structure, or surface) (see Matthew, 1993).

The more successful Canadian suburban downtowns include city halls, shopping facilities, hotels and restaurants, concentrations of offices, and high-density housing (see Coffey et al., 2000; Coffey and Shearmur, 2001; Matthew,1992, 2001). By 1991 the larger suburban downtowns had grown to employment concentrations of around 20,000 jobs (Mississauga City Centre, Scarborough Town Centre, Metrotown in Burnaby) or even 40,000 jobs (North York City Centre). Others, however, were far more modest, but still started to perform well as focal points of suburban municipalities.

Yet the attainment by suburban downtowns of some of their original planning objectives proved to be a challenge. In some instances, after initial success, efforts at attracting office space have been less than rewarding (Canadian Urban Institute, 2005; Royal LePage, 2005). This has been, for example, the case in Mississauga City Centre (Charney, 2005). In its early phase of development, in the 1980s, this suburban downtown was the site of multiple office developments. But, as indicated in Table 10.1, the trend has since been for offices to locate in other types of Mississauga locations, business parks predominantly.[5] Still, Table 10.1 shows that another suburban downtown, North York Centre, has performed much better in this regard. It is worth mentioning that high-density residential development has progressed rapidly in most suburban downtowns. Just like downtown Vancouver and Toronto, they are presently undergoing a high-rise condominium boom.

Another difficulty in reaching planning objectives concerns levels of public transit use. Despite the presence of rail transit in two of the three most important Toronto suburban downtowns and of a local bus terminal in the third, transit reliance remains low compared to that for downtown Toronto. Over a 24-hour period, public transit modal shares of all journeys to North York Centre, Scarborough Town Centre, and Mississauga City Centre are respectively 23.6, 17.5, and 9.8 per cent.

The equivalent for downtown Toronto is 46 per cent (2001 figures) (see Table 10.4). Finally, the objective of creating a pedestrian-conducive environment has often proven to be elusive, particularly where suburban downtowns have developed around regional malls and their abundant surface parking lots. Research has indicated that many office workers in such downtowns rely on the car even for intra-downtown journeys (Filion, 2001).

The Importance of Downtowns

The advantages for a metropolitan region of possessing a healthy downtown stem from the fact that the downtown operates in a different fashion from the remainder of its territory, which is mostly suburban in nature (on the importance of downtowns, see Rypkema, 2003). (The foregoing also holds for suburban downtowns, provided they have been successful in breaking from the dominant suburban low-density and automobile-reliant pattern). People are more likely to use public transit to reach

Table 10.4   **Per Cent Modal Shares to Different Types of Greater Toronto Area Destinations**

	Auto Driver	Auto Passenger	Public Transit	Walk and Cycle	Other
Downtown Toronto	32.4	7.8	46.0	11.9	1.9
North York Centre (suburban downtown)	57.7	13.0	23.6	4.9	0.7
Scarborough Town Centre (suburban downtown)	63.2	17.7	17.5	1.1	0.4
Mississauga City Centre (suburban downtown)	67.4	18.4	9.8	3.1	1.3
Mississauga Rd/Highway 401 (suburban business park)	83.5	11.1	3.2	0.8	1.4
Pearson Airport/Highway 401 (suburban business park)	85.0	9.3	4.9	0.6	0.1

Source: 2001 Transportation Tomorrow Survey.

downtowns than any other destination, and once downtown, journeys from one location to another are generally done on foot. In fact, stimulating walking environments consisting in continuous facades with store windows, cafés and restaurants, and animated sidewalks are trademarks of successful downtowns (Alexander et al., 1987; APA, 1982; Francis, 1984). The more pedestrian-hospitable downtown environments are, the longer are the distances people will be willing to walk and the larger will be the number of activities able to benefit from downtowns' economies of agglomeration (Thomson, 1977). Their walking environment is a major asset of downtowns in their competition with car-oriented suburban areas. It is noteworthy that while the vast majority of medium-size city downtown areas are struggling, the few that are performing well stand out by the quality of their pedestrian environment. This is indeed the case of Halifax, Kingston, and Victoria (Filion et al., 2004).

The first reason why vital downtowns are important stems precisely from their distinctiveness. They add to the range of lifestyle choices within metropolitan regions by offering an alternative to an urban activity pattern fully dependent on the automobile. In this sense, regions where downtowns have declined to the extent that all there is left is a limited number of low-order activities are disadvantaged in terms of the living options they offer their citizens, relative to those regions that can provide both car-dependent suburban and transit- and walking-oriented lifestyles. The presence of such a choice is especially important to the minority of households (perhaps 20 per cent) that seek alternatives to the suburban lifestyle (Bunting et al., 2000).

Another advantage of downtowns pertains most specifically to successful large-city downtowns. Variations in land values translate into the presence of a wide diversity of activities, all within walking distance. These range from high-fashion establishments to second-hand stores, from exclusive restaurants offering international specialties to fast-food outlets, from large, sumptuous theatres specializing in Broadway musicals to tiny experimental theatres. Suburbs, with their formulaic fare, have nothing comparable to offer. Diversity fosters a feeling of

spontaneity and unexpectedness to downtowns, which is absent from most suburban venues. Indeed, in the suburbs land use is far more specialized, and in the absence of pedestrian-oriented commercial streets shopping areas are privately owned and controlled. Downtown diversity of activities rests largely on social diversity and an inherent inclusivity. To generate diversity, downtowns need to be accommodating to people belonging to diverse ethnic groups, subcultures, and income categories.

Alongside social and aesthetic benefits there are also economic advantages accruing from a successful downtown. One is the advantage it provides to firms that depend heavily on face-to-face encounters to generate and transmit information. Because these linkages involve intangible forms of communication (as well as lending themselves to repetition and correction), they are deemed to be superior to those that rely on electronic vectors (Sassen, 1991: 90–125; 1994: 65–9). For many firms no other location offers such easy access to enterprises with which they interact. In larger downtowns various activity clusters are strongly related and provide for the functioning of networks that tie together finance, media, arts, retailing, public administration, health care, education, and research. Another economic advantage is the attraction a pleasant and activity-rich downtown exerts on tourists and conventions. Finally, such a downtown is likely to appeal to members of the social category Richard Florida refers to as the 'creative class', comprised of individuals who value highly the rich street life of diversified urban areas and who are characterized by a strong economic development potential by virtue of their knowledge, innovative capacity, and their propensity to launch businesses (Florida, 2002, 2005). According to this view, there is thus a substantial economic payoff to a diversified and lively downtown.

One should not underestimate environmental advantages associated with the high density as well as with the walking and transit conduciveness of successful downtowns. In a large metropolitan region, journeys to and within downtowns rely the least on the automobile. This feature of downtown areas is dramatically portrayed by changes in modal shares that ensue from the relocation of a downtown office to a suburban business park (Table 10.4). Typically, such a move translates into the shift from a predominant use of public transit to an overwhelming reliance on the automobile for commuting purposes. Similar observations can be made about distinctions between journey patterns of downtown residents relative to those of residents of metropolitan regions as a whole. The auto driver and auto passenger modal shares of downtown Toronto residents are half those of residents of the entire Transportation Tomorrow Survey area, which corresponds broadly to the Greater Toronto Area (33 versus 65 per cent for drivers and 8 versus 16 per cent for passengers). Meanwhile, walking and cycling are twice as high among downtown dwellers (12 versus 6 per cent) and transit use is more than four times greater (45 versus 10 per cent).[6] What is more, the large buildings and compact layout typical of downtowns reduce energy needs as well as the consumption of land at the periphery of metropolitan regions—hence the reliance on suburban downtowns as an instrument to contain sprawl. In intensely built and used downtowns, we confront the paradox that these districts are among places that generate the most pollution per square metre, but the least per person (Owen, 2004). So if our cities in their entirety adopted the same form and journey patterns as their downtowns, we would be much better off from an environmental perspective.

Finally, synchronicity between downtown and metropolitan region expansion can improve attitudes towards urban growth. If disconnected from downtown expansion, urban development happens by replication, whereby new sectors are largely self-contained, with their own business and industrial parks, shopping malls and big-box stores, and standardized forms of housing. For the most part, these sectors reproduce facilities already present elsewhere and thus add little to the diversity of the metropolitan region. On the other hand, when metropolitan development translates into downtown expansion, the outcome is a wider range and greater sophistication of activities. As they grow, downtowns tend to generate specialized districts and broaden the variety of their restaurants, theatres, specialized retailing, and cultural activities.

Threats and Options

Loss of Employment

How much of an employment critical mass does a downtown need to generate agglomeration economies? And can downtowns function without an important concentration of employment? In the best of circumstances employment has remained stable in downtowns; in most instances it has declined. Downtowns have difficulty competing with suburban employment districts, with their lower land cost and taxes, convenient automobile accessibility, and ample free parking. Suburban locations have proven to be particularly attractive to back offices specializing in more repetitive tasks and those head offices that have little need for elaborate downtown linkage networks—especially Canadian subsidiaries of international companies, which access many of their support services from their world headquarters (Gad, 1985). Even suburban downtowns find it difficult to attract office employment, since office buildings increasingly opt for scattered locations within suburban areas, generally along highway corridors (Lang, 2003). (See Table 10.5 for a summary of the respective advantages and disadvantages of downtown and suburban office locations).[7]

Downtown problems in attracting or maintaining office employment are not exclusively related to difficulties in competing with dispersed suburban locations. Downtown office employment is also victim of corporate mergers and downsizing, as well as of the spread of home-based work and, increasingly, the movement offshore of administrative support tasks (Illegems and Verbeke, 2003).

Different measures can encourage a downtown location of office employment. One consists in targeting sectors particularly compatible with the atmosphere of downtowns, such as those that rely heavily on individuals belonging to the 'creative class'. In Montreal, la Cité Multimédia, a public-private partnership, provides 120,000 square metres of office space in eight buildings located in what was a derelict industrial sector to the south of the downtown. It now registers 6,000 jobs in about

Table 10.5   **Advantages and Disadvantages of Downtown and Suburban Office Locations**

	Downtown Locations		Suburban Locations	
	Advantages	Disadvantages	Advantages	Disadvantages
For workers	Stimulating environment; combination of journeys (work, shopping, culture); possibility to choose between modes.	Long commutes and congestion; expensive parking.	Shorter commutes; less congestion.	Lack of stimulating environment; absence of nearby restaurants; absence of modal choice—even carpooling can be a problem.
For firms	Access to metropolitan-wide labour pool; high potential for face-to-face linkages; prestige of downtown location.	Need to pay more for workers because of long commute; higher rent and taxes; limits on expansion potential; difficult deliveries.	Positive corporate image with a distinctive architecture and landscaping; cheaper space; more expansion possibilities; easier deliveries; can combine administration with warehousing and production.	Must rely on car for face-to-face meetings.
From a metropolitan-wide perspective	Permits concentration of destinations; transit orientation and high transit modal shares; helps prevent sprawl; helps define a clear urban structure.	Expensive infrastructure needs in order to funnel large numbers of journeys towards one destination.	Tax revenues and employment creation attractive to local administrations.	When locations are scattered, in contradiction with some metropolitan planning objectives; automobile orientation.

100 computing multi-media firms, as well as 500 housing units.

A second measure to enhance the downtown's fortunes would involve the use of zoning regulations to prevent offices particularly well-suited to downtown areas from locating in the suburbs. A problem with this approach, however, is that suburban municipalities would justifiably be loath to forgo such lucrative and prestigious activities. In addition, the definition of downtown-suitable offices would be the object of endless debates. And finally, there may be worthwhile reasons for such

offices to prefer suburban locations. In these cases, proscription of non-downtown development may lead firms to cancel investments or perhaps to find suitable locations in other metropolitan regions.

The third measure, present to varying degrees in most Canadian metropolitan regions, consists in metropolitan-wide tax revenue-sharing. Because central cities generally register higher tax rates due, among other things, to a poorer population and more elaborate services than found in suburban municipalities and also because central cities are responsible for operation of extensive transit services, traditional downtowns face distinct cost disadvantages when competing with suburban locations for employment. Any bridging of the tax load discrepancy between central cities and suburban municipalities is thus favourable to downtown development (see Canadian Urban Institute, 2005).

A fourth measure lies clearly within the jurisdiction of central cities. Some of the planning policies and taxation practices clearly privilege residential development and discourage the maintenance and attraction of places of work. In a recent *Vancouver Sun* article, Trevor Boddy sharply criticized the 1991 policy of rezoning part of downtown Vancouver from office to residential space, the lack of interest in preventing the conversion of office space to residential, and the relatively high taxation of office in comparison to residential properties. Boddy claims that offices in Vancouver are taxed five times more heavily than condo residences; in Toronto the ratio is 3.3:1 and in Calgary 2.7:1 (Boddy, 2005: 3). Clearly, municipal politicians and planners need to pay some attention to employment in the city centre. (They would also do well to protect the remnants of industrial spaces.)

A fifth measure that could serve to encourage downtown development involves improvement and/or expansion of public transit services. As downtowns represent the unchallenged transit accessibility peak, interventions contributing to raise public transit use have the potential of stimulating downtown activity, including employment (see Cervero and Landis, 1997).

Loss of Diversity

The diversity of downtowns was threatened at different times over the past 60 years. Over the 1950s and 1960s, older structures were frequently torn down to make way for urban expressways, widened arterials, and parking lots. While US downtown areas were far more affected by these kinds of transformations, Canadian downtowns were also the object of major transportation projects. The vision that drove these interventions was that downtown should be highly accessible by automobile and also

specialized in a limited number of relatively high-order activity categories such as office employment and department store and chain retailing. For the most part, however, these policies came to an end in the late 1960s and early 1970s, victims of a tighter public-sector purse and enhanced support for heritage conservation. The change of urban policy direction is perhaps best illustrated by the virtual absence of urban expressway construction in Canada after the early 1970s. While it is true that this period marked the end of major highway projects, the creation of surface parking lots in response to rising levels of automobile commuting has persisted. It is important to realize that these various forms of automobile spaces have generally involved the demolition of older buildings similar to the ones that today house exclusive boutiques, restaurants, residences, or second-hand music stores and affordable housing. Either way, the presence of such buildings would have had the potential to contribute to the diversity of downtowns, something surface automobile space cannot do.

In the mid-1970s, after a decade of accelerated office expansion, downtown overgrowth and overspecialization became a major preoccupation (Aubin, 1977; Gutstein, 1975; Stein, 1972). In Toronto, there was a perception among politicians and planners that downtown employment was on the verge of outstripping existing transportation capacity and that further development would demand massive financial outlay in expanding and additional systems. Worries were also raised about dangers of downtown Toronto becoming exclusively an office employment centre, other uses being crowded out by office space (Toronto, 1974, 1975; for similar reactions in Vancouver, see GVRD, 1975). In the end, no long-term attempt at controlling downtown employment growth materialized, but this preoccupation nevertheless resulted in policies encouraging the erection of housing in and around the downtown (Nowlan and Steuart, 1991).

With hindsight, concern about an overconcentration of office employment in downtown Toronto seems to have been exaggerated. Some 30 years after their introduction, measures promoting downtown housing are yielding results beyond all expectations. In fact, there is talk of large-city downtowns eventually becoming primarily high-density residential areas as housing developments proceed apace while employment stagnates. The spectre of masses of downtown dwellers having to reverse-commute to suburban workplaces has already been raised (e.g., Boddy, 2005). Whereas the present condominium construction boom is generally beneficial to downtowns (24-hour use of downtowns; market for shops, restaurants, cultural venues; commuting on foot to downtown employment), it also causes problems. For one, an increased presence of housing raises issues of incompatibility between downtown land uses that were easily ignored in the past. A noisy nightclub beside offices is not a source of tension thanks to differences in hours of operation. But tempers will flare if the nightclub is adjacent to a new residential condominium building.

An added concern about downtown living is the household income and type imbalance introduced by the kind of housing development presently taking place in the downtowns of large cities. By virtue of their size and cost, these developments appeal to small households with above-average income. In the past, downtowns and surrounding neighbourhoods hosted a variety of residential forms accessible to low-income households: rooming houses, inexpensive apartments, and public housing. But very little public housing has been built in Canada over the last 15 years and rooming houses and cheap apartments have either been taken over by gentrifiers or have made way for parking or new structures such as residential condominiums. These housing tendencies obviously result in a reduced social diversity. There are two ways of interpreting this growing social segregation. One is to deplore the exclusion of poor people as a violation of their right to use the city, including the downtown (Lefebvre, 2003). They, too, value proximity to employment, in their case in the low-wage downtown service sector. And for the very poor, downtowns and surrounding areas offer shelter, social services, panhandling opportunities, and public space. Suburban environments, where much of the space is privately owned, are far less hospitable for the very poor (especially the homeless) than are downtowns with their abundance of public spaces (squares, parks, and wide and lively sidewalks). What is more, the presence of other people facing similar circumstances engenders a sense of community and solidarity among the destitute. The second perspective on the falling proportion of low-income residents in downtowns concerns the loss of activities associated with their presence. We can expect that over time downtown shops, restaurants, or places of entertainment will increasingly be in the image of the gentrifiers and residents of condominium towers.

Many medium-size city downtowns face an opposite problem. In their case an overconcentration of marginalized people causes difficulties. When added to the deteriorated appearance of these downtowns and their limited offerings, such a presence is perceived by many as a deterrent to visit this district. Meanwhile, many suburban downtowns experience accelerated condominium development not unlike their large-city counterparts. These do not perform as much as agents of social segregation, however, because they are typically less expensive than those found in large cities' traditional downtowns and are not a factor in lower-income household displacement.

These are clearly circumstances calling for government intervention. In the case of large-city downtowns one measure could consist in legislating the presence of a given proportion of affordable units in new developments. By contrast, in medium-size city downtowns the challenge would be to launch a market-driven residential development process, perhaps by creating an environment that would be adapted to the needs and tastes of the future residents of such developments. To produce such an environment, municipalities could, for example, subsidize for a limited period stores that new residents would patronize, such as supermarkets, pharmacies, and hardware stores.

Suburbanization of the Downtown Environment

Suburbanization here is not understood as the departure from downtown of activities such as offices, but rather as transformations of the downtown that make it increasingly similar to the suburb. The above-mentioned adaptation of downtowns to growing car use is an example of such a suburbanization process, as is, in some measure, the loss of social and activity diversity. Suburbanization of downtowns is an issue because their diversity, pedestrian hospitality, and densely built environment are their major competitive advantages relative to the suburbs. If these are lost, downtowns are deprived of important assets.

The worst examples of suburbanization are found in the downtowns of medium-size cities. In large-city downtowns the land value imperative results in high-density developments, distinctive from suburban built forms. It is not unusual in medium-size city downtowns to find continuous store facades broken by new developments set back behind parking areas. Meanwhile, street widening has both caused a deterioration of walking conditions and made it easier for car traffic to drive through downtowns (Filion and Bunting, 1993; Robertson, 1993b). In addition, and nearly invariably in such downtowns, attempts to compete with suburbs on equal terms by building indoor shopping malls have been disastrous not only for the malls themselves, but for downtowns in their entirety (Gillette, 1985; Lorch and Smith, 1993). By sucking activity from the main streets, these malls were a cause of blight. As a result, when they faltered due to their inability to compete with larger suburban retail facilities enjoying better car accessibility, little retail was left to attract shoppers downtown.

A reverse situation is faced by suburban downtowns, where the intent is to move from a suburban-style layout to a denser and less car-oriented development pattern. The land use of most suburban downtowns is still dominated by surface parking lots, however (Relph, 1991). The problems these downtowns face is related to the costs involved in de-emphasizing the presence of the car in a context where a large majority of people drive to access their activities. If these costs are passed on to building owners or parking users, chances are that many will opt for other suburban locations where parking is abundant and free.

Quality of Life

We are far from the situation that prevailed in the 1950s and 1960s when the planning priority was to facilitate downtown access for office workers and shoppers, often at the expense of amenities such as waterfronts. With their growing dependence on people with a taste for urban amenities—downtown and nearby residents, visitors from the metropolitan region, tourists and conventioneers—the emphasis has shifted to issues regarding quality of life. Over the last decades, we have moved from a narrow economic and functional approach to downtown planning to one that stresses its role as a place of enjoyment.

Consistent with this change of perspective, contemporary downtown policies emphasize diversity. Policies targeted at downtowns have turned their back on the concept of the CBD as a functionally highly segregated area. Interventions have been adapted to distinctive requirements of specialized sectors within downtowns: historical districts, recreation areas, theatre districts, new developments with a strong residential orientation, and, of course, office and different types of retail areas (Toronto, 2002: 14–19).

Moreover, the urban amenity aspect of the traditional commercial street has been rediscovered. Whereas in the 1960s and 1970s the focus was on below-grade or elevated pedestrian corridors, emphasis has shifted back to the street, consistent with the views expounded by Jane Jacobs and the new urbanism movement (Duany et al., 2000; Jacobs, 1961; Untermann, 1984). Planners now attempt to ensure that new developments provide unbroken sidewalk-aligned facades, preferably with store windows. For example, in Vancouver the massive residential condominium developments in False Creek North, adjacent to the downtown, are organized around new streets with continuous facades, in sharp contrast to the 'tower in the park' model (consisting of high-rise buildings surrounded by abundant green space) predominant until a few decades ago (Vancouver, 1990: 4–5; Punter, 2003). It is noteworthy that measures aimed at improving the pedestrian environment of downtowns accentuate distinctions between these districts and suburban areas, and thus enhance downtown comparative advantages relative to other locales (Robertson, 1995).

Attempts at restoring pedestrian links between different components of downtown areas often entail repairing damages inflicted to pedestrian environments by urban expressways built from the 1950s to the 1970s (Sokoloff and Ahtik, 1992). The Montreal Palais des Congrès (Convention Centre) was built over a depressed stretch of Autoroute Ville-Marie, in part to re-establish a pedestrian-friendly link between the new and old sectors of the downtown. In Toronto, similar concerns are driving debates about the future of the elevated Gardiner Expressway, which separates the downtown from the waterfront. The proposed options include a tunnelling of the expressway, its demolition without replacement, and reliance on design devices to alleviate its adverse impact on pedestrians.[8]

Regard for the quality of the downtown environment is also expressed in recent architectural achievements, especially in the case of public buildings. Presently in Toronto the Royal Ontario Museum and the Art Gallery of Ontario are undergoing major expansions designed by world-renowned architects, Daniel Libeskind in the first instance and Frank Ghery in the second. But perhaps the most remarkable Canadian example of innovative public architecture is the coliseum-style Vancouver library, designed by Moshe Safdie.

However, the most visible efforts at improving quality of life involved the creation of parks and recreational and cultural centres along waterfronts adjacent to downtowns. This has been the case in the major-city downtowns—Toronto, Montreal, and Vancouver—as well as in smaller metros such as Halifax and Kingston. On weekends or during the summer, these waterfronts take on a festive atmosphere, the outcome of the stirring of different categories of people attracted by their activities: visitors to museums and recreational activities, cyclists and in-line skaters, strollers and tourists. In large cities, the contrast with the work orientation of the nearby financial district is indeed stark.

Conclusion

This chapter has concentrated on the deep transformations affecting downtowns over the last decades. While still important in large cities, their employment function has lost emphasis relative to emerging cultural, recreational, tourism, and residential roles. In the case of medium-city downtowns, however, the situation tends to be one of decline, manifested in a net loss of activity. The chapter has stressed the need for new policy approaches to downtowns that focus on quality of life (especially pedestrian hospitality) and diversity of activities and populations, along with more traditional employment strategies.

Notes

1. The fact that downtowns occupied the uncontested summit of most activity hierarchies within metropolitan regions does not mean that neighbourhoods were deprived of services. Throughout the nineteenth century, stores, together with some entertainment facilities in the halls of various fraternal organizations, emerged along the principal arterial roads of large Canadian cities. By the 1910s they had been joined by bank branches, small-scale offices, and cinemas. Distinct neighbourhood centres provided a modest degree of competition with downtown.

2. Revealingly, among these downtowns, that of Edmonton, the metropolitan region with the shortest rail transit system (12.3 vs 42.1 km in Calgary), is arguably the least vital in terms of retailing and office employment.

3. The downtown Toronto employment data originate from the City of Toronto Planning Department (Toronto, 2002) and the CMA figures are from the 1991 and 2001 censuses.

4. A similar trend towards downtown living is observed in the downtowns of US cities (Birch, 2002; Knack, 1998).

5. Although Mississauga as a whole flourished and office development in this city made the City of Toronto envious, there was not a single new office building added in the City Centre between 1991

and 2005. Land zoned for office building was rezoned for 'temporary' low-density use, including a cinema complex and a go-cart track.

6. Compiled from 2001 Transportation Tomorrow Survey data. For information on the methodology, see <www.jpint.utoronto.ca/>.

7. The threat of terrorism may further advantage dispersed suburban locales. The tendency for terrorists to target downtowns and public transit services, where intense concentrations of individuals make attacks all the more deadly, may urge firms to select high-security suburban buildings, which are easily accessible by car (Jenkins, 2001).

8. While there may be some good reasons to eliminate an expressway, the cost of doing this can be horrendous and may border on immorality given the huge number of municipal responsibilities.

Chapter 11

The Inner City

David Ley and Heather Frost

It has been said that all classifications are useful rather than true, and this statement applies with particular force to the classification of geographical regions. So a regional study, like this one, should begin both by defining its region and also by acknowledging at once that any such definition is arbitrary. While there are, undoubtedly, important themes shared by the ring of old neighbourhoods around the central business district (CBD) that we call the inner city, no single criterion, nor even a combination of criteria, permits boundaries to be drawn around urban areas with any claim to total adequacy.

With this proviso, we review in this chapter the status of, and changes among, inner cities in Canadian metropolitan areas. Beginning with a brief overview of the historical development of the inner city, we move on to employ a fourfold classification that underscores the diversity of these old (though increasingly renewed) neighbourhoods. Following some consideration of the possibility of explaining the landscape and character of the inner city in a simple theoretical model, we end by outlining a narrative that moves towards an integrated and contextual account of the inner city as an expression of societal change.

The Inner City as Perceived: The Biography of a Concept

As well as a seemingly objective profile revealed in land-use maps or census data, the inner city has a subjective identity. As presently understood, the inner city dates back to nineteenth-century industrialization and the construction of often shabbily built housing for blue-collar workers around the factories, warehouses, and construction sites adjacent to railway and water transportation and offering semi-skilled and unskilled employment. The pace of growth, the limitations on mass transportation, and the paucity of municipal bylaws contributed to high residential densities, few public services, and little environmental regulation so that the blue-collar labour force lived close by their work in often unhealthy conditions. There was, of course, a geography to such conditions, and in the early 1900s the Pittsburgh Survey recorded a fourfold differential in mortality rates between wards of that city, with the gravest rates occurring in the immigrant districts flanking the iron and steel plants.

The deprivation, pollution, and pathologies of the inner city led to middle-class avoidance. The substance and often the rhetoric of nineteenth-century images of the inner city have continued to recent decades, most notably in the United States in the polarized separations between racial minorities in the inner city and the middle class in the suburbs (Ley, 1974). Tabloids in Canadian cities also sensationalized conditions in the inner city and provided regular reinforcement of an image bound around poverty, pathology, and otherness. Rapid urban growth, particularly in the 1901–11 decade, and the arrival of immigrants from a plethora of sources seemed to be imitating earlier American experience. As Superintendent of All Peoples' Mission in Winnipeg, J.S. Woodsworth reflected on the impact of this rapid and unregulated growth and found much he could recognize from Upton

Sinclair's chronicle of the evils confronting the poor in Chicago recounted in *The Jungle* (Woodsworth, 1972 [1911]: 45). His own mission visitors were reporting similar conditions in inner Winnipeg (ibid., 70):

Shack—one table and a lean-to. Furniture—two beds, a bunk, stove, bench, two chairs, table, barrel of sauerkraut. Everything very dirty. Two families lived here. Women were dirty, unkempt, bare-footed, half-clothed. Children wore only print-slips.

By 1911, with a population nearing half a million, Montreal was the largest Canadian city. The pattern of labour conflict, municipal corruption, and poverty led a businessman, Herbert Ames, to initiate a social survey and reform campaign (Ames, 1972 [1897]). As elsewhere, rapid urbanization accompanied industrialization and the city's population had nearly doubled in the 1850s and almost increased fivefold from 1852 to 1901 (Hanna, 1986). Factory hands flooded the city from the francophone hinterland, from Britain, and from Ireland, and housing demand and marginal wages increased densities while decreasing housing quality. Spatial sorting of residential districts occurred, of which the most striking was the social precipice in the city's west end, strongly correlated with elevation above and below an escarpment. The decisive statistic was the death rate, and with infant mortality at 293 per 1,000 births in 1859, Montreal's rate far exceeded the level in New York (Olson et al., 1987). Ames estimated that the overall death rate below the hill was 70 per cent greater than that of the middle-class district above it.

Not all of the inner city consisted of poorer households, nor were all poorer households inner-city residents—significant working-class suburbanization existed in early Canadian cities (Harris, 2004; Lewis, 2004), including Montreal (Lewis, 1985), Toronto (Harris, 1996), and Vancouver (Holdsworth, 1977). But a combination of working-class households, environmental degradation, and poverty converged on the inner city to create the popular stereotype of the slum behind the industrial waterfront and around the rail yards. Ethnic and racial status compounded ignorance of the inner city by the middle class. Whether the 'out group' was the Irish Catholics of Griffintown in Montreal, the Jewish garment workers in Toronto's Spadina district (Hiebert, 1993b), or the Chinese and Japanese in Vancouver (Anderson, 1991), the presence of 'exotic' populations added to the strange and menacing image of the inner-city slum.

This unsavoury image, reinforced by social scientists obsessed with social disorganization in the inner city, helped to motivate urban renewal and slum clearance programs in Canada, as in other Western nations in the post-1945 period. In city after city the presence of old housing and high densities justified the arrival of the federal bulldozer (Moore and Smith, 1993). But slowly, a new perception of the inner city began to form. In the 1960s two important American social planners, Jane Jacobs (1961) and Herbert Gans (1962b), published ethnographic accounts of the inner city that severely challenged the dominant wisdom. Age and density, they showed, could be an asset rather than a disadvantage, sheltering a community where tight social networks and local institutions sustained a supportive social milieu that was not equalled in the frequently brutal landscapes of urban renewal. When Jacobs moved to Toronto in the late 1960s she extended her optimism to the Canadian inner city (Jacobs, 1971). Old buildings, social and land-use diversity, ethnic neighbourhoods, pedestrian travel and public transportation, urban parks and waterfronts: Jacobs's broad vision celebrated the cosmopolitan character of the inner city. To it was opposed the blandness of the freeway, high-rise city of the renewal planner, or indeed suburban conformity. The sometimes romantic vision of cosmopolitan vitality in the inner city has proven attractive to a significant minority of the professional middle class in metropolitan Canada since 1970. City living has gained a cachet it had not enjoyed since the eighteenth century in the perceptions of gentrifiers who, in eschewing suburban lifestyles, have transformed many older neighbourhoods.

Inner-City Diversity

Both the progressive reformers of the early twentieth century and the social scientists who followed them erred in their perception of the inner city. Their portrayal of social disorganization was too one-sided, and it remained for a later generation to identify the social order that existed even in slum neighbourhoods (Suttles, 1968). Moreover, a second error was to generalize the conditions of the slum to the entire inner city. In reality, central-city neighbourhoods display considerable diversity. A thoughtful classification of inner-city districts in Canada recognizes such diversity (Table 11.1), categorizing areas according to the processes of identifiable change rather than their social characteristics. Four processes are specified: decline, stability, revitalization, and massive redevelopment.

Table 11.1   **A Typology of Inner-City Neighbourhoods**

	Decline	Stability	Revitalization	Massive Redevelopment
Population	Continuing loss of population	No significant losses or gains	Little change	Gain in population
Socio-economic status	Decreasing	Stable	Increasing	Increasing
Family status	Increasing proportion of non-family units and elderly	Maintenance of population mix	Maintenance of population mix	Loss of families, gain of singles
Ethnicity	Varies: can be influx of deprived ethnic group or breaking down of traditional community	Sometimes strong ethnic community	Sometimes loss of ethnic groups	Seldom important
Community organizations	Poorly organized, unstable	Varies	Increasingly well-organized	Usually unorganized
Physical conditions	Worsening	Stable	Improving	Improved housing, possible environmental problems
Housing/land costs	Increasing much less than metro average	Increasing at same rate as metro average	Increasing more rapidly than metro average	Increasing more rapidly than metro average
Tenure	Increasing tenancy	Varies, but often high ownership	Little change	Tenancy
Non-residential functions	Loss of commercial-industrial functions with no replacement	Maintaining a mix of functions gaining others	Maintaining a mix of functions	Losing some commercial functions, but gaining others
Pressure for redevelopment	Low	Low	Strong, but controlled	High

Source: McLemore et al. (1975).

Districts in Decline

In these districts, physical deterioration of the housing stock is associated with population loss, as well as poverty and social problems among the remaining population. Property values increase slowly, and may even decline; residents are primarily tenants and turnover may be rapid. This set of traits characterizes areas that in the United States reach the ultimate stage of deterioration—widespread housing abandonment. Where scattered examples of abandonment occur, such as in parts of the North Ends of Winnipeg (Hiebert, 1992) and Halifax, or Saint-Henri and Pointe Saint-Charles in Montreal, or the Lower Ward of Toronto up to the 1960s (Mann, 1970), they are found in working-class neighbourhoods where poor housing and the collapse of the local industrial economy has contributed to low levels of demand and property disinvestment.

The deindustrialization of Montreal's 'city below the hill' has been particularly devastating (DeVerteuil, 1993, 2004). By 1986, the collapse of the economic base in the industrial southwest resulted in unemployment of over 20 per cent and demographic flight, as the population fell by one-half from its 1961 level of 107,000. A similar economic catastrophe hit the francophone waterfront neighbourhoods east of downtown (Sénécal, 1995), and in each instance recreational and tourist initiatives have featured prominently in redevelopment plans. The Lachine Canal, a former industrial thoroughfare running through the heart of the southwest, has been declared a National Historic Park, while in the east, new tourist and leisure amenities have been constructed around the Olympic Stadium. Nonetheless, these initiatives have scarcely dented the most extensive concentration of deep poverty in any Canadian inner city (Figure 11.1). East of downtown Montreal is a solid block of over 20 census tracts in acute distress where more than 40 per cent of persons fall below Statistics Canada's low-income cut-off (Ley and Smith, 2000; Séguin, 1997; Smith, 2004).[1] Unlike the patterns in Toronto and Vancouver, Montreal's geography of poverty remained remarkably stable throughout the 1990s.

While no comparable regions of such extreme poverty exist in other major cities, smaller concentrations are evident, such as a compact set of five tracts in Vancouver's inner eastside. Expanding from the traditional skid row, the Downtown Eastside began a steady decline during the 1930s. By 1965, the neighbourhood housed the city's major concentration of residential hotels, over 40 cheap cafés, 26 beer parlours, two liquor stores, and 11 Christian missions, and by the late 1980s it contained 80 per cent of the city's premises with a full liquor licence (Ley, 1994). Today, poverty and deprivation in Vancouver remain concentrated here (Blomley, 2004; Smith, 2004). Many of the area's residents are service dependent (Smith, 2002). Although elderly men who have lived in single rooms or social housing units for some time still comprise the majority of residents in Vancouver's Downtown Eastside, over the past two decades the population has diversified to include younger transients and street kids, the mentally ill, some immigrants, and families with one or more children. Districts such as these are heavily supported by the state and voluntary groups; some 40 social service agencies operate in Vancouver's Downtown Eastside, and proximity to these services (including social housing) offers a strong locational tie for residents. The district's coherence is further strengthened by strong neighbourhood associations that challenge the permissiveness typical of skid row and work to improve social services (Ley, 1994; Smith, 2002).

In the Prairie provinces, a substantial number of Aboriginal Canadians live in such districts, at least on a seasonal basis (Peters, 1996, 2002); in Winnipeg older surveys suggested a figure of up to 60 per cent (Rowley, 1978). Unemployment may be high, around 85 per cent in the Winnipeg case, and may be associated with heavy drinking (over 70 per cent of men interviewed by Rowley in the 1970s had received treatment at a detoxification centre).

Other poverty-challenged areas in the inner city are associated with a more dispersed rooming and lodging house population living in group homes for deinstitutionalized psychiatric patients and other community-based facilities. This group is at considerable risk, comprising perhaps a third of

Figure 11.1   **Incidence of Low Income among Persons in Montreal, 2001**

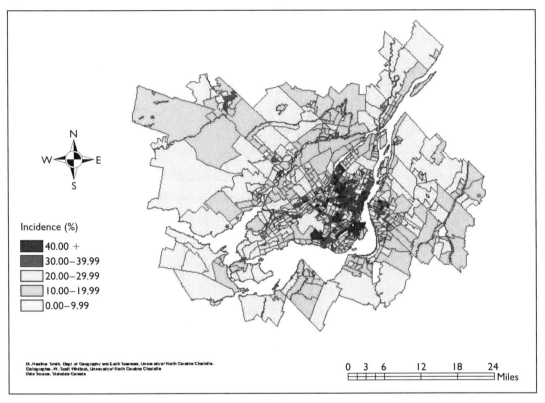

Source: Smith (2004).

the nation's homeless population, estimated in 1986 at between 130,000 and 250,000 (Dear and Wolch, 1993). Due to the availability of suitable housing, proximity to necessary services, and the presence or absence of exclusionary zoning, group homes are frequently concentrated in specific inner-city districts. South Parkdale in Toronto contained no fewer than 49 group homes, or more than a quarter of the city's total (Joseph and Hall, 1985). Such a concentration of poor and handicapped residents in aging lodging houses provides a local context for neighbourhood decline, as private reinvestment may be dissuaded by the locale's stigmatized identity (Slater, 2004).

Poverty districts are associated with other marginalized populations, including such historically persistent communities as the racial and ethnic minorities of Vancouver's Chinatown or the North Ends of Winnipeg and Halifax. During the 1990s, new immigrants have become far more prominent in districts of acute poverty (Ley and Smith, 2000; Smith, 2004). Relatively high entry levels of visible minority newcomers landing during a recession, who spoke neither official language, had limited or no Canadian job experience, and who were not the first hiring choice of employers, led to a troubling concentration of urban poor in the cheap apartment districts and public housing projects of Toronto, Vancouver, and Montreal in particular. As a result, the massive public housing projects of the 1950s and 1960s have become increasingly associated with deep poverty and where these were built in inner suburban sites, notably in Toronto, they contribute to the existence of significant suburban poverty nodes, often associated with the location of the most destitute immigrants and refugees (Murdie, 1994b, 1998). Poverty is linked as well to regional economies, for the structural unemployment of Atlantic Canada and parts of Quebec are manifested in a higher than average incidence of urban poverty. Montreal, Trois-Rivières, Quebec City and, above all, Saint John are all CMAs with twice as many census tracts showing extreme scores on an impoverishment factor as the national average (Davies and Murdie, 1993).

One reason why poverty may be less visible in urban Canada is that the various indicators of poverty do not necessarily overlap in the same district (Broadway, 1989). For example, the impoverishment factor mentioned above was dominated by the presence of female-headed families, but overlapped only slightly with two other poverty indicators, male unemployment and the presence of the elderly. But this generalization conceals considerable local variation. Indeed, in Winnipeg's North End, which has among the most extreme scores on impoverishment in urban Canada (Davies and Murdie, 1993), the geographical coincidence of poverty, female lone-parent families, and low educational attainment in neighbourhoods with a high Aboriginal population defines a state of multiple deprivation that approximates the conditions identified by the underclass theorists in the United States (Ricketts and Sawhill, 1988; Wilson, 1987). But this conjunction of events remains rare. In Toronto, Montreal, and Vancouver, analysis of the 2001 census revealed only a single census tract (in Toronto) where all four deprivation indicators used in American underclass studies (high levels of male unemployment, female-headed families, noncompletion of high school, and government transfer payments) overlapped in a single census tract (Smith, 2004).

Districts of Stability

In contrast are inner-city districts where the stability of the landscape suggests that the pressures for change are slight. Such areas have a stable population and socio-economic status, with limited land inflation and low pressures for redevelopment; home ownership rates may well be high, and property is well maintained; the presence of a cohesive social order is indicated by the objective and symbolic indicators of community, such as strong voluntary organizations and a well-defined sense of place.

Districts such as these in the inner city have been labelled 'urban villages', implying the existence of strong neighbourhood social networks, a complete range of local social institutions, and a tradition of mutual aid. The concept emerged from an ethnographic study of Italians in Boston's West End (Gans, 1962b), for despite a slum appearance associated with age and high densities, the district had a strong sense of local community. Its social fabric resulted from chain migration, which through kin networks had led immigrants of comparable socioeconomic status to the same area. Similarly, there is a significant voluntary component to the map of ethnic segregation in Canadian cities, though such communities have usually unfolded within the context of below-average economic status. But the formation of voluntary segregation has not always been evident, as racial discrimination played a decisive role in the residential distribution of Jewish and Asian immigrants in the early twentieth century (Anderson, 1991).

High levels of immigrant home ownership (Ray and Moore, 1991) contribute to a well-maintained housing stock, with substantial home improvement completed most often with family and friends. In Vancouver's Grandview-Woodlands neighbourhood, a working-class area with a well-defined Italian presence from the 1960s to the 1980s, interviews revealed a marked sense of pride of home; indeed, without government grants over 90 per cent of interviewees had made major repairs in the previous five years (Mercer and Phillips, 1981; Murdie and Teixeira, 2003). Canada's national policy of multiculturalism has encouraged such stable ethnic communities to express further their identity and pride in the built environment. Along the main business thoroughfare of Grandview-Woodlands, an earlier ethnic modesty has given way to the amplification of ethnic symbols in brightly coloured shop awnings, frequently with the green, white, and red motif of the Italian flag, distinctive signage, and Mediterranean design elements. Community solidarity appears in the distribution of ethnic churches, temples, mosques, or gurdwaras (Beattie and Ley, 2003), and the incidence of voluntary organizations (Owusu, 2000), demonstrates dense social networks.

The mutuality of identity and landscape, strengthened by the legitimating power of multiculturalism, has in some instances heightened the sense of ethnic proprietorship of neighbourhoods. This collective view of ethnic turf, aided by the icons of present and past cultural difference, may well be recognized by municipal councils and written into zoning and other protective bylaws (Anderson, 1991). Where older and less inclusive administrative styles have persisted, however, the status of ethnic communities has been precarious before more powerful interests; not untypical was the demolition of much of Montreal's Chinatown in the 1970s to accommodate a large complex of government offices.

In recent decades, examples of stable working-class communities of Northern European origin have been rare (Lorimer and Phillips, 1971), though stable francophone districts remain in Quebec City and the east island of Montreal. Until the 1980s, the bastions of stability of British-origin groups in the inner city were the upper-middle-class and elite districts close to downtown, which are such a persistent feature of the Canadian city (Beaudet, 1987; Ley, 1993). In the 1970s, close to 70 per cent of Shaughnessy residents in Vancouver claimed British origin. This inner-city district has been the wealthiest in Vancouver; it has over 70 per cent home ownership and, until the mid-1980s, enjoyed little population turnover. Households were stable—indeed, many adults were living in their childhood neighbourhoods. The district's landscape advertises its identity; curving streets, architect-designed homes in mainly European revival styles on spacious lots, and a supportive institutional cast of prominent churches, private schools, and social clubs, with a concentration of up-market shops on the district's edge.

The old elite neighbourhood is repeated as a type across the country from the Uplands in Victoria to Halifax's South End, and with few exceptions these districts have shown remarkable longevity in the twentieth century. By 1899, the southern half of Rosedale in Toronto was already a substantial elite community, and it has retained its status since. In Calgary the inner district of Mount Royal, developed before 1920 by the Canadian Pacific Railway as an exclusive neighbourhood, has upheld its social cachet. Since 1920 elite districts have expanded but they have rarely been displaced, and their locational stability is remarkable, considering urban growth and redevelopment pressures. The Toronto CMA, for example, grew sixfold from 1921 to 1981, with attendant pressures for residential redevelopment and downtown expansion, yet the innermost Rosedale tracts have experienced little decline in social stability.

Such stability has been accomplished through restrictive planning controls. In Westmount (close to downtown Montreal), municipal autonomy added political muscle to land use protection, while Shaughnessy, thwarted in its efforts at political secession early in the twentieth century, was nonetheless successful in acquiring protective zoning through a special act of the British Columbia legislature. Not unusual was a restrictive covenant, mandatory for homeowners in Calgary's Mount Royal, whose terms included a prohibition on commercial land uses, minimum lot sizes and house prices, and the requirement that single-family dwellings be the exclusive use (Beaudet, 1987). In each district vigilant homeowners' associations oversaw the conformity of the built environment with an elite protocol (Duncan, 1994).

In the acute land pressures of the 1980s some significant social and land-use changes influenced even elite districts. Modest infill increased densities, though it has not diminished prices or status. More substantial is an emerging transition in the complexion of the elite themselves. In Westmount, francophones are replacing the departing anglophone business elite, while in Shaughnessy new Asian wealth, particularly from Hong Kong, is evident (Ley, 1995; Mitchell, 2004). Other in-town elite districts similarly reflect the growing reality of multiculturalism and the diversity of Canada's international relations.

Districts of 'Revitalization'

In 1971 inner-city neighbourhoods in Canadian CMAs were 25 per cent over-represented by residents aged over 15 years with a university education, while during the 1970s the rate of expansion of degree holders in the inner city was double that of the CMA (Filion, 1987). Other socio-economic measures, notably occupations, tell the same story, for by the 1990s inner-city residents showed an over-representation of some 20 per cent in the proportions of professional and managerial jobs in the five largest cities; indeed, inner-city residents employed in these sectors grew by over 150,000 between 1971 and 1991 (Ley, 1996a). These changes are indicators of gentrification, the movement of middle-class professionals into lower-cost inner-city districts, accompanied by the renovation or redevelopment of the housing stock (Slater, 2005). Yet, despite gentrification, there has not been a marked elevation of inner-city household incomes relative to the CMA mean, except where there are double-income professional households (Bourne, 1993a; Rose and Villeneuve, 1998) (see Chapters 8 and 9). Of course, this is in part an outcome of the growing reality of two-wage-earner households in the suburbs, while the inner-city share of single-person households rises. However, in CMAs that have experienced slow growth and deindustrialization without significant downtown office development, the inner city has felt limited reinvestment pressure and persists as the home of a much broader grouping of poor households, including the unemployed, the elderly, and female lone-parent families (Broadway, 1992).

From meek beginnings in the 1960s, residential reinvestment by the middle class has expanded substantially in cities with a post-industrial service profile and a concentration of professional and managerial jobs in the core. In its original, and narrow, definition, gentrification described the renovation of older housing stock, such as has occurred in areas like Don Vale (Cabbagetown) in Toronto,

Plateau Mont-Royal in Montreal, and New Edinburgh in Ottawa. However, even in these districts, renovation is associated with infill and localized redevelopment. In cities like Vancouver and Victoria, where the building material of older homes is wood rather than brick, revitalization typically occurs as condominium redevelopment. Whether the dominant process is renovation or redevelopment, gentrifying districts are characterized by often spectacular short-term increases in land and housing costs, modest gains in home-ownership rates, and a well-educated and primarily childless population of young professional households with a growing population of empty nesters.

While up-filtering is discernible in smaller cities like Kitchener (Bunting, 1987), Saskatoon (Phipps, 1983), and Halifax (Millward and Davis, 1986), it is particularly evident in Canada's major cities (Caulfield, 1994; Ley, 1996a; Rose, 1996; Germain and Rose, 2000). The rate of change quickened appreciably in the 1970s, and during that decade the level of social status gain among inner-city residents was four times greater than it had been during the 1960s (Ley, 1988), so that by 1981 the inner cities actually contained a higher proportion of professionals and managers than the suburbs, a trend that has continued to the present. The location of reinvestment is not indiscriminate, and in major cities discernible patterns occur across the map (Figure 11.2). Trends in social status change are recorded by quintile and show clear tendencies towards concentration, with the highest rate of change in Toronto in the 1990s on the west side of downtown, in contrast to the eastward movements of the 1970s and 1980s around such early high-ranking cores as Don Vale (tracts 67 and 68 on Figure 11.2) and Riverdale (tracts 69, 70, and 71). During the 1970s, the best predictor of gains in social status was a census tract's proximity to an existing elite area; in the case of Toronto, for example, six of the seven locations of early gentrification wrapped around the downtown edges of Rosedale and the Annex, established higher-status districts (Ley, 1996a). By the 1980s, settlement by the middle class was more adventurous, occurring in areas some distance from established nodes.

Figure 11.2 **Changes in Social Status in the (pre-1998) City of Toronto, 1991–2001**

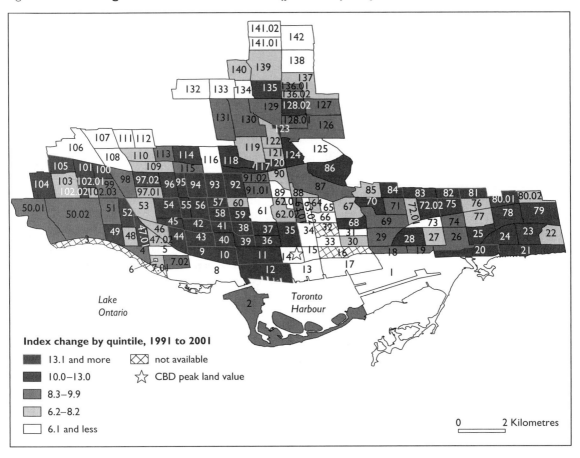

Particularly where the renovation (rather than redevelopment) of older houses is the dominant process, gentrification commonly—though not invariably—proceeds in stages (Gale, 1980). In the initial stage existing residents are joined by pre-professionals (students), artists, media groups, and certain other professionals, who are generally liberal or radical in their lifestyle and politics. This picture describes the character of Kitsilano and Cabbagetown in 1968–72 and Toronto's Queen Street West and Montreal's Rue St-Denis a decade later. Early gentrifiers are attracted to the socio-cultural diversity of the inner city and its affordable housing and while their incomes are modest, they help redefine the character of a district, paving the way for its commercialization and more substantial transition. Here artists have been especially instrumental.

In 1991 over half of Canada's artists were living in Toronto, Montreal, or Vancouver, and they have continued to concentrate in these metropoles, congregating in central locations with a 'marginal', 'gritty', 'authentic' feel, with relatively cheap rents and a tolerant and vibrant social scene (Ley, 1996a, 2003a). They seek out 'improvisational spaces', which have not been 'coiffed', homogenized, or 'cleansed to cater to middle-class sensibilities and consumptive tendencies', to stimulate and sustain their creative work and identities (Bain, 2003: 312). For these reasons, artists tend to live and work in older, low-income neighbourhoods. For instance, one artist estimated that over 600 artists presently live in South Parkdale in Toronto, a district that has included a large deinstitutionalized population of mentally handicapped residents (Slater, 2004). By locating in such neighbourhoods, artists render these places culturally desirable and target them for middle-class reinvestment. As the neighbourhood's image changes, subsequent purchasers are buying into an inflating market. Later buyers include wealthier professionals such as doctors and lawyers, who tend to be more protective of their investments and who regard the social mix more ambivalently or resist it altogether. At this stage pioneering professionals shift their focus to other districts, usually nearby, and a spatial diffusion of gentrification may be observed. In Toronto, for example, escalating prices in Don Vale caused middle-class demand to spill over to Riverdale to the east (Dantas, 1988). From there, by the 1990s gentrifiers had sought out cheaper neighbourhoods, moving for the first time to the inner western neighbourhoods (Figure 11.2).

The local impacts of gentrification are multi-faceted but the most dramatic impact is on the housing market, where in extreme cases prices have doubled in as little as two years (Don Vale, 1979–81; Fairview Slopes in Vancouver, 1980–1). There has been a predictable displacement of tenants and replacement of homeowners from affordable housing as a result (Ley, 1996a). Relocation occurs, if possible, nearby, though tenants typically pay higher rents for smaller units. The loss of affordable housing in the inner city has been precipitous. In Vancouver, some 7,500 rental units were demolished between 1973 and 1981, primarily in districts undergoing condominium redevelopment. The Toronto situation is even more serious; 18,000 tenancies were lost in the deconversion of joint owner-tenant properties back to single-family use in the 1976–85 period, while from 1981 to 1986 over 9,000 rental apartments were lost through various forms of upgrading (Howell, 1986). Housing at the bottom end of the market, including rooming houses and residential hotels, has been most vul-

nerable, and though gentrification is not the only factor implicated, it does play a major role. In Ottawa, municipal data record the loss of 40 per cent of the city's rooming house units in only three years, from 1976 to 1979, 70 per cent of which occurred in Sandy Hill and Centretown—wards where gentrification was the most marked. In this respect we can see how gentrification was implicated in the homelessness that appeared in the 1980s, in part due to the loss of inner-city affordable housing.

Retail upgrading and heritage revitalization commonly accompany gentrification. Retail landscapes are transformed as specialty clothing boutiques, ethnic restaurants, trendy cafés, and pubs emerge to satisfy the demands of an urbane middle-class clientele. In many instances, heritage restoration works to enhance a district's commercial appeal. The revitalization of Byward Market helped to galvanize reinvestment in Lower Town West, once the historic heart of Ottawa, which had declined into a 'zone of discard'. By the late 1990s, the Byward Market was the hub of the city's nightlife, shopping, and leisure activity; while an economic recession stalled commercial growth in other parts of the city during the 1990s, new restaurants and bars continued to vie for space in the market (Tunbridge, 1986, 2001). More recently, the Business Improvement Association in South Parkdale, Toronto, has sought to lure commerce to the area by evoking its more illustrious past, redesignating it the 'Village of Parkdale, 1879' (Slater, 2004).

Areas of Massive Redevelopment

Gentrification in the 1970s and 1980s followed, and was in many ways a reaction against the massive urban redevelopment that had taken place in inner-city districts in the 1950s and 1960s. In that earlier period housing stock was aging, and downtown employment growth sustained a lively demand, while permissive zoning allowed extensive apartment construction. Simultaneously, the public sector, motivated by its perception of urban slums, initiated a significant slum clearance and urban renewal program.

Massive redevelopment entailed population growth, but also a changing household composition. In districts like Vancouver's West End and St James Town in Toronto (Sewell, 1993), high-rise rental construction led to the replacement of families by one- and two-person households of somewhat higher social status. While the housing units were generally of good quality, high densities from a concentration of projects did not enhance cohesive social organization, particularly with rapid tenant turnover. In St James Town, the highest-density precinct in Canada in the 1960s, the 1971 census showed a population increase of 32 per cent, with over 70 per cent of residents (mostly tenants) having lived in the complex for less than two years. In recent years St James Town has become a major centre of initial immigrant settlement and experienced declining economic status.

The early location of apartment development, particularly high-rise development, was strongly site-specific. In Toronto, apartments were built in nodes with good access to the CBD, close to environmental amenities and biased towards higher-income sectors (Bourne, 1967). This trend was maintained in other cities also. The West End, adjacent to Stanley Park and the English Bay beaches, had been Vancouver's first elite district, as had Parliament Hill and Oliver in Edmonton, the sites of that city's major concentration of rental high-rise apartments (McCann, 1975). Even in smaller cities like Victoria, high-rises were drawn to in-town locations with generous amenities; despite above-average rents, waterfront settings boast the city's lowest vacancy rates (Murphy, 1973). The distribution of apartments constructed during the 1968–71 building boom in Victoria demonstrates the spatial regularities found in larger cities (Figure 11.3). A third of new units were built within a mile of the main downtown traffic intersection, while outlying concentrations tended to be built on major arteries. A strong locational bias south of downtown abutted ocean frontage and Beacon Hill Park, while the disproportionate concentration on the sector leading east to Cadboro Bay Road runs through the old, elite, Rockland district and towards the present high-status areas of Oak Bay.

Public-sector redevelopment also assumed a predictable, though somewhat different, pattern. While population densities generally rose, there was not necessarily a decline in the proportion of family households. Nor was there an increase in socioeconomic status. High levels of unemployment and poverty in concentrated locations rarely led to a positive social environment. Slum clearance by the state was empowered in the National Housing Act of 1944, and its first project was the clearance and redevelopment of Regent Park North east of downtown Toronto (Moore and Smith, 1993; Sewell, 1993). The 1,300 mainly medium-density units were joined by more than 700 additional units in row houses, low-rise apartments, and five high-rise projects in Regent Park South 10 years later. The result is a massive and demoralizing concentration of poverty, an outcome repeated in the vast Jeanne-Mance project in Montreal, as well as elsewhere.

The scale of urban renewal involved major dislocation of existing land uses and residents (Barcelo, 1988), with many residents reluctant to move. For instance, in Victoria, the Rose-Blanshard renewal project displaced 157 poor households (Robertson, 1973) and the city's relocation officer noted that he found 'many problem family units . . . the matter of relocating these persons will present a most formidable difficulty.' There were also obstacles in purchasing from some owners (Robertson, 1973: 55):

> With regard to the holdout realty owners still on the site, the majority of these are occupants who will not sell until they are offered sufficient money to be able to purchase comparable accommodation elsewhere. . . . This group of owners are unlikely to be intimidated by any means the Urban Renewal Authority can employ.

The insensitivity of slum clearance and the community mobilization it engendered, together with the social and design failure of massive renewal housing projects, led eventually to the suspension of these schemes. In 1969 a federal task force reported sternly on the public housing projects that were a

Figure 11.3 **New Apartment Units in Victoria, 1968–1971**

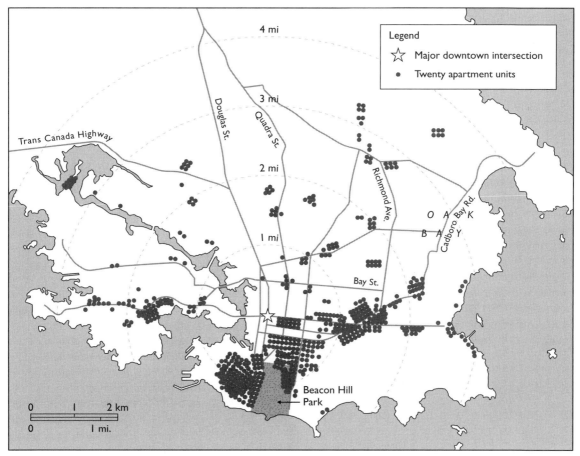

Source: Adapted from Murphy (1973).

common outcome of urban renewal, calling them 'ghettos of the poor' and places of 'stigma' and 'alienation'. During the 1970s federal policy shifted decisively away from large-scale clearance and rebuilding to more incremental policies of housing rehabilitation and neighbourhood enhancement; whereas in 1970 all federal monies were committed to renewal, by 1979 the ratio of rehabilitation and improvement funds to renewal was of the order of 50 to one.

This is not to say that publicly inspired residential redevelopment did not occur in the inner city in the 1970s and 1980s. Large schemes, both publicly sponsored and private, housing hundreds or even thousands of residents were undertaken in a number of cities, including Toronto (St Lawrence, Harbourfront) and Vancouver (False Creek South). But there were significant departures from the 1950s and 1960s in that densities were lower while design standards were higher, there was some social mixing, and most importantly, development of former industrial land meant there was no residential displacement (Hulchanski, 1984; Ley, 1987). During the 1990s, however, the construction of publicly subsidized and low-cost housing in cities across Canada was suspended by the federal government, tightening the housing market and intensifying housing affordability stress (Bunting et al., 2004; Moore and Skaburskis, 2004) (see Chapter 15).

In contrast, recent years have brought massive private redevelopment to Canada's emerging global cities. The construction of privately funded 'megaprojects' initiated the ongoing transformation of Toronto's and Vancouver's skylines by ushering in an era of transnational urban property development. Such projects are consistent with previous phases of private redevelopment in that they seek out amenity-rich central locations, and, consistent with earlier gentrification, they raise social status; however, they are distinct because they are commonly on brownfield sites and driven by global financial flows and social linkages. The development of Concord Pacific, a $3 billion condominium complex constructed on former industrial land and the site of the 1986 World Exposition on the edge of downtown Vancouver, is the purest example of this trend. In 1988 the government of British Columbia sold the 80-hectare section of waterfront land to the Li Group, presided over by Li Ka-Shing, 'Hong Kong's richest, most powerful and well-connected property tycoon' (Olds, 1998, 2001).[2] Concord Pacific Place—followed since by its Toronto sibling, Concord CityPlace, also built on a large, central brownfield site—is one of North America's largest redevelopment projects, a symbol of the deepening relationships between Canada and Pacific Asia, and exemplifying how contemporary inner cities are being shaped by global flows of people and capital (see Chapter 4).

The Inner City: Interpreting a Complex Region

The inner city becomes more diffuse as an object of study as we approach it empirically. There are no unequivocal grounds for delimiting it as a geographical region, and while we may set out objective or subjective indicators to establish a profile, both statistical and perceptual overviews obscure the diversity between districts and also overlook the dynamic elements of sometimes rapid urban change. Moreover, a variety of transitional processes occur within the same city and at the same time. Over a few square kilometres in inner Halifax, decline, stability, incumbent upgrading, and gentrification have been identified as present simultaneously (Figure 11.4). Nor is there any necessary relationship between household change and change in the housing stock; renovation, for example, occurs both in gentrifying and non-gentrifying districts.

There are nonetheless brave souls who have sought to contain this diversity within a single explanatory account. The Chicago School and neo-classical models maintain that urban land is sorted according to consumer demand, while more recent Marxist interpretations suggest that capital takes precedence in moulding landscapes. Still other explanations resist an economic emphasis. It is argued that the marketplace does not capture other dimensions along which urban land is valued, such as amenity, recreation, or heritage, or the political and legal processes through which public and private institutions (the state, the courts, land development corporations) interact with residents to influence urban landscapes.

Explanatory accounts of inner-city neighbourhoods, then, profitably recognize both the diversity of places and the range of processes that act on them. An assessment of reasons for inner-city decline identified nine more or less competing explanations (Table 11.2). A convincing case could be made for the salience of any of these explanations, while at different periods they have risen or fallen in importance. Moreover, there is a geographic specificity to the incidence of these processes; between regions, for example, we cannot expect cities to share a common age or economic structure; between nations, the explanations require certain institutional and inter-group relationships that are not constant, not even between Canada and the United States (see Chapter 2).

Theoretical explanations are not necessarily geographically portable; an attempt to assess recent inner-city trends in Canada using a primarily

Figure 11.4 **Process of Change in Single-Family Homes in Inner Halifax, 1977–1984**

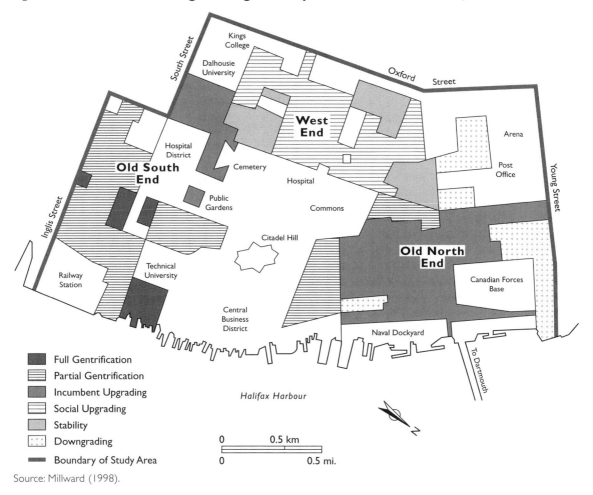

Source: Millward (1998).

American literature, which discusses centrifugal (suburbanization) versus centripetal (inner-city revitalization) processes, concluded that these competing arguments lose much of their explanatory power when faced with a Canadian object of study (Filion, 1987). A related study came to the same conclusion: 'immense regional and intraurban diversity remains. No single model of urban structure is sufficient to capture this diversity' (Bourne, 1987; see also Simmons et al., 2004).

The Inner City and Societal Change

The relative failure of any single-variable account to explain adequately inner-city landscapes and cultures suggests the wisdom of an integrated perspective, while the fact that the profile of the inner city is geographically and historically contingent indicates the necessity for fully contextual interpretation of the variable and evolving pattern of

---

Table 11.2   **A Typology of Explanations of Inner-City Decline**

Explanation	Dominant Process(es)
Natural evolution	Urban growth, ecological succession, down-filtering
Preference structure	Middle-class flight to the suburbs
Obsolescence	Aging of built environment and social infrastructure
Unintended effects of public policy	Suburban subsidies, including construction of freeways and aids to new single-family home ownership
Exploitation (1)	City manipulated by more powerful suburbs
Exploitation (2)	Institutional exploitation: redlining by financial institutions; tax concessions; suburbanization of factories
Structural change	Deindustrialization and economic decline
Fiscal crisis	Inequitable tax burden; high welfare, social, and infrastructure costs
Conflict	Racial and class polarization

Source: Adapted from Bourne (1982).

---

land uses and landscapes. Integration and contextualization together prescribe a distinctive regional geography of the Canadian inner city in transition.

What would that regional geography look like? It would recognize the nineteenth-century origins of the inner city in a rapidly industrializing and urbanizing society. In a largely unregulated urban milieu where industry promised rapid investment returns, industrial land use dominated, infiltrating almost any territory, even the neighbourhoods of the elite (Goheen, 1970). Until the adoption of the electric streetcar in the 1890s, mass transit was very limited, obliging the industrial workforce to live within a short distance of their work. Meanwhile, immigration depressed industrial wages while inflating housing demand. With sustained demand, incentives for improving the housing stock for the poor were limited, and municipal bylaws and enforcement standards were permissive.

But if the middle class withdrew they did not necessarily withdraw far. In the case of the elite, it was only a few kilometres before they put down roots. These high-status neighbourhoods were in turn quickly leapfrogged by the middle and respectable working classes as the electric streetcar and, later, mass-produced motor cars opened new territory. Following municipal reform during the early 1900s, a more active local state used zoning to regulate urban land use, providing the means to protect privileged districts from unwanted change. But urban boosterism remained the dominant ethos, and pro-development decisions came naturally to politicians who were also businessmen, sharing a common ideology of growth and progress.

In the post-1945 era the societal contexts impacting the inner city in Canada became more complex. Both suburbanization and the closure of old industries in the zone in transition around downtown were part of a restructuring of the central-city economy. Another element was the explosive growth of the service sector and the subsequent development of the CBD as the preferred location of corporate head offices and producer services, including finance and business services (see Chapter 10). Equally important were the burgeoning public sector and related non-profit professions, notably in teaching and health care.

This new middle class of professional and administrative workers has provided a key social group in inner-city restructuring of parts of the largest Canadian CMAs in the past 25 years. Through infill housing it has consolidated the status of the old elite districts, and from these bastions its more adventurous and non-conformist members have contributed to ever-advancing waves of residential renovation and redevelopment. As well as the housing stock, neighbourhood social infrastructure has been transformed; churches, schools, and thrift stores have been replaced by leisure and fitness centres, pubs and restaurants, and specialty and designer boutiques. The transformed retail landscapes of Spring Garden Road in Halifax, Rue St-Denis and Ste-Catherine in Montreal, Yorkville and Queen Street West in Toronto, and Granville Island and Fourth Avenue in Vancouver represent a broader transition towards the construction of landscapes of consumption in the inner city. New parks, new museums, refurbished theatres, concert halls and historic districts, casinos, the cycle of annual festivals and the periodic infusion of an Expo, the Olympics, or Commonwealth Games—all have transformed parts of the inner city into a consumption cornucopia. And in these landscapes, which proclaim so eloquently the power of the pleasure principle, the state is fully implicated.

At the municipal scale, civic politics underwent considerable change in the early 1970s in a number of major cities. The political power of the new middle class was expressed in their defence of neighbourhoods before the encroachment of freeways and high-density redevelopment, a curious, somewhat paradoxical mix of radicalism and NIMBYism. Inner-city districts faced the brunt of land-use change, and here locational conflict was most acute. Local councils down-zoned inner-city districts to lower densities, and senior government responded by abandoning urban renewal in favour of neighbourhood conservation and rehabilitation.

Pro-development councils were challenged, and urban politics and land-use decision-making entered a more plural and combative phase (Hasson and Ley, 1994).

Urban reform politics in the 1970s possessed a significant environmental and social justice edge, but in recent decades these gains have often been eroded as the federal and most provincial governments have retreated from their earlier involvement. Over the past 20 years, government deficits and the advancement of neo-liberal politics have meant a shift in political priorities, and throughout the 1990s cutbacks occurred in social assistance benefits, support services, and transfer payments to households. The effects of a shrinking welfare state have been particularly severe in Canadian cities as these changes have occurred in conjunction with post-Fordist economic restructuring. The shift towards predominantly service-based urban economies has resulted in a polarized occupational profile; while a significant minority of jobs offer good-paying employment in the quaternary sector of managerial, professional, and related fields, many well-paid manufacturing jobs have been replaced by low-wage employment in the unskilled or semi-skilled service sector. Historically, job market inequalities such as these were offset by social welfare measures so that income inequalities remained relatively constant (Bourne and Rose, 2001). Today, however, with less government support, there exists growing income polarization in the inner city.

Analyses of income distributions in the Toronto CMA (Bourne, 1993a, 1997; Walks, 2001) reveal an above-average incidence of low-income families in the (pre-1998) City of Toronto and the highest level of income polarization in the metropolitan area. A rough measure of economic disparity may be derived by comparing mean and median incomes. The disparity index in Table 11.3 shows that in the new suburbs income variation was modest, and while it was higher in the older municipalities, it reached by far its highest level in the old City of Toronto. Polarization, moreover, was intensifying during the latter half of the 1980s. Considerable evidence indicates that conditions have continued to worsen in more recent years; in every province

Table 11.3   **Variations in Household Income, Toronto CMA, 1985, 1990**

Municipality	Household Income ($)				Index of Income Disparity[1]		Per cent Low-Income Families[2]	
	Average		Median					
	1985	1990	1985	1990	1985	1990	1985	1990
Toronto CMA	100	100	100	100	16.6	18.8	10.6	14.6
	(59,450)	(36,890)	(50,049)	(43,025)				
Older central municipalities								
City of Toronto	91		79		34.1		16.5	
East York	81	83	81	77	16.2	31.7	11.8	21.7
York	75		75		16.6		15.6	
Older suburbs								
Etobicoke	102		102		17.2		9.6	
North York	101	95	94	94	24.3	22.7	12.9	17.5
Scarborough	95		103		8.4		11.7	
Newer suburbs								
Oakville	124		129		12.0		4.7	
Mississauga	109		114		10.8		7.5	
Brampton	105		117		4.8		6.5	
Vaughan	128	122	131	126	13.9	13.4	6.1	8.5
Richmond Hill	116		120		12.9		5.2	
Markham	140		143		14.8		4.3	
Pickering	118		131		5.2		5.9	

[1]An index of income skewness (I), where $I = \dfrac{(\text{Average} - \text{median income})}{\text{Median Income}} \times 100\%$

[2]Using Statistics Canada's definition of the minimum income needed to sustain a family.

Source: Adapted from Bourne (1993, 1997).

and CMA the low-income population grew proportionally between 1990 and 1995. In Vancouver, one of the nation's wealthier CMAs, the average family income was eroded by 10 per cent in constant dollars between 1990 and 1995 (GVRD, 1998). Within the City of Vancouver, the share of families who fell below the low-income cut-offs had risen from a fifth in 1986 to one-quarter in 1996, appreciably above the metropolitan level of 19 per cent. But most striking of all was the fact that despite the overall downturn in economic fortunes, the income category with the most pronounced growth through the first half of the 1990s was the top category, families earning in excess of $70,000 (Figure 11.5). Conditions improved somewhat over the most recent decade, but in recession the vulnerabilities of the poor were repeatedly bared.

The changing socio-economic circumstances, which have given rise to inequality and deepening impoverishment, have also served to generate a 'new' form of poverty (see also Chapter 25). Historically, poverty has been attributed to personal factors assumed to impede or prevent full employment, such as old age, disability, or health problems (including substance abuse and mental illness). Since the 1980s, inner-city poverty has broadened to include greater numbers of recent immigrants and refugees, young people, and families, particularly female-led, single-parent households.

While problems with housing affordability typically arise in the context of an inflated real estate market, where excessive demand has driven up housing costs, and/or in situations where housing costs outstrip incomes, the underlying causes for these circumstances vary from city to city. Compare,

for example, the growing divergence of housing and property markets in Vancouver and Toronto, the most internationalized of Canadian cities, with trends elsewhere in the urban system (Ley and Tutchener, 2001; Ley et al., 2002). Although housing prices rose steadily between 1971 and 1996 in all eight of the largest metropolitan areas, by the mid-1980s prices in Toronto and Vancouver, and their satellites, Hamilton and Victoria, began to diverge greatly. The rapid growth of immigration after 1986 and its concentration in Toronto and Vancouver have encouraged distinctive house price trajectories in these cities that reflect an international property market, unlike the regional and national processes that dominate other urban markets. Moreover, price inflation has been greatest in central neighbourhoods. Consequently, the stress on affordability in Toronto and Vancouver is uniquely related to their global status as Canada's leading destinations of immigrants. Throughout the 1990s this trend became more pronounced. In many ways, it is the pursuit of international status—to be distinguished as a 'world city'—that drives contemporary urban politics and best summarizes the present regime shaping inner cities. For the past 20 years,

Figure 11.5 **Average Family Income Groupings, Vancouver CMA, 1990 and 1995**

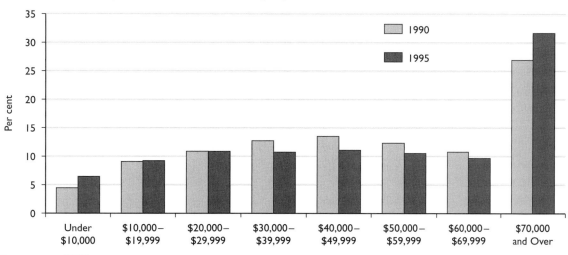

Source: GVRD (1988).

middle-class elites in Montreal have been allying with transnational capital in an attempt to 're-internationalize' the city, to sell it as a 'global city'. Montreal has been rebranded as the 'City of Festivals' and each year hosts and sponsors five internationally renowned events, among them the Montreal International Jazz Festival, which has become the largest tourist event in Canada (Paul, 2004). Similarly, the City of Ottawa sought to enhance its global profile through tourism; the city's calendar features 26 festivals and events, including May's Tulip Festival and Canada Day celebrations (Tunbridge, 2001). In the late 1990s, the City of Toronto supported a private bid for the 2008 Olympic Games, which, had it been successful, would have catalyzed a $12 billion waterfront revitalization strategy (Kipfer and Keil, 2002). Efforts such as these are founded on competition, entrepreneurialism, and image-making, and the inner city stands to be transformed most substantially as cities remake themselves in the pursuit of global aspirations and to secure a place in the global political economy.

Notes

1. The large concentration of poverty to the northwest of the City of Montreal boundary, visible in Figure 11.1, is an anomaly. It results from the assignment of the low-income level of a small apartment district to an extensive, predominantly non-residential census tract.

2. The development was overseen by Li's eldest son, Victor; it was his opportunity to earn experience and develop a reputation while diversifying his family's investment portfolio and securing a social and corporate base in Canada. Vancouver was chosen because of its supportive socio-cultural atmosphere, related to the strong and growing presence of ethnic Chinese immigrants and the city's political and economic ties to the Pacific Rim.

Chapter 12

Suburbs

Peter J. Smith

Of all the ways in which Canadian cities have been transformed since World War II, none has had such far-reaching effects, or wrought such immense changes to the Canadian way of life, as suburbanization. There were certainly suburbs before 1946, reaching back at least into the nineteenth century, but the era of large-scale suburban development and wholesale suburban living was very much a product of the new post-war economy (Bourne, 1993b).[1] Since then, urban growth has largely been *sub*urban growth, and the urbanization of Canada's population, which is one of the truly fundamental changes of the twentieth century, has actually meant its *sub*urbanization. Between 1951 and 2001, Canada's urban population increased by about 16 million, a threefold increase that accounted for 95 per cent of the country's total population growth. And where did all this growth take place? Mostly on the margins of existing cities: in their suburbs.

These few facts are enough on their own to make suburbanization a highly significant phenomenon, but suburbs are more than just a mechanism by which cities grow. They are profoundly important social phenomena as well, 'the fullest, most unadulterated embodiment of contemporary culture', as Jackson (1985: 4) puts it, and the prime arena in which cultural changes of all kinds play themselves out. And when cultural change is combined with rapid population growth, as has so often been the case in Canada, the consequences are enormous, for cities at large no less than for their suburbs. As suburbs grow and change, so, too, do the cities that house them, a pattern of mutual adjustment that goes far to explain why Canadian cities are 'in transition'. Indeed, the whole concept of

transition has particular relevance for the suburbs. There are, for example, the critical transitions that occur with the very act of suburban development, when rural land is first converted into urban use and environmental systems are irrevocably modified. In a rather different sense, suburbs themselves can be thought of as a transitional kind of development, which Rowe (1991), in a neat double entendre, calls the 'middle landscape'—a landscape that falls between the extremes of densely built-up urban core and open countryside, in form and appearance no less than in location. Then there are the temporal transitions to which suburban development inevitably gives rise, the transitions in metropolitan form and social organization as small, compact, essentially pedestrian cities evolved into vast sprawling agglomerations in thrall to the automobile. Established suburbs, too, go through complex transitions over time, a mix of demographic, social, economic, and physical changes that are constantly reshaping the suburban pattern. All have large geographical and planning implications, which this chapter aims to explore.

Suburbs in Metropolitan Context

Suburbs are an integral part of the modern city. Every city in Canada has its suburbs, and any model of city structure must express that reality. It also follows, thinking of cities as economic and social systems, that suburbs are inextricably linked with all the other elements that together make up the city. Although they serve their own particular purposes (otherwise, why bother to distinguish them?), those purposes are determined in relation to the larger whole. Suburbs cannot exist apart from the cities to which they belong.

These are extremely broad principles, of course, and for all their theoretical importance they do not begin to capture the complexity and variety of suburban experience. Moreover, they appear to be at odds with how suburbs are so often represented, especially in popular writing where cities and suburbs tend to be treated as separate entities—separate and quite different. Sometimes, suburbs are even described as parasites, implying that their relationship with cities is neither necessary nor healthy. And although this confusion can often be put down to a loose use of the words 'city' and 'suburb', there is a truly fundamental problem here as well, the conceptual problem of determining exactly what a suburb is and how it differs from other parts of the city. Suburbs today come in surprising diversity, including such 'a wide range of communities and landscape forms' (Pratt, 2000: 805) that their common properties are quite obscured. It is even hard to tell where reality ends and myth takes over, so hedged about are suburbs in popular perception with outworn clichés and inadequate stereotypes (Bourne, 1996a).

In contrast to the ambiguity that clouds the concept of the suburb today, its original usage was simplicity personified. 'Sub' in this context means near, and the English word 'suburb' derives from the Latin, *suburbanum*, meaning a villa or country estate near Rome. In similar vein, the first modern suburbs appeared in the eighteenth century, when wealthy merchants began to take up second residences within carriage drive of London and other large commercial cities.[2] Soon many of these merchants were living permanently outside the cities where their businesses were located. They were creating the first true dormitory suburbs, small communities of large, spaciously laid-out houses in a near-rural setting. Fishman (1987) has labelled them 'bourgeois utopias', living prototypes of the suburban ideal whose influence throughout the Anglo-American world has been both lasting and profound.

From this limited beginning, under the impact of urbanization and industrialization and the economic and social changes that followed in their wake, suburbs gradually came to be associated with a highly varied array of development forms and conditions. Ironically, however, the more diverse suburbs became, the more difficult it was to generalize about them on any basis except their location. Donaldson (1969: ix) affords a neat example: 'A *suburb*', he writes, 'is defined simply as a community lying within commuting distance of a central city.'[3] Yet the reality is far from simple, for while commuting distance has the advantage of being more technical than such vague descriptions as 'near' or 'close', it is still a misleading way of characterizing suburbs. With modern transport facilities, commuting distances can well exceed 80 kilometres and the potential commuting zone around any large city is likely to include at least some functionally-separate communities (see Chapter 13). Hamilton and Guelph, for instance, lie within commuting distance of Toronto, and people do indeed commute from both places, but neither would tolerate being counted among Toronto's suburbs (Statistics Canada, 2003a). Nor need they be. A location within commuting distance may be a *necessary* condition for suburban development but it is by no means a *sufficient* one.

What additional criteria might then be called on? One frequently mentioned is political independence, which relates back to Donaldson's remark about the central city. This is actually a technical term and refers to the city as an administrative unit with its own municipal government and precise territorial limits. As a general rule, as cities grow they try to expand their territories by annexing land from the counties or townships that surround them. When these moves are resisted, however, as they commonly are, development spills beyond the city's boundaries. Rural municipalities then become urbanized and new urban municipalities are established until the original city, now the *central* city, is more or less encircled by its outlying communities. But while these communities are quite properly described as suburbs, it does not follow that a suburb must necessarily be independent from its central city, certainly not in Canada where a great deal of suburban development actually falls under central-city jurisdiction.

As a matter of more general concern, if suburbs are to be characterized in relation to some well-defined areal unit, the central city is not the most appropriate choice; it is simply too arbitrary and inconsistent. A better, if still imperfect alternative is to be found in the concept of the *inner city*, which this book adopts. If the inner city is thought of as the city's core area, it is equally logical to think of suburbs as constituting an outer zone of development, regardless of the pattern of municipal government. This elementary observation is the basis for the model put forward in Figure 12.1, and although it does not sweep away all the conceptual fog it does at least seize on a characteristic that all suburbs share. It is also axiomatic that development in the outer zone will have occurred as a direct result of the need to accommodate the city's growth. For a century or more, Canada's cities have expanded chiefly by adding new suburbs, advancing ever further into their surrounding countryside and engulfing such towns and villages as lie in their path. Since local planning controls came into force in the 1950s, much of this expansion has been directed to the margins of existing built-up areas—the zone of contiguous suburbs in the model—but beyond that, in the rural-urban fringe, pockets of suburban development are typically spattered across an otherwise rural landscape. The boundary between suburbs and countryside is not a line so much as a broad indeterminate zone, over which the pressures of suburbanization are widely dispersed. This is especially true of the largest and most rapidly growing metropolitan regions, such as Toronto or Vancouver, though all Canadian cities, whatever their size or growth history, conform more or less to the pattern shown in Figure 12.1.

The demand for new suburbs, then, is primarily a function of population growth, a truism that masks a most complex reality. In the first place, suburban population growth is itself a complex phenomenon, driven partly by its own natural increase and the eventual creation of new suburban households and partly by net migration from a variety of sources: from the inner city, from rural areas and small towns, and from other cities and their suburbs

in Canada and elsewhere. In addition, established residents move frequently within the suburban zone, for many different reasons (Fairbairn and Khatun, 1989; Phipps and Cimer, 1994; Simmons, 1974). Their relocation patterns are extremely diverse as well, but the general tendency, when combined with the population growth factors, is towards outward movement—to the subdivision offering start-up homes for first-time homebuyers, perhaps, or the élite new community for older, upwardly mobile families.

On the inner margin of the suburban zone, meanwhile, there are growth pressures of a different kind. Sooner or later, the oldest surviving suburbs must expect to be absorbed into the inner city, except perhaps when they are in separate municipalities. Victoria's Uplands district, for example, originated in 1907 as a planned community within the newly created municipal district of Oak Bay (Forward, 1973b), and by that criterion is as suburban today as it ever was. But how about Mont-Royal, another planned community of almost identical age (McCann, 1996), which lost its autonomy in 2002 when forced to amalgamate with Montreal. Did it then cease to be suburban as well? Or how about places like Maisonneuve or Rosedale? Maisonneuve, too, was once independent but joined with Montreal as long ago as 1918 (Linteau, 1985), while Rosedale was annexed by Toronto in 1905 after having been 'plotted out as a high-class suburb' in the 1860s (Careless, 1984: 96). Then there is Shaughnessy Heights in Vancouver, which set out in 1907 to be 'the most prestigious residential suburb in the City' (Duncan, 1994: 60)—*in* the city, not outside it. Should any of these be considered suburbs today, or are they now part of the inner city? In terms of the indicators discussed by David Ley and Heather Frost in Chapter 11, the latter would seem to be the case, though Ley and Frost also make it clear that there are no agreed criteria for delimiting inner cities. Nor, whatever criteria are used, are their limits either fixed or definite. Boundaries, once again, are zones rather than lines, shifting zones of transitional character, no longer as suburban as they once were but not yet unmistakably of the inner city.

Figure 12.1   **Suburbs in the Generalized Structure of a Typical Canadian City (not drawn to scale)**

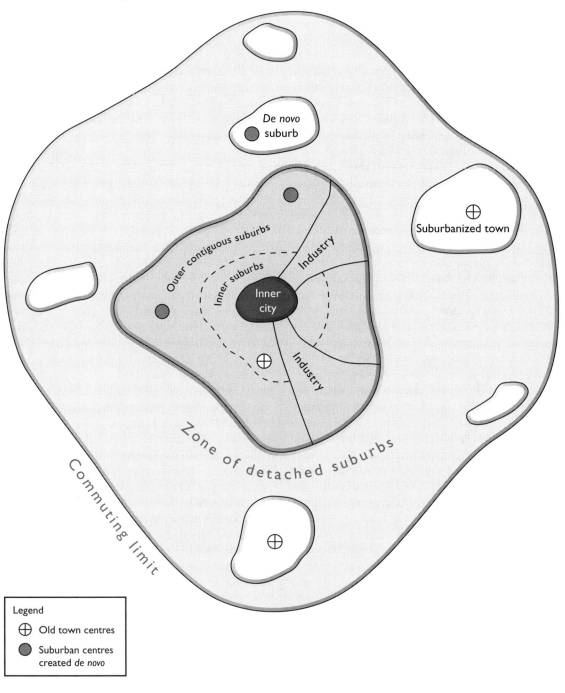

Of course, just to substitute 'inner city' for 'central city' in definitions like Donaldson's does not in itself throw much light on the nature of suburbs or their place in the constantly changing city. For this it is necessary to consider other characteristics, beginning with the widely stated view that suburbs are economically and culturally dependent on the cities that spawned them. Jobs are a crucial aspect of this relationship, so to that extent dependency is already implied in the concept of commuting. More generally, though, it relates to services of all kinds, and particularly those highly specialized services (medical, educational, retail, entertainment, and so on) that require large populations to support them and have traditionally been provided from a single central location. But while there is still much validity to these generalizations, they have long since ceased to be adequate characterizations of city–suburb relations. Already, more than a century ago, the greatest industrial expansion was occurring on the outskirts of cities, usually in separate municipalities. Thus was born the industrial suburb, a new kind of suburban community that simultaneously broadened and obscured the whole notion of a suburb (Lewis, 1991; Linteau, 1985). Although these new communities were physically close to their parent cities, and were usually connected to them by some form of rail transit that fostered commuting, they possessed a degree of economic independence that was not typically suburban: they were places to work as well as places to live (Lewis, 2004). Since then, as Chapters 6 and 14 explain, the suburbanization of jobs has accelerated enormously and commuting patterns have become more complex as a consequence (Statistics Canada, 2003a). For all that we think of suburbs as places where most of the residents work somewhere else—and the examples presented in Table 12.1 indicate this is still a reasonable view to take—that 'somewhere else' is not necessarily the inner city or even the central city; it could be anywhere within the greater metropolitan area. Nor are those who live in central cities immune to this effect; as Table 12.1 makes clear, more and more of them, too, are commuting to suburban workplaces.

At the same time, the suburbanization of jobs has not affected all suburbs equally. In some cases, especially among smaller suburbs with little or no local industry, almost all of the labour force will work elsewhere, mainly (but not necessarily) in the inner city. These suburbs function essentially as dormitories, with some local service employment. Larger suburbs, by contrast, tend to become increasingly independent and self-sufficient as they grow, a phenomenon known as the urbanization of the suburbs (Muller, 1976). The largest—and several in Canada have populations well in excess of 100,000—function much like cities in their own right, even to the extent of being structured around their own multi-purpose cores. In the contemporary dispersed city, these suburban downtowns act as major development nuclei, competing in many respects with the central business district (see Chapter 10), just as suburban locations are frequently preferred these days for specialized service facilities of all kinds, from airports to universities. These trends have given rise to a new generation of functionally diverse suburbs, typified by such places as Richmond, BC, and Mississauga, Ontario—suburbs that are significantly less dependent on their central cities, for either services or jobs, than was once the case, while yet being thoroughly integrated into their respective metropolitan economic systems.

A further weakness of the conventional dependency thesis is its implicit assumption that suburbs are mere appendages of cities, to which they contribute little in return. In fact, though, by supplying living space of generally good quality for a large and continually increasing population, suburbs perform a most vital function. They are also commonly thought of—and here they become ideological constructs as much as practical ones—as facilitating a much-desired lifestyle, a belief that has long set suburbs apart in popular imagining. The 'good life' may be no more certain in suburbia than anywhere else, but it is a compelling dream nonetheless (Wright, 1983).

At the historic core of the suburban mystique is the idea that suburbs are more akin to the country

Table 12.1 **Suburban Residence/Work Patterns in a Selection of Census Metropolitan Areas (CMAs)**

	% of CMA Workers Resident In Suburban Municipalities in 2001	Where in the CMA Workers Resident in Suburban Municipalities Worked in 2001			% of Workers Resident in Central City Who Worked in Suburban Municipalities	
		Suburb of Residence (%)	Central City (%)	Another Suburb (%)	1981	2001
All CMAs	46	32	35	33	10	14
St John's	44	18	72	10	4	8
Quebec City	76	23	36	41	34	40
Montreal	70	22	33	46	29	31
Toronto	49	38	34	28	9	18
Edmonton	28	30	52	18	6	8
Vancouver	71	33	23	44	24	32
Victoria	75	23	44	33	26	33

Source: Statistics Canada (2003a).

than to the city, and so permit a healthier, more satisfying, better adjusted way of life. There are clear overtones here of the Arcadian myth, a vision of a pastoral paradise that was one of the many offshoots of the great Romantic movement that swept the Western world after 1750.[4] In accordance with Romantic ideals, suburbs came to be associated with an environment that was both closer to nature, in the literal sense, and more 'natural', meaning more in harmony with people's physical, social, and spiritual needs. Where the city was the place of work and commerce, a place of great energy and busyness, crowds and noise, and in its residential quarters, poverty, squalor, and disease, the suburb was the blessed antidote, a place of respite and regeneration and wholesome domesticity (Mumford, 1938). These were powerful images and they had a profound influence on early planning theory, most notably in Frederick Law Olmsted's

concept of the Romantic suburb, which he pioneered at Riverside, Illinois (Fisher, 1986), and in its English counterpart, the garden suburb, as first devised by Raymond Unwin (Miller, 1992). Central to both, and of continuing importance ever since, was a vision of the suburb as a place where family life and social life would both flourish, a vision of healthy families living in healthy communities. This was the ideal that Olmsted, Unwin, and their many followers sought, in Canada as in the rest of the Anglo-American world (Carver, 1962; Delaney, 1991; Hancock, 1994; Purdy, 1997).

For a time, while suburbs were still small and exclusive and clearly separated from their parent cities, a quasi-rural atmosphere was readily maintained. This all changed, however, as the transition to the age of the 'mass suburb' took effect and suburbs began to appear in forms that made them accessible to ordinary people, in sociological terms, to the 'masses'. This change did not happen overnight, and in Canada did not become fully established until after World War II, but long before then the modern suburb had been set on a new and irreversible course that was itself the product of two overpowering forces (Doucet and Weaver, 1991; Hayden, 2003; McCann, 1999). The first was the explosive growth of urban population and the concomitant emergence of a huge new middle class. Combined with an increasingly affluent working class, this soon created a demand for new houses and new communities that only mass production could satisfy. On top of that, the second force, was the constant stream of technological innovations that helped bring suburban living within reach of the mass of the population: the many advances in construction methods, going back to the 1830s in Chicago, when the balloon-frame house was invented (Wright, 1983); the adoption of new and cheaper house styles, such as the bungalow, which was introduced into Britain from India in the 1860s (King, 1997); the increasingly sophisticated techniques of land development and capital financing even before Levittown became a synonym for the large-scale, 'corporate' suburb (Paterson, 1991; Sancton and Montgomery, 1994; Weaver, 1978);[5] and perhaps most important, from a geographical and planning standpoint, the successive changes in modes of public and private transportation, beginning with the horse-drawn omnibus in the 1820s and progressing from there to electrified streetcars and subway trains, to high-speed suburban railways, and, most overwhelmingly of all, to the automobile and its paraphernalia of highways and expressways, bridges and interchanges (Armstrong and Nelles, 1986; Doucet, 1982; Frisken, 1994b). All helped facilitate the spread of suburban development on an ever-expanding scale and gave rise, in the process, to an ever more complex social geography. As Olsen (1976: 236) explains, writing about Victorian London: 'The new suburb was a highly efficient means both of functional and social segregation: functional in that it enabled home-life and work to be carried out in two distinct and often distant places, social in that it enabled each class to be tidily sorted into its own homogeneous neighbourhood.'

For all its segregating tendencies, however, suburban development, then and since, has been shaped by tastes and values that are typically thought of as middle-class. During the Victorian period, in particular, the suburb was the very embodiment of bourgeois ideology and a highly visible metaphor for the cult of respectability that permeated Victorian life. What could be more respectable, after all, than owning one's own home on its own plot of ground, and providing there a secure place for one's family, a safe, quiet, and, above all, private place? What Boyer (1994) refers to as the privatization of urban space was one of the fundamental transformations wrought by the suburban revolution, and none better fitted the Victorian sense of rectitude and propriety. The quest for private space might be inherently paradoxical—'a collective attempt to live a private life' is how Mumford (1938: 215) described it—but it was of elemental importance to the geography of suburbia. Low-density development became the norm and the prime attribute of suburbia as a distinct kind of environment. The spaciousness of the suburbs, especially in contrast to the congested city core, was also a major factor in their rapid expansion and huge extent, since so much more land was needed to house a given number of people. In our own day that same spaciousness is often condemned as wasteful 'sprawl' (Bourne, 2001a), yet its appeal is as powerful as ever. The ideals of space and privacy and the freedom they convey, the sense of independence and personal control, are not easily forgone, certainly not by Canadians. They are core values that the suburban way of life seeks to satisfy.

At the same time, as the architect Moshe Safdie (1970: 224) has observed, there is a 'contradictory desire in our utopia', a desire for openness and for small communities on the one hand, and for the amenities and opportunities of the large city on the other. Herein lies what Safdie calls the 'paradox of suburbia', in that the larger a city becomes, and the further it spreads in a low-density form, the more difficult it is to achieve either desire. The transportation problems simply become too great.

In other respects also, patterns of suburban life have changed dramatically in recent years, forced to adapt to a host of new circumstances far removed from the original ideals. Falling birth rates, working wives, an aging population, single-parent families, corporate downsizing, immigration from the developing world—these are just some of the factors that have come into play. Suburbs now have to accommodate a much greater variety of people and lifestyles, household arrangements and housing forms, often at densities that make a mockery of the traditional notions of space and privacy. And although many suburban communities are as privileged and sheltered as ever (as evidenced, for example, by the growing popularity of 'gated communities' [Grant et al., 2004]), the picture is quite different for suburbs as a whole. The distinction

between suburbs and inner city has become increasingly blurred as well (Bourne and Louris, 1999). Even in a relatively new city like Edmonton, where suburban residents are definitely younger and more affluent on average than those in the inner city, and more likely to belong to conventional families living in their own detached houses, many people in the suburbs do not fit this description, while many in the inner city do (Table 12.2). Old people and poor people, single parents and immigrants, renters and non-family households, all are still found in higher proportions in the inner city, but in absolute terms there are many more of them in the suburbs. And all, in their several ways, contribute to the great changes that have occurred in suburban character.[6]

Table 12.2   Comparison of Suburbs and Inner City, Edmonton, 2001

	Suburbs	Inner City
% of population 0–14 years of age	20.9	10.9
% of population 65 years or older	10.4	13.8
Family households as % of all private households	75.0	40.6
Single-parent families as % of all family households	16.7	22.2
Mean household income per census tract (a) median	$59,880	$41,880
(b) range	$34,158–$139,791	$26,302–$57,102
% of population in low-income households	14.8	31.5
% of private dwellings owner-occupied	72.3	34.6
Single detached houses as % of all private dwellings	63.7	29.6
% of population whose mother tongue is a non-official language (single responses only)	18.9	23.1
Recent immigrants (1981–2001) as % of total population	9.2	11.5
Population increase 1996–2001	8.8	7.3
% of total CMA population	76.1	13.3

Note: In Tables 12.2, 12.3, and 12.4 suburbs are defined as (a) census tracts within the City of Edmonton largely or entirely developed since 1950, when neighbourhood unit planning was officially adopted; (b) census tracts that originally formed part of suburban municipalities subsequently annexed by Edmonton; and (c) large detached communities within Edmonton's commuter-shed.
Source: Statistics Canada (2004b).

The Variety of Canadian Suburbs: Order out of Diversity

'American suburbs', writes Jackson (1985: 5), 'come in every type, shape and size: rich and poor, industrial and residential, new and old.' So, too, do Canadian suburbs, except that their variety is greater even than Jackson suggests. This is brought out by Figure 12.2, which uses the device of the morphological matrix to identify basic variations on 15 key attributes of contemporary suburbs, grouped into five more general clusters. Each attribute is

Figure 12.2 **Morphological Matrix of Suburban Characteristics**

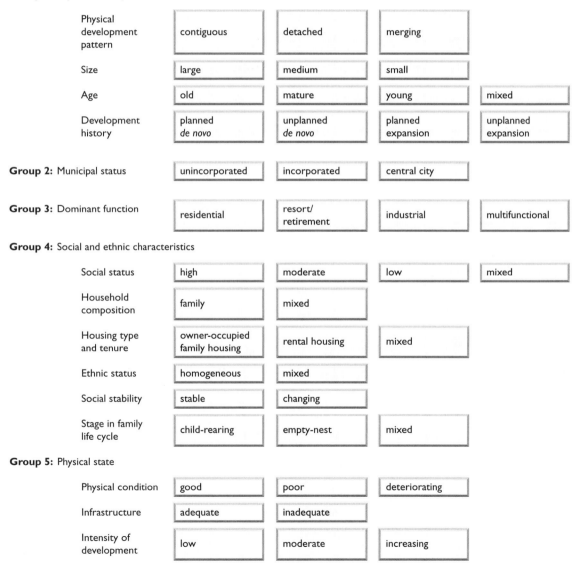

Group 1: Physical development characteristics

Physical development pattern	contiguous	detached	merging	
Size	large	medium	small	
Age	old	mature	young	mixed
Development history	planned *de novo*	unplanned *de novo*	planned expansion	unplanned expansion

Group 2: Municipal status

unincorporated	incorporated	central city

Group 3: Dominant function

residential	resort/ retirement	industrial	multifunctional

Group 4: Social and ethnic characteristics

Social status	high	moderate	low	mixed
Household composition	family	mixed		
Housing type and tenure	owner-occupied family housing	rental housing	mixed	
Ethnic status	homogeneous	mixed		
Social stability	stable	changing		
Stage in family life cycle	child-rearing	empty-nest	mixed	

Group 5: Physical state

Physical condition	good	poor	deteriorating
Infrastructure	adequate	inadequate	
Intensity of development	low	moderate	increasing

described in turn, bearing in mind always that every suburb is a composite of all 15.

1. Physical Development Characteristics

The first attribute, physical development pattern, harks back to Figure 12.1 and the distinction made there between 'contiguous' and 'detached' suburbs. The former lie within the continuous built-up zone that extends out from the inner city, while the latter are physically separated from other suburbs in a pattern of discontinuous or fragmented development that is a defining characteristic of the dispersed metropolis. The matrix also recognizes a third, transitional category called 'merging suburbs' to cover those situations where suburbs that were once clearly detached are being encroached upon as the city grows. Their eventual fate, of course, is to be absorbed into the greater mass of contiguous suburbs, though this process may take decades to complete. The mix of suburbs in individual cities also varies, which has important implications for metropolitan form. Edmonton, for example, where roughly one-fifth of the CMA population lives in detached suburbs, has a much more dispersed form than Calgary, which is the most compact of Canada's larger cities (Smith, 1991).

In addition to their differences in development pattern, suburbs also vary by size and age, though these are relative concepts. Thus, Mississauga, which had more than 600,000 people in 2001, is a large suburb by anyone's standards, but others, such as Burnaby (194,000) in Vancouver and Mill Woods (85,000) in Edmonton, can equally be considered large in their local contexts, especially when compared with the many suburban communities whose populations are a few thousand at most. In principle, then, the distinction between large and small suburbs is easily made, though it can be a source of confusion in another respect. This is illustrated by Mill Woods, a comprehensively planned district made up of 24 separate neighbourhoods. So, is Mill Woods one suburb or 24, since each neighbourhood can be considered a suburban community in its own right? In fact, both answers are correct, because the larger the suburb the more likely it is

to develop its own hierarchical structure: to form suburbs within suburbs within suburbs.[7] In both systems terms and planning terms, this makes eminent sense, but it also underlines the importance of scale to the characterization of suburbs. Early editions of *The Dictionary of Human Geography*, for instance, defined suburb as 'a socially homogeneous residential district within an urban area', a definition that would have disqualified both Mill Woods and Burnaby, let alone Mississauga. Although each contains many relatively homogeneous units—its 'small' suburbs—at the overall or 'large' scale, homogeneity is out of the question.

The significance of this point can be seen immediately with respect to the attribute of age. Every city has some suburbs that developed relatively early ('old' suburbs), others that developed quite recently ('young' suburbs), and some at an intermediate stage that the matrix describes as 'mature'. If a suburb is of a neighbourhood scale or less, and especially if it was developed after about 1950, it is highly likely that it will all be of the same age. For large suburbs, however, that is all but impossible. Even Mill Woods, where construction has been going on continuously since 1970, has neighbourhoods that are mature by Edmonton standards alongside others that are still quite new, while Burnaby, which one local planning official describes as a mature suburb when viewed as a whole (Ito, 1995: 122), has developments ranging from the 1920s to the present. The matrix would classify them both as 'mixed' suburbs, a mixture of young, mature, and, in Burnaby's case, relatively old communities.

Development history, the final attribute in this set, combines two characteristics. The first is summed up in the distinction between 'planned' and 'unplanned' suburbs, while the second distinguishes development that occurred *de novo* (meaning an entirely new community was created on what planners call a 'greenfields' site) from the 'expansion' and suburbanization of once-independent towns. Together these yield four types of suburbs, all of which are fairly common across Canada. It can also be observed that *de novo* development is normal for contiguous suburbs, though detached suburbs sometimes fall into this category as well. The

Ottawa suburbs of Kanata and Orleans are excellent examples. More commonly, detached suburbs grow around the nucleus provided by an existing town, usually a rural service centre that is utterly transformed in consequence (Evenden, 1991a; Sinclair and Westhues, 1974). Such growth is also likely to be spontaneous rather than planned, though there are certainly instances in Canada where metropolitan planning policy has supported the construction of detached suburbs (Millward, 2002; Wright, 1978). Generally, however, suburban development is a market-driven process that local planning systems attempt to control as best they can. In this pragmatic sense, a suburb can be considered planned if it adheres to established principles of community design and meets local standards of environmental quality, particularly as prescribed by zoning and subdivision regulations. This requires the suburb to have been built in accordance with an approved plan governing the arrangement of land uses, the layout of streets and other circulation facilities, the type, density, and appearance of the intended development, and the provision of physical and community services such as schools, playgrounds, shops, and sewers. By these criteria, virtually all suburban development in Canada today is planned, though evidence of earlier unplanned development still abounds.

2. Municipal Status

Whatever their physical development characteristics, all suburbs come under some form of municipal government. The actual forms vary from province to province, but the three categories adopted for the matrix are sufficiently broad to cover all situations.

The first category, 'unincorporated suburbs', refers to communities, mostly quite small, that have established themselves outside a central city in a rural municipality under whose jurisdiction they remain. In the past, this pattern was often associated with the worst characteristics of unregulated fringe development, rural municipalities then being poorly equipped to cope with the suburban invasion. This generally changed in the 1950s and 1960s, when even unincorporated developments came to be closely regulated by local planning authorities. The best of them, like Don Mills in the Toronto municipality of North York (Hancock, 1994) and Sherwood Park outside Edmonton, were carefully designed as well. Sherwood Park now has more than 45,000 people and many of the trappings of an independent city, yet it is still legally part of its surrounding county.

In the most extreme cases, fringe municipalities become so thoroughly suburbanized that a rural form of government is no longer appropriate. Burnaby, Mississauga, and the Montreal suburb of Laval are all examples of erstwhile rural municipalities that have been reconstituted as towns or cities. In the matrix they are classified as 'incorporated suburbs', though this category more usually applies to smaller places that have either expanded from a pre-existing town or obtained incorporation after the suburb became established. In an important variation on the Arcadian myth, the residents of these communities are often looking to protect a way of life they value for its imagined small-town similarities. Political independence gives them the control they feel they need.

The third category applies to suburbs that lie under central-city jurisdiction, a circumstance that comes about in one of two ways: either the suburbs originate within the central city or they are absorbed into it *ex post facto*. Calgary is the most striking illustration of the former situation, reflecting a two-pronged planning strategy that has been pursued since the 1950s. On the one hand, an aggressive annexation program provided ample land for the city's expansion; on the other, development in the surrounding municipalities was deliberately restricted (Brown, 1991; Brown et al., 1989). Saskatoon, Regina, and Edmonton adopted similar courses, though with less success in Edmonton's case (Smith, 1991). Even there, however, most of the largest suburbs, including Mill Woods, developed inside the central city.

In the second situation, suburbs form outside the central city and are then annexed by it, sometimes on the suburb's initiative but more usually because the city itself wishes to expand. All Canadian cities have grown in this way at some time, though none more spectacularly than Montreal, which annexed 20 suburban municipalities between 1883 and 1918 (Linteau, 1985). Some Canadian cities have also undergone comprehensive consolidations, though in these cases the initiative has come from above, from provincial governments (see Chapter 17). The earliest example was the so-called Unicity of Winnipeg that the government of Manitoba created in 1971 by amalgamating Winnipeg with all 11 of its suburban municipalities. Halifax had a similar reorganization imposed on it in 1996 (Millward, 1996). Then came the Toronto amalgamation of 1998, which introduced another variation. This time, only the innermost ring of municipalities was consolidated, while the more distant suburbs, which accounted for almost half of the metropolitan population, were left intact. The province of Quebec followed suit in 2002 by forcing mergers in Montreal and other urban areas (Fischler et al., 2004). In all these cases, however, the fact that once-independent communities were now incorporated into a central city did not necessarily mean that they ceased to be suburbs; their established character was not so easily erased.

3. Dominant Function

Throughout their long history, suburbs have been chiefly regarded as serving a dormitory or 'residential' function, and it is certainly true that any suburb must provide living space for its residents. In determining a suburb's functional type, however, other attributes have to be considered as well, particularly size and municipal status. A suburb that developed within a central city, for instance, is almost certain to be purely residential, because modern zoning practices will have ensured that living areas and work areas are clearly separated. Outside the central city the pattern is more diverse, especially among suburbs that are self-contained municipalities. All four of the matrix's functional types are represented in this group, though the distinctions are sometimes fuzzy. Thus, communities in the 'resort/retirement' category will function much like regular residential suburbs, except that they

have special amenities that attract recreationists and retirees as well. Usually, in fact, as typified by the Vancouver suburb of White Rock, such communities are known as resorts long before they become popular with commuters. 'Industrial suburbs', too, although distinguished by their independent industrial bases, depend on relatively high levels of commuting, both in and out, reflecting the complex pattern of economic relationships characteristic of modern metropolitan systems. Even the most highly industrialized suburbs, such as Edmonton's Fort Saskatchewan, function to some degree as dormitories.

So, too, do 'multi-functional suburbs', meaning those relatively large, urbanized suburbs that have broadly based economies of their own. Typically, in suburbs of this class, between a third and two-thirds of the local labour force will be employed somewhere else, but if none of these suburbs can ever be fully self-sufficient, they nonetheless house a diverse array of productive activities, serving not just their own populations but the larger metropolitan community.

4. Social and Ethnic Characteristics

Based on standard indicators of social status, such as income, occupation, and education, suburbs run a broad gamut, which the matrix simply divides into 'high', 'moderate', and 'low'. In practice, particularly at the neighbourhood scale, the great majority of Canadian suburbs fall into the moderate category, though in every city there are some that rank relatively high and some that rank relatively low. It is also to be expected, once again, that larger suburbs will themselves house communities of widely different status. These points are illustrated for Edmonton in Figure 12.3 and Table 12.3, and although the data refer to census tracts, which are not always a good fit with neighbourhoods or other recognized social units, they do substantiate the wide range of social characteristics that apply in Canada's suburbs today, as well as give evidence of the tendency to social segregation that has long prevailed in suburbs everywhere. Only one variable, average household income, is presented in

Figure 12.3   **Mean Household Income per Suburban Census Tract, Edmonton, 2001**

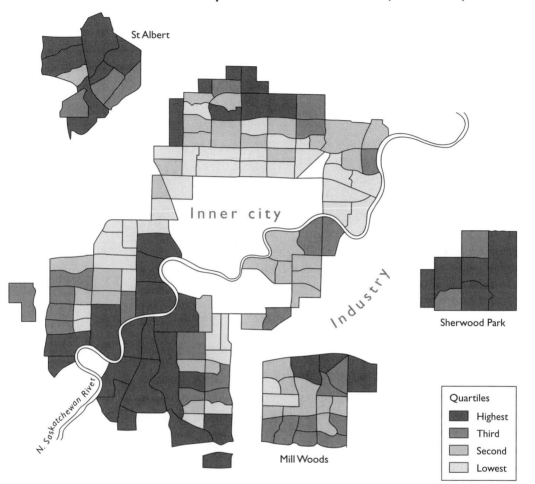

Note: Fifteen outlying census tracts defined as suburban (see Table 12.2) have been omitted.
Source: Statistics Canada (2004b).

Figure 12.3, but it correlates well with other indicators and so is a reasonable surrogate for social status in Edmonton's case. It certainly picks out the great wedge of neighbourhoods in the southwest sector, following the North Saskatchewan River, that are well-known as Edmonton's most prestigious, along with the exclusive detached suburbs of St Albert and Sherwood Park, outside the central city. Also clearly identified is the ring of older, low-status communities that almost encircles the inner

city. Needless to say, these are also the communities with the highest levels of suburban poverty (as indicated by percentage of population in low-income families: Table 12.3). Newer census tracts within the central city fall generally into the high and moderate categories, though larger units, such as Mill Woods in the far southeast, are best described as mixed.

The next pair of attributes, household composition and housing type and tenure, are closely

Table 12.3   **Indicators of Social, Household, and Ethnic Character for Suburban Census Tracts in Edmonton, 2001**

Indicator	Lowest	Quartile Second	Third	Highest
A. *Social characteristics*				
1. Average household income	$34,158–$51,984	$51,985–$59,799	$59,800–$72,999	$73,000–$139,790
2. % of population in low-income family units	1.7–8.6	8.7–15.5	15.6–20.9	21.0–38.6
3. % of labour force in professional, managerial, and related occupations	25.4–44.4	44.5–49.9	50.0–57.8	57.9–77.5
4. % of population 15 years and older with university degree	3.1–8.1	8.2–12.8	12.9–20.0	20.1–51.6
B. *Household and housing characteristics*				
1. % of private households in census families	43.6–67.2	67.3–77.4	77.5–83.2	83.3–93.8
2. % of private dwellings owned by occupiers	0–61.3	61.4–74.2	74.3–86.9	87.0–100
3. % of private dwellings in single detached houses	0–49.9	50.0–64.9	65.0–79.9	80.0–100
C. *Ethnic characteristics*				
1. % of population whose mother tongue is a non-official language (single responses only)	2.4–12.2	12.3–19.9	20.0–25.4	25.5–43.0
2. % of population who are recent immigrants (1981–2001)	0.5–3.7	3.8–8.7	8.8–14.3	14.4–24.7
3. % of population identified as visible minorities	0–5.3	5.4–14.9	15.0–22.4	22.5–48.3

Source: Statistics Canada (2004b).

related to social status, and, like social status, are more variable than conventional stereotypes allow. While suburbs at large certainly are still pre-eminently the domain of family households, not only is family more broadly defined these days (to include both married and common-law couples, with or without children living at home, and single parents living with at least one child), but non-

family households are also a large component of many suburban neighbourhoods. In Edmonton, for example, they account for more than a third of all households in about a quarter of suburban census tracts (Table 12.3). Housing type and tenure are even more variable, ranging from tracts that fit the conventional image of suburbs as places where families live in their own, mostly detached houses to those where most people live in rental accommodation of one form or another. The latter are also most mixed in household composition, as well as tending to have the lowest average household incomes. This suggests that the mixing of housing types that has become so typical of suburban neighbourhoods is largely market-driven, a sign of the market's adaptation to today's more varied household arrangements and housing needs. Yet it is a trend that urban planners have long supported as well. The particular housing mixes to be found in Canadian suburbs may not achieve the broad social balance that theorists like Lewis Mumford (1968) and Humphrey Carver (1979) aspired to, but the practice is nonetheless regarded as socially desirable.

Another characteristic of Canadian society with significant suburban ramifications is the ethnic diversity that has resulted from the changed immigration patterns of the past 25 years or so (Hiebert, 2000a). The effects are by no means uniform, however, and although many suburbs are now home to people of widely differing cultural, racial, and linguistic backgrounds, others have remained essentially untouched. The latter, which the matrix labels 'homogeneous', are typified by Beauport, an almost totally francophone suburb of Quebec City, and by Mount Pearl, a no less anglophone suburb of St John's; in both cases, immigrants accounted for a bare 1 per cent of the population in 2001. In 'mixed' suburbs, by contrast, substantial (though widely varying) proportions of the population will have been born outside Canada—53 per cent in the Toronto suburb of Markham in 2001; 49 per cent in Saint-Laurent, a Montreal suburb; 54 per cent in Richmond, BC, and 34 per cent in nearby Surrey. And while some of these people were brought up speaking either English or French as their native language, most were not. In Markham, 28 per cent of the population reported some foreign language as their mother tongue; in Richmond it was 34 per cent; and in Saint-Laurent 30 per cent. Saint-Laurent also has an unusually large anglophone population (29 per cent), making it perhaps the most polyglot suburb in Canada.

All of these examples have been taken from relatively large, politically independent suburbs, but

ethnic mixing occurs at a much smaller scale as well, in neighbourhoods and census tracts. Edmonton provides an example again, and although it is dangerous to reduce something as complex as ethnicity to simple indicators, those used in Table 12.3 and Figure 12.4 are highly suggestive. For one thing, they make it clear that suburban census tracts vary greatly in the degree to which they have been affected by immigration; for another, they establish that these differences have a definite geographical pattern. In other words, they suggest that recent immigration trends have resulted in an increased tendency to ethnic segregation within Edmonton's suburbs. Two particularly striking pieces of evidence are the relatively high concentration of people from foreign-language backgrounds in the northern and southeastern sectors of the city, including Mill Woods, and their virtual avoidance of the detached suburbs, not just St Albert and Sherwood Park but those that lie still further away, beyond the limits of Figure 12.4. In ethnic terms, most of Edmonton's nearly homogeneous communities are outside the central city.

The final pair of attributes in this fourth group introduces the complex issue of social and demographic change. First, and most broadly, the matrix distinguishes between suburbs whose social character is essentially stable, which most suburbs will be most of the time, and those that are changing in some vital respect. Inner suburbs, for instance, may increasingly become home to lower-income groups and to recent immigrants. We can see some indication of both tendencies in Figures 12.3 and 12.4. In addition, and regardless of any propensity to social change, all suburban communities undergo critical demographic changes as they age and the family life cycle runs its course. As children grow up and leave home, so the overall character of the suburb will shift from being strongly child-oriented to being primarily adult (the empty-nest stage). This effect may be offset to some degree by the natural turnover of population, since older families tend to be replaced by younger ones, but the demographic consequences are still substantial, in part because contemporary families are smaller on average than those of earlier generations. This is illustrated for

Figure 12.4   **Proportion of Suburban Census Tract Population Whose Mother Tongue Is Neither English nor French, Edmonton, 2001**

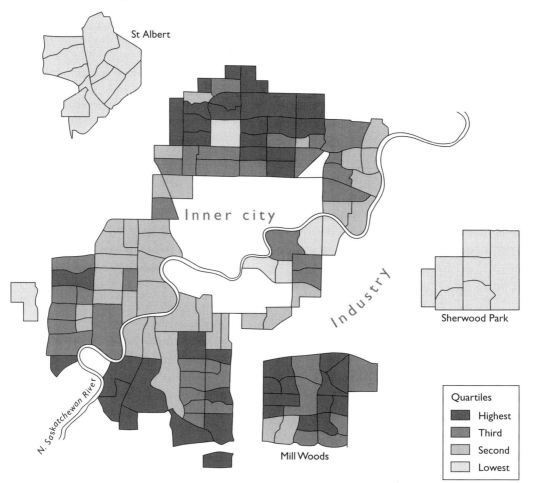

Note: Fifteen outlying census tracts defined as suburban (see Table 12.2) have been omitted.
Source: Statistics Canada (2004b).

Edmonton in Table 12.4, which shows how the family life cycle (as indicated by the increasing proportions of families without children living at home) manifests itself in a declining, aging, and increasingly immobile population. Eventually, of course, when none of the original residents remain, the whole cycle may begin again, and there is some evidence of that, too, in Table 12.4, in the relatively high proportions of census tracts developed before

1971 that experienced population increases between 1996 and 2001.

5. Physical State

The final set of attributes treats suburbs as built environment, especially in respect of those qualities that bear directly on family and community life. In the matrix, these have been narrowed down to

Table 12.4   **Indicators of the Family Life-Cycle Effect for Suburban Census Tracts in Edmonton, 2001, Stratified by Period of Development**

Indicator	Main Period of Development				
	1946–60	1961–70	1971–80	1981–90	1991–2001
1. % rate of population change 1996–2001					
Decrease	8	8	21	5	
Small increase (less than 3.0%)	9	6	16	3	
Moderate increase (3.0–10.0%)	10	11	9	7	1
Large increase (more than 10.0%)	2	3	11	5	15
Total	29	28	57	20	16
2. % of population living in same residence for at least five years (by quartile)					
Highest: 59.5–76.4%	10	9	13	2	3
54.5–59.4%	7	7	13	10	1
48.0–54.4%	7	6	19	5	1
Lowest: 17.7–47.9%	5	6	12	3	11
3. % of population 65 years and older (by quartile)					
Highest: 15.5–38.9%	19	12	3	3	1
9.0–15.4%	10	13	11	1	1
6.0–8.9%	—	2	28	4	5
Lowest: 2.2–5.9%	—	1	15	12	9
4. % of census families without children living at home (by quartile)					
Highest: 41.5–49.5%	16	13	6	1	1
33.5–41.4%	12	10	9	3	4
27.5–33.4%	1	4	25	3	5
Lowest: 19.9–27.4%	—	1	17	13	6

Source: Statistics Canada (2004b).

three, though the first two, 'physical condition' and 'infrastructure', commonly go hand in hand. Moreover, although the matrix divides both attributes into 'good' and 'poor' categories, this distinction was more important in the past than it is today. From the late nineteenth century on, many low-income families, a high proportion of them immigrants, sought cheap land outside the boundaries of towns and cities all across Canada. Here, beyond the reach of municipal regulations, they could build their own houses out of whatever materials they could obtain, on plots of land large enough to allow them to practise a semi-subsistence way of life. They had created their own Arcadia, though it came with a cost: houses were generally crude, often no more than shacks; there were no services of any kind; and access to the city and to jobs was a matter of walking or cycling to the nearest streetcar terminus or factory complex (Harris, 1992, 1996; Harris and Sendbuehler, 1992). Then, in the 1940s and 1950s, these working-class suburbs, as they are sometimes called, were overrun in the great surge of post-war expansion. Some, like Forest Lawn in Calgary and Jasper Place in Edmonton, incorporated themselves in a vain attempt to hold back the tide, but they were tax-poor, and amalgamation with a central city was the only way they could afford the environmental and servicing standards that residents and regulators were coming to demand (Smith and Diemer, 1978). Although they have left some mark on the suburban landscape—they account for several of the low-income census tracts in Figure 12.3, for example—the more rigorous enforcement of building codes and planning regulations normally ensures that contemporary suburbs at least reach acceptable standards of health, safety, and service infrastructure. Further physical changes may still occur, though, particularly under conditions of social downgrading or inadequate maintenance, and the matrix allows for this as well. The oldest and poorest suburbs are particularly at risk, not just of deteriorating but of losing their suburban status altogether.

This same issue, the transition of inner suburbs into inner city, also affects the last attribute, identified in the matrix as 'intensity of development' to avoid confusion with population density, which is a separate concept. Although changes in intensity (as indicated, for example, by an increased number of dwelling units per hectare) may lead to changes in population density, so, too, will demographic changes of the kind discussed earlier, where there is no change at all to the built environment.

Historically, suburbs have been associated with development of relatively low intensity, typified by spacious house lots, extensive community open space, and generously laid-out streets. That pattern has by no means been universal, however. Since at least the 1950s, particularly in planned neighbourhoods, standard practice has been to incorporate more intensive types of housing into the suburban environment: apartment buildings, both walk-up and high-rise; row housing in almost endless variety; and even more specialized forms of accommodation such as retirement villages and extended-care facilities (Holdsworth and Laws, 1994; Lucas, 2002). Sometimes these occur in sufficient concentrations for the overall intensity of development to be characterized as 'moderate' rather than 'low', though these are vague descriptions. It is also possible—and here the idea of transition comes into play—for a suburban neighbourhood to become more intensively developed over time. This can come about in several ways: owners may enlarge and upgrade their houses as family circumstances change (Evenden, 1991b, 1997); houses of modest size may be replaced by larger ones, again as a mark of social upgrading (Halseth, 1996; Majury, 1994); and additional housing units may be fitted into existing spaces, by breaking down large residential properties, perhaps, or adding 'granny flats' for elderly parents, or building over surviving fragments of open ground. When this last process, which is known as 'infilling', occurs in older, inner suburbs, it may also signal that the transition into inner city has begun, especially if it is accompanied by redevelopment; that is, if houses are being demolished and apartments or some other kind of multiple-housing structure erected in their place. In such situations, the increased intensity of development is a telling indicator of fundamental changes in neighbourhood character.

Planning Challenges of Suburban Growth and Change: Development Issues and Conflicts

Just as suburbs have been the prime arena for urban growth since the end of World War II, so, too, have they been the principal focus of urban planning activity. The sheer scale of suburban development, and its importance to Canadian society and the national economy, made that all but inevitable. It also gave planners of the post-war generation an unprecedented opportunity to refine the art of community design, which they had been schooled to think of as central to their discipline. In no other aspect of urban development have the interests of business and government, public and planners, coincided to such powerful effect. Indeed, considering that the suburban development system began from next to nothing in the 1940s, it is remarkable how quickly it was able to rise to the challenge of accommodating the mass of the new urban population in well-built houses and well-equipped communities. This was a huge achievement.

For all its material contribution, however, large-scale suburban development was no panacea, nor could the mass suburb deliver all that the Arcadian myth had seemed to promise. To the contrary, almost from the outset there were those who were highly critical of the new suburbs, seeing them as dreary and monotonous wastelands, petticoat ghettos that marginalized women, limited and limiting in all those aspects of life that make for a vital society (Clark, 1966). And although these particular concerns have faded somewhat over time, as suburbs and the development system both matured, there have always been others to take their place. It is one of the great ironies of the suburban experience that where earlier generations had condemned the city and looked to suburbs as the ideal escape, now the city was being idealized and suburbs condemned (Fowler, 1992; Sewell, 1984). In the eyes of contemporary critics, suburban development is unsound in every respect—environmentally, financially, and socially. In its stead, they wish to return to a form of city they regard as more truly urban,

a nostalgic and romanticized vision of a diverse, compact, endlessly interesting city that is as mythic in its way as the Romantic suburb ever was. It is also a vision that has powerful forces arrayed against it, not just the development industry in all its ramifications but the ordinary people of Canada, the vast majority of whom still see suburbs as providing their best choice of living place. The dilemma for our local planning systems—and it is but one manifestation of the universal dilemma of planning in democratic societies—is how best to ameliorate established suburban forms and patterns of expansion while maintaining the freedom of choice that is one of our most precious liberties (Grant, 1999).

Among the many problems that the processes of suburban growth and change have given rise to, the following are particularly noteworthy from a geographical and planning standpoint.

(1) Suburban growth is everywhere treated as though it can be sustained indefinitely, which is a logical impossibility. Indefinite expansion implies unlimited resources, above all, an inexhaustible supply of land on which to build. But no resource is more finite than land. In the vastness of prairie space perhaps the practical limits to development may seem remote enough to verge on the infinite, but elsewhere they are real and pressing. Where would future suburbs be built in a Vancouver of 5 million people or a Toronto of 10 million? The whole idea of limits to growth has received scant attention in Canada, and certainly no city has faced up to its long-term implications.

(2) Unchecked suburban expansion is invariably accompanied by environmental damage and the loss of irreplaceable natural resources. Natural hazards are often ignored as well, despite the risks to life and property and the high cost of remedial measures, such as Winnipeg's Red River Floodway. But even when prospective development areas are safe to build on, as they mostly are around Canada's cities, they may have other qualities that make development undesirable. They may provide critical wildlife habitat, for example, or may be ecologically significant in some other respect; they may pose a threat to nearby lakes, streams, and wetlands

through contaminated runoff or accelerated erosion; they may be the site of a valuable natural resource—an aquifer recharge area, or a sand and gravel deposit, or land uniquely suited to some agricultural specialty. Or they may just have great scenic value, offering those semi-wild landscapes that Canadians so prize in their urban environments. Why, then, are such areas not protected as a matter of course? There is no shortage of appropriate techniques: analytical techniques for identifying areas of special character and assessing their importance, and regulatory and design techniques for mitigating the impact of development on environmental systems. The general principle of sustainable development has gained wide acceptance, too, even if its practical implications are not well understood.[8]

The fundamental question always remains, however: Do the benefits of environmental protection outweigh the costs? The issue here is not just that protective measures are expensive in themselves, but that they may cause the cost of development to rise as well. There may even be long-term costs to the community at large, if a city is forced into a less efficient growth pattern, say, or if significant development opportunities have to be forgone. Protecting prime agricultural land is particularly problematic, because it is the easiest land to build on and the most economical to develop. This has huge implications for house prices and local housing markets, and while senior governments are sometimes willing to impose extraordinary protective measures, such as the Ottawa greenbelt and the Greater Golden Horseshoe greenbelt in the Toronto region, which is in the adoption process, or the special agricultural zoning that applies in Quebec and British Columbia, municipal governments are typically loath to take any action that might discourage development or add to its cost (Hossé, 1978; Wolfe and Glenn, 1992).

(3) Environmental considerations aside, the unit cost of low-density suburban development is already high when all the related costs for land and infrastructure are factored in. The situation is at its worst under conditions of unstructured dispersal such as prevail around most of the largest cities, but even moderately intensive, contiguous suburbs like those of Edmonton consume more in public expenditures than they generate in property tax revenues. This means that the suburban way of life, a privileged way of life in many eyes, is actually being subsidized by other taxpayers (Lewinburg, 1996). The planning problem, which is coming to receive a great deal of attention in Canada, is how to make suburban development self-supporting, or more nearly so, without pricing it out of the market for all but the most affluent.[9] One suggestion, which developers have favoured for many years, is that municipalities should lower their servicing standards: permit narrower streets, for example, or locate schools so as to draw on larger catchment areas. The general solution that has won most support, however, is intensification, meaning that suburban land could be used more efficiently and economically if it were more intensively developed (Tomalty, 1997). Sustainable development principles are often invoked as well, in the sense that higher housing densities are presented as a necessary trade-off if environmentally sensitive sites are to be spared. Whether these views will ever become popular is an open question, though. Intensification calls for trade-offs of its own, particularly in terms of space and privacy, those most valued features of suburban living (Leung, 1996; Simpson, 1996).

(4) A similar conflict of values bedevils the argument that intensification would help ease the transportation problems that are an inevitable and increasingly burdensome consequence of continuous suburban expansion. There is the sheer physical difficulty of moving ever-larger numbers of people and vehicles over ever-greater distances on ever-more congested facilities, to say nothing of the costs that then accrue. These are not limited to the construction and maintenance costs generated by a seemingly insatiable demand for new and improved facilities, especially for automobile traffic, but include all the associated costs in energy consumption and atmospheric pollution, in travel time and operating expenses, in injury, death, and property damage, and even in emotional well-being as stress and 'road rage' take their toll. But while a more

intensive pattern of suburban development could certainly achieve some improvement, by reducing travel distances, for instance, and by making mass transit more feasible, it is not likely to bring about the revolution in public attitudes and travel behaviour that the problems require. Suburban residents will not readily give up the freedom and convenience that the private automobile is still able to provide.

(5) A transportation problem of a rather different kind results from the suburbanization of jobs, and especially from their segregation in dedicated business parks and industrial zones. This pattern has definite advantages from a planning standpoint, but for the poor, living in the inner city or inner suburbs, the isolation of suburban workplaces is a serious obstacle—a geographical obstacle—in the way of employment. Women are particularly affected, because they are most likely to be at the mercy of inadequate and inconvenient public transit services (Mensah, 1994). One obvious solution would be to build low-income housing close to suburban industrial districts, but that is impractical with limited government involvement in social housing programs (see Chapter 15). Other possible approaches depend on jobs being provided at more accessible locations, such as suburban town centres, or even within certain residential districts, a practice that planners call 'mixed development'. Even with such measures, however, the spatial mismatch between employment opportunities and the homes of the poor seems destined to remain an intractable problem.

(6) Political fragmentation, such as prevails in most large Canadian cities, typically gives rise to unco-ordinated patterns of development that are both inefficient and inequitable. Not only are suburban municipalities free to compete, even fight, with each other and with their central cities—for territory, for development, for status—but they also vary widely in their resources and in their ability and willingness to share the burden of area-wide needs.[10] Welfare costs, for instance, are heavily loaded onto central cities where social problems are concentrated, while affluent residential suburbs deny any responsibility. Servicing standards and costs are also likely to vary among suburban municipalities, and there may be costly gaps and overlaps in service provision. As well, land-use practices prohibited in one community may be tolerated by a neighbour, adding yet another dimension to the basic pattern of spatial inequality. And although there are well-recognized mechanisms for coping with all of these problems, notably the various arrangements for metropolitan government (see Chapter 18), their effect has been undermined in recent years by increasingly vigorous demands for municipal autonomy and the subsequent 'retreat from regional planning' (Frisken, 1982). As far as most suburban municipalities are concerned, if there are costs and inefficiencies to political fragmentation, which they will almost certainly dispute, they are outweighed by the benefits that come from local control and self-determination. The right of local communities to govern their own affairs is cardinal in democratic politics, and fiercely defended whenever attacked. That lesson received one of its most dramatic demonstrations in 1997, in the fight that Toronto's inner suburbs waged against their enforced amalgamation with the central city. Similar sentiments were expressed in the 2004 'deamalgamation' referendums on the Island of Montreal, where residents of a number of suburbs, which had recently been amalgamated into an expanded City of Montreal, voted massively to recover their municipal autonomy.

(7) Suburbs are not static creations. Sooner or later, they all become subject to pressures for change: economic, social, and demographic pressures to which they adjust as best they can. Suburban life, suburban social relations, even suburban built environments, all will be affected in numerous ways. We might think, for instance, of the recent proliferation of home-based businesses, which is not only changing suburban work patterns but the very meaning of suburban residence (Gurstein, 1996); or the rapid increase in new-immigrant populations in suburbs such as Scarborough, Ontario, and Richmond, BC, and the social tensions to which that has given rise (Ray

et al., 1997; Rose, 2001); or the aging populations of the earlier post-war suburbs and the consequent imbalance between service needs and service facilities. Neighbourhoods designed for active families find themselves with half-empty schools and deserted playgrounds, while outlying neighbourhoods, where the school-age population is concentrated, wait for years for the same facilities. This is just one example, but it illustrates how difficult it is for suburban communities to keep up with changing needs and circumstances and to adapt their built environments to new activity patterns.

On technical grounds alone, coping with change is always a challenge, but when a political dimension is added, as it generally is these days, the problems become formidable indeed. Change is usually resisted, and often feared, in established communities, and political opposition and organized protest have become accepted means of giving vent to community concerns. This has been made manifest through a host of issues: the passion with which residents defend neighbourhood schools threatened with closure or resist the construction of 'monster' houses that would overwhelm a neighbourhood's established character (Halseth, 1996; Majury, 1994);[11] the prolonged fights that erupt when arterial roads become congested and grid-locked, and the residents of outer expanding suburbs seek relief at the expense of inner, long-established ones (Leo, 1977); and the regularity with which development proposals are attacked as LULUs (locally unwanted land uses), no matter how socially desirable they may be, and no matter how defensible they are under such rubrics as 'intensification' and 'smart growth'.

Meeting today's diverse housing needs in forms that are both appropriate and affordable is particularly problematical. To some extent, as evidenced by the growing popularity of such forms of living as retirement villages and adults-only condominiums, often in the form of gated communities, these needs are being accommodated in newly developing suburbs (Lucas, 2002), but a peripheral location is not suitable for everyone. If applied to disadvantaged groups, it becomes just another way in which they are marginalized in contemporary society

(Laws, 1994). Yet trying to provide for these people within established communities is rarely welcomed either. And while this can be condemned as self-interested NIMBYism, it is also every community's democratic right to try to prevent unwanted changes. The resultant conflict is something that local planning systems, through their elected bodies, must grapple with constantly. Where suburban planning was once seen as a relatively straightforward technical activity, focused on the design of good-quality environment, now it is a thoroughly political activity as well.

Suburban space has thus become contested space, far removed from those utopian images of bliss and harmony that were once its touchstone. In itself, however, this neither invalidates the suburb as a form of urban development nor robs it of its intrinsic appeal to the people it serves. On the contrary, it is a mark of the importance that most suburban residents attach to their homes and environs and the way of life they permit. For all their flaws—and they are large—there is no practical alternative to the suburbs for the mass of the urban population, nor will there be for as far as anyone can see into the future. The real challenge is not to do away with suburbs, as some critics seem to imply, but to adapt them more effectively to changing needs and circumstances and to changing public attitudes and expectations about suburban development, suburban environment, and the suburban way of life. In this respect, Canadian suburbs, and hence Canadian cities, must forever remain *in transition*.

Notes

1. For overviews and critiques of Canadian suburban development, see Baerwaldt and Reid (1986), Carver (1978), Evenden and Walker (1993), Linteau (1987), McCann (1999), Sewell (1977), and Smith and Moore (1993). There are studies of individual cities as well, including Vancouver (Evenden, 1978; North and Hardwick, 1992; Perkins, 1993), Calgary (Harasym and Smith, 1975), Edmonton (Smith, 1995; Wang and Smith, 1997), London (Sancton and Montgomery, 1994), Toronto (Lemon, 1985, 1996; Sewell, 1993), and Montreal (Charbonneau et al., 1994). The development of particular suburbs has

been the subject of studies by Cooper (1975), Delaney (1991), Elliott (1991), Evenden (1991a, 1995), Forward (1973b), Hancock (1961, 1994), Hanna (1980), Harris and Sendbuehler (1992), Lewis (1991), Linteau (1985), Martin (2001), McCann (1996), Paterson (1984), Smith (1962), Timusk (1976), Van Nus (1984a), and Weaver (1978).

2. As used here, the term 'modern suburbs' refers to suburbs as they developed in the Anglo-American world over the past 200 to 250 years. There is also a much older, largely European tradition best expressed in the French term 'faubourg'. This is medieval in origin and describes a pattern of exclusion and social marginalization in which unwelcome people and businesses were refused entry to the city but were allowed to congregate outside its walls and gates. By the nineteenth century, French faubourgs were largely working-class and industrial, often little better than slums and viewed with distaste and even fear by bourgeois society (Merriman, 1991). Their reputation, in fact, was much like that of North American inner cities today.

3. To give Donaldson his due, he did add two important qualifications, both of which are considered later in this section. The second part of his definition reads as follows: 'Usually, but not always, suburbs are dependent on central cities economically and culturally; usually, but not always, they are independent of these cities politically' (Donaldson, 1969: ix).

4. American authors usually refer to this as the Jeffersonian myth and relate it to a strong anti-urban tradition particularly associated with Thomas Jefferson; for examples, see Donaldson (1969) and Jackson (1985).

5. Terms like 'corporate suburb', 'corporate city', and 'corporate society' often have a pejorative connotation, implying that power is excessively concentrated in a few elite corporations, governmental as well as commercial, which are then able to impose their narrow self-serving values on an unwitting public. See, for example, Lorimer (1978) and Reid (1991). In more neutral terms, a corporate suburb is one developed as a unified project, in which all phases of planning and construction are controlled by a single corporation.

6. The following authors examine various aspects of the changing character and growing diversity of Canadian suburbs, though sometimes in the context of a broader study: Carlyle (1991), Dansereau (1993), Dowling (1996), Le Bourdais and Beaudry (1988), Ray et al. (1997), Rose (2001), Skaburskis and Geros (1997), Taylor (1987), and Vischer (1987).

7. The concept of hierarchically structured suburbs has been established in planning theory since at least the 1950s. Mill Woods, for example, is organized as a three-level hierarchy of neighbourhoods, communities, and district, corresponding to small, medium, and large suburbs in the matrix (Wang and Smith, 1997). See also Harasym and Smith (1975) and Smith and Moore (1993).

8. Although environmental protection and resource conservation in the face of suburban expansion are generally subsumed under the rubric of sustainable development these days, they have been major themes of the planning literature for many decades. For case studies of Canadian approaches and experience, see Crawford (1993), Grant (1994a), Livey (1995), Pierce (1981a), Reid (1990), Robinson (1995), Smith (1989), Tamminga (1996), Tomalty (1994), White (1996), and Yip (1994). Rees and Roseland (1991) provide a useful review of the sustainable development concept.

9. This issue is best illustrated in a series of reports commissioned by Canada Mortgage and Housing Corporation: *The Integrated Community: A Study of Alternative Development Standards*, 1996; *Changing Values, Changing Communities: A Guide to the Development of Healthy Sustainable Communities*, 1997; and *Conventional and Alternative Development Patterns—Phase 1: Infrastructure Costs*, 1997, and *Phase 2: Municipal Revenues*, 1997.

10. For case studies of the problems and conflicts resulting from political fragmentation in a variety of Canadian cities, see Batey and Smith (1981), Des Rosiers (1992), Frisken (1990), Millward (1996), and Smith and Bayne (1994).

11. 'Monster' or 'mega' houses are houses larger than normal for a particular neighbourhood. Usually they replace an existing unit by taking advantage of the circumstance that most houses are not built to the maximum size permitted under zoning regulations.

Chapter 13

The City's Countryside

Christopher Bryant and Clare J.A. Mitchell

Peri-urban areas—'urban fringes' and 'rural–urban fringes'—are a permanent part of our living space. Neither ephemeral nor transitory, they are definitely spaces undergoing transformations. During the twentieth century, the areas around most cities of the developed world have become an increasingly important component of urban citizens' living spaces. Thus, in Canada, the term 'city's country-side', first coined by Bryant, Russwurm, and McLellan (1982), has become even more appropri-ate. This phrase recognizes that these peri-urban areas have become an integral part of the evolving city form—a dispersed or regional city (Bryant et al., 2000). It also conveys the idea that the rela-tionships between the city and its surroundings are dominated by urban-oriented functions, activities that continue to evolve in the city's countryside.

The development of these functions has led to a variety of land-use and community conflicts, both at local and broader regional scales. Issues of gover-nance in the broadly defined urban and metropol-itan regions of the country have emerged over the last 50 years, and continue to do so. That no universal solution has been found—or is indeed possible—is testimony to the variety of geographic circumstances in which these urbanized regions have developed across the country, as well as to the variety of intra-regional geographic contexts.

In this chapter, we first present the range of forces that have shaped the city's countryside. We emphasize, through a relatively innovative framework, how these forces influence the decision-making processes of various actors at dif-ferent scales. We next present the major collective functions that have developed in the city's coun-tryside, and then move on to discuss the nature of its evolving form. We conclude the chapter with a discussion of some of the most important Canadian issues facing planning and management, as the future city's countryside is constructed.

Evolutionary Forces and the Dynamics of Change in the City's Countryside

The city's countryside has evolved in relation to a range of powerful forces. They can be identified as originating at the broad societal scale, and are often spoken of as mega-trends. Each of the major forces—economic, demographic, social, technolog-ical, political—have shaped the city's countryside, but their influence has changed over time as they themselves have evolved. The result has been the transformation of the countryside, its economy, and society as a whole from an industrial to post-indus-trial milieu.

Economic Forces

The industrial society that emerged from the tech-nological and economic transformations of production, beginning in the late eighteenth century and continuing through to the first half of the twentieth century, became associated with increasing levels of urbanization and industri-alization. With employment opportunities increas-ingly concentrated in urban and subsequently metropolitan areas, powerful rural–to–urban migration forces affected demographic patterns across Canada from as early as the late nineteenth century. This, together with important transformations in agricultural technology and productivity, led to massive declines in farm populations (e.g., in parts of rural Nova Scotia from the late 1890s).

To the production-based forces were added important and often related shifts in corporate structure, subsequently reinforced by globalization processes (see Chapter 4). Initially, corporate reorganization led to increased size of manufacturing plants, encouraging concentration of production, a trend that was later reinforced by scale economies in production technology. This had the effect of concentrating many economic activities in urban areas, especially in a number of metropolitan regions, located in the Quebec City–Windsor corridor (see Chapter 3). Larger firm sizes and the demands of large-scale industrial production drove many manufacturing firms to suburban locations and beyond in search of large tracts of inexpensive land. As global competition ensued, other firms, initially embedded in older industrial districts of the urban core, either closed or relocated capacity to other countries. At the same time, major office locations still remain important, absolutely and relatively, in the central cores of our cities. Some forms of tertiary employment have, however, become decentralized as telecommuting has become increasingly popular (Coffey and Trépannier, 2003; see Chapter 14). Recently, the growth in many sectors of smaller and often 'entrepreneurial' businesses has altered the prospects for many towns and villages, particularly those in fairly close proximity to major urban agglomerations.

Demographic and Social Forces

These forces have modified patterns of population change. The omnipresent decline in family size over the course of the last half-century has been associated with a slowing of Canada's population growth (Chapter 8). However, this slowing

is not evident where growth has been fuelled by rural-to-urban migration, and particularly by international migration (notably in the Toronto-centred region). These macro-scale patterns of migration at international and national scales became increasingly reflected in meso-scale processes as the population of major urban and metropolitan regions began to disperse rapidly. This trend reflects the permissive nature of technological developments in personal transportation. A variety of forces related to individual and family behaviour also contributed to this shift as some people sought out cheaper properties, peaceful living environments, and closer contact with 'nature', to name but a few of these lifestyle factors.

The influx of non-farm populations into peri-urban areas often has more than compensated for the fall in farm populations. The effects have included bolstering an otherwise declining economic base for many villages and small towns in the city's countryside (Bryant et al., 2000). Thus, this influx of different population segments has not necessarily been a negative phenomenon.

Technological Forces

Within the context of the urban and metropolitan region, population expansion moved from one of accretionary urban development in the early period when transportation was still a significant constraining factor to increasingly dispersed forms of residential development after the middle of the twentieth century. This was permitted by the rapid diffusion of the private automobile in Canada. While public transportation systems have become important in the latter part of the twentieth century and have permitted more peripheral urban growth in some regions, e.g., the Toronto region's Go Train system, they have never played the same role as suburban train systems did around many of the major European metropolitan centres. Rather, the private automobile, aided by massive pubic investment in highway construction, fostered a much more dispersed form of settlement in the city's countryside in Canada.

Political Forces

The variable political context provides yet another set of powerful forces that help to explain the particular forms and dynamics of the city's countryside. First, significant variations exist between provinces. For instance, the roles of provincial governments in intervening in—and even recognizing—the issues involved in loss and degeneration of farmland in the face of dispersed urban development pressures have varied considerably. Since the late 1970s, for example, Ontario has relied mostly on persuasion to encourage local and regional regulation. This contrasts significantly with the forceful approaches taken by the provinces of British Columbia and Quebec (Bryant and Granjon, 2005; Bryant and Johnston, 1992). Second, at the regional level, the techniques and impacts of public interventions also have differed considerably. These range from direct public intervention and purchase of land as early as the 1950s in the Ottawa region to create the greenbelt, to attempts at regulation through more traditional forms of land-use planning and the recent attempt by the Ontario government to create a greenbelt around the Greater Toronto Area.

Another powerful political force that has influenced both land-use transformations and our forms of governance is the increasingly important role ascribed to the citizen, who has become more vocal and present in many land-use debates. Today, it is inconceivable that major changes to the governance and management of specific communities could go ahead without the involvement of citizens' groups through various forms of participation (see Chapter 18).

The relationship between rural, peri-urban spaces and urban areas clearly has changed over the last century as technology, consumer preferences, and population needs have evolved. Relationships established much earlier in history have often intensified, and the interconnectedness between urban and rural has become more complex. Inevitably, the challenges to managing and planning the transformation of change in the city's countryside have become more complex.

A Framework: The Traditional 'Concentric Ring' Perspective versus the Mosaic of Peri-urban Spaces

Our way of conceptualizing these changes and their impacts on the spatial structure and dynamic of the city's countryside has evolved. Since the late 1940s and continuing until the early 1980s, the dominant conceptualization was based on a 'concentric ring' type of model. This derived from the notion that the dominant force shaping transformations in the city's countryside was the dispersal of urban functions, particularly residential development, into the countryside, which maintained strong ties to the urban core where employment opportunities were concentrated. Other factors were relegated to a secondary role. The logical consequence of this simplification was a sequence of land-use rings, driven by accessibility considerations to the central city and its suburbs—hence the various terms used: inner urban fringe, outer fringe, rural–urban fringe, urban shadow, and outlying rural hinterland. The framework was presented as a series of concentric land-use zones in various works (e.g., Bryant et al., 1982; Bryant, 1986; Russwurm, 1977) and the accessibility dynamic has been used in other publications (e.g., Bryant, 1984).

This framework, which was at the core of the chapters on the city's countryside in the first two editions of this book, did not discount other shaping factors and forces. Rather, their role was downplayed in the search for meso-scale regional patterns. They often led to statistical generalizations producing evidence of broad zonal differences; this is still a useful purpose (see below). But it often glossed over the fact that the actual content of these zones are the result of human agency—actors making decisions. These actors are not only associated with public planning—regional and local municipalities, government agencies and ministries, and planning and development professionals—but also with myriad private and community (not-for-profit) organizations, and include, as well, private citizens.

Recognition of this reality has been at the base of an analytic framework developed at the Université de Montréal since the mid-1990s to deal with the dynamic of rural localities in the city's countryside and elsewhere (e.g., Bryant, 1995; Bryant et al., 1996). The framework parallels and complements the work of Marsden et al. (1993). It is based on seven components (Figure 13.1). Understanding the development of a locality in the city's countryside requires identifying the actors (1) and their interests, values, and objectives (2). Actors pursue their interests and objectives through their actions (or non-actions) (3), often by mobilizing the resources in their networks (4). Networks reflect both formal organizational structures (e.g., the hierarchical governmental structures) as well as informal organizational structures (e.g., networks of friendship, family members, colleagues) (5a, 5b). Cumulatively, the actions give rise to a locality's profile, characterized by specific orientations (e.g., intensive agriculture, a strong farmland conservation orientation, agro-tourism, dispersed settlement patterns) (6a). Other orientations with potential to emerge remain latent (6b) (e.g., a natural environment conservation movement). All of these interactions and actions occur in different contexts, at different scales (7). At the provincial level within Canada, this would include the legislative context, the economic context in which agriculture finds itself, and the societal context, e.g., the acceptability of public intervention for protecting farmland.

This relatively new way of viewing the city's countryside in Canada since the early 1990s underscores the notion of this area as a mosaic of spaces that bear the stamp of decisions of actors operating at a variety of geographic scales; they do not translate into the same form for the city's countryside in each urban region. It also supports the idea that the

Figure 13.1   **A Conceptual Model of the Dynamic of Localities**

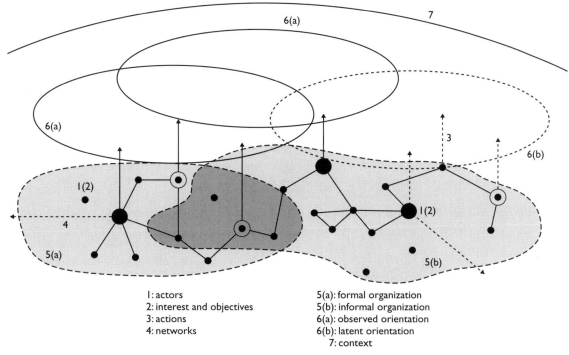

1: actors
2: interest and objectives
3: actions
4: networks

5(a): formal organization
5(b): informal organization
6(a): observed orientation
6(b): latent orientation
7: context

Source: After Bryant et al. (1996).

specific compositions of functions in each locality in the city's countryside are socially constructed.

Evolving Functions

The city's countryside is a multi-functional territory. Its evolving functions tie it ever more closely to the city, through various systems of interaction—journey to work, recreation and leisure, natural environment systems, political systems, social and cultural systems. The positive linkages between rural and urban milieus have long been recognized. The city's countryside contributes to healthier urban environments because of what it offers (e.g., support for leisure and recreation activities, farm produce for the city, and its roles in waste management, infrastructure support, and water supply for cities). Furthermore, cities provide support for healthy rural localities and communities in the countryside by creating a significant demand for various 'rural' products and services (e.g., farm products, tourism and recreation enterprises and facilities, and commercial services, especially ones such as antique stores that cater partly to the urban citizen's demand for contact with 'authentic' rural lifestyles). As well, the city offers significant services accessible to the people of the city's countryside, such as specialized medical services and cultural facilities. Of course, as rural communities see their own populations increase through an influx of new population segments, commercial services and public services such as schooling, medical services, and public libraries are stabilized and may even expand.

The various functions that rural localities and settlements can provide in the city's countryside are constructed by a variety of actors. Many are developed with a minimum involvement of public planning, but public planning and management do have

Table 13.1   The Principal Functions of Peri-urban Rural Spaces in the City's Countryside

Four Broad Categories of Collective Functions	Specific Collective Functions
Place functions based on the locational situation of peri-urban spaces	A place of residence and work
	A land reserve for management and control of urban growth
	A place for the development of recreation/tourism activities
Play functions or leisure and tourism functions	A place for the development of recreation/tourism activities
	A place for tourism development
	A place for appreciation of heritage and natural and cultural resources
Production functions based on peri-urban resources	A source of resources for supporting urban areas
	A place of agricultural production
Protection functions	The protection of resources for production, e.g., agricultural land, construction materials
	The protection of natural and cultural heritage resources
	The protection of zones with a particular educational and scientific interest

important roles to play. In all cases, we observe the development of a mosaic of localities with different functional profiles. Table 13.1, using Russwurm's (1977) four basic categories of functions (place, play, production, and protection), shows a categorization of 'collective' functions of rural spaces in the city's countryside. Each function is introduced, with examples of the issues involved, and comments are given regarding some of the conflicts, stresses, and management challenges associated with each.

Place Functions

Place functions develop in the city's countryside because of considerations of accessibility to the urban agglomeration. They include residential functions, work and employment functions, the control and management of urban growth, and the development of certain recreation-tourism activities (see the play function below).

The city's countryside has become increasingly important as a choice for residence by a diverse group of people. For instance, Bryant, Russwurm, and McLellan (1982) show how farm populations within commuting radius of Canada's major urban centres from the 1940s to the 1970s dipped below non-farm populations, the turning point varying from province to province but generally occurring during the 1960s.

The results in terms of population changes in the countryside have been dramatic. Tables 13.2 through 13.4 show the changing spatial distribution of Canada's population within and outside its larger urban areas, the census metropolitan areas (CMAs) and census agglomerations (CAs).

Table 13.2 reveals the distribution of population within Canada's CMAs and CAs. Using Statistics Canada (2005c) definitions, it shows that the vast majority of the population lives in the urban core (somewhat more than 75 per cent of the population of major urban centres). Notwithstanding some northern jurisdictions, the four provinces of Atlantic Canada exhibit the smallest percentage of population concentrated in this zone. In contrast, regions in central and western Canada have markedly higher percentages of their CMA and CA populations

concentrated in core areas. Similar differences can be observed in northern Canada. While the distribution in Yukon closely mirrors the situation in Atlantic Canada, the distribution of residents in the Northwest Territories approaches that of the western provinces.

Outside the urban core, the population is distributed fairly unevenly between the urban area and rural fringe. Less than 3 per cent of the population resides in small urban nucleations, with more than 8 per cent living in scattered farm or non-farm dwellings. Again, however, variations can be observed. The urban fringe is of somewhat greater importance in Nova Scotia and New Brunswick (housing nearly 10 per cent of their CMA and CA populations), but is not significant in the northern territories. Similarly, the rural fringe plays a much greater role in the provision of living space for residents of the Atlantic region than it does for those living in other parts of southern Canada.

The city's countryside thus plays a very important role in the provision of housing in certain parts of Canada. Over the course of the past 25 years, this influence has extended beyond the statistical boundaries of many Canadian urban areas. Evidence of this has been provided in the 2001 census where, for the first time, data on external commuting in all rural and small-town municipalities (i.e., those outside the CAs and CMAs) has been collected (Bourne and Simmons, 2004). This information has been used by Statistics Canada to classify all small municipalities according to their degree of metropolitan influence. Four such metropolitan influence zones (MIZs) are recognized, based on the percentage of the population commuting to work in any CMA or CA. Those identified as strong MIZs have more than 30 per cent of the municipality's residents commuting to work in any CMA or CA. When between 5 and 30 per cent commute, the census subdivision is identified as a zone of moderate influence. Those with a commuting population of between 0 and 5 per cent are classified as zones of weak influence, whereas those with fewer than 40 (where data suppression rules apply) or no commuters are designated as zones of no influence.

Table 13.3 reveals that the total population of all metropolitan influence zones was approximately

Table 13.2   **Distribution of 2001 Population within Canada's CMAs and CAs, Provincial and Territorial Totals**

	CMA/CA Population 2001	% Urban Core	% Urban Fringe	% Rural Fringe
Nfld-Lab.	238,538	81.3	4.5	14.2
PEI	74,558	70.7	3.0	26.3
NS	574,696	66.7	9.7	26.7
NB	381,169	63.7	9.7	26.7
Quebec	5,681,453	92.8	1.0	6.2
Ontario	9,925,949	88.5	3.5	8.0
Manitoba	746,184	92.8	0.6	6.6
Sask.	565,222	89.8	3.1	7.1
Alberta	2,244,336	91.0	2.8	6.2
BC	3,369,035	89.7	4.6	5.7
Yukon	21,405	78.7	0.0	21.3
NWT	16,541	97.1	0.0	2.9
Nunavut	0	—	—	—
Total	23,839,086	88.8	2.8	8.3

Note: In cases where a CMA or CA is divided between two provinces, the breakdown by core, urban fringe, and rural fringe is reported only for the province containing the greatest population. Urban core is a large urban area around which a CMA or a CA is delineated. The urban core must have a population (based on the previous census) of at least 100,000 persons in the case of a CMA, or between 10,000 and 99,999 persons in the case of a CA. Urban fringe includes all small urban areas (with less than 10,000 population) within a CMA or CA that are not contiguous with the urban core of the CMA or CA. Rural fringe is all territory within a CMA or CA not classified as an urban core or an urban fringe.

Source: Statistics Canada, *Population Counts, for Census Metropolitan Areas and Census Agglomerations, by Urban Core, Urban Fringe and Rural Fringe, 2001 Census—100% Data.*

6 million in 2001, representing a small decline (of 0.4 per cent) between 1996 and 2001. This trend largely reflects the continuing loss of rural residents in several provinces, particularly Newfoundland (Hamilton et al., 2004) and Saskatchewan (Stabler and Olfert, 2002), where employment in certain primary-sector activities is increasingly precarious. In contrast, only three of Canada's 10 provinces experienced a net gain in their MIZ residents—Manitoba (by 0.5 per cent), Ontario, and Alberta (1.5 and 5.5 per cent respectively). Thus,

when based on aggregate data, it appears that the majority of municipalities located outside Canada's largest urban centres are in a negative demographic situation, confirming earlier comments made about the macro-scale processes of migration towards major urban regions. The growth of the city's countryside in many urban regions, therefore, is confirmed as a meso-scale dispersal process.

The data in Table 13.4, however, show that population change is not consistent throughout the four MIZ categories. Population gains have, in fact,

Table 13.3   **Population of Canada's Metropolitan Influence Zones: 2001 and 1996 (%)**

	MIZ Pop. 2001	% MIZ Pop. 2001	MIZ Pop. 1996	% MIZ Pop. 1996	% Change MIZ Pop. 1996–2001
Nfld-Lab.	274,392	53.5	306,924	55.6	−10.6
PEI	60,736	44.9	61,332	45.6	−1.0
NS	333,311	36.7	341,220	37.5	−2.3
NB	348,329	47.7	357,980	48.5	−2.7
Quebec	1,556,026	21.5	1,569,153	21.9	−0.8
Ontario	1,484,097	13.0	1,462,242	13.6	1.5
Manitoba	373,399	33.3	371,454	33.3	0.5
Sask.	413,711	42.3	428,565	43.3	−3.5
Alta	730,471	24.5	692,185	25.7	5.5
BC	538,703	13.8	544,929	14.6	−1.1
Total	6,113,175	20.4	6,135,984	21.3	−0.4

Source: See Table 13.2.

occurred in two types of areas—in municipalities that lie beyond the area of urban influence (defined by Statistics Canada) and in those where more than 30 per cent of the population commute to a CMA or CA. This latter scenario, which is the one emphasized here, can be found in every province except New Brunswick and Newfoundland.

The growth of municipalities with high levels of commuting undoubtedly reflects the ongoing trend of 'exurbanization' that has been documented for more than 50 years (McRae, 1981). First recognized by Spectorsky (1955), this demographic movement has seen the migration of urban residents to the countryside in search of a bucolic setting, while still retaining their employment ties to the urban core (or suburbs). In Canada, this movement was first observed by Pearson (1961), who drew attention to the growth of the 'Mississauga conurbation' in the late 1950s. Before long, similar patterns were being recorded across Canada around Winnipeg (Carvalho, 1974), Montreal (Brunet, 1980), Edmonton and Calgary (Smith and Johnson, 1978), and Halifax (Bruce et al., 1999).

Although it is likely that population growth in these regions is fuelled to a large extent by the exurban cohort, other individuals also have taken up residence in the city's countryside. According to Mitchell (2004), two other groups of newcomers from the city (generally called 'counter-urbanites') can be distinguished according to their migration motivation and place of employment. First, 'displaced urbanites' are individuals who have moved out of the urban core either by choice or necessity, in search of cheaper housing, a lower cost of living, or employment. Evidence of this population cohort has been found in the village of Elora, located in proximity to three CMAs (Toronto, Guelph, and Kitchener–Waterloo) (Mitchell et al., 2004). Second, anti-urbanites are attracted to the countryside for its bucolic setting (see Bourne et al., 2003; Halseth, 2003). While some choose to retire here (Dahms, 1996; Joseph and Cloutier, 1991; Rosenberg et al., 1989), others seek out, or create, employment (Mitchell et al., 2004). In each case, the implications of these moves are growth of population and potential conflict within the city's countryside.

Table 13.4   **Distribution of Population within Canada's Metropolitan Influence Zones (MIZs): 2001 and 1996 (%)**

	Strong		Moderate		Weak		No	
	% 2001	% Change since 1996	% 2001	% Change since 1996	% 2001	% Change since 1996	% 2001	% Change since 1996
Nfld-Lab.	6.5	−10.7	45.6	−10.9	39.0	−10.0	8.9	−11.2
PEI	31.8	0.1	48.4	−1.2	19.2	−2.0	1.1	−5.8
NS	6.7	4.9	29.6	−2.1	62.4	−3.2	1.4	−1.3
NB	14.5	−1.6	41.8	−3.5	38.9	−2.9	4.8	3.0
Que.	28.3	2.3	50.8	−1.3	18.0	−4.4	3.0	−0.4
Ont.	46.9	4.1	33.0	−0.1	18.2	−2.9	1.9	11.6
Manitoba	13.1	3.1	31.2	1.8	44.8	−1.3	10.9	1.4
Sask.	6.3	0.8	24.3	−2.6	46.9	−4.4	22.6	−3.5
Alta	18.3	12.7	27.6	5.9	49.1	1.8	5.0	17.9
BC	13.2	2.5	35.0	0.7	44.0	−3.9	7.8	1.1
Total	24.8	3.7	37.4	−0.9	32.2	−2.9	5.5	1.0

Note: Strong MIZ: more than 30% of the municipality's residents commute to work in any CMA or CA. Moderate MIZ: from 5% to 30% of the municipality's residents commute to work in any CMA or CA. Weak MIZ: from 0% to 5% of the municipality's residents commute to work in any CMA or CA. No MIZ: fewer than 40, where data suppression rules apply, or none of the municipality's residents commute to work in any CMA or CA.
Source: See Table 13.2.

The residential development function has been associated with substantial conflict and stress (e.g., Bourne et al., 2003; Bryant et al., 1982). Certain resources may be withdrawn from their previous functions (e.g., agricultural land resources) and land-use conflicts can be generated between the evolving residential function and other activities. Examples of the latter include residential complaints about the odours and other forms of pollution from intensive animal farming operations, increased road traffic making agricultural machinery movement more difficult, and incidents of trespass and vandalism of farm equipment and crops.

Furthermore, the influx of newcomers can lead to change in the local power structure by causing shifts in the political weight of different population segments. It has been tempting to associate these political tensions with differences in values between newcomers in their search for alternative lifestyles and long-term residents. However, in reality, the situation is often much more complex. For instance, some newcomers may demand more 'urban' types of services, but others want to keep their new place of residence as 'rural' as possible.

One of the most important challenges facing many communities in the city's countryside is how to integrate successfully people with potentially different values, regardless of their origin. This is important in the resolution of many conflicts and the reduction of stresses, as these often arise from a lack of understanding by some people about the lifestyles and activities of others in the same community. Efforts at integration include the organization of social events to sensitize newcomers to the needs and traditions of the rural community.

The city's countryside is also a place of work. This is frequently forgotten because we have tended to focus on newcomers with strong commuting ties to the urban core or suburbs. However, in addition to small levels of employment in traditional activities such as farming, aggregate mining, and services, other commercial, industrial, and service activities have developed in some small towns and in some villages and greenfield sites in the city's countryside (Coffey and Trépannier, 2003). These new employment nodes in the outer parts of metropolitan regions thus expand the reach of the urban complex by spreading the focal points for commuting patterns over a wider area. This further contributes to the creation of a more diversified and balanced set of lifestyle opportunities in the city's countryside.

Some newcomers have been able to maintain their employment ties with the central city and suburbs because of the development of telecommuting. The ease of accessibility to the urban agglomeration has certainly also given a boost to the development of some types of traditional activities such as agriculture. Some relatively novel forms of farming have developed. Community supported agriculture (CSA), for example, sees some urban consumers 'contract' with farmers, principally organic farmers, to provide a relatively steady source of farm produce delivered at distribution points in the urban area or directly to the consumer. While still marginal, CSA does provide evidence of increasing integration between city and countryside.

Some of the management and control of urban growth (including infrastructure) functions overlap with the protection of certain rural peri-urban spaces (e.g., the development of greenbelts). While densification has become an important leitmotif in the management of urban areas, much urban growth still continues in the suburbs and beyond. Furthermore, demands for 'open space'—park space and the like—in urban areas may cancel out the

metropolitan-wide effects of a densification of living spaces. All of this implies that a demand for land for future development can be expected to continue on the edges of built-up areas and beyond.

The overall shape of the urban form partly depends on what growth control measures are put in place in the rural peri-urban spaces where 'no' or 'little' growth is desired. Thus, while greenbelts and the like have been more common in some European countries, certain Canadian cities have developed similar tools, such as Ottawa's greenbelt from the late 1950s and the newly announced greenbelt for the Toronto region (Ontario, 2004a).

Largely because of accessibility, but also because of availability of space, other urban development demands have often been placed on peri-urban spaces. Transportation infrastructure—major highways, airports—have naturally been attracted to the city's countryside due to available space and, concomitantly, lower population densities. Mirabel Airport, for example, has become something of a *cause célèbre;* located towards the periphery of the Montreal metropolitan region, it has faltered and had its passenger function transferred to the urban airport at Dorval, the Pierre Elliott Trudeau International Airport. One explanation is the inability to provide adequate ground transportation connections to Montreal and other cities in the region. Other types of infrastructure development attracted by available space, accessibility, and lower population densities have been the various waste management sites serving the nearby urban areas.

Almost all these infrastructure demands generate negative externalities for the local populations—hence the attractiveness of locales with smaller population densities. But their development raises difficult questions about governance of urban and metropolitan regions. Equity considerations are also important—who pays, who benefits?

Play Functions

The city's countryside is home to many recreational and tourism-type activities. In large part, they have been developed because of accessibility to the urban consumer. While resource factors also are involved (e.g., specific natural or cultural resources in the city's countryside), proximity to the city and the urban consumer is the key factor for activities such as agro-tourism. The leisure and recreational function of the city's countryside is multi-faceted. Activities are wide-ranging—from passive activities such as landscape appreciation, through certain types of educational activities (e.g., farm-based educational experiences, nature centres), to activities involving more active use of the environment and facilities, such as cross-country skiing, snowboarding and downhill skiing, and golfing. Thus, the city's countryside is both accessible to the urban consumer and provides a diversity of leisure-time activities. Day visitors from the city—and this includes tourists using the city as a base—can enjoy the 'rural' pleasures of eating in rural restaurants, hiking through the countryside, and shopping in rural villages and small towns (Dahms and McCoomb, 1999; Mitchell, 1998; Mitchell et al., 2001; Mitchell and Coghill, 2000).

Canada's large and medium cities all have attractive nearby areas accessible by car, and sometimes public transport, e.g., the Laurentians (Montreal), the Rockies (Vancouver and Calgary), the Niagara Escarpment that runs through the backyards of several southern Ontario cities, and the ubiquitous cottage country, such as the Muskoka and Haliburton regions in south-central Ontario. Participants benefit from their experiences, and the local communities involved may—though not always—benefit from additional consumer spending. Certainly, some segments of the urban population do not have the means for easy access to 'nature' and recreation/tourist activities in the city's countryside. But some opportunities, in the form of near-urban parks, have been developed to cater to an essentially urban population through the provision of public transportation. A good example of this in Canada is the near-urban provincial park of Bronte Creek between Toronto and Hamilton in southwest Ontario.

The resources for recreation and tourist activities in the city's countryside include components of the landscape that reflect aspects of cultural heritage, the natural environment, and open spaces. The landscapes of the city's countryside contain important vestiges of our culture and its historical development—architecturally in rural buildings and in the cultural landscape, as in the case of the long lots or rangs still visible in many agricultural areas in Quebec, which date to the early settlement of New France, and the dyked lands at the top of Nova Scotia's Annapolis Valley that reflect the early Acadian presence in the region. These resources can be valued by the urban citizen; in some cases, they are directly integrated into local land-use planning and management schemes, supported by other actors with an interest in the resources (e.g., the Centre de la Nature on Mont St Hilaire southeast of Montreal). In this way, certain localities in the city's countryside witness the construction of specific multi-functional profiles involving recreation/tourism activities, the whole characterized by considerable heterogeneity (Doyon and Frej, 2003; Frej et al., 2001; Granjon, 2004).

Inevitably, stresses and conflicts are associated with the development of the play function, including incompatibilities generated by overuse of certain natural environments (e.g., in sensitive ecological areas). And, of course, some activities are not pursued only on public lands or commercial recreational property (e.g., ski hills, fish farms); some people inevitably use the private property of others to satisfy their recreational needs, creating potential problems of trespass and property damage. Recognizing the importance of these types of activities has led to various management approaches, such as negotiating access agreements, such as along the Niagara Escarpment by the Bruce Trail Association. One of the more difficult challenges is how to respect the needs of local communities while still accommodating the demands and needs of the broader regional population. This becomes particularly important in many jurisdictions where more responsibility has been placed for land-use planning at the municipal level. It is important for the actors (municipalities, organizations, the public) involved in planning, managing, and using the different localities in the city's countryside to understand and account for these sometimes competing needs.

Production Functions

Other functions developed in the city's countryside depend as much, if not more, on the resources for production located there. These include resources for supporting urban areas (construction materials, water supplies) as well as agricultural land resources.

Water resources located in the city's countryside have been important for nearby cities in several urban regions, e.g., groundwater resources in the Kitchener–Waterloo region in southwest Ontario. Water is a critical component of a sustainable life support system, and is needed for both city and rural populations and activities. Urban water demands can sometimes compete directly with other water demands, such as agricultural needs for irrigation water. Furthermore, an adequate supply of water also implies an important quality dimension, and requires that attention be paid as well to agricultural runoff and pollution. This certainly became apparent in the aftermath of the horrendous situation that developed in 2000 in the Walkerton area in southwest Ontario.

The issues are complex. A large number of water users are affected, and the involvement of public actors is necessary because of the negative externalities generated by several users and their activities. Standard land-use planning practices are not enough to regulate the supply and use of water. For instance, in relation to the negative effects associated with farming, the possible tools range from on-farm waste management requirements and directives concerning fertilizer and other chemical applications, to specifications concerning the location of intensive animal husbandry operations (e.g., in Quebec) and to more persuasive, counselling approaches (e.g., in the agricultural land reserves in the Lower Fraser Valley in British Columbia).

In some regions, the city's countryside also contains significant aggregate resources used in urban development. Because of high transportation costs, deposits of such materials close to urban markets have been the first to be exploited, making deposits in the city's countryside prized locations. This inevitably brings industry into conflict with other activities, notably residential development.

Good examples come from the various quarries close to Montreal—Mont Saint-Bruno, for instance, located about 30 km from Montreal, has a history of quarry development but has also attracted up-market residential development and a conservation park. Similarly, in southwest Ontario, the Niagara Escarpment has attracted both quarrying and residential development. The significance of these aggregate resources in Ontario was deemed sufficiently important in the early 1970s that the provincial government took steps to prevent premature development, thus preventing them from being 'sterilized' (Bryant et al., 1982).

In several provinces, the agricultural land resource in the city's countryside has been given significant attention over the last 35 years. British Columbia and Quebec, for example, have developed particularly stringent provincial legislation to protect high-quality farmland. The transformation of transportation technology for agricultural products for over a century has rapidly reduced the locational advantages for agriculture in close proximity to cities. Agriculture in our cities' countrysides must now compete with other producing regions across North America and beyond. Nevertheless, the quality of the agricultural land resources and the frequently good farm structures still convey a certain advantage to farming in the city's countryside. This advantage is enhanced by changes in consumers' preferences—local, fresh, and, increasingly, organic farm produce is highly valued today. For instance, a relative concentration of organic farms in Quebec's metropolitan regions suggests the possibilities of increasing linkages between farming in the city's countryside and the urban consumer searching for 'improved' food produce and innovations in farming (Beauchesne and Bryant, 1999). Farm production close to our cities, especially in southern Ontario, southwestern Quebec, and the Vancouver region, is particularly diversified partly because of the size of the nearby urban markets and the varied urban demand.

Given the other transformations affecting the city's countryside, it is not surprising that significant stresses and conflicts impact the agricultural system. Most obvious has been the removal of high-quality agricultural land around the fastest-growing cities, such as in southern Ontario and the Vancouver region (see the summaries in Beesley, 1999; Bryant et al., 1982; Pierce, 1981b). There are also a series of more indirect impacts of peri-urban development on agriculture. On the negative side are impacts that reduce the ability of farms to operate efficiently. Examples include farm fragmentation related to highway construction, trespass and vandalism of fields and equipment, and higher property taxes in some jurisdictions. On the positive side, other impacts contribute to stability and even prosperity of farming in the city's countryside (e.g., the potential for participation in off-farm employment and market proximity).

In assessing conflicts and stresses for farming in the city's countryside, we must recognize that not all the 'problems' result from the urban side of the conflict. In addition, difficulties stem from the nature of modern productivist agriculture—the use of pesticides, herbicides, and chemical fertilizers that pollute the wider environment, damaging wildlife habitat and killing wildlife; large-scale reliance on farm machinery that both compacts and dries out the soil; monocrop production that exhausts the soil; factory farming practices that impact the environment both physically and aesthetically. Thus, for example, throughout the 1980s and well into the 1990s, the conflicts between hog production in Quebec and non-farm residential development were so severe that stringent environmental regulations have been put into effect to control the development of these enterprises.

To a certain extent, increases in farm productivity through the development of intensive agriculture over the last half-century have reduced the negative effects on food production capacity of the conversion of farmland. However, with increasing concerns for the sustainable development of agriculture, together with mounting preoccupation over genetically modified organisms (GMOs), it is quite possible that the level of intensity of agricultural production will diminish, leading to renewed pressures to retain the best-quality farmland. In pursuit of this, local municipalities will likely appropriate more responsibility, making it imperative that

provinces with farmland protection legislation ensure that their systems are sufficiently flexible and realistic to accommodate the different interpretations that local actors are placing on farmland protection (Dumoulin and Marois, 2003).

Protection Functions

Many rural spaces in the city's countryside also possess significant protection functions. Mostly, these are associated with the other functions already referred to. Thus, various resources have come under different degrees of protection from development pressures because they have been considered essential for:

- the maintenance and development of a private economic activity—e.g., farming, aggregate mining, recreation/tourism activities—important for sustaining the quality of life of the broader population, notably in the cities;
- the maintenance of significant resources whose contribution to the broader population is principally non-market driven—e.g., cultural and heritage resources, water resources;
- the management of the urban growth process leading to more desirable urban forms—e.g., the intended protection of rural land resources, including farmland, in the new greenbelt for the Greater Toronto Area (Ontario, 2004a).

Closely related to several of these protection functions are those related to the development of scientific and educational values associated with some resources of the countryside. Again, these tend not to be organized through the marketplace, though some are. In the Ottawa greenbelt, for instance, various research establishments (e.g., an experimental farm) have been put in place, as are ecological research facilities associated with McGill University on Mont St Hilaire near Montreal. Frequently, educational facilities are also associated with various public park or conservation facilities in the city's countryside, as is the case with the interpretative centres in Ontario's conservation areas, the Ottawa greenbelt, and the Centre de la Nature at Mont St Hilaire.

Evolving Form

Characteristically, the evolving localities in the city's countryside are becoming multi-functional. But they are constructed by many actors in different ways, resulting in a mosaic of spaces that affects not only the evolving form of the city's countryside, but also the overall urban form. Figure 13.2 depicts some of the relationships. Actors (see Figure 13.1) from a variety of scales pursue their interests and objectives. Sometimes, the interests and objectives of individual non-public actors also include collective interests and objectives. Thus, actors from different arenas and scales (e.g., community and municipality, region, province) sometimes work together in partnership (and sometimes work towards the same ends without any formal relationship to each other) to construct specific types of spaces. A good example is the development of agricultural activity by farmers working in concert with the city of Longueuil (on the southern periphery of the Montreal agglomeration) (Granjon, 2004). Here efforts were made to reintroduce farming into a zone that, although under the agricultural land protection law, had become increasingly abandoned by farming. The provincial legislation was important as context, but not sufficient to ensure continued agricultural activity. This space is now being constructed not only as an agricultural space, but also as an integral part of urban form, with landscape and leisure-related functions.

In other circumstances, actors from different arenas and/or scales may act in competition and in conflict with one another. Dumoulin and Marois (2003) describe how some municipalities developed relatively innovative plans to promote farming in agricultural reserves near Montreal only to have their plans rejected by the Agricultural Land Protection Commission because the projected activity was not 'real' agriculture (activities included horse farming and riding establishments). At the more local scale, residential development has often been in conflict with agricultural development, giving rise to continuous tensions and to difficulties in coexistence. Of course, there are many examples of different functions and activities

Figure 13.2   **Actors, Actions, and Process in Creating New City's Countryside and Urban Forms**

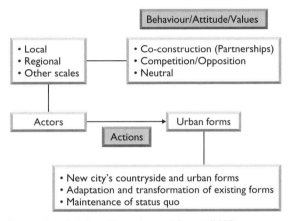

Source: Adapted from Desroches and Bryant (2005).

evolving in the same localities without any significant conflicts.

In all cases, the form of the city's countryside evolves, even though sometimes little change actually occurs. New forms may develop (e.g., a new greenbelt scheme). More generally though, existing forms are adapted and transformed—e.g., a new greenbelt form in which existing agricultural activities are intended to be maintained. The space needs to be co-constructed and local actors, including the farmers, need to appropriate the broader societal values implied in the greenbelt—otherwise, conflicts and stresses may prove difficult to manage. In all cases, the relationships that evolve contribute to a heterogeneous form for the city's countryside and, ultimately, to the evolving form of our urbanized regions.

Managing Change in the City's Countryside of the Future: Some Concluding Remarks

We have argued that the city's countryside has evolved as a series of multi-functional spaces, with all sorts of functions being intimately linked to the demands and needs of the nearby urban population.

In this sense, the city's countryside today performs strategic roles essential for the sustainable development and quality of life of urban citizens (Charvet and Bryant, 2003). Multiple actors have legitimate interests and operate at a variety of scales. These interests are not always in harmony, as is to be expected in any process involving changes in human behaviours within any environment.

Evidently, some form of management is necessary, but we see from experiences across the country that, by themselves, traditional approaches to land-use planning are not capable of dealing with most of the issues. The development of unitary forms of government linking city and countryside is not necessarily the answer either. All effective approaches, however, must link the needs of residents in the city's countryside with those of the broader regional population, and even beyond.

We have already argued that local actors—public, private, and community—construct their localities to a large extent. They are, of course, potentially influenced by the broader context—including wider structures of governance, provincial legislation regarding land-use planning, the environment, and resource protection. However, because of the trend towards local municipalities and communities acquiring greater responsibilities in managing their own space, local actors need to be associated with the development of broader schemes (e.g., greenbelts) if they are to appropriate the values embedded in these schemes and contribute to their effective construction and implementation. Because there are so few lines of direct authority between many of the actors involved, the rise of flexible and dynamic forms of governance with different forms of citizen participation appropriate to the varied localities present in the city's countryside is likely to be a major future trend. We will then likely see the growth of an even more highly differentiated countryside space, in which the only broad spatial generalizations will be associated with the statistical abstractions of the urban core, the urban fringe, and the rural hinterland.

Chapter 14

Employment in Canadian Cities

William J. Coffey and Richard G. Shearmur

Over time, an increasing share of Canada's economic activity is becoming concentrated in cities, particularly the largest city-regions. Several well-established perspectives on cities view their principal *raison d'être* as economic production; other perspectives emphasize the role of cities as the fundamental, most stable, units (rather than provinces or countries) of the emerging global economy (see Chapter 4). This chapter uses employment to explore changes in economic activity within Canada's cities. We first consider a series of changes occurring in the nature of employment itself. We then turn to the changing geography of employment, at both the inter-urban (urban system) and intra-urban scales.

The Changing Nature of Employment

Over a period of 30 years, *circa* 1971–2001, the nature of employment in Canada—and especially in its cities—has undergone significant change. An important *sectoral shift* has occurred as employment has increasingly shifted to the service sector. While about 35 per cent of all Canadian jobs were in the goods-producing sector (primary, manufacturing, and construction sectors) in 1971, with the remaining 65 per cent in the service sector, in 2001 the respective figures were 25 and 75 per cent.[1] And the vast majority (85 per cent) of service jobs are now located in cities. In the course of this 'non-industrial revolution' over 7.7 million jobs were added to the Canadian economy, with 84 per cent of these in services. Particularly striking has been the relative

decline of employment in the manufacturing sector (from 21.9 to 14.9 per cent over the period) and the increase in high-order service employment (principally business services and high-order financial services, from 7.2 to 16.1 per cent). While certain authors have interpreted these changes as deindustrialization (i.e., a loss of productive capacity), the majority of researchers now see it as a natural evolution of advanced productive systems. In other words, contrary to economic thought beginning with Adam Smith in the late eighteenth century and continuing with Karl Marx and Colin Clark in the nineteenth and twentieth centuries, it is now accepted that services—high-order services in particular—represent an important element of the economic base of urban and national economies. Just as much as the fabrication of goods or the extraction of mineral resources, services must be considered as 'productive' activities that have the capacity to contribute to—and, indeed, stimulate—economic growth. Further, in spite of the declining importance of manufacturing in Canada in terms of both GDP and total labour force, its growth has continued in absolute terms, albeit at a lower rate than that of services. Rather than being viewed as mutually exclusive activities, goods production and service production have come to be recognized as two essential elements of modern integrated production systems.

Second, from an occupational perspective, employment has become more *professionalized*.[2] Just as the economic sector is commonly classified using the simple typology of primary, secondary, and tertiary sectors, occupation is often classified in terms of activities that are white-collar (managerial and administrative, scientific and engineering, and health-care and educational), grey-collar (clerical, sales and service), and blue-collar (extractive, assembling and fabricating, construction and maintenance). Over the past 30 years, the trend in Canada and its cities has been towards a professionalization of the workforce: the percentage of workers in white-collar occupations has risen from 21.5 to 41.2 per cent, while those for blue-collar and grey-collar occupations have declined from 33.7 to 26 per cent and from 44.8 to 32.8 per cent, respectively. Out of each 100 new jobs created between 1971 and 2001, 56 involved white-collar occupations, 26 grey-collar occupations, and 18 blue-collar occupations.

The two trends—tertiarization and professionalization—are, of course, interrelated rather than simply occurring in parallel. The portion of the employed service sector labour force working in white-collar occupations has increased from 26 to 36 per cent over the 30-year period. Interestingly, the same phenomenon has occurred in the goods-producing sectors, where the proportion of white-collar workers has risen from approximately 10 to 20 per cent. This transformation has involved fundamental changes in what is produced, in how the production of goods and services is organized and carried out, and in the very nature of work. The latter point represents the next in our list of significant changes.

Third, there have also been significant changes in the *nature of work itself* and in the manner in which work is carried out. Over at least three decades, a new production system has evolved, variously termed the 'information economy' (Porat, 1977), the 'new service economy' (Gershuny and Miles, 1983), the 'new economy' (Alcaly, 2003) and the 'knowledge economy' (Neef, 1998). Thus, while employment in goods-producing sectors and in blue-collar occupations has declined, at least in relative terms, 'orientation' functions (design, planning, management, and control tasks) have risen in importance both within goods-producing firms and across all sectors of the economy. Manual labour is increasingly being replaced by mental work in

which human creativity, services, capital goods, and technology are more essential inputs than muscle power—the 'brawn to brains' shift. A related change is that the 'raw material' upon which the production of both goods and services is increasingly based is information (data, ideas, innovations, know-how, and so forth) rather than physical matter. Material inputs now represent a minor proportion of the value of virtually all manufactured goods. Meanwhile, across all sectors and occupations, work is becoming increasing sophisticated and technical. 'Production' workers, for example, are increasingly becoming operators of sophisticated machine tools and computers. There has been an up-skilling of the entire labour force and, in this context, the 'ideal' worker is one who is better educated, better trained, and more skilled in terms of social interactions. These changes have led Rifkin (1995) to predict the 'end of work'; Reich (1992, 2002) to speak of the increasing economic importance of the 'symbolic analyst' and 'the end of employment as we knew it'; and Florida (2002, 2005) to herald the rise of the 'creative class'.

Important changes have also occurred in the *form of employment*. Non-standard forms of employment—those that diverge from the traditional model of a full-time, year-round job—have been on the increase. These include part-time employment, short-term contractual employment, and self-employment. In 2001, 18.1 per cent of all Canadian workers were employed on a part-time basis (27.1 per cent of females and 10.4 per cent of males); part-time work currently accounts for approximately one-third of all new jobs created.[3] Short-term contractual employment is also on the increase, principally because of its advantages to the employer: greater flexibility, fewer or no benefits to pay, and an avoidance of unionized labour. Self-employment, too, is rapidly expanding, due in part to economic conditions and in part to the advantages to firms in shedding certain of their employees and then rehiring them as consultants or contractual workers. In 2001, approximately 15 per cent of all Canadian workers were self-employed. While non-standard forms of employment may be observed across all economic sectors, they are particularly concentrated in the consumer and personal services sectors and often involve females to a greater extent than males. Further, there is little doubt that these non-standard forms of employment have important implications for workers in terms of security of employment, level of remuneration, and benefits. Certainly the possibility exists that a portion of the labour force will be disadvantaged by the continuing 'non-industrial revolution' and that these non-standard forms of employment are dichotomizing the labour market into 'good jobs' (those that are full-time, stable, well-remunerated, and satisfying) and 'bad jobs' (those that are unstable, poorly paid, and devalorizing—often referred to as 'McJobs') (Economic Council of Canada, 1990).

Changes have also occurred in the *relative location* of employment. The next two sections of this chapter deal with the geography of employment at both inter-urban and intra-urban scales. The point here concerns the place where workers carry out their tasks, relative to the location of the firm or establishment that employs them. Increasingly, work is being accomplished outside of the physical confines of the traditional 'place of work'.[4] Recent advances in information and telecommunications technologies—everything from laptop and hand-held computers, wireless voice and data networks, call-switching technologies, and so forth—have enabled the development of both home-based telecommuting and a new generation of mobile workers: those who work from a combination of locations, including home, cars/trains/planes, customers' premises, and the central office of the company. One result of these trends is that the physical dimensions of the traditional workplace (the central office of a consulting firm or an insurance company, for example) have frequently been downsized due to 'hot-desking'—the practice of sharing a limited number of offices among a substantially larger number of mobile employees who use their offices on an occasional basis (Gillespie and Richardson, 2000). When the above-mentioned trend towards an increasing proportion of self-employed workers is factored in, it becomes evident that the traditional notion of a geographically fixed

'place of work' is undergoing a significant evolution. Unfortunately, few reliable statistics exist concerning the incidence or rate of growth of this phenomenon. The 2001 Census of Canada indicates that 8.3 per cent of the Toronto CMA (census metropolitan area) workforce had no fixed workplace, while another 6.3 per cent worked at home; for the Montreal CMA these figures are 6.4 and 5.5 per cent. It is clear that employment differs substantially from what it was as recently as two or three decades ago.[5]

As noted, Reich (1992) sees the rise of the 'symbolic analyst' and 'symbolic-analytic services' as the hallmark of the transformations occurring in the nature of work. The work of symbolic analysts includes problem-identifying, problem-solving, and strategic-brokering; their products are not standardized 'things' but, rather, the manipulations of symbols: data, words and ideas, and oral, written, and visual representations. Occupationally, this group includes a wide range of consultants, strategic planners, systems analysts, designers, and artists. Their manipulations are done with analytical tools (e.g., mathematical algorithms, legal arguments, financial manipulations, scientific principles), sharpened by experience. Some manipulations reveal how to deploy resources more efficiently, while others yield new inventions and innovations; still others serve to entertain their consumers. Reich notes that symbolic analysts are concentrated in specialized geographic zones, most of which are integral parts of selected large metropolitan areas (e.g., Wall Street, Madison Avenue, Hollywood, Silicon Valley); these zones represent a dense complex of institutions and skills that have evolved over time. Comprising 20 per cent of the US workforce in 1990, Reich notes that the symbolic analysts represent the fastest-growing segment of employment.

Florida (2002, 2005) conceptualizes these changes in terms of the rise of the 'creative class', which currently comprises one-third of the workers in advanced economies. Florida's arguments are founded on human capital theory, which posits that people, rather than firms or natural resources, are the motor of economic growth; a city's endowment of highly educated and creative people—talent, in

Florida's terminology—is the key to its success. When creative human capital clusters in certain urban areas, important productivity effects—'Jane Jacobs externalities' according to Lucas (1988), in acknowledgement of the contributions of Jacobs (1969, 1984) in this area—are the result. Florida's 'creative capital theory' extends traditional human capital theory by identifying a particular type of human capital—creative people—as the key to economic growth and identifying the underlying factors that shape the location decisions of the creative class. In Florida's view, the creative class gravitates towards places characterized by the '3 Ts of economic growth', each of which represents a necessary, but by itself insufficient, condition: technology, talent, and tolerance. He views the latter factor as particularly important; tolerance means diversity, openness, and inclusiveness with respect to all ethnicities, races, and lifestyles—in other words, low barriers to entry for all creative people. One of the most significant implications of Florida's conceptual framework is that traditional economic development efforts that seek to create a better environment for firms (often through improving the efficiency with which one can make things or do business) are misplaced; rather, in his view, greater emphasis needs to be placed on ways of making cities more attractive to the creative class through establishing an environment characterized by openness, diversity, and amenities of all types.

In sum, across the varying perspectives reviewed here, it is clear that in Canada and, most especially, in its cities, the nature of employment and of economic activity itself is undergoing profound modifications. We are developing both new economic activities and new ways of organizing and accomplishing traditional activities. Perhaps the primary theme underlying these changes is the evolution towards a 'new' or 'knowledge' economy in which knowledge, information, and know-how are both the principal factors of production and, increasingly, the final products of economic activity. Canadian cities are thus increasingly both important vectors and end results of this new knowledge economy (Lapointe, 2003). The follow-

ing sections document the geography of employment in the 'new' and 'old' economies, at both the inter-urban and intra-urban scales.

Inter-Urban Dynamics: Economic Activities within Canada's Urban System

The Metropolization of Economic Activity

Over the last three decades there has been a marked tendency for economic activity to grow in and around Canadian metropolitan areas. Over this period employment grew by 109 per cent in metropolitan areas and 80 per cent in the rest of (non-metropolitan) Canada. In 1971, 45.7 per cent of all jobs in the Canadian economy were already located within Canada's eight largest metropolitan areas; by 2001 this figure increased to 49.4 per cent (Table 14.1).[6] As one moves from manufacturing employment to that in all services—FIRE (finance, insurance, and real estate) services and business services—the proportion of national employment in the eight large CMAs increases successively. In 2001, 69.5 per cent of all Canadian business service employment is accounted for by the eight largest CMAs—which contain only 47.7 per cent of the national population. A counterpoint to the concentration of business services is provided by retail employment, where the proportion is slightly lower (47.5 per cent) than that of the population.

The difference between population growth in metropolitan and non-metropolitan areas emphasizes the rising weight of metropolitan areas—as markets and labour pools—in the Canadian economy. Population grew by 53.7 per cent in metropolitan areas, whereas it grew by only 25.3 per cent in non-metropolitan areas. Between 1971 and 2001, metropolitan areas have grown over twice as fast in terms of population.

One important factor driving metropolitan growth (demographic in nature, but closely connected to economic opportunities) is migration. Migration within Canada and migration from abroad both tend to converge upon or around the largest metropolitan areas. With Canada's natural growth

Table 14.1   **Metropolitan Concentration of Population and Employment, 1971 and 2001**

	Population	Employment	Manufacturing	All Services	FIRE	Business Services	Retail
	% Canada	% Canada	% Canada	% Canada	% Canada	% Canada	% Canada
1971							
Toronto	12.5	14.9	18.1	15.6	23.7	23.9	15.4
Montreal	12.8	12.3	15.7	12.8	17.2	17.6	11.9
Vancouver	5.0	5.4	4.4	6.2	7.8	9.4	6.0
Ottawa–Hull	3.0	3.2	1.2	4.2	3.2	3.6	2.9
Calgary	1.9	2.0	1.1	2.3	2.6	4.0	2.1
Edmonton	2.5	2.7	1.6	3.2	2.7	3.0	2.9
Quebec City	2.4	2.1	1.3	2.6	2.2	2.2	2.1
Winnipeg	2.6	2.9	2.6	3.3	3.6	2.8	3.3
Total	**42.6**	**45.7**	**45.9**	**50.1**	**63.0**	**66.5**	**46.8**
Rest of Canada	**57.4**	**54.3**	**54.1**	**49.9**	**37.0**	**33.5**	**53.2**
2001							
Toronto	15.7	16.4	17.8	16.9	26.6	25.2	15.3
Montreal	11.1	11.1	12.9	11.3	11.6	14.1	10.8
Vancouver	6.6	6.7	4.5	7.3	8.8	9.6	6.6
Ottawa–Hull	3.5	3.7	1.9	4.2	3.0	6.5	3.3
Calgary	3.2	3.6	2.4	3.8	4.0	6.4	3.4
Edmonton	3.1	3.4	2.2	3.6	3.1	3.7	3.4
Quebec City	2.3	2.3	1.5	2.5	2.6	2.4	2.4
Winnipeg	2.2	2.3	2.2	2.4	2.3	1.7	2.2
Total	**47.7**	**49.4**	**45.4**	**52.1**	**61.9**	**69.5**	**47.5**
Rest of Canada	**52.3**	**50.6**	**54.6**	**47.9**	**38.1**	**30.5**	**52.5**

Note: The CMAs are ordered by population size in 2001.

rate approaching zero, at the national scale internal migration is a zero-sum game benefiting metropolitan areas at the expense of non-metropolitan areas. International migration is thus both the only source of net national population growth and a major source of metropolitan population growth. Since, as noted, migration is often related to economic decisions that reflect employment opportunities, migration trends that benefit metropolitan areas should perhaps be viewed as a consequence, rather than a cause, of metropolization (see also Chapter 24).

The term 'metropolization' must be qualified. Many analysts have pointed out that some rural areas and small cities in Canada are experiencing rapid employment and population growth, and this is sometimes put forward as evidence that the trend towards metropolization is either illusory or, at the very least, no longer occurring. However, a closer look at the evidence suggests that it is rural zones within about an hour's drive from metropolitan areas—especially the peri-urban zones surrounding Montreal, Toronto, and Vancouver—that have been experiencing the fastest growth (Polèse and Shearmur, 2002; see also Chapter 13). These areas have benefited from a number of economic trends. The crowding out of lower value-added manufacturing employment from Canada's largest cities, as more knowledge-intensive activities have taken their place, has benefited communities where space is available, where there is easy access to services and transport infrastructure, and where costs are lower. Further, in many peri-urban zones, the number of residences of professionals is growing markedly; these 'knowledge workers' often combine physical commutes on several days a week with telecommutes on the remaining days. The tourist and leisure markets generated by metropolitan areas also spill out into surrounding small towns and rural areas, with areas such as Whistler (BC), Georgian Bay (Ontario), and the Laurentians (Quebec) benefiting from nearby metropolitan markets. Thus, metropolization of economic activity in Canada should be understood as not exclusive to metropolitan areas per se, but to metropolitan areas and their immediate hinterlands, loosely defined as all urban and rural areas within about an hour's drive from a metropolitan region. In other words, there is a strong tendency for the Canadian economy to reorganize itself in *and around* its largest metropolitan regions.

Regional-scale metropolization comes in marked contrast with growth trends in the 1950s, 1960s, and 1970s when remote areas were being opened up and settled for resource exploitation, and people believed that these regions would eventually develop to the point of becoming fully urbanized (Pomfret, 1981). In the 1960s, for example, the city of Sept-Îles in the remote Côte-Nord of Quebec was planned to accommodate about 500,000 people. It was to be the regional city in which mining, logging, and other resource-based operations would flourish, bringing with them longer-term and more varied development. This growth did not occur: from the early 1980s it became evident that rising productivity in most resource sectors, limits to the resources themselves, and evolving ideas about the best way to develop and manage resource-exploitation operations would limit employment growth in such cities, many of which have entered a phase of marked decline. Sept-Îles, whose population peaked in the early 1980s at 33,000 people, now has a population of 27,000.

The question of how to deal with declining cities and regions in non-metropolitan parts of Canada has not yet been resolved. The trend towards metropolization is strong, and rests on the well-understood location requirements of non-resource-based firms. All else being equal, such firms tend to locate in proximity to labour markets, to clients and suppliers, and—increasingly—to points from which global markets can easily be accessed. These requirements are met in and around metropolitan areas. In this regard Canada, with its vast and sparsely populated—but not empty—land base, is faced with an economic development challenge that has not yet been addressed.

The Spatial Concentration of High-Order Functions at the Top of the Urban Hierarchy

A few years ago, as the shift from a manufacturing-based to a service-based economy was being observed and documented, there was much discussion about the growth of 'footloose' industries that could easily locate in non-metropolitan regions, thereby forestalling the decline of these areas. Specifically, high-order services (by which we mean knowledge-intensive services usually produced as intermediate inputs in the production processes in other economic sectors) were envisaged as possible motors of growth for stagnating or declining regions in Canada. (New Brunswick, for example, tried to attract growth with an economic development package that showcased the province as the country's 'information highway'.) Such hopes were recently renewed with the arrival and rapid proliferation of the Internet in the late 1990s. The argument went as follows: one of the problems facing non-metropolitan areas is their distance from markets and the difficulty of transporting goods to and from remote regions. High-order services, one of the fastest-growing sectors since the early 1970s, do not need to be located close to their markets; their main input is information, and their main output is knowledge, both of which can be transmitted at virtually no cost.

High-order services have grown rapidly since the early 1970s in Canada: employment in these activities has increased by 244 per cent to reach 1.77 million jobs in 2001. Although high-order services have grown throughout the Canadian economy, they have generally tended to grow faster in metropolitan areas (Table 14.2). Further, all metropolitan areas have not performed equally. Whereas high-order service growth in Montreal and Winnipeg (156.4 and 105.5 per cent respectively) has been slower than in the 'rest of Canada' (Canada minus the eight largest metropolitan areas—a growth rate of 225.8 per cent), growth in the six other CMAs has been very high, varying between 273 and 500 per cent.

Notwithstanding the changes occurring within the set of Canadian metropolitan areas, there has been a remarkable stability over time with respect to the relative location of high-order services across Canada. Indeed, the location of these services is very closely related to the urban hierarchy: there are relatively more high-order services in Canada's largest cities, and as cities become smaller their presence is less felt. This is in accordance with central place theory, which suggests that high-order functions—those that are relatively specialized and are required only intermittently or those for which only a few providers exist—will tend to agglomerate in the larger central cities. It can be argued that the Internet, far from diminishing the attraction of

metropolitan areas for high-order services, has in fact increased it as the larger and better-connected firms in Canada's largest cities can now more easily compete for contracts in smaller and more remote regions.

Over the most recent period for which we have data (1996–2001), the gap in high-order service growth rates has widened between metropolitan and non-metropolitan areas, after a period of stability between 1981 and 1996. There are therefore signs that high-order services, in particular 'high-tech' services, are tending to concentrate further in Canada's largest cities.

This in turn fuels the metropolization of Canada's economy: as increasing numbers of firms require access to the type of knowledge and advice that high-order services provide, and as it becomes more important to interact with advisers who are part of international or global networks, access to this type of high-order service is becoming a location factor in its own right. Location within an hour's drive of a large metropolitan area ensures ready access to the knowledge and connections provided by high-order services. In turn, as the market for high-order services concentrates in and around metropolitan areas, so will high-order services. Although this circle may eventually be broken, it will most probably be peri-urban areas and smaller cities within easy reach of metropolitan areas that will attract high-order service functions; it is unlikely that such 'footloose' sectors will be a vector of economic revival for remote cities and regions.

A final and more general point can be made about high-order service functions. In spite of the rhetoric, these types of service require intense and frequent face-to-face interaction between clients and service providers: 'co-production', as it is often called. The services rendered are often complex and unique, devising a publicity campaign or exploring the possible liabilities of a new product, for example, and require personal contact for knowledge to be transmitted. Thus, two types of service provision exist. The first is proximity-based service provision, where the service provider is located within easy reach of the client. Clearly, the best location from which to maximize such access is close to the centre

Table 14.2 Employment and Growth in High-order Services, 1971–2001

	1971				2001			
	Professional	High-Tech	FIRE	Total	Professional	High-Tech	FIRE	Total
Toronto	21,654	14,726	85,912	122,291	76,615	161,840	218,240	456,695
Montreal	15,244	11,549	62,225	89,018	40,165	93,105	94,995	228,265
Vancouver	7,073	7,162	28,126	42,360	27,735	63,015	72,070	162,820
Ottawa–Hull	2,321	3,165	11,657	17,143	10,135	51,715	24,890	86,740
Calgary	2,372	3,648	9,534	15,553	14,415	46,190	32,710	93,315
Edmonton	2,298	2,225	9,874	14,397	9,980	24,900	25,355	60,235
Quebec City	1,811	1,590	8,058	11,459	5,960	16,620	21,660	44,240
Winnipeg	2,603	1,582	12,981	17,167	5,965	10,360	18,945	35,270
Total	**55,376**	**45,646**	**228,367**	**329,389**	**190,970**	**467,745**	**508,865**	**1,167,580**
Rest of Can.	**30,429**	**20,508**	**133,904**	**184,840**	**104,195**	**185,085**	**312,950**	**602,230**

	% of Canada 1971				% of Canada 2001			
	Professional	High-Tech	FIRE	Total	Professional	High-Tech	FIRE	Total
Toronto	25.2	22.3	23.7	23.8	26.0	24.8	26.6	25.8
Montreal	17.8	17.5	17.2	17.3	13.6	14.3	11.6	12.9
Vancouver	8.2	10.8	7.8	8.2	9.4	9.7	8.8	9.2
Ottawa–Hull	2.7	4.8	3.2	3.3	3.4	7.9	3.0	4.9
Calgary	2.8	5.5	2.6	3.0	4.9	7.1	4.0	5.3
Edmonton	2.7	3.4	2.7	2.8	3.4	3.8	3.1	3.4
Quebec City	2.1	2.4	2.2	2.2	2.0	2.5	2.6	2.5
Winnipeg	3.0	2.4	3.6	3.3	2.0	1.6	2.3	2.0
Total	**64.5**	**69.0**	**63.0**	**64.1**	**64.7**	**71.6**	**61.9**	**66.0**
Rest of Can.	**35.5**	**31.0**	**37.0**	**35.9**	**35.3**	**28.4**	**38.1**	**34.0**

	Growth Rates 1971–2001			
	Professional	High-Tech	FIRE	Total
Toronto	253.8	999.0	154.0	273.4
Montreal	163.5	706.2	52.7	156.4
Vancouver	292.1	779.9	156.2	284.4
Ottawa–Hull	336.6	1534.1	113.5	406.0
Calgary	507.8	1166.1	243.1	500.0
Edmonton	334.3	1019.1	156.8	318.4
Quebec City	229.1	945.6	168.8	286.1
Winnipeg	129.1	554.7	45.9	105.5
Rest of Can.	**242.4**	**802.5**	**133.7**	**225.8**

Note: Professional services: legal services, accounting, marketing.

High-tech services: computer services, architectural and engineering consultants, management consultants.

FIRE services: finance, insurance, and real estate.

of a large market area. The second is delivery of the service over long distances, where a consultant (or the client) travels. The most accessible locations, both nationally and internationally, are metropolitan areas towards which air and road transport routes converge. These more general arguments further emphasize the point that, in Canada as elsewhere, high-order services are likely to continue their rapid growth in metropolitan areas, the Internet or other communications technologies notwithstanding.

Functional Specialization and Complementarity within the Urban System

It is already clear from the two previous sections that all cities do not play the same role within the Canadian urban system. A variety of 'city types' can be identified, many of which resemble those identified by researchers in other developed countries (Coffey and Shearmur, 1996). One method of identifying sets of urban areas that are most similar in terms of their employment profiles is to use statistical analysis. For present purposes, we performed a *cluster analysis*, a hierarchical grouping algorithm, using location quotients (measures comparing the spatial concentration of employment in a given sector in a given city to that sector's level of concentration in the Canadian economy) for each economic sector in each city as the basic data. (See Coffey and Shearmur, 1996, for a detailed description of this method.) Using 2001 data for all 152 CMAs, census agglomerations (CAs), and census subdivisions (CSDs) of over 10,000 people, the cluster analysis results in the identification of eight groups of urban areas (Table 14.3).

Four basic types of cluster emerge:

- Group 3 corresponds to cities with a diversified economic structure.
- Group 4 gathers cities that are highly specialized in public administration.
- Groups 5, 6, and 8 include cities specialized in the primary sector and one or two other sectors (transport and public administration for Group 5;

low-order services and public administration for Group 6; and first-transformation manufacturing and services for Group 8). Cities in these clusters are primarily located in peripheral areas.
- Groups 1, 2, and 7 encompass cities specializing in manufacturing and one or two other sectors (public services for Group 1; low-order services for Group 2; and retail and public administration for Group 7). Cities in Groups 1 and 2 are principally in central areas, whereas those in Group 7 are mainly in the periphery.

Most of Canada's large metropolitan areas, with a few notable exceptions, fall into Group 3. They tend to have very diversified economies, with an emphasis on high-order services and on certain government and medical sectors. Within this broad class of cities, Toronto stands out as being relatively specialized in high-order services and Montreal in manufacturing activities. The presence of many resource-related office functions in Vancouver biases its economic structure towards resources, as does, to a lesser extent, the oil-based economy of Calgary. In fact, a key question relating to Calgary is whether, given its recent very fast growth, its economy will become more diversified and independent of its resource sector. Some smaller places such as Regina, Moncton, and Rimouski (with about 50,000 to 300,000 people) also have a diversified industrial structure similar to that of larger metropolitan areas. These are small metropolitan areas (and census agglomerations, in the case of Moncton and Rimouski), distant from Canada's principal CMAs, that play an important role in providing a range of specialized economic functions at a regional level. It is particularly interesting to note that Guelph and St-Jean-sur-Richelieu, both within the zone of influence of major CMAs—Toronto and Montreal, respectively—are the only cities in Group 3 that were not a part of the group in 1991, when both were in Group 1 (manufacturing and public services). Their economies have diversified significantly in the last decade.

Among Canada's metropolitan areas Ottawa–Hull (now Gatineau) and several provincial capitals, such as Halifax, Victoria, and Quebec City, stand out

Table 14.3   **Sectorial Typology of Canadian Urban Areas, 2001**

Group 1: Manufacturing and Public Services

New Glasgow, NS	Montmagny, Que.	Shawinigan, Que.
Cornwall, Ont.	Saguenay, Que.	Drummondville, Que.
Hawkesbury, Ont.	Saint-Georges, Que.	Granby, Que.
Brockville, Ont.	Thetford Mines, Que.	Saint-Hyacinthe, Que.
Belleville, Ont.	Sherbrooke, Que.	Joliette, Que.
Cobourg, Ont.	Cowansville, Que.	Salaberry-de-Valleyfield, Que.
Port Hope, Ont.	Victoriaville, Que.	Lachute, Que.
Lindsay, Ont.	Trois-Rivières, Que.	Saint-Jérôme, Que.

Group 2: Basic Manufacturing and Low-Order Services

Strathroy, Ont.	Woodstock, Ont.	Wallaceburg, Ont.
Bracebridge, Ont.	Tillsonburg, Ont.	Sarnia–Clearwater, Ont.
Huntsville, Ont.	Stratford, Ont.	Collingwood, Ont.
St Catharines–Niagara, Ont.	Chatham, Ont.	Orillia, Ont.
Brantford, Ont.	Windsor, Ont.	Midland, Ont.

Group 3: Diversified Economy

Calgary, Alta	Toronto, Ont.	Barrie, Ont.
Edmonton, Alta	Hamilton, Ont.	Rimouski, Que.
Vancouver, BC	Kitchener, Ont.	St-Jean-sur-Richelieu, Que.
Winnipeg, Man.	Guelph, Ont.	Montreal, Que.
Moncton, NB	London, Ont.	Regina, Sask.
Saint John, NB	Owen Sound, Ont.	Saskatoon, Sask.
Oshawa, Ont.		

Group 4: Public Admin., Primary, & Services

Victoria, BC	Halifax, NS	Whitehorse, Yukon
Fredericton, NB	Ottawa–Hull, Ont.-Que.	Yellowknife, NWT
St John's, Nfld	Quebec City, Que.	

Group 5: Primary, Transport, & Public Admin.

Prince Rupert, BC	Gander, Nfld	Moose Jaw, Sask.
Thompson, Man.	Kenora, Ont.	

Table 14.3   **(continued)**

Group 6: Primary, Low-Order Services, & Public Admin.

Lethbridge, Alta	Edmundston, NB	Thunder Bay, Ont.
Camrose, Alta	Kentville, NS	Charlottetown, PEI
Wetaskiwin, Alta	Truro, NS	Summerside, PEI
Cranbrook, BC	Sydney, NS	Amos, Que.
Penticton, BC	Pembroke, Ont.	Rivière-du-Loup, Que.
Kelowna, BC	Kingston, Ont.	Alma, Que.
Vernon, BC	Peterborough, Ont.	Dolbeau, Que.
Kamloops, BC	Simcoe, Ont.	Sept-Iles, Que.
Duncan, BC	North Bay, Ont.	Val-d'Or, Que.
Nanaimo, BC	Sudbury, Ont.	Rouyn-Noranda, Que.
Courtenay, BC	Elliot Lake, Ont.	Yorkton, Sask.
Campbell River, BC	Haileybury, Ont.	Swift Current, Sask.
Terrace, BC	Kirkland Lake, Ont.	Weyburn, Sask.
Prince George, BC	Timmins, Ont.	North Battleford, Sask.
Dawson Creek, BC	Sault Ste Marie, Ont.	Prince Albert, Sask.
Brandon, Man.		

Group 7: First-Transformation Mfg., Retail, & Public Admin.

Port Alberni, BC	Campbellton, NB	Roberval, Que.
Kitimat, BC	Grand Falls–Windsor, Nfld	Matane, Que.
Selkirk, Man.	Corner Brook, Nfld	Baie-Comeau, Que.
Portage la Prairie, Man.	Kapuskasing, Ont.	La Tuque, Que.
Bathurst, NB	Gaspé, Que.	Sorel, Que.

Group 8: Primary, First-Transformation Mfg., & Services

Medicine Hat, Alta	Matsqui, BC	Haldimand, Ont.
Red Deer, Alta	Powell River, BC	Nanticoke, Ont.
Lloydminster, Alta	Williams Lake, BC	Leamington, Ont.
Grand Centre, Alta	Quesnel, BC	Sainte-Marie, Que.
Grande Prairie, Alta	Fort St John, BC	Magog, Que.
Fort McMurray, Alta	Labrador City, Lab.	Estevan, Sask.
Chilliwack, BC	Dunnville, Ont.	

as having a highly specialized economic structure dominated by public administration (Group 4); the only other cities with such an economic structure are small administrative outposts in peripheral regions, i.e., Yellowknife and Whitehorse. Other cities, such as Saguenay (Group 1) and Sault Ste Marie (Group 6), while still playing the role of regional service centres, tend to have a more distinct economic specialization. Saguenay and Sault Ste Marie, for instance, are heavily dependent on resource extraction and on manufacturing.

Smaller cities in Canada's periphery often have strong resource sectors, and some also have high concentrations of first-transformation manufacturing (such as wood or fish processing, Groups 7 and 8). Small central places can also be found in the periphery, often characterized by high concentrations of government, health, education, and retail services, and sometimes associated with a specialization in one other industry. These central places provide lower-order services to their immediate, resource-dependent hinterland. Depending on their size and the economic trend in the hinterland, such cities are either thriving or in decline. Decline—which has been more common since the 1990s—is usually initiated by loss of economic opportunities linked with dwindling employment in resource-based sectors: it is often associated with out-migration and the closing down of certain services (such as schools or health facilities). Other services, such as durable product retailing, can increasingly be delivered over the Internet, leading to closings even in the absence of population decline. Thriving service centres in the periphery are in areas benefiting either from resource development (such as certain parts of Alberta and Newfoundland) or from in-migration from their hinterlands as population and economic activity decline in rural areas and migrate towards regional central places.

Small cities surrounding large metropolitan areas have a variety of functions. Some specialize in traditional or medium value-added manufacturing. Others are more specialized in construction—an activity closely associated with the nearby metropolitan markets. Yet others—usually small ones—specialize in leisure and entertainment activities.

Such specialization reflects their dependence for many services (whether government, high-order, or personal services or even certain types of retailing) on larger cities. An increasing number of such cities, especially those surrounding Toronto, are specializing in certain types of high-order services (often those that require sizable back-office operations, such as insurance).

There is some evidence that, in certain parts of the country, retirement-related migration is beginning to play a role in determining population levels (and hence low-order and health service levels); in some cases, especially in those places with high amenity value, retirement migration may be weakening the link between economic opportunity and population growth. An interesting example of this is Elliot Lake (Group 6), a formerly active mining community in northern Ontario that has managed to market its vacant apartments and houses to young retirees. The health and community facilities, initially built for the mining community, are now being used by the more elderly population. However, evidence also indicates that elderly people are migrating from peripheral areas towards cities and metropolitan areas in more central regions to be close to services and to their children. Counter-trends such as those observed in Elliot Lake, while they should not be ignored, are unlikely to reverse the general trend towards metropolization.

Intra-Metropolitan Changes in the Location of Economic Activities

Although the suburbanization of some manufacturing employment was already occurring in Canadian cities prior to World War II (Lewis, 2000), most economic activity remained concentrated in or around the central business district (CBD) until the early 1950s. This was in large part attributable to the limited mobility of the workforce and to the requirement that most industries be located in areas with good access to transport infrastructures such as railway lines and port facilities.

The end of World War II witnessed a massive wave of suburbanization, led by residential development, itself often fuelled by two types of government policies. First, mortgage guarantees (especially for the purchase of *new* houses) encouraged new development. Second, the rapid building of intra- and inter-urban highways—which occurred in large part during the 1950s, 1960s, and early 1970s—enabled this development to encroach on land further and further away from the city centre. Rising affluence—and, specifically, car ownership—was a necessary condition for such development. Population was also increasing rapidly during this period due to both in-migration and high birth rates. Therefore, a certain physical expansion of cities was inevitable in the absence of increasing density—a form clearly not favoured by the North American lifestyle.

From an economic perspective, the first type of activity to follow the population to the suburbs was final demand services—retail and consumer service functions. The hallmark of this suburbanization was the shopping mall, serving either a neighbourhood or a subregional market.

Next, in response to the dispersal of the workforce and to the better accessibility and lower cost of suburban land, manufacturing activity began to locate further from the urban core, either as freestanding factories or in industrial parks. Other types of activity such as warehousing, distribution centres, and wholesaling moved to similar locations; these functions have similar land requirements (low costs, accessibility, large lots) and are often subject to similar zoning requirements.

The increase in job opportunities in the suburbs is not only a consequence of the suburbanization of the population, but must also be regarded as a cause of this phenomenon. With the creation of suburban economic activities, it became possible for developers to implant housing even further from the city centre while ensuring adequate access to employment opportunities for the residents. Thus, although the initial impetus behind suburbanization may well have been the centrifugal movement of population, Lewis (2000) indicates that it very quickly became difficult to disentangle the demographic from the economic processes occurring in the urban periphery.

The New Suburbanization and Edge Cities

From the 1970s onward, a new phenomenon began to be observed in many cities across North America: the suburbanization of office employment. Initially, this involved mainly *back-office* functions—those more standardized and routinized activities not involving direct contact with the client (e.g., data entry, credit card billing). These activities were attracted to suburban locations that provided good access to certain types of labour (e.g., relatively well-educated women), inexpensive land costs or office rents, and good access to the CBD where head offices often remained (Nelson, 1986).

In the 1980s, a new wave of decentralization began to be observed in North American metropolitan areas: the suburbanization of head offices and other high-order *front-office* functions that, previously, remained concentrated in the CBD of the central city. Stanback (1991) refers to this phenomenon as the 'new suburbanization' and Garreau (1991) identifies the creation of 'edge cities' as its principal result. Edge cities, large concentrations of office functions (involving a minimum of 5 million square feet of office space and a minimum of 20,000 employees, according to Garreau's criteria) that are located at the intersections of major highways and often associated with large shopping centres, may be regarded as 'suburban downtowns' (Chapter 10), offering many of the advantages of traditional CBDs: retail, entertainment, and leisure facilities, possibilities for face-to-face contact with clients and complementary high-order services, and, above all, economies of agglomeration made possible by the density of economic functions.

Suburban Downtowns and the Decline of the CBD

Edge cities are increasingly in direct competition with the CBD as centres of high-order office activities and their growth has incited a debate concerning the possible decline of the economic primacy of the CBD in North American metropolitan areas. Garreau (1991) identified three possible scenarios for edge city development: the CBD retains its economic primacy, with edge cities playing a secondary role; edge cities and the CBD share the role as the locus of high-order office functions; and one or more edge cities become the centres of high-order office activities as the traditional CBD enters into a phase of decline (see also Chapter 10). Most often, it is in fact unclear whether edge cities, or suburban downtowns, are competing with, or complementary to, the traditional CBD. In a context of extremely fast growth in high-order functions across the whole economy, it is normal that segmentation should occur: the 'lower-ranking' high-order services are possibly being pushed out of the traditional CBD towards suburban locations, while only the 'highest' high-order services remain in the traditional centre. Current methods of classifying employment (often based on the final product of an establishment, not on the complexity of the tasks performed) make it difficult to distinguish between different functions within the general category of high-order services. Notwithstanding this limitation, there is evidence that high-order services in suburban locations have a propensity to serve the local (i.e., intra-metropolitan) market rather than to be export-oriented; as well, suburban service establishments are often back-office functions of strategic downtown service activities (Coffey et al., 1996; Harrington and Campbell, 1997; Shearmur and Alvergne, 2002).

Evidence from some US cities, such as Detroit and Baltimore, clearly indicates that the traditional CBD has suffered a process of long-term decline, and that growth of all sorts—retail, manufacturing, and high-order service—has only been occurring in suburban locations. In these cases, it would appear that edge cities are indeed supplanting the urban core. This is not the case in all cities, however. In New York, for example, growth in the suburbs is attributable to the very high costs of locating in Manhattan and to the lack of space there. Manhattan itself has not been supplanted as a high-order service centre, although only the 'highest' high-order services are prepared and able to pay Manhattan rents.

Agglomeration and 'Scatteration'

The growth of edge cities was well-documented by the early 1990s. Even if these agglomerations of office-based activities were located in the suburbs, they remained recognizable as relatively dense spatial concentrations of employment. More recently, Fujii and Hartshorn (1995) and Gordon and Richardson (1996) have suggested, after studying the Atlanta and Los Angeles metropolitan areas respectively, that economic activity—and high-order services in particular—is no longer agglomerating; the polycentric metropolitan form induced by edge cities may be entering a phase of decline. These authors suggest that employment is increasingly dispersed across the entire urban region (the phenomenon of 'scatteration', in the words of Gordon and Richardson). The increased mobility attributable to ever rising car use, combined with the possibility of conducting routine communications via electronic means, may be rendering obsolete the need for close proximity at the intra-urban level. We have emphasized that, at the inter-urban level, proximity and agglomeration continue to play a vital role in understanding the location of economic activity. Gordon and Richardson (1996) are suggesting that this may no longer be the case at the intra-metropolitan scale. The implications of this viewpoint are quite significant, calling into question the validity of the concept of agglomeration economies at the intra-metropolitan scale. As we have observed elsewhere (Coffey and Shearmur, 2002), however, in the Canadian context, 'reports of the demise of agglomeration economies have been greatly exaggerated.'

In a variation on the scatteration theme, Lang (2003) introduces the concept of 'edgeless cities': widely scattered office developments, often consisting of single buildings at very low densities. Lacking the density and cohesiveness of edge cities, edgeless cities are almost imperceptible on the metropolitan landscape—they can be qualified of 'stealth cities'. Lang notes that while edge cities and traditional downtowns continue to play an important role in providing the conditions necessary for the location of many types of high-order services and office activities, in the US context edgeless cities now contain more office space and office jobs than do edge cities: two-thirds of all non-downtown office space in most metropolitan areas, as opposed to only one-third in edge cities. In addition, the growth of office space and employment in edgeless cities is much more rapid than in edge cities. According to Lang, edge cities may be on the way to becoming the exception rather than the rule.

Intra-Metropolitan Employment Distribution: A Tale of Four CMAs

So far, at the intra-metropolitan scale, little specific mention has been made of Canadian cities, primarily because many of the ideas just reviewed have been developed in the context of US cities. Already, we have pointed out that some differences exist between US cities themselves: Baltimore and Detroit, with declining CBDs, differ from New York and Chicago, which have strong CBDs (together with growing edge cities), and all four differ from Los Angeles and Atlanta, in which economic activity is tending to scatter. Thus, while the processes described above are indeed occurring, they are often playing out differently in different urban contexts.

In a previous study (Shearmur and Coffey, 2002) we conducted a detailed analysis of the intra-metropolitan geography of employment in Canada's four largest CMAs—Toronto, Montreal, Vancouver, and Ottawa–Hull (now Ottawa–Gatineau)—over the period 1981–96, seeking to answer two questions. First, do large Canadian CMAs follow a similar pattern of spatial development? Second, do these Canadian CMAs follow patterns similar to those described for US cities? We used two principal approaches in attempting to answer these questions: an analysis of employment centres (identified using a methodology applied at the census tract level based on an employment threshold of 5,000 jobs and an employment-to-resident worker (E/R) ratio greater than 1.0), and on an analysis of employment by concentric rings. Looking first at employment

centres, Figures 14.1–14.4 identify the location and relative size of employment centres in the four CMAs in 1996. Table 14.4 presents the distribution of employment in 1996 in three metropolitan zones: the CBD (itself an employment centre), employment centres outside of the CBD, and the remaining metropolitan zone (not in an employment centre). Perhaps the most notable aspect of this table is the percentage of CMA employment outside of centres in Montreal (59.3 per cent), a figure that is significantly higher than in the other three metropolitan areas. Table 14.5 focuses on employment growth in the four CMAs. In each case, the CBD is the zone that has seen the slowest employment growth; with the exception of Ottawa–Hull, the most rapid growth occurred in the non-CBD employment centres.

Figure 14.5 presents the results of the analysis of total employment by concentric rings centred on the CBD. Two distinct urban forms emerge. On the one hand, both Ottawa–Hull and Montreal display essentially monotonic distance decay patterns with a strong central area (significantly stronger in relative terms in the case of Ottawa–Hull), a high number of jobs close to the centre, and fewer jobs as one moves further away. Toronto and Vancouver display a different pattern, with a relatively strong central area (proportionally stronger in the case of Vancouver) surrounded by a ring with fewer jobs. In these CMAs, the highest proportion of jobs is found in the rings beyond 10 km from the CBD. In Toronto, in particular, the third and fourth rings each contain more jobs than the central zone; 68 per cent of all jobs are located more than 10 km from the centre. In Montreal, in contrast, 59 per cent of all jobs are located within 10 km of the centre. Similar analysis for manufacturing, consumer services, FIRE, and business services reveals that the domination of the central ring is particularly evident in the case of FIRE and (except in the case of Toronto) producer services. Finally, Figure 14.6 indicates changes in the distribution of total employment across the concentric zones over the period 1981–96. The distribution of growth in total employment differs markedly across the CMAs. In

Figure 14.1 **Montreal Employment Centres, 1996**

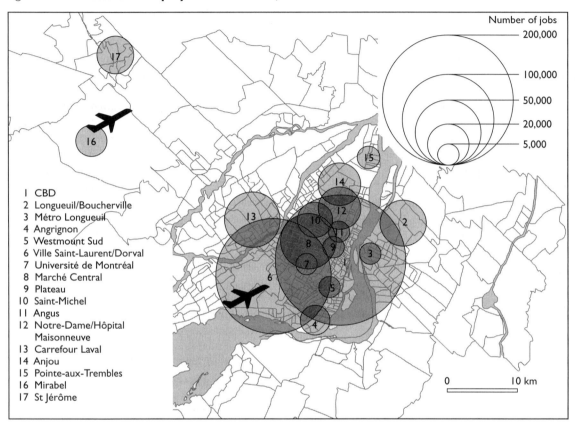

Montreal, over 70 per cent of employment growth occurred within 20 km of the centre. In Toronto, the first two rings experienced absolute decline in employment and 91 per cent of job growth occurred more than 20 km from the centre. Ottawa's pattern is relatively similar to that of Montreal, while Vancouver represents a hybrid characterized by strong growth in the central ring and the outer suburbs.

What do these analyses tell us about Canada's four largest CMAs, especially as compared to their US counterparts? In Canada, there is little evidence that CBDs are declining, at least over the 1981–96 period when many of the 'new suburbanization' changes described above were taking place. This may partly be due to the fact that in no Canadian city has there been major social or racial unrest to compare with

that occurring in the US. While the fortunes of city centres may have waxed and waned, in Canada there has been no compelling reason for people or for economic activity to flee the city centre. Suburban growth has been a natural consequence of overall population and employment growth, as well as of the changing needs in certain economic sectors. Economic activity has tended to overflow from the CBD into new—often suburban—locations without bringing about a decline of the CBD. More often than not, certain types of suburbs (for example, the traditional industrial suburbs in east-end Montreal) have declined at the expense of the more 'high-tech' manufacturing suburbs (such as Ville St Laurent and Dorval in Montreal's west island).

This does not mean that Canadian cities are not changing: in fact, different spatial patterns of devel-

Figure 14.2   **Ottawa–Hull Employment Centres, 1996**

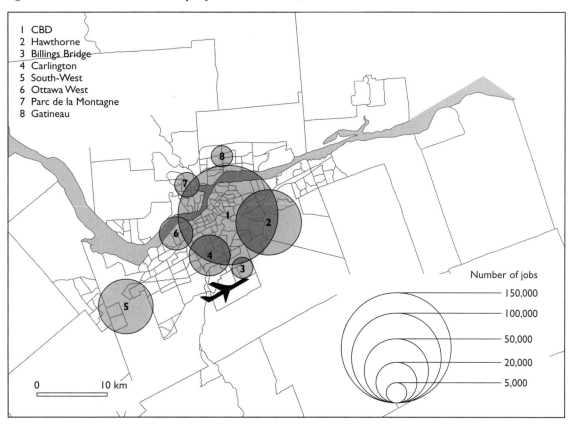

opment are observed in each of the major metropolitan areas. Toronto is developing along lines similar to New York and Chicago. Its CBD (which is not synonymous with the central ring discussed above) remains strong and is not declining, but most employment growth, whether manufacturing or high-order service, is occurring in suburban employment centres situated at highway intersections over 20 km from the CBD. These centres tend to be complementary to each other, with some having a marked manufacturing specialization (such as Markham) and others being more service-oriented (such as Mississauga).

In Montreal, on the other hand, most high-order service growth is occurring in and around the traditional CBD, with very little evidence of growth at any distance from the CBD. Manufacturing employment has declined almost everywhere across the metropolitan area, except in certain suburban employment centres (mainly Ville St Laurent/Dorval) where it has grown strongly. Retail growth is more dispersed and tends to agglomerate less than other activities. Recent evidence from Montreal, covering the 1996–2001 period, shows that the CBD and the major employment centres have reinforced their positions: growth has been faster in employment centres than in the zones outside of centres; employment has not undergone a general dispersal across the metropolitan area. Having said this, about 50 per cent of all employment growth has occurred outside of employment centres, principally along the major highways; linear centres are thus being created.

Figure 14.3 **Toronto Employment Centres, 1996**

Vancouver has a strong CBD and only one medium-sized employment centre (Richmond). However, it has a large number of small—mainly service-oriented—subcentres. Here, too, the CBD retains strong high-order functions, although some of the very smallest subcentres seem to be attracting some of these functions. Most of the subcentres are located at some distance from the Vancouver CBD. Unlike Toronto, but like Montreal, Vancouver's CBD remains clearly dominant in terms of its high-order functions. Unlike Montreal, but like Toronto, Vancouver's subcentres are located at some distance from the CBD.

There is no simple intra-metropolitan model that can describe the space economy of Canada's

major cities. Furthermore, it is unlikely, given their evolution between 1981 and 1996 (Shearmur and Coffey, 2002)—and up to 2001 in the case of Montreal (Terral and Shearmur, 2005)—that Canadian cities are merely at an earlier stage of a general development towards edge cities and the scatteration of employment. Rather, elements of new and older spatial processes are intertwined in the economies of each city, with each city developing along recognizable, but independent, lines. This is underscored by policy decisions: in Montreal, for instance, the strong CBD has been further strengthened by government underwriting of three major office developments since the mid-1990s (the Cité du Multimédia, the Cité

Figure 14.4   **Vancouver Employment Centres, 1996**

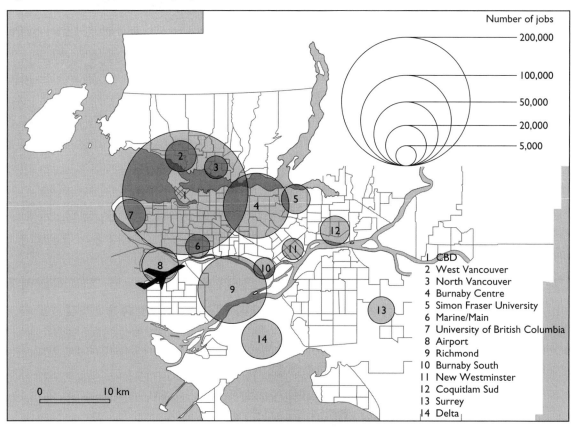

Table 14.4   **Employment Distribution in Montreal, Toronto, Ottawa–Hull, and Vancouver, 1996**

	Montreal		Toronto		Ottawa–Hull		Vancouver	
	Employment (000)	% of CMA	Employment (000)	% of CMA	Employment (000)	% of CMA	Employment (000)	% of CMA
CBD	203.0	14.0	362.2	17.9	121.3	25.1	187.1	22.7
Other employment centres	386.7	26.7	714.3	35.4	142.3	29.4	219.4	26.6
Remaining (non-centre) zone	859.7	59.3	942.9	46.7	219.7	45.5	417.4	50.7
Total	1,449.4	100.0	2,019.4	100.0	483.3	100.0	823.9	100.0

Table 14.5   **Employment Growth in Montreal, Toronto, Ottawa–Hull, and Vancouver, 1981–1996**

	Montreal		Toronto		Ottawa–Hull		Vancouver	
	Growth (000s)	Rate %	Growth (000s)	Rate %	Growth (000s)	Rate %	Growth (000s)	Rate %
All centres	117.5	24.8	224.3	26.3	70.0	36.19	130.1	47.1
CBD	15.0	8.0	1.0	0.3	18.5	18.03	25.5	15.8
Other employment centres	102.6	35.9	223.3	42.4	51.5	56.76	104.6	91.1
Remaining (non-centre) zone	123.8	26.2	260.2	9.3	74.0	69.77	158.9	74.3
Total	241.3	19.8	484.6	31.3	144.0	42.1	289.0	53.6

Figure 14.5   **Concentric Rings: Percentage of CMA Total Employment, 1996**

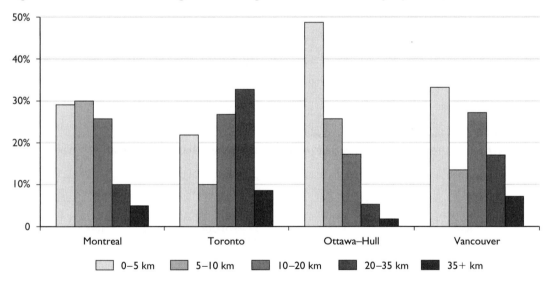

Internationale, and the Cité du Commerce Électronique). Prestigious residential developments in and around Vancouver's downtown strengthen its image and attractiveness for high-end services. And ongoing policies such as subsidized suburban transport (the GO train in Toronto and the expand-ing commuter train system in Montreal), under-ground transit (Montreal and Toronto), and the Sky Train in Vancouver also structure these cities' spatial economy.

The general patterns observed across US cities certainly help in understanding the patterns

Figure 14.6 **Concentric Rings: % of Total Employment Change, 1981–1996**

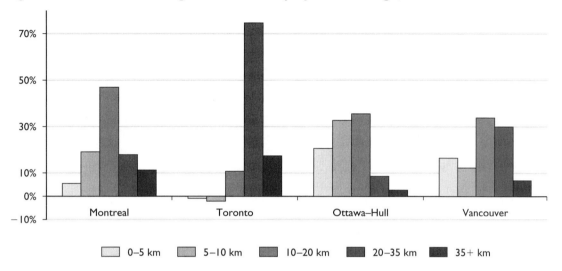

observed in Canada; however, just as patterns differ quite substantially between US cities, they also differ between those in Canada. These patterns reflect certain general processes linked to the historic development of cities during the twentieth century and to recent changes in metropolitan economies. They also reflect specific policy contexts, differing social and geographic contexts, and decisions relating to transport and land-use planning at the regional level.

Conclusion

In this chapter we have examined employment in Canada's cities from several perspectives. The 'what' and the 'where' of employment—its very nature and its location at both inter-urban and intra-metropolitan scales—have been changing significantly over the past several decades. In terms of the nature of employment, we have seen that Canada's cities, particularly those at the top of the urban hierarchy, have increasingly become centres of 'knowledge economy' activities involving high-order services and the manipulation of information rather than physical material. Further, those tradi-

tional economic activities that continue to thrive in cities have been organized in new ways, often involving new forms of employment. At the inter-urban scale, we have noted a marked tendency towards metropolization and towards the functional specialization and the increasing economic complementarity of individual elements of the urban system. At the intra-metropolitan scale, the principal trend observed is one of the decentralization of economic activities, in general, and high-order services, in particular, away from the traditional CBD towards 'edge cities' and 'edgeless cities'. The magnitude of this phenomenon in Canadian cities appears to be less significant than in their US counterparts, however.

It is important to recognize that the trends identified here all have important implications for public policy. The changing nature of work has created a demand for a new type of labour, particularly in urban areas: workers who are better educated, better trained, and better able to 'manipulate symbols'. At the same time, less-specialized jobs for workers with lower levels of educational attainment or lacking 'modern' (e.g., information technology) skills are in decline. Thus there is a strong possibility not only that a portion of the labour force will be severely disadvantaged by the continuing 'non-industrial revolution', but that the labour market will continue its polarization into 'good jobs' and 'bad jobs'. A major problem that society—urban society, in particular—must face, then, is that of integrating into the economic system those persons, whether young high school dropouts or laid-off middle-aged factory workers, who do not possess the educational and skill attributes that allow them access to suitable employment. A related issue, raised by Rifkin (1995), is that of the economy's ability to continue to create jobs in the face of technological change that appears to be rendering obsolete many traditional jobs.

At the national scale, the continuing metropolization of Canada's employment (using a broad definition of metropolization that includes the peri-urban zone beyond the boundaries of CMAs) has created problems of uneven spatial development. The traditional view of regional disparities involving differences between provinces has largely been recast in terms of differences between metropolitan and non-metropolitan areas. It is now widely recognized that the major disparities are not those between Toronto (in a 'developed' province) and Halifax (in a 'lagging' province), for example, but between each of these CMAs and their non-metropolitan rural hinterlands. While certain researchers and policy-makers have occasionally expressed optimism concerning the combined ability of service activities and telecommunications technologies to provide economic development opportunities for Canada's non-metropolitan zones, it is clear that the rise of the 'new, service-based knowledge economy' has not benefited urban and rural (or central and peripheral) areas equally. Even more than in the case of manufacturing activity, the forces of spatial concentration acting on high-order services are very strong. What, then, can be done to address this uneven development and to better use cities in peripheral areas to stimulate growth in their hinterlands? The search for solutions continues.

Finally, the intra-metropolitan dynamics of Canada's large city-regions are also associated with a broad range of policy issues. To begin with, the basic building blocks of Canada's urban economies are spatially extensive city-regions rather than municipalities or even the CAs or CMAs. The Toronto economy does not stop at the administrative boundaries of the CMA but extends over a much wider area that, arguably, includes adjacent non-metropolitan areas and even other CMAs. Similarly, the Montreal economy arguably extends into the Laurentian and Eastern Township zones to the north and east of the CMA. Thus governance becomes an important question when addressing any specific policy issue. Governance at a metropolitan-wide scale is certainly more effective than at a municipal scale, but it may not sufficiently reflect the realities of evolving urban economies. In addition, the federal government's evolving 'Cities Agenda' raises all sorts of jurisdictional questions involving the local, metropolitan, provincial, and federal levels of government. Next, and more specifically, a whole set of significant policy issues involve job creation, economic development, transportation, and land-use planning. For example, as residences and places of work become increasingly dispersed, transportation systems—the link between place of residence and place of work—become more and more important. Should these systems simply link work and home or, rather, be used to influence the location of one or the other? Similarly, to what extent should public policy attempt to influence the spatial form of urban economies, for example, by trying to limit the scatteration of employment and promoting a polycentric structure? Researchers choosing to study Canada's urban economies will certainly not be idle in the coming decades.

Notes

1. Note that the Canadian urban system (defined here as all municipalities, census agglomerations, and census metropolitan areas with more than 10,000 inhabitants—152 geographic units in all) represents slightly more than 80 per cent of all Canadian employment.

2. While the concept of 'economic sector' is based on the nature of a firm's final product, that of

'occupation' reflects the nature of the work accomplished by an individual worker, irrespective of the kind of business (economic sector) in which the work is accomplished; a person whose occupation is 'lawyer' does 'legal work' regardless of whether he/she is employed by a law firm or an oil refinery.

3. It is important to distinguish between part-time employment that is voluntary versus that which is involuntary (i.e., the worker would prefer to work full-time); in 2001, 25 per cent of all part-time work was involuntary.

4. A portion of the workforce has long been classified as having 'no fixed workplace'; this group includes workers in the employ of a firm with one or more fixed addresses but who, themselves, are rarely on the premises: taxi drivers, truck drivers, certain employees of public utilities, and so forth.

5. Some observers, such as Rifkin (1995), have gone so far as to predict the 'end of work', the destruction of employment by a host of new technologies involving both hardware and software. Others have focused on the spatial implications of these changes, heralding the 'end of geography', the 'death of distance', and the 'loss of the city' through the 'decline of physical presence in favour of an immaterial phantom presence' (Virilio, 1996) as the workplace is displaced by electronic shared workspaces.

6. These are the following census metropolitan areas: Toronto, Montreal, Vancouver, Ottawa–Hull, Calgary, Edmonton, Winnipeg, and Quebec City. Unless otherwise stated, all figures are drawn from Statistics Canada census data, and the 1991 geographic boundaries are used.

Chapter 15

Housing: Dreams, Responsibilities, and Consequences

Richard Harris

Housing occupies 30 per cent of the land area of Canadian towns and cities. As a result, houses help define the character of cities: the urbane row 'plexes' of Montreal, the graceful limestone homes of old Kingston, the comfortable bungalows of Vancouver, the ambitious condominiums of Toronto. Dwellings such as these have all kinds of significance (Harris and Pratt, 1993). Housing is the largest item in most people's budgets. Including furnishing and household expenses (such as heat and property taxes), it absorbs a quarter of household income. For homeowners, the dwelling is the household's largest capital asset. Canadians value the comfort, privacy, and personal autonomy that housing provides. But four walls can hide the misery of loneliness and, for some women and children, the daily degradation of battery and abuse. For better or worse, we spend most of our lives at home and we care a lot about how we are housed.

This chapter surveys the way Canadians are housed. It considers how housing has been produced, financed, and sold and how it is occupied and used by different types of people. In addition, geographical variations at the regional and local scales are highlighted. Housing has long been a concern of public policy, and this concern, as well as issues of affordability, energy use, and public health that will keep it in the public eye, is also examined here.

The Production, Financing, and Sale of Housing

Critics have complained that housing is produced in much the same way as a century ago (Harris and Buzzelli, 2005). True, most dwellings are still erected on site (McKellar, 1993). The rate of technological change has not been spectacular: in a century electrical wiring became the norm; iron pipes were replaced by plastic; lath and plaster by wallboard; insulation has improved; roof truss assemblies are now produced off-site; power tools are ubiquitous. None of these developments, however, has dramatically changed the production process. Then, too, builders remain relatively small enterprises. In Ontario in 1998, for example, more than 98 per cent of them erected fewer than 100 units per year and were responsible for 74 per cent of all housing starts (Buzzelli, 2001). Builders still rely on subcontractors, both for physical tasks such as digging basements and for professional services such as accounting (Harris and Buzzelli, 2005). For this reason they operate with little capital equipment: a truck, some power tools, and a cellphone. This means it is still easy to become—and to fail as—a builder: during the 1990s in Ontario, on average one-third of the builders active in any year had entered the industry in the past 12 months; another third would be gone in 12 months' time (Harris and Buzzelli, 2003). Construction has always been a favoured source of employment for immigrants with limited capital, and it still is (Walton-Roberts and Hiebert, 1997). And yet the building industry is surprisingly efficient. Subcontracting enables entrepreneurs and workmen to specialize, reaping economies of scale. Suppliers deliver to sites just-in-time, and with builders and contractors they form a dense and flexible production network, akin to those found in other industries that operate in industrial districts.

Continuities in house building have been balanced by significant changes in building, finance,

Figure 15.1   **The Structures of Residential Building Provision**

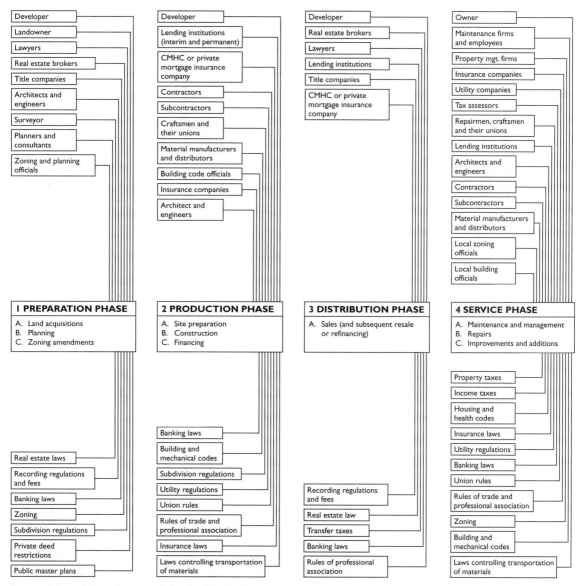

Source: Adapted from Report of the President's Committee on Urban Housing (the Kaiser Committee), *A Decent Home* (Washington, 1968), 115.

and land development (Figure 15.1). Three developments are noteworthy. First, speculative builders (those who build first and then try to find buyers) have grown in importance. Many households once commissioned homes from architects and/or custom builders. Low-income households built their own homes with help from family or neighbours. In the building boom at the beginning of the twentieth century about a third of all new homes in Toronto were self-built, and in western Canadian cities the proportion was probably higher (Harris, 2004). Today, custom work makes up a modest fraction of new construction and owner-building is important, chiefly in the Atlantic region (Rowe, 1989).

A second change has been the growth of housing finance. As late as the 1940s, many households relied largely on savings to buy their first home. Few buyers borrowed more than half the value of their property (that is, mortgage ratios were below 50 per cent). Borrowers obtained credit from other individuals, including family, friends, or people contacted through local lawyers or, in Quebec, *notaires publiques* (Harris, 2004). In the 1930s, to encourage new construction and pull the economy out of Depression, the federal government passed the first in a series of Housing Acts that revolutionized home finance. In 1946 the Central (now Canada) Mortgage and Housing Corporation (CMHC) was set up, mainly to grant and insure mortgages. Buyers were encouraged to borrow; mortgage terms were relaxed to allow 25-year loans on high ratio (80–90 per cent) mortgages. This helped to restore and then exceed the high level of urban home

ownership that had already been achieved before World War II (Figure 15.2). With federal encouragement, institutional lenders soon dominated the mortgage market, except among some immigrant groups (Murdie, 1991). Insurance companies and, after 1954, banks dominated the mortgage scene. By 1990, the banks were owed 40 per cent of the residential mortgage debt held by lending institutions, and by 2003 they held 64 per cent.

A third change has been the rise of the developer. A century ago, land was subdivided, sold in parcels to speculators, sold again to small builders, built upon, and eventually sold to the first occupants. The result was a varied landscape in which small and large dwellings might be juxtaposed. Some housing in some areas is still built this way. But, especially in large metropolitan areas, much is now built by developers who control the process from land subdivision through to final sale. Developers emerged in the 1920s, shaping areas like Kingsway Park in Etobicoke (Toronto) (Paterson, 1984) and Westdale in Hamilton (Weaver, 1978). After World War II, they became dominant in building offices, shopping centres, apartments, and

Figure 15.2 **Urban Home Ownership in Canada, 1901–2001**

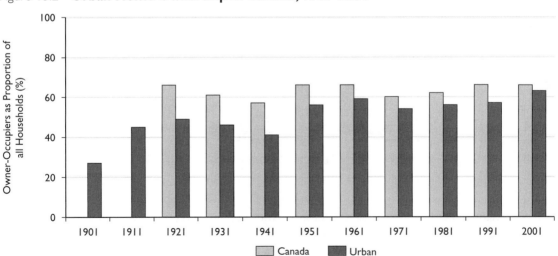

Note: Values for 1901–21 are estimates.

condominiums, as well as suburban homes. From coast to coast, the result was the planned subdivision (Harris, 2004).

Balancing the trend towards large-scale development has been the growth of home renovation. In 1966, renovations and repairs to the existing housing stock accounted for 18 per cent of housing investment. (The remainder was for new construction.) By 1976 this proportion had increased to 23 per cent and by 2002 to 47 per cent (Fallis, 1993). If the land component of new housing is excluded, renovation expenditures exceeded new construction by 1981 (Clayton Research Associates, 1988: 6). Renovation is more significant than published data suggest since much of this is done by homeowners themselves. This is supported by building suppliers who are oriented to consumers, not contractors. They stock a variety of materials and offer advice. Home Depot, a US chain, has made incursions into Canada, but is being resisted by Rona, a Quebec-based company (Yakabuski, 2004). Other renovations are done by contractors whose receipts are unrecorded and not declared for tax purposes: the underground economy accounts for about 15 per cent of new construction, 56 per cent of renovations, and 67 per cent of repairs (Canadian Home Builders' Association, 2003). Demand for the services of small contractors and subcontractors will remain strong.

The growth of speculative builders has made marketing more important. In the early decades of the twentieth century, builders and homeowners used the classified section of the local newspaper to sell houses. Starting in the 1920s, speculative builders began to build model homes. Today, many offer variations on a few basic models, and build only when a client has signed a contract. (This blurs the line between speculative and custom building.) Some new homes and most existing homes are sold, and some apartments are rented, through agents. In major cities, 'multiple listing services' (MLS) record and display information on the price and characteristics of each dwelling. Real estate agents use these listings to identify properties that might interest their clients. Using the MLS guarantees that a property will be seen by many agents and potential buyers. This advantage comes at a price to the seller: a commission of 5–6 per cent of the selling price. This major cost is one reason why homeowners move less often than tenants.

The Occupation of Housing

By definition, housing units are occupied by households (Miron, 1988, 1993c). The household may be a social entity—an individual, a couple, or a nuclear family—but not always. In the past, many families took in lodgers or lodging families, though this became uncommon after the 1940s (Harris, 1994: 35) Then, too, 'the family' might include grandparents or siblings of the parents, especially among immigrants. The household is malleable, responding to changes in economic circumstances, social mores, and market conditions.

Household formation depends on incomes and the age composition of the population. High rates of household growth after 1945 were due to rising incomes: one-third of the increase in households from 1951 to 1981 resulted from the changed living arrangements that affluence made possible (Miron, 1988). In time, this increase also reflected the emergence into adulthood of the baby-boom generation. This age cohort sought rental accommodation and fuelled the apartment boom of the 1960s. As they married, saved, and had children (though fewer than their parents) they acquired homes, pushing prices up rapidly, but ensuring that ownership rates remained high (Foot and Stoffman, 1996: ch. 2). In the 1990s, as the 'echo' generation entered the housing market, high prices compelled many to stay or return home (Mitchell and Gee, 1996). Between 1991 and 2001, the proportion of 20- to 29-year-olds living at home increased from 33 per cent to 41 per cent. Incomes and demographics still determine how dwellings are occupied.

Filtering and Neighbourhood Change

New households rarely occupy new housing. Most are formed by young people with modest incomes and savings. Except in inaccessible locations, new homes are not cheap, costing at least as much as the average home in any given city. In 1996, for example, a new single-detached home cost an average of $125,760 while existing homes ($99,534) were cheaper.[1] The cheapest houses and apartments are older, lack some conveniences, and may be deteriorated, and it is these that are occupied by new households and by lower-income households in general.

For decades, experts and policy-makers assumed that markets worked effectively to house low-income households. Supposedly, new homes were occupied by the affluent, who freed up older homes for those on moderate incomes, leaving modest homes for the poor. A house in an expensive suburb would generate a 'chain' of moves:

households moved up-market while units 'filtered' down (Bourne, 1981: 149–60) (Figure 15.3). The concept of filtering (although not at first the term) was used from the 1920s by Chicago sociologists, who assumed that immigrants occupied inner-city housing that had filtered down.

The filtering model assumes that boundaries between submarkets are permeable. Submarket implies that in price and quantity the housing market has discrete segments. Units within each submarket are equivalent, but those in different submarkets are not. Since housing is immobile, each urban area defines its own submarket (see below). Locally, tenure, house type, and, in large metropolitan areas, location define further subcategories. For a low-income family with children that needs to

Figure 15.3   **Patterns of Urban Filtering in Canada, 1945–2006**

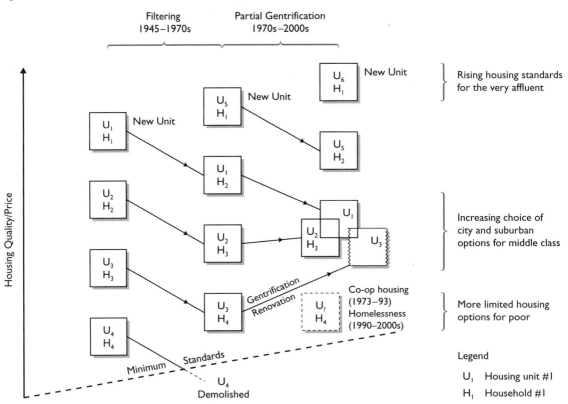

rent an at-grade dwelling in the city's east end, the availability of new housing for purchase, or of vacancies of any sort in the city's west end, is unhelpful. Filtering can link submarkets: a family may move from an older east-end townhouse into a new west-end home. But when filtering is blocked, slowed, or reversed then problems arise, especially at the low end of the market.

Filtering has become less common over the past 30 years. Until the 1970s it was the norm. In the first half of the twentieth century, for example, it characterized the city of Toronto, though not always the suburbs. Older districts housed low-income people and immigrants. In Vancouver the Chinatown and eastside districts, in Toronto the Kensington–Spadina neighbourhoods, and in Montreal the St Urbain corridor all exemplify this process. In cities like Hamilton and Winnipeg this pattern continues. Elsewhere the gentrification of inner-city neighbourhoods, including those just mentioned, has slowed or reversed the process (Ley, 1996a). One consequence has been the loss of cheap rental housing and the displacement of immigrants and others with low incomes (Toronto, 1986). Some demand for cheap housing is now met by bungalows and apartments built in the 1920s and by apartments built in the 1950s and 1960s. Toronto's St Jamestown is a case in point. But the growing ranks of the homeless testify that this is insufficient. Reverse filtering has disrupted the fragile market mechanism for providing housing to the poor.

Residential Mobility and Neighbourhood Change

People move when they perceive their existing dwelling to be much less desirable than an alternative. Many factors can contribute to dissatisfaction (Brown and Moore, 1970). These include job relocation, changes in income or family size, or a deteriorating neighbourhood. In moving to the suburbs after 1945, Canadians often moved closer to suburbanizing jobs, and usually acquired the larger homes that growing families needed and that rising

incomes could support (Clark, 1966). The decline of some inner-city neighbourhoods added a push.

Gentrification, too, may be explained by changes in job location and household structure (Ley, 1996a). Its more visible aspects—singles and gay bars, upscale specialty stores, cosmopolitan restaurants—reflect a new lifestyle of discriminating consumerism. These patterns have also been shaped by office growth in central cities and by the desire of employees to live close by. Then, too, changes in household structure have caused a new generation to re-evaluate inner-city living. More households now contain two earners and/or no children, and to these a central location makes sense, even if neither person works downtown. It may be a compromise location for those working at opposite ends of the city, and thus may offer a safer bet should one or the other become unemployed. A central location also makes sense for single parents, since inner areas are better served by transit and the community services (notably daycare) that such households need (Rose, 1989; Rose and LeBourdais, 1986).

The growth of two-earner families has complicated the household's decision about where and when to move (Hanson and Pratt, 1995; Jarvis et al., 2001). With two earners and two workplaces, adults must compromise about where to live. Women still compromise more than men. Many are employed part-time and/or in jobs—such as clerical work—that are available in many locations (Armstrong and Armstrong, 1994). Most households decide where to live mainly on the basis of where the man works. The woman then seeks employment nearby to avoid interfering with her responsibilities for housework and child-rearing (Michelson, 1984). Of course, more women now have full-time work or careers, often in the central business district (CBD). Single or married, they have an incentive to live close to work. Without someone else at home they minimize commuting to leave time for household chores and are attracted to easily maintained downtown condominiums or apartments (Rose, 1989). For various reasons, then, women do not commute as far as men.

Social Differences in Housing Occupancy

Social groups differ in the housing they occupy. The major social groups in Canada are those defined on the basis of class (or socio-economic status), ethnicity, and gender. These determine a person's housing situation, chiefly through income. Professionals, for example, earn more than clerical workers, and a male professional earns more than his female counterpart (Armstrong and Armstrong, 1994). Some 'social' housing is provided to the needy (below), but the market allocates on the basis of price. Differences in household income (and wealth) determine what type of housing—and in what location—a person can afford.

Business owners, managers, and, to a lesser extent, middle-class professionals live in relatively large and well-equipped homes, and tend to own. In Canada there are strong tax incentives for home ownership. Unlike other assets, homes are exempt from capital gains tax, an aggregate tax subsidy that is much larger than the amounts channelled to social housing (Dowler, 1983). Except for those who move often or who find property maintenance to be a burden, households prefer to buy rather than to rent. Since they can afford to, most business owners and managers do in fact own their own homes. Levels of home ownership among manual workers are lower, although higher than their income might suggest: workers have especially strong aspirations to own their own homes. Vulnerable to layoff and with little control over their work environment, they view the home as a source of financial security and a place of personal autonomy (Harris, 2003). Those with the lowest incomes, including the unskilled and welfare poor, occupy the worst, typically rental, accommodation. Some districts of such housing are badly deteriorated. Slums that result in housing abandonment, however, are uncommon in Canada.

Differences in the housing situation of men and women began to receive serious attention in the 1980s (McClain and Doyle, 1983). In the 1950s, when most adults lived in husband-wife households, men and women occupied the same dwellings. The home meant something different to the woman than to the man: she experienced it as a (sometimes isolated) domestic workplace and as a showplace for homemaking talents, while he viewed it as a haven from work (Harris and Pratt, 1993; Strong-Boag, 1991; Strong-Boag et al., 1999). But both lived in the same structure. With rising divorce rates and more single-parent households, mostly headed by women, this is no longer true. An increasing proportion of households living below the poverty line, typically in poor-quality rental housing, are headed by women (Rose and Wexler, 1993; Watson, 1986).

Immigrants and ethnic minorities also differ in their housing situation. In the past—although not always today—immigrants had low incomes and occupied modest housing. They brought a strong desire to establish themselves in their adopted country, and tolerated crowding to save capital to acquire property. The same is true today. In Hamilton, Ontario, in 2001, for example, only 26 per cent of recent immigrants (those who arrived between 1996 and 2001) owned their own homes. Those who immigrated between 1991 and 1995 were in a better position (48 per cent), while those who came to Canada before 1985 had a higher home ownership rate (72 per cent) than the Canadian-born (69 per cent) (Schellenberg, 2004). The same pattern was apparent across the country. But it can be misleading to generalize. Some recent immigrants, notably those from Hong Kong, are affluent. Some groups, including Italians and Portuguese, have attached special value to home ownership. Observers have suggested the existence of a cultural difference between Canada's two 'charter' groups, and that Montreal once had a lower home ownership rate than Toronto because French Canadians did not value home ownership to the same extent as Anglo Canadians. Recent research has challenged this view (Choko and Harris, 1990), but in general cultural as well as economic factors influence the types of housing people aspire to and occupy.

The Meaning and Uses of the Home

Once built and occupied, houses are used daily and acquire meaning. Consumers use material goods to construct and express their personal identities, and also to signal their membership in socially distinct groups (Bourdieu, 1984; Jackson, 1999; Miller, 1987). Dwellings are especially important in this regard because they are valuable and permanently visible. Front exteriors present the social self; interiors embody personal traits, especially for women (Belk, 1988; Sadella et al., 1987; Leslie and Reimer, 2003). Over the past century the balance has shifted as the home has become more important for recreation. Gas barbecues and swimming pools testify to the recreational uses of the backyard. Radio, television, computers, and the Internet have made leisure based in the home more attractive. Homes have grown and developed new rooms, in part to house this technology (Simon and Holdsworth, 1993). As feminists have emphasized, however, the home is also important as a place of work.

Unpaid Work

The home has always been a workplace, especially for women (Bradbury, 1993; MacKenzie and Rose, 1983). Just running a household requires a lot of labour. People, clothes, floors, and dishes have to be kept (fairly) clean. Food has to be bought and cooked. Children create tasks: changing diapers, teaching, ferrying, and consoling. Some technologies have reduced the amount of housework done in the home: doing the wash by hand, or fetching water from a well, was time-consuming. But the differences between past and present may be overstated (Cowan, 1983). There is more to keep clean: single-detached homes built in the 1990s were 50 per cent larger than those built in the 1946–60 period, even though households have declined in size, from an average of 3.9 persons in 1961 to 2.1 in 2001. Appliances have raised standards—of cleanliness and culinary expertise—and created new work. Dishwashers must be bought and maintained. Automobiles have encouraged us to build at lower densities, and modern sprawl compels us to buy and maintain cars in order to live. Today we spend less time cleaning, but more time shopping, than our parents. To consume more than earlier generations we have to work hard.

Unpaid work is also performed on the home, chiefly by men. As late as the 1950s, many families built homes with their own hands (Harris, 2004). Today, more modest forms of do-it-yourself are common. Some maintenance is carried out by almost every household, including tenants when their landlords offer rent discounts (Krohn et al., 1977), but owner-occupiers have the greatest opportunities and incentives to do such work. Many buyers hope that doing repairs and renovations themselves will save them money, build capital, and allow self-expression. Then, too, ownership can change people's lifestyle, encouraging do-it-yourselfers as part of a more home-centred life (Michelson, 1977: 268–9).

Paid Work

The home has also been a place of paid employment. Historically, many women earned income by taking in lodgers. Recently, other types of home employment have increased. Licensed daycare has lagged behind the number of young mothers in the labour force, and many children go to home daycare, an important part of the underground economy (MacKenzie and Truelove, 1993). There has been a resurgence of industrial 'homework', especially in the garment industry in Toronto and Montreal, while technology has made possible new types of home employment. The recent growth of small businesses, many run out of the home, has been supplemented by telework. In 2001, 11 per cent of employed Canadians worked primarily from their homes, while 40 per cent worked at home at least part of the time (EKOS Research Associates, 2001). The number of teleworkers alone rose from 600,000 in 1991 to an estimated 1.5 million in 2004 (Canadian Telework Association, 2004; Gurstein, 1995: 31).

Homeworkers place new demands on homes and neighbourhoods. Many households alter homes to accommodate work needs, typically by improved lighting and wiring (Gurstein, 1995: 34). Almost a third of respondents to a survey in 1994 had renovated existing space, while 12 per cent had added a new room for home-based work. Use of neighbourhood facilities also changed. Home-based workers make more use of post offices, and copy centres, while many contravene local zoning regulations. In terms of public health and safety, paid work in the home is a growing issue.

Work at home is part of a gender division of labour. Since the nineteenth century, men have commuted, and worked on the home, while women have laboured in it, whether for love or money. This pattern is weakening but still persists. Women spend a good deal of time working outside the home, but surveys show that they do most of the housework, even in households where both adults work full-time (Armstrong and Armstrong, 1994; Michelson, 1984). In 1998, for example, employed men spent 2.8 hours/day on unpaid domestic tasks while employed women spent 4.1 hours. More than men, women juggle work to accommodate domestic responsibilities (Hanson and Pratt, 1995). Some are attracted to teleworking for this reason: in the mid-1990s women made up about 45 per cent of the labour force but 55 per cent of those who worked for pay at home (Gurstein, 1995: 12). The persistence of differences between men and women is nowhere more apparent than in the use of the home.

A Geographical Perspective

Especially in Canada, it can be misleading to generalize about housing. It is true that Canadians occupy some of the best, and best-equipped, housing in the world: almost all urban dwellings are structurally sound and have the basic conveniences of piped water, electricity, and central heating. But the form these houses take, and how much they cost, varies greatly from place to place.

The Uniqueness of Each Place

The size of Canada, and the immobility of housing, guarantees that housing market conditions vary enormously from place to place (Bourne and Bunting, 1993). A local shortage cannot be met from a surplus elsewhere, especially since most major urban areas are beyond commuting distance of one another. Prices in Calgary rose rapidly during the OPEC-induced oil boom of the 1970s and

slumped in the early 1980s. In Vancouver they spiked during speculative booms in 1980–1 and the early 1990s, falling briefly thereafter (Figure 15.4). In Toronto and southern Ontario they boomed in the prosperous 1980s, but dropped by a quarter in the early 1990s. In Montreal, prices were depressed for a generation. Recently, economic growth and very low interest rates have pushed prices up everywhere but this is unusual, and average prices vary widely from place to place: they are currently twice as high in Toronto as in Montreal. Single-industry towns have the most volatile housing markets, but even the largest centres are susceptible to price variations, booms, and busts.

The progression of European settlement in Canada has helped distinguish urban housing sub-markets. Eastern cities have the highest proportion of older housing, developed before the automobile, and hence a higher proportion of dense, multi-occupancy housing with higher levels of tenancy. In western cities, neighbourhoods of single-detached homes may be found close to the CBD. As each city was settled by different immigrants, varying architectural styles predominate. Nineteenth-century Montrealers favoured 'plexes', superimposed dwellings with separate entrances; Torontonians favoured gabled row houses, while Vancouverites drew on California bungalow and British 'Tudorbethan' models (Holdsworth, 1977). The historical geography of the country has helped to create a unique housing stock, and different housing markets, in each centre.

Generic Differences between Places

If each place is unique, some geographical variations are generic, being specific to certain types of places. The most basic difference is that between rural and urban areas. Property is more expensive in urban centres, where housing requires a high proportion of residents' incomes, is less likely to be owner-occupied, and contains a high proportion of attached, multi-family dwellings. In 2001 the home ownership rate was lower in CMAs (61 per cent) than in smaller urban centres (68 per cent), and

Figure 15.4   **House Prices in Selected Metropolitan Areas, 1988–2003**

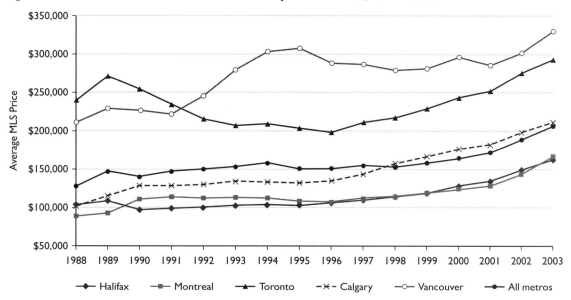

much lower than in rural areas and places with a population of less than 10,000 (76 per cent). Contrasts in the proportion of multi-unit dwellings—respectively 52, 36, and 18 per cent— were even more striking.

The difference between urban and rural housing is one of degree, and suburbs lie in between. Suburbs contain, and are defined by, a high proportion of detached, owner-occupied homes (Harris, 2004: ch. 2). This is due to lower land prices and the fact that post-war suburbs developed when incomes were relatively high. City–suburban differences in home ownership are associated with variations in the uses to which the home is put. Owners do more unpaid work around the home than tenants, partly because they are more likely to have children, and are more likely to become active in the community (Cox, 1982). Generic differences between city and suburban housing are bound up with different ways of life.

Because of urban–rural differences, urbanization affected the types of housing that Canadians

occupied until the trend tapered off in the 1970s.[2] It raised the proportion of multi-unit structures, notably during apartment booms in the 1920s and 1960s. It also depressed the level of owner occupation, though this was counteracted by rising incomes and the suburban trend. In Canada as a whole, the home ownership rate fell from 66 per cent to 62 per cent between 1951 and 1981, after which it rebounded to 66 per cent in 2001 (Figure 15.2). One reason for the recent growth in home ownership has been the popularity of condominiums, which enable households to own real estate in multi-unit structures. By 2001, condominiums accounted for 8 per cent of the housing stock in CMAs as a whole, the highest rate (17 per cent) being in Vancouver. Trends in housing are still being shaped by changing patterns of population settlement.

After 1945, suburban development eroded the character of each place. Everywhere, suburbs looked the same: the first appearance of the generic term 'suburbia' in the *Globe and Mail* was in 1946 (Harris, 2004). A new National Building Code, the growth of municipal planning and of large land developers, and the popularity of ranch and split-level styles, produced a standardized environment (Relph, 1987). Today, much of Mississauga, Kingston Township, and Richmond, BC, look alike. Since the 1970s, however, there has been a resurgence in the popularity of historical and regional styles. In Toronto, more 'Victorian' homes date from the late twentieth century than from the late nineteenth century. This shift in taste may reflect a popular need for symbolic reassurance at a time when divorce has become common and career paths increasingly uncertain. Because ornamentation in architecture is often read as 'feminine', the new popularity of historic styles may also symbolize the growing public presence of women in Canadian society (Bondi, 1992; Devlin, 1994). Beneath the surface variety, however, methods of land development have become more streamlined than ever.

Housing and the State

In Canada housing is produced by the private sector and mostly owned by private corporations or individuals, but its character and use are profoundly influenced by the state. The social meaning of the basic categories 'owner-occupation' and 'tenancy', for example, are defined in law and enforced by the state. Moreover, as the enforcement of rent controls and the emergence of condominium tenure show, these social meanings can change, in part through the initiatives of federal and provincial governments (Hulchanski, 1993).

The Growth, and Faltering, of Government Activity

All three levels of government have played a growing role in the housing market over the past century. Municipalities were the first to become involved because conditions in inner cities were worst and the municipal level of government, obviously, had the most direct concern and responsibility. Industrial urbanization, coupled with low wages, led to overcrowding and poor sanitation and the spread of infectious diseases threatened everyone.

Frame construction led to serious fires. Municipalities began to control how houses were built, maintained, and occupied (Hodge, 1998). Suburbs, especially those of immigrants and workers, adopted controls slowly, but most had done so by the 1950s (Harris, 2004).

After 1900, municipalities also took control of land use. A century ago land was developed piecemeal, with stores or small factories built in many residential areas. A merchant might build a fine brick home only to have his investment threatened by a shack next door. Subdividers perceived a demand for regulated subdivisions where undesirable users were prohibited. They used legal covenants to prohibit certain uses or building materials, and also certain residents. On the west coast the Chinese were sometimes targeted; in Nova Scotia, African Canadians were excluded from some areas and funnelled into others; frequently, Jews were prohibited from buying property in specified areas (Harris, 2004). In 1948, the Supreme Court declared ethnic covenants illegal, and in the same period the provinces began to require municipalities to develop systematic land-use plans. Recently, these have been supplemented by a new wave of private covenants, although not to the same degree as in the US (Filion and Alexander, 1994). Today, municipal zoning controls specify how each piece of land may be used (Hodge, 1998). They are not always followed to the letter. In older districts, 'non-conforming' uses persist. Anywhere, zoning can be changed in response to pressure from developers or local residents. Such changes require public hearings, which are a staple of local politics.

Permanent federal involvement in housing dates from the Great Depression (Bacher, 1993; Harris, 2004: ch. 5) (Figure 15.5). In 1935 the government passed a Dominion Housing Act (DHA) that provided insured mortgage loans. Its purpose was to revive the building industry; most buyers were affluent (Belec, 1997). In 1938 the DHA was folded into a National Housing Act (NHA), and in 1946 a Crown corporation, CMHC, was made responsible for administering federal housing policy. The mortgage loan activity of CMHC has shaped suburban development ever since (Harris, 2004; Poapst, 1993).

Figure 15.5   **Evolution of Federal Housing Programs, 1945–1993**

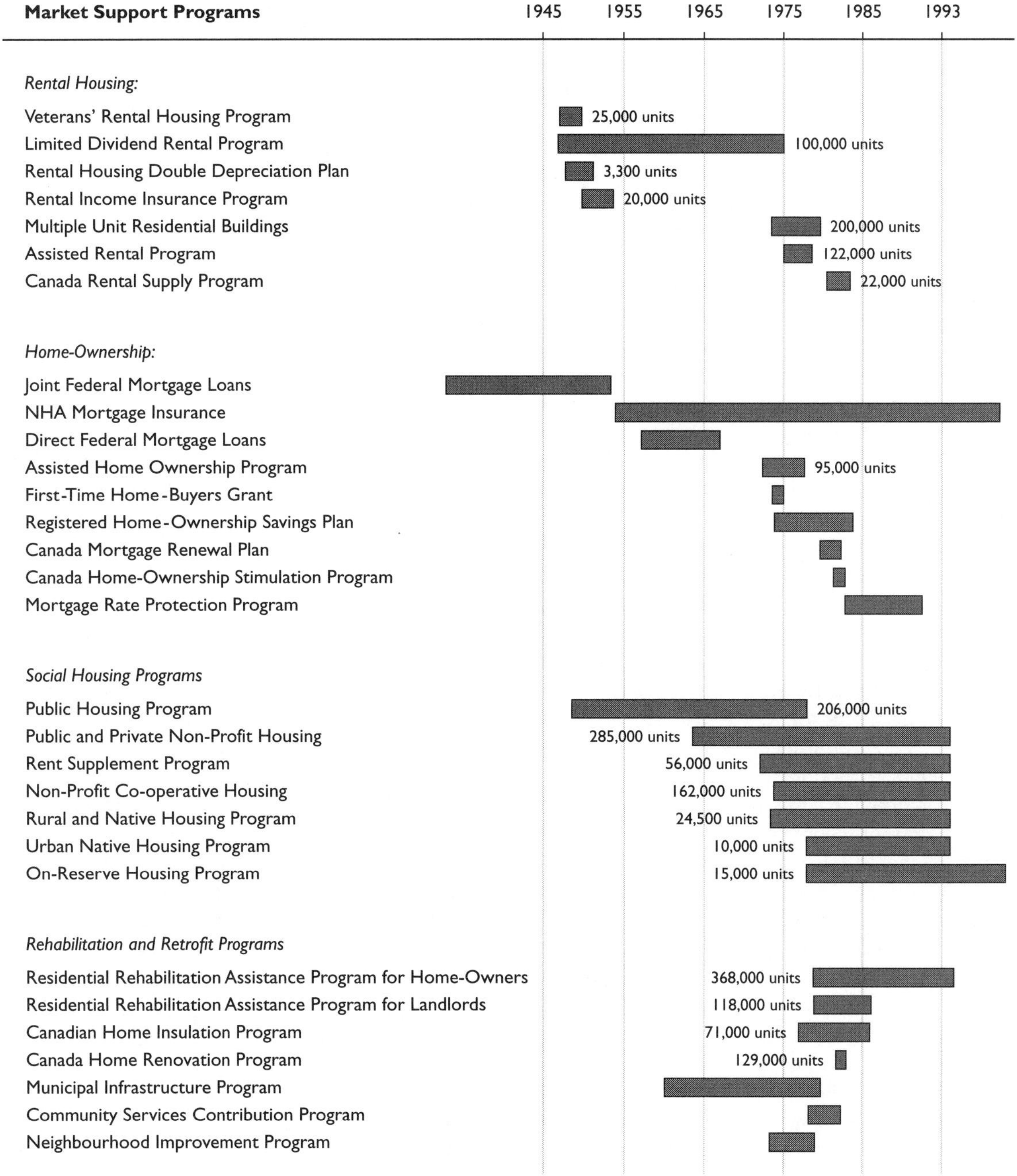

Market Support Programs	1945	1955	1965	1975	1985	1993

Rental Housing:

Veterans' Rental Housing Program — 25,000 units

Limited Dividend Rental Program — 100,000 units

Rental Housing Double Depreciation Plan — 3,300 units

Rental Income Insurance Program — 20,000 units

Multiple Unit Residential Buildings — 200,000 units

Assisted Rental Program — 122,000 units

Canada Rental Supply Program — 22,000 units

Home-Ownership:

Joint Federal Mortgage Loans

NHA Mortgage Insurance

Direct Federal Mortgage Loans

Assisted Home Ownership Program — 95,000 units

First-Time Home-Buyers Grant

Registered Home-Ownership Savings Plan

Canada Mortgage Renewal Plan

Canada Home-Ownership Stimulation Program

Mortgage Rate Protection Program

Social Housing Programs

Public Housing Program — 206,000 units

Public and Private Non-Profit Housing — 285,000 units

Rent Supplement Program — 56,000 units

Non-Profit Co-operative Housing — 162,000 units

Rural and Native Housing Program — 24,500 units

Urban Native Housing Program — 10,000 units

On-Reserve Housing Program — 15,000 units

Rehabilitation and Retrofit Programs

Residential Rehabilitation Assistance Program for Home-Owners — 368,000 units

Residential Rehabilitation Assistance Program for Landlords — 118,000 units

Canadian Home Insulation Program — 71,000 units

Canada Home Renovation Program — 129,000 units

Municipal Infrastructure Program

Community Services Contribution Program

Neighbourhood Improvement Program

Source: CMHC, *Canadian Housing Statistics,* various years, from Carter (1997).

Unlike the US, Canada did not build public housing during the Depression, and it was not until 1964 that it made the financial terms attractive enough to encourage the provinces to participate. In the next five years there was a short boom in public housing construction, that is, of subsidized rental accommodation owned by public agencies (Patterson, 1993).Units for seniors were accepted but those for families were opposed. Large schemes exacerbated social problems and attracted stigma, especially as projects increasingly housed visible minorities. In Toronto, for example, blacks at first occupied only 4 per cent of units managed by the Metro Toronto Housing Authority (Murdie, 1994b). By 1986 the figure had soared to 27 per cent, five times this group's proportion of the Toronto population. By the early 1970s opposition, and high unit costs, caused the government virtually to halt construction of public housing for families (Patterson, 1993).

In the early 1970s, new programs encouraged the rehabilitation of existing housing and the construction of new types of social housing, chiefly co-operatives and municipal non-profits (Patterson, 1993). (Social housing refers to units provided on the basis of need to lower-income households.) In co-ops, ownership is shared and projects are socially mixed. Since most projects were built in older, mixed neighbourhoods they avoided social stigma (Skelton, 1994). However, project mix reduced the number of low-income families housed (CMHC, 1984). In the late 1980s, the federal government reduced support for social housing and in 1993 froze funding for new social housing projects, except on Aboriginal reserves. Few provincial governments picked up the slack, and Ontario devolved responsibility for the management of public housing to local municipalities. Commonly, the construction of social housing ceased (Carter, 1997; Shapcott, 2004;Wolfe, 1998). In Hamilton, Ontario, for example, no units were built between 1996 and 2003 (Hamilton, 2004: 37–9).

One consequence of funding cuts was the growth of homelessness (see Chapter 25). Rates of homelessness have been consistently highest among Aboriginal Canadians: for example, in 2002 Aboriginal people made up 6 per cent of the population of Edmonton but about 43 per cent of the city's homeless population (Edmonton, 2002). In part for this reason, in 1998 the federal government developed an Urban Aboriginal Strategy, but this initiative involved more consultation and research than action. More generally, in 2001 the federal government re-entered the housing field by committing $680 million over five years for affordable housing; in 2003 this figure was raised to $1 billion, and $1.5 billion more was promised by the Liberal government during its successful election campaign in 2004. To access these funds, provinces have entered cost-sharing agreements, with varying consequences. Quebec and BC acted promptly: by 2003 they had cost-shared 30 per cent and 27 per cent of their original allocations, respectively. Montreal initiated a Solidarité 5000 campaign to erect 5,000 affordable units by 2005; by June 2005 it had subsidized 5,122 units. Other provinces lagged. By 2003, the Conservatives in Ontario had spent only $1 million of their $245 million allocation; by 2004 a new Liberal government appeared more proactive. Even so, although Canadians pride themselves on their social safety net, their governments build less social housing than those of other industrialized nations—including the United States (Harris, 2000; Shapcott, 2004).

Figure 15.5 portrays the evolution of federal housing policies and their impact in terms of units built until the mid-1990s. If its coverage were extended to 2006, it would show a considerable reduction in the number of programs and in units erected, with a slight increase in housing policy activity in the mid-2000s.

The Purposes and Consequences of Housing Policy

In Canada, housing policy has had a strong economic purpose, as distinct from a social purpose, a fact implied in the name of CMHC: it is a 'corporation' concerned as much with 'mortgages' as with housing. Federal policy has flirted with social housing, but has consistently sought to strengthen the private sector, and especially corporate land development (Bacher, 1993). Actions during the 1930s sought to revive the building industry and facilitate mortgage lending. The first president of CMHC had been an executive at Sun Life. After 1945, policies favoured large developers over small builders (Lorimer, 1978) and financial institutions over the individual lender, although the latter held half of all mortgage debt in the early 1950s (Harris, 2004). CMHC consistently makes a profit, chiefly from its mortgage operations, one of the few Crown corporations ever to have done so (Shapcott, 2004).

The market bias of policy has been a mixed blessing. It has helped produce safe, energy-efficient, and roomy housing for most Canadians, but at a price. The promotion of mortgages has created a nation of debt-encumbered consumers living in low-density suburban homes. This has boosted demand for other goods and credit (Belec et al., 1987), but with unfortunate environmental and health consequences. Policy has also been socially regressive. Subsidies to owner occupation, through the non-taxation of capital gains and imputed rent, have outweighed spending on 'social housing', and those with the most valuable homes receive the largest subsidies (Dowler, 1983; Steele, 1993). Housing policy has not been part of Canada's social safety net. Instead, unwittingly and through design, it has neglected those who cannot help themselves. Past biases have become self-perpetuating. Most Canadian households own their own homes—a large constituency that would resist attack on the subsidies they enjoy. Indeed, politicians court them with the promise of new subsidies: during the Ontario election campaign of 2003, the Conservatives offered to allow homeowners to deduct mortgage interest payments from their income tax. The constituency for the status quo is both numerous and powerful.

Current Issues

Currently, and for the foreseeable future, four issues dominate the public debate about housing in Canada: affordability, a rental housing shortage, environmental effects, and health. Until the 1950s, the housing problem was one of poor housing con-

ditions and overcrowding. Since then, municipal regulations have raised standards of construction and maintenance. Today, Aboriginal Canadians are the only group who commonly experience substandard or crowded housing, notably on reserves. In 2001, only 2.5 per cent of the units occupied by non-Aboriginal households were inadequate (in need of major repairs), and 1.4 per cent failed the National Occupancy Standard (NOS) (CMHC, 2004b).[3] The equivalent ratios for Aboriginal households off reserves were 6.8 and 4.9 per cent, respectively; for those on reserves the proportions were 22.5 and 10.3 per cent.

Mostly, however, the key issue is affordability. 'Core housing need' exists when a household must spend at least 30 per cent of before-tax income for an adequate, uncrowded dwelling. On this criterion, 16.6 per cent of all Canadian households were in need in 2001, up from 14.3 per cent in 1991. Increasingly, the problem of affordability is concentrated among tenants, and the private rental sector is becoming marginalized (Federation of Canadian Municipalities, 2004). Low-income tenants are unattractive to builders. During the early 1970s more than 20,000 rental units were being built each year; by the late 1990s the figure had fallen to less than 2,000 (Shapcott, 2004). In Hamilton, between 1991 and 2003, units for rent accounted for under 2 per cent of new construction (Hamilton, 2004: 37–9). Unless recent policy initiatives bear fruit, and unless builders re-enter the rental market, the affordability problems of tenants will worsen and more Canadians will end up homeless (Hulchanski and Shapcott, 2004; see Chapter 25).

Canadians have long viewed larger houses, and a growing array of electrical appliances, as signs of progress, but this view is now counterbalanced by other considerations. Oil price increases in the early 1970s made the cost of energy an issue. The federal government funded a short-lived program to promote energy conservation in existing dwellings; in 1973 the criterion of energy conservation was introduced to the National Building Code; in 1981 the National Home Builders' Association, with National Resources Canada, initiated the 'R2000' building program for new homes (Canadian Home

Builders' Association, 2004). International awareness of the links between global warming and the burning of fossil fuels led to the 1997 Kyoto Accord, to which Canada is a signatory. Oil and gas are the main fuels used for home heating, and home energy consumption is an environmental as well as an economic issue. A federal 'Energuide' program offers property owners loans and grants to improve energy efficiency. Between 1990 and 2001, energy use per household declined by 13 per cent, due to retrofitting, more efficient windows, appliances, and heating systems, but on a global scale we are energy gluttons. Most Canadian dwellings are detached and on average they use 50 per cent more energy than multi-unit structures (Climate Action Network, 2002: 7; CMHC, 2000; Sierra Club, 1998). New Urbanist suburbs that include multi-unit and row dwellings are more environmentally friendly, but consumption of fossil fuels will remain a prominent housing issue in Canadian cities (Gordon and Tamminga, 2002).

Larger single-family homes and reliance on the automobile are associated with low-density suburban development. In recent years we have become aware that together they have brought health as well as environmental problems (Frumkin et al., 2004; Gurin, 2003). Homes and residential environments are designed to save labour: we drive to the store for a carton of milk; purchase fast food without leaving the driver's seat; and change channels from the couch. On average Canadians do less, eat more, and grow fatter by the year, with predictable consequences for the incidence of heart disease and other health problems. Such problems will not be solved but they can be addressed through better urban design that promotes walking, cycling, and public transit. These changes require higher densities and will affect the size and type of dwellings that are built. In addition to the challenge of building more affordable and energy-efficient housing, Canadians will have to change their expectations. More is not always better.

Notes

1.   These figures relate to homes sold and financed under the provisions of the National Housing Act. In general, NHA homes are a little cheaper than the average. These, and comparable data for specific cities, are reported in Canada Mortgage and Housing Corporation, *Canadian Housing Statistics 1996* (Ottawa: CMHC, 1997).

2.   The number of people living in cities, of course, continues to grow, but the proportion has changed little since the 1970s.

3.   The definition of the NOS is complex. See CMHC (1991: 4).

Chapter 16

Dynamics of the Canadian Retail Environment

Ken Jones and Tony Hernandez

The retail landscapes of urban Canada reflect the immense diversity of social classes, incomes, ethnicity, lifestyles, and business formats that comprise our cities. Strips, neighbourhood streets, suburban plazas, power centres, downtowns, and revitalized boutique districts are some of the most visible elements of the metropolitan landscape. Names like The Bay, Wal-Mart, Canadian Tire, Club Monaco, Harry Rosen, and HMV are instantly recognized by most Canadians.

Retailing is a major component of the Canadian economy. In 2004, total retail sales (including automotive) measured $346.7 billion or 25.7 per cent of the gross domestic product (Statistics Canada, 2005d). Thirteen per cent of the Canadian workforce, 1,754,885 persons, are employed in the retail sector (Statistics Canada, 2001a). In our society, retailing is pervasive. For many, shopping is a major leisure activity. Retail sales absorb approximately one-third of our disposable income and the image of our cities is shaped in large part by the nature and vibrancy of their retail environments.

This chapter will describe and interpret the various elements that comprise and shape our urban retail system, stressing geographical, locational dimensions. First, we will briefly review the literature associated with intra-urban retailing. Second, we examine the evolution of the Canadian intra-urban retail system, focusing on the development of the shopping centre, the rebirth of the central city, the growth of the big-box and power retailers, and the role of the specialty retail area. Next, a general morphology of the contemporary urban retail

structure will be introduced. The chapter concludes by presenting an integrated framework for evaluating the intra-urban retail system and outlining a series of trends related to the future of retailing in Canada.

Intra-Urban Retailing: A Review

The literature in geography on urban retailing can be grouped into four research perspectives: (1) the identification and classification of various structural elements of the retail landscape; (2) the spatial dynamics of retail change; (3) the development and operation of various retail structures—shopping centres, central area retail districts, retail strips, and specialty retail areas; (4) applied research investigations. In applied research, geographers assess new retail locations for major retail firms and use various spatial models to analyze shopping centre impacts.

The development of a systematic classification of retail structures is based to a large extent on the pioneering works of Proudfoot (1937) and Berry (1963). These studies differentiated shopping environments on the basis of their locational and functional characteristics. The literature related to urban retail change can be traced back to the empirical work of Simmons (1966). Simmons's conceptual model of retail change examined how socio-economic conditions and elements of urban growth influence the development of the intra-urban retail system. In this model, temporal and spatial variations in income, technological development, and urban demographic growth and change affect consumer mobility and preferences, and eventually cause an adjustment in the nature and distribution of retail structures. In this and related, more recent analyses, the final disposition of the retail system is viewed as the outcome of the spatial strategies of, and interplay between, developers, retailers, and planners—the actors who ultimately shape the future form of the urban retail landscape.

Retail structural analysis has had a long tradition in urban geography. In the 1950s and 1960s, North American studies of retail structure dominated the literature. These studies explored suburban retail strip development, retail mix and usage patterns, inner-city retail decline, the emergence of the shopping centre, and the specialty retail phenomenon. More recently, applied studies have tended to focus on particular elements or projects associated with the retail system. Because of their nature, most of these studies adopt a micro-based, case study approach. Typically, these analyses are undertaken to provide advice to retail corporations concerning the investment potential of particular locations or to aid government agencies in assessing the social, economic, or environmental impact of a specific development. In the literature, the works of Applebaum (1968), Davies and Rogers (1984), and Lea (1989) illustrate these forms of study.

Evolution of the Canadian Urban Retail System

The contemporary retail landscape of urban Canada is the product of a series of complex structural changes. Retail structure is perhaps the most responsive element in the urban landscape. A high degree of volatility was confirmed by an analysis of aggregate failure rate of retail enterprises along 175 major retail streets in Metropolitan Toronto, 1994–6—a staggering 33 per cent (CSCA, 1998). In some categories, such as fashion, the failure rates over the three-year period were in the 40–4 per cent range, while the lowest turnover rates were experienced by pharmacies (24.5 per cent) and laundries (19.7 per cent). Very minor shifts in the income, demographic, lifestyle, and/or competitive

Figure 16.1   **The Determinants of Retail Structure**

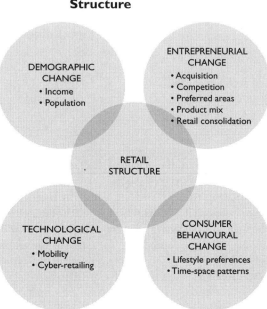

characteristics of an area will lead to quite rapid changes in both form and structure of the retail environment. Conceptually, the retail fabric of our cities has been created in response to the dynamic interplay of demographic, technological, behavioural, and entrepreneurial change (Figure 16.1).

The spatial pattern of retail groupings relates to the technology of the time. When mobility is low, retail activities concentrate; when mobility increases, retail activities disperse. At a finer level, consumer and entrepreneurial decisions can determine which retail areas grow and which areas decline. Consumer preferences for both retail goods and destinations can reflect a whole set of considerations that can be broadly defined as lifestyle-related (see Chapter 8). Certain urban shopping areas move in and out of fashion for particular consumer groups. On the supply side, investment decisions are based on the entrepreneur's assessment of the future disposition of the retail system. Will a certain downtown redevelopment project be successful? How will the competition react? What will be the demographic composition and demands of a community in 10 years? What demographic cohorts will experience growth, and what demographic cohorts will experience decline?

The Pre-World War II System

The intra-urban retail system has experienced several transformations in the last 60 years. These transformations were tied to successions in types of urban structure and transportation: the compact pre-automobile city; the dispersed automobile city; and the emerging information city.

In the pre-war city, both aggregate consumer mobility and car ownership were low. In response, many consumers shopped daily for food and going downtown to shop was viewed as a normal activity. An examination of the pattern of retail activities in urban Canada prior to 1950 reflected this reality. Nearby corner stores were a necessity and downtown retailing flourished. It was the age of the department store. To illustrate, in 1930 all divisions of the T. Eaton and Robert Simpson companies controlled an impressive 10.5 per cent of total retail sales in Canada (Royal Commission on Price Spreads, 1935). Because of the reliance on public transit along major arterials, inner-city retail strips were a significant element in the retail landscape. These strips extended into the residential portions of the city and consisted of almost continuous rows of shops that served essentially local convenience-oriented needs.

Relatively low mobility in the pre-war city explains retail location patterns. Day-to-day shopping was carried out close to the home. High-order goods were typically purchased downtown, the uncontested public transit accessibility hub at a time when transit was the dominant form of transportation (Jones and Simmons, 1993).

The Emergence of the Shopping Centre

In 1950, the next era of retail development began with the opening of Park Royal Shopping Centre in Vancouver. For the next 40 years, the planned shopping centre, the automobile, and suburbanization were the major forces shaping retail structure. By 2003, shopping centre sales accounted for approximately 60 per cent of non-automotive retail sales in the country (ICSC, 2005a) and for almost all the growth in shopping goods activity.

Shopping centre development in Canada has undergone four periods of evolution since its inception. In the 1950s, shopping centre developers adopted a *consequent* development strategy where the shopping centre was constructed after the housing stock in a given area and the details of the market were known. Most were small, unenclosed 'plazas' that were automobile-oriented, and developed independently to serve community convenience needs. During this period, retail planning controls were in most cases non-existent and often a form of uncontrolled retail sprawl resulted. The major Canadian department store chains were reluctant to move to the suburbs. Both Eaton's and Simpsons adopted a wait-and-see attitude and were content to remain securely located in the downtown cores of Canadian cities.

The 1960s saw a shift with the emergence of *simultaneous* shopping centre development where both the centre and the housing stock were built at the same time, with the shopping centre viewed as the centre of the 'planned' community. In Canada, the first development to adopt this approach was Don Mills Plaza in Toronto (1959). This linkage between residential and commercial land uses helped to foster the emergence of several large development companies. These included Cadillac Fairview, Bramalea, and Trizec. The philosophy of simultaneous development became accepted at all levels, from the large regional complexes (e.g., Fairview Mall, Bramalea City Centre, and Scarborough Town Centre in Toronto) to the neighbourhood plazas that form the centre of small residential communities.

By the end of the 1960s, the shopping centre industry in Canada was well established and a level of corporate control over the prime shopping centre locations in Canada had been assured. Table 16.1 lists selected major shopping centre and power centre developers in Canada, most of which are a

Table 16.1   **Selected Major Canadian Shopping/Power Centre Owners and Management Companies, 2004–5**

Owner/Management Co.	Headquarters	Total # Centres/ Properties	Total Gross Leasable Area (sq. ft.)
Ivanhoe-Cambridge	Toronto	50	31,486,055
First Professional	Toronto	132	29,420,465
RioCan	Toronto	190	24,189,987
Cadillac Fairview Corp.	Toronto	31	21,569,000
Oxford Properties Group	Toronto	32	13,564,798
20 Vic Management Inc.	Toronto	22	13,174,816
First Capital Realty	Toronto	103	12,700,000
Crombie Properties	Stellarton, NS	78	9,722,944
Trinity Dvlp. Group Inc.	Toronto	33	9,300,000
Calloway REIT	Calgary	56	8,302,376
Canadian Real Est. Inv. Trust	Toronto	24	5,695,428

Source: Maclean-Hunter Web site (2005).

legacy of this period. These developers are arguably the most important players in determining the spatial structure of the retail distribution system in Canada. It is important to note that the shopping centre system that emerged from the 1960s was essentially homogeneous in nature. One shopping centre at any one level of the hierarchy looked much the same as the next, with the same layout and design, and the same range of goods, services, and tenants in the same standardized environment—a style of development very much in keeping with the meta-narrative of rational comprehensive planning (see Chapter 19).

In large part, this sameness was the product of the corporatization of the shopping centre based on synergy between corporate, chain retailers and shopping centre developers that continues to the present. Throughout North America, the planned shopping centre provided the principal vehicle for the entry of and ultimate dominance of the retail chain in the urban marketplace (Doucet et al., 1988). By 1986, slightly more than half of all retail chains and department stores in Canada were located in shopping centres—51.7 per cent or 17,795 outlets. Certain types of retail chains were disproportionately shopping centre-oriented. In terms of total sales, women's clothing (91 per cent), luggage and leather goods (89 per cent), children's clothing (87 per cent), jewellery stores (85 per cent), and shoe stores (83 per cent) were the retail activities that showed the greatest propensity for shopping centre locations.

The relationship between the retail chain and the shopping centre is reflected in the redistribution of retail space in many metropolitan environments. For example, in Metropolitan Toronto (since 1998, the City of Toronto), which has kept an inventory of retail space since 1953, the share of the total retail space found in planned shopping facilities rose from 2.4 per cent in 1953 to 40.8 per cent in 1971, 54.5 per cent in 1986, and 55.3 per cent in 1994 (Simmons et al., 1996).

The early 1970s saw a gradual shift to a third stage in some larger metropolitan markets—the 'catalytic' shopping centre. In this case, the shopping centre was viewed as a growth pole that would stimulate future development. Typically, a super-regional shopping centre built in a 'greenfield' at the intersection of two major expressways would precede residential development by three to five years. Scarborough Town Centre and Mississauga's Square One are prime examples of this trend in the Toronto region. In part, these developments were in keeping with the 'bigger is better' philosophy that permeated North American business decision-making in this period. The success of these centres was also contingent on both the presence of large development companies with extensive land banks and the willingness and ability of national chains to enter a location and wait for the market to develop.

The 1960s and 1970s were also characterized by the commercial revitalization of central cores. In Canada, the first attempt at a downtown shopping centre was in London, Ontario (Wellington Square, 1960). By the end of the 1970s, most major cities in Canada had an enclosed downtown shopping facility. Most were joint ventures that involved the developer, a major department store (often Eaton's), and an important financial institution. Over 30 city centres in Canada experienced this form of development, which reshaped the retail form of Canada's downtowns (see Table 16.2 for a list of the major shopping centres in Canada).

The end of the 1970s saw market saturation of the suburban shopping centre in Canada. Developers pursued a series of alternative growth strategies. First, a number of selected shopping centres were rejuvenated. This process generally involved the enclosing and 'remixing' (i.e., changing the store types to accommodate new trends in consumption) of first-generation regional shopping centres constructed in the 1960–5 period. Second, through a strategy termed 'infilling' a number of smaller towns became targets for enclosed regional or community malls on their periphery. (As a consequence, a number of downtown cores in these

smaller communities experienced severe decline.) A third option adopted by major developers such as Cadillac Fairview, Olympia and York, Bramalea, Oxford, Cambridge, Trizec, and Daon was to become active in the high-growth markets of the United States—Canadian retail-commercial developers became major players in Los Angeles, New York City, Dallas, Minneapolis, and Denver.

The 1980s saw the emergence of a fourth form of shopping centre development—the shopping centre as an *entertainment or tourist attraction*. The overt mixing of retailing and recreation in a major shopping centre is an innovation peculiar to Canada. The 350,000-square-metre (3,800,000-square-foot) West Edmonton Mall is by far the most ambitious example of this type of megaproject, with dozens of tourist attractions including an ice skating rink, wave pool, submarine rides, marineland, aviary, Fantasyland Hotel, children's amusement park, and a mock 'Parisian' shopping boulevard.[1] In these environments retailing and entertainment go hand in hand. Also in the 1980s, many inner-city shopping centres and redeveloped waterfront properties have been targeted partly at tourists and recreational shoppers. Over the last decade, the entertainment component has become a more important component of many shopping destinations as multi-screen theatres or virtual-reality complexes become shopping centre anchors and key tenants within power centres.

By far the most active form of shopping centre development in Canada during the 1980s was the revitalization of existing properties. Developers have found that shopping centres have a distinct life cycle. After approximately 10–15 years, most centres are in need of renovation. Since their initial construction, the demography and income level of their trade area may have changed, their competitive environment altered, and their 'book value' depreciated to zero. Revitalization offers a number of advantages to the developer. Existing shopping centres are well situated in a known market, they experience fewer zoning or environmental regulatory problems, and renovation typically involves lower construction and financial costs than does the construction of new complexes. Most of these

Table 16.2   **Major Shopping Centres in Canada**

Centre/Node	Market	Gross Leasable Area
West Edmonton Mall	Edmonton	3,800,000 sq. ft.
Heartland Town Centre	Mississauga, Ont.	1,800,000 sq. ft.
Toronto Eaton Centre	Toronto	1,624,000 sq. ft.
Square One Shopping Centre	Mississauga, Ont.	1,600,000 sq. ft.
Yorkdale Shopping Centre	Toronto	1,544,165 sq. ft.
Les Galeries de la Capitale	Quebec City	1,400,000 sq. ft.
Pacific Centre	Vancouver	1,390,000 sq. ft.
Place Laurier	Ste-Foy, Que.	1,340,000 sq. ft.
Scarborough Town Centre	Scarborough, Ont.	1,313,137 sq. ft.
Le Carrefour Laval	Laval, Que.	1,243,000 sq. ft.
Polo Park Shopping Centre	Winnipeg	1,202,000 sq. ft.
Vaughan Mills	Vaughan, Ont.	1,200,000 sq. ft.
Chinook Centre	Calgary	1,175,000 sq. ft.
Bramalea City Centre	Brampton, Ont.	1,155,201 sq. ft.
Oshawa Centre	Oshawa, Ont.	1,120,800 sq. ft.
Les Promenades St-Bruno	St-Bruno-de-Mont., Que.	1,084,000 sq. ft.
St Laurent Centre	Ottawa	1,073,560 sq. ft.
Devonshire Mall	Windsor, Ont.	1,055,955 sq. ft.
Le Centre Fairview Pointe Claire	Pointe-Claire, Que.	1,020,000 sq. ft.
Les Galeries d'Anjou	Anjou, Que.	1,013,000 sq. ft.
Twin Oaks Town Centre	Windsor, Ont.	1,000,000 sq. ft.

Source: Rogers Media Publishing, 2005.

renewal projects involve the re-tenanting of the centre and result in an increase in the total number of retail units. Even if no additional retail space is added, because of the reduction in the space requirements of most retailers, the actual number of stores in a centre can increase dramatically. Revitalization has taken a number of forms. These include expansions, enclosures, re-tenanting, renovations, or various combinations of the above.

Figure 16.2 illustrates the process whereby shopping centre maturation contributed to major shifts in the growth of new retail forms. In essence, the intra–urban shopping centre hierarchy that was developed between 1950 and 1970 led to a dichotomous retail system. The new suburban system was planned, functionally homogeneous, and the domain of the retail chain. In contrast, the older inner-city areas remained unplanned and were dominated by independent merchants. By the mid-1970s, shopping centre developers recognized that they had created a series of standardized, often overly sanitized, shopping environments. Their

Figure 16.2 **Shopping Centre Maturation and Urban Retail Change**

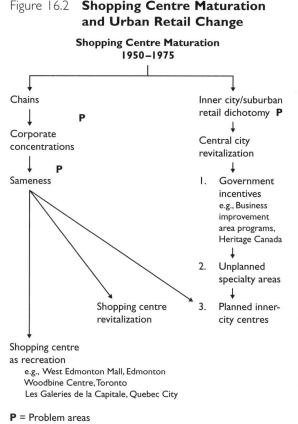

**Shopping Centre Maturation
1950–1975**

Chains
↓ **P**
Corporate concentrations
↓ **P**
Sameness
↓
Shopping centre as recreation
  e.g., West Edmonton Mall, Edmonton
  Woodbine Centre, Toronto
  Les Galeries de la Capitale, Quebec City

Shopping centre revitalization

Inner city/suburban retail dichotomy **P**
↓
Central city revitalization
↓
1. Government incentives
   e.g., Business improvement area programs, Heritage Canada
↓
2. Unplanned specialty areas
↓
3. Planned inner-city centres

P = Problem areas

programs. Grant programs, often subsidized by a property tax levy, were used to upgrade the physical appearance of retail strips, improve public parking, and provide assistance for a wide range of business activities such as advertising, marketing, and financial management (Holdsworth, 1985). In part, these programs were used to offset some of the consequences of shopping centre competition on traditional retail areas. In other cases, inner-city areas rejuvenated 'naturally'. In this scenario, selected inner-city strips in major metropolitan areas developed a specialty focus. These areas provided an alternative shopping environment to the shopping centre. They stressed assortment and quality of merchandise and merchant expertise and offered the vitality of an uncontrolled shopping environment. In some districts, such as Toronto's Yorkville and Vancouver's Gastown, this process was initiated in the 1960s.

The Arrival of the Big-Box Retailers and Power Centres

The 1990s will be remembered as a decade where virtually no shopping centre growth took place in Canada (Doucet and Jones, 1997; ICSC, 1997). Indeed, Vaughan Mills Shopping Centre, opened in 2004, was the first major shopping centre built in Canada since 1989. Shopping centre sales decline stems from a variety of factors—recession in the early 1990s; high cross-border shopping, 1990–2; decline in consumer real incomes; aging of the Canadian population and corresponding shifts in retail expenditures (Foot and Stoffman, 1996)— have led to a downturn in consumer spending (Kidd, 1996). The introduction of major competition in big-box retailers and power centres and the arrival of Wal-Mart precipitated a consumer shift to the free-standing discount department store/superstore. In response, shopping centres' share of retail sales declined and some shopping centres have been closed and/or changed to other land uses. Table 16.3 provides a selected list of the store portfolios of major big-box retailers in Canada between 2001 and 2004.

response was threefold. First, through shopping centre renovation, they instituted new, upscale design features in many of their major centres. Second, they began to experiment with new marketing approaches such as the shopping centre as an entertainment vehicle. Third, they returned to the inner city, often with the assistance of local government authorities, to develop planned central city shopping centres (e.g., Pacific Centre, Vancouver), festival retail developments in waterfront locations (e.g., Market Square, Saint John), or historic properties (e.g., Le Vieux Port, Montreal; Warehouse District, Winnipeg).

Lately, in many cities across Canada, provincial authorities reinvested in old inner-city shopping districts through a variety of business improvement

	No. Units (2001)	No. Units (2004)
Table 16.3 **Big-Box Retailers in Canada, 2001–4**		
Category		
Discount Department		
Wal-Mart	196	234
Warehouse Clubs		
Price Club/Costco	60	62
Automotive		
Canadian Tire (not all big-box)	451	456
Home Improvement		
Home Depot	76	109
Rona Home & Garden	3	25
Office Products		
Business Depot/Staples	183	229
Office Depot/Office Place	37	33
Computers/Electronics		
Future Shop/Best Buy	91	130
Books		
Chapters	76	72
Indigo	9	12
Sporting Goods		
Sport Chek	91	113
Sportmart	46	99
Home Furnishings		
Brick	61	82
Ikea	9	12
Toys and Games		
Toys R Us	64	64
Arts and Crafts		
Michaels	24	34
Bedding Supplies		
Linens & Things	8	19
HomeSense	9	36
Home Outfitters	14	46

Changes in the competitive environment have altered the tenant mix of the regional shopping centre. Hardware, food, sporting goods, toys, electronics, furniture, office supplies, arts and crafts, pet stores, and optical wear have been under the most pressure from the invasion of big-box retailers, mostly US-based (Hernandez, Jones, and Maze, 2003). Large retailers, such as Home Depot, Sports Authority, Toys R Us, Office Depot, Chapters, Business Depot, Michaels, Lenscrafters, and PetStuff, which stress competitive pricing, assortment, and brand merchandise, increasingly dominate our retail markets (Jones et al., 1994). In the Greater Toronto Area (GTA), between 1995 and 2002, the number of big-box retailers increased from 267 to 695, accounting for approximately 33 million square feet of retail space (Hernandez, Birsiotto, and Jones, 2003). During the same period, shopping centres in the GTA grew by only approximately 90,000 square metres (one million square feet) (CSCA, 1998). Exacerbating the problem for the shopping centre is the higher sales productivity of the big-box retailer. In 2003, it has been estimated that big-box retailers control approximately 10 per cent of total retail selling area, but account for nearly 20 per cent of all non-automotive sales (Simmons and Hernandez, 2004a; 2004b). These

---

Defining Power Retail

Big box: Big-box outlets are typically three or more times larger than other comparable stores. The definition of 'big box' varies by sector and is determined by gross leasable area.

Power centre: Three or more big-box retailers with shared parking lot and, typically, ancillary commercial services.

Power node: One power centre with additional big boxes or other power centres/major malls within a one kilometre radius, typically centred on a major intersection.

---

big-box retailers have clustered into what have been termed power centres and power nodes (see Tables 16.4 and 16.5).

Table 16.4 **Power Retail across Canada, 2003**

Measure	Total	Average
Power Centres	204	
Total stores	3,936	19.3
Big-box stores	1,465	7.2
Big-box share (%)	26.9	26.9
Total floor area (sq. ft.)	77,435,000	379,600
Big-box floor area (sq. ft.)	65,887,000	323,000
Big-box share (%)	85.1	85.1
Ancillary stores	2,471	30.6
Retail	1,530	19.0
Food	534	6.6
Services	407	5.0
Power Nodes*	103	
Total stores	6,828	66.3
Big-box stores	1,541	22.6
Total floor area (sq. ft.)	93,991,000	912,500
Big-box floor area (sq. ft.)	74,240,000	720,800
Big-box share (%)	79.0	79.0
Power Centres in Power Nodes	162	1.57
Total floor area (sq. ft.)	55,274,000	536,600
Power centre share (%)	58.9	58.9

* Some power nodes also include conventional shopping centres not included in this database.
Source: CSCA (2004).

In 2003, more than 200 power centres operated across Canada, mostly in the fastest-growing retail markets. Table 16.6 provides a list of the top 20 retail hotspots across Canada, based on the *Small Area Retail Trade Estimates* released by Statistics Canada. As a result of power retail, the regional shopping centre has become marginalized and increasingly dominated by fashion merchandisers and personal services. In response, in many shopping centres, rents have fallen, vacancies have increased, many shopping centre properties have become overvalued, and the ownership has changed hands.

The Role and Positioning of Specialized Retail Areas

There have always been specialized retail clusters within metropolitan areas. It is the growth in the importance of these types of districts that is new. Several reasons account for this, including: general reaction to the sterility of suburban plazas; an expansion of consumer demand; and changes in demographics and lifestyles (see Chapter 8). Specialty retailing tends to be an inner-city phenomenon and is often spatially associated with gentrified residential areas or waterfronts.

The pattern of specialty retailing can be either dispersed or concentrated. The former includes merchants who offer a highly specialized product (e.g., model trains, comic books, historical documents) and who rely on consumer motivations that can be best described as esoteric. These retailers have no need to form specialty clusters since they offer one-of-a-kind merchandise and their customers will travel long distances to purchase the product. The other group of specialty retailers clusters in order to attract a certain set of consumers, e.g., antique and art dealers, furniture stores, high-fashion retailers, suppliers of electronic equipment, restaurants, and automobile showrooms.

Jones and Simmons (1993) have identified five distinct types of specialty clusters: specialty product areas; fashion centres; factory outlets/off-price centres; historic or theme developments; and ethnic strips. In addition to these five clusters, lifestyle centres geared to the higher-income shopper can be added as a new variant of specialty retail.

Specialty product areas provide an environment for comparison shopping, where choice offered by a group of stores selling similar goods attracts consumers. Some areas, such as Granville Island Market in Vancouver and Harbourfront Antiques in

Table 16.5   **Major Power Nodes in Canada (over 1 million total store sq. ft.)**

Power Node	Market	Total No. of Stores	Total Store Sq. Ft.	Total No. of Big Boxes	Total Big Box Sq. Ft.
Hwy 400 & Hwy 7	Vaughan, Ont.	163	2,744,354	74	2,309,559
Sunridge	Calgary	201	1,968,594	53	1,651,357
Langley	Langley, BC	194	1,924,244	58	1,625,232
Coquitlam	Coquitlam, BC	85	1,897,349	44	1,661,449
Stoney Plain/Terra Losa	Edmonton	201	1,704,123	48	1,331,740
Bayers Lake	Halifax	73	1,442,620	36	1,258,900
Westhills Town Centre	Calgary	145	1,366,360	35	1,032,133
Polo Park	Winnipeg	49	1,356,911	33	1,350,911
137th Ave. NW	Edmonton	135	1,354,897	39	1,104,013
Heartland Town Centre	Mississauga, Ont.	142	1,329,923	43	1,091,723
Quebec City	Quebec City	58	1,305,289	22	1,188,989
Shawnessy Town Centre	Calgary	127	1,276,765	29	966,560
Saint-Bruno	Saint-Bruno, Que.	42	1,269,000	24	1,170,900
Barrie 400	Barrie, Ont.	84	1,204,027	28	1,058,865
Hwy 2 & Harwood Ave.	Ajax, Ont.	72	1,189,508	33	1,067,356
Calgary Trail and 34th Ave.	Edmonton	94	1,159,677	38	979,570
Yonge St. and Davis Dr.	Newmarket, Ont.	71	1,151,252	35	1,011,553
Eglinton Ave. E. & Warden Ave.	Toronto	98	1,137,987	24	914,902
Regent Ave. & Lagimodiere Blvd	Winnipeg	41	1,136,305	21	1,073,855
Hwy 403 & Dundas St. E.	Oakville, Ont.	74	1,102,936	36	968,876
Trans-Canada Hwy and Victoria Ave. E.	Regina	53	1,056,900	27	1,002,800
Kanata	Ottawa	111	1,004,680	24	701,572

Source: CSCA National Power Centre Database, 2004.

Toronto, serve the entire metropolitan market (and enjoy high tourist appeal); others serve a more limited market. Those areas that serve the whole metropolitan market tend to locate near the city centre, though automobiles and furniture districts, because of space requirements, locate at the periphery in low-rent areas. The neighbourhood specialty strip is typically found in older residential areas that have experienced gentrification (e.g., The Beaches, Toronto; Rue St-Denis, Montreal; Old Strathcona, Edmonton), providing quality food and fashion goods and new forms of personal services.

Fashion and factory outlet centres are on the opposite sides of the spectrum. Fashion outlet

Table 16.6 Retail Hotspots in Canada: 2001

Rank 2000	Rank 1999	FSA*	Market	Sales Score	Sales/Location ($000)**	Power Centre	Major Shopping Destination	#Shopping Centre	#Power Centre
1	2	T2H	MacLeod Trail, Calgary	11.29	4106.675	Heritage Towne Ctr/Chinook Crossing	Chinook S.C.	9	2
2	1	L3R	Markham/ Unionville, Ont.	8.67	1761.110	Woodside Centre	Markville S.C.	19	1
3		S7K	Saskatoon, CBD	7.15	2445.530	River City Centre	Midtown S.C.	4	1
4	7	M6A	Toronto (North York)	5.68	2374.757		Yorkdale S.C.	4	
5	3	L4L	Woodbridge, Ont.	5.62	2388.820	Seven & 400 Power Ctr/ Colossus Power Ent Ctr/Weston Rd. & Hwy 7	Woodbridge Town Centre	13	3
6	4	L4M	Barrie, Ont.	5.52	2751.654	Bayfield St & Livingstone St	Bayfield St./ Georgian Mall	5	1
7	8	M5C, M5B	Toronto, CBD	5.43	2207.020		Eaton Centre/ The Bay	5	
8	11	H9R	Pointe Claire, Que	5.30	2815.577	Trans-Canadienne & Blvd St-Jean Power Centre/Hwy 40 and Blvd Des Sources	Fairview Centre	6	2
9		N8X	Windsor, Ont.	5.15	3138.092	Devonshire Power Centre	Devonshire Mall	7	1

(continued)

Table 16.6 **(Continued)**

Rank 2000	Rank 1999	FSA*	Market	Sales Score	Sales/Location ($000)**	Power Centre	Major Shopping Destination	#Shopping Centre	#Power Centre
10	13	V5H	Burnaby, BC	5.15	2393.892		Metrotown	6	
11	6	M1P	Toronto (Scarborough)	5.03	2475.664	Kennedy Commons	Scarborough Town Centre	7	1
12	9	H3B, H3A	Montreal, CBD	5.00	1421.243		Place Ville Marie/Eaton Centre	10	
13	10	V6X	Richmond, BC	4.71	1595.487	Hwy 99 & Bridgeport Rd	Lansdowne S.C.	11	1
14	14	T1Y	Calgary, Alta	4.54	3274.663	Sunridge Towne Centre	Sundridge S.C.	7	1
15		L5B	Mississauga City Centre	4.54	2290.726	Square One Power Ent. Ctr	Square One	8	1
16	15	T2E	Calgary	4.47	2213.750		Deerfoot Mall	4	
17		T5T	West Edmonton, Alta	4.36	1706.216	Terra Losa Power Centre	West Edmonton Mall	5	1
18		T3A	Calgary	4.34	2813.041	Dalhousie Station/ Country Hills Blvd NW & Sarcee Trail NW	Market Mall	5	2
19	18	M9W	Toronto (Etobicoke)	4.34	2808.752		Woodbine Shopping Centre	9	
20		T2J	Calgary	4.23	2137.998		Southcentre Mall	15	

*Forward sortation area. FSAs correspond to the areas covered by the first three characters of the postal code.

** Sales/Location calculated as retail sales in FSA/# of locations in FSA.

Source: Statistics Canada (2001b).

centres deliver designer products in an upscale environment (e.g., Bay-Bloor/Yorkville, Toronto; Sherbrooke West/Crescent, Montreal); factory outlets offer perhaps last year's styles or imitations in a low-overhead store. Both forms of retail development attract the recreational shopper. Fashion streets are often the most expensive and visible shopping locations within the metropolis (e.g., Fifth Avenue, New York City; North Michigan Avenue, Chicago), with close links to the high-income sectors and/or executive employment locations. These high-fashion streets have been particularly attractive to European chains and sometimes have been incorporated into mixed-use projects that integrate offices, hotels, and entertainment.

The factory outlet, or off-price centre, is a relatively recent variant of the suburban shopping centre. In these locations costs are reduced by strategies such as less glamorous mall design, reduced customer service, minimal mall/store fixtures, and a reliance on merchandise that is end-of-the-line, overruns, or seconds. The Cookstown Manufacturers' Outlet Mall located on the outskirts of Barrie, Ontario, provides an excellent example. The 200,000-square-foot mall located on the major highway linking Toronto to Barrie and surrounding 'cottage country' is positioned to capture tourist shoppers. It houses 57 tenants, including Tommy Hilfiger, Nike, Paderno, and the Cadbury Chocolate factory outlets. In Canada, these centres are not as prominent as in the United States.

Historic redeveloped properties or theme malls have become a feature of revitalization in older parts of the city, especially waterfront and warehouse districts. Historic Properties in Halifax, Quebec City's Lower Town, Toronto's Distillery District, and Winnipeg's Warehouse District suggest that a variety of developments are possible. Historic or architecturally important buildings provide the focus. In some developments existing building stock is used, and in others new structures are created. In either case, these environments take on the appearance and function of planned shopping centres.[2]

Specialized retailers capitalize on another amenity: small towns and villages in attractive rural settings. Unplanned versions of these recreational retailing clusters have also emerged in smaller communities near large metropolitan regions that provide close-by markets: Niagara-on-the-Lake, Elora, and St Jacobs in Ontario and Knowlton in Quebec are examples. These retail environments are seasonal and are comprised of independent merchants, although in certain instances land costs/rental rates have put extreme pressure on the traditional character of these areas.

Ethnic strips are normally associated with the point of entry of an immigrant group in the city. At first, the retail component adjusts to serve the needs of the immediate neighbourhood. In this phase certain types of products dominate, in particular food and fashion retailers, restaurants and personal services linked to the community's cultural heritage. Eventually, the strip evolves to cater to members of the ethnic group throughout the metropolitan area, and over time these areas may also become tourist attractions, as is the case with Kensington Market and Chinatown in Toronto.

The rapid growth of specialty retailing areas has added a new aspect of competition within the urban retail system. The addition of a shopping goods function to the retail strip presents the consumer with an alternative to the conventional shopping centre. It also has generated a series of negative externalities based on the growing retail traffic in certain inner-city neighbourhoods. Independent merchants have normally satisfied specialty retail demands but more specialized chains now are taking aim at the market niches that such unplanned street environments and theme malls provide. In response, some conventional malls are attempting to develop more distinct images and in some of our major urban areas (e.g., Toronto and Vancouver) ethnic shopping centres are emerging (Wang, 1996) (see Chapter 24).

Lifestyle centres have been a key element of new retail development in the US over the last decade. In Canada only a small number of centres can be identified as 'lifestyle-type' centres. According to the International Council of Shopping Centers, a lifestyle centre is:

most often located near affluent residential neighborhoods ... caters to the retail needs and 'lifestyle' pursuits of consumers in its trading area. It has an open-air configuration and typically includes at least 50,000 square feet of retail space occupied by upscale national chain specialty stores. Other elements differentiate the lifestyle center in its role as a multi-purpose leisure-time destination, including restaurants, entertainment, and design ambience and amenities such as fountains and street furniture that are conducive to casual browsing. These centers may be anchored by one or more conventional or fashion specialty department stores. (ICSC, 2005b)

The Village at Park Royal adjacent to the Park Royal Regional Shopping Mall on North Shore in Vancouver provides a Canadian example of a lifestyle centre. The 238,000-square-foot centre houses a number of major big-box stores including Home Depot, Urban Barn, Old Navy, and Michaels. Opened in 2004, the Village provides winding streetscapes in an architecturally themed environment. Parking is directly in front of stores and limited to one-hour only along the main street, which is lined with trees, street furniture, and ornate lighting. Located next to the 1.2 million-square-foot Park Royal Shopping Mall, the Village at Park Royal provides an up-market unenclosed retail spur to the existing mall, serving the relatively high-income demographic of North Shore, Vancouver.

Downtown

The downtown constitutes a distinct retail environment (see Chapter 10). Once the unchallenged centre of high-order retail activity, downtown has had to adapt to successive retail transitions over the past century. This area's high-density built environment distinguishes it from the remainder of the metropolitan region. The premium on downtown space forces all establishments, including retail, to be parsimonious with their use of land. Also, downtown's unparalleled transit access sets it apart from suburban locales, though the area is less accommo-

dating to cars than suburbs where parking is free and plentiful.

The central business district of a city combines almost all the retail types described above: it is the highest-order unplanned centre serving the entire metropolitan region. Usually, it incorporates a series of diverse retail areas. These can include skid row that features bars, cheap restaurants, and adult entertainment; high-fashion streets; major inner-city shopping centres; entertainment districts; traditional shopping streets; underground retail concourses; ancillary malls associated with mixed-use developments; and historic redeveloped specialty retail areas.

In many major US cities, and in many smaller centres in Canada, the downtown retail environment has been threatened by the continued development of planned suburban shopping destinations within an essentially no-growth market. In other places, including most major Canadian metropolitan areas, the downtown has been viewed as a retail investment. In a retail context, the former T. Eaton Company was the major player in the redevelopment of over 20 Canadian cores. Yet despite these investments, the relative share of CBD retail sales is declining. In Toronto, the central core now accounts for 9.7 per cent of the retail floor space and 6.9 per cent of retail employment in the Greater Toronto Area (Simmons et al., 1996).

In both Canada and the US, the key to downtown survival is the vibrancy of the economic base of the community or region as a whole. The downtowns of blue-collar industrial cities, such as Hamilton, Sudbury, and Windsor, are most vulnerable. Downtowns are more successful in cities, like Halifax or Saskatoon, that act as regional service centres. Factors that contribute to the success of downtown retailing include a strong public transit system that focuses on the core, a concentration of office/government employment in the downtown area, inner-city high-rise apartment or condominium development, a safe, unthreatening inner-city environment, and the willingness of major retailers (normally department stores), developers, and financial institutions to invest in the central area.

Towards a Classification of the Urban Retail System

The retail landscape within metropolitan areas is difficult to categorize. Neighbourhoods change, access patterns evolve, consumer preferences are modified, and new retail forms are developed. New retail typologies emerge daily as retail stores and districts are continuously undergoing change. If a store does not work, the retailer can shift the product mix or alter the image or advertising. It is not uncommon for the same location to go through dozens of variations in function and/or form over a 20-year period.

Four different approaches have been taken to classify the urban retail structure. These relate to the *morphology* or spatial form, the *functional composition* of the business types, the composition of the *market* served, and *ownership*.

In this chapter, a revised version of the taxonomy developed by Jones and Simmons (1993) differentiates urban retailing according to morphology, location, and market size and type (Figure 16.3). Each urban retail area initially is defined as either a centre or a strip. Then, in sequential stages, all areas are placed into inner-city and suburban categories and centres are further subdivided into planned and unplanned classes. Each retail area is assigned a position in the intra-urban retail hierarchy reflecting the size of its market and is further classified as satisfying either spatial or specialized markets.

Inner-city retailing has been dominated historically by the unplanned shopping area. Three unplanned forms are possible—the CBD, specialty product areas, and larger retail clusters at major intersections served by public transit. The first two serve metropolitan markets, the latter more community demands. Planned inner-city shopping areas, a recent phenomenon, have become a common feature in urban Canada since the mid-1970s. Downtown we find the central city fashion mall, which often has been the focus of major urban revitalization projects, and the ancillary retail

Figure 16.3   **A Typology of the Contemporary Urban Retail System**

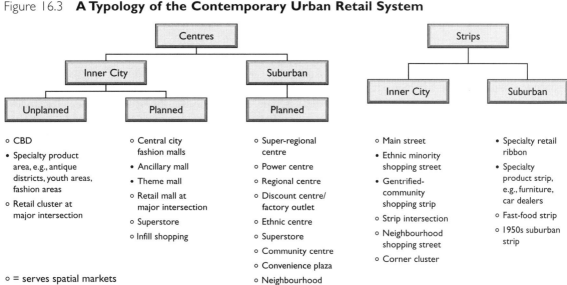

Note: In this classification the term 'planned' refers to a retail environment that is developed, designed, and managed as a unit and where the tenancy and common areas are under corporate control.

complex that has become the normal underground use in major office, hotel, and condominium developments in Montreal and Toronto.

Since the 1970s, four inner-city planned centre types have emerged: theme malls, infill shopping centres, retail mall developments at major intersections, and superstores or hypermarkets. Theme malls are normally tourist-oriented, occupy waterfront locations, and promote a distinct specialty product theme and atmosphere. The infill centre is a typical suburban shopping centre transplanted to the city. The development of planned centres at major inner-city intersections represented a modernization of traditional retailing at these shopping nodes that took advantage of established public transit linkages and the traditional regional shopping focus. The superstore represents the return of the major supermarket chains to previously abandoned inner-city locations—typically, single retail units occupying a minimum of 4,500 square metres (50,000 square feet), offering discount prices and wide product assortment, and relying on extensive trading areas.

Planned suburban shopping centres are essentially hierarchical—ranging from neighbourhood plaza to super-regional shopping centre. They can be classified by several criteria such as number of stores, number of establishments, floor surface, total selling area, number of parking spaces, customer volumes, trade area size, rental rates, and sales per square foot values. Since the 1960s there have been three additions to the planned suburban retail system. First, during the late 1960s the super-regional shopping centre, anchored by a minimum of two major department stores, comprised over 90,000 square metres (a million square feet) of gross leasable area and served a market of approximately 500,000 customers. Next came the discount or off-price centre with 'no-frill' shopping catering to the bargain-oriented market. This discount trend is reflected in the growth of three other retail forms— the factory outlet, the flea market, and the warehouse/superstore. Other variants of the suburban shopping centre include the mega-mall/recreational complex (e.g., West Edmonton [Johnson, 1987])

and new suburban complexes that are increasingly directed towards market segments—the family, the young urban professional.

The retail strip is effectively differentiated according to location in the inner city or suburbs. In the inner city, six retail forms can be identified. Main streets (the downtown strip), strip intersections, neighbourhood shopping streets, and corner store clusters have served essentially the same functions since the early 1900s. The main street still remains the foremost focus of retail activity for most large Canadian cities, although its proportion of total urban retail sales has declined. In smaller metropolitan regions, high vacancy rates attest to both relative and absolute retail decline. Neighbourhood retail areas continue to serve the daily needs of local populations and reflect the cultural and lifestyle characteristics of the resident population of the areas they serve. These neighbourhood strips are some of the most volatile elements in the urban retail landscape. In ethnic and gentrified communities some serve specialized, metropolitan-wide markets, particularly with respect to restaurants, fashion goods, and specialized products (e.g., art and antiques).

In the suburbs, four distinct forms of strip retailing have evolved, all auto-dependent. The first comprises unplanned 1950s suburban strip shopping on major suburban arterials. Normally, they are characterized by a series of small centres, with limited parking abutting property fronts. Some suburban arterials have taken on a specialty focus. Typically, these specialized clusters include fast-food restaurants, automobile dealers, furniture warehouses, home improvement retailers, and discount merchandisers.

Since the late 1980s, big-box retailers (also known as category killers) and power centres have been added to the urban retail system. These can include a variety of retail forms, all based on low margins and high sales per square foot and supported by low land costs and labour inputs—hence high volumes and low unit prices. Typically, these retailers occupy industrial lands and prefer highly accessible, expressway/highway locations. In the

Figure 16.4 **Typical Power Centre**

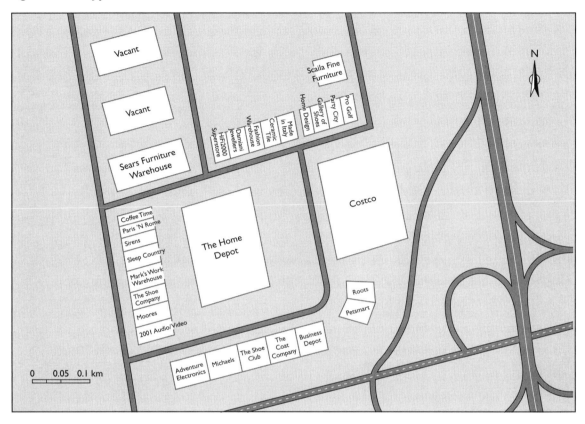

typical power centre, one would find a free-standing Price Club/Costco and Home Depot, and a variety of other category killers (Chapters, Business Depot, HomeSense, and Michaels) (see Figure 16.4).

This classification provides a conceptual framework for understanding the complexity of the urban retail environment. It should be remembered that the downtown makes up between 10 and 15 per cent of stores and the outlying shopping centres perhaps another 20 per cent, accounting for close to half the sales in the metropolitan region. However, approximately two-thirds of urban retailers operate in a variety of other shopping environments where they serve both specialized and convenience-oriented needs.

Conclusion

The urban retail system is structurally complex. In attempting to understand this environment, three distinct approaches should be integrated (Figure 16.5). First, it is necessary to describe, and develop an inventory of, the functional characteristics and spatial distribution patterns of the retail structure using basic dimensions such as retail type, number of stores, employment, ownership, and store turnover rates. The second and third approaches examine the retail system as demand and supply. Geographers have been more comfortable examining spatial aspects of demand—retail expenditure patterns, journey-to-shop, distance decay relationships,

Figure 16.5   **An Integrated Framework for the Study of the Intra-Urban Retail System**

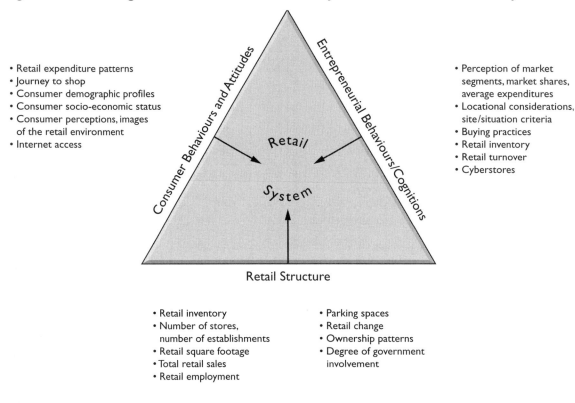

* Retail expenditure patterns
* Journey to shop
* Consumer demographic profiles
* Consumer socio-economic status
* Consumer perceptions, images
  of the retail environment
* Internet access

* Perception of market
  segments, market shares,
  average expenditures
* Locational considerations,
  site/situation criteria
* Buying practices
* Retail inventory
* Retail turnover
* Cyberstores

Consumer Behaviours and Attitudes

Entrepreneurial Behaviours/Cognitions

Retail System

Retail Structure

* Retail inventory
* Number of stores,
  number of establishments
* Retail square footage
* Total retail sales
* Retail employment

* Parking spaces
* Retail change
* Ownership patterns
* Degree of government
  involvement

and images of various retail environments with markets typically assessed in terms of location, areal extent, income level (market size), demographic composition, and lifestyle characteristics. The third component, retail supply, has been overlooked in most geographic appraisals of the urban retail landscape. Important questions to be addressed include: How do particular retailers react to specific market segments? How does the retail firm decide what retail merchandise to stock in a particular area? How are locational strategies formulated? What is the relationship between the retail chain and the shopping centre developer? What determines the retailer's ability to pay for a particular location? What is the role of retail planning control on investment activity?

This chapter concludes by speculating on some of the changes that most probably will impact the Canadian urban retailing system over the next decade. First, as our population ages, new retail types and forms will target increased convenience, new merchandising mixes, and the growth of new specialty chains that specifically cater to the 'greying' population (e.g., nutrition and health food stores). The 'baby-boomer' market seems likely to demand higher-end retail venues (e.g., lifestyle centres) and generally to be less inclined to shop in 'big-box' formats. Second, corporate concentration throughout the Canadian retail system will continue to increase—two retailers tend to dominate each retail category. This retail consolidation will occur both through acquisition and by the arrival in Canada of major American and European retailers, reflecting growth of an international retail system (Yeates, 1998) and the realities of the North American Free Trade Agreement. (Most effected will be department stores and fashion retailers.) Third, the dichotomy between inner-city and suburban retailing will increase. Certain areas will cater exclusively to particular market segments, and shopping environments will be developed to serve distinct lifestyle groupings—normally the affluent. Structurally, either large power centres or free-standing destination retailers will continue to grow, as will small convenience centres (as witnessed by the growth in food-anchored shopping centres). The established enclosed mall environment will continue to be challenged by demands for large operating square footage. The demise of the traditional department store has raised issues relating to the definition and operation of 'anchor' stores. Who are the new 'anchor' stores or 'anchor clusters'? As increasing numbers of malls integrate big-box format stores within and/or on their out-pads, how are consumer behaviours changing, and what does this mean in terms of retail lease rates? Finally, new issues will influence the operation of our retail system. These may include property rights and shopping centre access; the consequences of 'over-storing' on new retail development; the role of planning legislation on the final disposition of our urban retail future; the long-term impact of e-retailing; and privacy issues related to the proliferation of large databases that capture the purchasing patterns of the individual consumer.

The retail environment is continually washed by waves of innovation. New products, new store types, new technologies, new locations emerge, and new market segments are identified. There is constant interplay among categories of actors—retailers, consumers, developers, all levels of government, and, increasingly, technology providers. In this system winners and losers are quickly identified as the retail landscape constantly evolves.

Notes

1. The Eaton Centre, the most popular tourist destination in Toronto (Toronto, n.d.), further illustrates this phenomenon.

2. In the United States, these forms of inner-city shopping areas have become commonplace and have added a new, upscale dimension to the retail fabric of central cities. One developer, James Rouse, has been prominent in this form of retail renewal. Examples of the 'Rouse Model' include Faneuil Hall, Boston; The South Street Seaport, New York City; HarborPlace, Baltimore; and The Gallery on Market Street East, Philadelphia. In other cases, a property of some importance is renovated as a specialty theme mall. Examples of these forms of development include Trolley Square, Salt Lake City; Union Station and Georgetown Park, Washington, DC; Jax's Brewery, New Orleans; Old Colony Mill, Keene, NH; and Ghiradelli Square, San Francisco.

Chapter 17

City Politics: Municipalities and Multi-Level Governance

Andrew Sancton

Canadian politicians at all levels of government are talking a great deal about a 'New Deal for Cities'. By this they usually mean that they aspire to spend significantly more public money to improve urban infrastructure and that they want urban municipalities to be granted more legal authority to make autonomous decisions about the quality of urban life. The former objective is probably easier to achieve than the latter, because spending money is always easier than making major changes to the basic structures of governance. As our cities increasingly become the focus of economic, social, and cultural activity in Canada, is it likely that the municipal will be the most significant level of government in determining the quality of life in our cities? Or is it more likely that federal and provincial governments will become even more involved with cities than they already are, thus entrenching a multi-level perspective as the main lens through which we must understand urban governance?

We cannot understand or evaluate new deals for cities unless we understand the basic principles on which our cities have been governed in the past. The main objective of this chapter is to explore these assumptions and to analyze how they are being affected by the constant barrage of change that now faces everyone—from mayors to bus passengers—in any way connected to Canadian municipal government. The chapter is divided into four sections: the historical background and constitutional status of Canadian local government; functions and funding; politics and parties; and issues relating to the government of metropolitan areas, those large urban areas in which we usually find

many municipalities and the greatest pressures for growth.

History and Constitutional Status

Canada's municipal system—even in Quebec—is grounded almost entirely in British law and practice, with some later additions from the United States. Prior to the nineteenth century in Britain the first municipal corporations were established by royal charter or Act of Parliament in order partially to remove certain defined urban territories from the control of traditional feudal authorities. By this device urban property-holders were able to set up their own taxing system, to build their own streets and public markets, and to enforce their own regulations concerning local trade and commerce. In these early days, attaining municipal status was often a major victory, if not for the whole community, at least for established merchants and property-owners. During the nineteenth century, Parliament extended the municipal system throughout Britain. The central government had become increasingly strangled by hundreds of its own local boards and commissions, which had been created to cope with the multitude of problems resulting from rapid industrialization. A comprehensive system of municipal government was seen as a valuable mechanism for helping finance, implement, and co-ordinate central policies at the local level.

Reasons for establishing municipal government in Canada were similar to those that emerged over the centuries in Britain (Isin, 1992). Municipalities met the needs of both local elites and central governments. As in Britain, early Canadian municipal governments were not particularly democratic. The franchise was generally restricted to male property-owners or leaseholders. Much of the impetus to democratize Canadian local government—including the idea of holding direct elections for the office of mayor—came from the United States.

The Constitution of Canada[1] establishes two orders of government: federal and provincial. By Section 92(8) of the Constitution Act, 1867, 'Municipal Institutions in the Province' are included as one of the 'Classes of Subject' for which 'In each Province the Legislature may exclusively make Laws.' Municipal institutions are mentioned in the 1867 Act because they were already established in the three British colonies—Canada (Ontario and Québec), New Brunswick, and Nova Scotia—that initially comprised the Canadian federation.

The oldest incorporated municipality in Canada is Saint John, New Brunswick, which received a royal charter in 1785. The legislature of Lower Canada incorporated Montreal and Quebec City in 1832; Hamilton and Toronto were incorporated by the legislature of Upper Canada in 1833 and 1834 respectively. Following the unification of Upper and Lower Canada in 1840, the new legislature established comprehensive systems of municipal government for both parts of the colony. The Municipal Corporations Act of 1849 (the Baldwin Act) was the most important legislation for what is now Ontario; the equivalent legislation for Quebec was approved in 1855 (Higgins, 1986: 40–7).

In both Ontario and Quebec each distinct urban area was to be governed by a single municipality, usually called a city but sometimes a town. Rural areas were to be governed by both counties and smaller units contained therein: townships or parishes, towns, and villages. This system survived intact for more than a century in both provinces. It still exists in many parts of Ontario. Other Canadian provinces have generally adopted similar systems of municipal government, except that they have generally done so without counties as upper-tier units of rural government.

When an area is incorporated as a municipality under provincial legislation, it acquires a legal personality, just as a business does when it is incorporated as a limited company. Incorporation necessarily involves the specification of three features essential to a municipality's existence: a precisely defined territory; a mechanism, usually an elected council, by which the municipality can make legally enforceable decisions; and a list of governmental functions that are legally within its jurisdiction. Because municipalities owe their existence to provinces while the federal and provincial governments owe theirs to the Constitution, the municipal level of government in Canada is in a legally inferior position. Such a position is reflected by the fact that, legally speaking, the federal and provincial governments are directly linked to the Crown and carry out their activities in the name of the reigning monarch while municipal corporations act legally only on their own behalf; they are not acting for Her Majesty the Queen.

In 1997, the constitutional status of Canadian municipalities was tested in the courts. Five of the six municipalities that were being merged by the Ontario legislature challenged the constitutionality of the Act in question. In his judgement rejecting the municipalities' case, Mr Justice Borins clearly stated 'four principles which apply to the constitutional status of municipal governments':

1. Municipal institutions lack constitutional status.
2. Municipal institutions are creatures of the legislature and exist only if provincial legislation so provides.
3. Municipal institutions have no independent autonomy and their powers are subject to abolition or repeal by provincial legislation.
4. Municipal institutions may exercise only those powers conferred upon them by statute (Borins, 1997).

Unlike the provinces, the federal government has no legislative authority with respect to municipalities. Nevertheless, the federal government is an extremely important institution for determining the quality of our urban life (Tindal and Tindal, 2004:

207–14). Through its monetary, fiscal, and trade policies, it plays a central role in defining the nature of urban economic activity. Its policies concerning taxation and intergovernmental transfers have much to do with determining the capacity of provincial governments to respond to municipal demands for additional funds for urban services. Federal jurisdiction over railways, ports, and airports is of crucial importance to many aspects of urban development; so is the fact that the federal government is the biggest single landowner in urban Canada. For some of our urban neighbourhoods, the most significant determinant of their future character will be federal immigration policy.

The importance of provincial governments for cities goes far beyond their constitutional responsibility for municipal government. Provinces control health care, education, and social services. Hospitals, schools and universities, and daycare centres providing special services to the young, the old, or the handicapped are all important features of urban life. Although provinces usually do not operate such institutions directly, they have become responsible for assuring their financial survival. Provincial highways are crucial arteries for urban transportation; their extension and expansion often determines the future direction of urban development. Provincial policies relating to the subsidization of housing (Carroll, 2002), sewage treatment, water-supply systems, public transit (Fowler and Layton, 2002), and other urban services can have a huge influence on large-scale strategic land-use decisions usually made at the local level.

Functions and Funding

The exact functional responsibilities of municipalities vary widely across the country. Even within the same province, municipalities of similar size and character often do not have the same list of functions. In Quebec, municipalities have virtually no involvement with hospitals or social services. In Ontario, municipalities operate homes for the aged, provide child daycare for low-income families, and are responsible for the delivery of welfare payments. They have no formal responsibility for local hospitals but are sometimes expected to make significant contributions to their capital fundraising campaigns. Most urban municipalities in Canada have direct control over parks and recreation, but in Vancouver this task is performed by a directly elected local commission. In Quebec, local police forces are generally under the direct control of the municipality. In Ontario and other provinces, the municipalities generally pay the bill while the forces themselves are controlled and directed by commissions not directly accountable to the municipal government (Martin, 1995).

Almost without exception, Canadian provinces have assigned the following functions to municipalities: fire protection; local roads and streets; the collection and disposal of residential solid waste; sewage systems; the taxation of land and buildings; and the regulation of local land use. The common thread in this list of functions is property. This has led many in Canada—practising municipal politicians, journalists, and academics—to conclude that municipalities are the units of government concerned with regulating, servicing, and taxing our built environment. For many politicians, other functions are at best frills and at worst the unjustifiable result of provincial policies aimed at unloading costly social functions on unwilling municipalities and their overburdened taxpayers.

Land-use planning is often considered the government function that best exemplifies the close connection between municipalities and the built environment. It is almost impossible to generalize about land-use planning procedures in the various provinces. All provinces provide for municipal adoption, in one form or another, of an overarching plan intended to provide a framework for future development and detailed land-use regulation (Leo, 2002). Similarly, they all provide for some form of municipal control on the subdivision of land for new development and on the uses to which land can be put. However, the degree of provincial control over these processes varies widely. Regardless of legal arrangements in the various provinces, the political agendas of municipalities throughout the country are dominated by land-use issues. In the real world of inter-municipal competition for investment, and provincial regulations aimed at ensuring affordable housing or co-ordinating the development of large-scale infrastructures, there is little room for radical differences in land-use policies among municipalities sharing similar characteristics within the same province. Nevertheless, there are important decisions to be made in each locality about such matters as the number, size, and location of suburban shopping malls; the preservation of heritage buildings and streetscapes; the extent to which downtown business and commercial functions will be allowed to spread into adjoining residential neighbourhoods; the timing and density of new suburban development. All these matters relate to land-use planning. They are at the heart of Canadian municipal politics. (For fuller discussions of planning in Canada, see Chapters 18 and 19.)

One of the major difficulties in attempting to describe municipal functions in Canada is that, in most cities, the municipal government does not have direct responsibility for many important functions of government that are subject in some degree or other to local control. Instead, such functions are under the control of what are generally known as special-purpose bodies. Exact definitions of such bodies are notoriously difficult. In their purest form they are very much like municipalities. They are established by provincial legislation; they have a defined territory; they have the right to raise their own revenues; members of their governing body are directly elected by the public. The main difference is that, while municipalities are responsible for a number of governmental functions, special-purpose bodies only deal with a particular function or set of closely related ones. School boards are the best Canadian examples.

Most other special-purpose bodies lack one or more of certain key characteristics. They have no taxing authority or legal right to claim municipal funds; their members are appointed rather than elected; or certain of their decisions are subject to approval by municipal councils. In assessing the real political power of various special-purpose bodies, it is important not to rely exclusively on an examination of their legal status. For a wide range of reasons, municipal councils might be extremely reluctant to attempt to change police, transit, or library policies, even though in some circumstances they might be legally entitled to overrule the relevant special-purpose body.

Funds for services delivered by municipalities and special-purpose bodies come from three main sources: an annual tax on the assessed value of real estate; grants—either conditional or unconditional—from provincial government; and user fees. The relationship between the property tax burden and the level of provincial grants has in recent years become a significant political issue in most Canadian provinces. In principle, there seems to be less disagreement about the desirability of user fees, especially for environmentally sensitive services such as water supply and sewage (Kitchen, 2002: ch. 6). Nevertheless, there are serious practical problems to extending them further. For example, charging user fees for garbage collection seems to work out satisfactorily in smaller communities where people tend to know each other. No large Canadian city has attempted such charges, presumably because of the fear that some city residents will attempt to avoid the charge by dumping their garbage in unauthorized locations.

Issues relating to property taxes, provincial grants, and special-purpose bodies all come together in attempts to 'disentangle' the provincial–municipal relationship. Quebec experienced a massive disentanglement in 1980: the province cancelled most grant programs to its municipalities and drastically restricted the authority of school boards to levy property taxes, thereby allowing municipalities to make up for the lost grants by taking over the property tax revenues previously collected by the school boards. Municipalities were quite happy with this arrangement until 1990, at which time the province decided that school boards would henceforth be expected to cover much of the cost of maintaining school buildings by increasing their property tax levies (Kitchen and Auld, 1995: 14).

More recently, other Canadian provinces, including British Columbia, Alberta, New Brunswick, and Newfoundland, have all taken significant steps to reduce the authority of school boards to levy taxes. Nowhere, however, has the disentanglement process been more wide-ranging and controversial than in Ontario. When the Progressive Conservative government of Mike Harris came to office in 1995, one of its objectives was to gain control of the educational system by drastically reducing the authority of school boards. Eliminating their right to levy taxes was a crucial element in this plan. Property taxes for education remain in Ontario, but rates are determined by the province. Reductions in education taxes on residences have been countered by the need for municipalities to pay a higher proportion of total welfare costs (Siegel, 2005). Nowhere else in Canada do municipalities face such a heavy financial commitment for welfare-related programs.

This state of affairs is demonstrated in Table 17.1, which shows 2005 revenues and expenditures for London, Ontario, a single-tier unit of municipal government not forming part of the political and administrative structure of any of Ontario's counties or regional municipalities. The table has a number of significant features. Its main object is to show, in descending order, the extent to which each of the various functions of local government in London draws on the general revenues of the municipal corporation, that is, proceeds from the property tax and from other municipal revenues not tied to a particular municipal function.

Two kinds of local special-purpose bodies (conservation authorities and the local public health unit) serve areas extending beyond London's city limits. For them it is impossible to determine the extent of their total expenditures and revenues relating only to London. What is known, and what is reported in the third column of the table, is the extent to which different functions are funded from London's general revenues. For purely municipal functions and for functions performed by

Table 17.1 **Budgeted Local Government Expenditures in London, Ontario, for Selected Functions,[1] 2005 ($000s)**

Function	Total Expenditure	Revenue from Conditional Grants and User Charges	Expenditures from Property Tax and General Revenues
*Police	65,859	2,794	63,065
Welfare and employment services (OntarioWorks)	113,968	66,261	47,707[2]
Fire protection	40,734	241	41,492
Road maintenance, traffic control, and parking	27,670	7,081	25,703
Housing	37,496	20,472	17,024[3]
Parks and recreation	28,426	13,920	14,506[4]
*Public transit	39,450	25,050	14,400
*Library	15,457	1,405	14,052
Land ambulance	n/a	n/a	8,800[5]
Solid waste management	9,242	1,245	7,997
*Public health	n/a	n/a	6,195

(continued)

Table 17.1   **(continued)**

Function	Total Expenditure	Revenue from Conditional Grants and User Charges	Expenditures from Property Tax and General Revenues
Child daycare	27,732	21,585	6,147
Property assessment	n/a	n/a	3,636[6]
Services for the handicapped	2,769	298	2,471[7]
Land-use planning	2,791	543	2,428
Long-term care	15,049	12,711	2,338
*Economic development and promotion	2,362	65	2,297
*Watershed conservation	n/a	n/a	2,182
*Art gallery & museums	2,379	1,003	1,375
Animal control	n/a	n/a	1,011[8]
Building controls	4,534	3,544	990
*Convention Centre	4,331	3,662	669
Centennial Hall	658	563	95[9]
Sewage collection and treatment	48,411	48,411	0
Water	46,940	46,940	0

*This function is not under the direct control of city council but rather under the control of a local special-purpose body of one type or another.

n/a: Expenditures and revenues relating only to the City of London are not available because the relevant special-purpose body operates beyond the city's boundaries.

1. Excluded from this table are all costs related to general municipal government, community grants, general management of some departments responsible for multiple functions, and all debt charges, capital levies, and contributions to reserves.
2. The municipality pays 20 per cent of approved payments to individuals and 50 per cent of administration costs.
3. Includes social housing within the Planning and Development Department and the costs of the London and Middlesex Housing Corporation.
4. Includes parks and recreation facilities from the Environmental and Engineering Services Department and recreation and neighbourhood Services from the Community Services Department.
5. This is the amount billed to the City of London by the County of Middlesex for the city's share of this service, which is managed by the county.
6. This is the city's 1998 share of province-wide assessment costs expended by the Ontario Property Assessment Corporation.
7. Transportation services for the physically handicapped and the blind.
8. This is the net amount paid to a contractor for this service.
9. A multi-purpose hall owned and operated by the city.

Sources: City of London, *2005 Corporate Operating Budget Reports*, 25 Jan. 2005, together with more detailed information provided by city staff; City of London, *2005 Water Budget*; City of London, *2005 Sewer Budget*. The research assistance of Tracy Zhou for this table is gratefully acknowledged.

special-purpose bodies operating only within the city boundaries, the table reports in the first column the total expenditures for each function. The second column shows the revenues—mainly user charges and conditional grants—generated by each function. For these functions, the figure in the third column is the result of subtracting the figure in the second from that in the first.

It is an article of faith among Canadian municipal politicians that they have been the victims of fiscal 'downloading', that is, federal and provincial governments have reduced grants and/or expected municipal governments to take over functions for which higher levels of government were previously responsible. Such beliefs are especially strong among politicians in Canada's largest cities. They point to federal retreat from the funding of social housing, lack of sufficient federal and provincial assistance in helping Aboriginal Canadians and new immigrants adjust to urban life, and decreased provincial support for urban infrastructure and public transit as especially egregious examples. After intensive efforts to draw their concerns to the attention of the federal government, they believed they were making considerable headway as federal politicians began to talk about a 'New Deal for Cities'. When the 'New Deal' turned out to apply not just to large cities but to all Canadian 'communities', there was considerable disappointment.

If municipalities in general and cities in particular have indeed been the victims of downloading and if municipal governments have not otherwise reduced spending, we should expect local government spending to increase as a proportion of total government spending. The truth of this claim depends almost entirely on what year is chosen as a reference point. For example, in 1913 local governments accounted for 36 per cent of government spending in Canada; provinces for only 17 per cent. By 1948 the percentages were 14 and 18 respectively (Crawford, 1954: 59). It would appear that a rather dramatic form of 'uploading' occurred between 1913 and 1948.

Table 17.2 presents annual data from Statistics Canada showing the percentage of total government expenditures accounted for by each level of

Table 17.2   Per Cent of Total Expenditures (Excluding Transfers) by Canadian Governments, for Each Level of Government, 1989–2003

Year	Federal	Provincial	Local
1989	50.1	38.0	12.0
1990	50.1	37.7	12.2
1991	49.5	38.5	12.0
1992	50.6	39.1	12.8
1993	48.7	39.7	11.6
1994	48.0	40.3	11.7
1995	48.2	40.2	11.6
1996	48.1	40.4	11.5
1997	46.2	41.5	12.3
1998	45.7	43.2	11.1
1999	44.2	44.4	11.4
2000	44.7	43.0	12.2
2001	45.0	42.9	12.1
2002	44.1	43.7	12.1
2003	44.0	43.5	12.4

Sources: Percentages calculated from Statistics Canada CANSIM II data, at: <http://datacentre.epas.utoronto.ca>, Table Number, 385002, Series V156163, V206449, V206447, V206448, V644256, V644254, V644255.

government for the period 1989–2003. In order to eliminate double or triple counting, transfers from other levels of government to a particular level are deducted from total expenditures for that level. Readers are reminded that expenditures of school boards are included as local government expenditures. The main story told by this table is that, since 1989, the federal government's share of total expenditures has declined from about 50 per cent to 44 per cent while the provincial share has increased from about 38 to 43 per cent; the local share of expenditures has remained relatively constant around 12 per cent. Despite the frequent claims of municipal politicians that their financial burdens have increased significantly in recent years, this table provides little or no evidence to support them. It is always possible, of course, that the statistics do not tell the real story. Perhaps the federal government and the provinces have indeed withdrawn from a significant number of essential functions and/or reduced their grants to local governments for such functions. Perhaps local governments have absorbed the additional burdens with minimal increases in costs by eliminating frills and becoming more efficient. If this is in fact what has happened—and many local politicians make precisely such a claim—then the reality of downloading would not be reflected in the percentages shown in Table 17.2. Determining the validity of the claim is virtually impossible. For every alleged example of downloading, a counter-example of increased provincial financial responsibility can usually be found; for every example of increased local efficiency, there are similar examples at other levels.

Now that federal and provincial budgets are generally balanced, it is doubtful that local spending will continue to increase faster than spending at other levels. The level of property taxes in Canada is already the highest among OECD countries.[2] Provincial governments seem as unwilling as ever to widen the variety of taxes available to local governments. Grants to local governments might begin to grow again in relative terms, but it is unlikely that total local expenditures (exclusive of transfers) will. This is especially true in light of projections that the greatest demands for increased government expenditures in the foreseeable future will result from the aging of the population. Health, pension, and long-term care costs are generally not local responsibilities.

While municipalities might not have significantly increased their functional and fiscal capacities in recent years, there is little doubt that they have fared better than school boards, whose outright decline in authority is especially obvious. But, significantly, school boards in Canada have generally lost authority to provincial governments, not to local municipalities. Similarly, hospitals, long-term care institutions, and personal social services are still almost completely insulated from municipal control and funded directly by provinces. In short, municipalities are a long way from having complete control over local public services within our urban areas. They are still, above all, the agencies of government that look after property.

Politics and Parties

During the 1970s in many Canadian cities it seemed that municipal politics was going through a period of fundamental change. Citizen groups were mobilizing against developers and were often winning their battles to protect neighbourhoods and green space. Their political representatives were being elected to council and were occasionally in control. Although adherents of the so-called 'new reform movement' might have had a relatively clear conception of the ideal urban environment, they had no common view concerning the role of municipal government in bringing it about. Some were genuinely committed to various forms of neighbourhood self-government. Others wanted to use local issues primarily as a way of mobilizing the working class for larger and more important battles to be fought out in the national arena. Most were concerned only with the particular issues at hand and became involved in municipal politics simply because it was the municipal government, in the first instance at least, that would be making the relevant decisions (Caulfield, 1988). Nobody in the new urban reform movement argued in favour of the principle that decisions by municipal governments should be considered final and should not be appealed to provincial supervisory bodies. Nobody articulated a vision of a genuinely multi-functional municipal government, the control of which would be contested at election time by competing political parties. Such views were more often expressed by academics (Plunkett and Betts, 1978: 147–52) and authors of provincially sponsored reports (Manitoba, 1976: 61–7). In fact, many new urban reformers seemed profoundly suspicious of any political institutions, including municipal governments and local political parties, with the potential to overrule the expressed preferences of local neigh-bourhoods and their leaders (or delegates).

The new urban reformers were successful in changing the way many Canadians viewed their cities. They were responsible for the implementation of elaborate new mechanisms to ensure that indi-viduals and citizen groups had ample opportunity to express their views about proposed changes to the physical environment in their areas—i.e., participa-tory democracy. They helped change the style of the municipal political process such that sensitivity to neighbourhood concerns became an avowed objec-tive of just about everybody, including municipal managers and engineers. But the functions and capa-bilities of municipal government changed very lit-tle. If anything, new provincial regulations relating to such matters as environmental assessments had the effect of reducing the capacity of municipal gov-ernments to manage their own affairs.

Sharp divisions between new reformers and old-guard pro-development municipal politicians are now hard to find. This means that we seem fur-ther away now from municipal party politics in Canada than we were in the 1970s. Outside Quebec, Vancouver is the only major Canadian city whose council is in any way controlled by a polit-ical party. Because of Vancouver's at-large election system, the 'right' organizes itself as the Non-Partisan Association (NPA) in order to finance expensive city-wide contests and present a com-plete slate of candidates. Its counterpart on the 'left' is the Committee of Progressive Electors (COPE).

In Montreal, a municipal party system has been in place since the mid-1950s (Quesnel, 1994). The most successful municipal political party in Canadian history is Jean Drapeau's Civic Party, which completely controlled Montreal city coun-cil from 1960 to 1986. By embodying Montrealers' intense civic pride, Drapeau remained firmly in control through the turbulent late 1960s and early 1970s. By the time the Montreal Citizens Movement (MCM) took over in 1986, the provin-cial legislature had amended municipal election law to provide for public funding of recognized munic-ipal political parties and to allow the printing of their names on the ballot. Since the defeat of the MCM in 1994, two quite different municipal parties (led by mayors Bourque and Tremblay respectively) have controlled the Montreal city council.

During the 1960s and 1970s there was a widely held belief that the emergence of political parties at the municipal level in Canada was both desirable and inevitable (Masson and Anderson, 1972). In the early twenty-first century, it is clear that increasing urbanization and complexity of urban problems do not themselves create and nurture local political parties. We are no closer to having established party systems in our major cities now than we were 25 years ago. Why were the earlier expectations never realized?

The answer seems to lie in the fact that, notwithstanding the growing importance of cities and their problems, municipal government remains limited in its functions and autonomy (Peterson, 1981). The great societal issues that create and sustain political parties in our national politics—building the Canadian nation on the basis of the National Policy for the Conservatives, establishing our independence from Britain and bilingual iden-tity for the Liberals, and building the welfare state in response to the Great Depression for the CCF/NDP—are not present in local politics.

This is not to say that there are no divisive issues in local politics. In recent decades we have become increasingly familiar with the NIMBY syndrome—not in my backyard. Residents of par-ticular areas fight bitterly with municipal govern-ments and other public and private institutions trying to build potentially dangerous, noisy, disrup-tive, or ugly installations in their immediate areas. Citizens rarely become more aroused politically than when someone wants to turn their quiet neighbourhood street into a multi-lane thorough-fare or the nearby vacant field into a landfill site. Important as such issues are at the time, they are rarely capable of building an ongoing city-wide coalition of like-minded people sharing similar interests and political priorities. Without such coali-tions there can be no indigenous local political par-ties. Whether Conservatives, Liberals, and New Democrats decide to become more openly involved in local politics will probably have more to do with the exigencies of national and provincial politics than with their assessments of the need for change in our municipalities. There is every reason to believe that municipal politics in Canada will continue to focus on issues relating to the use and development of land. Depending on the economic circumstances of the particular community in question, there will be more or less pressure to accommodate the wishes of particular developers who invariably will promise that their proposed projects will improve the community, attract further investment, and provide jobs. In prosperous economic times, citizen groups opposing particular developments are in a relatively strong position (as they were in Toronto in the early 1970s and the late 1980s); in times of economic downturn, pressures for growth and development are irresistible and the political leverage of citizen groups all but disappears.

Municipal Reorganization

Major Canadian municipalities such as Montreal, Toronto, and Vancouver were originally incorporated as a result of specific legislation relating only to them. Montreal and Vancouver remain legally isolated from the general municipal systems subsequently established in their provinces. The City of Toronto is now negotiating with the provincial government to again have its own distinct legislative status among municipalities in Ontario. The more common arrangement has been for cities to be incorporated according to procedures outlined in such general legislation. The important point, however, is that cities in Canada, until the 1950s at least, were not linked in any legal or political way to the towns, villages, and countryside that surrounded them. Conventional wisdom held that city problems and rural problems were different. Arrangements for municipal government were structured accordingly.

In the early twentieth century Montreal was unquestionably Canada's pre-eminent city. Municipal incorporation of parishes surrounding the City of Montreal was relatively easy. As the residential and industrial property market boomed, new municipalities sprang up by the dozens. As

many sunk into bankruptcy (in some cases by design) because of excessively optimistic investment in expensive infrastructure, they were annexed by Montreal. The territory of the central municipality grew dramatically; so too did its debt, because the standard condition of annexation was that the city absorb all outstanding financial obligations of its new component parts. In 1920, when four more suburban municipalities were in desperate financial straits, the city refused to solve the crisis through annexation. As a result, the provincial legislature established Canada's first metropolitan government, the Island of Montreal Metropolitan Commission. The Commission's main initial function was to control the borrowing of the member suburban municipalities. Optional functions were added later, including the building of a 'metropolitan boulevard', but most municipalities resisted and progress was virtually non-existent (Sancton, 1985: 26–30).

As in Montreal, the City of Toronto's boundaries also grew dramatically as a result of annexation in the early twentieth century. But in Ontario, the provincial government itself moved in to control the problem of excessive borrowing by the remaining Toronto suburbs as well as for all Ontario municipalities. Toronto did not get metropolitan government until 1953 with the creation of the Municipality of Metropolitan Toronto. The Metro level of government in Toronto soon became much more important than its equivalent in Montreal. Metro Toronto was charged with providing the roads, sewers, water supply, and overall planning for the gigantic suburban expansion of the 1950s and 1960s. It did its job well and became known worldwide as a Canadian success story (Rose, 1972). In 1960, the Manitoba legislature implemented its version of metropolitan government by creating the Corporation of Greater Winnipeg (Brownstone and Plunkett, 1983: 21–5). In 1969 the Quebec legislature greatly strengthened and enlarged Montreal's system of metropolitan government by creating the Montreal Urban Community (Sancton, 1985: 116).

The essentials of the metropolitan government systems in Montreal, Toronto, and Winnipeg were the same. The central city and surrounding municipalities kept their existing boundaries. They each gave up some of their functions to the new level of government, which was controlled by its own council. In Montreal and Toronto (until 1988), members of the metropolitan council came from the local councils, while in Winnipeg they were directly elected. Costs of the new metropolitan functions were apportioned to each member municipality in proportion to its share of the total taxable property assessment in the area covered by the metropolitan authority.

Constituent municipalities in the metropolitan authorities surrendered the relevant functions with varying degrees of reluctance. Some of them correctly calculated that a modest loss of authority was a small price to pay to maintain their existence and their ability to continue to control such matters as local zoning, streets, and parks and recreation. Rapidly growing areas, especially in suburban Toronto, experienced real gains from metropolitan government. Infrastructure to support new development was built on a scale far surpassing the financial capabilities of the municipality itself. Using the established tax base of the central city, Metro Toronto effectively created vast portions of what became the cities of North York, Scarborough, and Etobicoke.

From the mid-1960s until the late 1970s, provincial governments in many provinces made dramatic changes to the organization of municipal government. Ontario, British Columbia, and Quebec introduced new upper-tier structures, the structures in Quebec being known as 'urban communities' and in British Columbia as 'regional districts'. The Greater Vancouver Regional District (GVRD) remains in place as a key governance institution for the Vancouver urban area. At the same time as it created 'regional municipalities', Ontario merged numerous towns and villages at the lower tier. In 1972, the Manitoba legislature amalgamated the Corporation of Greater Winnipeg and its 12 constituent municipalities into one 'Unicity' (Brownstone and Plunkett, 1983).

Policy-makers justified this dramatic assault on traditional structures for municipal government on three main grounds. First, they argued that, especially in fast-growing areas, a local political authority was needed to plan future development around existing population centres. The main implication of this belief was that, contrary to previous practice, city and countryside would now have to be joined, for planning functions at least.

Second, they believed that economies of scale could be captured both by moving services from lower-tier municipalities to the regional or metropolitan level and by merging lower-tier municipalities into larger units so that even the most local of services could be delivered by larger units. Associated with this belief was the argument that more highly trained administrators were needed at the municipal level and that their inevitably hefty salaries could only be paid for by relatively large units.

Third, many policy-makers in this field were convinced that larger municipal units would increase equity as measured both by relative tax burdens and levels of service. Municipalities that benefited from abnormally high concentrations of revenue-producing industrial and commercial property would now have to share their good fortune. Those that might have been unable to afford such items as sophisticated sewage treatment facilities or good public libraries would find their service levels upgraded, probably to the standards in place in the best-served community with which they had been merged.

Unfortunately, each of these arguments contained inherent flaws, which caused serious problems for those politicians making them (Sharpe, 1981). Merging city and countryside caused significant problems for both sides. If the central city were relatively strong within the new region, outlying areas felt that effective regional government would inevitably serve the city's interests and not theirs. If suburban areas seemed to be politically stronger, as was the perception in Winnipeg's Unicity, then the central city felt its concerns always took second place behind those of suburban shopping centres or new residential subdivisions. On the other hand, if boundaries for the region extend far out into the countryside, the different concerns of both sides are all too obvious. If they are tightly drawn around largely built-up areas, which became the case for

Metropolitan Toronto, then genuine regional planning is impossible.

No structural arrangement is likely to mitigate the inherently different interests of city, suburb, and countryside; hence, democratic regional planning is likely to be exceptionally difficult regardless of structural arrangements. There are obvious problems with the traditional municipal system in Canada in which city and countryside are kept separate. But this system at least has some inherent flexibility in that both sides recognize the inevitability from time to time of annexations of rural land to the city for purposes of new urban development.

The 1990s brought a dramatic resurgence of interest in municipal reorganization, especially in eastern Canada. In Cape Breton and Halifax in Nova Scotia, in Miramichi in New Brunswick, and in Ottawa, Hamilton, Sudbury, London, Kingston, and Chatham–Kent in Ontario, single-tier municipal governments have been created that include vast expanses of undeveloped rural land (Sancton, 2000). Western Canada was not much affected by all this amalgamation activity. For example, the 2001 Canadian census tells us that the population of the City of Vancouver is only 546,000 while the total population of the 21 constituent municipalities of the GVRD is 1,987,000.

During the 1990s, the established two-tier systems of municipal government were under attack in both Montreal and Toronto, and for similar reasons. Both were seen—especially by elected politicians in the constituent municipalities—as unduly complex and rigid. More importantly, the upper-tier authorities covering the central cities, the Montreal Urban Community and the Municipality of Metropolitan Toronto, only included 56.8 per cent and 53.7 per cent of their respective 1991 census metropolitan areas (Sancton, 1994: 76). With such limited territorial scope they could hardly be expected to perform some of their main original objectives, notably strategic land-use planning and economic development for the entire metropolitan area.

In April 1995, the NDP government in Ontario appointed a three-person task force chaired by Anne Golden to make recommendations about municipal government in the Greater Toronto Area. The task force reported to the Conservative government headed by Mike Harris and recommended the establishment of a Greater Toronto Council having a much larger territory than Metro, but fewer functional responsibilities (Ontario, 1996). The Harris government was reluctant to establish a Greater Toronto Council that would clearly link the outer suburbs of the GTA, the source of much of its political support, to the problems of the central city. Since Premier Harris had promised during the election campaign that 'one way or another the metropolitan level of government in Toronto had to go' (Ibbitson, 1997: 244), he felt obliged to do something. The decision in late 1996 to merge the constituent units of the Municipality of Metropolitan Toronto into one new City of Toronto was highly controversial. Because the government announced its decision only a few weeks before proclaiming its new regime for allocating provincial and municipal responsibilities (the 'megaweek' announcements in January 1997), many have concluded that amalgamation was a financial necessity flowing from downloading. In fact, the notion that the amalgamation would save money was more a justification after the fact for a decision that had already been made on other grounds. In any event, the amalgamation did not save money. In April of 2003, the Toronto City Summit Alliance, 'a coalition of over 40 civic leaders from the private, voluntary and public sectors in the Toronto region' (Toronto City Summit Alliance, 2003), argued that Toronto needed 'a new fiscal deal' in part because:

> The amalgamation of the City of Toronto has not produced the overall cost savings that were projected. Although there have been savings from staff reductions, the harmonization of wage and service levels has resulted in higher costs for the new City. We will continue to feel these higher costs in the future. (Toronto City Summit Alliance, 2003: 4)

In 2000, the Quebec government decided to follow Ontario's lead by introducing legislation to force all the municipalities within each of the two-tier metropolitan governments of Montreal, Quebec, and Hull to merge with each other. There were also provisions for mergers in other urbanized parts of the province, including Chicoutimi–Jonquière and Sherbrooke. Hostility to the mergers was so intense that the opposition leader, Jean Charest, promised to create a mechanism to undo them if he were elected premier. When he was elected in 2003, he surprised many by going at least part way to implement his promise. His government introduced legislation stating that a referendum on demerger would be held if 10 per cent of the eligible voters in a merged municipality signed an official petition. For a demerger to be implemented, it had to receive the support of more than half the people voting in the referendum and this group had to comprise at least 35 per cent of all eligible voters. In June 2004, 89 such referendums were conducted. In only 32 cases were the requisite numbers of votes obtained to bring about a demerger. Fifteen of these were within the territory of the newly amalgamated City of Montreal and two within Quebec City (Hamel, 2005: 154–6).

The result is that, for both Montreal and Quebec City, the current system of municipal government is almost indescribably complex, especially because there is to be an 'agglomeration council' established to link the demerged municipalities with the municipality that they have chosen to leave. In both Montreal and Quebec City, there is also a council for the 'metropolitan community' that covers approximately the same territory as the census metropolitan area. Within the City of Montreal, there are also borough councils with decision-making authority for local issues, including zoning. Montreal residents effectively have four tiers of local government: borough, city, agglomeration, and metropolitan community. The outcome of the amalgamation process in Montreal was dramatically different from what it was in Toronto.

Conclusion: A New Deal for Cities?

Over the past 10 years much attention has been focused on the governance and financing of

Canada's urban municipalities. This has been caused by a growing concern that perhaps our cities are losing ground in the increasingly competitive global marketplace. After decades of being smug about how Canadian cities are much better off than American ones, there is now ample evidence that American cities are recovering, and perhaps even surpassing their Canadian counterparts in promoting creativity, innovation, and economic growth. Concern about the state of our urban municipalities has manifested itself at each of our three levels of government.

At the federal level, Paul Martin had promoted his 'cities agenda' before he became Prime Minister, while he has been Prime Minister, and, most dramatically, in May 2005, as part of his bid to save his faltering minority government. One of the most important reasons Belinda Stronach gave for her decision to cross the floor of the House of Commons and join Martin's beleaguered government was that she wanted to save the provisions in the 2005 budget that provided new urban infrastructure funds for her constituency in Newmarket–Aurora, an area of rapid suburban growth north of Toronto. More funds for cities were also part of the deal that Martin made with the New Democrats in order to gain their support for his 2005 budget. In addition to its increased funding of urban infrastructure, the Martin government has also relieved municipalities of their obligation to pay the Goods and Services Tax and initiated negotiations with the provinces to funnel a share of the federal gasoline tax to their respective municipalities. In this regard, it is important to note that, although the Prime Minister is clearly committed to providing new federal support for cities, he is only doing so to the extent that the provinces approve. Whatever we might think of the federal 'cities agenda', no one can claim that it violates the basic tenets of Canadian federalism.

If urban municipalities in Canada are to get more than increased grants, it will be as the result of provincial action, not federal. Here the signs about future directions are conflicting. On the one hand, provinces in eastern Canada have created populous, amalgamated urban municipalities that some say have the potential to rival the provinces themselves in political power. In Winnipeg such a municipality has existed since 1972 and in Calgary constant boundary changes have enabled the territory of the municipality to keep up with urban expansion. By any standards, Canada has the kind of large, territorially comprehensive municipalities that have the potential to be major forces in urban governance. But, as we have seen earlier, their functions are limited because they have little or no jurisdiction over public education or over most social services, functions that are the bedrock of municipal strength in many parts of the democratic world. Their taxing authority is limited almost exclusively to the property tax, unlike municipalities elsewhere with much more diverse revenue sources.

Some of Canada's largest municipalities—notably Winnipeg and Toronto—have launched major initiatives to obtain new authority and tax resources from their respective governments. In these cases, however, it does not look as though they are getting access to much sought-after income and sales taxes, although there is still significant room for various provincial controls to be removed without fundamentally altering the provincial–municipal relationship. But, as urban municipalities in Canada do gain increased revenues and legal authority, it is difficult to imagine the demise of the provinces in relation to urban issues. This is especially so in Ontario, where the current provincial government has recently launched a massive initiative to protect a designated greenbelt area around Toronto and to ensure that projected future growth takes place in a much more intensified manner than has previously been the case. Indeed, the provincial government of Ontario is essentially now acting as the regional planning authority for the wider Toronto area, an authority that the Golden task force called for more than a decade ago. The main difference is that the area covered by the province's new planning policies—labelled the Greater Golden Horseshoe and extending from Barrie to Niagara Falls and including Kitchener–Waterloo to the west—is much larger than the area of the Greater Toronto Council contemplated by the Golden task force.

Urban municipalities in Canada need new sources of revenue and more authority to deal with the increasingly complex problems of urban life. They are beginning to make minimal progress in getting what they need. But there is no evidence that their own power and importance are gaining at the expense of the provinces. Nor is there evidence that the new initiatives from the federal government are displacing the provinces with respect to the governance of Canadian cities. For the foreseeable future, Canadian cities will continue to be the subject of a complex web of multi-level governance in which provincial governments will be dominant.

Notes

1. The Constitution of Canada is defined (partially at least) in Section 52(2) of the Constitution Act, 1982.
2. As reported by the Canadian Tax Foundation in *Canadian Tax Highlights*, 1–11 (16 Nov. 1993), 83. The report uses 1992 data from the Organization for Economic Co-operation and Development (OECD), whose membership includes 24 countries with the world's most productive economies.

Chapter 18

Shaped by Planning: The Canadian City Through Time

Jill Grant

Cities are intentional artifacts created through innumerable individual and collective decisions about what to build, what to destroy, and what technologies to use. To understand the role of planning—that is, collective intent—in shaping Canadian cities, we must situate practice within the context of cultural values, processes, and choices. Planning has become embedded in Canadian society as one of the means by which we transpose cultural values onto our townscapes and landscapes: its strengths and weaknesses mirror those of the societies that employ it. This chapter briefly explores the history of planning in Canada, beginning with colonial settlement. It describes the context and process of planning and considers how the contemporary urban landscape reflects more than a century of policies, regulations, and practices.

Early Settlements

While archaeologists continue to search for evidence of the earliest human occupation of North America, consensus indicates that people had arrived in Canada by at least 12,000 years ago. Early sites were small and temporary, near good sources of food and water. Millennia later, when Europeans traversed the Atlantic to claim Canada as their possession, they found the land populated with a diverse array of settlements. In the agricultural heartland around the Great Lakes and along the fish-rich west coast, substantial communities housing hundreds of people greeted the newcomers.

Extending their political and military domain to the New World, Europeans soon began their own settlements in Canada. Arriving by sea, the newcomers made their settlements on protected harbours near abundant natural resources such as fishing grounds or close to routes for the fur trade. Some of the earliest communities developed in an essentially organic fashion, with no evident plan. These settlements, including Quebec City (see Figure 18.1), reflected the patterns of medieval towns and villages: paths and roads followed the lay of the land to serve necessary economic and social functions, while commercial areas developed near port facilities.

Figure 18.1

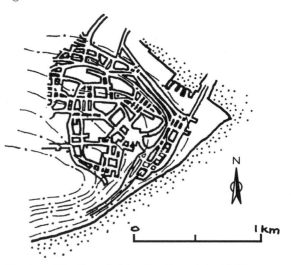

Quebec City, founded by the French in 1608, offers an example of an organic layout. Streets followed lines that connected sites of work, commerce, and housing, and reflected the rough topography of the site.

By the eighteenth century, England and France enhanced control of their North American colonies. Planting towns became a keystone of colonial policy: establish military control of the land through new settlements. True to the popular renaissance and baroque traditions of the time, the Europeans designed streets, squares, and markets in an elegant geometry: eastern cities such as Halifax, Charlottetown (see Figure 18.2), and the French fortress at Louisbourg reveal such influences. This approach to planning reflected the triumph of political authority over landscape; despite the grade of the hill or the presence of waterways, the formal pattern laid out by military engineers dominated. Legal systems provided for private property ownership, imposing an economic order that would continue to influence the shape and development of communities for centuries to come.

As settlers moved westward, settlements developed at key junctures along trade and travel routes. Industries that required power located along fast-flowing streams. Corporate decisions about building trading posts and government's choice of locations for military forts created nodes for urban development. As western settlement expanded, the surveyor applied the pragmatic rigour of the grid in laying out the landscape, whether on the flat

Figure 18.3

Vancouver, first settled in 1862, illustrates the rigidity of the survey grid (which changes orientation and grain from time to time). From the Ontario–Manitoba border westward, the surveyor set the template for the Canadian city.

Figure 18.2

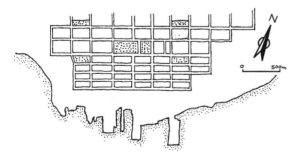

Charlottetown was laid out in a Renaissance design (similar to that of Philadelphia) by British soldiers in 1768. Like Halifax and Saint John, it shows the simple elegance of narrow blocks, central square, and survey baseline along the harbour.

meadows of the prairies or the rocky knolls of the Canadian Shield; cities such as Winnipeg, Edmonton, and Vancouver (see Figure 18.3) illustrate the standard patterns that resulted. By the end of the nineteenth century, the grid covered most of the West, with land divided for sale to new immigrants. New railway lines carried immigrants westward to fill the land, bringing growth to towns chosen as stations along the route. Early in Canadian urban history, the rationality of the market and of the engineer had a dramatic effect on the shape of settlements in Canada; later comprehensive community planning and land-use regulation would provide additional mechanisms to reinforce the impacts of economic imperatives and technical specifications (Gunton, 1991; Hodge, 2003; Kemble, 1989; Wolfe, 1994).

When people generate communities through the course of their everyday lives, form generally follows function. In other words, the layout of the organic settlement reflects the traffic patterns people create in going to work, market, or worship on foot or with their animals. Such patterns are found in early Canadian indigenous settlements and fishing villages and in the areas outside the planted cores of eastern colonial cities. The obverse is also clear in Canadian planning history: authorities plan settlements according to abstract principles where form controls function. The military and civic authorities of the early colonial period imposed rigorous and rational grids on the land in patterns that reflected centralized control. By the end of the nineteenth century, innovations in transportation and other technologies contributed to the perceived need for controlled urban forms. The twentieth century would see governments turn increasingly to formal town planning.

Town Planning

The modern town planning movement in Canada gained its impetus from the urban problems of the late nineteenth and early twentieth centuries. National immigration policies brought a million newcomers to Canada, increasing pressure on local governments to respond to the stresses created in cities ill-equipped to accommodate the inflow. The urban population of Canada increased from 1.1 million (25 per cent of the total) to 4.3 million (50 per cent of the total) between 1881 and 1921 (Rutherford, 1984). Housing conditions proved abysmal, with intense crowding, poor sanitation, and considerable risk of fire. Poor immigrants flocked to the cities, creating an urban working class of meagre means and diverse backgrounds.

A survey of working-class conditions in Montreal in 1897 illustrated the prospects faced by many: high mortality rates, long work hours, no access to education, subsistence wages (Copp, 1974). Epidemic diseases presented a risk, not only to the poor but to other urban residents. Investigative journalists exposed poor urban conditions, convincing many Canadians that remedial action was necessary.

Industrial districts grew in suburban areas with good access to rail networks and newly available electricity (Lewis, 2002; Rae, 2003); workers followed the factories. Railways often cut off port cities from their waterfronts, redirected development patterns, and sometimes created neighbourhoods 'on the bad side of the tracks'. Cities in eastern Canada declined as the railways carried capital and immigrants west.

Street railroads encouraged suburban and strip development radiating out from the core. As early as the 1860s, streetcars offered affluent urbanites fast access to suburban villas (Sanford, 1987). By the end of the century, even the working classes took advantage of extended streetcar lines to buy cheap land outside cities like Toronto; there they built small homes in fringe developments that typically lacked water and sewer services (Harris, 1996).

Other than building roads, local governments provided few services until late in the nineteenth century. However, interest in the newly popular germ theory of disease increased recognition that inadequate sewer services, poor water supply, and uncollected garbage contributed to epidemics. Consequently, after the 1870s many municipalities began programs to ensure clean water and to remove waste from streets and yards. Cities invested in massive infrastructure projects for sewers, piped water systems, and garbage collection, often providing excess capacity in anticipation of future population and economic growth (Rutherford, 1984; Sanford, 1987). Municipalities began broadening their mandates to encompass a wider range of responsibilities, thus setting the context in which planning would become an integral part of their activities.

As wealth concentrated in large corporations, cities became nodes of power and prosperity, with pockets of extreme poverty. Centralization of industry and wealth in the largest cities led to growth in some settlements at the expense of others. The Maritime economy, once the backbone of the Canadian colonies, collapsed by the late nineteenth century as industries rode the rails westward. Montreal and Toronto became the economic hubs of the nation, centres of manufacturing and commerce. Cities across Canada sought strategies either to enhance their economic prospects or to maintain their influence. The urban reform movement reacted against the corruption and inefficiency of city governments; in response, many municipalities changed their administrative systems, bringing in a city manager structure and implementing a career public service model (Rutherford, 1984). With new structures in place and experts on hand to advise council members on appropriate interventions, cities had the tools to build on their strengths to tackle the most pressing problems.

Popular interest in urban reform, scientific management (as used by Henry Ford in developing the production line in America), and garden cities (as constructed by Ebenezer Howard and his colleagues in Britain) generated support for the idea of town planning: a rational way of dealing with urban problems. Facing the end of the open frontier, national leaders became anxious to conserve resources for future prosperity. Confronting competition from other cities (and countries) to attract investment and residents, local government leaders sought to promote their communities as the best places to live and work (Ward, 1998). With the advent of the private automobile, governments faced new demands for road development and improvement and concerns about keeping residential streets safe. At both the national and local levels, by the 1910s government leaders came to see town planning as a tool they could use to achieve their economic, political, and social aims.

Planning schemes for Canadian cities began to appear in the first decade of the twentieth century. For instance, the Ontario Association of Architects and the Toronto Guild of Civic Art commissioned a plan for Toronto in 1906, and John Lyle prepared another in 1911 for the central city (Sewell, 1993). Plans were drawn for other cities, including Calgary and Regina, but not implemented (Gunton, 1981). Beautification leagues appeared across the country, even in small communities. (Readers of the L.M. Montgomery novels about Anne of Green Gables may recall that even tiny Avonlea, PEI, had a village beautification society.) In larger cities, civic art groups prepared schemes for elaborate urban beautification projects inspired by the American city beautiful movement (Van Nus, 1984b).

As early as 1912, several provinces adopted legislation to allow towns to prepare planning schemes. Responding to the interest in town planning, the Commission of Conservation (established in 1909) invited Thomas Adams, veteran of British garden city planning, to visit Canada in 1913. The same year, following a decade of boosterism and wild speculation, western land markets collapsed, saddling cities with acres of serviced but valueless suburban land. The national government became convinced that Canada needed town planning: in 1914 the government appointed Adams to lead a planning division in the Commission of Conservation. For the next several years Adams toured the country writing planning legislation, promoting town planning, and developing model suburbs (Armstrong, 1959; Simpson, 1985; Stein, 1994a, 1994b).

Adams came to town planning through his activities with the Garden City Association in Britain. Inspired by Ebenezer Howard's (1985 [1898]) vision of a self-sufficient community that offered the best of town and country, the garden city movement grew rapidly at the turn of the twentieth century. A former farmer, councillor, and journalist trained in surveying, Adams saw in the garden city an answer to inner-city congestion and regional sprawl (Adams, 1974 [1934]). As manager of the first British garden city project at Letchworth, Adams helped translate the vision into reality. His pragmatic approach contributed to the success of the project, but sacrificed some of Howard's idealistic tenets (like public ownership of land) to secure project financing (Simpson, 1985).

While war raged in Europe, Adams visited almost every province (most several times). He developed a model town planning act and assisted several provinces in their attempt to adopt it into law. He designed plans for new and renewed communities, including Temiscaming (1917, northern Quebec), Lindenlea (a proposed suburb in Ottawa), and the Richmond district in Halifax (1918). Adams's plans reveal his interest in diagonal streets (efficient routes to connect destinations) and boule-vards (which provide more open space). While some critics dismiss his designs as uninspired (Perks and Jamieson, 1991), Adams's clean lines show his commitment to efficiency, economy, and functionality.

Adams's plan for the Richmond district in Halifax created a unique urban experiment. In 1917, an ammunition ship exploded in the narrows of Halifax harbour, killing 2,000 and razing 325 acres. The Halifax Relief Commission brought in Adams and other planning experts in March 1918. Adams and his team, including Horace Seymour, prepared a planning scheme that featured residential boulevards and diagonal streets to direct traffic through the area (see Figure 18.4). Architects designed row housing in an old English effect (similar to styles favoured in the early British garden cities). Although the Relief Commission had hoped to provide low-cost housing for displaced families, construction delays and mate-rial costs put the rents for new housing above the means of most (Weaver, 1976).

As town planning activity proliferated under Adams, surveyors, architects, and engineers were increasingly drawn to the practice. In an effort to professionalize their activities, in 1919 a small group gathered in Ottawa to establish the Town Planning Institute of Canada (Sherwood, 1994), with Adams as president. The Institute grew rapidly, publishing a journal and organizing conferences to share knowledge and develop professional standards.

Changes in government and shifting national priorities undermined the commitment to town planning in the 1920s, although not before zoning had gained a foothold as a tool for protecting property values. In the wake of the Russian Revolution, and in view of the faith of socialists in long-term planning, the Canadian government reassessed its agenda. Even Adams's assurance that planning supported the

Figure 18.4

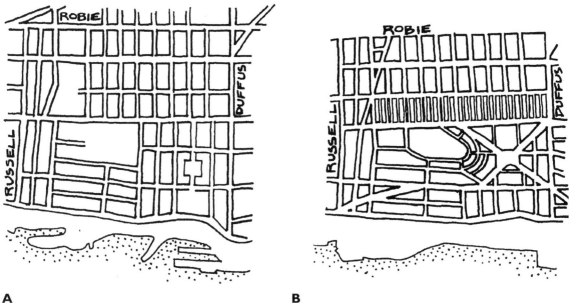

A   **B**

Thomas Adams's 1918 plan for the Richmond district of Halifax brought together elements of the British garden city and the American City Beautiful, while exemplifying Adams's unique commitment to pragmatic functionality. (Plate A shows the district before the explosion; Plate B is Adams's design.)

market failed to persuade a government increasingly fearful of socialism. The Commission of Conservation was disbanded in 1921; Adams headed to New York in 1923 (Armstrong, 1959; Simpson, 1985).

The most significant planning tool initiated by planners in the 1920s did catch on, only to further undermine town planning efforts for the next three decades. The first zoning bylaw in Canada was prepared for Kitchener in 1924 by Horace Seymour (Bloomfield, 1985). By the 1920s, zoning dominated American cities as a way of controlling land use (and land values) and increasing the predictability of development. During the mid-1920s through to the early 1950s, zoning effectively replaced local planning in Canada. Instead of developing overall town planning schemes for cities, local politicians adopted zoning bylaws that confirmed the status quo while providing mechanisms to enable land-use changes under specific conditions. As Moore (1979) argues, zoning worked well with patronage and populist politics and thus proved attractive to business interests, ratepayers, and councillors. By contrast, attempts to adopt plans in cities like Toronto were ignored or defeated during the 1920s. Planning vision yielded to property interests.

Economic growth in the late 1920s led to a brief resurgence of interest in planning. Vancouver hired the American planner, Harland Bartholemew, to craft a plan influenced by city beautiful principles (Todhunter, 1983). With the economy in collapse after 1929, however, town planning generally fell into abeyance. Through the Depression the government reaffirmed its faith that the market could create wealth and thereby shape good cities.

The Great Depression of the 1930s led to government interest in planning in the United States, but not in Canada. The federal government consistently refused to finance planning schemes or to take initiatives that might challenge the market. In 1935, the League for Social Reconstruction, a group of prominent Canadians, published *Social Planning for Canada*, the framework for a welfare state (League for Social Reconstruction, 1935). While that document did not immediately influence government, the ideas it incorporated began to percolate into public discussion as Keynesian economics grew in popularity. Beginning in 1935 the government took small steps towards addressing housing need by adopting the Dominion Housing Act, followed by the National Housing Act in 1938; finally, as war loomed in Europe, the federal government began to accept a limited role in remedying urban problems.

Post-War Reconstruction

With World War II underway, the federal government reasserted its leadership role in managing resources. In this context, it began planning at national and local scales. It established the Wartime Housing Corporation to address the pressing needs of military and munitions workers. Various committees and agencies planned for post-war reconstruction and reintegration of returning soldiers into the economy and society. The federal government laid the groundwork, first in housing and then in other spheres of activity such as road and infrastructure building, for urban planning following the war (Hulchanski, 1986; Sewell, 1994; Wolfe, 1994).

The post-war period saw a rapid expansion in community planning activities. The national mood of post-war optimism for a better future, faith in science, and trust in government service created an atmosphere in which city planning seemed logical, appropriate, and necessary. The 1950s and 1960s witnessed the rise of rational comprehensive planning (an expert-based planning process making large use of scientific methods) in Canada and the revival of the planners' professional organization, renamed the Canadian Institute of Planners. Many communities prepared master plans, long-range documents to govern future growth. Governments at all levels hired experts to study problems and offer rational solutions in a climate of popular support for public-sector interventionism. While some of the work in this period set the stage for the modernization of Canadian cities, some of the decisions taken appear, in hindsight, deeply flawed.

Mortgage insurance policies established through the Central Mortgage and Housing

Corporation (CMHC, later renamed Canada Mortgage and Housing Corporation) indirectly encouraged cities to prepare plans and to adopt approved site planning standards and zoning practices: homes built according to CMHC guidelines received speedy mortgage approvals. CMHC guidelines set the parameters for minimum site planning standards nationwide. During the 1960s, many cities established planning departments and hired staff planners (often trained in the new university planning programs funded with federal and provincial assistance). City planning became institutionalized within the local civil service (Carver, 1962, 1975; Hodge, 2003).

Meanwhile, developers actively explored housing markets created through the purchasing power of a growing middle class. Outside Toronto, Macklin Hancock built Don Mills, a suburb of ranch-style houses, looping streets, neighbourhood units, and open spaces with pathways. Drawing on the popular garden city precepts of the 1950s, Don Mills presaged a new era in suburban design in Canada (Figure 18.5). Developers nationwide copied elements of the award-winning and economically lucrative project. Within a generation, the features of Don Mills became the hallmark of Canadian suburbia, a landscape dominated by the values of privacy, family, amenity, growth, and progress (Hancock, 1994; Sewell, 1977, 1993).

Don Mills represented the epitome of modernist garden city principles: separated uses; low-density development; a hierarchy of streets; shopping concentrated in retail malls and strips; loops, crescents, and culs-de-sac; buffers of green space or high-density residential housing to protect single detached housing; extensive open space systems. The neighbourhood unit, developed by Clarence Perry (1929), formed the basis of spatial and community organization. Although no other community experienced quite the same level of success and fame as Don Mills, communities across Canada entrenched the principles into their plans and land-use regulations. Developers endlessly cloned the suburban form, boiled down to its essentials (wide lots, winding streets, and shopping strips). Several new resource-based towns, such as Kitimat,

Figure 18.5

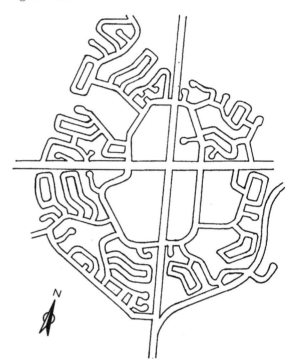

Don Mills in Toronto became the paradigmatic Canadian suburb. From the late 1950s onward, developers across the nation copied its winding streets.

BC, and Thompson, Manitoba, employed garden city principles to create a new urban standard.

The success and replication of the suburban model through the 1960s and 1970s reflects a confluence of factors. The federal government promoted suburban design elements and regulations through its site planning guidelines and mortgage insurance programs; with programs to support the development industry, the federal government encouraged the mass production of housing by companies committed to economies of scale in servicing land and building homes. Local governments eager to facilitate development adopted CMHC standards in their local land-use and subdivision regulations. Planners trained in the new planning schools and reading the latest planning journals and books believed in the principles of the garden city and neighbourhood unit, and tried to promote them in their work. Builders recognized the profit potential and popularity of the new suburban model, and thus sought to meet demand. Householders influenced by the visual imagery and rhetoric of the new medium of television saw in suburbia a reflection of their own middle-class aspirations. Rising affluence and widespread car ownership facilitated suburban living (see Chapter 12 on suburbs).

The modernist project, as shown in the development of post-war suburbia, had a 'flip side' in the approach taken to dealing with the central city. Journalists and activists had complained about abysmal conditions in the slums of the larger cities since the late nineteenth century, but governments rarely responded. With the optimism of reformers and the resources of the expanding welfare state in the post-war period, governments finally addressed urban blight. In the 1950s and 1960s, the federal government provided loans and grants to encourage cities to clear slums. Commissioned studies identified the worst areas, and plans were developed to renew cities. Faith in progress and science, and growing nationalism, enhanced confidence that Canadians could improve their cities and the lot of their inhabitants. Planning provided an essential tool in the arsenal for the war on the slums.

The first slum clearance project began in Toronto in 1948, at Regent Park North. During the 1947 Toronto election, residents approved the project by a three-to-two margin in a plebiscite; taxpayers generally supported such improvements, as did major newspapers' editorials. The project resulted in more housing units than had been on the site, but a reduced diversity of use. In this and dozens of neighbourhoods across the country, land was expropriated, dilapidated buildings demolished, and new multi-family housing constructed. Plans for the renewed sites reflected popular planning principles of the time: large amounts of open space (predominantly grass or pavement), high-rise apartment towers and townhouse clusters, separation of pedestrian and vehicular traffic, no through streets. The 'towers in the park' of Le Corbusier, the

great French architect and modernist planner, featured strongly in the site plans. Public subsidies kept the cost of new housing affordable, creating the first substantial amounts of public housing in the nation (Sewell, 1993).

The federal government provided funds for redevelopment studies through the 1950s, seeing slum clearance as part of a strategy of national development of urban infrastructure. Many of the redevelopment studies were elaborate and scientific, in the fashion of the day. Gordon Stephenson, professor of planning at the University of Toronto, completed several. His Halifax report (1957), for example, examined and mapped substandard housing, fire calls, instances of tuberculosis, children in foster care, cases of juvenile delinquency, and other 'indicators' of urban blight. He overlaid maps of these indicators and through rational analysis identified areas of the city that, he argued, warranted redevelopment. Halifax designated a 'central redevelopment area', secured funds from the federal government to expropriate land and demolish structures, and laid waste to large tracts of the city core. Unfortunately for Halifax (and several other cities that destroyed old neighbourhoods based on such analyses), the land sat vacant for the better part of a decade awaiting a developer (Collier, 1974).

Through to the early 1960s, support for urban renewal projects remained strong in Canadian communities. Newspaper reports from the time show little evidence of protest even by those forced to relocate. However, as municipalities expanded the renewal net to ever more neighbourhoods and people realized that these projects rapidly generated new communities of poverty, resistance began to develop. By the mid- to late 1960s, homeowners and tenants began to fight to try to save older neighbourhoods. Governments had already invested millions in redevelopment projects that seemed slow to produce much of a return. Public housing providers had planned or constructed nearly 20,000 units between 1960 and 1966, but the backlash from private-sector builders was significant. 'Slum clearance' and 'urban renewal', which at first seemed such hopeful concepts, had become dirty words by 1970. Planners often found themselves carrying the blame for urban projects they had facilitated in their roles as municipal civil servants.

As suburban growth blanketed the nation, many cities planned new urban expressways during the 1960s. Increasing automobile ownership and resulting traffic jams convinced highway engineers of the need for better routes across town and from suburb to downtown. Federal and provincial governments invested massively in highways. Planners worked with the engineers in identifying optimal routes and in trying to persuade city residents of the viability of the plans. By the late 1960s many neighbourhoods resisted the relocation and segmentation associated with expressway construction. Planning projects became the focus of civic action and protest; in communities like Toronto and Winnipeg, reform-minded councillors were elected on platforms opposing planning projects (Higgins, 1986). With the defeat of the Spadina Expressway project in Toronto, Canadian communities had a model that proved that citizen action could stop unwanted developments and thus affect the future shape of the city (Sewell, 1993).

Democratizing Planning

While originally the preserve of civil servants and developers' experts, the planning process opened in the early 1970s to provide room for public involvement. Governments responded to the new social context in which citizens were taking to the streets to insist on the right to participate in decision-making. Planning issues became public battles as residents fought to protect neighbourhoods threatened by urban renewal, development projects, and highway alignments. Inspired by media images of the American civil rights movement and protests over the Vietnam War, citizens marched for a variety of causes in the late 1960s. Planning projects soon faced considerable opposition. Author Jane Jacobs (1961) gave focus to the criticisms of modern planning, decrying the open spaces, high-rise towers, and formless street patterns that planners promoted. Rising commitment to civic action and interest in planning issues were felt strongly in most of the developed nations at this time (Grant, 1994b).

The extent of urban public action overwhelmed politicians and led to revisions to planning acts and local planning practices to provide for public participation in the planning process (Grant, 1988). Citizens received new rights to participate in plan development and administration, and to appeal decisions. Many cities established neighbourhood planning offices to bring planning to the people. CMHC funded the Neighbourhood Improvement Program (NIP) to allow municipalities to assist run-down neighbourhoods to plan their own infrastructure improvements. People across the country began to learn about planning and worked in partnership with politicians and planners to formulate plans for their communities (see Figure 18.6).

The late 1960s also witnessed resurgent interest in cities and a commitment to regional development. The federal government established the Ministry of State for Urban Affairs (MSUA) with a mandate to conduct research and promote vibrant cities. Other federal agencies encouraged regional planning for economic development through programs to help disadvantaged regions establish industrial infrastructure and economies of scale in various sectors (such as agriculture and fisheries).

Figure 18.6

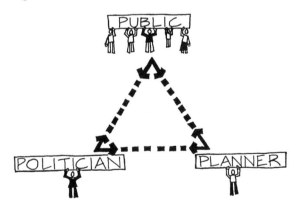

Harry Lash's (1977) 'triangle of participation' illustrates the partnership between planners, politicians, and the public in planning. Lash's study was among many published by the Ministry of State for Urban Affairs to encourage new approaches to promoting urban vitality.

Several provinces initiated regional planning for urban regions. While some planning strategies were changing, the basic national goals of growth and rational development remained paramount in efforts at all scales, from national to local (Gertler and Crowley, 1977; Lang, 1972).

Planning Under Attack

By the late 1970s, many of the initiatives of the participation era had come under attack. Citizen involvement had fallen off dramatically, yet developers argued that vocal members of the public had too many opportunities to delay viable projects. Costly regional development initiatives had not yielded expected returns; regional disparity grew apace. Extensive government investments in urban and regional development during the 1960s and early 1970s contributed to heavy debt burdens and growing tax levels. The federal government dissolved the MSUA in 1979, ended the NIP, and reduced its regional development expenditure. In the shifting political climate of the late 1970s and early 1980s, Keynesian economics came under attack. Conservative opinions grew in influence, thus undermining support for participatory and interventionist planning.

The 1980s and 1990s brought economic reassessment: recession, debt crisis, and 'downloading'. Planning faced attacks by those who argued that government regulation dampens a rational and free market. Some jurisdictions (e.g., Prince Edward Island and Alberta) reduced provincial and regional planning functions. 'Strategic planning', modelled on business approaches, replaced comprehensive planning. Municipalities were amalgamated to create new mega-cities in several provinces (including Nova Scotia, New Brunswick, Quebec, and Ontario). The context of planning changed dramatically as the values of rationality, individualism, and entrepreneurship became increasingly powerful and as governments yielded authority to market forces.

Although planning found itself under attack from many sides in the 1990s, its early principles proved so well entrenched within Canadian culture (and congruent with mainstream values) that they continued to dominate built form. Development interests suggested that planning regulations and processes slowed needed growth (despite clear evidence that growth has long been a planning goal). Governments looking to reduce operating expenses cut planning positions, restructured operations, and streamlined procedures. Critics accused planning of destroying cities, of promoting exclusionary values, and of constructing urban spaces with no sense of place or character (Duany and Plater-Zyberk, 1992; Kunstler, 1993). The very term 'planning', suggestive of government control, has often been replaced in municipal administrations by labels meant to evoke a pro-development attitude. For example, in Toronto planning functions are now lodged in the department of Urban Development Services. 'Modernist' planning was blamed for many of the problems of the city, from traffic jams to abandoned inner cores. Yet, despite the criticisms of postmodernists, ordinary Canadians continued building and buying suburban forms that replicated many planning principles of the garden city. At the end of the twentieth century, fiscal realities and cultural values continued to exert powerful centrifugal forces on urban development: suburbia spread while downtowns faced serious problems. Planning has become a well-established function of government, although its profile waxes and wanes in response to the volume of criticisms levelled against it. It seems clear, though, that most Canadians accept that government should play some role in setting the rules and regulations for urban development.

The history of urban planning in Canada reveals the nexus between planning and growth in public consciousness. In times of growth, Canadians turn to planning as a means to control and channel change in ways that benefit the community. In times of economic decline, Canadians blame planning for creating urban problems and preventing development. Our society has a love/hate relationship with planning and zoning. On the one hand, we want the security and predictability control offers for neighbourhoods; on the other hand, we resent the way in which applying rules can produce outcomes

The Newfoundland Resettlement Program: An Experiment in Urbanization and Regional Planning

Although Newfoundland is one of the smaller provinces, it hosted a bold experiment in regional planning and urbanization during the late 1960s and early 1970s. Eager to turn around a legacy of poverty and unequal opportunity, the provincial and federal governments planned a major project to resettle the residents of remote fishing outports into 'growth centres'. Communities designated for growth would be provided with education, health care, and other government services unavailable in smaller settlements.

The resettlement project provided government with an opportunity to test theories of regional planning and economic development being promoted internationally at the time. Third World countries eager to share the wealth enjoyed by developed nations were encouraged to stimulate urban industrial centres. Foreign aid supported investment in infrastructure, such as dams, ports, roads, and power projects, that would integrate Third World economies into the global system. In planning the resettlement program, Canadian governments applied principles advocated by international experts, bankers, and diplomats.

While many of the objectives of the resettlement scheme were well intentioned, the impacts on outport communities and their residents proved tragic. Growth centre communities often failed to receive the promised upgrades on services and facilities. People mourned the identity and heritage they left behind. Moreover, the project did not improve the circumstances of many of the relocated residents. Trends that undermined local self-reliance and the resources upon which it depended continued unabated. Within a few years critics saw the project as a dismal failure (Matthews, 1976).

and landscapes that some find offensive. We have come to rely on planning to regulate a complex set of economic and physical processes with partial knowledge and limited tools. The outcomes often disappoint us.

Planning has become institutionalized as a cultural apparatus for shaping change in the built environment, for imposing cultural values and preferences on the landscape. In times of changing values, planning stands condemned for its adherence to mores that are becoming outdated. Some in society are poised to 'throw the baby out with the bath water' and give up on planning: they would let the market govern land use. Others argue for new planning approaches and values that respond to contemporary problems: they prefer to transform planning and those it serves. Few proclaim that planning is working quite effectively, although some hold that view. The debates between these differing positions occur not only within the profession but increasingly within the public arena. Regardless of the position we take in this argument, we must

acknowledge that in participating in the shaping of the built environment, the planning process generates particular types of outcomes. In the next section we discuss the planning process and the type of cities that planning contributes to produce.

Changing Processes

Through a century of planning in Canada, the planning process has become more bureaucratic, legalistic, expensive, and esoteric. Planning is now deeply embedded in the philosophy and the mechanics of government. Planning and its regulations provide the ground rules that enforce dominant values on the landscape; they have shaped the typical urban and suburban forms we find in Canadian cities in the early twenty-first century. Because of its utility as a tool in the management of the land market, planning has been widely accepted (although extensively criticized). As it became more deeply entrenched in Canadian society and economy, planning lost much of its original vision and settled on a more constrained range of values than when originally promoted (see Table 18.1).

Planning operates within many contexts: legal, political, economic, social, organizational, and technical. Each of these domains exerts pressure and influence on those participating in the planning process. The legal context involves laws and regulations at national, provincial, and local levels. National legislation on issues such as environmental protection, environmental impact assessment, and fisheries and oceans can limit local planning options or require compliance with particular procedures. Federal standards, such as the building code or CMHC requirements for mortgage insurance, also influence local planning outcomes. Provincial laws set out the framework for local planning practices through enabling statutes and provincial land-use policies (on themes such as agricultural land and mine-land protection). Provincial legislation also regulates such matters as public participation rights, appeal processes, engineering standards, and environmental protection requirements. Municipal decisions result in plans, land-use bylaws, subdivision regulations, site planning standards, design guidelines, and minimum standards (upkeep requirements). As creatures of the provinces, however, municipalities may find their bylaws subject to review by provincial authorities (see Chapter 17).

The political context within which planning operates is highly contentious. Local politicians search for issues that will garner popular support. To be elected they need both the support of voters and the financial assistance of those with resources. Planning issues often feature into campaigns: growth and development have proven a populist strategy through the years, although heritage conservation also becomes a convincing option in some communities. The economics of campaign financing often forges alliances between politicians and development interests. Land development companies seek to create an environment sympathetic to their applications and hence may contribute to local political campaigns. In the absence in certain provinces of laws requiring candidates to disclose financial contributions in local elections, suspicion of undue influence from 'special' interests runs rife.

As the early advocates of planning realized, the economic context plays a key role. In a society that values private property, and where home ownership is the major investment for most households, regulating the land market is essential. Planning and zoning have provided tools to achieve this goal. As a prime component in the national economy the development industry has considerable influence over the process and the principles guiding planning practice. With the recent decline in the welfare state and a diminishing role for government intervention, planning finds itself even more affected by market factors.

The social context brings dominant cultural values and expectations to planning. Values related to privacy, family, domesticity, democracy, consumerism, and convenience shape the perceptions of the players in the planning process, and thus influence the outcomes of planning decisions. Planning and zoning produce landscapes and townscapes that reflect those societal values.

The organizational context of local government also affects planning processes and outcomes. Municipal bureaucracies develop their own cultures and logics that favour particular approaches to planning. Mechanisms for advancement within the organization may encourage some actions more than others. Where councils are most responsive to citizen involvement, planners prove eager to promote active participation; for instance, planners and politicians in Vancouver found themselves accused of 'planning by polling' (Howard, 1995; Seelig, 1995). Some organizations seem disposed to innovation and experimentation while others discourage deviation from the status quo.

Finally, the technical context also influences planning process and outcomes. As new tools and approaches appear, they offer planners alternative techniques for dealing with problems and issues. With science and rationalism continuing to dominate notions of professional competence, however, radical changes in approaches seem unlikely.

Table 18.1   Professional Values in the History of Planning in Canada

Key Values Associated with Planning	Early Town Planning Movement (1890s to 1920s)	Depression Era (mid-1920s to late 1930s)	Wartime and Recovery (1940 to 1965)	Reflection and Citizen Action (1965 to 1979)	Postmodernism and Neo-conservatism (1980 to 2000)
Efficiency	Planning legislation first promoted planning schemes to improve conditions; later zoning became the favoured practice.	Zoning spread across the country as an efficient (and politically acceptable) strategy for controlling land.	Comprehensive planning gains popularity. Plans and regulations adopted. Economies of scale implemented.	Regional planning projects initiated to encourage growth. Neighbourhood planning to accommodate protest.	Fiscal crisis led to fewer resources for planning. Planning seen as 'inefficient' and impeding market flexibility.
Health	Sanitary reform led to the adoption of codes and practices to improve health.	Few improvements made. (Some declines due to poverty.)	Established building codes and land standards. War against urban blight.	Expansion of welfare state benefits. Concerns about pollution but limited action.	Healthy communities project promoted. Interest in 'sustainable development'.
Amenity	Parks advocates promoted parkland development. The city beautiful movement inspired art and architecture. The neighbourhood unit promised a good family environment.	Little interest from government. Consultant planners were unable to sell their services.	Established standards for open spaces, parks, playgrounds. Land standards ensured open environment, wide streets. Highways and roads to accommodate traffic.	Established environmental assessment procedures. Expanded parks. Neighbourhood improvement program for infrastructure.	Interest in downtown revitalization and nostalgia for tradition led to strength of New Urbanism movement. Heavy focus on amenity and aesthetics.
Equity	Housing advocates unable to convince government to	Few resources committed by government. Fear	Social housing projects implement small homes and	Created opportunities for greater citizen	Promoting mixed-use and mixed housing type

	provide low-cost housing. Planning separated from housing interests.	of socialism.	'towers in the park' in limited numbers. Mass-produced housing for the middle class.	involvement. Reaction to urban renewal; neighbourhood protection.	developments to provide diverse housing. Affordability remains a problem.
Dominant pattern	The garden city movement effectively brought these values together in a comprehensive theory (but partial practice).	Planning virtually disappeared as a government activity.	The 'modernist project' sought to use planning tools to reshape the urban environment to meet the goal of progress.	While modernist trends continued, there was greater reflection on the nature of planning and how citizens should participate in it.	Planning finds its major approaches and codes under attack as urban design and free market come to the fore.
Planning models	Common planning models in this period included garden city, city beautiful, and public health.	While some advocated regional planning, cities focused their attention on putting zoning in place.	After the war rational planning led to master plans. Modernism contributed to interest in urban renewal.	Protests led to participatory and neighbourhood planning. Regional development initiatives sought to spread the wealth.	Strategic planning and sustainable development heralded new approaches. New Urbanism and smart growth arrived.
Notable developments	New resource towns like Temiskaming and rail towns like Dauphin appeared. Adams redesigned the Richmond district of Halifax.	Planning took a back seat in Canada, but *Social Planning in Canada* had an impact, and national housing legislation appeared.	The government established CMHC. Renewal projects like Regent Park competed with new towns like Don Mills for attention.	Protests stopped the Spadina Expressway but not the removal of Africville residents in Halifax. Redevelopment of inner-city neighbourhoods began.	The new towns of the late century featured New Urbanism principles: higher density, mixed use, and mixed housing types.

Thus we find that the land planning process occurs within many contexts that influence its players. The steps in the process are relatively straightforward. The provinces set the general rules for planning and zoning, and municipalities prepare and implement the plans and regulations. While the rules and procedures vary somewhat across the country, the basic processes are quite similar.

Provincial planning legislation enables municipalities or regions to prepare plans to regulate the development and use of land. Plan preparation typically involves a range of background studies documenting themes such as demographic trends, land-use patterns, traffic analysis, housing need, and commercial and industrial capacity. Public participation allows members of the community to share responsibility for developing the plan, for example, through planning advisory committees or in public meetings. Staff members synthesize the inputs from the process into a policy document variously called an 'official plan', 'community plan', or 'municipal planning strategy', and prepare the accompanying land-use regulations or zoning bylaw and subdivision regulations. Plans and bylaws take effect upon motion of local councils and after review by provincial authorities.

Once councils adopt plans, planning and development staff administer the regulations to ensure that developments comply with the plan and bylaws. For example, are the proposed uses allowed within this zone? Is the proposed building appropriately placed? Staff normally approve projects that comply with the regulations. Projects that meet most but not all of the technical specifications may merit a 'minor variance'. Larger or more complex projects may need additional reviews to ensure compliance with health, environmental, or traffic engineering regulations and to assess capacity of schools, fire, police, infrastructure, and commercial facilities. When developers assemble large parcels of land and apply for subdivision permits or comprehensive development districts, the development officer reviews the site plans and schematics for compliance with subdivision regulations, then circulates them to appropriate departments and government agencies for evaluation and feedback.

Projects that require changes to permitted uses or that demand a comprehensive site plan receive more detailed analysis and usually need council approval. Proponents of such projects often retain consultants to provide background studies demonstrating the need for, and suitability of, the project. Community members have an opportunity to air their concerns and suggestions at public meetings or hearings. Planning staff review the project against plan policies and offer council advice on the suitability of the request. If they believe that the project fulfills the intent of the plan, they may recommend rezoning or acceptance of the development agreement. Council then decides whether to approve or reject the project. Because planning policies are often vague (and sometimes even contradictory), the approval process offers many opportunities for contention and dispute (Grant, 1994b).

Urban Outcomes

The planning process, operating within its complex context of legal, economic, political, social, technical, and organizational influences, generates the outcomes that shape urban and suburban realms. In the post-war period it created central cities with high skylines, concrete plazas, asphalt parking lots, and one-way street systems. It produced cookie-cutter suburbs and radiating strip commercial districts featuring corporate outlets with parking in front. While economic, transportation, and social factors generated the forces driving the post-war Canadian city, planning and land-use regulations provided the ground rules that forged spatial structures and patterns.

The shape and fate of central cities in the second half of the twentieth century tended to reflect the growing influence of the automobile and the internationalization of the economy. Traffic patterns changed considerably. In the 1950s and 1960s, cities built highways to bring commuters downtown and to facilitate transport activities around rail, air, and water. Traffic engineers often converted streets into one-way systems in an effort to reduce traffic jams and improve flow; the indirect effect was to make the network opaque and to discourage visits downtown.

Seeing an opportunity to purchase inexpensive land on the urban periphery, and thus to provide abundant parking within an easy journey for affluent consumers, developers built shopping malls at key traffic junctions. The malls caught on quickly with consumers, providing a new recreational shopping experience. One by one, major retailers in the city centre moved to the malls, leaving central commercial areas weakened (see Chapter 16 on retail location trends). While office functions continued in central business district skyscrapers, retail facilities declined markedly in most central cores. Abandoned buildings and growing parking lots changed the feel of downtown. The bustle of the central city in the early 1950s had, by the late 1970s, given way to clear signs of malaise. By the 1980s and 1990s, even office uses began to move to the periphery, lured by inexpensive land and less traffic congestion (see Chapter 10 on downtowns). The shift from rail to truck transportation enhanced the attraction of the suburbs to many industries.

In the 1950s and 1960s, planning facilitated many of these changes by providing land-use regulations and policies that reflected modernist ideals. Attempting to respond to the symptoms of urban blight, cities regulated height, massing, open space, parking, use, and, in some cases, design. By adopting policies and regulations on these matters, cities streamlined and 'depoliticized' the process of considering applications. At the same time, the planning process tended to standardize outcomes, with developers seeking the 'highest use' for their properties that the rules would allow. Thus high-rise towers in the park or plaza proliferated, and urban design accommodated the automobile and truck.

As political and social concerns about the effects of planning on the central city grew in the late 1960s and early 1970s, municipalities adjusted processes (and thus outcomes). They provided processes with more opportunities for public input, and revised their regulations to modify the size and density of structures and uses allowed in the central city. Incentive programs tried to save or revitalize the 'main streets' of Canadian downtowns. Planners worked with neighbourhoods to renew infrastructure and reverse the process of decay. While some areas experienced gentrification and revival, others continued to endure the loss of economic strength and function. The numbers of schools, stores, and hospitals in inner-city areas continued to diminish as cities found it difficult to reverse the economic and cultural factors disposing people to move to the suburbs. Plan policies designed to protect and rebuild urban cores seldom managed to repel the centrifugal forces that transferred industry, commerce, and housing to the urban periphery. Although planning has great influence on urban form, land-use tools lack the power to solve many contemporary urban social problems.

As products of an era in which planning regimes facilitated built form, the suburbs and the commercial strip developments of the post-war period aptly illustrate how planning and land-use regulation contributed to creating standardized landscapes. Suburbia represented the post-war rejection of the industrial city: spacious lawns and winding streets replaced the narrow lots and grid layout of the central core (see Figure 18.7). The myths of the middle-class nuclear family, homemaker mom, two cars in the driveway, and neighbourhood school were embodied in building practices and land-use regulations that resulted in look-alike suburban areas from coast to coast. Governments even built Arctic and Aboriginal settlements with similar houses and layouts, despite extreme differences in culture and climate. Zoning standards demanded wide lots, significant setbacks, and separation of housing types and uses. The market called for ranch-style bungalows and grassy lawns. Commercial uses were segregated to arterial roads to prevent through-traffic from penetrating residential environments: in the process, the regulations generated the visual wasteland of strip development. A market shaped by corporate concentration and heavy brand-name advertising, and a regulatory environment seeking to protect neighbourhoods from commerce, led to rapid expansion of this urban form. Thus suburban and new town maps from cities across Canada show similar patterns for areas built between the 1950s and 1980s, which contrast markedly with building trends of an earlier era (see Figure 18.8).

Figure 18.7

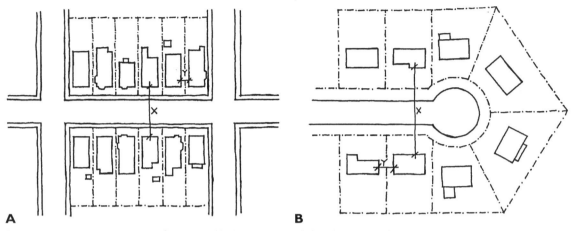

A   B

Planning standards adopted after World War II reduced the density and changed the characteristics of residential areas. Plate A shows pre-war development patterns in the old city: they resulted in narrow lots, narrow streets, grid layouts, and a mix of uses. Plate B indicates that with the adoption of new engineering and planning standards in the post-war period, development patterns tended to feature wide lots, broad winding streets, and separated uses. The distance between facing (x) and abutting (y) homes almost doubled with the new standards, creating spacious but sprawling suburbs.

Figure 18.8

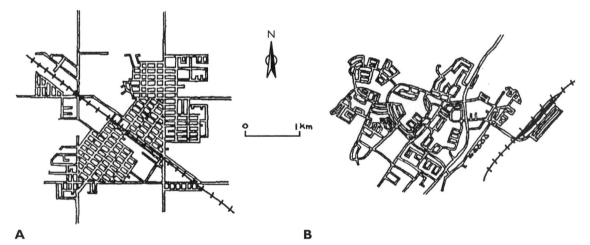

A   B

Two new towns in Manitoba contrast planning styles. Built in 1896, Dauphin (Plate A) follows a grid that reflects its raison d'être: The railway line. Thompson (Plate B), constructed in 1957 to house workers at an Inco nickel mine, follows the garden city principles so popular at the time.

Conclusion

Canadian cities reveal the legacy of several centuries of conscious choices about how to plan our settlements. Colonial interests in the early years shaped location choices and the formal elements of urban centres. In the last century, national initiatives to establish codes and standards increasingly influenced the materials, patterns, and relationships of structures, while provincial governments facilitated municipal efforts to regulate development and land use. The result of government interventions is considerable consistency and commonality across the nation, despite local control over planning. Common values and interests have induced a degree of conformity across the country.

While planning shares responsibility for exacerbating the problems of the city, it is not the driving force behind the changes witnessed during the twentieth century. Planning provides the tools to shape cities, but political leaders and community members decide whether and how to use planning. Canadian governments have chosen to rely on planning tools in a typically Canadian way: less intrusively than is the case in Britain, but with more insistence than is found in the United States. Institutionalized planning and land-use regulation support the market and political realities. Professional planners gave communities the expertise needed to impose cultural and economic values on landscapes. Despite decades of change, many of the dominant assumptions underlying planning remain strong; planning promotes efficiency, health, and amenity. Ideals related to family, domesticity, privacy, and growth continue to influence planning outcomes and thus affect the shape of the city.

Canadian cities are far from perfect: they consume too much land, energy, and resources and condone too much inequity. However, Canadian cities improved in the twentieth century. Planning contributed to the processes whereby cities became better managed and for the most part healthier. Change has become somewhat more predictable, with its effects subject to some control. Residents have confidence that they will not (or should not) face noxious uses in their neighbourhoods: cities that experience environmental contamination, such as Hamilton, Ontario, and Sydney, Nova Scotia, see it as a serious issue for community action and government investment. Canadian cities cannot claim to enjoy the best features of European or Asian cities with their wealth of heritage and character; indeed, planning shares responsibility for perpetuating the ugliness of strip development and the repetitiveness of suburbia for which our cities are known. Still, Canadian cities have avoided the worst problems of American cities: viz., racism and wholesale abandonment of neighbourhoods. We cannot credit planning alone with either the successes or the failures of our urban landscapes. Instead, we must conclude that our artifacts (such as our cities) reflect our cultural values and commitments as do the instruments (such as planning) that we use to create them.

Note

Thanks to Neil Emms for the illustrations for this chapter.

Chapter 19

Contemporary Planning

Raphaël Fischler and Jeanne M. Wolfe

Planning may be defined as the collective management of development, that is, the use of foresight to influence the evolution of society through the built, natural, and, to a lesser extent, social environments, according to shared values and collective interests. It is a political activity in which communities, from the local to the national scale, enunciate visions of a better future, elaborate policies, plans, and programs to realize them, and organize processes and institutions to facilitate decision-making and implement decisions. Planning activities include formal plan-making and public regulation but also informal networking and stakeholder deal-making.

Planners provide expert advice on decision-making processes, alternative futures, possible courses of actions, expected outcomes, and techniques of implementation. They perform this task in the public sector as advisers to elected officials, in the private sector most notably for real-estate developers, and in the not-for-profit sector usually for environmental groups and community development organizations. In these various settings, planners generally are employees fulfilling a mandate given to them by a superior or a client, but they can help to set that mandate by contributing to the definition of the problems at hand (Jacobs, 1980; Krumholz and Forester, 1990). In plan preparation and implementation, planners must contend with inefficiencies in the public sector, most notably the lack of co-ordination among different levels and agencies of government, and with pressures from business and civil society, especially from developers and resident associations. Thus the gap is often wide between an initial perception of the issue and a resulting action or between plans and actual implementation.

Planning allocates resources such as public investments, subsidies, and development rights in urban and regional space. It is therefore an eminently political activity, and its evolution in time must be understood in light of shifts in the ideas and institutions that frame politics, most notably in the wake of globalization and liberalization. Public, private, and community players are aware of the increasing importance of cities as creators of wealth and centres of innovation and, hence, as a country's champions in the global economy. Fostering a good 'business climate', building an efficient transportation and communication infrastructure, providing high-quality public education, and enhancing local quality of life serve to attract private investment and members of the creative class. At the same time, government is redefining itself as enabler and mediator rather than as top-down decision-maker and is working alongside the business sector and civil society in defining common objectives specific to time and place. The growing distrust of government and the increasing heterogeneity of urban populations are fostering the adoption of more flexible modes of planning that give greater leeway to actors on the ground, greater voice to citizens and to organized groups, and greater attention to the specific needs of cultural or ethnic communities. The shift of economic and social policy to the right, away from the principles of the welfare state and towards neo-liberalism, has undermined the redistributive function of planning (Wolfe, 2002), but the belief in sustainable development is providing a new planning ethos with its own equity considerations.

This chapter is divided into two major sections. The first examines institutional and administrative frameworks, responsibilities of each level of government, and interactions between government and the business sector, civil society, and the population at large. The second explores some of the most pressing planning problems of today and reviews the present state of planning in the light of the 'New Deal for Cities and Communities' put forward by the Canadian government in 2004.

Institutional Framework of Planning

Although planning is largely a local affair, responsibility for the management of urban and regional development lies at the provincial level. Municipal and regional bodies have no constitutional powers; their existence, territory, rights, and responsibilities are set by the province in which they are located and they derive their ability to plan from a delegation of provincial power.

The federal government does not have direct authority over planning, but it influences local and regional development in many ways: it controls monetary policy and largely sets economic and social policy; it broadly controls housing policy through the Canada Mortgage and Housing Corporation, which also disseminates research to improve development and regulatory practices; it is the largest landowner in the country, with a portfolio including ports, airports, canals, railroads, military bases, national parks, office complexes, post offices, and the like; it is the biggest employer in Canada; and it participates, with provincial and municipal governments, in tripartite agreements to tackle specific local issues, generally pertaining to infrastructure development and to social welfare. Still, the provinces and territories hold the key to the planning system.

In each of the 10 provinces and three territories, the Municipal Act, or similar legislation with a different name, sets out the rights, duties, extent, and modes of operation of municipalities (Lidstone, 2004). The Planning Act—again the terminology varies—determines the responsibilities of local and regional bodies in matters of plan preparation and land-use regulation. Under this system, municipalities are required to adopt detailed plans of development and to enforce a variety of planning bylaws with respect to the use of land, the density and quality of development, land subdivision, building safety, housing quality, transportation networks, and environmental protection. In addition, most provinces issue policy directives to municipalities on major issues such as housing, economic development, environmental protection, historic preservation, and transportation to frame local decision-making. With varying levels of strictness, they ensure the conformity of municipal plans and regulations with these policy frameworks, as they do with respect to plans that may have been adopted at the regional level. They also influence local practices by providing technical assistance to municipalities and disseminating research findings among public and private actors. Last but not least, they are themselves participants in the process of urban development as builders of infrastructure networks, largely highways and electricity grids, and of public facilities such as hospitals and schools.

To deal with problems that extend across municipal boundaries, provinces have also delegated planning powers to regional bodies (Hodge and Robinson, 2001). Regions, districts, counties, or Regional County Municipalities in Quebec bring together several municipalities for the purposes of planning, infrastructure development, and service delivery. Metropolitan authorities such as the Greater Vancouver Regional District and the Montreal Metropolitan Community adopt plans, develop infrastructure, and even deliver some services for whole urbanized regions. Provincially sponsored special planning bodies also exist for regions with particular geographic characteristics or environmental problems, such as the Niagara Escarpment of Ontario, for river-basin conservation areas, such as that of the Grand River, or for sensitive regions such as the Georgia Strait (Mitchell, 2005).

Planning Instruments

Despite the concentration of political authority at the provincial level, the bulk of planning activity is to be found at the local level. Elected municipal officials (e.g., city councillors, mayors, reeves, alderpersons), local planning boards and consultative committees, and the professional planners who advise them are the principal actors in formal planning practice. Their plans, prepared by planners and approved by officials, set out schematic structures of development, specifying preferred areas of growth, axes of major infrastructure investment, and areas of natural or agricultural conservation. Municipalities that are part of a region must prepare their plans in conformity with the regional plan. In general, plans prepared at the local level will be revised and sanctioned by regional districts, counties, metropolitan communities, conservation authorities, or provincial bodies.

The main instruments of planning at the municipal level are the General Plan (or Master Plan, Official Plan, Strategic Plan, Comprehensive plan, Integrated Plan; the terminology varies) and the zoning bylaw. The former sets out the municipality's goals and objectives; the latter helps to reach these by controlling the location, nature, and quality of development. Regional and municipal plans are prepared on the basis of both technical studies and participatory procedures. Technical studies include analysis of the biophysical and built environments and growth projections for population and economic activity. Expected changes in the number and types of households and in the number and types of jobs are translated into required additions or subtractions to the land area devoted to housing, commerce, industry, open space, and transportation, and into new public facilities needed to service households and businesses. Growth projections and estimates of needed land and services are generally extrapolated for a time horizon of 20 years. Given the uncertainty inherent in such forecasting, plans have to be revised periodically; provincial statutes usually call for five-year revisions, using the results of the most recent census, itself a five-year exercise.

Originally focused on the physical growth of the municipal territory, with blueprints for its land use, infrastructure, and public facilities, the General Plan today can be a multi-faceted policy document that deals with economic, social, cultural, and environmental issues. Most plans contain chapters dealing not only with land use and infrastructure, but also with the conservation of natural and cultural resources, the revitalization of declining neighbourhoods, the enhancement of architectural quality, and the stimulation of economic activity. Municipal plans may also include a transportation plan and an economic development plan, and possibly a social development plan, which may be presented as separate documents. Most of these are now available on Web sites (see, for example, Ottawa, 2003). Figure 19.1 lists the goals of the new Master Plan for Montreal. For some districts within the municipality with specific problems, a very detailed plan may be prepared. Such a district plan, also known as a secondary plan or special-area plan, is usually made for an area requiring large new investments, such as a waterfront, an obsolete industrial district, a downtown, or for a neighbourhood that requires particular attention.

Figure 19.1   **Goals of the New Master Plan of the City of Montreal**

- High-quality, diversified, and complete living environments
- Structuring efficient transportation networks fully integrated into the urban fabric
- A prestigious, convivial, and inhabited centre
- Dynamic, accessible, and diversified employment areas
- High-quality architecture and urban landscape
- An enhanced built, archaeological, and natural heritage
- A healthy environment

Source: Montreal (2004).

Planning can thus be thought of as a nested function cascading from provincially designed policy, through regional structure plans, to municipal general plans, and sometimes to local area plans. Most important, plans are translated, more or less faithfully, into land-use regulations and other controls that subject development to close scrutiny before it is allowed to proceed. It must be emphasized that land-use control is mostly the responsibility of local governments, not upper-tier bodies. (But see also the discussion on greenbelts and agricultural zoning below.) Also, the approval of zoning maps and supporting bylaws is the responsibility of the elected municipal council, not planning professionals and not advisory commissions, even though their advice is no doubt very important.

Public Participation

Participatory processes are written into every provincial planning act. In Quebec, for instance, consultation with the population must take place at least three times during the preparation of a plan, once at the beginning when goals are being formulated, again when alternatives are being considered, and finally when the plan is prepared (Québec, 2002). Ideally, participatory processes are run concurrently with the technical studies, so that the knowledge thus generated may also inform public discussion.

Most provincial legislation either permits or insists that municipalities appoint a planning board or planning advisory committee, such as the Comité consultatif d'urbanisme in Quebec. This body usually includes one or two elected council members and a number of appointed residents, often with expertise in community and building matters, to advise the council on planning matters. Larger municipalities may also appoint a design review board, made up of experts in architecture and urban design, to examine development proposals for their aesthetics and fit in the built environment. Some municipalities constitute similar expert panels to advise on heritage issues and on projects subject to Site Plan Control (see below) (Kumar, 2002). In all cases the committees are advisory: final decisions are taken by the elected council.

Mechanisms for citizen participation in planning include: public media campaigns to disseminate information and call for ideas; community meetings, surveys, focus groups, workshops, and charrettes (a participatory process focusing on the sketching of design solutions to a given problem) to elicit ideas and set priorities for a new policy or plan; formal public hearings to present draft plans and projects and receive input about them; working groups from the business, social, and education sectors, and from other levels of government to gather knowledge and opinions. Some cities have created special units to manage public participation processes; such is the case of the Office de consultation publique de Montréal. The extent to which these means are used and the specific manner in which they are being applied depend on political will: some provincial and municipal administrations seek out public input more eagerly than others; some officials take that input to heart more than others.

Plan Implementation

Although goals listed in General Plans display a diversity of concerns, the tools that municipalities have at their disposal to reach these goals lie mainly in the realm of physical development. *Bylaws* concerning land use, development density, site planning, and building design will serve to shape development projects, whether they are on undeveloped land or in existing urban areas. *Capital expenditures* in underground infrastructure (water, sewage, cable, etc.), transportation infrastructure (roads, bicycle lanes, public transit), and public facilities (promenades, parks, libraries, etc.) will help to improve urban areas directly, by enhancing the quality of the urban environment for current residents, and indirectly, by attracting private investment in land made ready or made more attractive for development. Although general plans have 20-year horizons, most municipalities cannot venture far into the future in their budgeting exercises and prepare three-year rolling capital expenditure budgets.

Fiscal measures, such as the imposition of development fees or the granting of subsidies, can also influence the pace and location of development, in particular in the realm of housing. Development fees, which are applied by a growing number of cities and suburbs to cover the cost of providing public infrastructure and facilities for new subdivisions, make housing less affordable and may push development into more peripheral regions, where such fees do not apply (Skaburskis and Tomalty, 2001; Tomalty and Skaburskis, 2003). Subsidies, on the other hand, may encourage development in desired locations, such as brownfield sites, and may help to make housing more affordable, for instance, by targeting first-time homebuyers or developers of rental units. *Allocations of public services*, finally, can help to improve an area. Community development efforts, through grassroots organization or municipal bodies (often with financial support from the province), can help attract households and businesses in poorer neighbourhoods.

Development Regulation

Public intervention in private development in Canada is facilitated by the fact that property rights are not constitutionally protected as they are in the US, where they are staunchly defended in the courts. Though private property is held dear in Canada as well, public constraints on its development are generally well accepted. One widely accepted principle is the need for intervention to limit the negative impact that one person's use of land may have on other people's enjoyment of theirs—the nuisance principle. Hence, creating different zones for incompatible activities and limiting their intensity are key objectives of municipal planning bylaws.

Traditional zoning designates different sections of the municipal territory for residential, commercial, and industrial purposes, and for green space, public facilities, and transportation infrastructure. In rural areas, the classification of uses will also contain agriculture, forestry, resource extraction, recreation, tourism, and conservation, along with the urban activities of towns and villages. In large urban areas, land-use classifications can grow very complex when different housing types (single-family homes, semi-detached houses, townhouses, small apartment buildings, large apartment buildings) and different types of commerce (from local to regional) and of industry (from totally clean to highly noxious) are distinguished from one another.

Aside from segregating land uses, zoning bylaws also determine the density, height, bulk, shape, and quality of development by means of the floor area ratios and standards for land coverage, building height, setbacks from lot lines, size of courtyards, parking, and presence and location of ancillary buildings. Design can also be regulated by means of standards for facades, roofs, and building materials or for greenery, parking, and loading areas (Kumar, 2002). More discretionary controls, which call on subjective evaluation on the part of professionals, can also help to regulate development where specification standards, which set fixed numerical thresholds, are found wanting. Sites for large mixed-use projects, for instance, are often reviewed under Site Plan Control bylaws that set overall density levels but leave many details to be hammered out by negotiation between developers and officials. Where development involves the subdivision of land into legally separate properties, site planning is also regulated by means of subdivision controls that impose standards on the design of streets and building lots.

Over the years, new regulatory techniques have appeared in response to changing needs. One trend is the growing importance of environmental and aesthetic considerations in development control. Another is the shift from a strict segregation of land uses towards the integration of residential and other uses, particularly in downtowns and central neighbourhoods. As long as they meet certain performance criteria with respect to noise and vibrations, many quasi-industrial activities are now deemed compatible with residential uses, as in Toronto's redevelopment areas along King Street (Bedford, 1997). Flexibility has also increased with respect to housing types. More and more municipalities are now allowing secondary suites in single-family residential areas or are welcoming condominiums in formerly low-density zones (Kraehling, 2004). A third noteworthy trend is the greater reliance on incentives rather than constraints in order to reach public objectives through private development. Under so-called 'bonus zoning', developers are allowed to build at higher densities, or are given another benefit such as fast-track project review, in exchange for including public amenities or facilities in their projects (e.g., more park space than normally required; a daycare centre) or for contributing residential units, land, or money to increase the affordable housing stock (Punter, 2003). In fact, negotiations over development, starting well before the actual design process begins, have become much more frequent in many cities. Developers, city officials, designers, and future users confer at the beginning of the conceptual process in most successful projects (Beasley, 2003).

Although it contains more and more elements of discretionary review, the Canadian system of development control, as in the US, is generally of an administrative type, whereas the British system, for example, with its focus on plans and relative paucity of regulations, is discretionary (Booth, 1996). Conformity of a project with the zoning plan is checked against the specific regulatory norms contained in local bylaws, rather than against the overall planning objectives that the plan spells out. Where conformity with regulations is established, a building permit is issued. Where a departure from regulations is requested, projects may still be approved under a system of minor variances (exceptions) or by modifying the regulations. These two mechanisms provide flexibility but also lend themselves easily to abuse.

Planning decisions can be appealed by residents, owners, and developers if they are considered unfair or imprudent. In most provinces there is a planning appeal board of some sort. In Ontario, complaints are heard by the Ontario Municipal Board, a body that operates in a quasi-judicial mode and that has come under severe criticism in recent years for the apparent capriciousness of its decisions

(Chipman, 2002). In Quebec, proposed planning and zoning changes can be contested by citizens if a certain proportion of residents in an affected area request a referendum. The costs of the referendum are borne by the municipality and the results are binding on the council. Otherwise, individual complaints are usually heard in court.

Contemporary Planning Issues

In the past 10 years, Canadian planning has confronted a variety of issues, some of which have existed for a long time—indeed, for as long as modern planning has existed—and some that have appeared more recently on the public policy agenda. At the federal level, the most hotly debated issue is the inability of cities to meet their needs with their current sources of revenue (Simmons and Bourne, 2003), especially in light of the looming crisis in infrastructure due to deferred maintenance and repair. Mayors of large cities and the Federation of Canadian Municipalities have started calling explicitly for granting cities a greater share of the nation's fiscal pie.

The forced amalgamations of so many municipalities to create mega-cities, especially in Ontario, Quebec, and Nova Scotia, which were undertaken to save costs, did not solve their financial shortcomings: in fact, total expenditures are up in all cases (Jerret et al., 2002; Sancton, 2000; Vojnovic, 1999a). However, the changes did create a new political force in the form of a big-cities caucus, with members whose population is larger than that of the smaller provinces (see Chapter 17). This coalition of big cities has received the support of the business community in applying pressure for change.

At the regional and local levels, the enduring issues include transportation problems, the continued spread of formless sprawl around cities, the decline and regeneration of central areas, the concentration of poverty and its attendant problems for immigrants and members of minority groups, and the destruction of natural assets. Newer problems include the demographic renewal of older suburbs and the decline of cities in non-metropolitan and peripheral regions, as well as the search for more effective public participation, multicultural outreach, and community empowerment in planning processes.

Transportation and Infrastructure Planning

Automobile use spawns two major sets of immediate problems: road congestion, which is high on the urban policy agenda, and the compounding problem of pollution, i.e., greenhouse gas emissions, their public health impacts, and Canada's obligations under the Kyoto agreement (NRTEE, 2001) (see also Chapters 7 and 20). Clearly, progress can be made in both of these areas with greater use of collective and alternate forms of transport (NRTEE, 2003). There may, however, be no solution as long as the private automobile remains as popular and its use remains as concentrated at certain times of day (Downs, 1999). The shift of much goods transport from rail to truck, in part in answer to just-in-time (JIT) requirements from industry, also helps to explain the increase in road congestion in the 1980s and 1990s. Road congestion problems are discussed in Chapter 6.

An approach to these problems is to improve the quality of infrastructure for non-motorized travel to encourage people to get out of their cars. Bicycle lanes, with safe lock-ups and showers at major destinations, and pedestrian pathways offering shade and safety are much needed but have not been placed high on planners' agenda, except in the context of recreation (Blair, 2004). Another approach, which is appealing but the efficacy of which has yet to be demonstrated, is to increase urban density and foster the mixing of land uses to get people to run certain trips on foot. That people walk more in denser, mixed-use neighbourhoods is a given; that they might also use their cars less to commute to work or to taxi their children to soccer games is not evident (Price, 2002). One of the most telling arguments for densification is shown in the following facts from a Quebec government study of the Montreal region, where, for an average

household choosing to live close to a metro station, the following gains are made each year:

- 1,050 fewer automobile trips are taken;
- 15,000 fewer kilometres are driven (the equivalent of one less auto);
- 6,000 fewer kilograms of greenhouse gases are produced;
- 650 extra journeys are made by transit;
- 425 extra journeys are taken by foot or bicycle (Québec, 2001: 59).

Another direct problem with traffic is pollution. The transport sector contributes about 30 per cent of greenhouse gases generated by human activity, and much of that share is produced by private automobiles (Canada, 2002; NRTEE, 1997). Not only does this have implications for climate change, it leads to the formation of urban smog, deteriorates the environment, and has serious consequences for public health.

Studies in various cities, for instance in Toronto (Filion, 2001; reviewed in Chapter 10) and in Montreal (Sénécal et al., 2002), indicate that proactive interventions could improve matters in transportation. A more pedestrian-friendly environment and the intensification of residential development on underused sites in the vicinity of employment centres could help to increase the share of non-motorized trips in daily movement. Planning to reduce dependence on the automobile must also target the location and concentration of employment, the provision of parking spaces in new projects, and the adoption of programs of carpooling and privately organized collective transport. A particular concern in transportation planning, too, has been to ensure the mobility and safety of women and of the elderly, especially in suburban areas.

Suburban Sprawl

The label 'sprawl' is generally attributed to urban growth that exhibits the following characteristics: (a) low building and population density, (b) discontinuity of the urban fabric or 'leapfrogging', (c) separation of land uses and, therefore, (d) dependency of people on the private automobile for their daily trips, and (e) the waste of agricultural land through fragmentation. The typical suburban environment of single-family residential areas, shopping strips, and industrial parks, all separated one from another by empty, unused pieces of land and remnant agricultural holdings, is considered the paradigm of sprawl (Bourne et al., 2003).

While most observers focus on the wastefulness of low residential densities, contemporary research suggests that densities seem to be increasing, perhaps due to market forces. But the other forms of fringe development—big-box stores, warehousing and trucking, manufacturing, commercial recreational centres, and the like—are gobbling up the land in huge quantities (Bourne, 2001a). Moreover, defenders of current patterns of growth argue that the remedies proposed by critics of sprawl will do more harm than good. They maintain, for instance, that limiting the supply of land for new construction in the periphery will drive up housing costs, hence worsening the problem of housing affordability for the poor (JAPA, 1997). Some professional planners, large numbers of politicians, and the majority of the public at large would seem to fall into this camp.

The direct containment of sprawl has been tried by two means—the designation of greenbelts and agricultural zoning. Ottawa has a greenbelt, identified in the Gréber Plan and purchased outright by the National Capital Commission in the early fifties (Gyton, 1999). Since the late sixties, urbanization has been jumping over it, but it has become a wonderful, defining local amenity and should be designated a heritage site. Two provinces, British Columbia and Quebec, have agricultural zoning, which, while protecting agriculture, effectively marks the edge of urbanization. The British Columbia Land Commission Act was first passed in 1973, and there have been constant contestations over the extent of the Agricultural Land Reserve ever since (ALR-PEC, 2005; Garrish, 2002–3). The Quebec Act to Protect Agricultural Land dates from 1978 and has been similarly contested through the years. Recognizing that there is no point in

protecting agriculture unless it is a highly competitive occupational option, the Quebec government has recently introduced proactive programs to improve the farming economy. It insists that the Regional County Municipality plans must include positive methods for upgrading agriculture and that the Commission de protection du territoire agricole must not allow any further removals of land from the *zone verte* unless the proponent of such an exclusion can prove that there is no vacant space in the area zoned for urban uses in the municipality concerned (Québec, 2002a).

The Ontario government, recognizing the twin problems of urban sprawl and loss of the province's best farmland in the Greater Golden Horseshoe (GGH)—the area centred on the Toronto conurbation, extending from Niagara Falls to Peterborough and as far north as Georgian Bay—has recently published a plan combining the notions of both a greenbelt and agricultural zoning (Ontario, 2004b). The region contains a population of 7.8 million and this is expected to increase by another 3.8 million by 2031. A greenbelt has been proposed to encircle the existing urban area, where development is to occur by intensification and infill; new peripheral development will only be permitted in designated settlement areas adjacent to existing built-up areas. The Places to Grow Draft Growth Plan was released in February 2005 and the Greenbelt Plan approved at the same time, and they are likely to become the 'foundational core' of all future planning in southern Ontario (Ferrigan and Ghent, 2005).

Critics of sprawl have put forward various alternatives to traditional suburban development. Andres Duany and his colleagues in the New Urbanism movement that has swept across North America are calling for the replacement of endless cookie-cutter subdivisions by well-designed, medium-density communities that group various housing types and land uses in close proximity to a town or neighbourhood centre (Duany and Plater-Zyberk, 1992). Though New Urbanists have had some success in building such new communities, their track record so far is rather modest. Two well-known Canadian examples are Cornell in

Markham, Ontario, and Mackenzie Towne in south-east Calgary (Thompson-Fawcett and Bond, 2003; Toderian, 2004). Although both of these neo-traditional projects display a real mixture of housing types and include commercial and institutional facilities, they are located on peripheral land, are automobile-dependent, and cater only to the well-heeled.

Closely allied with New Urbanism, but taking on a more regional approach, is the movement for transit-oriented development (TOD) (Calthorpe, 1993). Here, the goal is to link land-use planning and urban design, on the one hand, and transportation planning, on the other, in the creation of higher-density, nucleated urban clusters around mass-transit stops, whether bus, transit, or rail. The Town of Mount-Royal, an inner suburb of Montreal laid out by Frederick Todd for the Canadian National Railway in 1912, is the finest example of a TOD ever built, 80 years before the term was invented. Another approach to curtailing sprawl has been the adoption of alternative development standards (ADS). Typical post-World War II subdivisions were laid out in 50- × 100-foot lots (approx. 16 × 33 metres) for single-family housing, with 60–66-foot (approx. 20-metre) road allowances, a pattern that has persisted and been unfortunately propagated through bylaw standards. These norms are now being reviewed and modified all across the country, not only in an effort to prevent the wasteful use of land, but also to save on the cost of services (a 35-foot lot obviously saves 30 per cent on all linear installations) and to control costs in the face of skyrocketing housing prices, since smaller lots are cheaper (Paul, 2000; von Hausen, 2002).

A more comprehensive approach to the problem of sprawl, one in which fiscal considerations figure more prominently, is that of the Smart Growth movement (Filion, 2003; Onyschuk et al., 2001). The expression 'smart growth', like that of 'sustainable development', is vague enough to be used by people holding very different opinions of what constitutes appropriate government intervention in urban change. In general, it denotes practices of planning, regulation, and construction that aim to economize on land, natural resources, and public monies by promoting greater densities, preventing leapfrog development, establishing an urban perimeter and restricting development to areas within that boundary (i.e., more infill development, intensification, re-urbanization), and fostering the reuse of brownfield sites, already serviced by public infrastructure (CUI, 2001). As discussed earlier, decisions on what roads and water and sewer lines will be built, and where, are critical to managing growth. Proponents of smart growth argue that before new public investments are made, existing investments must have been fully exploited by proper infill development. The government of British Columbia has fiercely embraced smart growth under its Growth Strategies Act of 1995, which resurrected regional district planning and has wide support through the activities of Smart Growth BC, a provincial NGO that works with communities for responsible development (Smart Growth BC, 2005). However, a study of the Capital Regional District, Victoria, suggests that integrated growth management still faces substantial challenges (Boyle et al., 2004).

Not only new suburbs but also existing ones are target areas of smart growth action. The low-density suburbs of the 1920s to 1970s, with their aging housing stock and, often, aging population, offer great potential for consolidating development in urbanized areas. Deprived of the advantages of older residential communities, with their quality homes and easy access to urban amenities, and of the advantages of newer ones, with their contemporary construction and easy access to nature, mid-twentieth-century suburbs face an uncertain future (Fortin et al., 2002; Friedman, 2002). One strategy here is residential densification, an objective that can be pursued by permitting the inclusion of secondary suites in private homes or adjacent to them, by encouraging infill development on empty lots or parts thereof, or by allowing demolition and higher-density reconstruction on major thoroughfares. Another, complementary, strategy is improvement of the public realm, to make the area more attractive to new residents. This objective can be served by investments in public transit and in public facilities such as parks, libraries, and community and sports centres, as well as by public–private partnerships to redevelop old shopping malls and industrial sites. At the same time as the public realm of the suburb is receiving more attention, however, the privatization of public space continues in commercial developments and in gated communities (Des Rosiers, 2002; Grant, 2004).

Obsolete Industrial and Commercial Sites

Brownfield sites, which are abandoned industrial parcels and military bases, rail corridors and rail yards, and industrial waterfronts and old harbourfronts, constitute so many 'lost spaces' in the urban fabric and so many occasions to reconnect different parts of the city with each other or the city with its waterfront (Trancik, 1989). Additional challenges and opportunities lie in greyfield sites, such as old shopping malls, which do not have the same degree of contamination.

One of the key obstacles to the reuse of brownfield sites is the need to remove the toxic deposits that industrial activities have left in the soil. Decontamination can be expensive and can therefore limit the feasibility of some kinds of development (Sénécal and Saint-Laurent, 2000). Various programs in Canada have subsidized site preparation work, though sums allocated have been insufficient to the task at hand. Other obstacles include: liability to potential risk, especially for housing, and the consequent reluctance of financial institutions to lend; the lack of streamlined technology for cleaning sites; the perceived stigma of their reuse; and strict regulations (CMHC, 2005; Delcan and McCarthy Tétrault, 1996; de Sousa, 2000; NRTEE, 1998). Still, examples of large, successful brownfield conversions exist in various cities. False Creek in Vancouver, Garrison Woods in Calgary, the Angus Shops in Montreal, and the Moncton Railyards show that, once properly cleaned up, a large industrial site, a decommissioned military base, a locomotive works, or a railway yard can be reborn as a complete neighbourhood.

Waterfronts have been the object of special attention, in part because of the amenity value of water, in part because of the scale of the urban territory involved, and in part because the federal government has primary ownership. Many cities in Canada, from coast to coast, have worked in the past two decades on more or less ambitious waterfront reclamation plans (Hoyle, 1995). Key issues addressed in these plans are the public's access to the water, the uses to which land is to be put and their densities, and the integration of continued port activities and rail service along the waterfront. Questions of access arise when barriers, such as Toronto's Gardner Expressway, exist between the waterfront and the rest of the city and when waterfront land is being privatized. A general rule is to ensure that the public domain extends all the way along the water's edge and that this linear park or walk be accessible at many points, both physically and visually. Questions of use and density concern the nature and amount of construction to take place. Although early plans for Montreal's waterfront called for high-rise development, as occurred in central Toronto, the plan that was ultimately adopted, after a lengthy public consultation process, allowed only for the renovation of existing structures and for the erection of a few pavilions directly related to the public function of the waterfront as a recreation and tourism area. Most of the land was to be left open as promenade or park. But the whole transformation has taken over 30 years to unfold and is not yet complete (Courcier, 2005).

A recent phenomenon that preoccupies planners is the obsolescence of older shopping centres and strip malls. Due to increased competition from big-box stores and category killers including Wal-Mart, Costco, Staples, Toys R Us, and Future Shop, sometimes grouped as power centres, traditional suburban malls, not to mention traditional commercial streets, have seen their fortunes decline (Jones and Doucet, 1999; see Chapter 16). Responding to bankruptcy or acting to prevent it from happening, strip malls and shopping centre owners or their creditors are working either to improve their property or to rebuild it altogether.

Choosing the first strategy, they may add new recreation activities in their tenant mix, attract public facilities inside the mall, or add new structures on their site for a hotel and/or convention centre, for offices, or even for residences, often seniors' housing. Adding new buildings generally requires that some of the surface parking gets transferred to a multi-storey garage. Opting for the second strategy, rebuilding, owners demolish the mall to make way for a new neighbourhood or for a power centre, much as would be the case on a brownfield site, save for the fact that soil remediation is generally not a consideration. In the development of power centres, whether on greyfield or on other sites, developers and local officials are increasingly concerned with the provision of a humane, attractive, even truly urban-looking environment. To create 'place' (see Chapter 26), they are trying to adopt design strategies and public guidelines to 'tame' the large buildings and parking lots and to include inviting public spaces in their midst.

Declining Cities and Regions

Historically, urban planners have worked to anticipate the needs of a growing population for housing, commerce, industry, recreation, and other uses. Yet many small towns in remote regions are declining in population (Bourne, 2004; Simmons and Bourne, 2003). Outside the major growth areas of Toronto, Vancouver, Edmonton–Calgary and Montreal–Ottawa, growth may be fairly modest, as it is in Winnipeg and Halifax and many other mid-size places, or even negative, as it is in many small towns and some larger places across Canada. Polèse and Shearmur (2002) have shown how in Atlantic Canada and Quebec, urban centres that are further than about 150 km from a major metropolitan area become stagnant. Even with the advent of information technology (IT), small remote centres cannot compete in the knowledge economy. In general, such towns have birth rates below replacement levels, receive few if any immigrants, and lose population through migration to large cities. Their authorities have to manage a process of shrinkage

that involves a loss of population and jobs, a decline in property values, and a consequent reduction in the municipal tax base. The problem is structural: fundamental geographic and economic factors—the remoteness of some regions from the major hubs of the global economy, their dependence on the exploitation of scarce resources, the lower levels of skills of their population, and, hence, their lower attractiveness to new investment—conspire to create a negative feedback loop of population loss and economic decline. Ultimately, the future of economically peripheral regions is rather bleak, and planners there, with their counterparts in provincial and federal governments, must learn to plan for urban contraction rather than growth.

Demographic change in the long run is also a preoccupation in large urban centres. The new development plan of the Montreal Metropolitan Community (MMC, 2005) anticipates that the population of the region will stop growing and start declining in mid-century. The MMC proposes to consolidate already urbanized areas, to rationalize regional infrastructure investment, and to arbitrate the inter-municipal competition for households and businesses by restricting development on greenfield sites (MMC, 2005). The City of Montreal's goals, meanwhile, as expressed in its Master Plan of 2004, are precisely about that: to prevent a larger number of households from leaving for the suburbs, to improve the older neighbourhoods where poorer residents live, to populate underused and vacant sites, and to increase or at least maintain transit ridership (Montreal, 2004). For many planners, the challenge now is to maintain or improve their city without the benefit of vigorous growth (which is itself a challenge).

Social Sustainability: Minority Groups and the Poor

Ensuring social sustainability has also become an important part of the urban planning mandate (Clutterbuck and Novick, 2003). Although living conditions today are in general vastly superior to what they were a century ago, when the modern planning movement was born, planners must still contend with social problems in our cities. Most pressing are the lack of affordable housing and the special difficulties experienced by recent immigrants, members of visible minorities, and First Nations people. Polarization in incomes makes matters worse—see Chapters 8, 9, and 25—and levels of homelessness are a national disgrace (Layton, 2000; see also Des Rosiers, 2003; Hulchanski and Shapcott, 2004).

Planners' most important weapon in the fight against poverty and marginalization has been the construction of subsidized housing. Since the federal government essentially stopped building new social housing in 1988 (except for special groups and Native people), provinces have been left to their own devices (Carter and Polevychoc, 2004). They have responded to this challenge in an uneven and generally weak manner; Quebec and British Columbia are the only provinces with significant, albeit modest, programs of support for affordable housing, mostly in the form of subsidies for setting up housing co-operatives and non-profits. Carter and Polevychoc (2004) remind use that, traditionally, housing has not been seen as an integral part of the package of social policies required to secure public well-being in Canada; no doubt it should be.

The enormous number of recent immigrants to Canada and their preference for the major cities is well known (Ley and Germain, 2000). Planners have not been very responsive to the new mix of lifestyles, customs, and needs, a major theme in Chapter 24 (see also Wallace and Moore Milroy, 2001). The Metropolis project, a massive cross-Canada research initiative, has provided much information in recent years about the problems of immigrants. However, while this research has produced little direct guidance for planners on thorny practical matters, it has probably raised their sensibilities to the difficulties faced by newcomers (Andrew, 2004). A practical problem confronting planners in neighbourhoods with high concentrations of immigrants is the difficulty in communi-

cating with residents because many of the newcomers do not belong to community groups, have no tradition of local democracy, are too shy or insecure in a strange language to express opinions, and, especially for women, may be culturally conditioned to remain silent and lack knowledge about their rights. New means to foster meaningful dialogue must be found along with ways to promote empowerment and to nurture citizenship (Sandercock, 1998).

The problems of social exclusion are also severe for First Nations peoples, especially in the cities. Pushed to urban centres by poor housing and lack of educational or job opportunities on reserves, First Nations households face problems of cultural dislocation, loss of identity, and discrimination (Peters and Walker, 2005). In the prairie cities, Aboriginal people make up a sizable proportion of the inner-city populations; their poverty rate is over 50 per cent and they are disproportionately subject to homelessness. Here, too, mutual learning is necessary for understanding and resolving problems (Brown, 1999). On the other hand, after more than a century of struggle, some progress is being made by Indian bands where land settlement treaties have been negotiated and a degree of self-government has been instituted (Usher, 2003). The passage of the First Nations Land Management Act (1999) has put the management of lands and resources on reserves into local hands in order to improve local governance and planning for economic and social development. An alliance has been made between the First Nations Land Management Resource Centre and the Canadian Institute of Planners to assist in this process (Leach, 2005).

The problems in deprived neighbourhoods are multi-faceted. The first need is a robust social and physical infrastructure—education, health, child care, affordable housing, and transit—which requires special financing from senior governments (Séguin and Germain, 2000). Integrated interventions, which bring together physical and social planners, hold the most promise, but their implementation is often thwarted by administrative rigidities.

Environmental Planning and Sustainable Development

All polls show that the state of the environment consistently remains one of the major concerns of Canadians. Sustainable development, however this is defined, has become the major dogma and focus of planners' work (Wolfe, 2002). Planning used to be called upon to help face three main environmental challenges: the restoration of a richer ecology in already urbanized areas; the protection of sensitive and valuable natural areas from urban and industrial development; and the modification of planning practices to reduce energy consumption. Today, as evidenced by the ratification of the Kyoto accord and the adoption of the *Climate Change Plan for Canada* (Canada, 2002), growing concerns with water and air quality, energy depletion, toxic contamination from persistent organic pollutants (POPs), and public health disasters have placed environmental considerations at the heart of public action. The definition of sustainability most widely used among planners is the resolution of the conflict between the needs of the environment, of the economy, and of people, along with the intergenerational responsibility of providing for the needs of future populations.

The problems of the urban environment and the possible means of tackling them have been well researched and documented in recent times. The Prime Minister's Caucus Task Force on Urban Issues, the *Climate Change Plan*, the National Round Table on the Environment and the Economy, scores of government departments at all levels, university and research think-tanks, and numerous environmental and transportation NGOs have all produced reports and proposals (e.g., Canada, 2002; NRTEE, 2003). The federal government has set up a research program on adaptation to climate change and municipal responses (Canada, 2005).

Under its 'New Deal for Cities and Communities', the federal government has made more money available to the provinces for sustainable development by sharing revenues from the gasoline tax to support public transit, rescinding the GST (Goods and Services Tax) for municipalities to improve their fiscal situation, and allocating $800 million a year for the next two years for affordable housing. It will also generally take a proactive stand on improving the energy efficiency, environmental friendliness, and responsible management of all its own operations. The amounts of money to be made available on a municipal basis are hard to calculate, since they are spread out over a number of years, are subject to negotiation by each of the provinces, and are allocated under various rules and performance criteria. John Sewell (2005) has estimated that for Toronto the amount received will average $500 million per year.

At the local level, planners are trying to promote sustainable development in all areas, but progress is slow. Resistance to densification is high, especially in areas where large homes on large lots are popular. In addition, retrofitting existing suburbs to bring them up to densities where they can support transit is an almost impossible task. Municipal infrastructure renewal is creating opportunities for alternate forms of transport, green building, and life-cycle costing, but the actual 'greening' of municipal operations (adoption of fuel-efficient vehicles, refitting public buildings and facilities, finding viable solutions to solid waste disposal problems, etc.) is progressing slowly (Robinson and Gore, 2005). Likewise, residential communities have been slow to pursue green building techniques and other alternatives, such as energy-efficiency retrofits.

Industrial areas are another matter: environmental regulations have historically been applied to limit emissions, noise, and nuisances. Today, much of this control is done by negotiation, by trying to find ways in which processes can be modified to reduce pollution. One promising approach is the start-up of eco-industrial parks, a European invention now applied in Canada, for instance in Dartmouth, Nova Scotia (Côté, 2000). In these industrial areas, the waste of one process becomes an input for another: steam, heat, and residual materials from one plant are taken up by others, evidently to mutual benefit. Entry into such a park requires demonstration of the symbiosis anticipated. In a similar vein, district heating and cooling are known to be efficient and environmentally friendly, and are gaining ground. Toronto has just completed a deep lake heat exchange system to cool some of its central area buildings. In Montreal, part of the newly renovated Benny Farm property, a former veterans' housing project, will be heated by geothermal means.

Planning for open space in communities has become a much more sensitive process than it was when the point was to obey standards for the provision of playing fields and parks. Most plans for new areas follow the McHarg (1969) technique of 'Plan with Nature' and assiduously map out watercourses, wetlands, special habitats, forested areas, areas of outstanding natural beauty, and land that floods or is too steep, too boggy, or too unstable for development. These are then designated for protection before design begins (see Chapter 21). Within built-up areas, landscapes are analyzed in a similar manner, with a view to the remediation of past errors. It is now recognized that biodiversity is important for a healthy ecosystem, that indigenous plants are more likely to be sustainable than imports, and that linear open space offers protective buffer zones, reduces wind speeds, provides shade, and can be employed for pedestrian and bike paths. Open space planning has thus turned much more to greenways and greenbelts linking park spaces, waterfronts, and natural areas (Taylor et al., 1995). Trail-building can also lead to economic returns (Go for Green, 2005). Re-naturalization of degraded wetlands and of riverbanks, as has been done along the Bow River in Calgary, is very common. Urbanized watercourses are also receiving attention: there is a movement to 'bring back the Don' in Toronto, and the rehabilitation of the Lachine Canal in Montreal, which has taken about 30 years, is a delight (London, 2003). But, as Chapter 22 points out, there are still too many unknowns and much remains to be learnt.

Conclusion

Canadian planning at the opening of the twenty-first century displays great diversity. Differences abound, for instance between small-town planning and metropolitan planning, but practices and ideas show many similarities irrespective of location and scale. The most remarkable change in planning in these first years of the twenty-first century is the move towards integrated activity: the sharing of ideas, programs, projects, and financing between the three layers of government; the partnerships between governments and NGOs and other civil society organizations in program design and delivery; and the partnerships between governments and the private sector. Urban scholars in the US and UK have described this particular approach as collaborative planning and communicative/interactive planning, respectively (Healy, 1997; Innes, 1995). In Canada, it has been best labelled by one of Vancouver's chief planners as co-operative planning (Beasley, 2003). However, reaching consensus on urban problems is not simple despite the easy optimism of some analysts (Cormick et al., 1996).

Communication among officials, planners, and residents is now rapid and vivid thanks to information technology. Many municipal planning departments have their plans, regulations, and studies on the Web for the benefit of their citizens and also for the benefit of professionals and interested people from around the world. Policies, programs, and plans, together with studies of planning outcomes, analyses of best practices, and handy hints, fill the ether. One can only wonder why good planning ideas are not adopted more rapidly and why planning is not more successful. For instance, it is disappointing to note that only over 100 municipalities, among the more than 4,000 that exist in Canada, have taken action towards emissions reductions, despite enormous interest in the Partners for Climate Protection Program of the Federation of Canadian Municipalities (Robinson and Gore, 2005). Reasons given for the lack of action are insufficient finances, human resources, capacity, and knowledge.

Despite the inertia, urban affairs, and thus planning, are back on the public policy agenda in a substantial way (Andrew et al., 2002). The Canadian Policy Research Network and other organizations are working to make clear why cities matter and why place-based policies, rather than wall-to-wall programs irrespective of location, are essential (Bradford, 2002, 2004). The Law Commission of Canada has bemoaned the continued infantilization and dependency of municipalities as creatures of the provinces, the inadequacy of institutions in the face of new challenges and functions, and the continued prevalence of 'one size fits all' thinking in policy circles (Valverde and Levi, 2005). No doubt Canadian municipalities need a 'New Deal' from the federal government.

Still, in the effort to tame the forces that make and break cities, the key player in Canada, historically and functionally, is the province. How well planning is being practised today in a given Canadian city or region depends to a large extent on how supportive the provincial government is of good planning, how well it leads by example, and how high its expectations are for planning work done at the local level. The province's behaviour in these matters, in turn, depends largely on political leadership. Where the government places the wise use of space high on the provincial policy agenda, officials can spend attention, effort, and money to study problems thoroughly and devise feasible solutions. Local political leadership is also very important, and much that is good in the history of the planning profession can be ascribed at least in part to the vision of a mayor, a senior bureaucrat, or a leading citizen advocate.

The fate of Canadian cities is uncertain. In the face of economic, social, and environmental challenges, planners have the mandate to advise elected officials and private developers on the best ways to allocate land, to design the built environment, to lay out infrastructure, to distribute public facilities, and to protect natural and cultural assets so as to make our settlements fairer, more competitive, more enjoyable, and more sustainable. However, it is clear that sprawl and its nefarious attendant problems or the decline of certain regions can only be attacked by strong provincial policies (and with federal funding). Provincially mandated or supported spatial planning that encompasses the whole urban dynamic—central city, suburbs, and rural fringe—is equally important in order to achieve stated objectives in social, economic, and environmental sustainability.

Where does all this leave planning professionals? As advisers, planners do not hold any of the political and financial levers that must be moved to ensure sustainable urban development. Their tools are analysis and vision, research and persuasion. Yet they surely get blamed for inevitable failures and will not likely receive much praise for possible successes. Such is the fate of urban planning: to be the object of high hopes and the subject of constant attacks, to have visible effects and to be kept in the shadow. It is a task at once thankless and undeniably rewarding.

Chapter 20

Canadian Cities and the Sustainability Imperative
Kevin S. Hanna

Contrary to the romantic image of a land of loggers and cowboys, Canada is now mostly a nation of city dwellers commuting daily across settled landscapes to urban-based employment. While the global movement from rural to city is certainly a major demographic event, it also symbolizes, as Rees and Wackernagle (1996: 223) suggest, a human ecological shift. Urbanization reflects the utmost collision of humanity and nature. Few processes are as seemingly permanent. Urbanization conquers landscapes; even more so than logging or agriculture, which, though certainly land-altering, are in many respects temporary processes. A fallow field or logged landscape may not immediately yield a new forest, meadow, or prairie like the previous one, but will usually rebound to become some stage in a sequence of ecological succession. When cities expand, the impact is usually permanent and more intense than most other human processes. The city is an entirely human construct; there is nothing 'natural' about it—it exists in opposition to nature and at the expense of it. Indeed, cities have evolved as economic entities, and over time they have unfolded largely to meet the demands of growing economies.

Since the Industrial Revolution, at least, urban dwellers have tended to see nature as being external to the city. Natural and rural spaces have often been treated as land waiting to be urbanized. Nature has been seen as an obstacle to overcome as cities grow, and when it was considered, nature was viewed as an amenity to be preserved in reduced form or replicated as snippets of 'green' space. Developers, even today, do not view the preservation of nature as especially desirable. Preservation is a nuisance; when it occurs it is frequently placation, perhaps a modest requirement of the approval process, or even the product of acrimonious negotiations.

This chapter uses the concept of sustainability to introduce the broad interrelationships and impacts of built-up urban form on the natural environment. Sustainability can have variable definitions and interpretations, but at its core it is about sustaining human and ecological well-being. At the level of the city sustainability is, by necessity, planning- and design-focused. The way we have constructed our cities reflects our ability to manipulate landscapes and nature. We have not grown within the limits and needs of nature; instead, we subdue it. When developers build suburbs they remove trees and flatten the land, take out the undulations, and remake the natural qualities of the landscape. It takes little time to remove all traces of farm, forest, streams, or other earlier features. What is emphasized here, within the context of a 'natural' image, is that sustainability planning requires that 'we' work with and not against nature (Williamson et al., 2003: 27). We must design our communities, our cities, in ways that enhance and maintain natural features, rather than erode or destroy them; this is not rocket science, but it does require political, corporate, and societal will. As McHarg (1969: 7) wrote: 'If one accepts the simple proposition that nature is the arena of life and that a modicum of knowledge of her processes is indispensable for survival and rather more for existence, health and delight, it is amazing how many apparently difficult problems present ready solution.'

The discussion that follows has three parts. The first briefly introduces the image of the city and nature, and the second provides a brief review of four environmental dynamics—or problems—common to Canada's cities. These serve to create an image and set the stage for the third part, which explores and critiques the notion of the sustainable city as an imprecise, halcyon concept but nevertheless an important semantic device in the discourse responding to environmental change. As the locales where most people in the developed world live, cities have great promise to affect the changes needed to reduce resource consumption and realize a sustainable society.

Nature and the City

Though they provide a tempting target, cities are hardly the sole cause of contemporary global environmental change. Deforestation, desertification, the degradation of freshwater resources, and the seemingly imminent collapse of marine ecosystems are major factors in global environmental decline. The roots of present-day catastrophic environmental change are sunk deep into the neo-liberal ideas that dominate national politics and the global economy. The direct impacts of urbanization in processes of physical change are complex and variable. Globally, urban regions have grown in different ways; they have varying densities and quite different patterns and rates of resource use and waste generation. It is accurate to say that cities can be an important, indeed primary element in regional environmental change. They are also significant as the locales where most globally altering decisions are made and where those who make such choices live—often isolated from the impacts of their decisions. As Canadians have become more urbanized, it may be that they have lost a connection to the Canadian landscape. Few Canadians have a strong sense of the rural areas where their food is produced. There may be occasional visits to a lake or campground, and many consider themselves 'environmentalists', which often means opposing logging, hunting, or other traditional land-based

activities. But this relatively recent *disconnect* makes many urbanites oblivious to the impacts that consumption and urban-based ideologies have on Canada's rural communities and natural areas.

Urbanization has four main impacts on nature. First, as urban areas grow they consume landscapes—forests, fields, wetlands, or shorelines are changed in ways that will most often render them unable to support natural systems. Second, even in those instances where landscapes are not wholly altered, fragmentation will occur. The transportation and utility corridors, and banal swaths of residential, commercial, and industrial development that characterize contemporary Canadian development, separate natural places and compromise the integrity of ecosystems. This leads to the eventual collapse of ever smaller islands of nature. Third, since cities are the places where more people increasingly live, they are the pre-eminent places of consumption. They require large quantities of global resources to maintain infrastructure, fuel growth, and support their inhabitants. Consumptive impacts are felt far beyond urban or even national boundaries. And fourth, the end result of consumption is pollution, which cities generate in increasing quantities as solid, liquid, and airborne wastes. These are rarely if ever managed within the city. The city externalizes the impacts of consumption, and may impose these on rural communities often quite distant from the places of waste generation.

In 1969 Ian McHarg stated that we must accept that nature is process, an interacting one that responds to laws and represents certain values and opportunities for human uses, albeit with definite limitations and even prohibitions. The present dominant form of urban growth largely disregards this fundamental reality. But this wilful ignorance marks a shift in the relationship between nature and community that has evolved quite rapidly over the last century, and most significantly, it can be argued, within the last five decades. As Calthorpe (1993: 25) comments:

> Communities historically were embedded in nature—it helped set both the unique identity of each place and the physical limits of the

community. Local climate, plants, vistas, harbours and ridgelands once defined the special qualities of every memorable place. Now, smog, pavement, toxic soil, receding ecologies, and polluted water contribute to the destruction of neighbourhood and home in the largest sense. We threaten nature and nature threatens us in return: sunlight causes cancer, air threatens our lungs, rain burns the trees, streams are polluted and poisonous, and soil is too often toxic.

We have entered an era where environmental issues are paramount, even though many choose not to acknowledge this and instead pursue actions that hasten global environmental decline. As places with great potential for realizing environmental efficiencies and effecting change for huge numbers of citizens within relatively small areas, cities hold promise for helping to achieve an imperative—the meaningful move towards an environmentally sustainable society—but such movement is slow.

Four Environmental Dynamics

The general vision of Canadian cities is one of livable, well-run urban areas with few substantial social, economic, or environmental problems. But as other authors in this book have shown, Canada's cities face substantial challenges in maintaining and enhancing their livability. If we consider the state of four common environmental dynamics that affect urban regions across Canada—air quality, clean water, waste water, and solid waste (garbage)—we see few reasons for being smug, and, indeed, have to conclude that we are far from achieving sustainability. In addition to the four dynamics outlined here, many important environmental issues affect Canada's cities—transportation, sprawl and growth management, and urban ecology. Most of these are addressed by other authors in this book (see Chapters 6, 12, 13, 19, and 21).

Air to See, Taste, and Touch

At the moment Canadian cities may not be facing conditions quite like the noxious brown clouds of Beijing, or Mexico City's legendary toxic air; but those who live in the orange/green air of a Toronto July or the thick grey haze that spreads from Vancouver up the Fraser Valley know that urban air quality in Canada is far from good. Most urban air pollution comes from our cars, factories, industrial plants and power stations, and even home furnaces. Levels of airborne particles can vary quite a bit depending on time of year and quantity of emissions from local or long-range sources. Summer can be especially bad. While smog is commonly associated with urban areas, nitrogen dioxide, volatile organic compounds, ozone, and fine particulate are transported by air currents from cities, impacting rural and even other urban areas over distances that range from several hundred to a few thousand kilometres (Environment Canada, 2001).[1] Toronto sometimes likes to blame the US Rust Belt for its air woes, but Ontario produces enough home-grown air effluent to account for a fair portion of Toronto's poor air quality.

Smog is now a common problem in major Canadian cities. Smog is the combination of ground-level ozone and airborne particles mixed with other atmospheric pollutants. While there have been modest improvements in air quality over the last decade, in the summer, cities such as Toronto, Waterloo, and Hamilton experience particularly poor conditions, causing warnings to be broadcast calling for the elderly and children to remain indoors. Environment Canada notes that the fine particles, those with diameters less than or equal to 2.5 micrometres ($PM_{2.5}$), pose the greatest threat to human health—they travel deepest into the lungs. Over the last 10 years ground-level ozone levels have not changed significantly across Canada, although they tend to be higher in eastern Canada. Levels are heavily dependent on the weather, with the highest levels occurring in the warmer months. Ground-level ozone is a concern principally in the Windsor–Quebec corridor and in the Lower Fraser Valley of British Columbia, areas where Canada's three major cities are found. While the ambient levels of several important pollutants (nitrogen dioxide, sulphur dioxide, carbon monoxide) have dropped between 1980 and 2000, emissions of volatile organic compounds have not shown improvement. The data indicate that many urban areas record daily particulate levels with great potential to cause adverse health effects. Improvements in clean air technology have occurred, but these are offset by rising urban populations and increases in the number of automobiles.

Car emissions are perhaps the most important contributor to urban air pollution. In some cities, such as Vancouver (which has little heavy industry), cars certainly account for the lion's share of air pollution. But driving is part of the daily lives of most Canadians. Reliance on the car is made essential by the way most communities are planned. Car use by Canadians has grown by about 10 per cent over the last decade, so much so that by 2000, for every 100 kilometres Canadians travelled, 74 kilometres were travelled by car. Between 1990 and 1999 fossil fuel used by cars had increased by 21 per cent. Canadians have also been buying greater numbers of fuel-inefficient pickup trucks and sport utility vehicles. The amount of kilometres travelled in these vehicles has almost tripled over the last two decades, from 10 per cent of personal vehicle travel in 1976 to 27 per cent in 2000.

Clean Water

Of all the surface water and groundwater used in Canada, 11 per cent is taken by municipalities. High water use has its costs, not just environmental but also economic. The cumulative costs of supplying drinking water (which in many cases must be treated), processing wastewater, and maintaining, expanding, and upgrading infrastructure are a heavy burden on municipal budgets. Many municipalities have been putting off costly infrastructure investments, but with time these costs will only increase. Canadian cities have aging water systems, which results in substantial losses of water. These 'leaks' can account for as much as 30 per cent of municipal water use. Water shortages are the result of drought, inappropriate uses, and demand that grows beyond the capacity of natural systems. When water is drawn down below recharge rates, especially in drought-prone areas, decreases in groundwater levels and stream flow will result. Such changes in turn affect ecosystem functions and impact aquatic and terrestrial habitat. But lower water levels and poor water quality not only have direct impacts on aquatic ecosystems and biodiversity, they can affect human health. Some Canadian municipalities have been plagued with 'boil water' advisories; in the Ontario community of Walkerton in 2000, polluted surface water and poor water quality management had catastrophic consequences for human health, and the same was true in the James Bay Native community of Kashechewan in northern Ontario in 2005. While these have been high-profile incidents, they are not isolated.

After Americans, Canadians are the highest water users in the world, using roughly twice as much per person as other industrialized countries.[2] In Canada, household water use accounts for more than half of all municipal water consumption. One factor contributing to high residential consumption rates is the lack of financial incentives for Canadians to conserve water.[3] The tendency in Canada has been to react to demand, not by managing it through pricing or other *consumption disincentives*, but rather by increasing water supply capacity. Demand management cannot negate all the impacts of growing urban populations, but it is an essential tool for addressing the limits imposed by supply and environmental degradation. Without decent funding Canadian cities will not be able to finance adequate water infrastructure. One funding source is volume-based pricing. It could help pay for clean water, and since water consumption is price-responsive it can lead consumers to use water more carefully. But there is resistance to such measures, and implementation will itself require new infrastructure investments.

Used Water

Most garden shops, hardware stores, and big-box home repair retailers sell a range of chemical fertilizers, herbicides, fungicides, and insecticides. Canadians apply these with varying degrees of skill. Cars leave tire and fuel residue and oil and other lubricants on our streets. A walk through most municipal parks reveals feces from pets whose owners will not 'stoop and scoop'. After each rain a good portion of these leavings will end up in the storm sewers of Canada's cities. Coupled with the wastewater drained from our homes, factories, and shops, Canadians deliberately or unthinkingly send a great array of polluting substances to their streams, rivers, lakes, and sea coasts.

The sewage and stormwater discharged from Canada's cities is a mix of disease-causing pathogens, decaying organic wastes, suspended solids, nutrients, sediment, and hundreds of measured chemicals, and no doubt hundreds more that are not routinely tracked. Each year Canadians generate 3 trillion litres of sewage (Sierra Club, 2004). Environment Canada (2003) says that municipal wastewater effluents represent one of the greatest threats to the quality of Canadian surface waters. The release of untreated or inadequately treated municipal wastewater effluents may put Canadians at risk from drinking water contaminated with toxins, bacteria, and protozoans. Canadians in many cities face health risks if they choose to swim in rivers or lakes that are part of their urban region. After a day or so of rain, storm sewers release an array of pollutants that make Toronto's beaches unusable for swimming. Few would swim in the Fraser River near Vancouver, and in Winnipeg the Red River no longer offers a clean respite from summer heat.

Depending on the level of treatment they provide, wastewater treatment plants can remove a good portion of some contaminants. By 1999, 78 per cent of Canada's municipal population sent their wastewater through secondary or tertiary treatment.[4] While this marks an increase from only 56 per cent in 1983, in a nation as affluent as Canada, with access to the best available technology and engineering experience, the rate should be 100 per cent. For over a decade the Sierra Club has conducted an evaluation of sewage treatment in 22 Canadian cities based on level of sewage treatment, volume of raw sewage discharged, compliance with laws and regulations, the type of disinfection used, sludge disposal method, state of combined sewer overflows, and the city's commitment to improvement. The Club publishes the results as a *Report Card*. The third *Report Card* came out in 2004 (Sierra Club, 2004) and provides a review of publicly available data for 22 Canadian cities. The image it imparts is a diverse one. Calgary, Edmonton, and Whistler, BC, are the best. Each has 100 per cent tertiary treatment with UV disinfection. But these are hardly Canada's major cities. Among the three largest, Montreal still discharges 3.6 billion litres of raw sewage into the St Lawrence River and produces more sewage per person than any other Canadian city—900 billion litres per year with only primary treatment. By 2001, Vancouver, despite years of improvement, was still discharging approximately 22 billion litres of untreated wastewater from combined (sanitary and storm) sewer overflows into Georgia Strait and the Fraser River.

Combined sewer overflows (where the contents of sanitary and storm sewers get mixed) are a management headache for Canadian cities and will require substantial infrastructure investments—something many cities have been delaying. The *Report Card* also notes that although Halifax has committed to building an advanced primary sewage treatment plant, the city still dumps 65.7 billion litres of raw sewage per year into the Atlantic. St John's has made a commitment to construct primary sewage treatment facilities, but it still puts 33 billion litres of raw sewage per year into the sea. The surprise is Victoria. Despite its genteel tidy image, Victoria annually pumps more than 34 billion litres of untreated effluent into the Strait of Juan de Fuca. Victoria is the only large Canadian city that discharges *all* of its sewage *raw,* with no real commitment to upgrade.[5]

Solid Waste

Garbage, or solid waste, is the by-product of consumption. Packaging in its many forms, food waste, paper, and a range of other waste materials all reflect the ability of humans to consume greater amounts of resources in unsustainable ways. Canada's largest city, Toronto, has struggled with solid waste management for several decades. Toronto generates about 2.9 million tonnes of household waste, but only about 32 per cent is recycled and some 1.25 million tonnes are trucked to Michigan (120 trucks a day) (Toronto, 2005a). Heavy transport trucks loaded with Toronto garbage are now a common feature on the drive between Toronto and the Michigan border.

Environment Canada notes that in just a two-year period (from 1998 to 2000) the per capita generation of waste increased by 10 per cent. Approximately 50 per cent of non-hazardous solid waste is produced by households, while the other 50 per cent comes from the industrial, commercial, and institutional sectors as well as from construction. Of all this waste, about 25 per cent is diverted from disposal and thus reused or recycled. Though disposal levels (waste not diverted to recycling or composting) remain high, there have been modest improvements in municipal waste management. Across Canada, during the same period waste diversion also increased by 10 per cent, though the waste diversion *rate* (total waste diverted divided by total waste generated) actually remained constant at 24 per cent.

The richer humans become the more they consume, and Canadians may well be the leading per capita producers of solid waste in the world. Excessive packaging, inefficient production processes, shoddy goods and poor durability, and rising consumption patterns all support waste generation that echoes trends in affluence and economic growth. North Americans love disposable goods. Our cities offer a glut of consumption opportunities; shopping has indeed become entertainment for many urban dwellers (see Chapter 16). Excessive waste generation is not limited to cities— people everywhere produce garbage. But for Canada's cities waste management is a particular problem because of the scale of garbage production, the challenge of finding a place to put it, and the cost of handling and disposing of it. Managing solid waste consumes land, material, and energy resources, and generates a range of toxic emissions and greenhouse gases. Waste management costs Canadians billions of dollars a year. In Toronto, from curbside pickup to final dumping, it costs about $117/tonne to ship garbage to Michigan (Toronto, 2005a). This adds up to an annual cost of $146.25 million. Even when we account for revenue from recycling, it costs about $80/tonne to recycle paper, glass, and plastics, which means that Toronto spends about $12 million per year to process 150,000 tonnes of recyclables (Toronto, 2005a).

Progress in Addressing Environmental Dynamics

The picture to emerge from the above discussion of the four dynamics is one of stagnating environmental conditions. Few environmental aspects of our cities have been substantially improved. Air quality, for instance, leaves little room for optimism. In an earlier edition of this book, Larry Bourne (2000: 42) commented that Canada's urban areas, on balance, continued to be pleasant places to live due in part to the relatively high standard of public services, which have been largely equitably distributed. While this remains true for the moment, the environmental quality of Canada's cities and their contribution to larger, diffused impacts on the environment are major sources of concern. Managing growth and moving away from the dominant suburban form poses perhaps the greatest challenge to Canada's cities. Canadians seem unable to break from patterns of development and consumption that cannot be sustained.

Urbanization now means the sprawl of low-density developments characterized by tract housing, parking lots, strip malls, big-box retailing, stale architecture and poor construction quality, ever wider roads, and few pedestrians.[6] Urban growth has fallen short of its promise; suburban post-industrial culture is now seen as the root of many urban environmental and social ills (Calthorpe, 1993: 18). In order to maintain the urban quality of life that Canadians take for granted and to achieve the enhancements that are necessary, significant changes will have to be made to the way we plan our cities and consume resources. The current attention given to the idea of sustainable cities is in part recognition of this. But sustainability is a difficult notion to apply—largely because it requires fundamental changes to the way the most affluent humans live their lives.

The Sustainable City

The present interest in the sustainable city emerged almost two decades ago, after the Brundtland Commission's (WCED, 1987) report popularized the expression 'sustainable development'. Sustainability is now commonly presented as melding ecological, social, and economic imperatives, while ensuring a degree of equity in terms of access to opportunity (Dale, 2001; Robinson et al., 1996; Serageldin, 1995; Voinov and Smith, 1998). Notwithstanding variances in definitions, sustainability is about creating a setting where balance governs action among the needs and means of the human and non-human environment. What has proved to be contentious is the word 'development' (Davies, 1997; Shearman, 1990). Sustaining development has taken precedence over sustaining nature, so that many in the environmental movement today speak of 'sustainable livelihoods' and 'environmental justice', leaving 'development' out of the equation.

Planning for urban sustainability also lacks a universal model and there are few good applied or operational examples. Some may interpret sustainability as promising something that may ultimately be unattainable—a sense that conditions can stay the same, or that a particular type of growth will always be possible. So if sustainability is such an illusive objective, how do we make it tractable? One answer may be in accepting that sustainability is not about keeping certain unnatural systems as they are; sustainability is a call for change cloaked in a term originally adopted to comfort those who would like things to continue as they are. Ultimately, we should be seeking to sustain only one element—the integrity of natural systems. The current nature of economic growth is unsustainable, and many aspects of our social systems should not be sustained but

should instead be made genuinely equitable and pluralistic. Reducing the consumption of natural resources is a key imperative in planning for urban sustainability. In this respect, certain tangible practicable actions can bring us closer to a state of sustainability:

1. Reduce landscape consumption (Figure 20.1). Increase densities for housing, industry, retailing, and services; more people living on less land translates into more efficient use of public transit, roads, water, energy, and waste services.
2. Design buildings and urban systems to minimize the waste of energy, water, and land (Figure 20.2). Improve building quality; integrate sustainability into building codes and ensure adequate enforcement of codes. Blend uses and build for longevity. Growth in a sustainable city requires innovation in *new* development for the blending of retail, services, residential, and even manufacturing uses within the same buildings, neighbourhoods, or blocks.
3. Greatly reduce reliance on the car.
4. Create incentives to reduce the consumption of goods that lead to undue waste production. While this issue is largely beyond the municipal mandate, local governments can support waste reduction by advocating policies and laws that require reduced packaging and better recycling.
5. Plan strategically by investing in public infrastructure and engaging in genuinely proactive thought about the cities we need and want, rather than following the reactionary processes that have led to the fractured, uninspiring landscapes that characterize so much of new urban development in Canada. We must also accept that some places simply should not be developed.

The many facets of the built environment play a major role in the human impact on the natural environment and on the quality of life. Sustainable design integrates resource efficiency, healthy buildings and materials, and ecologically and socially sensitive land use with an aesthetic sensitivity that inspires and ennobles (UIA/AIA, 1993). Instead, despite much talk about sustainable cities, the

Figure 20.1   **Innovative Densities**

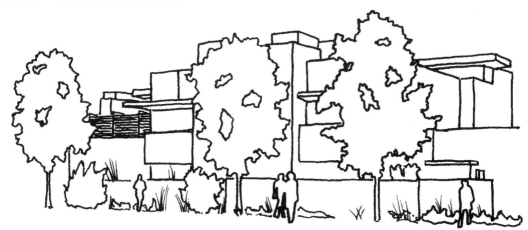

Architect Duncan Bates suggests that increased densities and mixed use do not have to mean large towers. Higher densities can be achieved through innovative and engaging design, with quiet streetscapes woven into contiguous and connected green space. *(Drawing by Duncan Bates)*

dominance of suburban form in the growth of Canadian cities tells us that sustainability rhetoric lacks applicability. Canadians have quietly accepted a sort of 'lowest common denominator' in urban design, where the best that can often be said of new development is that it is ordinary.

While sustainability may seem a strategic concept, in reality it is a reactive notion; it emerges when it appears that business as usual is no longer possible (Hanna, 2005). Despite this, it has gradually become a more complex idea—one that has moved beyond an initial, simple emphasis on accommodating *development* while maintaining nature as capital stock. Today, sustainability is a nuanced idea subsuming a broader, more systemic recognition of the environment as encompassing the intertwined ecological, economic, and socio-cultural values and ethics, as well as the political dimensions, of society (Bryant, 1999; Dale, 2001; Shearman, 1990). Hempel (1999: 44) comments that sustainability, like other transformative ideas, promises change through a process of reflection and then choice, but ultimately the potential and influence of the concept are more a product of its ambiguity, rather than of any conceptual precision or clarity. There may be no value in aiming for a

universal meaning; rather, sustainability has a contextual rationality that depends on where it is applied and the needs and values of those seeking it (Shearman, 1990).

The permeable nature of sustainability makes it an attractive theme in planning because it excludes no one; environment, development, and social interests and the agendas they represent all find comfort in its vagueness and potential (Hanna, 2005). Yet despite some equivocation, sustainability maintains just enough coherence to spur diverse interests to move in a certain direction, even though the path is rarely well marked (Hempel, 1999). For planners, moving in this certain direction requires an integrative approach that melds social theory and environmental thinking with conflict resolution skills (Campbell, 1996). Although many would like to move in this direction, in *truth* few really know how to, some feel that it cannot be done within existing political bureaucratic structures, and others see sustainability in terms of sustaining growth. For example, in a case study of a Calgary planning initiative that resulted in the report 'Sustainable Suburbs', Davies (1997: 365) wryly notes that the objectives of the report were clearly stated in the subtitle, 'creating more fiscally, socially and

Figure 20.2 **Communal Spaces/Communal Gardens**

Sustainability proposes a different urban lifestyle, where community spaces can even become food gardens based on systems that recycle wastewater and large-scale composting. *(Drawing by Duncan Bates)*

sustainable communities', which was to be achieved within the context of accommodating growth and reducing costs. This is hardly an image of sustainability with nature in mind.

All this poses challenges for urban planners and the politicians and bureaucrats who work within the tensions created by competing interests. The difficulty for policy-makers is that if sustainability is a reactive concept, then thoughtful deliberation about responding to change, or anticipating it, becomes a challenge. When sustainability does become part of the planning and public policy discourse, planners and political decision-makers find that they are reacting to environmental degradation or conflict rather than engaging in strategic proactive thought. The sustainability discourse has become an extension of a reactionary process brought on by panic about the impacts of growing urban regions and attendant declining environmental quality.

The commitment to sustainability needs to be considered as more than an improbable ideal; it should form the basis of planning, development, and the renovation and construction of buildings. Sustainable cities must be seen in terms of their individual components—the buildings, streets, parks, and retail and industrial ingredients that make up communities and the cities that communities form in the aggregate. Though there are scattered examples of success, in practice architecture, development, and planning have yet to evolve in a way that embraces such a vision. The state of the four environmental dynamics outlined above suggests that Canadian cities have a long way to go before they reach sustainability. But there is reason for hope. Many Canadian cities are struggling with the need to develop and articulate new ideas about improving their social and environmental characteristics, but they are trying. Gradually, a range of pragmatic tools is emerging: innovative standards for building and community design; snippets of new funding for infrastructure investments; greenfield retention; new mixed-use development; affordable housing; and, in a few instances, some cities are making tough decisions about growth management. There is an increasing understanding that present forms of growth cannot be sustained and that nature is imposing very real limits on consumption. As places where the great majority will soon be living, cities will play an integral role in achieving a sustainable society.

Notes

1. Unless otherwise noted, the information and data I use in describing these four dynamics are taken from Environment Canada's *National Environmental Indicator Series* (Environment Canada, 2003). This source was chosen because it is readily accessible and provides a decent synopsis of current conditions. Environment Canada tends to be cautious; so if its information points to worsening conditions, which it does, then we know such problems exist.

2. While Canadian daily water use per person declined by about 4 per cent between 1991 and 1999, Canada's municipal population also increased, so the total daily municipal water consumption actually went up by 5 per cent during the same period.

3. Research has shown that households paying a flat rate for water used 50 per cent more water than households paying for water by volume used. But in order to charge for consumption by volume a water meter must be installed. As of 1999 only 57 per cent of Canada's municipal households had water meters.

4. Primary treatment removes some material through settling ponds. Secondary treatment removes suspended material and organic matter, and tertiary treatment removes target substances, such as phosphorus or pathogens. These additional levels of treatment use biological and/or chemical processes to further remove organic material, suspended solids, and other substances from the water. One of the impacts of improved treatment levels has been a reduction in phosphorus loadings. Even though there has been a 24 per cent increase in Canada's urban population (1983 to 1999), estimated loadings of phosphorus dropped by 44 per cent.

5. Neighbouring Washington state has denounced Victoria for pouring its raw sewage into Puget Sound.

6. There are those who make a clear distinction between that which is urban, by which they mean the central, dense, and usually older parts of the city, and suburban, which they define as low-density sprawl beyond the urban core and inner city. Originally, suburban was a locational designation—those areas at the edge of the city. Now 'suburb' evokes sprawl, a form that dominates urban growth in Canada.

Chapter 21

Metropolitan Form and the Environment
Hugh Millward

As cities grow, they mould themselves to their sites and settings, but in turn completely transform those environments. Both the moulding process and the subsequent environmental impacts can be viewed, analyzed, and planned at a range of spatial scales. Certain facets of urban-environmental interaction, however, are of particular concern at the mid-range or meso-scale. In planning terms, this meso-level focus corresponds to that of the metropolitan regional plan and to a lesser extent those of individual municipal or community plans.

Though geographers and planners have long studied the morphology or form of cities, there has been renewed interest in the topic over the past decade and recognition of its practical significance for the planning of efficient, livable, and environmentally sustainable metropolitan areas. This chapter begins with a brief review of the components of urban form, and their measurement and significance. Environmental controls on evolving urban form—operating both as constraints and attractors—are then reviewed, and typical patterns of laissez-faire development are considered.

The bulk of the chapter is devoted to the phenomenon of urban sprawl and attempts to control it or at least mitigate its negative impacts. Two interrelated approaches to its mitigation are considered. The first is watershed-based ecological planning ('designing with nature'), which aims to optimize the location and pattern of development. The second is 'smart growth', in which the emphasis is primarily on reduction of the urban footprint through 'growth management' and densification.

The Components of Urban Form

Urbanized areas may be defined in a variety of ways—usually as 'built-up' or developed area—with the intent being to differentiate their characteristic land-use and land-cover patterns from those of natural or rural areas.

Environmental and visual impacts of urban development are strongly related to the three components of urban form: land cover, land use, and built form. As development proceeds, land cover is converted from 'rough', many-layered vegetative surfaces to smooth artificial surfaces, which greatly decrease stormwater retention and increase surface wind speeds. Land cover also shifts from pervious to impervious surfaces. At least one-third of the surface is impervious, even in a low-density suburb—impervious surfaces include roofs, driveways, and roads. It follows that overall surface runoff is increased and retention of runoff is further reduced. Peak stormwater flows are thus several times higher than in the pre-development state and well beyond the capacity of the natural drainage systems. The proportion of impervious cover increases according to the density or intensity of land use: high-density housing areas (whether low- or high-rise) are often two-thirds impervious, and commercial or industrial areas have until recently been allowed to be close to 100 per cent impervious.

Land-use type and intensity also have environmental effects through the generation of vehicular traffic, which in turn causes various atmospheric pollutants, greenhouse gases, noise, and congestion.

Commercial areas and high-density employment nodes such as the downtown have particularly high trip-generation rates, and the planned separation of residential and employment areas has exacerbated both the number and length of vehicular trips. Strategic planning of the mix, density, and regional location of land uses can provide considerable control over not only the volume and location of trips, but over the mode employed: specifically, whether or not a large percentage of trips are by environmentally friendly public transport.

The size, shape, and massing of buildings, collectively termed 'built form', also have visual and environmental consequences, though primarily at a localized scale. Bulky and/or tall buildings can create severe wind-funnel effects (*venturi* effects), especially in the downtown 'concrete canyons' of Canada's major cities. Conversely, large and massed buildings are amenable to the environmental and economic advantages of district heating, produce lower per capita heat radiation, and allow the high densities necessary for transit-oriented development.

Environmental Influences on Urban Form

Broad patterns of urban development are shaped by four sets of factors. Classic models of urban growth have focused on the economic and technological sets, with particular emphasis on the land market as influenced by transportation technology. A third set concerns environmental processes (whether natural or modified) and a fourth set relates to the political process. Political influences—including land planning—tend to be derivative, in that they mediate between the other sets and attempt to resolve conflicts and incompatibilities.

In localized areas environmental factors may place absolute constraints on development, but at the metropolitan scale they should be viewed in a more probabilistic manner, as increasing or decreasing the likelihood of development, and advancing or retarding its timing (De Chiara, 1994; Ewing, 1996; McHarg, 1969; Thomas, 2002). Some metro-

politan areas face few major environmental barriers (e.g., Edmonton, London, Ottawa), while others are tightly constrained (e.g., Vancouver, Halifax, Hamilton).

In considering environmental influences on development patterns, we should be aware of at least five differing—and at times opposing—viewpoints: those of developers, urban households (the main 'consumers' of development), planners, politicians, and environmentalists. However, household preferences are indirectly factored into developments through both the market mechanism and the political process, while the concerns of environmentalists often dovetail with those of municipal planners, engineers, and politicians. Major environmental factors and their spatial impacts are illustrated in Figure 21.1.

Bedrock geology (Figure 21.1a) is seldom a major concern, but takes on great significance where hard bedrock appears at or near the surface (as in glacially scoured areas of metamorphic or intrusive rock, such as those surrounding Halifax, St John's, and Sudbury). Developers' costs for roads, sewers, and foundations are greatly increased, as are some municipal costs. Another consideration is the permeability of bedrock, particularly where large-lot subdivisions are serviced by on-site wells and septic fields.

Surficial geology and soils can be important in several ways: developers will gravitate to areas with sufficient overburden to minimize the need for blasting, while planners and environmentalists will seek to minimize construction on clay soils, which are unstable and produce severe sedimentation problems.

Topography affects developer costs through the need for land-grading in steep areas and drainage in flat areas (Marsh, 1998). Flooding is of concern to all parties in flat areas. Prestige residential areas are attracted to areas of topographic contrast ('scenic edges' on Figure 21.1b) or to waterfront areas, while industry prefers large tracts of flat land and will tolerate flood hazards. In Greater Vancouver, for example, prestige housing climbs the mountain slopes of North and West Vancouver, while industry lines the Fraser River and its North Arm.

Figure 21.1   **Environmental Influences on Urban Development Patterns**

a) Geology (bedrock & surficial)

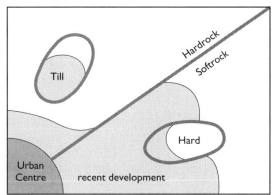

b) Topography & Scenery

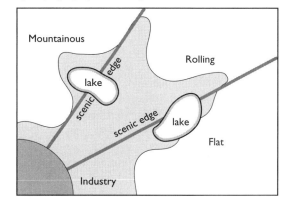

c) Watersheds & Sewersheds

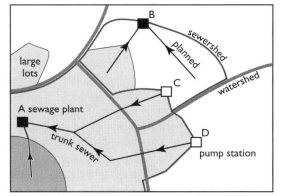

d) Reserves

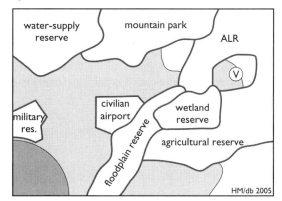

NB: maps show unrelated cases

Groundwater can be very important in areas where drinking water is provided by private 'on-site' wells. Low-density housing development is attracted to areas with sufficient and reliable supply (e.g., permeable sedimentary rocks such as sandstone), and avoids areas of impermeable rock, deep water table, or poor chemical qualities (e.g., arsenic or other toxins). The latter has been an issue around Halifax.

Surface waters (rivers, lakes, and wetlands) are important in relation to flooding, recreation, and scenery, but also often provide municipal water supply. When they do, development is often disallowed from lake margins or even the entire watershed.

Wetlands, though still often viewed as a nuisance by developers, are increasingly protected by planners and municipal engineers as an important functional component of the storm drainage system. Environmentalists treasure them for their special habitat.

Watersheds and sewersheds strongly affect where and when development can occur, since municipal trunk sewers and treatment plants are expensive to provide and, as far as possible, must rely on gravity drainage. Central sewer services require a large drainage area, with the treatment plants (A and B in Figure 21.1c) located downstream at locations where effluent can be fully diluted (on the coast, or a large lake or river). Sewage from smaller watersheds can be pumped over low drainage divides (C and D in Figure 21.1c), while in unserviced watersheds 'large-lot' development has been the main option (though 'cluster development' using shared septic fields is increasingly used).

Along and to either side of the Oak Ridges Moraine north of Toronto, the construction of trunk sewers has both followed and led high-density development. Of particular significance have been the Newmarket and Aurora force-mains, which pump sewage south over the moraine, and the King City connector, which has enabled development in Nobleton and King City.

Flora and fauna increasingly are considerations shaping urban form. Developers now recognize that retention of mature trees (particularly hardwoods) can enhance the marketability of residential communities. Municipal planners and engineers are conscious of the need for vegetation retention to minimize erosion and flooding, and feel pressure from environmentalists to identify and protect habitats of endangered or rare species.

Figure 21.1d suggests how a variety of government-designated reserves can strongly shape patterns of development. Some reserves are largely ecological (such as wetlands), some have more direct utility (water-supply reserves, floodplains), and some are multi-functional. Agricultural land reserves (ALR) protect prime agricultural lands (typically defined as Canada Land Inventory classes 1 to 3) from development, but they are also deliberately employed as greenbelts to contain and shape the evolving urban form. Note on the figure that lands surrounding the village (v) are exempt from the ALR and have attracted leapfrog development. In Canada, agricultural land reserves were first used forcefully and extensively in the Fraser delta and became an important factor in the Greater Vancouver Regional Plan.

Environmental Consequences of Urban Sprawl

The historical links between transportation technology and urban form are well known. In 1970, John Adams presented a four-stage graphic model of urban structural evolution related to personal modes of transportation, to which enhancements and a fifth stage were added in 1992 by Truman Hartshorn (Adams, 1970; Hartshorn, 1992). The five stages of the Adams-Hartshorn model describe the typical scale and shape of urban development as it evolves in an unconstrained or laissez-faire land market. In Canadian terms the key form characteristics are as follows:

1. Walking/Horsecar Era (to *c.* 1890): small, compact, very dense.
2. Electric Streetcar Era (*c.* 1890–1925): star-shaped, dense centre, medium-density spokes.
3. Motorbus and Early Automobile Era (*c.* 1925–55): star-shaped with light exurban scatter.
4. Early Freeway Era (*c.* 1955–80): extensive low-density tract suburbs, plus discontinuous exurban halo.
5. Beltways and Suburban Downtowns (*c.* 1980–present): pockets of suburban concentration, with continuous exurban halo.

In all but the last era, metropolitan areas have been expanding outward far more rapidly than population growth alone would warrant, so that the overall density gradient has declined in height and slope, and average land consumption per capita has increased. Judged by average lot size, the heyday of sprawl in North America was during the 1950s and 1960s, when most households acquired a car, and zoning constraints on development in the peri-urban zone barely existed. In the United States sprawl was often exacerbated by the push of 'white flight' (see Chapter 2), but in Canada sprawl was less severe and mostly fuelled by the pull of cheap land and housing. Sprawl has continued almost unabated in the United States, but has moderated in most Canadian urban fringes.

In physical terms, sprawl is automobile-dependent development characterized by low net densities and extremely low gross densities, which proceeds piecemeal and in leapfrog fashion, without overall co-ordination. Such development discourages extension of piped water and sewer services. On-site services (wells and septic systems) are thereby often necessitated; their use locks in a cadastre of large lots and precludes subsequent densification. Figure 21.2 shows the process around Halifax, where extremely low land values and lack of planning controls promoted an exaggerated form of sprawl after 1950. Already by 1960 ribbons of lots were emerging along the sparse rural road network. By 1980 these ribbons were continuous, and 'backfilling' was creating subdivisions behind the main routes (Millward, 2000), notably at Lake Echo, Fall River, and Hatchet Lake. Bedford, Lower Sackville, and Cole Harbour grew as more compact nodes, since they were selected in 1962 for planned communities based on central sewer and water services

(their deep till overburden promising low development costs) (Millward, 2002). Between 1980 and 2000, lot creation was rampant on all privately owned lands (i.e., those not reserved as Crown lands, provincial parks, military reserves, or water-supply areas), but particularly close to paved roads and in areas with a scattering of till, such as Fall River and Hammonds Plains. Shorelines at the head of St Margaret's Bay and on larger lakes also attracted subdivision activity.

While sprawl is almost universally condemned by academics, planners, and environmentalists (Bourne, 2001a), it is worth reminding ourselves that it occurs for reasons and must therefore be

Figure 21.2 **Time Periods of Large-Lot Subdivisions in the Halifax Urban Fringe**

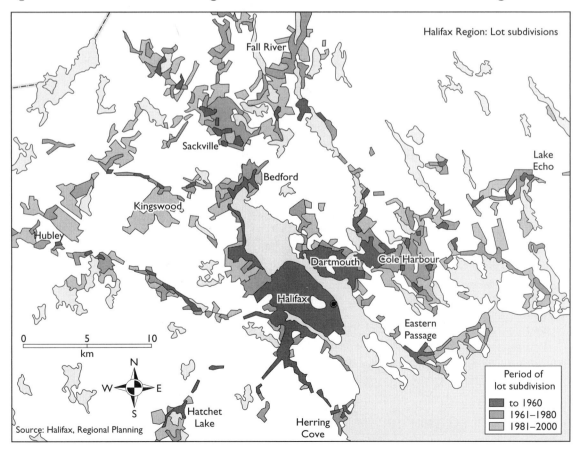

perceived by some as beneficial. The creators of sprawl are rural landowners (often farmers), land speculators (often banks or insurance companies), and developers, often encouraged by local politicians and chambers of commerce in the small towns and townships of the rural–urban fringe. Their market is the upwardly and outwardly mobile middle class, each household seeking their personal acre of the Canadian or American dream, in fulfillment of Frank Lloyd Wright's vision of Broadacre City.

Sprawl may be more empathetically re-labelled as 'country-estate' or 'large-lot' development, and does indeed have specific advantages for individuals, if not for society or the environment (Table 21.1). It is economically efficient, since it works through the 'hidden hand' of the housing market to provide households with maximum choice (of location, lot size, and house type) at minimum dollar cost (Ewing, 1997; Gordon and Richardson, 1997). It allocates farm and forest land in the urban fringe to its 'highest and best' economic use (i.e., that providing highest return), and imposes no restrictions on the rights of landowners. The commercial and industrial variants of sprawl provide merchants and industrialists with plenty of cheap space in peripheral locations adjacent to major highways.

It can of course be argued that urban sprawl's advantages, even to individual households or firms, are often short-term or illusory. The country atmosphere and slow pace of life are rapidly eroded, as more and more exurbanites seek their rural idyll (Kunstler, 1993) (see Chapter 13). Though those arriving early try to block further development (Walker, 2003), a kind of 'tragedy of the commons' is played out, and all suffer from increasing traffic congestion, overcrowded schools, loss of heritage features and community charm, landscape degradation, and a variety of pollution issues.

Two impact categories amenable to measurement and quantification have received particular attention in the planning literature. The first relates to provision of urban infrastructure and services, which can be excessively expensive or totally impractical when densities fall below critical thresholds (Burchell et al., 2002; Carruthers and Ulfarsson, 2003; Speir and Stephenson, 2002) (see Chapter 7). Several studies in both Canada and the United States have assessed municipal costs per capita of housing developments at varying net densities, dividing them into infrastructure capital costs (roads, sewers, sewage plants, and water supply), infrastructure operating costs, social services capital costs (for schools, fire halls, and police stations), and social services operating costs. In general, both capital and operating costs increase linearly with lot road frontages (if we include private well and septic costs in exurban areas), and hence decrease in negative exponential fashion against density (Burchell et al., 2002; Nelson et al., 1995).

A second set of quantifiable impacts from sprawl concerns its negative effects on the environment. A large literature documents a host of environmental costs (e.g., Frumkin et al., 2004; Hasse and Lathrop, 2003; Johnson, 2001), against which we can set only a few questionable benefits (Table 21.1). Sprawl produces high rates of per capita land consumption (a large 'footprint' on the land), leading to unnecessary loss of prime farmlands, areas of high scenic value, and wildlife habitats. Since it is characterized by piecemeal development, it also leads to fragmentation of remaining habitats, farmlands, and green spaces, which downgrades their viability or functionality.

Of particular concern are the impacts of sprawl on woodlands, wetlands, and surface water bodies, all of which perform vital natural functions. Woodlands sequester carbon and help to reduce global warming, while also providing useful habitats. Wetlands filter pollutants and also act as natural sponges to absorb storm water and help regulate stream flows. Some argue, however, that in eastern North America sprawl has encouraged vast acreages to revert from agricultural crops or grasses back to woodland and that intensive agriculture is considerably more polluting than extensively managed estate lots. Regarding degradation of surface water quality and hydrological flow regimes, it is also arguable that sprawl spreads or dilutes the impact of urban development. In contrast, intensive

Table 21.1   **Costs and Benefits of Residential Sprawl**

Affected Groups or Resources	Costs	Benefits
Participating landowners/farmers	Rise in assessments and property taxes, incompatibilities with farming	Capital gains (potential or actual), maximum land rights
Land speculators/ developers	Larger developers disadvantaged	Large and open land market, lack of planning controls, maximum land rights, small developers advantaged
Participating households	Lengthy commutes, high transport costs, lack of public transit, on-site sewage costs, crowded schools, lack of public and private services	Low-cost housing, privacy, personal space, fresh air, rural lifestyle, perceived lack of crime and social problems
Pre-existing rural communities	Breakdown in social cohesion, loss of heritage landscapes and buildings	'Fresh blood', enhanced service provision, new local employment
Peri-urban (fringe) municipalities	Capital and operating costs for enhanced services (schools, roads, police, fire, etc.)	Increased property tax revenues, new service industry
Central city/inner suburbs	Loss of population and tax base, loss of employment, rise in crime and social problems	Less need for expansion of central water and sewer services
Society at large	Spatial separation of social and cultural groups (social polarization), inter-municipal inequities, loss of valued common resources, 'hidden' subsidies to road transport	Land rights, freedom of consumer choice, use of 'hidden hand' to minimize housing costs overall
Land resources	Excessive land consumption (footprint), loss of prime farmlands, habitat loss, scenic degradation	Growth in private forest and bush on estate lots
Water resources	Degradation of water quality (sediments, nutrients), loss of wetlands, degraded flow regimes (increased flooding)	Impacts of development spread widely (diluted)
Atmospheric resources	Increased output of exhaust gases, greenhouse gases, increased smog, highway noise	Impacts of development spread widely (diluted)

developments—characterized by high proportions of impervious surfaces—concentrate impacts in a small number of watersheds but can have drastic localized impact in those areas.

By definition, urban sprawl is associated with a highly scattered pattern of land uses and activities, and thus with excessively long journeys to workplace, shopping, school, and recreation. Low settlement densities cannot support public transit, so almost all journeys are by automobile. Exurbanites undertake more motorized trips than central-city dwellers, and average trip length is longer, so total vehicle kilometres are three to four times higher, resulting in large dollar and time costs to exurban households (Burchell et al., 2002: Part 3). The environmental impacts of all this unnecessary travel are also large, and are borne by society as a whole. There are increases in polluting exhaust gases such as carbon monoxide, ozone, sulphur dioxide, and nitrogen oxide, and in particulates, which combine to produce toxic smog. There are similar increases in greenhouse gases, thus contributing to global warming (20 per cent of carbon dioxide in the United States is produced by vehicles).

Ecological and Landscape Approaches to Urban Development

All forms of urban development—including sprawl—can benefit from sensitive planning, whether the primary aim is to reduce land-use incompatibilities, minimize development costs, or curtail environmental degradation (a balance of the three is normally sought). The ecological and landscape approaches to planning are concerned specifically with the environment, and increasingly underlie land-use planning at all scales. While the term 'ecology' implies concern with vegetation and habitat, the term 'landscape' suggests a broader focus, bringing in landforms, hydrology, and scenery. Urban environmental planning has a long pedigree, going back at least to Patrick Geddes, and is particularly associated with Ian McHarg's 'design with nature' approach (Baldwin, 1985; Daniels and Daniels, 2003; Hough, 1995; Marsh, 1998; McHarg, 1969). The concept of sustainable development is integral and central to such planning, and in practical terms the key planning unit is the watershed.

We can split environmental planning techniques into three broad categories, although in practice various combinations and hybrid techniques are employed.

Economic land capability analysis (or land suitability analysis) focuses on greenfield development costs for specific types of urban development. It employs geologic, topographic, hydrologic, soil, and vegetation data to estimate and map full development costs to the developer or municipality, including costs associated with risks (e.g., floods, earthquakes).

McHargian landscape analysis is concerned both with the land's suitability for development and with its intolerance to it. McHarg selected key natural conditions/processes and noted that development suitability was inversely related to intolerance (e.g., flat lands are both suitable and tolerant; marshes are neither suitable nor tolerant). While McHarg refined his techniques over time, his analysis employed transparent overlay mapping of up to 30 natural factors, with high intolerance shown by dark tones. When all factors are superimposed, the most suitable areas for development are graphically revealed by the lightest tones.

Resource value assessment may be viewed as an attempt to quantify McHarg's graphic approach. It employs econometric techniques to estimate the value to society (say, per hectare per year) of land, water, and even atmospheric resources and the costs of their destruction or impairment. Shadow-pricing is employed to translate all costs and benefits into a common unit of account (usually dollars). Such pricing is fraught with difficulties, and the technique is (literally) much less transparent than McHarg's.

All three approaches to environmental planning have benefited from modern computing power, but McHarg's overlay technique in particular is suitable for use with geographic information systems. Though McHarg avoided explicit weightings for his physical factors (relying instead on colour tones), we can easily employ such weightings using a GIS and produce composite maps of development costs and benefits. Figure 21.3 shows generalized results from an early GIS study for the 1975 Halifax regional plan—the Metropolitan Area Planning

Figure 21.3 **Natural Land Capability Ratings in the Halifax Urban Fringe**

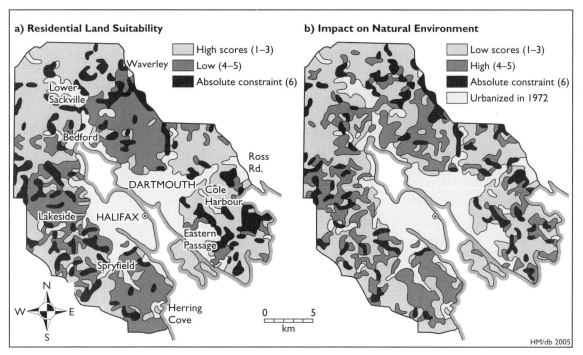

Source: Generalized from Nova Scotia, Department of Development (1973).

Commission (MAPC) plan. This *Natural Land Capability* study (Nova Scotia, 1973) compiled maps both for development suitability and environmental impacts, with each map showing ratings for small quadrants (each 14.6 ha) on a six-point scale. The worst-case rating (6) on each map represents an absolute constraint to development, such as lakes, marshes, bogs, and floodplains. Low scores indicate either low development costs (high development capability) or low environmental impacts.

Six physical factors were used to compute the composite ratings for residential development suitability (Figure 21.3a), with particular emphasis given to depth of overburden and slope. Extensive areas of low suitability (high costs) occur to the west and south of the Halifax peninsula and between Bedford and Dartmouth (areas of harder rock,

minimal till, and/or more rugged topography), while areas of thicker till around Lower Sackville and east of Dartmouth have high suitability.

Figure 21.3b was derived using only four variables (soil type, slope, tree density, and surface hydrology), with the composite index representing expected degrees of erosion and sedimentation produced by development. In keeping with McHarg's observations, areas of lower environmental impact tend also to have higher development suitability. MAPC planners selected large blocks of land with these two characteristics that could also be serviced with central sanitary sewage at low cost. The 1975 regional plan thus recommended major residential expansion in Bedford–Sackville and in Cole Harbour, and minimal development to the west and south of Halifax.

A second example of the regional impact of ecological planning is the Oak Ridges Moraine Conservation Plan (Ontario, 2002). This is an ecologically based plan for land use and resource management in a 160-km-long band of territory north of Toronto, from Caledon in the west to Coburg in the east. It is designed to protect and manage ecological, hydrological, and agricultural resources in this important 'headwater' drainage area, and to severely limit urban and exurban encroachment, with the dual purposes of ecological sustainability and urban growth management. The Oak Ridges plan was prepared and adopted in 2001 by the Ontario provincial government. It overrides existing municipal plans and requires municipalities to prepare detailed watershed plans (which relate environmental management to land use) and water budget plans (to maintain the sustainability and quality of ground and surface water resources).

Figure 21.4 shows the plan area due north of Toronto, the portion that is most contested in terms of urban expansion. This section contains about one-quarter of the total moraine area. The figure shows the four broad categories of land use designated by the plan, with existing areas of development superimposed. In order of development restriction (most to least) the categories are as follows:

- *Natural core areas* (38 per cent of total plan area): well-forested areas of important habitat and

Figure 21.4   **Central Section of the Oak Ridges Moraine Conservation Plan**

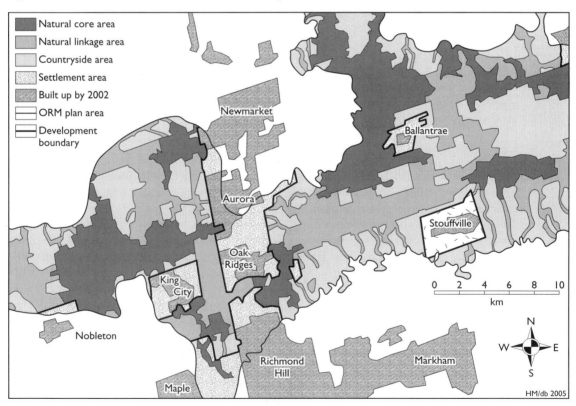

Note: White area is both outside the ORM plan area and non-built-up.
Source: Ontario, Municipal Affairs and Housing (2002).

water resources, within which only conservation, forestry, and agriculture are permitted.

- *Natural linkage areas* (24 per cent): less fragile areas adjacent to or linking core areas, within which forestry, farming, and aggregate-quarrying are allowed.
- *Countryside areas* (30 per cent): largely agricultural areas, within which prime agricultural lands (Canada Land Inventory categories 1 to 3) are fully protected from development and other lands may be developed for residential subdivisions only with strict restrictions.
- *Settlement areas* (8 per cent): areas adjacent to existing towns and suburbs, delineated 'to focus and contain urban growth' through the use of central sewer and water services and 'transit-supportive densities'.

As Figure 21.4 suggests, much of the area designated for settlement expansion in the Oak Ridges plan lies due north of Toronto, where development pressures are greatest and where existing sewer, water, and transport infrastructure can be used most cost-effectively. The plan allows Richmond Hill, Maple, and Aurora to expand onto the moraine and provides limited growth for smaller communities lying on the moraine. Conversely, it strongly protects two large 'core' blocks, plus almost all lakes, wetlands, ravines, and valleys. The Oak Ridges conservation plan embodies and exemplifies most 'best-practice' policies regarding ecological protection on metropolitan margins.

Smart Growth: Urban Containment and Transit-Oriented Development

The strategies for containment of sprawl are various in their details but similar in essentials. The main ideas were proposed by Ebenezer Howard and the Garden City movement around 1900 and were fully implemented in the Greater London (England) Plan of 1944 (Hall, 1988: 164–73): a tight development boundary surrounded by an extensive greenbelt, within which development would be severely curtailed. Development needs would be met by high-density infill within the development boundary

and the building of free-standing new towns beyond it. The plan was largely successful, owing to the negation (through nationalization) of most land development rights and their replacement with a development permit system (DPS).

The two-pronged development boundary and greenbelt approach has been widely adopted in Britain and elsewhere (Grayson, 1990), but has only recently taken hold in North America, owing to its need for 'un-American' restrictions on land rights. The state of Oregon led the way in the United States by fixing an urban growth boundary (UGB) for metropolitan Portland in 1979 (Harvey and Works, 2002). In Canada, the British Columbia government initiated restrictions on Vancouver's expansion through its agricultural land reserve legislation (1973), and a comprehensive strategy for urban containment was central to the Livable Region strategy developed in 1992–5 by the Greater Vancouver Regional District (Tomalty, 2002).

Strong control of peri-urban development is increasingly labelled and promoted as *growth management* (Carruthers, 2003; Daniels, 1999; Heim, 2001; Nelson et al., 1995), and is a major component in the related concepts of smart growth (Alexander and Tomalty, 2002; Daniels, 2001; Danielsen et al., 1999; Filion, 2003; Pim and Ornoy, 1996) and transit-oriented development (TOD) (Dock and Swenson, 2003). Of 12 major planks in the loosely assembled smart growth platform, seven may be realized or enhanced through urban containment: principles 1 through 5 (Table 21.2) relate primarily to planning at the regional and/or municipal scale, whereas principles 9 and 10 apply only at the local scale (though note that principle 9 works in tandem with principle 4). Principles 2 and 3 are directly related to the tenets of ecological landscape planning: higher-density development and compact urban form help minimize the urban footprint and preserve farmland, scenery, and environmentally valuable landscapes. Principles 1, 4, 5, 9, and 10, in contrast, require compact and higher-density development primarily to promote public transit and 'active transportation' (walking, bicycling, rollerblading, etc.). These principles are best realized when employment and residential areas are

Table 21.2 **Key Principles of Smart Growth**

No.	Applicable Scale (Regional, Municipal, Local)	Principle
1	R	Undertake broad regional planning that integrates land use and transportation.
2	RML	Preserve green space, environmentally sensitive areas, scenery, and farmland.
3	RM	Make full use of existing urban land and infrastructure (high densities).
4	RM	Emphasize the use of public transit (and de-emphasize the private auto).
5	RML	Ensure all development is compact and directed primarily to existing communities.
6	ML	Create a range of housing choices (type, price, location).
7	ML	Mix compatible land uses within each neighbourhood.
8	ML	Encourage community collaboration in plan-making and development decisions.
9	L	Create neighbourhoods that promote walking and bicycling.
10	L	Foster attractive communities with a strong sense of place.
11	L	Encourage innovative, attractive, and environmentally friendly civic design.
12	L	Make the development approval process predictable, timely, fair, and cost-effective.

Source: After Pim and Ornoy (1996).

proximate or co-extensive, a high proportion of the population lies within easy walking distance (500 metres) of both bus stops and linear trails, and (for high-capacity transit routes) large concentrations of people, jobs, and services are clustered around transit stations.

Urban containment strategies normally involve the delineation of an urban growth boundary, defining a growth zone or 'urban envelope' sized to accommodate anticipated development needs over the time horizon of the plan and within which central sewer and water services will be extended. Beyond these essentials, however, a range of options is available, as illustrated in Millward (2005). The tightness of the UGB may vary greatly, depending on the accommodation period, plan-revision period, rate of household growth, planned density levels, and desired degree of land oversupply. In Japan and Britain, sufficient land is supplied to accommodate only five years of growth at high densities, with no provision for higher rates of growth. In Canada, those metropolitan areas with UGBs typically set them more loosely, to accommodate 15 to 40 years of growth at moderate densities, with some allowance for oversupply (and hence market competition). Within such long-term growth boundaries, interim boundaries may be set in order to phase development in a logical and coherent pattern.

Variations are also possible in strategic patterns of growth. The main options (Hodge, 1998: 333) are (1) a single *compact* built-up area, with new development designed to 'round off' the perimeter and minimize the length of the city/country edge, (2) *axial growth* along one or more high-capacity transit routes, leading to a star-shaped urban form, with interstitial 'green wedges', and (3) a *city with satellites* pattern, in which the main urban envelope is accompanied by several secondary envelopes—encircling neighbouring towns or villages, or even entirely new overspill communities. In practice, elements of all three strategic patterns are typically considered (e.g., the three alternative growth patterns developed for the Halifax region [Halifax Regional Municipality, 2004a]) and a hybrid metropolitan plan emerges.

Strong containment requires strict development control outside the growth boundary, either through widespread zoning of 'rural reserves' for agricultural, environmental, or scenic protection, or through the blanket use of a development permit system with no as-of-right development allowed. In Canada, the latter approach is difficult to justify legally or to achieve politically, so that various types of rural reserve are more typically employed. In addition to rural reserves, there is also the notion of an 'urban reserve', lying beyond the current growth boundary in an area with long-term suitability for centrally serviced development. In the absence of controls, such areas frequently attract large-lot development, with widely spaced roads and on-site services. These 'country estate' subdivisions effectively pre-empt the provision of central sewer services, since they cannot later be retrofitted to urban or suburban lot sizes and density levels. Urban reserves disallow such pre-emptive large-lot development and provide for long-term expansion of the UGB. They may be realized through municipal land banking (as practised by Saskatoon, Regina, and Edmonton) or through zoning policies (e.g., the draft Halifax regional plan: Halifax Regional Municipality, 2005).

In all Canadian provinces the norm in the city's countryside is still as-of-right development, albeit typically with large minimum lot sizes or with controls on the timing and size of subdivisions. However, the trend is to the increasing use of rural

reserves. Ontario recently moved furthest in this direction, with legislation of its Greenbelt Plan (Ontario, 2005c). This plan builds on earlier protective legislation for the ecologically sensitive Niagara Escarpment and Oak Ridges Moraine, but incorporates these areas into a much broader greenbelt to contain and manage growth in the Golden Horseshoe conurbation (the adjacent metropolitan areas of Oshawa, Toronto, Hamilton, and St Catherines–Niagara). Beyond a tightly drawn UGB, the greenbelt arcs in a 10- to 40-km-wide belt, and consists of:

1. the Oak Ridges Moraine plan area;
2. the Niagara Escarpment plan area;
3. protected countryside lands, divided into natural system lands, agricultural system lands, and settlement areas.

Natural and agricultural system lands are further subdivided according to their features and functions, and have varying degrees of protection from development. Settlement areas comprise hamlets, villages, and small towns within the greenbelt, which are allowed modest growth, but only on the basis of central sewer and water services. The plan is a key environmental and growth management tool, since all municipal planning decisions must be in conformity with it. It will be complemented by the Greater Golden Horseshoe Growth Plan (Ontario, 2005b), a conceptual strategy for economic, transportation, and land-use patterning within the growth boundary.

Figure 21.5 presents growth management strategies for two medium-sized urban areas that have recently completed regional plans. The Waterloo and Halifax plans each employ growth boundaries to delimit areas within which central services will be extended and beyond which very little development will be allowed. In Waterloo Region's plan (approved in 2003) the UGB is termed the 'Countryside Line' and is drawn to accommodate 40 years of population growth (Waterloo Region, 2003). The boundary restricts development to the three cities of Kitchener, Waterloo, and Cambridge and to the airport area in the intervening township of Woolwich. Encroachments onto

Figure 21.5 **Growth Management Strategies in the Waterloo and Halifax Regional Plans**

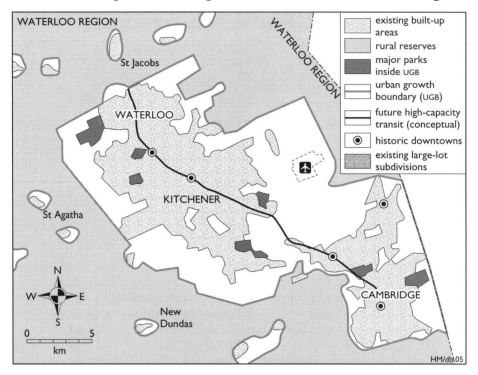

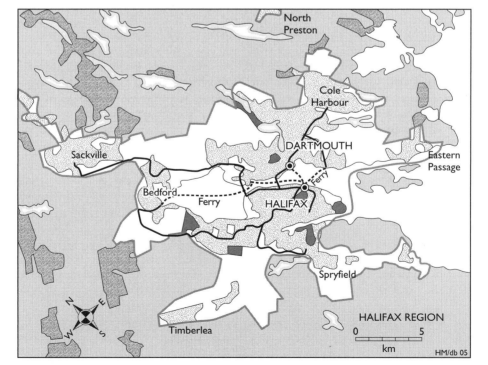

Class 1 farmland (mostly north and west of Waterloo) are minimized. Within the UGB, extensions to built-up areas will be made entirely by development permit and will maintain sharp and compact edges to surrounding agricultural lands. Beyond it, larger villages will have their own central services and be allowed some growth, but large-lot subdivision in the open countryside will be disallowed (with minor exemptions for farm kinship lots).

In the Halifax area, large-lot subdivisions have already spread widely (see Figure 21.2) and the emphasis is on limiting damage to forests and lakes rather than on preservation of farmlands. The draft regional plan (endorsed in 2005) draws a tight UGB by zoning 'urban reserve' lands, within which central water and sewer services will be provided over the 25-year life of the plan, and large-lot subdivision is disallowed. Within the UGB, an even tighter service-area boundary (not shown) delimits service extensions within 10 years. Urban development will be severely restricted in the Spryfield area, partly because of environmental sensitivity (Figure 21.3) and partly to avoid the expense and disruption of a bridge across the Northwest Arm. Beyond the UGB, strict environmental conditions will limit further large-lot development, and all but the smallest subdivisions must use shared septic systems and cluster design.

The Waterloo and Halifax regional plans are both strongly oriented to transit-oriented development (TOD) for environmental, fiscal, and quality-of-life reasons. Environmentally, TOD enables (and requires) intensification/densification along high-capacity bus or rail lines, thus reducing greenfield development. It also helps to shift people from private cars to public transport and reduce emission of pollutants and greenhouse gases. Fiscally, high-density corridors of development allow municipalities to save considerable capital and operating costs (for roads, sewers, waterlines, fire, police, etc.). Politically, TOD can be promoted as an important strategy for increasing the livability and attractiveness of Canadian cities, along European lines.

Waterloo region may have sufficient population (430,000 in the urban area) and growth rate

(1.5 per cent per year) to enable a viable light-rail transit (LRT) system within a decade or so. A single tramline is envisaged, connecting the city centres of Cambridge, Kitchener, and Waterloo (Figure 21.5). Within walking distance of this, the 'central transit corridor' will be re-urbanized and intensified, making full use of many brownfield industrial sites. As an interim measure, in 2005 the regional transit authority initiated a lower-capacity bus rapid transit (BRT) line along a similar route.

The Halifax urban area has less population (290,000) and a slower growth rate (0.7 per cent per year) than Waterloo region, so a rail system will be impractical for some time. Instead, regional planners have focused their growth centres along a radiating set of BRT lines, starting with routes to Cole Harbour and Sackville (initiated in 2005) and expanding later to Spryfield and Bedford West (Figure 21.5). A fast ferry will also connect Bedford to downtown Halifax.

Too Much Development or Too Little?

This chapter has explored interrelationships between urban form and the environment, viewed at the metropolitan scale. Even in the absence of planning, environmental factors attract or constrain development and thus help shape the metropolis. Fortunately, market mechanisms tend to direct development away from many sensitive environments, such as wetlands or mountains, but they also lead development towards lakes, scenic areas, and environmentally fragile water recharge areas. The advent of mass automobile ownership after World War II greatly magnified the destructive potential of market-led development, creating fragmented, unco-ordinated, low-density patterns of suburban and exurban sprawl. Though sprawl benefits some, policy-makers now agree that its social and environmental costs are excessive and that it must be tamed.

Sprawl *has* been tamed to a considerable degree in Canada, both through mitigation of its more pernicious impacts and, more recently, through outright prevention. The main mitigative tools have been (1) zoning bylaws requiring very large lots to prevent the creation of subdivisions; (2) subdivision and environmental regulations disallowing development in sensitive areas; and (3) provincial or regional designation of agricultural and/or environmental land reserves. When comprehensively applied, land reserves lead to (4) urban containment (or growth management), which combines use of an urban growth boundary and a greenbelt or no-growth zone.

Will urban containment (and its partner, transit-oriented development) prevail in Canada? It has been fully and effectively applied in only a few metropolitan regions, most notably in Vancouver, and to lesser degrees in Ottawa–Gatineau, Calgary, and Edmonton. More recently, it has been introduced in the Greater Toronto Area, Waterloo Region, and (in draft form) Halifax. These urban regions typically have had severe development pressure on valuable or sensitive resource lands, and political mechanisms allowing for a strong metropolitan planning authority (whether a unitary metropolitan government, a provincially supported inter-municipal body, or provincially imposed planning).

Smart growth principles have now become mainstream in urban planning, and are likely to be employed in all metropolitan and urban plans going forward. They will promote densification of our existing urban fabric, provide clear city-country edges, and minimize large-lot development in peri-urban areas. They will help to save and protect our farmlands, forests, waters, and habitats, and to reduce greenhouse gas emissions. But their benefits will not be free; growth management in particular may have socially and economically unacceptable consequences if applied too enthusiastically. Limitations on land supply are likely to increase land and housing prices (Evans, 1991; Knaap, 1998; White and Allmendinger, 2003), and may lead to British or Japanese levels of 'town-cramming' (Hall, 2001b; Millward, 2005). Do Canadians really need to make such sacrifices of space and privacy, and if so, can they be persuaded to do so?

Chapter 22

Why Micro-Scale Urban Ecology Matters

Stephen D. Murphy

At the micro scale, individual plants and animals interact with the soil, air, and water to form the basis of ecological communities, such as forests, wetlands, and meadows. The direct impact of exchanges of oxygen and carbon dioxide (gases), nitrates and phosphates (nutrients), and water (liquid) is the sustenance of life. Other compounds, such as sulphur dioxides, methane, low-altitude ozone, and dioxins, can harm life. Ecosystems are complex because they are composed of so many components (individuals of each species present within the system, including humans) and ongoing small-scale processes such as the metabolism of nutrients, gases in air, and water. All of this—individuals and processes—can interact, and while it is rare that any individual or individual-scale ecosystem process is indispensable, the ecosystem will depend on the cumulative impact of all these small-scale processes and individuals.

Ecologically, the fundamental issue is to understand how these compounds and organisms interact. Humans are a huge part of this process because ecosystems are changed by building cities. The chemical environment is altered by the use and venting of compounds from industry and transportation, and all organisms will respond to changes wrought by human development. Often the impacts are subtle, as they accumulate for many years before a sudden change occurs. A forest may slowly die and then change within a year or so into a meadow, or a stream once teeming with a diversity of organisms may become permanently imbued with excess nutrients and then saturated with a few species of algae. These are noticeable impacts but

their origin—and prevention—lies in micro-scale interactions.

When discussing how something works, the unspoken corollary is what do you do with this knowledge? This issue is controversial because it often challenges existing cultural norms, e.g., how should an urban area be managed? Analyzing how urban ecosystems work becomes controversial because 'evidence' can be challenged. It is usual to encounter disagreement over whether enough data have been gathered, whether the methodologies and analyses were appropriate, how comparable data are between locations or between sampling times, how risk to urban environments should be measured, and what standards of risk are acceptable. Science offers a valuable framework to test ideas but it can require long-term studies of decades or more—too long a time before critical decisions need to be made.

Essentially, the extensive literature—and only a representative sample is provided in this chapter—points to the conclusion that sound urban governance requires measuring micro-scale ecosystem structures and processes and projecting how they respond to urban development. If a city contemplates building single detached housing ever farther from the core, what ecological structures will be harmed? Will forests disappear directly and will pollution from all the cars added to the city indirectly harm terrestrial and aquatic systems? Will this diminish the quality of life, including that of the human inhabitants? Such questions are now being directed regularly at Canadian urban planning and governance authorities (Chipman, 2002; Gerber and Howard, 2002). (One must also consider the financial implications of such development: will development charges cover its true cost?)

As yet there are no easy answers because cities create such extreme impacts. If urban sprawl triumphs, then much of the diversity and function-ality of the displaced ecosystems vanishes. Conversely, if there is less sprawl and more intensi-fication of cities around urban cores, the current transportation systems and building designs help to create a dome of pollutants trapped in the core that harm humans and other organisms. There is much work to be done and at this point it is impor-tant merely to acknowledge the complexity of the problem—a first step that can lead either to defeatism or to the political will to address the challenges.

This chapter comprises three main sections. In the first section I describe and discuss some signif-icant examples of micro-scale problems as a way of introducing the kinds of initiatives that will need implementation at this scale. Second, I turn to the short-term future and consider interventions already being implemented in some Canadian settings—these are the kinds of initiatives with which we will hopefully become more familiar in the immediate future. Measures associated with the short-term horizon can be expected to be prima-rily reactive in tone because they are mainly preoccupied with restoring what has been lost. Very different are the more proactive, innovative, and challenging local measures that will emerge if we truly embrace the sustainability ethic. This is the topic of the final part of the chapter. These sorts of measures cannot be accomplished overnight because they will involve significantly changing the way we live, think about, and build urban settlements.

Micro-Scale Measures

'Micro-scale measurements' is a hard expression to define simply because the distinction between small- (micro-) scale and larger- (meso-, macro-) scale measurements can often be artificial. Pragmatically, micro-scale measurements refer to variables collected from local sources—a population of animals, reaches along creeks, point sources like rooftop sampling stations within the airshed of a city. However, these variables must be placed in the context of larger scales—the landscape the animals live in, the watershed the creeks are part of, the entire airshed of the city and the surrounding area. Municipalities carry out measurements and plan at different scales; these approaches are referenced in Table 22.1.

Pollution

Pollution is the result of unwanted excess of chem-ical compounds and particulates (like dirt). The compounds and particulates can be both natural and created by humans, but usually they become pollu-tants because too much has been used, e.g., fertiliz-ers, the products of combustion engines. In cities, pollution comes from internal and external sources (e.g., Brook et al., 2002). Contributors include industry and transportation, which add dioxides (nitrous, sulphur, carbon), ground-level ozone, and heavy metals (Kaye et al., 2005; Sharma and McBean, 2002). These help form the smog that is visible in urban areas, and the compounds can harm organisms via cumulative toxicity or mutagenesis and alter ecosystem functions.

It is relatively easy to measure ambient concentrations of pollutants, but harder to measure their impact. Because chemicals interact with one another, individuals and species respond differently to varying concentrations. Moreover, because cumulative impacts may take a long time to create a measurable impact, it is often too late to repair the damage by the time the effect becomes observ-able (Chen et al., 2001; Keller et al., 2001; Theobald et al., 1997; Yauk et al., 2002). Road salts, fertiliz-ers, and pesticides are examples of subtle pollutants that cumulate over a considerable time period before their presence registers (Mayer et al., 1999). Most pollutants create problems ranging from individual changes, such as in frogs that become anatomically hermaphroditic, to changes in nutrient cycling that alter the species and the processes that characterize an urban ecosystem.

Table 22.1   **Examples of Canadian Municipal Environmental Initiatives for Urban Habitat Protection**

Initiative	Examples
Comprehensive environmental planning	• Burnaby (Mountain Land Covenant Agreement) • Calgary (Environmental Planning) • Edmonton (Environmental Strategic Plan Policy Document) • Halton Region (State of the Environment Reporting) • Hamilton–Wentworth (Vision 2020) • Kamloops (KamPlan) • London (Environmental Plan) • Nanaimo (Plan Nanaimo) • Ottawa (State of the Environment Report) • Peel Region (State of the Environment Reporting) • Montreal (Plan of Action for a Local Agenda 21) • Port Moody/Anmore, BC (Naturscape) • Red Deer (Ecospace Evaluation) • St Catharines (Green Plan) • St John's (Comprehensive Environmental Management Plan) • Toronto (Healthy City 2000) • Victoria (Healthy City Strategy) • Waterloo Region (State of the Environment Reporting) • Winnipeg (Plan Winnipeg) • York Region (Greening of York Region Initiative)
Development permit areas/zones	• Kelowna (Development Permit Guidelines for ESAs) • Halifax (Comprehensive Development Districts & Development Plan)
Environmentally sensitive areas studies	• Calgary • Edmonton • Halton Region • Niagara Region • Ottawa • Richmond, BC • Surrey • Toronto • Waterloo Region
Greenways and green zones	• Edmonton (Ribbon of Green Master Plan) • Greater Vancouver Regional District (Green Zone Program) • Montreal (Green Network)

(continued)

Table 22.1   **(*continued*)**

Initiative	Examples
	• Ottawa (Greenspace) • Regina (Open Space Management Strategy) • Toronto (Waterfront Plan) • Waterloo Region (Proposed Natural Habitat Networks)
Integrated pest management plans/pesticide reduction bylaws	• Burnaby (Integrated Pest and Vegetation Management Program) • Halifax (pesticide reduction bylaw) • Hudson, Que. (pesticide reduction/elimination bylaw) • Nepean (integrated turf management/pesticide reduction bylaw) • Ottawa (IPM policies) • Victoria (IPM policies) • Waterloo (city only—pesticide reduction bylaw)
Natural area management plans	• Calgary (Natural Areas Plan) • Richmond BC (Natural Areas Acquisition/Planning & Protection Programs) • Hamilton–Wentworth (Greenlands Study) • Mississauga (Natural Areas Study) • Montreal (Ecosystem Management Program) • Oshawa (Second Marsh) • Ottawa (Natural and Open Spaces Study) • Quebec City (Ecological Program for Municipal Land)
Park plans with conservation priority/community involvement	• Abbotsford (Wildlife Habitat Enhancement Through Parks Maintenance) • Edmonton (Whitemud Nature Reserve) • Greater Vancouver Regional District (Parks Plan) • Guelph (Comprehensive Park Naturalization) • Kitchener (Huron Natural Area Master Plan) • Mississauga (Naturalization Program of Park & Open Space) • Nanaimo (Neck Park Master Plan) • Nepean (Park Naturalization & Adopt a Park) • New Westminster (New Westminster Parks and Sustainability) • Ottawa (Park Naturalization Program) • Surrey (Volunteers in Parks) • Toronto (Parkland Naturalization Compendium) • Vancouver (City Park Board Strategic Plan [Draft]) • Victoria (Beacon Hill Park Management Plan) • Whitehorse (Adopt a Park) • Windsor (Ojibway Park Plans)

Table 22.1   **(continued)**

Initiative	Examples
Restoration & rehabilitation	• Burlington (McNichol Project Waterfront Restoration) • Guelph (Naturalization of Road Allowances [suspended 1999]) • Kitchener (gravel pit rehabilitation [Kolb & Stanley Park Optimists Parks] & stormwater catchment naturalization) • St Albert, Alta (wetland naturalization) • Toronto (restoration of High Park savanna)
Urban forest/native vegetation programs for protection & promotion	• Barrie (Trees 2020) • Cambridge–Kitchener–Waterloo (Trees for Our Future) • Halifax (Biological Tree Spraying & Sackville Streetscape Design Study) • Medicine Hat (New Homeowner Tree Program & Urban Forest Program) • Montreal (Urban Forest Program) • Ottawa (Protecting Trees on Private Property & Urban Forest Program) • Quebec City (Urban Tree Planting & Protection Techniques Programs) • Red Deer (Trees by 2000 Program) • Richmond, BC (Heritage Trees Preservation and Tree Policy) • Trois-Rivières (Greening Initiative & Landscaping of Parking Areas project) • Surrey (Re-Leaf Program/tree preservation & replacement bylaw) • Vancouver (Street Tree Planting & Tree Protection Program) • Whitehorse (Boulevard Beautification Program) • Winnipeg (Urban Habitat Stewardship Network) • York Region (Urban Forest Program)
Watercourse protection	• Nanaimo (Aquatic Habitat Protection Committee/Plan Nanaimo) • Surrey (Watercourse Protection Signs Program)
Watershed planning/stewardship	• Hazelton, BC • Peel Region • Waterloo Region • York Region
Wildlife planning	• Fort Saskatchewan, Alta (Urban Flock Park Maintenance Program)

Sources: See relevant municipal Web sites.

There are often unnoticed changes to the fungi and invertebrates in soils and water that ultimately alter the plants and animals visible to humans (Cousins et al., 2003; Pickett et al., 2001; Reeder et al., 2005).

Impervious Surfaces Cause Flooding, Erosion, and Spreading of Pollutants

On a sub-watershed scale, the wider problem is how the replacement in recharge areas of vegetation and porous soils with impervious roads, sidewalks, and buildings affects surface and groundwater and the organisms living within these areas (Brander et al., 2004; King et al., 2005). Even lawns can add to this problem, as they cause the soil structure to become so inverted that water capacity can be compromised and biological activity reduced. Impervious structures tend to increase the impact of storm events in terms of sediment loading, making runoff an efficient carrier of pollutants. The addition of stormwater management ponds to urban developments has been intended to reduce this impact and it is clear that such ponds do mitigate storm events, but it is not so simple. Storm management ponds may only delay the release of pollutants into the storm drain system. If the ponds remain connected to riparian zones, for example, they can leach into groundwater. These factors, alongside other misguided treatments of riparian zones (e.g., zones that are canalized or even buried as storm drains or sewers), mean that sub-watersheds may not drain properly and thus fail to support ecological functions and mitigate natural hazards, and may become sources of contamination (Donohue et al., 2005; Kominova et al., 2005). Runoff also carries health risks (Beck, 2005). For example, groundwater sources may become polluted and pose considerable risk for human consumption. Such pollution can result from inorganic or organic industrial contaminants, but it can also originate from fertilizers, which promote the growth of pathogens like *Escherichia coli*—a phenomenon more commonly recognized in agricultural regions.

Exotic Species

Two of the most visible changes brought about by urban development are interrelated: some native species are endangered, die off, and become rare; meanwhile, exotic species come to dominate some ecosystems. Most of the species that become extinct are not likely to attract much attention or sympathy as they are protozoans, fungi, and micro-invertebrates and probably never were identified or classified before they vanished. However, more visible species are recognized as being endangered,

threatened, or otherwise at risk in urban areas. Of the 500 Canadian species at risk listed in 2005 (COSEWIC, 2005), up to 5 per cent of these are in urban areas (Table 22.2). This table does not consider non-vertebrate and non-plant species beyond the mandate of the Committee on the Status of Endangered Wildlife in Canada. It also does not address the indirect impacts of urban areas, e.g., demand for energy means that some species in non-urban areas are at risk because of resource extraction to meet this demand. The variation between numbers of species at risk in urban areas probably reflects the fact that some cities are built at the terrestrial-aquatic ecotone, i.e., the transition zones where these meet and where terrestrial, aquatic, and transitional species are found and can be at risk. Other cities, such as St Catharines–Niagara Falls, are in climates that are hospitable to a greater diversity of species.

Pollutants favour some exotic species and harm some native ones. The cumulative impact of changes to the landscape and nutrient and water cycles does likewise. Property owners deliberately or accidentally introduce exotic species. Again, these are late symptoms of problems that needed to be solved long before (Mortberg, 2001). By the time researchers can successfully measure changes in species' populations, as well as in the larger communities and ecosystems, and link these changes to impacts such as urban development or pollution, it may be too late, or at least very expensive and difficult, to solve the problems.

Some native species need no assistance as urbanization favours them, but some of these are regarded as nuisances or pests, e.g., deer, coyotes, raccoons, skunks, muskrats, field mice, gulls, Canada geese, foxes, and perhaps bears and wildcats. Their presence is associated with problems of garbage foraging, property damage, fecal matter, and rabies (Atwood et al., 2004; Broadfoot et al., 2001). Indeed, even conservation efforts may create habitats that favour new pests or disease vectors such as ticks that carry Lyme disease (Slingenbergh et al., 2004). However, interrelationships are complicated and causes may be hard to pinpoint. For example, West Nile virus is encouraged less by conservation

Table 22.2   **Numbers of Species at Risk in Canada's Twenty Largest Cities**

City	Population	Number of Species at Risk
Calgary	821,628	6
Chicoutimi–Jonquière	160,454	5
Edmonton	862,597	4
Halifax	332,518	4
Hamilton	624,360	11
Kitchener	382,940	7
London	398,616	15
Montreal	3,326,510	13
Oshawa	268,773	8
Ottawa–Hull	1,010,498	11
Quebec City	671,889	7
Regina	193,652	7
Saint John	125,705	6
Saskatoon	219,056	9
Sherbrooke	147,384	5
St Catharines–Niagara Falls	372,406	23
St John's	174,051	2
Sudbury	160,488	3
Thunder Bay	125,562	3
Toronto	4,263,757	10
Trois-Rivières	139,956	7
Vancouver	1,831,665	10
Victoria	304,287	11
Windsor	278,685	12
Winnipeg	667,209	11

Source: Statistics Canada, 1996 census; COSEWIC, 2005.

efforts, such as storm ponds, than by negligence as regards waste materials—tires, empty containers, and pop cans—left lying around for the mosquito vectors to breed (Carlson et al., 2004; Medlock et al., 2005; Rainham, 2005).

Fragmenting the Urban Ecosystem

Possibly the largest challenge in an urban ecosystem is the fact that, at the macro scale, development has proceeded largely unplanned and so has fragmented the ecosystem into small remnant pieces (e.g., they may be only a few dozen or hundred metres in area). Species that dwell within fragments cannot survive if they move from one fragment to another, hence impairing the necessary process of mixing genes from different local populations and creating genetic variation to allow for future responses to changing environments. Barriers to local migration between safe fragments are usually related to the presence of large inhospitable areas, where species can be exposed to starvation, predators, and death and injury caused by human activity. Even on a watershed basis, it is relatively easy to see the impacts of urban areas. Figure 22.1 shows the remnants of once-extensive forest cover in the Grand River watershed. The relative absence of woodlots in cities is noteworthy.

Fragmentation also creates problems because much of the habitat is juxtaposed against urban structures, leaving abrupt transitions between habitat and urban features. In such cases, the large exposed perimeter is affected by drastic changes in temperature, humidity, light, and nutrient and water exchanges. In addition, physical features such as wind can punch 'holes' in this perimeter. The perimeter influences are called 'edge effects', meaning that there is exposure and transition between a habitat and its external landscape. This area is often hostile to species associated with the original habitat and attractive to exotic or different native species that will invade. Through reproduction and metabolic wastes, invading species enlarge this perimeter, and in consequence even more area becomes hostile to the original habitat's species. It is hard to predict how small a fragment has to be or what the ratio of edge to interior can be before a habitat irreversibly shrinks to nothing (or more properly, becomes so altered that none of the original habitat remains). This is because many variables influence the outcome of fragmentation. However, without intervention, many of the natural habitat fragments in cities may be doomed to vanish or become undesirable from an ecological or even aesthetic perspective (e.g., a woodland becomes a weedy meadow). Some fragmentation has been caused by interventions that turned out to be devas-

tating, even when the actions themselves were based on what was assumed to be correct practice, e.g., filling in wetlands to permit additional development or to allay fear of disease. Generally, across most Canadian cities waterfront and watercourse areas have been altered for a variety of purposes. Dams, berms, and channels have been built along watercourses for (intended) flood protection, sewage, stormwater management, or power generation; low-lying areas have been raised to reduce flooding; wetlands have been filled for development or because of perceived threats to human health; ravines have been filled for development and traversed or used as rail, power, and road corridors. The eventual proliferation of buildings, yards, parking lots, and transportation and utility corridors has meant that little of the natural environment remained.

Shrinking natural areas in cities did inspire early attempts to conserve what was left. Such initiatives took the form of the creation of parks and housing planning in a fashion that encouraged open space. But consistent with a pervasive Victorian influence in North American cities, the focus was on open, mown areas (Zmyslony and Gagnon, 2000). More recently, this approach has changed somewhat as more truly 'natural' areas were saved and restored. To some extent, these have provided an outlet for people to enjoy what is left of 'natural' fragments, though not everyone sees the benefits of living near open naturalized green spaces (Hobden et al., 2004; Manuel, 2003). Even these fragments, however, remain at risk, as people trample through, bring exotic species on their clothes, encroach on natural areas with lawns, and allow their pets to roam and kill small organisms (Murphy and Martin, 2001).

The Short-Term Future: Restoring What Was Lost

Awareness of problems is a necessary first step in attempts to correct them. However, listing problems does little good in the absence of a strategy laying out systematic (and systemic) solutions. In terms of micro-scale ecology, an immediate challenge is to

Figure 22.1 **Forest Cover in the Grand River Watershed, Including the Cities of Kitchener, Waterloo, Cambridge, Guelph, and Brantford, Ontario**

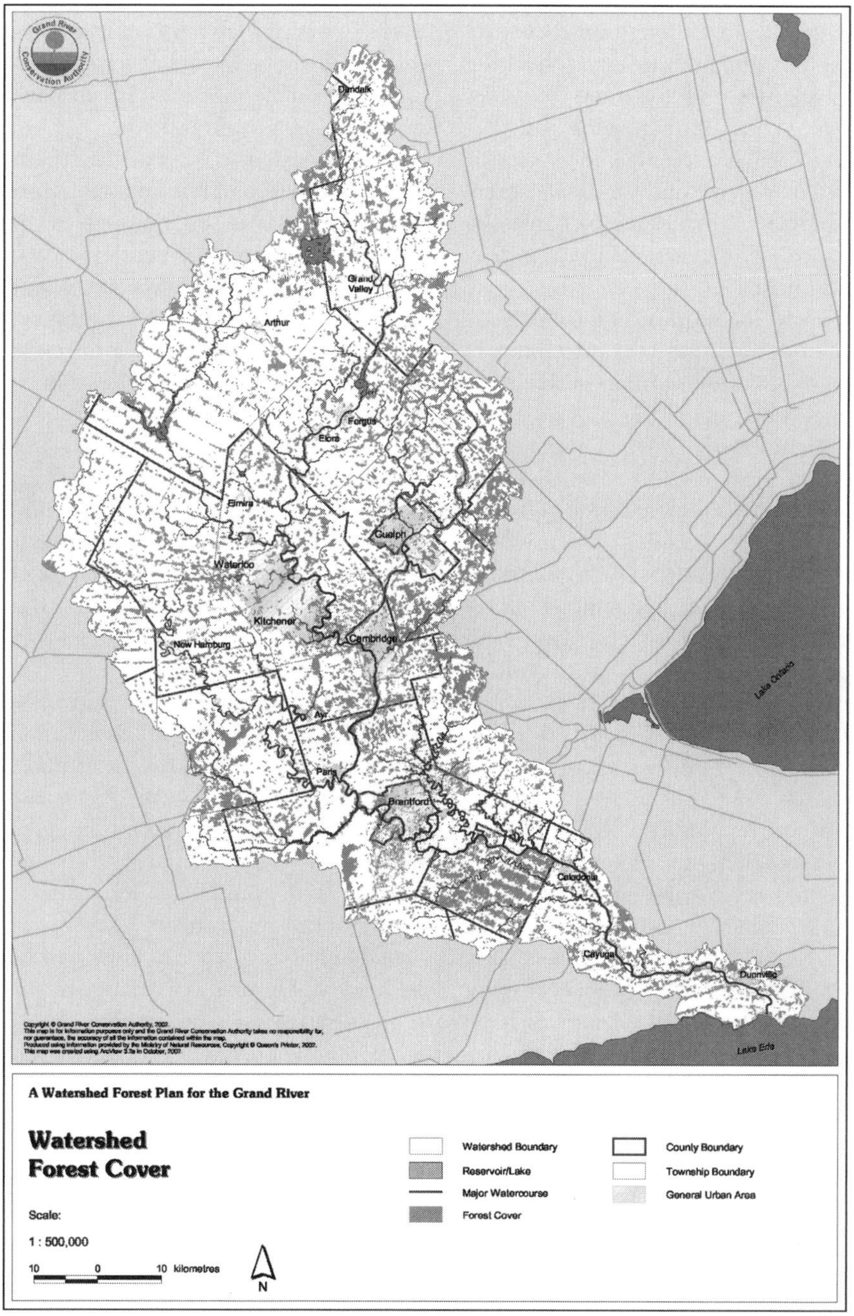

Source: <www.grandriver.ca/Forestry/images/ForestPlan_Map_Cover.jpg>.

mitigate problems and repair as much damage as possible. This means restoring native species and ecosystem processes. One important approach is via ecological restoration. In the strictest sense, ecological restoration would attempt to re-establish all the key ecological structures and functions of times past and so return us to a self-organizing and self-sustaining system. Normally, the reference state or ideal is interpreted to be a pre-industrial landscape. But the essential problem is that cities so change the landscape and its ecology that restoration is probably impossible on this scale.

Most urban efforts focus on what is called ecological rehabilitation. The thrust here is to mitigate the worst impacts of pollution or other problems so that some ecological functions and structures might be restored (Sartori and Assini, 2001). For example, long-abandoned gravel pits could be reshaped and species reintroduced so the pits become small, deep ponds that would support a reasonable ecosystem. On former contaminated industrial or 'brownfield' sites, heavy metals or organic pollutants could be removed via chemical or biological remediation and acidification may be mitigated to promote reintroduction of native species (Colombo et al., 1996; Gunn et al., 1995). Also on brownfields, old concrete foundations could be pulverized and turned into urban alvars, rocky outcrops with shallow soils or artificial rocks for reptile habitat (Webb and Shine, 2000). If properly designed, stormwater management ponds could remove pollutants and perhaps maintain some ecological functions (Anderson et al., 2002; Helfield and Diamond, 1997; Kennedy and Mayer, 2002). In more serious cases, ecological reconciliation may be practised. Reconciliation consists in humans learning to share habitats with other species (Rosenzweig, 2003). Examples can be as benign or even inspiring as encouraging peregrine falcons to nest on tall buildings or as 'boldly radical' as accepting field mice in our backyards or native plants in what used to be manicured lawns.

Regardless of the approach taken, ecologists work at micro scales to mitigate urban impacts and redress imbalance and so return ecological health. Micro-scale experiments and knowledge are needed to ensure that we know how to restore eco-logical functions and structures. Soil is restored by removing excess nutrients and by planting cover crops that are harvested and then key fungi and invertebrates may be reintroduced (inoculated) into soil. Plants can be seeded or transplanted from commercial or public nurseries. Streams may be restored by removing channels, taking old mill ponds or reservoirs 'off-line', bypassing them with new stream channels, and reintroducing historical meanders. Wetlands can be restored by removing tile drains, as most cities are built on old farmlands that used such drains to make land arable. Integrated pest management can be used to mitigate exotics and give native species the chance to re-establish structure and natural ecosystem function.

All of the approaches listed in the preceding paragraph are often started on local scales. In fact, an excellent start is right in people's own (literal) backyards (Rudd et al., 2002). Students and professionals do experiments or demonstration projects on the scale of a few hundred metres of habitat (see Figure 22.2). A neighbourhood adopts a forest. Boulevards and yards are planted with low-growing native species once bylaws are passed to allow this. The grounds of schools, commercial blocks, or industries are planted with natives. Trails may be closed. Isolated habitats may be reconnected. In this latter case, however, the risk of facilitating disease and pest transmission must be acknowledged. Innovations like green roofs may increase energy efficiency and reduce ecological impacts by impounding water or air pollutants. A green roof features mainly shallow-rooted plants seeded or transplanted into a low-density substrate of shallow soil. The goal is to reduce stormwater runoff to abate storm drain surges that can cause erosion, create sediment dams, or overwhelm water treatment plants and foul rivers.

Even 'backyard' restoration can be relevant to the larger scale as there may be a cumulative impact of smaller nodes of restoration and conservation, provided species or ecological functions can connect across these nodes. For example, a series of backyard naturalizations can benefit native species such as birds. Local focus often fosters ownership and a sense of care for these projects and may inspire other projects as they convince people that small

Figure 22.2

Transformation of a former lawn into a natural garden with native plants, Dorney Garden at the University of Waterloo. (*Photo by Pierre Filion*)

steps can result in large beneficial effects. Local projects are also the most feasible in terms of politics, funding, and maintenance. However, too much focus on micro scales means the projects can be also become disconnected ecologically (Naveh, 2005; Quon et al., 1999, 2001). Indeed, the outcome may be that the easiest projects to fund or initiate get done, but at the expense of the larger critical ecological issues, which are ignored. Ecologically, this backyard-style restoration could mean that a whole series of fragmented habitats are created, but ultimately cannot be sustained without continual human maintenance, contrary to the goal of creating an ecosystem that is self-organizing and sustaining over the long term. Fragments never create a landscape that supports metapopulations and larger-scale ecosystem functions of nutrient and water cycling. There is also a social learning issue with overreliance on micro-scale projects. Because of a limited awareness of each small-scale effort, we may never learn from successes or mistakes and thus continually reinvent the wheel and repeat errors.

The main point to all this is that short-term, micro-scale interventions are important but not sufficient. Ongoing efforts to date beg for policies that encourage a priority-driven and integrated approach to local restoration and conservation efforts so that the needs within the city are connected. Likewise, since ecosystems have been artificially bounded by municipal and other political borders, new designations will be required to interconnect cities—ecological restoration should also be a regional/county, provincial, federal, and international responsibility. There is the promise of better co-operation, but the danger looms that such co-operation will fall victim to an overriding spirit of municipal, entrepreneurial-style competition.

The Long-Term Future: What Canadian Cities Might Become

At the heart of the restoration ecology concept are the challenges inherent in the reconciliation of natural and built environments (see Czerniak, 2001). Key to these challenges is the 'fragmentation' problem, which is pervasive in urban areas. Generally, Canadian cities today are primarily comprised of relatively low-density older suburbs, outer newer suburbs of often still lower density, and an outer rural zone constituting the edge of census metropolitan areas. These rural portions tend to disappear rapidly as suburbs expand (see Chapter 21). Prevailing forms of development have led to advanced fragmentation in terms of both natural areas and human habitation. The human habitation fragmentation is a consequence of urban sprawl and forces residents to travel far and often by single-occupancy vehicle to school, work, shopping, and recreation (see Chapter 6). In response to sprawling development, new models are presently considered. These would involve mixed-zoned areas, much higher density, and better planned transportation corridors and journey patterns from residence to other destinations. Much disagreement remains, however, over how well all this might work from an ecosystems perspective (Byun and Esparza, 2005; Irwin and Bockstael, 2004; Jim, 2004; McAvoy et al., 2004; Robinson et al., 2005; Stone, 2003). A critical question is thus, what kinds of innovations might be favourable to urban ecology at micro scales?

In the context of the longer-term future, micro-scale interventions might improve the energy efficiency of individual buildings, thereby reducing overall energy requirements and the pollution originating from coal-fired and other power plants, which ultimately finds its way to cities. Dovetailing with the goal of energy efficiency are innovations that may serve multiple functions. For example, green roofs and living/green walls may attenuate absorption and re-radiation of sun-generated heat (urban heat island effects), resulting in lower energy use for cooling over summer months. They would also provide additional insulation to buildings and thereby reduce energy loss throughout the year. A further environmental advantage would be reduced water loss to storm sewers. Green buildings also promise to intercept and bioremediate or impound airborne and precipitation-borne pollutants. In addition, they provide local nodes of 'ecosystems in the air' that serve as homes and sources for sub-populations of organisms from fungi to birds and mammals (Del Barrio, 1998; Kim, 2004). This is an impressive list of promises and it remains to be seen whether green roofs are able to deliver all of these. Still these promises do warrant hope that micro-scale approaches at the building roof level can be a worthwhile first step in terms of the environmental restoration of cities, especially in their densely developed sectors (Monterusso, Rowe and Rugh, 2005; Niachou et al, 2001).

Other innovations might consist in efforts to green an entire building or neighbourhood, rather than just the roof. The simple act of planting native trees and shrubs near buildings may reduce energy use in buildings and a neighbourhood's urban heat island effect (Carver et al., 2004; Simpson, 2002). New renewable energy sources may become viable and operate on a smaller scale, e.g., each building could have an independent power source or a neighbourhood could share such a source. 'Living machines' involve constructed, self-contained (usually) aquatic ecosystems used to treat wastewater; they provide an alternative to treating wastewater by chemical means in a waste treatment plant or impounding storm runoff in a management pond. Those who design and operate living machines probably will improve their efficiency and these may become an increasingly viable option for treating wastewater and perhaps all household organic waste (Todd et al., 2003). A neighbourhood-scale version of a living machine might operate on the same principles as a neighbourhood stormwater management pond, which captures runoff. Ultimately, the improvement of water quality at a neighbourhood level rests on more sophisticated predictive modelling of how water balances are likely to be altered by development changes (Graham et al., 2004).

At both a property/lot and community scale, work on greyfields and brownfields offers some possible direct and indirect benefits (De Sousa, 2003). Greyfields are normally abandoned or underused commercial buildings, such as early shopping centres or big-box stores that have closed. Brownfields are normally old industrial or heavy commercial sites that are contaminated, e.g., gasoline from service stations or heavy metals from tanneries. Brownfields require action since owners may be legally required to remove toxins before new development can proceed. Physical removal of toxins is generally rapid but expensive (it involves chemical methods or some forms of microbial remediation). Such removal is often used in cases of heavy metal contamination, because the elements in the compounds must be immobilized and removed, not detoxified. Slower and cheaper methods may also be used. This is the case of phytoremediation, wherein plants might detoxify organic compounds so that a temporary ecological community may provide habitat for remediation with relatively low ecotoxicological risk, i.e., low risk of inadvertently making the problem worse by making toxins mobile and able to spread to other parts of an ecosystem. By no means is there agreement on which approach is better, and the choice of remediation options rests on the preferences of policy-makers after consideration of factors related to site hydrology, geomorphology, and the chemicals involved (Zhou and Hua, 2004).

Sites such as brownfields could be more fully ecologically restored if they were located in a landscape that would allow connection with otherwise isolated natural fragments. Alternatively, the sites may be economically attractive, so that housing or commercial development can cover remediation costs. In such cases, some ecological restoration may occur in the form of building design (like a green roof) or landscaping, but the main environmental impact might be that infill sites such as these save peripheral greenfields from development. Greyfield redevelopment may also prevent greenfield development (see Ferrante and Mihalakakou, 2001, for a good overview).

Canadian provinces (in particular) have modified their municipal and planning acts so as to introduce legislation specific to brownfield sites and other kinds of 'infill' redevelopment projects. Cities themselves have also adopted infill-friendly bylaws and incentives. Overall there appears to be increasing interest in infill development (De Sousa, 2003), perhaps stemming from the ideal of a more sustainable city. Again, the most valuable impact may not be felt at the site of micro-scale restorations, but may result from the ensuing preservation of greenfields further away. If most of the restored sites are near the city core or inner suburbs, there might be an ancillary benefit of intensification: less need to develop roads and subdivisions, and thus avoidance of some of the environmental damages these developments cause.

Environmental and, more importantly, integrated urban planning from the scale of the neighbourhood to that of an entire urban watershed must go beyond the innovations suggested above, though the objectives of more density and reduced dependence on long-distance travel by car are likely to be part of most urban environmental strategies. There may be more emphasis on co-housing wherein individually owned units are clustered around shared amenities, including playrooms, full kitchens, and clusters of offices, separated from the living areas (Stewart, 2002). Co-housing may reduce the ecological footprint of home ownership by providing more incentive for reduced commuting to work, promoting a willingness to engage collectively in initiatives like native species landscaping or energy-efficient buildings, and fostering a sense of community co-operation and education that helps people reduce their resource use and waste production (McCormick, 1994).

Some observers perceive co-operative housing as well as neo-traditional or New Urbanism styles of development as being equally beneficial from an environmental perspective. However, these efforts are not without critics (cf. Berke et al., 2003; Southworth, 1997; Zimmerman, 2001). Some of the shortcomings they raise might be overcome by planning in conjunction with other efforts such as greenways. It has been argued that successful implementation of a range of alternative, community-based, ecologically friendly arrangements, whether greenways or green roofs, is more likely because those living in co-housing, co-operative, or New Urbanism housing units may be intellectually predisposed to further implementation of non-status quo ideas, though this is not always the case (Walmsley, 1995). Alternative housing developments may also spur adoption of other innovations, such as altered street patterns to increase foot and bicycle transportation and make auto trips less wasteful (Song, 2005; Southworth, 1997). Other critics call for a more ambitious or even radical approach, which involves actively discouraging dependence on autos and encouraging more reliance on public transportation.

The preceding paragraphs have stressed the role of locally based urban environmental measures, for cities are becoming one place where citizens may make a direct difference in combatting large-scale issues like climate change (Kousky and Schneider, 2003). However, the message is clear that the ecological future at micro scales will depend on meso- and macro-scale political, social, and economic efforts, many of which are related to personal and institutional preferences and ethics (e.g., Filion et al., 1999). By no means will the adoption of such initiatives be simple, as they entail sociological challenges, political battles, and economic shifts that have not been addressed here; other chapters will do so (see, e.g., Chapters 4, 8, 14, 25). The crucial point is that urban ecology, micro-scale or otherwise, is not a silo wherein ecologists can happily do science ignorant of the non-ecological factors that affect the city system. Ecologists must continue advancing scientific knowledge, but we also must link this to the changes in the urban milieu (Bessey, 2002; Grimm et al., 2000; Hough, 2004; Li et al., 2005; Murphy, 2004; Naveh, 2005; Niemala, 1999; Pickett et al., 2001; Pickett et al., 2004; Platt, 2004; Venn and Niemala, 2004). Otherwise, urban ecology will become a mere curiosity while real innovation will happen in other domains.

Chapter 23

Being Realistic about Urban Growth

Christopher Leo and Kathryn Anderson

Growth is to North American civic leaders what publicity is to Hollywood stars: there is no such thing as bad growth, and no such thing as too much of it. If we take local media seriously, we may come away with the impression that growth is the elixir that cures all ills, from potholes to poverty, and that any city that is not growing rapidly is being 'left behind' and is 'off the map'. The city is seen, first and foremost, as a 'growth machine' (Logan and Molotch, 1987) and is valued only if it conforms to that image.

This growth fixation is a North American peculiarity, and it has deep roots. In both Canada and the United States, the settlement of the West and the Industrial Revolution were marked by boosterism, as expanding cities competed for investment (Artibise, 1981; Wade, 1959). Within metropolitan areas, a similarly growth-oriented and competitive environment was evident. From the earliest days of suburban development, much of the outward expansion of cities took the form of competition among urbanizing municipalities vying for residential, commercial, and industrial development (Binford, 1985; Logan and Molotch, 1987: 179–99; Lucy and Phillips, 2000; Markusen, 1984). Cities that are growing rapidly, or have grown to a great size, are the 'successful', desirable, and admired ones, while residents of 'Nowheresville' struggle with a diminished sense of self-worth.

Europe is less afflicted with the growth fixation. European metropolitan areas that would be classified by American urban policy analyst Anthony Downs (1994) as growing slowly or declining include Vienna, Brussels, Copenhagen, Cologne, Frankfurt, Hamburg, Florence, Genoa, Milan, Naples, and Rome (Leo and Brown, 2000). Listening to the growth talk, one might also forget that slow growth is more nearly the rule than the exception, even in North America. Downs (1994: 60–9) classifies cities growing less than 10 per cent a decade as growing slowly. He refers to cities that—like Copenhagen, Hamburg, Florence, Genoa, Milan, Naples, and Rome—are losing population as declining. According to the United States Census Bureau, 118 of America's 280 metropolitan statistical areas (MSAs) are growing slowly or declining (see Table 23.1). As for Canada, if we consider that 10 per cent growth in a decade is the equivalent of 0.96 of 1 per cent per year, assuming a constant growth rate, we can see that Table 23.2 shows an even higher rate of slow growth or 'decline' for Canadian metropolitan areas. For example, of 26 metropolitan areas in the year 2000, 13 were growing slowly or losing population. For 2004 the figure is 17 out of 28 (see also Chapter 3).

Adding to the air of unreality around growth talk, therefore, is the fact that, for many cities, rapid growth, though tirelessly discussed and repeatedly advanced as the cure for all ills, remains tantalizingly out of reach. Our prescription for North America's civic leaders is a stiff dose of realism. We recommend that they resist the seduction of growth talk and build policy on the reality of their situation. In a discussion of the importance of growth rates in setting the conditions for urban policy-making, Leo and Brown (2000) made the case that slow growth is not a malaise, but that it does impose a different set of conditions on policy-makers than rapid growth does. There are advantages and disadvantages to both slow and rapid growth. Moreover, most cities

Table 23.1   **United States MSAs and CMSAs*: Selected Growth Rates, Top, Middle, and Bottom**

Rank	Metropolitan Area Name	Census Population		Change, 1990 to 2000	
		1 April 2000	1 April 1990	Number	Per cent
1	Las Vegas, Nev.–Ariz. MSA	1,563,282	852,737	710,545	83.3
2	Naples, Fla MSA	251,377	152,099	99,278	65.3
3	Yuma, Ariz. MSA	160,026	106,895	53,131	49.7
4	McAllen–Edinburg–Mission, Tex. MSA	569,463	383,545	185,918	48.5
5	Austin–San Marcos, Tex. MSA	1,249,763	846,227	403,536	47.7
6	Fayetteville–Springdale–Rogers, Ark. MSA	311,121	210,908	100,213	47.5
7	Boise City, Idaho MSA	432,345	295,851	136,494	46.1
8	Phoenix–Mesa, Ariz. MSA	3,251,876	2,238,480	1,013,396	45.3
9	Laredo, Tex. MSA	193,117	133,239	59,878	44.9
10	Provo–Orem, Utah MSA	368,536	263,590	104,946	39.8
154	Macon, Ga. MSA	322,549	290,909	31,640	10.9
155	Lynchburg, Va. MSA	214,911	193,928	20,983	10.8
156	Bloomington, Ind. MSA	120,563	108,978	11,585	10.6
157	Corvallis, Ore. MSA	78,153	70,811	7,342	10.4
158	Fayetteville, NC MSA	302,963	274,566	28,397	10.3
159	Portland, Me. MSA	243,537	221,095	22,442	10.2
160	Johnson City–Kingsport–Bristol, Tenn.–Va. MSA	480,091	436,047	44,044	10.1
161	Fort Wayne, Ind. MSA	502,141	456,281	45,860	10.1
162	Florence, SC MSA	125,761	114,344	11,417	10.0
163	State College, Penn. MSA	135,758	123,786	11,972	9.7
271	Anniston, Ala. MSA	112,249	116,034	−3,785	−3.3
272	Johnstown, Penn. MSA	232,621	241,247	−8,626	−3.6
273	Wheeling, WV–Ohio MSA	153,172	159,301	−6,129	−3.8
274	Alexandria, La. MSA	126,337	131,556	−5,219	−4.0
275	Elmira, NY MSA	91,070	95,195	−4,125	−4.3
276	Pittsfield, Mass. MSA	84,699	88,695	−3,996	−4.5
277	Binghamton, NY MSA	252,320	264,497	−12,177	−4.6
278	Utica–Rome, NY MSA	299,896	316,633	−16,737	−5.3
279	Grand Forks, ND–Minn. MSA	97,478	103,181	−5,703	−5.5
280	Steubenville, Ohio–Weirton, WV MSA	132,008	142,523	−10,515	−7.4

*Metropolitan Statistical Areas and Consolidated Metropolitan Statistical Areas.
Source: United States Census Bureau (2001).

Table 23.2   **Canadian CMAs: Population Growth Rates (% change), 2000–4**

	2000	2001	2002	2003	2004
Total census metropolitan areas	*1.4*	*3.2*	*1.6*	*1.2*	*1.1*
Toronto	2.2	2.9	2.8	1.9	1.7
Montreal	1.0	1.0	1.1	0.9	0.8
Vancouver	1.4	1.8	1.7	1.4	0.9
Ottawa–Gatineau	2.0	2.3	1.4	1.1	1.0
Calgary	2.6	2.5	2.6	1.7	1.8
Edmonton	1.7	1.5	1.9	1.1	1.1
Quebec City	0.4	0.5	0.7	0.6	0.7
Hamilton, Ont.	1.4	1.5	1.3	1.0	0.8
Winnipeg	0.6	0.5	0.5	0.5	0.8
London	1.2	1.0	1.1	0.7	0.5
Kitchener	2.0	1.9	1.7	1.4	1.2
St Catharines–Niagara	0.6	0.4	0.4	0.3	0.1
Halifax, NS	0.9	0.8	1.3	0.8	0.8
Windsor, Ont.	2.1	2.2	1.6	0.8	0.7
Victoria	0.5	1.1	0.4	0.4	0.6
Oshawa	2.5	2.2	2.4	2.6	2.5
Saskatoon	0.1	0.2	0.4	0.3	0.6
Regina	−0.3	−0.6	−0.1	0.4	0.7
St John's	0.4	0.1	0.8	0.6	0.7
Sherbrooke	0.8	0.9	1.1	1.1	1.2
Greater Sudbury	−1.0	−0.4	−0.3	0.1	0.0
Abbotsford, BC[1]	n.a.	n.a.	1.0	0.7	2.5
Kingston[1]	n.a.	n.a.	1.2	0.8	0.5
Saguenay	−1.0	−1.0	−1.0	−0.8	−0.5
Trois-Rivières	−0.3	−0.3	−0.1	0.3	0.6
Saint John	−0.1	−0.5	0.1	0.2	0.2
Thunder Bay	−0.7	−0.1	−0.3	0.5	0.3

n.a.: Not available.
[1]Abbotsford and Kingston became census metropolitan areas in 2001.
Source: Statistics Canada (2005e).

will not change their rate of growth appreciably, no matter what policies they institute. They can, however, tailor their policies to capture the benefits of their city's slow or rapid rate of growth while minimizing the constraints. Leo and Brown pressed their case by compiling a catalogue of typical slow-growth policy failures. These originated in the determination of policy-makers in slow-growth cities to induce faster growth or, failing that, to pretend to it. In this chapter we carry thinking about slow growth a step forward by comparing policies in a slow-growth city, Winnipeg, with those in a growth magnet, Vancouver, in five policy areas. What is the significance of the Winnipeg and Vancouver cases? There is no such thing as a typical city, but Vancouver is a Pacific Rim metropolitan area with a population of almost two million, which grew 8.5 per cent between 1996 and 2001, and Winnipeg is a prairie metropolitan area of almost 700,000 that grew 0.6 per cent over the same time period (Statistics Canada, 2001c). One, therefore, is growing slowly, the other quickly. It seems reasonable to assume that many of the observations we make of those communities will resonate elsewhere.

Vancouver

Vancouver is located on the Pacific Ocean, in the southwest corner of British Columbia, known as the Lower Mainland. The city is surrounded by both suburban sprawl and the fertile farmland of the Fraser Valley. Vancouverites' attitudes towards urban development have been influenced by a strong public attachment to the city's spectacular natural setting, with the ocean never far away and mountain vistas in the background. The setting, a mild climate, and many other attractions and amenities have made Vancouver a highly desirable place to live and have helped it to grow 2.6 per cent annually, a rate comparable to such developing-world mega-cities as Cairo, Jakarta, and Rio de Janeiro (Northwest Environment Watch, 2002: 3). Vancouverites' attachment to the city's natural setting has produced widespread dismay at any developments that seem to threaten a valued milieu. That dismay, together

with the confidence engendered by the aura of rapid growth, has stiffened the spines of politicians and planners and produced a system of careful planning and strict land-use development policy.

Economic Development

British Columbia's economy has been marked by the decline of resource extraction—forestry, mining, oil and gas—and the growth of tourism, advanced technology, financial services, educational services, and film production (Table 23.3). This transformation has worked to the detriment of much of British Columbia but to the benefit of the Lower Mainland. Vancouver's 2001 unemployment rate of 7.2 per cent was markedly lower than province's 8.5 per cent (Statistics Canada, 2001c), and employment grew from 1991 to 2000 by 2.6 per cent annually (Vancouver Economic Development Commission, 2001).

Vancouver's favourable location provides the entrée to economic advantage and rapid growth. This opens a wealth of opportunity that can be seized or lost. It also brings with it, for many Vancouverites, a great deal of adversity, which can be ameliorated or left to fester.

Infrastructure and Services

Infrastructure and services refer to the building and maintenance of all the facilities needed to serve the city, including roads, public transit, sewerage, water, parks, education, library branches, community centres, and police and fire protection. These facilities represent a potentially ruinous financial burden, as the case of Winnipeg will demonstrate, but Vancouver is avoiding ruin, partly through good fortune and partly by policies that take advantage of the city's good fortune. The good fortune is a product of both burgeoning population and geographic situation, which have combined in the production of a population density high enough to sustain the cost of infrastructure and services.

Vancouver's fortunate geographic situation is marked by the fact that mountains, an ocean, and

Table 23.3   **Growth Sectors in Vancouver in 2000**

Advanced technology	61,000 jobs (16 per cent growth in 2000); 7,800 establishments operating; contributed $3.8 billion to GDP (up 17 per cent); exports of high-tech/biotech almost $1 billion (up 15 per cent).
Information technology	Contributed $1.1 billion to GDP in 1999. This subsector accounted for 21,000 of 61,000 of advanced technology jobs.
Biotechnology	Supports health care, agriculture, food production, forestry, mining, and waste treatment. Sixty per cent of biotech results from growth at universities and hospitals. Biotech at UBC alone grew from $560 million in 1998 to $1.35 billion in 2000.
Environmental	Becoming a world leader in environmental conservation. Location is ideal for environmental technology to expand and for increased investment. Vancouver engineers maintain a world reputation.
Tourism	Tourists spent $2.7 billion, supporting 114,000 jobs in industry. Growing for past nine years. Ranked by World Tourism Organization as seventh ideal destination with 2.7 million visitors surveyed.
Film and television	Third largest film production centre in North America employs 35,000 people; industry spent $1.18 billion generating $3.3 billion in economic impact. Three major film companies, 26 studios, 70 post-production facilities, 50 shooting stages, and 200 movies and television features shot annually in Greater Vancouver.
Finance, insurance, and real estate	30 foreign banks, 15 international financial institutions, several major banks and regional headquarters for Canadian institutions. As a designated International Financial Centre, Vancouver offers tax and regulatory exemptions for ease of foreign trade and banking.
Education	Education accounted for 67,800 jobs: two international universities, strong community colleges, and various public- and private-sector schools.

Source: Vancouver Economic Development Commission (2001).

an Agricultural Land Reserve surround the metropolitan area. These factors alone encourage dense development, at 690 persons per square kilometre (calculated from Statistics Canada, 2001c). This means that, on average, each component of infrastructure within the metropolitan area, whether a square kilometre of sewerage or the transit lines and community centres serving that area, is shared by 690 taxpayers. With the flabby land-use policies such as those that represent the North American norm, the mountains, water, and Agricultural Land Reserve might well have had the opposite effect—

encouraging more sprawl, with low-density subdivisions straggling on past land reserves and around mountains. However, the *Official Development Plan* guidelines have determined minimum densities for the various districts of the Vancouver region. Intelligent policy has pushed the market to develop more infill, dense, and mixed-use development. This is achieved by taking advantage of the fact that a burgeoning economy and a favourable location produce an intense demand for development and put developers in the mood to accept strict conditions, if necessary, in return for a cut of the profits to be made (Leo, 1994).

Vancouver's infrastructure and services are in good shape, operating to a substantially higher standard than those in Winnipeg. Well-maintained roads and sidewalks, good transit connections throughout the metropolitan area by bus, automated rapid transit, and catamaran ferries, a wealth of well-kept parks, attractively designed, pedestrian-oriented public places, with lots of park benches, and well-maintained bus shelters are among many signs of a prosperous city that values its public realm and can afford to pay for it. But the city goes well beyond high-quality provision of the basic infrastructure and services. A conspicuous example in the public realm is a system of greenways (Vancouver, 2004a), which act not only as natural pathways for leisurely Sunday walks but as commuter routes for bicycles and pedestrians connecting stores, parks, neighbourhoods, and cultural sites. In addition, public waterfront development and park space are maintained and expanded where possible. In 1991 the Urban Landscape Task Force was appointed to promote and monitor the use and development of the urban environment (Vancouver, 1992). Density, however, is at the heart of Vancouver's success in managing its infrastructure and services, and density is a matter of land use.

Land Use

Vancouver's concern with the creation and maintenance of an attractive milieu includes strict regulation of private property and its development. In Vancouver's case, two sets of land-use measures have been important in raising average densities throughout the Vancouver metropolitan area. One of these, design guidelines, is discussed in the following section. The others are regulations established for Agricultural Land Reserves.

In 1972, in the face of growing concern that BC's meagre supply of high-potential agricultural land was threatened by sprawl, the provincial government halted urban development on agricultural land. Lands excluded from urban development were designated as the Agricultural Land Reserve (ALR) and an Agricultural Land Commission (ALC) was appointed to oversee their management (Smart Growth BC, 2003). Planning control within the ALR remains in the hands of local governments, but the ALC, under its mandate to encourage and support agriculture, reviews local plans, issues guidelines, and, where necessary, works with local governments to revise plans.

The ALC enjoys strong public support, which appears to relate more to its conservation of open space than to its somewhat mixed success in agricultural land preservation (Garrish, 2002–3).

Planning for Growth

By definition, the exclusion of land from urban development limits options for the location of new suburbs, but whether those limits have the effect of concentrating development or simply triggering a search for ever more distant parcels of land for low-density sprawl depends on the presence or absence of effective urban planning controls. Planning controls have been a major concern of Vancouver's civic leaders since 1972, when a reform party focused on the concept of 'livable' cities initiated extensive and highly restrictive planning controls, broadly aimed at encouraging people to live and work downtown while providing a variety of opportunities for medium- and high-density living in neighbourhoods where both amenities and job opportunities are close at hand. Considerable emphasis was given to preserving the character of single-family neighbourhoods.

A foundation of the downtown plan was the decision, in the 1970s, not to develop freeways and thereby 'to let congestion be an ally' (Beasley, 2000: 2) in influencing the choice between downtown and suburban living. Innumerable details are prescribed to ensure that medium or high residential densities are combined with convenient and attractive shopping, a pedestrian-friendly street environment, plenty of grass, trees, shrubs, and flowers, and recreational and community amenities. Other measures are designed to facilitate living close to one's place of work. These include: underground parking and related measures to minimize the encroachment of automobiles on pedestrians; measures that encourage the creation of private courtyards offering relief from the hubbub of the street; and measures to preserve views of the water, the mountains, and landmark buildings (Vancouver, 2005). Developers are also required to provide parks, fully developed for recreational use, a sharp contrast with the slivers of land nobody wants that often pass for a developer's park allowance elsewhere in Canada. Downtown Vancouver acquired 65 acres of new parks in the 1990s alone. Most significantly of all, the city insists that the costs of the many facilities and amenities it demands be borne primarily by the developer.

In implementing such regulations, Vancouver is breaking all the rules. Many an 'expert' has advised city councils across North America that refusal to accommodate automobiles is not feasible; insistence on high-density family living in a mixed-income environment will drive development away, and innumerable demands for design refinements and amenities at developer's expense will demonstrate that the city is not open for business or will provoke ruinous legal action. Conventional growth talk includes the frequently voiced belief that any restrictions placed on developers will drive growth away. Vancouver planning regulations give lie to that notion and direct our attention to what ought to be an obvious corollary of the law of supply and demand: if there is money to be made, someone will be found to make it. Vancouver takes care to keep its exactions economically viable, and its regulations, though strict, are clear and transparent. As a result, developers complain, but they comply (Leo, 1994) because Vancouver is a good place to do business and because, at the end of the day, a market for housing or local commerce is one that will be developed locally by Developer Z if Developer Y takes a pass. Being a magnet for development puts the city in the driver's seat and gives it the confidence to regulate firmly. All of this is good news, partly caused by rapid growth. But growth also brings bad news.

Housing

It is a matter of common experience that a growth-driven hot housing market produces expensive housing. This is not a concern for those who attain the top jobs, but it can be a hardship for the middle class and a nightmare for the poor. A Vancouverite trying to make a living as a cleaner or receptionist in one of the downtown glass towers may be forced to choose between a long commute he or she cannot afford or a residence in a decaying central neighbourhood. Others, unable to pay for housing, may find themselves homeless. According to the 2001 census (Statistics Canada, 2001c), the median household income in the Vancouver CMA is $49,940. The average renter pays $814 per month or 20 per cent of the median annual income. The average owner-occupied dwelling is valued at $294,847 and the homeowner spends $1,057 per month or 25 per cent of median annual income on mortgage payments alone. Moving from Winnipeg to Vancouver increases one's average income by only 12 per cent, but the cost of owning a home skyrockets by 182.6 per cent (calculated from Statistics Canada, 2001c). Renters and homeowners are paying 50.7 per cent and 40 per cent more per month respectively in Vancouver, with only a 12 per cent increase in average income (Table 23.4).

The gap between wages and housing costs is a direct consequence of rapid growth. The demand for housing is high because of rapid population growth and because the supply of affordable housing is limited by the costs of development and land value (Chapter 5) and by the profits to be made in

Table 23.4   **Cost of Living and Housing, Vancouver and Winnipeg, 2001**

	Vancouver CMA (2001)	Winnipeg CMA (2001)	Van. > Wpg. by:
Median household income	$49,940	$44,562	12%
Average home value	$294,847	$104,331	183%
Rent: $/month	$814 (20% of income)	$540 (14.5% of income)	51%
Mortgage: $/month	$1,057 (25% of income)	$755 (20% of income)	40%

Source: Calculated from Statistics Canada (2001c).

the top-tier housing market. City policy-makers have worked hard to overcome these disadvantages. Despite their persistence, they have not been entirely successful. Punter, for example (2003: 197–212, 227–40), relates a series of developments around an ocean inlet called False Creek where affordable housing attempts have been fraught with difficulty. Where housing is concerned, rapid growth is more a curse than a blessing, because all of the planners' efforts do not free Vancouver, and especially Vancouver's poorest residents, from the growth-induced high cost of housing.[1] In Vancouver, the resources of service providers to the homeless are stretched to the limit. Winnipeg, meanwhile, has the good fortune to be able to give the top priority not to street people but to prevention of homelessness through the provision of more affordable housing (Leo and August, 2005).

Winnipeg

Winnipeg has a very modest growth rate and, in terms of collective self-image, an ego to match. The word 'decline' is often, and inaccurately, used in describing the city. In self-characterizations, harsh winters and mosquitoes are invariably mentioned, salubrious summer weather and Winnipeg's acknowledged status as the 'performing arts capital of Canada' (Everett-Green, 1996) almost never. If self-deprecation is charming, Winnipeg is Charm City. In fact, neither Winnipeg's population nor its

economy is in decline. As Table 23.2 shows, its population growth ranged between five-tenths and eight-tenths of 1 per cent per year in the five years from 2000 through 2004; a bit slower than Frankfurt, the primary financial centre of continental Europe (0.91 per cent annual average, 1985–95), but much faster than Milan, a powerhouse of the Italian economy (−1.59), and Copenhagen, a city of legendary attractiveness and livability (−0.28) (Leo and Brown, 2000).

Economic Development

The population growth rate gives still less cause for concern when we consider it in conjunction with economic growth and when we compare Winnipeg with Vancouver on both dimensions. As Table 23.5 shows, Winnipeg's economic growth from 1994 through 2003 outpaced its population growth in all but two years and never fell behind. Vancouver did not fare as well, with the result that Winnipeg's per capita GDP steadily gained on Vancouver's.

Nor does a comparison of unemployment rates show that Winnipeg is in greater trouble than Vancouver. On the contrary, Winnipeg's average unemployment rate was the same as or lower than Vancouver's in eight out of 10 years—substantially lower most of the time (Table 23.6).

Instead of being characterized as decline, Winnipeg's slow growth could easily be seen as an asset since it stems, at least in part, from the fact that

Table 23.5   **GDP and Population Change, Vancouver and Winnipeg**

	1994	1995	1996	1997	1998	1999	2000	2001	2002	2003
Vancouver CMA										
Real GDP at basic prices (million $1997)	$50,881	$51,838	$53,316	$55,313	$55,589	$57,960	$61,810	$62,393	$65,385	$68,227
% change from previous year	5.3	1.9	2.9	3.7	0.5	4.3	6.6	0.9	4.8	4.3
Total population (000s)	1,788	1,845	1,907	1,958	1,985	2,013	2,040	2,076	2,111	2,141
% change from previous year	3.2	3.2	3.3	2.7	1.4	1.4	1.4	1.8	1.7	1.4
Real GDP per capita	$28,464	$28,093	$27,962	$28,246	$27,999	$28,799	$30,295	$30,053	$30,969	$31,873
Winnipeg CMA										
Real GDP at basic prices (million $1997)	$16,636	$17,197	$17,340	$18,131	$18,983	$19,078	$19,744	$20,354	$20,929	$21,040
% change from previous year	2.4	3.4	0.8	4.6	4.7	0.5	3.5	3.1	2.8	0.5
Total population (000s)	677	680	679	678	679	682	686	690	694	697
% change from previous year	0.3	0.4	−0.2	−0.1	0.2	0.5	0.6	0.5	0.5	0.5
Real GDP per capita	$24,567	$25,299	$25,551	$26,740	$27,956	$27,961	$28,763	$29,494	$30,171	$30,183

Note: Real GDP has inflation factored out; it is in constant 1997 dollars.
Source: Conference Board of Canada, Metropolitan Outlook data set.

the economic base is a well-balanced mix of agriculture, manufacturing, government (provincial capital and a major regional centre for the federal government), and education (two universities and a community college) and therefore is not subject to booms and is also relatively well-insulated from busts. However, when growth talk dominates the public agenda, such evidence is discounted.[2]

A decade ago Winnipeg's economic development efforts were undertaken in a mood akin to that of an addicted gambler, simultaneously desperate and hopeful. Leaving no stone unturned to induce

Table 23.6	**Unemployment Rates, Vancouver and Winnipeg (%)**									
	1994	1995	1996	1997	1998	1999	2000	2001	2002	2003
Vancouver	8.8	7.9	8.0	8.3	8.1	7.7	5.8	6.6	7.8	7.2
Winnipeg	10.4	7.9	8.3	7.3	5.8	5.9	5.3	5.2	5.2	5.2

Source: Conference Board of Canada, Metropolitan Outlook data set.

faster growth, Winnipeg's economic development strategies included competing to attract companies in aerospace and high technology and making Winnipeg a 'world grain centre' (Price Waterhouse, 1990: 93–7).[3] The nadir of that phase came in 1995, when the governments of Winnipeg and Manitoba spent some $55 million in a failed attempt to save the Winnipeg Jets NHL hockey team, since renamed the Phoenix Coyotes (Silver, 1996). Such actions are a product, not of rational economic calculations, but of the irrational fears produced by a growth-driven perspective in which 'smaller' also means 'less valuable' and 'less significant' (Leo and Brown, 2000).

In the new millennium, however, Winnipeg's decision-makers have emphasized the identification of existing areas of economic strength, building on them and seeking opportunities for the export of local production in preference to luring producers from elsewhere to relocate to Winnipeg. This finds direct expression in the City of Winnipeg's *Homegrown Economic Development Strategy* (Winnipeg, 2001) and the business plan of the newly reorganized economic development agency, Destination Winnipeg (Destination Winnipeg, 2003).

Infrastructure and Services

In looking at infrastructure and services in Vancouver, we referred to the relationship between development density on one hand and the cost of infrastructure and services on the other, noting that higher average densities across a metropolitan area produce more taxpayers to share the costs of what can then be higher-quality or lower-cost services.

The case of Winnipeg gives us an opportunity to examine the issue of density and cost more closely.

Much has been written about the urban development industry as a growth machine (Logan and Molotch, 1987), but relatively little attention has been paid to urban development as a machine for the production of empty spaces. In the typical North American city, empty spaces appear in both suburban areas and the inner city. In the suburbs this happens because farms, forests, or fields at the edge of the city are rarely developed in strict sequence, with the land nearest to existing urbanized tracts ahead of more distant ones in the development queue.

A parcel of land separated from the rest of the city by greenfields will require roads, sewerage, water lines, and transit service. These expensive services will have to be extended across lands that generate the low levels of taxation typical of farmland, rather than the much higher taxes that come from urban development. Once occupied, a new subdivision requires conveniently located community centres and library branches, the same response times for firefighters, police, and paramedics that more densely populated areas of the city enjoy. Street cleaning, snow removal, grass cutting, insect control, and everything else the municipality does will have to serve empty parcels of land as well as full ones. It is easy to see that Vancouver, with 690 persons per square kilometre, has an easier time paying its bills than Winnipeg, with 162. Even if everyone in Winnipeg lived in expensive homes and everyone in Vancouver in modest bungalows—which is decidedly not the case—Winnipeg would have trouble keeping pace.[4] Winnipeg and

Table 23.7   **Comparative Population Densities, Vancouver and Winnipeg**

Jurisdiction	Population 2001	Area sq. km.	Density per sq. km.
Vancouver CMA	1,986,965	2,878.52	690
Winnipeg CMA	671,274	4,151.48	162
City of Vancouver	545,671	114.67	4,759
City of Winnipeg	619,544	465.16	1,332

surrounding municipalities are forced to spread their services far more thinly than Vancouver-area municipalities[5] (Table 23.7). Suburban development in and near Winnipeg is one of two empty space machines that inflate the costs of infrastructure and services.

The second empty space machine is the decay, followed possibly by abandonment, of many inner-city neighbourhoods adjacent to the commercial heart of the city. In a city that is growing rapidly, development pressure tends to produce rapid gentrification or expansion of downtown towers. In slow-growth centres, the decay simply continues, and empty lots sprout, producing more untaxable land that must be serviced. Slow, sprawling growth carries a heavy price tag for Winnipeg, and the most readily quantifiable part of what amounts to a structural deficit is the deterioration of older infrastructure. A meticulous 1998 survey of Winnipeg's infrastructure found a massive disparity between the amount needed to maintain existing infrastructure and the amount actually being spent. Regional streets, for example, were found to be $10.2 million a year short of the required amount. Even more drastic was the situation of residential streets, which were found to have benefited from an average annual budgeted expenditure of $2.5 million, compared with a requirement of $30 million, a disparity of $27.5 million each year (Winnipeg, 1998: ch. 3). Although there has been no careful study since 1998, no one imagines that the situation has improved. Estimates of the total infrastructure deficit vary between $1 and $2 billion. Both academic commentators and the popular imagination

tend to associate the problem of sprawl with rapidly growing cities (Downs, 1994: 152), but a comparison of Winnipeg and Vancouver suggests that slow-growth cities pose the biggest sprawl problem (Lennon and Leo, 2001).

An understanding of how the production of empty spaces piles up liabilities also provides insights into the matter of Winnipeg's alleged decline. The word 'decline' springs to mind when Winnipeg is mentioned, not because of anything to do with either economic or population growth, but because of a proliferation of empty storefronts and decaying houses in a number of downtown districts, a profusion of potholes, and a sewer system so badly deteriorated that sinkholes open up in the streets and swallow automobiles and construction equipment. A good share of this deterioration stems from the willingness, indeed the determination, to spread the city so thinly as to deplete the resources available for the maintenance of existing infrastructure and services. Winnipeg's problem is not slow growth, but mismanagement of growth. The visible deterioration, in turn, eats away at the self-confidence that would be needed to enforce some sensible measures for better management of growth. The vicious cycle is not one of decline, it is one of mismanagement, leading to loss of confidence and, in turn, to unwillingness to correct the mismanagement.

Land Use

While Vancouver benefits from the densification induced by the provincial Agricultural Land

Reserve, Winnipeg struggles on without the benefit of serious regional controls over land use. Municipalities near Winnipeg are in a position to offer semi-rural lifestyles at much lower tax rates than those Winnipeg must charge, because it is up to the city to pay for policing, a transit system, public libraries, community centres, schooling for low-income children, and the many other services that are necessities in a major metropolitan area. At the same time, the residents of adjacent municipalities are only a short commute from enjoyment of city jobs, theatres, restaurants, concerts, sophisticated shopping, and other amenities of city life.

Small wonder that the adjacent municipalities are burgeoning, despite the fact that large tracts of land within the city remain undeveloped. Population growth within the city was 3.7 per cent from 1986 to 1991, 0.3 per cent over the next five years, and 0.17 from 1996 to 2001. Meanwhile, the 1996–2001 percentage growth for exurban areas was 6.41, 38 times faster. (East St Paul, home to the most expensive real estate in the metropolitan area, saw a population increase of 19.3 per cent during the same period. The municipality actually had more *absolute* population growth than Winnipeg, even though Winnipeg's 2001 population was about 620,000 to East St Paul's 7,700. Headingly, another formidable competitor for Winnipeg's urban growth, grew by 20.2 per cent.) In meeting exurban competition, Winnipeg not only suffers from the tax imbalance imposed on the deliverer of metropolitan-style services for the whole region, but also lacks Vancouver's drawing power as a growth magnet. The situation obviously calls out for some form of regional land-use regulation, or perhaps tax equalization, to right the imbalance, but there seems to be little chance of that. Manitoba's idea of dealing with regional issues is something called the Capital Region Committee, consisting of the mayors and reeves of 16 municipalities in the metropolitan area and the provincial Ministers of Intergovernmental Affairs and Conservation (Figure 23.1). This is supposed to be a body for the discussion and resolution of regional growth issues, but its composition tells the whole story of its capacity to exercise control over regional growth.

The 15 municipalities, with a population of about 52,000, that stand to gain by siphoning development away from the city have 15 votes, and the city itself, with 620,000 people, has one vote.[6]

Planning for Growth

At less than 8 per cent of the CMA population, the number of persons who have so far opted for tax havens outside the city is not in itself alarming. More worrisome for Winnipeg is the fact that there are now locations outside the city with the necessary service infrastructure, as well as the political will, to compete with the city on all fronts: residential, commercial, and industrial. Commercial and industrial development is flourishing in Headingly, immediately west of the city, and seems imminent north of the city. Residential development is blooming on all sides. Even more significant, however, is the degree to which the existence of this competition has watered down the political will of city residents and decision-makers to control sprawl within the city. A recent case in point is City Council's quick approval of an application to rezone a large parcel of farmland known as Waverley West for neighbourhood development. It is estimated that Waverley West will ultimately accommodate some 40,000 residents (Winnipeg City Council, 2004), more than 37 times as many as were added to Winnipeg's population between 1996 and 2001. The approval came in the face of an estimate by city planners that more than 20,000 greenfield lots could be brought on stream in areas of the city already zoned for neighbourhood development (Winnipeg, Planning, Property and Development, 2004: 13).

The decision on Waverley West very succinctly sums up the dilemmas facing slow-growth cities in a growth-obsessed society: Winnipeg's decision-makers, eager for faster growth, grasp at every development proposal, heedless of the fact that the inappropriate locations, densities, and neighbourhood designs of many of the proposals will have the cumulative effect of steadily undermining the city's ability to provide quality services and infrastructure. The wish for growth defeats rational planning,

Figure 23.1 **Manitoba's Capital Region**

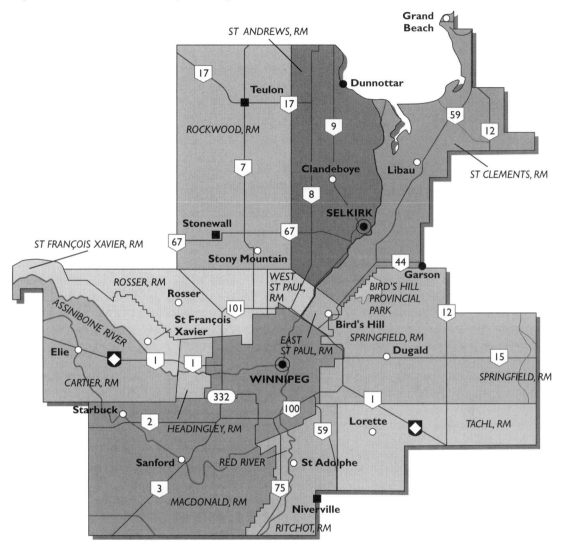

becomes the source of ill-considered policy, and undermines first the city's collective self-confidence and ultimately its viability.

Housing

One of the advantages of slow growth is that it keeps housing prices down. Vancouver's housing affordability problem, therefore, is mirrored in Winnipeg

by a policy opportunity. With single-family homes available for $60,000 or less, government incentives for the provision of moderate and low-income housing do not come at a high price to the taxpayer. Since decaying inner-city neighbourhoods are a problem that accompanies slow growth, affordable housing provision can bring the added benefit of stabilizing threatened neighbourhoods, all at a much lower cost in Winnipeg than in Vancouver.

Table 23.8	**Winnipeg Housing and Homelessness Initiative Funding Commitments: Levels of Government**
Level of Government	WHHI Funding over Three Years (2000–3)
City of Winnipeg programs	$4.2 million
Province of Manitoba—NHA	$6 million
Federal NHI programs	$23.5 million

Source: Leo and August (2005).

In Winnipeg all three levels of government have recognized these opportunities. For decades, the federal government's Residential Rehabilitation Assistance Program (RRAP), with the help of a 25 per cent provincial contribution, has been subsidizing the renovation of older homes. The provincial government also pays for home renovations through its Neighbourhood Housing Assistance program (NHA), which targets inner-city neighbourhoods, and the city has its own home renovation fund.

But there have also been squandered opportunities, growing directly out of a failure to appreciate the policy implications of growth rates. The federal government's National Homelessness Initiative (NHI), for example, only provided funds to deal with the problems of street people, i.e., for shelters, transitional housing, and services to homeless people but not housing development or renovation (Leo and August, 2005). This was reasonable for Toronto and Vancouver, where housing is expensive and the numbers of street people substantial, but not for Winnipeg, where the problem of visible homelessness is much less serious but where decaying inner-city neighbourhoods contribute to an acute problem of inadequate housing.

Slow and Fast Growth

Vancouver and Winnipeg are facing very different challenges and opportunities. Our findings show that Vancouver has created many of its opportuni-

ties for itself. Policy-makers have used Vancouver's drawing power as a lever for good planning. Vancouver has been growing rapidly, as the growth-imperative model anticipates, but has enjoyed much success in shaping the growth of the region. Winnipeg is not faced with intense population growth, yet its decision-makers cannot muster the courage to control the dispersal of the region's population. Meanwhile, the low collective self-confidence that North Americans typically associate with slow growth produces an exaggerated sense of powerlessness. City councils in such cities as Winnipeg become accustomed to accepting that mobile businesses can demand concessions based on their ability to locate, or relocate, elsewhere (Leo, 1994). Often, this distasteful knowledge is generalized into the belief that it is impossible ever to refuse a developer's demands.

Winnipeg, it seems, has overlooked the difference between mobile development, which could do business from various cities, and one tied to a particular locality, such as a retail business or a residential subdivision. While Winnipeg is unquestionably subject to limitations in the terms and conditions it can dictate to a corporate branch office, or branch plant, it could be in substantially the same position as Vancouver with respect to residential and retail development, on one condition. That condition—unfortunately a big one—is that the provincial government take action to ensure relief for the City of Winnipeg from the one-sided competition it faces from surrounding municipalities. As we have shown, these municipalities are able to offer a spacious, semi-rural environment and low taxes, with the added benefit of access to the services and economic opportunities of Winnipeg, without the obligation to share the costs borne by residents of the city. Relief from this competition could take the form of either a tax-sharing arrangement or, more constructively, some growth management rules to ensure that the entire region develops in such a way as to safeguard the environment and the viability of the region's network of infrastructure and services.

Some things are overdetermined by the rate of urban growth. As long as the contrast in the two cities' rates of growth persists, Vancouver will not have the benefit of Winnipeg's affordable housing and Winnipeg will not enjoy Vancouver's impunity in dictating terms to mobile corporations; the contrasts between wealth and poverty will remain more glaring in Vancouver, but the streets will be livelier and the economic opportunities more numerous and varied. However, given intelligent management and sensible intergovernmental cooperation, there is no serious reason why both cities cannot enjoy high-quality services and infrastructure, safeguards for air, water, and soil, both within the city and surrounding it, a significant amount of affordable housing, attractive, functional, well-designed neighbourhoods, and a lively, diverse core. Slow growth will make some of these boons easier to achieve and rapid growth will be an advantage in the pursuit of others. The only unqualified bane is growth talk and the policy illusions it brings.

Notes

1. According to two censuses of homeless people, their number in Greater Vancouver doubled, from 1,049 in 2002 to 2,112 in 2005 (GVRD, 2005). Another report suggested that 125,000 people are at risk of becoming homeless in that they pay 50 per cent or more of their income for shelter (Ladner, 2004).

2. This was the public mood in the 1990s, when Winnipeg was caught up in a kind of collective growth panic. The media vacillated between pessimistic warnings of a clouded future and declarations that the 'big break' was just around the corner. If the Winnipeg Jets go, $50 million will be lost to the economy; if the Canadian Wheat Board is abolished or relocated, 5,000 jobs will be lost; Winnipeg is about to become a major North American transportation hub, thousands of jobs will be created, and millions added to the economy. These are samples of what amounted to a steady stream of journalistic manic depression.

3. Drawing on the microeconomics literature, Leo and Brown (2000) made a case—which need not be repeated here—that global-scale changes in technology and the economy were reducing many of the advantages that large, diverse companies once enjoyed,

while opening new opportunities for smaller enterprises. They argued that, today more than ever, cities that are not major economic players are best advised to support and promote smaller enterprises and to build on the local economy, not to throw subsidies around in an attempt to compete with the Vancouvers, Torontos, and New Yorks of this world for major companies.

4. Various studies that have calculated the infrastructure costs associated with different densities and settlements patterns, as well as the differences between uniform and mixed-use developments, make it clear that the low-density, single land use typical of North American suburbs and exurban areas carries a heavy price tag (Essiambre-Phillips-Desjardins Associated et al., 1995; Isard and Coughlin, 1957; Leo et al., 2002; Real Estate Research Corporation, 1974; Wheaton and Schussheim, 1955). Studies that go beyond infrastructure to calculate the costs of other services (Blais, 1995; Greater Toronto Area Task Force, 1996) similarly demonstrate that higher densities and greater proximity of different types of development (houses, stores, offices) produce substantial savings compared with the isolated residential districts, shopping centres, and industrial areas typical of North American suburban development.

5. By sheer force of numbers and distance, cities necessarily densify as they get larger, even if they are badly planned, and if they are growing rapidly, they densify more quickly. As a practical matter, that means that when leapfrog development takes place at the edge of metropolitan Vancouver, the empty spaces that represent a taxpayer liability get filled in quickly; in Winnipeg, they languish for a long time as empty spaces and taxpayer liability.

6. Another sign of Manitoba's 'steadfast commitment' to regional growth rules is the fact that the Capital Region Committee's Web site is, at this writing, about two years out of date (Manitoba, n.d.). Effective action to deal with regional growth issues is not on the political agenda, and there is no relief in sight. Successive Progressive Conservative and New Democratic governments have had similarly permissive attitudes towards regional urban growth, and slow-growth Winnipeg suffers acutely as a result. For a concrete example of the results of failure to regulate regional growth effectively, see Leo (2002: 229–31).

Chapter 24

Immigration and Urban Change: National, Regional, and Local Perspectives

Heidi Hoernig and Margaret Walton-Roberts

In this chapter we examine national, regional, and local policy responses to the geography of immigrant settlement. At the national scale we broadly consider immigration policy as it relates to immigrant settlement patterns, particularly urban concentration. At the regional scale we interpret both the nature of immigrant concentration in certain core urban regions, particularly the Greater Toronto Area and its surroundings, and the emergence of recent policy debate regarding immigrant dispersal to regions beyond the largest cities. At the local scale we interpret how urban areas with significant immigrant communities have managed service provision and municipal land-use planning under conditions of increasing ethnic diversity and urban change. This chapter is therefore intended to provide a broad overview of the interconnections among immigration, ethnic diversity, and urban change at various scales.

Federal Policy, Immigration, and Canadian Cities

Immigration and Urbanization

As the country's default population policy (Ley and Hiebert, 2001), immigration plays a central role in determining Canada's social, economic, and cultural future. In the current context of declining fertility and population aging, immigration has become a vital component of Canada's population and labour force growth. In 2003 immigration accounted for 65 per cent of population growth and over the decade of the 1990s represented almost 70 per cent of the total growth of the Canadian labour force. If current immigration rates remain constant, by 2011 immigration will account for virtually all labour force growth (Statistics Canada, 2003b). Recent immigration also contributes to social transformation through increased ethnic diversity. Since the 1960s the origins of Canadian immigrants have shifted from Europe and the United States to Asia, the Pacific, Africa, and the Middle East. For example, in 2002 over 50 per cent of immigrants came from Asia and Pacific realms, while only 17 per cent came from Europe (Citizenship and Immigration Canada, 2002).

The geographical outcomes of immigrant settlement since the 1980s have also changed. Immigrants, especially those from Asia, exhibit a far greater propensity to settle in large urban centres. The impact of immigration is therefore most visible in the largest Canadian cities, especially the Greater Toronto Area (GTA), the Greater Vancouver Regional District (GVRD), and the Montreal CMA, Canada's modern gateway cities.[1] Table 24.1 identifies the settlement patterns of immigrants by country of birth and, with some European-origin exceptions, reveals a general pattern of immigrant concentration in the nation's three largest cities. While research has tempered concern over the possibility of US-style connections between immigrant concentration and poverty (Ley and Smith, 2000), immigrant concentration has nevertheless been subjected to several negative assessments linked to urban growth, environmental sustainability, and social relations (Collacot, 2002; Stoffman, 2002). Daniel Stoffman (2003), for example, argues that the federal government's immigration policy is in effect an urban growth policy, particularly for the Greater

Table 24.1   **Place of Residence in 1996 by Place of Birth, Immigrants Who Landed During 1991–6**

Place of Residence	Three Largest Cities (%)	Next Five Largest Cities (%)	Other CMAs (%)	Non-CMAs (%)	Number (000s)
Canadian-born	27	13	18	43	23,390
Immigrants	74	13	7	6	1,039
Immigrants born in:					
USA	41	14	16	29	29
UK	44	17	13	25	25
Germany	34	12	13	41	8
Netherlands	18	14	5	61	3
Switzerland	23	7	3	65	3
Italy	69	13	10	8	3
Portugal	81	8	7	4	9
Yugoslavia	54	19	19	7	22
Russian Fed.	77	14	4	5	11
Poland	64	17	13	5	37
Bosnia/Herzegovina	45	23	27	6	9
Hong Kong	89	8	2	1	109
China	78	13	5	3	88
India	75	12	4	9	71
Philippines	72	19	4	4	71
Jamaica	83	11	4	2	21

Source: Citizenship and Immigration Canada (2001).

Toronto Area. During the 1990s and early 2000s almost 40 per cent of all immigrants to Canada settled in Toronto, up from 28 per cent in the early to mid-1980s (Walton-Roberts and Smith, 2005). Toronto now has the second highest percentage of foreign-born population globally, after Miami (see Table 24.2), and is most likely the most ethnically diverse city in the world.[2] As a result Toronto is considered 'the world in a city' because it is home to immigrants from over 170 countries who speak over 100 languages (Anisef and Lanphier, 2003).

Immigrants are also increasingly settling in suburban regions surrounding large cities (Hiebert, 1999). This is especially evident in the nation's core urban area, the extended Golden Horseshoe that comprises the GTA and extends east to Oshawa, southeast to St Catharines–Niagara, west to Kitchener, and north to Barrie. Home to 22 per cent of Canada's population, this region experienced half of Canada's total population growth in the period between 1996 and 2001. Driven by its integration into the North American auto

Table 24.2   **Top 10 Cities by Share of Foreign-Born Population, 2000–1**

City	% Foreign-Born
Miami	59
Toronto	44
Los Angeles	41
Vancouver	37
New York City	36
Singapore	33
Sydney	31
Abidjan	30
London	28
Paris	23

Source: United Nations Human Development Report (2004: 99).

manufacturing system, the region boasts a regional median household income of $62,252, over $7,000 higher than the national median of $55,016 (2001 census). While immigrants are certainly attracted to the area's economic success—between 1994 and 2003 close to 50 per cent of all immigrants to Canada settled in this area—recent research indicates that the most important factor in immigrant settlement decisions is the presence of family or friends (Statistics Canada, 2003c). Extensive social networks, therefore, can act as immigrant conduits and resulting chain migration processes become centred on immigrant gateway cities such as Toronto and its surroundings.

Current Immigrant Policy and Urban Settlement

Both humanitarian and economic criteria shape Canada's current immigration policy. Refugee/asylum policies together with family reunification comprise the humanitarian aspects of immigration policy, but the overwhelming share of immigrants who have come to Canada in the last decade have been selected through economic criteria. Federal policy-makers assume that Canada must compete in the global economy through an export-led economic strategy that depends on foreign capital and skilled and professional labour capacity. Thus, in an age of low domestic birth rates, these needs must be met through immigration (Simmons, 1999: 46).

Current Canadian immigration policy is designed according to such assumptions and targets economic immigrants such as skilled workers and entrepreneurs. Skilled workers are assessed according to language ability, skills, education, and employment experience. These applicants and their families have provided the majority of Canada's recent immigrants, but their economic integration has been hindered by widespread credential recognition problems (Bauder, 2003). Business immigrants include entrepreneurs and investors who make economic investments in Canada in exchange for entry. Despite the positive rhetoric accompanying this policy, the economic success of this immigrant stream has been mixed (Ley, 2003b). Federal policy has changed to increasingly favour economic immigrants, so that in 2001 they made up over 61 per cent of the total intake compared to 36 per cent in 1986 (Citizenship and Immigration Canada, 2002). Over the same period landings to the three largest cities have increased from around 52 per cent of all immigrant arrivals in the early 1980s to over 74 per cent in the late 1990s. Settlement in Toronto accounted for a substantial part of this shift. Indeed, in 2002 Toronto received over 50 per cent of all the economic-class immigrants who landed in Canada during that year (Citizenship and Immigration Canada, 2002). Large urban cities are the staging posts for the new global economy; they are the sites that accommodate the economic demands Canada has sought to satisfy by importing skilled labour and immigrant capital. Therefore the geographical concentration of immigrants in Canada's largest urban regions should not be too surprising.

Despite the positive economic and cultural benefits that accompany immigrant concentration in the nation's largest cities, such growth is also accompanied by certain costs. Critics of Canada's immigration policy claim that the numbers of immigrants and rates of admission have negatively influenced integration (Stoffman, 2002) and may result in social tension and civic dysfunction (Collacott, 2002). However, by focusing solely on the nature and number of newcomers, critics fail to examine the broader political context of settlement, which during the 1990s consisted of sustained high levels of immigration accompanied by severe federal and provincial government fiscal cutbacks. Federal program spending as a share of GDP declined by one-third from the early to the late 1990s, ending the decade at rates lower than any time since World War II (Stanford, 1999). These cutbacks, when combined with significant immigrant settlement, create huge challenges for managing urban growth and providing urban services, particularly those required by immigrants. The Toronto experience is illustrative of this dynamic (Frisken and Wallace, 2003; Hanna and Walton-Roberts, 2004). The concerns expressed by Collacott and Stoffman, therefore, must be read as concerns over the *context* of settlement, rather than solely a concern with the nature and scale of immigration (Walton-Roberts, 2005).

With its strong emphasis on Canadian economic needs, federal immigration policy has also neglected to consider carefully social behaviour and organization within the context of immigrant settlement, as evidenced by the lack of parallel investment in adequate settlement services throughout the 1990s. Once immigrant newcomers settle in Canada they often turn to their co-ethnic community for social support and cultural security—hence, increasing ethnic concentration can be a reflection of positive voluntary community-building processes (Qadeer, 2003). However, such concentration is also reflective of constrained choices faced by immigrants, and this is particularly evident in a context of fiscal restraint where services are reduced and newcomers use the informal assistance of friends and family to help them access housing, employment, and other resources. In Toronto this has been linked to the increasing presence of a 'shadow state' where voluntarism evolves into a

two-tier system of mainstream and co-ethnic immigrant settlement services (Sadiq, 2004).

Regardless of this wider policy and political context there have been highly publicized critiques of immigrant concentration, and these critiques have contributed to a broader policy debate regarding how immigration policy could be altered to produce a more balanced regional settlement pattern. This debate has also been propelled by regions and provinces that do not contain gateway cities. Provinces such as Manitoba and Alberta, as well as northern and rural regions across the nation, have expressed an interest in using immigration to fill their demographic and labour needs. This has led to new developments in federal-provincial relations as regions outside of the major urban cores seek a greater share of Canada's immigration intake.

Immigration, Regionalism, and Intergovernmental Relations

Until recently the federal government was the primary authority in immigration matters, with little provincial involvement. Over the past few years several provincial governments have expressed support for immigration policies that would lead to greater regional development outside the main metropolitan growth centres. Quebec was the first province to seek more control of immigration, and subsequent provincial involvement has targeted settlement services funding and Provincial Nominee Program (PNP) agreements. (PNP agreements allow provinces to identify applicants who fulfill provincially designated labour market needs, exempting them from meeting certain federal immigration policy criteria.) Faced with declining populations some prairie and Atlantic communities see immigration as a tool to increase population and to fill labour market gaps. PNP agreements have helped Prairie provinces attract skilled professionals and may mark the beginning of a slight shift in immigrant settlement patterns. For example, in 2002, 1,527 PNP immigrants went to Manitoba, which represented over 70 per cent of all Canadian PNP arrivals. Although the actual numbers are small, we are seeing shifts in immigration trends. Indeed, in 2004 the Prairie provinces experienced the first relative increase in their share of immigrants since 1988, receiving 11 per cent of the national immigration total (Vineberg, 2005). Many of these immigrants are settling in Calgary, Edmonton, Winnipeg, and Saskatoon.[3]

Immigration, Metropolitan Regions, and Urban Policy

Our third level of analysis addresses the local context, which certainly has the greatest impact on the day-to-day lives of Canadian immigrants. Here we see the consequences of the intersection of the social geography of immigration with national immigration policy and municipal urban policy.

Municipal Approaches to Immigration

Immigration has been largely responsible for Canadian urban economic and population growth, creating a reciprocal relationship between cities and immigrants. Research in this area has evaluated what Ley (in Edgington and Hutton, 2002: 13) refers to as 'multicultural readiness', that is, the capacity of municipalities to address issues associated with high recent immigrant populations: cultural accommodation, equity, and accessibility. While all levels of government share responsibility for immigrant settlement and integration, the federal and provincial governments act as co-ordinators and funders, while local governments and the not-for-profit and private sectors are primarily involved in service delivery. This results in a municipal policy context that includes hierarchical and lateral policy networks across federal, provincial, regional, and local government and includes non-governmental and private organizations (Edgington and Hutton, 2002).

Municipalities face several challenges in addressing immigrant issues (Frisken and Wallace, 2003: 157–8). They have no constitutional obligation to address immigration, and are largely constrained by the dictates of their provincial masters. Municipal revenues depend on property taxes and thus are sensitive to economic trends and beholden to new development to finance programs and services. Furthermore, national and provincial multicultural policies provide almost no practical guidance on handling local issues related to immigration.

Understandably, central cities with high immigrant populations, such as Toronto, Vancouver, and Montreal, have made greater investments in inclusionary municipal services than their adjacent, outer suburban communities, which have hosted comparatively lower numbers of immigrants in the past (Edgington and Hutton, 2002; Frisken and Wallace, 2003; Germain et al., 2003; Wallace and Frisken, 2000). Municipal-wide policies that promote and support the multicultural communities accommodate cultural diversity, promote equity and difference, and make strong statements against racial discrimination. Examples include the City of Vancouver's Civic Policy on Multicultural Relations (Vancouver, 2004b), and the City of Montreal's 1989 *Declaration against Racial Discrimination* (Germain et al., 2000).[4] However, as Germain et al. (2003) observe, formal policies alone do not guarantee their effective implementation. Municipalities demonstrate their commitment to their newcomers' needs through program and service delivery. Many municipalities have focused on improved communication in service delivery, including translation services, multilingual Web pages or literature, and the use of community-based ethnic organizations and media to distribute information (Edgington and Hutton, 2002; Frisken and Wallace, 2003; Siemiatycki et al., 2001). For example, Vancouver's CityPlan project implemented its neighbourhood visioning process with the use of facilitators, the ethnic media, the translation of key documents, and a multilingual telephone line (Edgington and Hutton, 2002; Lee, 2002). Other municipal endeavours have included staff training in cultural sensitivity and race relations and concerted efforts to develop a multicultural municipal workforce (Frisken and Wallace, 2003). Municipalities have also developed specific programs in such areas as affordable housing and sports and leisure (Germain et al., 2003).

Critics observe that despite some gains in municipal responses to immigration, municipal actors continue to respond to many problem-solving and decision-making scenarios in an ad hoc or 'trial and error' manner (Germain et al., 2003; Moore Milroy and Wallace, 2002). They also note the critical role that local community organizations have played in determining the extent to which municipal responses to newcomer issues are implemented.

Settlement Services

Observers of immigrant settlement and integration note the multiple challenges that immigrants face upon arrival in Canadian cities. Immigrants must find housing, secure employment, improve language skills, upgrade their education or obtain Canadian professional credentials, access health care, help their children settle into schools, and cope with the general challenges of adapting to a foreign culture, a different climate, and a new urban environment (Mwarigha, 2002; Omidvar and Richmond, 2003). For refugees fleeing dangerous circumstances, these challenges are further compounded by their need for emotional and psychological recovery.

The two main phases of immigrant incorporation into Canadian society are settlement and integration (Canadian Council for Refugees, 1998). Settlement is the initial period during which immigrants acclimatize to their new surroundings, find work and housing, and adapt to a new way of life. Integration refers to the long-term process through which immigrants gradually come to participate fully in their new society. Settlement services develop immigrants' skills and knowledge, respond to specialized needs, strengthen relationships between newcomer and host communities, and help host communities adapt to newcomers (Canadian Council for Refugees, 1998). Federal and provincial funding is allocated through two main programs: Language Instruction for Newcomers to Canada and the Immigrant Settlement and Adaptation Program.

The current need for settlement services is compounded by recent trends showing that immigrant labour market rewards have decreased over the last decade (Human Resources Development Canada, 2001; Reitz, 2001), while immigrant poverty has increased (Basavarajappa and Jones, 1999; Kazemipur and Halli, 2001; Ornstein, 2002). Furthermore, these trends are more noticeable for most visible minority groups. For instance, Ornstein's (2002: 97) study of ethno-racial inequality in Toronto based on 1996 data reveals that the incidence of poverty in non-European ethno-racial groups is much higher than it is for European ethno-racial groups (36.9 per cent of all families in Toronto are non-European, yet they account for 58.9 per cent of all poor families). Responding to the broader context of economic fluctuation, rising social polarization, and the increase and geographical concentration of urban poverty (see Chapter 25), immigrant policy advocates and immigrant-serving agencies have pressed for the use of settlement services to mitigate economic disadvantage (Omidvar and Richmond, 2003). With the neo-liberal shift towards the contracting out of governmental services, NGOs have become the principal agents of settlement service delivery. Yet the NGO sector is increasingly under pressure due to growing service demands, diminished, unstable, and short-term funding sources, increased competition for funding, greater accountability reporting requirements, fewer volunteers, and often insufficient staff and administrative support (Richmond and Shields, 2004).

Geographic issues are particularly important in ensuring accessibility to settlement services. Earlier models of immigrant settlement depicting new immigrants as landing and residing in ethnic enclaves in the inner city have given way to increasingly suburban settlement, particularly in Vancouver and Toronto (see Chapters 9 and 12; also Hiebert, 2000b). These new patterns require the simultaneous suburbanization of settlement services (Ley and Murphy, 2001; Hiebert, 2000b). Similarly, recent trends concerning the spatial concentration of poverty resurrect the question of whether a spatially sensitive policy approach targeting disadvantaged neighbourhoods would be effective as a means of serving those most in need and of mitigating the negative neighbourhood effects of poverty (Séguin and Divay, 2002). The underlying challenge of matching the location of services and infrastructure with communities of need is shared by many immigrant settlement service providers.

Municipal Land-Use Planning

The ethno-racial diversity that immigration brings to cities results in a number of land-use planning issues. These issues challenge planners (and communities) 'to define, in locally relevant ways, the meaning of Canadian multiculturalism' (Hiebert, 2000b: 32). They also require municipalities and planning professionals to reconsider their definitions of 'public interest', the hidden cultural values embedded in planning practice, and the degree of community participation within their planning practices (Qadeer, 1997; Sandercock, 2003).

Planning within the context of ethno-racial diversity raises issues that can be categorized into two key areas: the accommodation of cultural difference and the demand for equity. Two central questions related to cultural difference have been succinctly articulated by Wang (1999: 34) in his discussion of ethnic commercial activity:

must ethnic minorities adapt to the [land-use] conventions of mainstream society or should mainstream society show flexibility to accommodate innovative . . . practices transplanted from other cultures?

As such, Wang is asking: to what degree should Canadian municipalities with high ethno-racial diversity define a *margin of flexibility* within their land-use planning practices? In the area of equity, most issues are related to planning processes and their accessibility to immigrant participation. Process is important because it defines how community needs are identified and incorporated into planning activities. In most cases, planners are reactive, responding in an ad hoc manner as issues emerge (Moore Milroy and Wallace, 2002; Qadeer, 2001). Planning processes become particularly salient in situations of conflict because cross-cultural communication and inter-ethnic interaction further complicate the identification and resolution of

issues. Issues of places of worship, ethnic retailing, and land-use conflict illustrate the intersection of land-use planning and ethno-cultural diversity.

Places of Worship

Many recent immigrants belong to religious communities that are relatively new to Canadian society. The first major task of these communities is to develop appropriate places of worship. Places of worship are important because they provide spiritual services that can assist individuals and families through the difficult integration process. They also fulfill other social needs, providing sites for cultural and religious ceremonies and activities, support services for children and seniors, and personal support in such areas as housing, employment, and counselling (Ebaugh et al., 2000; Germain and Gagnon, 2003).

As recently as the 1980s Canadian urban planning issues related to places of worship were primarily concerned with Christian and Jewish communities. The most recent decades of immigration, however, have brought a proliferation of minority religions to Canadian cities, particularly world religions such as Buddhism, Hinduism, Islam, and Sikhism (Bramadat, 2005). Religious communities of these faiths organize time, space, and social relations in ways that differ from Christian and secular Canadian traditions. Many of these cultural patterns have implications for land-use planning.

In the movement to address emerging places of minority worship some municipalities, such as those in the Greater Toronto Area, have had to address several basic policy issues (Chaudhry, 1996; Qadeer and Chaudhry, 2000). Policy references to churches have been replaced with inclusive wording such as 'places of worship' or 'places of religious assembly'. Planners have had to include provisions for alternative architectural features such as domes and minarets. In addition, they have had to redefine parking formulas for places of worship that do not use conventional seating—i.e., pews or chairs—and therefore accommodate more people per square foot of interior space.[5] Municipalities have conducted special studies to deal with places of worship, examining issues such as parking requirements, traffic impacts, and the location of places of worship in residential areas and industrial areas (Brampton, 2000; Macaulay Shiomi Howson Ltd, 2002; Mississauga, 2000).

Some issues related to places of worship are not exclusive to minority religious communities. Both majority and minority religious communities carry out multiple social functions and frequently construct large social facilities in conjunction with worship areas. Further, with the mobility of households and the proliferation of types of religious communities, many places of worship, regardless of size, function as regional facilities rather than local parishes (Macaulay Shiomi Howson Ltd, 2002). These issues have resulted in traffic and parking impacts that depart from those of previous decades, and again, have required municipalities to adjust community plan policies and zoning bylaws (Mississauga, 2000; Mississauga, 2002; York, 2004).

Ethnic Retailing

Studies of recent Asian immigrant settlement and commercial activity illustrate the relationship among changes in immigrant policy, immigrant origins and characteristics, settlement and integration patterns, and subsequent commercial activities. The outcomes of these interactions have had significant implications for municipal land-use policy (Li, 1992; Lo and Wang, 1997; Wang, 1999; Preston and Lo, 2000).

Chinese immigration to Canada increased substantially over the past two decades due to both changes in Canadian immigrant policy and the political economy of East Asia (Lo and Wang, 1997). Unlike earlier waves of Chinese immigrants, those arriving in Canada during the 1990s entered through business immigration programs, were wealthier and better educated, and, rather than settling in central-city Chinatowns, located in suburban areas such as Richmond, BC (Li, 1992), and Markham and Richmond Hill, Ontario (Preston and Lo, 2000). Chinese commercial activity shifted from being primarily an inner-city phenomenon to become suburban. For example, in Toronto during the 1980s, Chinese commercial activity was located in three Chinatowns: Old Chinatown (Dundas Street West), central Chinatown (Spadina Avenue and Dundas Street West), and East Chinatown (Gerrard Street East and Broadview Avenue). The gradual suburbanization of Chinese commercial activity took place first in the Agincourt area in Scarborough, expanding out to Markham, Mississauga, Richmond Hill, and Vaughan (Wang, 1999). The central-city Chinatown has been dominated by small-scale family-operated businesses that specialize in food retail and dining. Newer suburban shopping centres feature an expanded spectrum of businesses and services, many of which belong to globalized overseas corporations with headquarters in Hong Kong, Taiwan, or China (Wang, 1999: 30).

The development of Asian malls has forced several Toronto region municipalities to address this new form of ethnic commercial development (Preston and Lo, 2000; Wang, 1999). First, suburban Chinese commercial development has broken loose from the conventional three-tiered retail hierarchy of neighbourhood, community, and regional shopping centre and has formed clustered districts of Chinese shopping centres. This development pattern has challenged orthodox Canadian retail conventions and has come into conflict with official plan policies. Municipalities have had to study and reconfigure existing land-use policy to adjust to, and prepare for, similar future developments. Municipalities have also had to develop regulations to control retail condominiums. Community opposition to the new malls pushed municipalities to further investigate uncertain parking and traffic impacts.

Ethnic retail and its associated services have the capacity to boost economic activity and inject commercial variety into faltering or homogeneous urban landscapes. Zhuang (2003) observes how ethnic business owners transform retail districts into unique urban places through the combination of land use, urban design (e.g., street furniture, sidewalk stalls, and festival space), decorations (e.g., banners and facades), and architectural elements such as materials (e.g., stucco, ceramic tiling, or wrought iron), cultural symbols (e.g., colours or iconography), and the creative uses of space (e.g., markets, patios, stalls, plazas, awnings, and gardens). These features are sometimes further enhanced by district business retail associations or municipal governments that, in their attempt to create official municipal tourist or heritage districts, promote the development of infrastructure, public art, parks, landscaping, marketing, or street maintenance projects or programs. Examples include sidewalk mosaics in Vancouver's Downtown Eastside Footprints Community Art Project (Moss, 2003) and the many Canadian inner-city Chinatowns marked by arches, lamps, street furniture, gardens, and parks, which promote a traditional image of Chinese culture and heritage. These districts strengthen ethnic community identity and contribute to a local, spatial multiculturalism.

Land-Use Conflict

Despite the potential for community and urban enhancement, land-use issues also include conflict involving cultural and equity issues. Land-use conflicts can arise when differences in behaviour, values, or needs result in disagreement over the best way for urban development to take place. They also occur when residents cannot accept differences taking place in their community and resist outsiders because of fear, ignorance, or discriminatory attitudes. Of course, conflict is not always entirely negative and can be a catalyst for positive change in the planning system.

A land-use planning conflict that exemplifies the role of culture and difference in urban planning is the mega- or 'monster' home debate that took place in Vancouver during the late 1980s and early 1990s in the long-established Anglo-Canadian neighbourhoods of Kerrisdale and Shaughnessy (Ley, 1995; Ley, 2000; Li, 1994; Mitchell, 1997). While conflicts over so-called 'monster' homes are common to many communities across Canada (see, e.g., Ontario Municipal Board, 2001, 2002), this particular controversy stands out because of the scale and duration of the debate and its polarization of opponents and proponents largely along ethnic

lines. The conflict developed as wealthy Hong Kong immigrants purchased properties in pre-existing well-to-do neighbourhoods and rebuilt the original properties in a fashion suited to the newcomers' preferences. These new homes were large, usually more than 4,000 square feet, with narrow setbacks, large windows, and minimal vegetation. The size, architectural style, and site design of these homes departed significantly from the neighbourhoods' 'leafy, landscaped streets and gardens with character homes, including mansions frequently of Georgian, French, Dutch, or especially Tudor revival styles' (Ley, 2000: 28).

Opposition to this development from existing homeowners rapidly became a public and political debate and was reported widely in the local, national, and international media. Accusations of racism and intolerance were made on both sides. Many questioned whether the debate was really about neighbourhood design, or if 'unwanted Chinese neighbours' (Li, 1994) were at the core of the issue. Several community-based groups of both long-term Anglo-Canadian and recent Chinese-Canadian residents were formed and became politically active in the debate. After several political and bureaucratic interventions the issue was finally resolved through planning regulations. Over time a facilitated process involving both residents groups developed zoning bylaws with specific design criteria to accommodate new residential development and also address long-term residents' concerns.

One frequent observation has been that issues such as that regarding the Chinese 'monster' homes in Vancouver reveal the conservative nature of urban planning (Isin and Siemiatycki, 1999; Qadeer, 1997; Sandercock, 1998). The Canadian planning system is highly effective at maintaining the status quo and responds easily to those who fear or oppose change. Thus, many scholars question the ability of municipalities to implement Canada's claimed multiculturalism at the local level (Germain and Gagnon, 2003; Ray et al., 1997). They ask how meaningful multiculturalism is in a society that only permits one cultural interpretation of urban development. Such questions concerning urban, spatial multiculturalism reveal contradictions in the supposed neutrality of urban planning principles and practice (Mitchell, 1997; Qadeer, 1997; Qadeer, 2001; Sandercock, 1998). Debates about land-use compatibility, streetscape character, harmonious design, acceptable rates and degrees of urban landscape change, and social mix illustrate the cultural basis for many essential planning concepts. Land-use conflicts typically include differing ideas about what is appropriate and compatible land use. They illustrate the dynamic and heterogeneous nature of community perceptions and valuations of land and land use.

Another important reading of these issues considers the role of discrimination, racism, intolerance, and fear of 'the other'. Opponents to immigrant-related development rarely openly exhibit intolerant views. However, some people do make blunt public statements that expose their fears of difference and outsiders through their attempts to preserve the dominance of Anglo-Canadian cultural norms and their faulty assumptions that immigrant settlement will result in the creation of ghettos (Isin and Siemiatycki, 1999; Ley, 1995; Li, 1994; Wang, 1999). Many victims of this intolerance have publicly identified the discrimination and successfully leveraged it to force municipalities to use a more inclusive planning process, as seen in both the Asian mall and mega-home debates.

It is also important to avoid hasty overgeneralizations in these debates, as they can be further complicated by inter- and intra-ethnic diversity. At least two studies show that the division of people for or against certain developments is not exclusively drawn along ethnic lines. For example, Rose's (1999) study of Anglo-Canadian and Asian-Canadian responses to neighbourhood change in Richmond, BC, reveals that sometimes length of residence, not ethnicity, was associated with common reactions to new development. Similarly, concerning both the support of and opposition to Asian malls by Chinese Canadians, Preston and Lo (2000: 188) point out that:

> the differences in opinions about the proposed mall expressed by Chinese-Canadians remind us that there is no single Chinese-Canadian identity. Length of residence in Canada, social class, occupation and many other social characteristics differentiate Chinese-Canadians from each other. These differences are overlooked and disregarded when . . . immigrant groups mark their presence by concrete changes in the landscape.

These observations demonstrate the complexity of social phenomena at work in land-use planning conflicts.

Conclusion

Immigration to Canada over the last two decades has resulted in shifting settlement patterns and increased ethnic diversity and cultural transformation in the nation's largest cities. The benefits and challenges of this demographic change have been the subject of numerous commentaries. In assessing the impact of immigration we have argued that the political and policy *context* of settlement, locally, regionally, and nationally, as well as the composition and consistency of immigrant flows, must be considered. Such an approach encourages a sharper awareness of the challenges of immigrant integration during a time of rapid urban growth and severe government fiscal retrenchment. We also suggest that the geographical patterns of immigrant settlement are in some ways an outcome of both the economic criteria of immigration policy and the limited presence of extensive formal systems of settlement integration. In such situations immigrants' needs are satisfied through informal channels of chain migration and social networks, and these tendencies contribute to ongoing concentrations of immigrant settlement in core urban regions.

Despite this pattern, a recent policy debate has emerged concerning regionalization of immigrant settlement, driven by the demographic and economic needs of urban regions beyond the largest cities. In developing immigration plans for these regions the experiences of larger cities in dealing with cultural diversity and urban change provide vital information. Successful immigrant settlement requires numerous support services that have to be co-ordinated and funded via increasingly complex and challenging financial arrangements, policy networks, and organizational environments. It further demands adaptation across the entire municipal public sector, spanning a range of issues such as retail development, places of worship, and neighbourhood change.

It is possible that the emerging regionalization debate over immigration will shift the debate from one of concern over immigrant concentration to one of building coherent frameworks to enhance immigrant dispersal. However, that being said, there are still important factors to consider in making immigrant settlement work across Canada, whether in cities, towns, or rural areas. Future policy responses to immigration need to direct appropriate resources to facilitate settlement and integration and ensure that all levels of governments give thoughtful consideration to planning for diversity, rather than merely reacting to it.

Notes

1. The term 'gateway city' refers to those urban areas that have acted as entry points, regional nodes, and reception centres for immigrants. Traditional immigrant gateway cities were port cities (e.g., Halifax) or regional centres (Winnipeg). They are now those cities hosting major international airports and large tertiary and quaternary employment sectors.

2. Over 60 per cent of Miami's population is Hispanic, half of which are Cuban (US Census Bureau, 2002).

3. Small communities have also looked to immigration to address declining populations and labour shortages. For example, the local municipal government of Steinbach, Manitoba (with a population of just under 10,000 in 2001), instigated its own community immigration plan and began recruiting Russian/German Mennonite immigrants. Sharing similar cultural backgrounds to community residents, these immigrants brought appropriate economic skills and provided a much needed demographic boost to the region (Rural Development Institute, 2005). Cases like Steinbach are unlikely to significantly alter dominant urban immigration trends; nevertheless, interested smaller communities should consider the full spectrum of challenges and opportunities experienced by larger metropolitan regions with regard to immigration.

4. See also the City of Toronto's vision statement on access, equity, and diversity and a *Plan of Action for the Elimination of Racism and Discrimination*. Toronto's plan reaffirms its post-amalgamation (1997) official motto 'Diversity our strength' (Toronto, 2003a).

5. Qadeer and Chaudry (2000) observe that this has resulted in a tremendous range of parking standards across the Greater Toronto Area.

Chapter 25

Homelessness, Housing Affordability, and the New Poverty

R. Alan Walks

'To eat, homeless steal, trade sex' screamed a headline detailing a recent study of homelessness in Canada (Porter, 2005). The study found that homeless women are regularly taken advantage of in their search for shelter and that more than half of all homeless youth get their food from garbage cans. Such is the current tragedy of homelessness in Canada. Homelessness is a more serious issue in Canada than elsewhere, due to the life-threatening temperatures experienced during the winter months when many homeless die of exposure.

This chapter examines the problems of homelessness and affordability in Canadian cities. It begins by comparing definitions of homelessness and the forms it takes, and then discusses the range of perspectives characterizing the literature on homelessness and housing provision. Changes in housing affordability and the rise of homelessness in Canadian cities are examined in terms of economic, social, and policy shifts. Attempts at measuring homelessness in Canada are explored and compared, and the geography of housing affordability stress and services for the homeless in Canadian cities are examined. The chapter concludes by discussing the government record of addressing homelessness and looks to future challenges.

Forms and Definitions of Homelessness

The United Nations defines homelessness as either (1) having no place to call home and being forced to sleep either outside or in a temporary shelter, or (2) having access to housing that is lacking in one or more of: sanitation, protection from the elements, safe water, security of tenure, affordability, personal safety, and accessibility to daily needs (particularly employment, education, and health care). This definition thus embodies not only those who literally have no home, but also those who do have some form of shelter but whose present housing situation is precarious and insufficient. The difference between these situations is often conceptualized as one between *absolute* (or '*literal*') *homelessness* (not having any home) and *relative homelessness* (precarious or insufficient housing). Discrepancies in precise definitions employed by various agencies and institutions are important because alternate definitions can yield wildly diverging estimates of the extent of homelessness; they also support different courses of remedial action. Those whose housing is sufficient but who are paying so much on housing that it cuts into their ability to meet other daily needs are experiencing *housing affordability stress*, and thus are considered *at risk of homelessness*. Stone (1993) calls this situation *shelter poverty* because, in such cases, housing costs alone are the cause of the households' current poverty situation and of their risk of falling into absolute homelessness.

Absolute homelessness can be distinguished by its duration, with three archetypical forms identified by Kuhn and Culhane (1998). (1) *Chronic homelessness* involves those who remain homeless over extended periods of time. (2) *Episodic homelessness* concerns repeated forays into and out of homelessness, and is the most difficult form of homelessness to treat. (3) *Temporary homelessness* typically entails only one or two brief periods of homelessness and is the easiest form to target with preventive or emergency services. While the temporarily homeless make up the majority of all homeless persons taking beds in shelters, the chronic homeless consume the majority of shelter resources and public services targeted to the homeless.

Even these distinctions, however, cannot grasp the complexities involved in the experience of homelessness. Most experts now acknowledge the existence of a *continuum of residential security* between 'homefulness' at one extreme and absolute homelessness at the other. The relative level of homelessness can thus be discerned as the degree to which key aspects of having a home are lacking (Murray, 1990: 17). Such a continuum is shown in Figure 25.1. Home ownership is the housing situation that best characterizes 'homefulness' in Canada, and indeed this form of tenure is exactly what federal housing policy has attempted to maximize for much of its history (Bacher, 1993; see also Chapter 15). At the other extreme is the situation most stereotypical of the homeless—'sleeping rough'. This is the housing option of last resort. Those who find themselves in this situation may take refuge on park benches, under bridges, in tents, in bus shelters, in parking garages, or in their cars. In between are found varying levels of relative homelessness/homefulness. These housing forms can be further distinguished by the level of state or community involvement in their provision (including that provided by non-governmental organizations). State and community forms of housing (emergency, transitional, supportive, and

social/co-operative housing) provide significant options for households to help prevent them from falling into absolute homelessness, particularly those that face acute problems in the labour and housing markets and those with special needs.[1]

Perspectives on Homelessness and Housing Provision

There is considerable debate on the ultimate causes of homelessness and, thus, on the types of policies that should be enacted to deal with it. The traditional lines of debate run between individual and structural explanations of homelessness. Recently, more nuanced explanations attempting to mediate between these extremes have appeared.

The Individual Model

Explanations under the individual model assume that personal failings—some problem with the individual—cause homelessness. Such failings may include physical disability, mental illness, substance abuse, criminal behaviour, delinquency, family breakup, domestic violence, inability to work, or poor job skills. In this model, it is assumed that housing is available for such persons but that they cannot find a place to live due to their inability to find work, pay rent, care for themselves, or access social resources (Jencks, 1994). Policy recommendations thus include more targeted mental and physical health services, job training, substance abuse programs, family counselling, etc.

The implicit assumption in this model is that individuals are homeless, at least at some level, due

Figure 25.1   **Continuum of Homefulness to Homelessness**

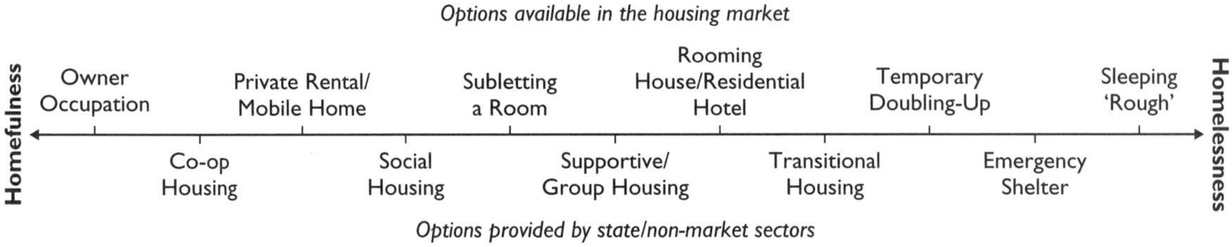

Options available in the housing market

| Homefulness | Owner Occupation | Private Rental/ Mobile Home | Subletting a Room | Rooming House/Residential Hotel | Temporary Doubling-Up | Sleeping 'Rough' | Homelessness |
| | Co-op Housing | Social Housing | Supportive/ Group Housing | Transitional Housing | Emergency Shelter | |

Options provided by state/non-market sectors

to the choices they have made or failed to make in life. Because of this, such perspectives are often accused of 'blaming the victim' and perpetuating stereotypes about those in poverty (Layton, 2000: 23–4; Ryan, 1976). More recent studies in this vein seek to avoid this appearance and instead concentrate on the 'risk factors' such as gender, race, poverty, depression, substance use, and child abuse that together increase the chances one will become homeless (e.g., Early, 1999; Herman et al., 1997; O'Toole et al., 2004; Susser et al., 1991). Yet, these studies all share a focus on the individual and tend to lack any critique of the housing or labour markets as systems helping to produce homelessness.

Such explanations fit best within *neo-classical* and *demographic* perspectives on the supply of housing—viewing housing outcomes in terms of the supply of, and demand for, housing as a result of choices made by free agents in the housing market. In such a perspective, intervention into the self-regulating 'invisible hand' of the market is counterproductive, since the market is assumed best at allocating scarce housing resources to those who need (demand) it most. Rent controls, for instance, are seen to depress profits and limit new construction, in turn leading to shortages that provoke rather than reduce homelessness (Early and Olsen, 1998; Fallis, 1985). Invariably, studies in this vein see intervention in the housing market, either through 'misplaced' government policies or 'irrational' (inefficient) discriminatory practices, as the main problems limiting choices for low-income earners (e.g., Early, 1999; Early and Olsen, 1998).

The Structural Model

Structural models explain homelessness not as the result of personal failings but as an inevitable outcome of the main structural features of modern capitalism, such as unemployment, high rents, wage inequality, uneven development, and a housing system set up to benefit homeowners at the expense of tenants (Bacher, 1993). Homelessness in its various forms would result from a faster rise in rents than in either wages or state benefits. The 'invisible hand' of the market, therefore, does not benevo-

lently allocate scarce housing resources efficiently to those most in need, but instead only to those who can afford it.

These explanations provide examples of a *political economy* perspective on housing provision. Such perspectives are mostly advocated by Marxists and neo-Marxists, and often see housing decisions as made within the framework of class interests and class struggles over control of housing resources. Under capitalism, wage inequality means that some will be able to consume far more housing than they need whereas many poorly paid workers cannot afford to occupy even the housing that is produced for the low end of the market. Indeed, it has long been argued that Canada has more than enough existing housing stock to house everyone. It is just that the bulk of the housing space is horded by wealthy homeowners (Blumenfeld, 1979). The problem is thus not one of production, but of distribution. It follows from this analysis that homelessness will not be solved until structured inequalities in society are dealt with. Policies advocated under this model include state intervention into the labour and housing markets to reduce wage inequality and to subsidize the construction of state-run permanent housing for low-income households.

Combining Individual and Structural Perspectives

Evidence confirming either of the two above models is at best mixed, and such confirmation depends largely on the type of data examined. When individual-level data are analyzed, the importance of individual attributes such as gender, race, substance abuse, and mental health—but not rent levels or housing market conditions—is usually confirmed (Early, 1999; Early and Olsen, 1998; Main, 1996; O'Flaherty, 2003). Conversely, when city-level data are examined, macro conditions and rent levels invariably prove to be significant while individual-level indicators show minimal effects (Applebaum et al., 1991; Lee et al., 2003; Quigley et al., 2001; Ringheim, 1990; Wright and Lam, 1987). This apparent paradox suggests that neither model best captures the complexities involved in causing homelessness.

Recently, a number of authors have sought to provide more holistic perspectives on homelessness and housing that link the individual agency and structural models. The most conceptually simple are economic explanations that stress the combined effects of tight rental markets and the relative inability of individuals with multiple risk factors to compete effectively for scarce housing (O'Flaherty, 2003). Thus, while combinations of individual-level factors may be ultimately responsible for exactly *who* ends up without a permanent home in any given place, the *proportion* of such persons left without market housing is dependent on local housing market conditions, particularly the median rent level and the relative number of households competing for each unit available (Lee et al., 2003; O'Flaherty, 2003). While a step forward over previous thinking, this perspective still assumes that individual-level risk factors are exogenous (not related) to the housing market. Yet evidence suggests that individual risk factors are indeed related to housing conditions. For example, research has found that the experience of being homeless is as much an outcome of depression and mental illness as its cause (Kozol, 1988; Timmer et al., 1994) and that the move out of homelessness is a major factor bringing an end to substance abuse (Sosin et al., 1995).

More nuanced explanations focus on the intersection between various structural constraints (including high rents and income inequalities, but also gender and ethnic inequalities), individual aspects and agents (both personal liabilities, substance abuse, etc. and also the role played by family members, real estate agents, developers, institutions, and landlords), and life transitions (e.g., out of the workforce, into and out of marriages, relocation for education, etc.). Such explanations most closely relate to what are loosely referred to as *humanist* and/or *postmodern* perspectives on the social production and provision of housing. These examine, among other things, the meanings provided by the home, the motivations of different actors operating within the housing system, and the importance of social and political arrangements (Kellet and Moore, 2003). Similarly, *feminist* perspectives examine the relationship between gender relations and the different housing experiences faced by women and men (Hayden, 2002; MacKenzie, 1988).

Homelessness Pathways

Nuanced explanations are best articulated in the literature on the pathways in and out of homelessness. Such pathways are shaped through the changing expectations of individuals, households, and institutional agents (Clapham, 2002). The greater vulnerability of single mothers to homelessness, and greater victimization and stigmatization rates for single homeless women, for instance, can thus be partly explained as resulting from pathways conditioned by unequal gender relations, violence in the family, discrimination against women in the labour and housing markets, the different needs and conceptions of 'home' that lead women to prefer couch-surfing to emergency shelters, public policies that are ill-prepared to deal with the needs of poor women and children living without men, and the implicit and explicit acceptance of the unequal treatment of women in liberal society (Burrows, 1997; Evan and Forsyth, 2004; Takahashi et al., 2002; Zugazaga, 2004).

Homeless pathways are associated with particular geographies, as in the move from couch-surfing at friends or family, to living in one's car, to sleeping under a bridge or in an emergency shelter. Also, the homeless typically follow a coping strategy of remaining in touch with multiple social networks across time and space in order to meet daily needs, with significant movement beyond the reaches of local concentrations of homeless populations and homeless services (Rowe and Wolch, 1990; Wolch et al., 1993). Recently, DeVerteuil (2003) has shown how life events intersect with public policies concerning shelter time limits and state benefits in a context of high rents to produce a number of distinct geographies of homelessness for single homeless women. In particular, in what DeVerteuil calls the *new poverty management*, an increasing number of the poor and homeless are cycled between institutional and non-institutional settings that extend across space, even to other cities. The availability of subsidized shelter and being able to draw on the resources of family, friends, and state service providers, have been found important for enabling paths out of homelessness (Stojanovic et al., 1999; Thompson et al., 2004). This remains an under-researched area in the Canadian literature.

Housing Affordability, Homelessness, and the New Poverty in Canada

Housing affordability and homelessness are growing concerns in Canada. Over the 1990s (CMHC, 2004c), the proportion of households in *core housing need* significantly increased, particularly for renters (from 26.6 per cent to 30.4 per cent of tenant households, versus 6–8.7 per cent for owners) (England et al., 2005: 45). While these levels of core need are lower than the even higher levels witnessed in 1996, in absolute terms there are now more households paying greater than 30 per cent of their income on shelter (2,224,085 in 2001) than at any time in the past, up from 1,877,240 in 1991, and 2,223,480 in 1996 (CMHC, 2003). Thus, while overall housing affordability would seem to have improved for the *average* Canadian since 1996 due mainly to growth in employment incomes, there are now more low-income households than ever facing housing affordability stress.

A number of specific factors have combined to produce greater levels of housing affordability stress and to create new paths into poverty and homelessness in Canada over the 1980s and particularly the 1990s (Figure 25.2). First, broad-based economic changes have produced greater income inequality and, consequently, more low-income households and greater upward pressure on rents. Globalization and economic restructuring are linked to relative declines in stable middle-income manufacturing employment in Canada, with the balance taken up by growing numbers of low-paying and insecure service jobs, on one hand, and, on the other, highly paid and more secure professional occupations (Walks, 2001). Globalization and uneven urban systems dynamics (see Chapter 3) mean that incomes have grown rapidly in a few CMAs, leading to overheated real estate markets and housing price inflation in such places. Finally, the demise of the family-supportive wage (a wage earned by one 'head' of the household sufficient to support all dependent family members, including a spouse) has forced more family members to compete in the labour market, pushing wages down for low-income jobs and increasing household income inequality.

Linked to such changes are shifts in the demographic makeup of households vying for housing (Jarvis, 1999). Polarization in household incomes derives from the simultaneous growth of both dual/multi-earner households and no-earner households. This has occurred as a result of more seniors living alone and of higher divorce and family dissolution rates, which have led to rapid increases in female lone-parent households (by 2001, these comprised 9.2 per cent of all Canadian households). Importantly, greater numbers of single-person households are competing in the housing market. According to the national census, in 1951 only 7.4 per cent of all households in Canada were one-person households. This had grown to 25.8 per cent by the 2001 census. The greater range of household types has led to growing numbers of households with special needs and a more segmented and competitive housing market. Finally, high rates of immigration into Canadian cities have buffeted housing demand and exacerbated income inequalities in the short run, particularly in the immigrant 'gateway' cities such as Toronto and Vancouver (see Chapters 8 and 24), because new immigrants tend to have low incomes, though in the long run many immigrants are able to surpass native-born Canadians in prosperity (Wang and Lo, 2000).

Increasing income inequality at the household level and greater competition in the housing market translate into greater polarization between those who own their homes and those who rent. Since the mid-1970s, homeowners have become richer, while tenants have become poorer (Figure 25.3). Polarization in wealth is even starker. While

Figure 25.2   **Factors Inducing Homelessness and Housing Affordability Stress**

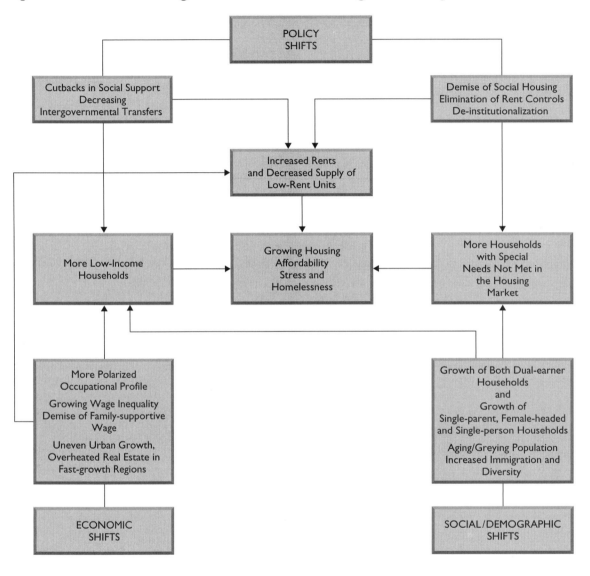

homeowners saw their median net worth increase (in real terms) by 24 per cent between 1984 and 1999, renters saw their net worth decline by 48 per cent (Hulchanski, 2004: 83).

Greatly exacerbating the effects of economic and social processes are shifts in public policy. Most important has been the reduction in support for new rental construction, both of private rental units

and social housing. The result is a precipitous drop in both the absolute number of rental housing units and their proportion of the total stock (Figure 25.4). First, legislation passed in 1970 allowed for the construction of condominiums—apartments that are owned rather than rented. Builders of high-density housing (often on lands too expensive for single-family dwellings) then switched from rental

Figure 25.3 **Owners Becoming Richer, Tenants Becoming Poorer: Median Income by Tenure, 1977–2000 (trend lines added)**

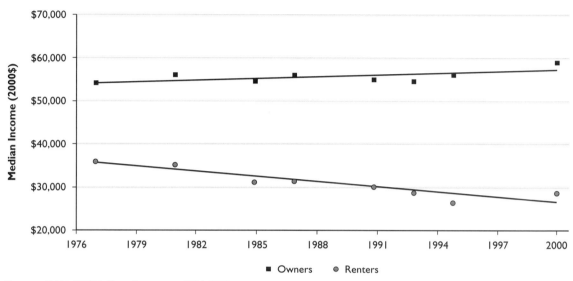

Sources: CMHC (2001); Canadian census, 1996, 2001.

construction to the condominium market, which produced greater profits under shorter time frames. In turn, the supply of private rental housing dropped from a high of 63,545 new units in 1970 to a low of only 4,290 units in 1996. During the 1990s, minuscule amounts of new construction were swamped by the conversion of rental apartments to condominium tenure and by gentrification of low-rent inner-city districts, which displaced many of the poor from the cheapest housing and reversed the filtering process that traditionally provided housing for low-income households (Begin, 1994; see Chapter 15). It is estimated that in Ontario over 45,000 rental units were lost to conversion between 1995 and 2002 (Shapcott, 2004: 202). Furthermore, the removal of rent controls by many provinces over the 1990s did not lead to greater investment in rental housing as anticipated, but merely allowed landlords to drive up rents (ibid.).

Meanwhile, social housing programs have felt the brunt of deficit fighting by the federal and most provincial governments. New social housing construction has fallen from a yearly average of over 20,000 new units in the 1970s and 1980s to under 2,000 units per year after 1995, with virtually all of the latter built in Vancouver or in the province of Quebec, the only places left with active social housing programs (Pomeroy, 2004).[2] The loss of social and supportive housing options has been particularly difficult for those with special needs, whose numbers have grown following the policy of deinstitutionalization of psychiatric patients and services in the 1970s.

The declining supply of both private and socially rented housing in the face of continued urban population growth and rising income inequality has led to escalating rents and affordability problems, particularly in rapid-growth CMAs. Even during the recessionary period between 1991 and 1996 when incomes remained stagnant, Canada lost a total of 310,000 low-rent (below $500/month) units (Pomeroy, 2004: 277). In addition, cutbacks in social supports have meant that the growing ranks of low-wage and special-needs households have

Figure 25.4   **Annual Number and Proportion, Social and Private Rental Housing Units Built in Canada, 1970–2001**

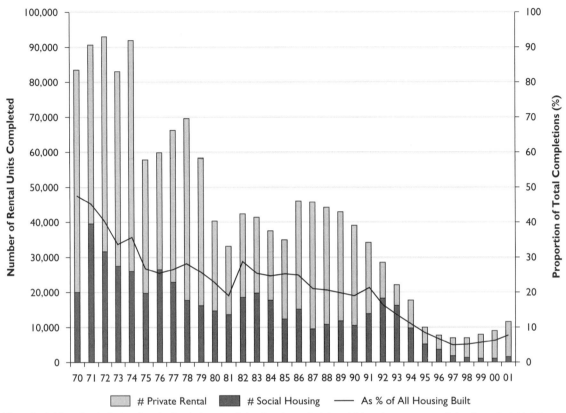

Note: Social housing includes all units funded under federal and provincial social housing programs, federal-provincial joint non-profit, co-operative, and provincial non-profit and co-operative housing programs. Data for completions of social housing over the years 1970 to 1981 are lacking, so data for social housing starts begun in the previous year have been substituted in their place. Source: CMHC, *Canadian Housing Statistics*, various years; CMHC (1999).

even fewer resources with which to compete for existing housing. Both Ontario and British Columbia, for instance, cut welfare rates significantly (upwards of 22 per cent) since the mid-1990s. Unable to afford market rents, increasing numbers of low-income households end up on waiting lists for existing social housing, for which average wait times have expanded rapidly since the early 1990s (in Toronto the minimum wait time in 2005 was seven years) (FCM, 2005). Low-income households unable to afford or maintain, and in

some cases even simply to find, adequate rental housing, and who cannot access social housing, then join the swelling ranks of the homeless. Federal and provincial policy has thus directly contributed to the growth of homelessness (Table 25.1).

The literature on poverty makes a distinction between traditional forms (the 'old' poverty) and the 'new' poverty. The former, many note, seemed to ebb and flow with the business cycle and was particularly associated with problems that prevented the poorest from working—chronic health

Table 25.1   **Number of Households on Waiting Lists for Social Housing**

City/CMA	Number	Date
Calgary (City)	3,000	2001
Edmonton (City)	2,400	2001
Hamilton (City)	4,213	2002
Kitchener–Waterloo RM	3,800	2001
Ottawa–Carleton RM	15,000	1998
Saskatoon	1,600	1998
Toronto (City)	71,625	2003
Vancouver (City)	13,000	2001
Winnipeg (City)	2,000	1999

Sources: NHHN (2001); Toronto (2003b); SPRC (2003).

problems, disability, mental illness, substance abuse, lack of skills, and discrimination in the labour force (Grabb, 1996). The 'new' poverty, however, is qualitatively different. It continues to grow in good times and bad, with little regard to the business cycle. Social and economic changes have meant that women and children, youth, immigrants, and families (particularly female single-parent families) increasingly constitute the poorest of our society (Cheal, 1996; Lochead and Scott, 2000). Perhaps most important to this discussion, this 'new' poverty is often *shelter poverty*—resulting directly from the growing inaffordability of housing for low-income tenants (Stone, 1993). It is most visibly articulated in the establishment of absolute homelessness—the epitome of deep-seated poverty—as a seemingly permanent and ubiquitous feature of the Canadian urban landscape.

Measuring Homelessness in Canadian Cities

Homelessness is very difficult to measure. Not only do different definitions produce wildly varying estimates, but the homeless typically lack an address where they can be reached. Thus, counting the homeless presents many practical problems. Partly as a response, the majority of the research that has sought to measure homelessness has employed a highly restrictive definition, close in spirit only to the first part of the United Nations definition above denoting 'absolute' homelessness.

Until recently, only scant information was available about the homeless in Canada as data derived from national surveys attempted in the 1980s and 1990s were not considered accurate or statistically significant. Increasingly, however, Canadian municipalities and regional governments are conducting their own studies of the extent of homelessness. This has either taken the form of enumerations (or 'snapshots') of the homeless on a single night (Table 25.2) or annual numbers of unique individuals using the shelter system (Table 25.3). In most cases such data are only available for those using shelters receiving funds from government sources, though a number of recent studies (in Calgary, Edmonton, Halifax, Sudbury, and Greater Vancouver) have also sought to count those sleeping rough. Yet, even when those sleeping outside are included, most studies consider the true level of absolute homelessness to be at least 50 or 60 per cent greater than the official counts. Regardless of the method employed or the actual level recorded for any given day or year, what is plainly evident is the growth in the numbers of the homeless across Canadian cities. In Toronto, increases are acute in the most recent years, with over 30,000 people accessing the shelter system annually since 1999 (Figure 25.5). Likewise, single-day snapshots from Calgary reveal the degree to which the problem of homelessness has escalated rapidly in that city (Figure 25.6).

What is also disconcerting is the appearance that homelessness is growing more rapidly in Canadian cities than in their US counterparts. Yet, despite the apparently faster growth of the problem in Canada, when the range in the proportion of the population estimated to be homeless (per 10,000 population) is compared between US and Canadian cities, lower levels of homelessness are found in Canada, even taking into account the broader

Table 25.2   **Single-Day Snapshots of 'Absolute' Homelessness in Previous and Current Decades**

City/ CMA	Number (Date of Count)		Average Annual Change (%)	Source
	1990–2000	2001+		
Calgary (City)	615 (May 1996)*	1,737 (May 2002)*	30.4	Calgary (2002)
Edmonton (City)	836 (1999)*	1,200 (2001)*	21.8	ETFH (1999); NHHN (2001)
Halifax RM	n.a.	234 (June 2003)*	n.a.	HRM (2004b)
Hamilton	160 (1995)	396 (2002)	21.1	SPRC (2003)
London (City)	400 (1998)	n.a.	n.a.	NHHN (2001)
Ottawa–Carleton RM	492 (1996)	932 (2004)	11.2	RMOC (1999); ATEH (2005)
Sudbury (Greater)	407 (July 2000)*	485 (July 2002)*	9.6	Kauppi (2003)
Toronto (City)	3,136 (1996)	3,735 (2005)	2.1	Springer et al. (1998); Toronto (2005b)
Vancouver (GVRD)	363 (1999)	792 (2002)/ 1,121 (2002)*	59.1	GVRD (2002)

Notes: These data represent actual counts of the total number of unique individuals sleeping in government-funded emergency shelters, overflow hotels, and transitional housing facilities, either on a single night or annually, except for (*), which also includes counts of those found sleeping 'rough' in accessible places. Those sleeping in private hostels and residential/single-rate occupancy (SRO) hotels are not included. Figures for single-day snapshots are for winter dates except where noted. Sudbury figures represent 'verified unduplicated cases' only (Kauppi, 2003: 11); n.a. = data not available.

sampling frames of many of the Canadian cities, which include those sleeping rough as well as in shelters (Table 25.4). Of the cities under study, Sudbury exhibits the highest levels and Vancouver the lowest. The relatively lower rates of homelessness in Vancouver likely relate to the fact that social housing is still being built there, as well as the presence of a large (over 8,000 units) single-rate occupancy (SRO) hotel sector that provides the bulk of Vancouver's lowest-cost housing.

Characteristics of the Homeless Population

The recent profusion of homeless surveys provides us with a glimpse of both the predominant socio-demographics of the homeless population and the geographic diversity of the homeless experience across Canadian cities. Table 25.5 provides information from those studies that sought to enumerate both those sleeping rough and those using food banks and shelters. While single men traditionally dominate the ranks of the homeless, and indeed constitute up to three-quarters of the samples listed here, women and children, and families, are the fastest-growing subset of the homeless (FCM, 2005). First Nations peoples are significantly over-represented among the homeless population—while only making up 3.3 per cent of Canada's population, those claiming Aboriginal identity or ancestry constitute between 14 and 42 per cent of

Table 25.3   **Annual Number of Unique Individuals Accessing Official Shelters**

City/CMA	Number (Year)		Average Annual Change (%)	Source
	1990–2000	2001+		
Calgary (City)	11,000 (2000)	14,181 (2002)	14.5	Perras and Huyder (2003)
London (City)	n.a.	3,900 (2001)	n.a.	Ginsler and Associates (2001)
Montreal Region/CMA	8,253 (1996)	n.a.	n.a.	Fournier et al. (1998)
Ottawa–Carleton RM	4,477 (1996)	8,664 (2004)	11.7	RMOC (1999); ATEH (2005)
Peel (RM)	3,403 (2000)	4,420 (2001)	29.9	Region of Peel (2002)
Quebec City	2,118 (1997)	n.a.	n.a.	Fournier et al. (1998)
Saskatoon	6,700 (1998)	n.a.	n.a.	NHHN (2001)
Toronto (City)	25,846 (1996)	33,399 (2001)	5.8	Toronto (2003b)
Victoria (City)	2,050 (1997)	n.a.	n.a.	BCMSDES (2001)
All Canada—shelters for abused women & children only	90,792 (1998)	101,248 (2002)	2.9	Transition Home Survey (accessed in CANSIM II, table 2560012, vector V10748)

Notes: See Table 25.2.

the homeless enumerated in shelters and on the street in the sampled studies. Visible minorities, on the other hand, would appear over-represented among the homeless only in some cities (particularly Halifax), and under-represented in others (Vancouver and Edmonton).

Perhaps the most stereotypical image of the homeless is of the panhandler on a street corner. However, the research suggests that the vast majority of the homeless do not panhandle and few rely on such activities for their income. Instead, a majority of the homeless depend on state benefits in the form of welfare, pensions, and disability payments.

Table 25.6 provides information about the homeless experience from those studies using *representative* samples of the homeless in Canadian cities. The reasons given by the homeless for their condition vary. Domestic abuse and family breakdown are clearly important precursors to becoming homeless, as is eviction and the simple lack of affordable accommodation. Release from jail or a treatment program, addiction problems, unemployment, and those in transit tend to make up most of the rest. Except in Calgary, those originating locally make up the majority of the homeless. Between one-quarter and one-half of the homeless say they are suffering from depression or mental illness, and between 14 and 39 per cent reveal past or current problems with substance abuse. The homeless also disproportionately suffer from physical disabilities and other medical conditions.

Figure 25.5   **Annual Number of Individuals Accessing Toronto Shelters, 1988–2003**

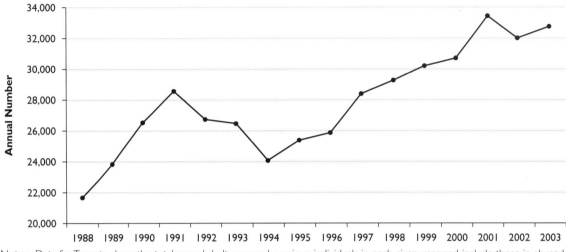

Notes: Data for Toronto show the total annual shelter usage by unique individuals in each given year and include those in abused women's shelters, transitional housing, and overflow motels. The drop in 1994 is based on a different method for collecting the data in that year and does not necessarily reflect a drop in usage.
Source: Toronto (2003b: 38; 2005b).

Figure 25.6   **Single-Day Homeless Counts in Calgary, 1992–2004**

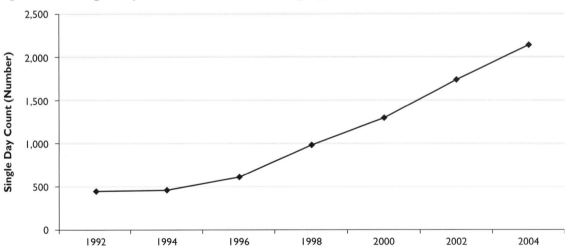

Notes: Data for Calgary reflect counts of both shelter users and those sleeping rough on a single night in November of each study year. The figures shown here are those determined using the constant methodology and leave out the additional transitional shelter facilities added for the 2004 study. If these facilities were included here, the number of homeless measured in Calgary in 2004 would be 2,597 (Calgary, 2004: 53–4).
Source: Calgary (2004: 53).

Table 25.4   **Comparison of Canadian and US Cities: Estimated Proportion of the Population Counted as Homeless on a Single Night (Persons per 10,000 Population)**

Canadian City/Date	Est. Range, # per 10,000	Mid-Point	US City/Date	Est. Range, # per 10,000	Mid-Point
Calgary (2002)*	18.3–19.8	19.0	Austin, City (2000)	35.9–60.6	48.3
Edmonton (2001)*	12.8–18.0	15.4	Boston, City (2003)	11.1–105.9	58.5
Halifax (2003)*	6.5–n.a.	6.5	Chicago, City (2004)*	11.0–33.4	22.2
Hamilton (2002)	5.9–8.1	7.0	Denver, Metro (2004)	36.7–n.a.	36.7
London (1998)	9.2–11.9	10.6	Los Angeles County (2002)	67.6–86.2	76.9
Ottawa–Carleton (2004)	8.7–12.0	10.4	Miami–Dade County (2003)	24.7–n.a.	24.7
Toronto (City) (2005)	8.8–15.1	11.9	New York City (2002)	18.9–47.5	33.1
Greater Sudbury (2002)*	29.5–n.a.	29.5	Seattle (2002)	5.9–36.2	21.1
Vancouver, GVRD (2002)*	5.6–n.a.	5.6			

Note: Calculated as the proportion (expressed in persons per 10,000) of either the CMA/CMSA (consolidated statistical metropolitan area) population (low end of the range) or the central city population (high end of the range) enumerated as sleeping in government-funded emergency shelters, overflow hotels and transitional housing facilities, on a single night, except for (*), which also includes counts of those found sleeping 'rough' in accessible places. Those sleeping in private hostels and single-rate occupancy (SRO) hotels are not included. In effect, the low end/left side of the range assumes that there are no homeless people living outside the central city (an unlikely scenario) while the high end/right side of the range assumes that homeless proportions are equally high in suburban as in central city municipalities (also an unlikely scenario). The more accurate figure is likely somewhere in between these extremes (hence the mid-point); n.a. = not applicable. (Both the total counts and the comparative base population are measured at the regional/metropolitan scale.)

Sources: Canadian homelessness data and sources listed in Table 25.2; American data from the following: Austin (1986, 2001); USCOM (2002); Rossi et al. (1987); CCC (2004); Morrow-Jones and van Vliet (1989); MDHI (2004); ISHP (2004); FDCF (2003); CFTH (2003). Census data from Canadian census, 1996, 2001; United States census, 2000. Calculations by the author.

The survey data suggest that chronic homelessness besets only a minority of the total, particularly in eastern Canada, where durations of homeless spells were shorter on average. However, difficulty acquiring space in an emergency shelter is an increasing problem, and many shelters have to turn prospective clients away because they are full or because they do not have enough beds of the appropriate type (particularly, beds for women and children). On the night that Calgary collected its 2004 snapshot, for instance, 159 (of 2,597 homeless) individuals had been refused entry to a shelter, and in Vancouver 13 per cent of those counted as sleeping rough could not get into a shelter. Surveys conducted in Halifax and Greater Vancouver asked those enumerated on the street where they had slept the previous night. The most common response was that they had slept at someone else's place (28 per cent and 56 per cent in Halifax and Vancouver, respectively), followed by sleeping outside, squatting in another building, staying in a shelter, and/or sleeping in a car, garage, or public building (HRM, 2004b; GVRD, 2002).

Table 25.5	**Demographic Characteristics of the Homeless, Selected Canadian Cities (%)**						
	Calgary 2004	Edmonton 1999	Halifax 2003	Montreal 1996–7	Quebec 1996–7	Sudbury Jan. 2003	Vancouver 2002
Gender							
Women	23.2	27.0	33.0	25.6	22.0	44.0	32.0
Men	76.8	73.0	67.0	74.4	78.0	56.0	68.0
Age							
Children under 18	8.4	23.0	25.0	4.6	11.7	28.2	13.0
5 or younger	3.4					5.7	
Adults 18–64	89.1	67 (19–54)	52.0	93.2	86.4	69.7 (19–59)	87.0
Ages 18–24	8.9		16.0				15.0
Ages 18–29				34.3	25.7		
Ages 25–44	46.7		36.0				52.0
Ages 29–44				40.0	42.5		
Ages 45–64	33.5		17.0	18.9	18.1		19.0
Seniors	2.0	9.0 (55+)	5.0	2.2	1.9	2.1 (60+)	1.0
Marital status (adults)				(1991)			
Single/div./widowed	n.a.	87.4	89.0	87.1	n.a.	87.0	90.0
Married	n.a.	12.6	11.0	12.9	n.a.	12.8	10.0
Race/ethnicity				(1991)			
White	75.8	53.0	63.0	94.2	n.a.	62.0	69.0
Aboriginal	14.7	42.0	14.0	n.a.	n.a.	27.0	17.0
Other visible minority	8.4	5.0	17.0	n.a.	n.a.	2.0	14.0
Source of Income	(2002)			(1991)*			
Panhandling/begging	4.7	n.a.	5.0	4.7	n.a.	n.a.	6.0
State benefits	5.7	n.a.	48.0	73.3	n.a.	42.3	51.0
Pension	n.a.	n.a.	7.0	9.7	n.a.	2.8	2.0
Disability	n.a.	n.a.	18.0	n.a.	n.a.	12.2	9.0
Welfare/training	n.a.	n.a.	23.0	63.6	n.a.	28.3	40.0
Employment or EI	52.0	n.a.	12.0	24.1	n.a.	6.5	13.0
Employment	52.0	n.a.	n.a.	16.0	n.a.	3.6	11.0
EI	0.0	n.a.	n.a.	8.1	n.a.	2.9	2.0
No income	n.a.	n.a.	23.0	8.9	n.a.	48.3	21.0
Other	9.4	n.a.	11.0	6.7	n.a.	1.4	8.0

Note: Only those studies enumerating the homeless are included here. The 2002 Calgary study only provided sources of income for unemployed respondents, implying that employment income was the main source for the 52 per cent of respondents who were employed in some fashion.

*Multiple responses were allowed.

n.a. = not available.

Sources: BCMSDES (2001); Calgary Homeless Foundation (2002); Calgary (2002, 2004); Fournier (1991); Fournier et al. (1998); GVRD (2002); HRM (2004b); Kuappi (2003).

Table 25.6   **Characteristics of the Homeless Situation, Selected Canadian Cities**

	Calgary	Halifax	Ottawa	Sudbury	Toronto	Vancouver
Date of study	2002	2003	2002–3	Jan. 2003	1996	2002
Reasons for situation						
Evicted	7.2	7.0	29.0	15.8	11.8	12.0
Moving/stranded	3.5	14.0	5.0	11.2	30.7	13.0
Can't afford to rent	17.5	19.0	23.0	15.2	n.a.	10.0
Can't find accommodation	8.1	12.0	n.a.	n.a.	n.a.	n.a.
Lost job/unemployed	12.5	n.a.	n.a.	10.3	n.a.	1.0
Abuse, family breakdown	16.3	19.0	28.0	19.1	19.3	26.0
Addiction (incl. gambling)	5.1	11.0	8.0	9.5	n.a.	5.0
Mental illness/disability	n.a.	n.a.	33.0[1]	9.7	n.a.	2.0
Out of jail/treatment	n.a.	3.0	n.a.	7.1	5.2	6.0
Other (transient, fire, refugee, not said, etc.)	7.4	14.0	n.a.	2.2	33.1	25.0
Home community						
% from local area	27.4 (>15 yrs)	62.0	46.0	n.a.	53.3 (> 5yrs)	71.0
% from elsewhere	72.6	38.0	54.0	n.a.	46.7	29.0
Health conditions					(1992)	
Physical/disability/injury	12.5	6.0	*	29.1	*	15.0
Addiction (alcohol/drugs)	18.0	26.0	27.0/39.0	34.8	14.0	39.0
Depression/mental illness	48.3	21.0	31.0	51.5	37.0	23.0
Other medical condition	*	16.0	*	*	13.0	30.0
Length of stay in shelter						
Less than 6 months	n.a.	79.0	68.0	n.a.	78.6	68.0
2–7 days	n.a.	31.0	n.a.	n.a.	40.3	12.0
1–4 weeks	n.a.	28.0	n.a.	n.a.	18.5	26.0
1–6 months	n.a.	20.0	n.a.	n.a.	19.7	30.0
6 months–1 year	n.a.	5.0	13.0	n.a.	4.9	12.0
Greater than 1 year	32.4	16.0	18.0	n.a.	16.5	20.0

Notes: Data on health conditions are for current health status in all studies except Sudbury, in which respondents were asked to list any health conditions experienced in the previous year.

*A number of health conditions were listed but data were insufficient to determine accurate statistics for these categories for all homeless in the sample.

[1]Overlapping responses.

n.a. = not available.

Sources: Aubry et al. (2003); BCMSDES (2001); Calgary Homeless Foundation (2002); GVRD (2002); HRM (2004b); Kauppi (2003); Springer et al. (1998).

The Geography of Inaffordability

During the televised mayoral debate for the amalgamated Toronto mega-city election of November 1997, then North York mayor Mel Lastman declared emphatically that there were no homeless people in his municipality. The next morning, a 48-year-old homeless woman, Linda Houston, was found dead while attempting to sleep in a gas station bathroom not far from Lastman's city hall office in the suburban municipality (Layton, 2000: 28). This awakened Canadians, not to mention Lastman himself, to the growing reality of homelessness in Canadian suburbs, an issue that hitherto had been considered an inner-city problem. Even now, the vast majority of shelters, facilities, and agencies serving the home- less are located in the inner city. Yet, it remains unclear whether or not there are more homeless in Canadian inner cities or suburbs.

While the intra-urban geography of absolute homelessness has yet to receive sufficient attention, data collected for the Canadian census allows tracking of the geographic locus of the *risk of homelessness* stemming from *housing affordability stress*, as indicated by households paying 30 per cent or more of their income on rent (one indicator of 'core housing need'). Although upward of 9 per cent of homeowners are in core housing need, they are one more level removed from absolute homelessness than tenants because they have the option of using the proceeds of the sale of their home to enter the rental market. Tenants suffering from affordability

Table 25.7 **Tenant Households Experiencing Housing Affordability Stress (Paying 30% or More of Income on Rent), as Proportion of All Households in Each Urban Zone, 2001**

CMA	Whole CMA	Inner City	Inner Suburbs	Outer Suburbs	Exurbs
Calgary	10.7	21.6	15.4	5.6	3.3
Edmonton	12.5	25.6	16.6	8.4	4.4
Halifax	16.6	31.9	22.1	12.7	4.1
Hamilton	13.8	24.2	15.5	7.8	3.7
Kitchener	12.1	22.2	15.0	8.6	4.2
London	16.4	25.0	18.4	15.1	3.9
Montreal	18.0	28.0	22.0	9.6	9.8
Ottawa–Gatineau	13.9	22.8	19.6	8.3	5.7
Quebec City	15.6	29.4	22.4	8.2	3.6
Saskatoon	15.8	26.1	19.2	10.7	2.6
Toronto	15.4	22.7	20.0	8.3	6.5
Vancouver	16.6	26.2	18.2	11.7	6.8
Victoria	16.3	27.2	16.4	8.4	8.5
Winnipeg	13.0	20.7	12.0	8.6	1.5
Average	14.7	25.3	18.1	9.4	4.9

Source: Calculated by the author from Canadian census, 2001.

problems, on the other hand, are at risk of eviction—one of the main triggers of homelessness.

As seen in Table 25.7, households paying 30 per cent or more of their income on rent are most prevalent in the inner cities of the largest Canadian CMAs, where the rate is almost twice that for the CMA as a whole. However, this is mostly due to the concentration of rental housing in the inner cities. There is much less spatial variation when the proportion of *tenants* in core housing need is examined (Table 25.8). Indeed, there is a greater proportion of tenants in core housing need in the post-war inner suburbs of four of the selected CMAs (Toronto, Saskatoon, Ottawa–Gatineau, and Calgary), and

zonal differences are marginal in three others (Vancouver, Montreal, and Edmonton). Yet, these proportions mask the fact that more households in core need are found in the suburban portions of Canadian CMAs than in the inner cities (Table 25.9). Of the 14 major CMAs under study here, only Victoria and Winnipeg have a majority of their households in core housing need living in inner city (pre-World War II) neighbourhoods. In the other CMAs, close to two-thirds of all tenant households experiencing housing affordability stress are located in either the inner suburbs (developed between 1946 and 1970) or the outer suburbs (built up after 1970). The suburban locus of shelter poverty is

Table 25.8   **Proportion of Tenant Households Paying 30% or More of Income on Rent, in Each Urban Zone, 2001**

CMA	Whole CMA	Inner City	Inner Suburbs	Outer Suburbs	Exurbs
Calgary	36.5	35.7	36.9	36.8	32.4
Edmonton	37.3	39.4	39.1	34.9	31.1
Halifax	43.7	49.7	45.9	38.3	36.1
Hamilton	43.8	48.0	41.8	40.9	34.1
Kitchener	36.6	40.4	36.9	34.5	29.2
London	44.3	47.0	45.7	42.7	33.3
Montreal	36.4	38.0	37.0	32.9	35.2
Ottawa–Gatineau	36.4	36.2	38.5	32.8	39.2
Quebec City	35.1	40.3	37.9	28.2	19.7
Saskatoon	45.3	48.9	49.5	39.3	23.3
Toronto	42.2	41.3	43.8	41.2	38.5
Vancouver	43.2	43.9	43.2	42.6	38.6
Victoria	44.6	47.1	43.1	40.7	44.7
Winnipeg	37.9	40.6	37.2	34.3	23.5
Average	40.2	42.6	41.2	37.2	32.8

Source: Calculated by the author from Canadian census, 2001.

Table 25.9   **Spatial Distribution of Tenant Households Paying 30% or More of Income on Rent, 2001**

CMA		Whole CMA	Inner City	Inner Suburbs	Outer Suburbs	Exurbs
Calgary	Share (%)	100	27.4	41.3	27.1	2
	Number	37,980	10,410	15,690	10,290	770
Edmonton	Share (%)	100	28.7	37.2	27.5	6.2
	Number	44,425	12,745	16,505	12,210	2,750
Halifax	Share (%)	100	39.5	23.5	32.6	4
	Number	24,045	9,495	5,640	7,840	950
Hamilton	Share (%)	100	44.1	32.7	20.3	2.5
	Number	34,880	15,390	11,400	7,080	880
Kitchener	Share (%)	100	23.4	39.7	34.9	2
	Number	18,565	4,345	7,365	6,480	375
London	Share (%)	100	29.4	27.4	38.1	2.6
	Number	28,360	8,330	7,775	10,805	730
Montreal	Share (%)	100	38.1	38.2	18.7	4.4
	Number	255,595	97,405	97,710	47,825	11,325
Ottawa–Gatineau	Share (%)	100	28.8	40.5	23.3	5.7
	Number	57,845	16,655	23,445	13,500	3,315
Quebec City	Share (%)	100	33	40.7	24.6	1.6
	Number	45,940	15,165	18,700	11,320	755
Saskatoon	Share (%)	100	36.4	36.3	25.5	1.8
	Number	14,015	5,095	5,085	3,580	255
Toronto	Share (%)	100	33.7	42.4	20.6	2.8
	Number	251,100	84,535	106,435	51,735	6,930
Vancouver	Share (%)	100	38.1	28	31.8	2
	Number	125,945	47,990	35,225	40,070	2,465
Victoria	Share (%)	100	54.7	23.5	18.5	2.9
	Number	22,060	12,060	5,190	4,090	630
Winnipeg	Share (%)	100	51	24.9	23.4	0.6
	Number	35,190	17,945	8,775	8,230	220
All 14 CMAs	Share (%)	100	35.9	36.6	23.6	3.2
	Number	995,945	357,565	364,940	235,055	32,350

Source: Calculated by the author from Canadian census, 2001.

particularly evident for family households, both female lone-parent families and couple-family households, whereas single-person households suffering from excessive rents are concentrated in the inner cities (Bunting et al., 2004). Since families, particularly female lone-parent families, are increasingly prevalent among the absolutely homeless, and since family households are limited in their ability to move to lower-rent accommodation and face difficulties related to the relocation of children (to new schools, daycares, etc.), the unique geography of affordability stress among such households warrants specific policy attention. Simply put, there would seem to be an emerging need for more facilities serving poor and homeless families in Canadian suburbs.

Solving Homelessness

Homelessness and shelter poverty have clearly grown as a result of neglect by upper levels of government of the needs of low-income renters, and of the cities that try to house these people. In November 1998 the situation became so bad the Federation of Canadian Municipalities (FCM) proclaimed homelessness a 'national disaster requiring emergency humanitarian relief' (Shapcott, 2004: 203). The response thus far, however, has only been to treat the symptoms, either with meagre new allocations of resources for emergency services or with shelter allowances to help low-income tenants make up the gap between what they can afford and the rent charged by the market. Neither of these stop-gap measures addresses the real problem—the lack of rental housing affordable to low-income Canadians. Unless the drastic reduction in new rental construction (as evidenced in Figure 25.4) is reversed, market rents will continue to be prohibitive for low-income renters, social housing waiting lists will continue to expand, and homelessness will increase.

It is widely agreed that upper levels of government must get back into the business of building new affordable rental housing. The FCM has advocated what is known as the '1 per cent solution'. If the federal government were to spend just one additional per cent of its annual budget on the construction of new rental housing (which would double its current level of expenditure), it would be able to build upward of 10,000 new rental units per year. This would bring social rental construction back in line with the levels produced in the late 1980s. Yet, for even such a modest measure there would appear to be little political will. The challenge thus facing Canada is not one related to a lack of knowledge—we know what has to be done and how to do it—nor is it a technical one—the housing industry is well equipped and prepared to build new rental housing. Instead, it is a political challenge. In particular, Canadians need to be educated about the severity of the problem, and governments need political pressure exerted on them to act. If they do not, homelessness will continue to grow, and many more lives will be lost.

Notes

Special thanks to Steve Pomeroy of Focus Consulting, Roger Lewis of CMHC, and Harvey Low and Maura Lawless of the City of Toronto.

1. While not shown in Figure 25.1 due to the rather different circumstances surrounding entrance and exit requirements, prisons and hospitals may also be seen as constituting state and non-market housing options for particular subgroups of the population.
2. There is a change with federal funds being earmarked for social housing, but requiring matching provincial contributions. In the spring of 2005, Ontario finally delivered funds and announced a series of new social housing initiatives.

Chapter 26

Re-Placing Canadian Cities: The Challenge of Landscapes of 'Desire' and 'Despair'

Ute Lehrer

Canadian newspapers today abound with articles about making cities more attractive to inhabitants and visitors alike. Mostly, they centre on improvement to the built environment—e.g., on world-renowned architects, hired in the hope that designs for new museums, waterfronts, and office buildings will enhance the appearance of places and hopefully contribute to attract outside investment. But the importance of how cities look has implications that reach far beyond appearances and economic development. Issues relating to where and how we choose to live, what we like, and what we identify as 'good places' to be in are intricately bound up with how we engage in civil society and how we impact the environment through our daily activities. Moreover, how we interpret urban space is informed by dominant ideologies, and is an outcome of political and discursive practices.

This chapter explores the evolution in the perception of different types of spaces in the Canadian urban environment and how these spaces oscillate between being attractive and repellent; between being 'places' and 'non-places', variously referred to in the literature as 'landscapes of desire', 'landscapes of despair', and 'landscapes of fear' (Ellin, 1997; Hough, 1990; Lefebvre, 2004; Pocock and Hudson, 1978; Relph, 1976). To this end, the chapter considers four approaches to re-'placing' urban landscapes—urban renewal, gentrification, new urbanism, and neo-liberal urbanism—each discussed and illustrated with concrete examples from the metropolitan region of Toronto. These include: a 1950s inner-city public housing project; an inner-city neighbourhood; a greenfield development; and

the downtown condominium boom. All four relate to housing, one of the basic necessities of cities. Each of these approaches sought to transform old repellent places and/or to create new attractive places within the urban environment.

This chapter further illustrates how social construction of place is important since what is attractive and what is repellent vary from one time to another. As in the case of Regent Park, detailed below, we have little assurance that an award-winning project will remain an attractive place for long. It is probably impossible to avoid entirely future landscapes of despair. We might nonetheless improve on how urban space has been designed, developed, and refurbished over the course of the twentieth century. However, if we want to make cities better 'places', we first need to understand how space, place, meaning, and time interrelate.

Space, Place, Meaning, and Time

Much has been written on the meaning of space, the images we associate with it, and the importance of ideology in interpretation (Goonewardena, 2005). The idea that space is socially constructed and that our relationship to space is defined through social practices has been made repeatedly (e.g., Lefebvre, 1991). Along similar lines is the argument that a reciprocal relationship exists between individuals and the environment. Yi-Fu Tuan (1973, 1974, 1979, 1990) helps us to understand the importance of cultural positioning that comes with the social production of space. The place of an individual, both socially and spatially, defines how she/he perceives, conceives, and lives spatial relations.

Socialization influences how we experience the environment around us. Thus, individuals brought up in a similar social, economic, and cultural environment read certain urban situations differently from those who grew up in another environment. This means that the same physical space can be read in very different ways—while for one spectator a neighbourhood looks safe and clean, for another it feels uncomfortable and watched (e.g., Buck-Morss, 1991; Hough, 1990: 68–76). For this reason, the visual interpretation of any particular point in space, or as John Berger (1972) calls it, the 'different ways of seeing', is in relation to our own socialization. Much has been written about how people perceive space differently, how human psychology and cultural values lead to different interpretation of the same space, and how important it is, through both design and the discourse about design, to create spaces to which people will develop attachment.

Although differing somewhat in the scale at which they carry out their reflections, and without denying socio-cultural differences, noted urbanists such as Jane Jacobs (1961), Kevin Lynch (1960, 1981), and Christopher Alexander (Alexander et al., 1977) all argue that fundamental principles of good urban form can be learned and practised through urban design and planning. They all agree that because of a well-designed physical environment, some cities or parts thereof are attractive to almost everyone while others have manifest features that render them nearly universally shunned. Both professionals and scholars who engage in and write about urban design believe that spatial features of the landscape can be manipulated to create areas that will be valued by a wide variety of people who live in or pass through them.

As mentioned above, space is a social construct that can have political, economic, social, and cultural qualities. The most common understanding of space, though, is in relation to its physical materiality, as a three-dimensional expanse that encompasses and separates objects and activities, measured in distance from one point relative to others. Place, on

the other hand, is about subjective feelings and attachment that human beings develop for the spatial environments that surround them. There is a close relationship between space and place. 'Place-making' is an activity through which members of society make sense of a particular space, their own positioning within, and their own relationship to that space (Shibley and Schneekloth, 1995). In this process, space is turned into place through meaning. The meaning created can be on an individual or collective level, and it changes within different cultural and temporal contexts. Sometimes this process is deliberate, for example, when a city supports strategies to bring new meaning into a previously industrial district, as was the case of the redevelopment of the former Distillery District in Toronto. Other times, place-making may be unintentional. Ironically, the best examples of unplanned place-making pertain to neighbourhoods in the inner city that were abandoned by households seeking new and pleasant-looking suburban developments during the 1960s and 1970s. Negligence and lack of investment in spaces—houses, yards, schools, streets, industrial areas—in these neighbourhoods contributed to their perception as unwanted and unattractive, so they became 'places' perceived to have been left behind.

Depending on one's expertise and values, a given place can evoke positive or negative sentiments, irrespective of whether this place was the outcome of concerted efforts or of an absence of such efforts. Moreover, there is no guarantee that the message to be conveyed by a place will be perceived as such by individuals or the public at large. The urban landscape is strewn with failed attempts to use place to transmit messages; these are ignored (sites being perceived as meaningless 'non-places') or misinterpreted, as in the case of structures meant to transmit a message of elegance and power that are dismissed as unsightly and arrogant.

Like space, place is a physical location, but place is also a mental construct. Hence, a place is not necessarily the same for two individuals. Much of Yi-Fu Tuan's work has been about the question of how humans develop a relationship to a place—

referred to as a 'sense of place'—and about how place becomes an important part of individuals' identity. Tuan uses the term 'topophilia' to describe the need humans have of attaching themselves with a particular place, filling it with emotions and meaning, and in this process making a particular place an extension of themselves. Tuan (1974) laments that this physical and emotional connection to a place, which needs time to evolve, seems to be diminished in today's fast-paced cities, where so much new development is generic in design—designed primarily with cost savings and ease of access in mind.

Place is often referred to as a space filled with meaning; it has an identity and a history. 'Non-place', on the other hand, is the absence of distinct meaning. The dominant argument put forward to explain the proliferation of 'non-places' in today's sprawling metropolitan regions is a critique of modernism, maintaining that modern design stripped places of their identity, history, and meaning and hence that space was turned into generic places.[1] Relph's treatises (1976, 1987) on non-places within the urban landscape are classic in this regard, while Kunstler's *Geography of Nowhere* (1993) echoes this in a popularized version. Jacobs and Appleyard (1987: 114) attribute placelessness to loss of meaning and roots: 'cities are becoming meaningless places beyond their citizens' grasp. We no longer know the origins of the world around us. We rarely know where the materials and products come from, who owns what, who is behind what, what was intended.' Whether they are places or non-places, some parts of the cityscape seem to defy solution. Parks can provide comfort and relief from highly engineered built form and high-paced activity, but they can also induce fear in some people, particularly when the sight is obstructed. And parking lots are predominantly perceived as inevitably unstimulating and unattractive places despite the fact that they occupy a great deal of space in today's cities; after dark, parking lots can become veritable landscapes of fear.[2]

Not every place is perceived as attractive or repellent at all times. Places can change their meaning. Further, certain places appear attractive to some people, while others find these exact places repellent. This brief introduction to issues associated with cities as places illustrates that the combination of physical features of our environment, alongside socially constructed realities and individual experiences, shapes the interpretation of place. The chapter now turns to the four case studies.

Case Examples

Urban Renewal: Regent Park

Rapid urbanization during the nineteenth and early twentieth centuries went hand in hand with Canada's increased industrialization and led to conditions that included pressures on local housing markets through high rates of in-migration, speculative development, and low maintenance of existing housing stock. These factors joined with the lack of well-paying jobs, resulting in poor housing quality and overcrowding. The low-income, ethnic, and racial composition of inner-city populations added to the perception of these areas by outsiders and urban reformers as 'slums'. Therefore, in the post-World War II era, neighbourhoods, such as the original community where Regent Park now stands, came under pressure. Senior governments, supported by local elites, developed a program—urban renewal—that legitimized the bulldozing of these areas.

Urban renewal purported to integrate those parts of society that had been excluded from the project of modernity. Improvement of standards of housing was seen as a fundamental condition needed to transform people living on the edge of survival into law-abiding and tax-paying citizens. Renewal was enthusiastically supported by the modernist architects who became obsessed with the belief that new and more efficient building techniques in combination with new design formulas—the modern style—could redress existing inequalities and move towards a more just society. At the same time, urban reformers, who often saw old, crowded neighbourhoods as breeding grounds for social and physical ills, supported the replacement of older urban forms with new ones (Relph,

1987). They, too, assumed that clean urban forms would improve the social conduct of the inhabitants in areas that had been the object of renewal. Consequently, a peculiar alliance of architects, planners, urban reformers, and housing activists gave rise to urban renewal as a housing program.[3] A dark side, however, deserves mention. Urban renewal in general was also about bringing speculative development to parts of the city where residents lacked the power to resist.

In the Toronto case, the city was very concerned about its role of providing jobs for new suburbanites and a place of capital accumulation (Goldrick, 1982). The city therefore was primarily interested in keeping up the inner city's appearance as a safe location for both employment and capital investment. With the Housing Act of 1944, Toronto was in a position to go ahead with plans for clearing out an area that 'had long been singled out as a nefarious "slum" by urban reformers, the media, state officials, and other "slumologists"' (Purdy, 2004: 522). Regent Park, as the project that replaced almost all of the old and stigmatized neighbourhood, represented the premier Canadian attempt at social transformation based on improving the built environment. While not avant-garde in design, Regent Park nevertheless tried to follow the paradigm of modern urban design known as 'city in the park'. There were clear setbacks from the street and no thoroughfares; density was reached through high-rise buildings.[4] Once built, Regent Park was acclaimed for turning a dilapidated neighbourhood into an attractive modern and sanitized housing complex. It won the Massey Medal, an architectural award for modern design. In 1960, approximately 10,000 people lived in Regent Park (Rose, 1958). Today, the numbers are about 7,500 tenants in 2,000 rent-geared-to-income units (Toronto Community Housing, n.d.) (see Figure 26.1).

The triumphant media reports of the early days of Regent Park, calling the development 'heaven', shifted within a short period; henceforth the project was described as a 'hopeless slum' (Purdy, 2003: 45). There were a number of reasons why the original acclaim of Regent Park quickly turned sour. Milgrom attributes the failures of this project to the lack of options for resident involvement right from the beginning: 'What little concern might have existed for the interests of the neighbourhood's residents, was overshadowed by the paternalistic attitudes demonstrated in the planning and design of the Park, the preference for abstract design ideas over concerns for everyday life, and the establishment of management structures that were not accountable to the residents' (Milgrom, 2003: 212).

Other reasons for the failure of Regent Park include disinvestment and poor maintenance by the municipal and provincial governments, which rapidly caused the development to be perceived as a place of despair, repellent to outside viewers. The spatial layout of the complex also contributed to such perceptions. As Rowe (2004: 20) notes, 'most Torontonians have not seen inside Regent Park.' Because the street layout disallows through-traffic, people's 'perceptions are principally shaped by its less attractive fringes.' The public's view has been mainly shaped by the media, politicians, and 'experts' (the social workers, planners, architects, etc.), and not by direct experience of the place. However, despite undeniable problems, many of its residents have developed a strong sense of community and attachment to Regent Park as a 'place' they want to inhabit.

Today, Regent Park is just about to be replaced by a new development that promises to do away with the mistakes of the past and remove its stigma (see Toronto Community Housing, n.d.). The new plan calls for a gradual demolition of Regent Park and its replacement by a much higher-density mixed-use development. A combination of mid-rise apartments as well as townhouses—most of them offered at market rents, but with the promise to keep enough housing units available for low-income groups—has been proposed. In order to reintegrate the area with the rest of the city, most of the streets will be opened up as thoroughfares. Also planned for the area is a large park, as well as several smaller ones. Still, nothing is said in the plan about providing the new development with a community centre, a pool, or a rink—all of which have been on current inhabitants' wish list for a long time. In contrast to the heyday of the urban

Figure 26.1

A sign announces the redevelopment project that will replace Regent Park. One of Regent Park's original buildings stands in the background. *(Photo by Ute Lehrer)*

reformers in the late 1960s and early 1970s, the social agenda has now changed: today's redevelopment seems to be more motivated by the city's constant search for new ways to make itself attractive to outside investment and to lure highly paid inhabitants who will contribute positively to tax revenues through raised property values. Due to its close proximity to downtown, it is a speculative project that fits well into the current, entrepreneurial urban agenda (see Chapter 4). This, of course, diverges from the original ideal of creating democratic places for everybody—as, at least in theory, Regent Park in its modernist form was trying to achieve.

Today, when the bulldozers are being activated again for 're-placing', the argument is heard that this time the people in charge know what they are doing and that the right balance between private-market housing and rent-geared-to-income housing will transform this neighbourhood into an attractive place to live close to downtown Toronto—a landscape of desirability. Critics of this most recent redevelopment scheme, however, point to the fact that the mistakes of the past should not be corrected by the wrecking ball but instead by proactive social policies. To replace Regent Park, they argue, is to place, once more, too much emphasis on the power of the built form.

Gentrification: Parkdale

A combination of technological progress, speculative activities, and rapid demographic and economic growth alongside shifting political ideologies led to the massive suburbanization from the 1950s on, resulting in disinvestment in many inner-city neighbourhoods (see Chapters 11 and 12). Subsequently, gentrification became an ideological, practical, and political reaction to suburbanization (Ley, 1996). Caulfield suggests that, for the Toronto case, gentrification can be seen as an emancipatory process by a portion of the middle class and the outcome of its desire to escape from suburbia with its 'routine of placeless space and mono-functional instrumentality' (1989: 624). Whereas this interpretation casts a positive light on gentrification, others see gentrification as primarily a speculative strategy, pushing out low-income households from affected inner-city neighbourhoods (Smith, 1996b). Either way, gentrification has entailed massive and ongoing renovation and redevelopment of old inner-city neighbourhoods that lead not only to changes in the appearance of a place, but also to inflated real estate prices as wealthier professionals buy into overheated markets. The usual gentrification story is one of a once dilapidated neighbourhood of low socio-economic status, with a relatively poor image and low attraction value, that becomes transformed—via pioneers such as artists and bohemians, followed by speculators—into a reasonably homogeneous enclave of professionals with high levels of attraction and secure real estate values. Parkdale seems to be somewhat different, however.

Gentrification, which has been going on in several of Toronto's neighbourhoods—e.g., Don Vale, The Beach, Cabbagetown—has captured the interest of a range of urban scholars (Bourne, 1992; Caulfield, 1994; Filion, 1991; Ley, 1996; see also Chapter 11). The example of Parkdale, which is currently Toronto's most studied case of gentrification, is interesting from several angles, including what constitutes an attractive or a repellent place. Before World War II, Parkdale was a wealthy neighbourhood (Filey, 1996). It offered comfortable Victorian and Edwardian houses on large lots, in close proximity to the waterfront and with easy access to one of the first streetcar lines in Toronto. However, with the construction of the Gardiner Expressway, the

neighbourhood was cut off from the waterfront and a large share of its housing stock fell victim to high-rise redevelopment. By the 1960s, Parkdale had lost almost all of its former glory. Real estate prices plunged, leading to speculative activities by absentee landlords and investment firms. Large homes—former 'mansions'—were converted into rooming houses or what the media of the day called 'illegal bachelorettes' that were rented to poor people, including low-income immigrants. The deinstitutionalization of psychiatric patients from the Queen Street Centre for Addiction and Mental Health in the early 1980s brought more than 1,000 ex-psychiatric patients into the Parkdale neighbourhood, which added to its already strong presence of single households. Over the 1990s, the media conveyed the image of a neighbourhood stigmatized by crack houses, prostitutes, and mental patients in a 'little ghetto of misery' where 'children are afraid to play outside' (Slater, 2004: 313). This stigmatization kept property values very low for a considerable time.

Since the late 1990s, however, gentrification pressures have intensified and Parkdale has become a trendy place with hip bars, galleries, and boutiques. Redevelopment of the neighbourhood has so far been mostly based on the decisions of individuals and not, as in the other places, on large-scale redevelopment strategies. Indeed, at the same time as the city was encouraging upgrading, a coalition of rooming-house landlords and tenants and anti-poverty activists became active, calling what the city was doing 'social cleansing' and also pointing to the fact that zoning and building bylaws were responsible for driving poor people out on the streets (Lyons, 1998, 2000; Weinberg, 2000).

Compared to the rest of the city, this neighbourhood is unique—half of the occupied dwellings were built before 1946 (for the city, the ratio is 1:5), and there are three times as many tenants as owners (for the city, the ratio is close to 1:1). In contrast to other neighbourhoods where the gentrification process took off rapidly, Parkdale seems to be partially resisting quick transformation of its socio-economic conditions as well as its physical appearance. Currently, it is home to a mix of housing types, land uses, and social groups. The area includes many low-income residents and, especially, single-person households, but also an economically vulnerable and socially creative arts community, as well as a steady and alarming increase of affluent professionals. For some, a 'place' like Parkdale would epitomize the kind of urban setting that attracts the 'creative class' (Florida, 2002) and relies on 'place' to foster innovation and economic development. Market mechanisms (see Chapter 5) would suggest that the present mix is not likely to be maintained for long and will succumb to competitive real estate pressures for increased gentrification. Present observation suggests that the newcomers are winning the 'gentrification war' by pushing out low-income tenants and replacing them with new buildings and retailing and services geared towards the middle class. In the long run, it remains to be seen whether Parkdale's distinctive 'place' attributes will be sufficiently entrenched to resist complete transformation.

New Urbanism: Cornell

Like gentrification, New Urbanism is in many respects a reaction against the modern suburb with its homogeneous landscapes comprised primarily of large-lot, single-family homes, wide streets (often in the form of culs-de-sac and without sidewalks), and heavy dependency on automobiles, as well as a distinct absence of systematic design or 'place-making' concerns. New Urbanism's postmodern approach uses a different point of reference by going back to architectural forms that predate the modernist style. While forceful in its critique of sprawl and in its attempt to overcome the lacunae of modernism by creating a sense of place, New Urbanism is mainly known for its effort to reintroduce architectural forms such as smaller lots, front porches, back lanes with garages, mixed land uses and housing types, narrow through-streets, picket fences, and so on. Hence, New Urbanism has to be understood as an answer to both modernist inner-city projects, such as Regent Park, and monotonous subdivisions around today's cities. One of the key arguments of New Urbanists is that cities have to become attractive places again and that design guidelines can help

to counter the lost sense of place and community (Duany et al., 2000).

In the 1990s, the rapidly growing Town of Markham, northeast of Toronto, became a site for New Urbanist development. The most prominent project, Cornell, has 'served as the major New Urbanist precedent in Ontario' (Gordon and Tamminga, 2002: 331). Designed by the Miami-based architects Andres Duany and Elizabeth Plater-Zyberk, the respected masters of New Urbanism and in particular of the so-called traditional neighbourhood development approach, this suburban development of 980 hectares achieved an increased density, up to 80 per cent higher than that of conventional suburban developments (Figure 26.2; see also Chapter 5).

Cornell and other such communities that follow neo-traditional design (e.g., MacKenzie Town in Calgary) try to 're-place' the traditional suburbs and create a more 'urban' sense of place in the hope that this will stimulate lifestyle changes (e.g., pedestrianism, social tolerance) and ultimately move cities towards better development practices. This design approach draws on ideas that Jane Jacobs (1961) addressed a long time ago when talking about the 'death and life' of the American city: the need for social and economic heterogeneity and good urban design that would also provide a certain amount of social control, e.g., 'eyes on the street'. New Urbanism is further fuelled by the belief that current forms of sprawl are not just unsustainable (Calthorpe, 1993; Calthorpe and Fulton, 2001; Van der Ryn and Calthorpe, 1986) but also create unnecessarily non-places (Kunstler, 1993, Relph, 1976).

However, Cornell has noted limitations, the same as have been described for other New Urbanist developments. Lehrer and Milgrom (1996), for example, argue that it perpetuates sprawl and, in fact, creates exclusionary and homogeneous communities. So far, it can be said that Cornell is not very different from other bedroom communities. With the exception of density and design standards, it works much the same. Diversity is reached more through architectural ornaments than through different ways of life.

Figure 26.2

Cornell in Markham illustrates attempts by neo-traditional developments to replicate styles from the past. In Cornell, inspiration came from late nineteenth-century Toronto neighbourhoods. *(Photo by Pierre Filion)*

Neo-Liberalism: The Downtown Condominium Boom

Toronto's most recent wave of development involves a heavy concentration of condominium-building activity in the downtown area, in particular on former railway yards and along the waterfront. While urban renewal and New Urbanism can be related to a clear understanding of how to design cities, both gentrification and the current condominium boom are of very different nature. They are not about employing principles of

a particular design approach; they are rather about the creation of built environments that look attractive as individual buildings but do not adhere to an overall design approach. Turner (2002) calls it 'privatization of design'. Whose interests are being represented by this current phase of urban development is the question that needs to be addressed. Thus, whereas urban renewal was presented as taking care of the basic needs of poor people and fostering their integration into mainstream society, the condo boom presents itself as the fulfillment of a need created by its advertising campaign—the desire for an urban lifestyle. It caters to high-end markets and fits well into neo-liberal urban entrepreneurialism (Kipfer and Keil, 2002; see also Chapter 4).

Over the past five years, Toronto has seen a dramatic growth of condominium towers all over the city (Figure 26.3). From the mid-1990s to 2005, annual completion of condos quadrupled to more than 12,000 new units. These new developments are particularly striking in the downtown core, where construction was almost non-existent during most of the 1990s. This boom is transforming the urban landscape in ways that will have a long-term impact on social and spatial conditions. Continuous pres-

sures in the housing market as well as speculative activities in the real estate business are the driving forces turning former industrial and 'underused' land into high-density neighbourhoods. Up to now, the city has been very supportive of new investment in this particular form of housing, expressing hardly any concern for social, economic, and cultural issues, let alone environmental problems, that this spatial transformation will cause in the long run. The argument can be made that the condos change the morphology of the city in unprecedented ways. For one, they form a spatial barrier between the city and the waterfront. They also alter the social and cultural composition of downtown residents.

Figure 26.3

High-rise condominium developers are selling a lifestyle wherein downtown cultural events and physical activity play a major role. (Photo by Ute Lehrer)

Table 26.1 Four Approaches in the Transformation of Toronto's Built Environment, Early Twentieth Century to Present

Approach	Time Frame	Example	Socio-Spatial Effect	Design Basis	Impact of Design on Land Value and Perception of Dangerous Spaces	Landscapes of Despair and Desire Over Time
Urban renewal	1940s–50s	Regent Park, Toronto	Inclusion	Modernism: • Democratic society	Decreases land value; increases perception of high crime rate	From landscapes of despair to landscapes of desire to landscapes of fear/despair and perhaps again to landscapes of desire?
Gentrification	1980s on	Parkdale	Transformation	Rediscovery of the city: • Creative and capital-intensive	Increases land value; perception that crime rate is reduced with improvement of built environment	From landscape of despair to landscape of desirability?
New Urbanism	1990s on	Markham (Cornell)	Exclusion	Postmodernism: • Design guidelines • Built environment as social regulator	Increases land value; perception of low crime rate	Landscapes of desirability
Neo-liberal urbanism (or "new pragmatism")	From mid-1990s	Condominium boom in Toronto	Polarization	The Creative City: • Urban lifestyle	Increases land value (for now); decreases perception of areas as dangerous places	From landscapes of despair to landscapes of desirability

While the increase of population, particularly its concentration in the downtown core, is helping to alleviate some of the pressures on the housing market, the condo boom has also created new fragmentations. Because of their highly speculative nature, the condo towers are geared towards a certain clientele: singles, or couples without children. The billboards and brochures promise an urban lifestyle that, by advertising special amenities such as spas, gyms, and swimming pools as part of the development, is centred on the body, culture, and consumption. They thus propose a landscape of desire that coalesces with present middle-class values. The boom will also have an impact on the socio-economic conditions in which Toronto finds itself (see Chapter 25). Indeed, the heavy concentration of condominium towers in downtown Toronto may well accentuate social and political cleavages by creating a large island of wealth in a core area that used to be socially diverse (Walks, 2004a).

Conclusion

For purposes of synthesis and conclusion, all four case examples discussed in this chapter are summarized in Table 26.1. The four chosen examples of urban transformation have in common that they address housing needs within their specific time period and come up with a different set of policies and practices. In the case of both the original Regent Park project and Cornell we witness apparently good design features with insufficient concern for social context. Thus we come to understand that a repressive and paternalistic social context has been primarily responsible for public perception of Regent Park as a landscape of despair. Equally, one can worry that in the absence of a strong social milieu, places like Cornell or the complex that will replace the bulldozed Regent Park will ultimately be found wanting as places of distinction, no matter how much they are marketed today as landscapes of desire. In contrast, another landscape of desire, the result of downtown Toronto's ongoing condo-

minium boom, seems to be all about constructing a sellable image of a lifestyle alternative to suburban living—but with no co-ordinated concern for spatial and design issues, let alone for social and environmental matters. Finally, in Parkdale we have a community where there has been little in the way of concerted physical design and no conscious social construction of community. Yet in Parkdale alone do we sense that real 'place-making' has occurred, brought about by the political and grassroots struggle against the forces of gentrification and by the recognition of being a socially and culturally mixed community, which sets this community apart from many other Toronto inner-city neighbourhoods.

We need also to understand that what constitutes a good 'place' varies with the times and that, as an intangible construct, place is especially vulnerable to change. As seen in this chapter, places are particularly exposed to bulldozers and the dictates of the competitive marketplace. What we can conclude from this study is that 'place' matters; yet there are no easy solutions. Likewise, there must always be balance—between a well-orchestrated physical environment and socially constructed healthy communities—but we cannot say exactly what that balance will entail or how it should look because it will vary greatly from one place to another. Urban design is only one important part of why a neighbourhood appears to be attractive or not. Just as important as the physical appearance, if not even more so, is the way that attractive or repellent images are socially constructed.

Notes

1. A second argument has its origins in neo-Marxist reasoning. From this point of view, non-places are defined as parts of the cityscape that have not been recipients of capital (re)investment (Lefebvre, 2003).
2. Repulsive reactions to certain spaces have led to the application of technical methods such as safety audits in cities (Wekerle, 1995). While these don't provide complete solutions, they do go some way towards helping us deal with spaces that repel or are perceived to elicit despair or fear.

3. As a new urban policy, this approach had been prac-
    tised throughout the major industrialized cities in
    the United States (Harris, 2000). While first greeted
    emphatically as the modern way of providing decent
    living conditions to the poor, public housing com-
    plexes built under urban renewal programs became
    the symbol for what was wrong with modernism. In
    1972, one of the most highly praised public housing
    complexes in North America, Pruitt-Igoe in St
    Louis, Missouri, was dynamited 'after having been
    flogged to death remorselessly for ten years by crit-
    ics such as Jane Jacobs' (Jencks, 1984: 23). This literal
    implosion presented in Jencks's strong words 'the
    death of modernism', which 'has the fault of an age
    trying to re-invent itself totally on rational grounds'
    (Jencks, 1984: 24).

4. This design approach had its foundation in the
    modern movement of architecture, in particular of
    Le Corbusier, who in 1925 suggested having inner
    Paris bulldozed to the ground and then replaced
    with high-rise towers, an elaborate highway system,
    and open green spaces.

Chapter 27

Alternative Future for Urban Canada: Challenges and Opportunities

Larry S. Bourne

Looking Ahead: Setting the Stage

For anyone interested in charting the future of urban Canada, the place to begin the voyage is with an understanding of the present and the immediate past. The future, indeed, several possible futures, is embedded in the here and now. A portion of the firms, infrastructure, institutions, housing stock, and much of the population of, say, 2026 are already now in place. Thus, it is imperative that we carefully assess the present state of our cities, identify the factors that produced those characteristics that distinguish the cities today, and document the paths of growth and change that will carry forward through the first decades of the twenty-first century.

This chapter offers a look ahead to the emerging trajectories of urban change and the challenges and opportunities that these trajectories will generate. It does so by drawing heavily on the empirical analyses and insights provided by the previous chapters. There will be no attempt here at forecasting the future; rather, the purpose is to set the stage for anticipating alternative futures for Canada and its cities. First, the chapter acknowledges the elements that have shaped the transformation of urban Canada in recent decades and will continue to do so in the future. Second, it looks at the challenges for public policy that flow from these trends at different spatial scales: the entire urban system, the regional scale, and the intra-urban scale. These challenges, in turn, generate not only political interest but in some instances policy responses, which, explicitly or implicitly, mirror an image or 'vision' of what the future city should be and what policies are necessary to support that vision. The third

section outlines the variety of such visions of the new (good) city and offers examples of recent proposals for new policy initiatives. The concluding section returns to a broad speculation on the ways that urban Canada and its individual cities may evolve in the future.

It is worth reminding readers how complex cities, large and small, really are and the difficulties they pose for those trying to understand their character and growth, and especially for those trying to manage or shape that growth. Cities are simultaneously complex social, economic, ecological, and political systems. They are real places, each distinct in its history, setting, and sense of itself. They are physical landscapes and built environments. They are machines for production and vehicles for private consumption. Those environments are embedded with externalities, which means simply that everything is interrelated—change in one use or activity or place has impacts on everything else. Cities are obviously the outcome of capital investment decisions and a means of furthering capital accumulation. They are markets but they also have meanings that extend beyond markets. Cities are also collective public goods, in the sense that they could not exist without appropriate institutions and public services. They are, moreover, social spaces, places for living and social reproduction, characterized by dense networks of social interaction and social support, and at times intense social alienation. They are, finally, places in which many sharp contrasts—innovation and tradition, cohesion and conflict, change and stability—coexist. It is not surprising, then, that it is difficult to describe, let alone understand and manage, such complex systems.

Components of the Urban Transformation

It is equally important at the outset to remind readers, especially students new to the study of cities, how recent the transformation of Canada into an *urban nation* has been. It is generally agreed that Canada became an urban nation, in the sense that more than 50 per cent of its population resided in urban places, only in 1920. It became a predominantly *metropolitan nation* at the time of the 1966 census when over 50 per cent of the national population resided in large urban centres with populations over 100,000. By the time of the 2001 census the country had become *mega-metropolitan* in that over 50 per cent of the population lived in just six major urban regions. At present, only 20 per cent of Canadians now live outside of the country's cities and towns, and only 3 per cent are actively engaged in agriculture. Canada's future clearly lies in its cities, notably its metropolitan areas and emerging city regions.

At least five major transformations have impacted on Canadian cities and urban Canada generally since the mid-twentieth century. These include: (1) economic restructuring (the shift to services), which has meant recessions, trade liberalization, and the effects of globalization writ large; (2) the demographic transition, notably recognized in an aging population and immigration; (3) technological innovation; (4) the changing nature and roles of government and, more broadly, the state; and (5) changes in household and family structures and gender relations. The details of these transformations are outlined in previous chapters and need not be repeated here. What is important to stress is that each of these components of change has its own geography—i.e., its own patterns of impacts—across the country and within cities. Yet all are interrelated. Changes in the urban economy, for example, cannot be divorced from changes in the labour force. Changes in the labour force are driven by the demographic transition (e.g., low fertility and an aging population), household composition, and immigration. In turn, immigration flows influence rates of household formation and thus alter the demand for public services. Technological change, including Internet-based e-commerce and e-government, could make peripheral regions more accessible, more plugged in, but to date the effect has been the reverse: to strengthen the role of the larger metropolitan areas as the command centres of the country's economy.

The geography of growth also evolves over time, and both demography and sectoral shifts in the economy play a role. The country's changing demography is a crucial factor. Over 50 per cent of the country's population growth and over 70 per cent of its labour force growth are currently attributable to immigration, and these proportions will increase in future decades. Cities able to attract new immigrants will grow; others will decline as their population ages. In parallel, the economy continues to evolve: an upward shift in commodity prices (e.g., oil, forest products) moves growth to western cities (Calgary, Edmonton, Vancouver); the growth in the services sector benefits large cities; a growth in manufacturing stimulates the growth of cities in southern Ontario and Quebec. On the other hand, a growing retirement population will stimulate the growth of some smaller places located in amenity-rich environments, but there are not many of these places and most are located near the larger metropolises. The federal and provincial governments will attempt to soften the impacts of this combination of economic and demographic change, for example, through equalization payments and regional development incentives, but they will not be able to reverse these trends.

The Challenges: Urban Concerns and Policy Issues

From these ongoing transformations flow a number of political concerns and policy issues. At the scale of the country's urban system the principal concern, as documented in Chapters 3 and 4, is the increasingly *uneven geography* of urban growth and change. As the earlier blanket of growth due to fertility has been removed, the overall rate of population growth has dropped, and many more cities and small towns have started to decline. The differences between Canadian urban places have increased accordingly. Although slow growth or even decline is not necessarily a problem, as Chapter 23 argues, decline in population is also associated with other attributes—fewer job opportunities, reduced public services, limited commercial services, and depreciated housing assets. If these contrasts continue for a period of time we may well see the appearance of new fault lines separating growing and declining places (Bourne and Simmons, 2003; Reed, 2003). The challenge for the federal and provincial governments is to try to ameliorate the consequences of excessive growth in some locations and decline in others. In some situations it will be necessary to find the means and legislative tools to manage urban decline in a humane fashion.

Individual cities, and especially the metropolitan areas that are the principal focus of this chapter, face a similar set of challenges. On balance, Canadian cities provide relatively high-quality, safe, and pleasant environments for living and work, at least for most people (Chapter 2). Nonetheless, there are groups left behind, and conflicts and tensions, some old and some new, are more or less common to all places. The present section, again drawing on the preceding chapters, summarizes the major issues facing our cities today and in the near future.

The Local Economy: Economic Growth, Technological Change, and Global Competitiveness

A dominant theme in the current planning and policy literature, especially since the recession of the early 1990s, has been the vulnerability of local economies and the need to maintain or improve each city's business climate and ability to compete—nationally and globally—for new investment and jobs (Brotchie et al., 1995; Savich and Kantor, 2002). Even in growing urban regions the last recession in Canada left its mark on the productive capacity and labour force of cities, as well as on social conditions and the local tax base. Widespread economic restructuring, the introduction of new technologies,

and increased global competition for markets and talent have added to the uncertainty of continued growth. Some observers put the blame on free trade and the lack of investment in infrastructure and skills training for relatively weak productivity improvement, while others cite the effects of high commercial taxes, neo-liberal government policies and/or political inertia, and administrative red tape.

Whatever the argument, governments at all levels have responded by creating new institutions (e.g., economic development agencies) and marketing strategies designed to attract new investment and to stimulate local entrepreneurship and innovation. For many planning initiatives, with one example being the Greater Toronto Area Task Force (1996), the overriding emphasis was on improving the competitiveness of the urban economy. In concert, pressures have increased to lower commercial taxes, raise public investment, reduce bureaucratic regulations, and encourage collaborative networks and clusters of innovative firms (Wolfe, 2003). Most recently, proposals to enhance competitiveness have been expanded beyond traditional factors of production to include the quality of local public services, education, the health of the environment, and cultural facilities (Bradford, 2005). Even small cities are looking at their futures in cultural terms (Garrett-Petts, 2005). All of these policies are designed to attract investment and to attract or retain the elite, the innovators, those Florida (2005) calls the *creative class*. Whether these strategies will work remains to be seen; but what is clear is that they will not work everywhere. While urban regions may be the engines of economic growth and the focal points of the knowledge economy, their local governments are not the managers of that growth.

Urban Sprawl and Inner-City/ Suburban Decline

For many observers the principal challenge facing urban planning and policy in Canada, or at least physical planning, is the seemingly unending spread of urban development into the rural countryside and into areas of environmental sensitivity or heritage value. This process of suburban and exurban development is often associated with the loss of population, jobs, and tax revenues in the inner city and older suburbs. It has also become the rationale for many environmental groups concerned with the loss of agricultural land, heritage sites, and recreational space. These concerns, in turn, have led to a plethora of recent policy initiatives designed to encourage more 'compact' urban forms through 'smart growth' and/or growth management schemes, the imposition of growth boundaries, and the reurbanization of underused sites within the built-up areas of cities.

The problem here is that the term 'urban sprawl' is itself problematic. There is little doubt, as several previous chapters have demonstrated, that Canadian cities have become more suburbanized and development has become more dispersed. Yet there is confusion between suburban expansion, which is necessary to accommodate new populations and activities, particularly in rapidly growing city regions, and the scattered, unplanned, and discontinuous development that is the traditional textbook image of sprawl. Around most Canadian cities there is relatively little unplanned growth, due largely to tight planning controls, and development seems to be re-concentrating in new suburban nodes and in outlying communities. Yet some growth continues to disperse, especially non-residential uses, for which densities have continued to fall. There are, on the other hand, instances of continued suburban expansion even in urban areas that are not growing and that have substantial acreages of vacant land within their existing boundaries. The latter is due in part to the ease and lower costs of development on the fringe. What seems obvious is that appropriate full-cost pricing practices for new infrastructure on the fringe (see Chapters 5 and 7) might achieve the same goals of encouraging a more efficient use of land than would the imposition of growth boundaries. The challenge for policy-makers is to find the means to use existing land and infrastructure more efficiently while not reducing consumer choice or raising the costs of land and housing for the next generation.

Marginalized Groups: Low Income, Poverty, and Social Polarization

One of the challenges posed by the rapidity of economic restructuring and social change in cities is the need to address the problems of those left behind, those marginalized in the competition for living space, services, and jobs. These contrasts are most apparent in the large global cities that provide high-order services for the world economy and attract large numbers of new immigrants (Chapter 4), but they occur in all cities. The most common examples, however, are drawn from New York, Paris, and London (Hamnett, 2003).

There is still continuing debate on whether or not Canadian society has become more unequal in terms of access to resources, specifically income and wealth. The evidence is mixed, at least for national income distributions, but clearly the gap between rich and poor has widened. Within cities the evidence is stronger; levels of spatial polarization in income have increased (United Way, 2004). Perhaps the most visible of the groups affected (Chapters 8, 9, and 25) are the homeless and street people, the mentally ill, and transient youth. More broadly, neighbourhoods have been moving further apart in terms of average incomes, especially within the larger cities. New concentrations of low-income populations have emerged, some associated with the suburban locations of social housing, which is often deteriorating. Still other groups are 'at risk' of falling into poverty—including those on fixed incomes, some recent immigrant and refugee populations, Aboriginal groups, single mothers, and the frail elderly.

These groups are caught in the grip of rising living and housing costs, especially in the larger metropolitan areas, and reduced job opportunities. These pressures were augmented by cuts in levels of social assistance (in some provinces) and more restricted unemployment benefits introduced during the 1990s. The challenge of reducing these levels of marginalized and at-risk populations is primarily the responsibility of senior governments, which control the financial resources and income tax systems, but local governments face the difficult tasks of ensuring a greater social mix within neighbourhoods and maintaining an equitable distribution of housing and services across the city. Specifically, the issue is how to maintain economic competitiveness while also ensuring social equity and cohesiveness. If we do not do so, our future cities will become more highly polarized and less pleasant places to live.

Congestion and Accessibility

In most cities, the trend to more dispersed urban forms, combined with the increasing separation of jobs and housing (propelled by multi-worker households), has increased the demand for transportation more rapidly than new facilities and infrastructure can be provided (see Chapters 6 and 7). The growth of information technology (IT) systems and the Internet does not appear to have stemmed the rise in travel demand. Increases in telework and work at home have also not—at least to date—reduced either traffic or congestion. As with previous telecommunication revolutions (e.g., the telephone), people are consuming more of both IT and travel. In parallel, truck traffic has increased dramatically; many firms now depend on far-flung suppliers, larger labour catchment areas, and just-in-time deliveries.

Two variables, however, may change this scenario—another deep recession and rising energy costs. If the latter costs continue to rise, people and firms may begin to make different travel and location decisions, either to reduce the length or the frequency of trips. The challenge for policy-makers is that high travel expectations, ease of highway access, dispersed jobs, and low energy costs are built into the current urban fabric and will be very difficult to change. We will have to find a more appropriate balance between the need for new infrastructure investment and the desire to manage growth through intensification, and between investing in highways and transit. Are mixed-use developments the answer? Or is full-cost pricing (e.g., toll roads, taxes on parking) the best solution? Or four-day workweeks? Perhaps higher energy costs

will achieve more compact development where growth boundaries are likely to fail. Whatever the specific approach, future decades will require massive investment in infrastructure and proactive government intervention in shaping land-use decisions.

Adapting to Social Change and Cultural Diversity

Almost all Canadian cities have become more socially diverse in recent decades, and this diversity is certain to increase in the future, as suggested earlier (Chapters 8, 9, and 24). Driven by demographic change, notably an aging population, and the increasing importance of immigration as a source of population growth, most cities are faced with the challenges of adapting services to new and older populations whose needs may be different and more costly to accommodate. These challenges are most evident in cities with large Aboriginal populations, such as Winnipeg and Regina, or those with aging populations, such as most small towns, and in the immigrant gateway centres such as Vancouver, Montreal, and Toronto (Aniself and Lanphier, 2003). How should governments, planners, and social service agencies respond to these challenges? How is this to be achieved in a time of fiscal restraint and strong interest-group politics in local governments?

Access to Housing: Rising Housing Costs and Homelessness

Concerns with poverty, economic prosperity, and suburban sprawl are invariably linked to changes in housing conditions and costs. Although most urban Canadians are well housed, and the housing market has been highly productive over the last decade, those living on the edge of the market or in social housing have seen their situation deteriorate, especially in the large and growing metropolitan areas (Chapter 15). Rising housing prices, combined with welfare cutbacks, residential conversions, and the lack of new rental and social housing construction, have reduced accessibility for many in the marginalized groups. Even in slow-growth urban areas average rent increases have exceeded the growth in incomes.

Addressing these shortfalls is made more complicated by rising building standards, tighter regulations—including environmental regulations, zoning restrictions, greenbelts, growth boundaries—and neighbourhood resistance to change. Although well intentioned, many of these regulations often become bottlenecks, adding to the cost of producing and consuming housing. There are no easy solutions here, but governments must do more than pay lip service to the need for an enhanced supply of reasonably priced housing while they address other policy concerns.

Environmental Quality and Urban Sustainability

There is little doubt that urban development places severe strains on the natural environment and local ecosystems (Chapters 20, 21, 22). The media are full of horror stories of smog days, water pollution, leaking toxic dumps, contaminated soils, and a host of other ecological problems, as well as disappearing green space and farmland. The obvious challenge is to minimize the negative impacts, but how? It is now common to assign priority to creating the 'sustainable city', which typically means environmentally sustainable but is often expanded to encompass economic and social sustainability. Despite the vagueness of the concept, there is a clear argument here—the need for society to make decisions that give greater weight to the environmental impacts of growth (and decline). Should the environment be priced? And if so, who should pay? Can the obvious need for collective action on improving environmental quality be balanced against—or, ideally, integrated with—the requirement for economic competitiveness, ease of travel, and affordable housing?

Social Cohesion, Crime, and Violence

All cities are undergoing a social transition, and Canadian cities are no exception. Most have become more heterogeneous and most face increasing social tensions emanating from both internal and external sources. In light of this transition the issue of maintaining social cohesion—that is, the collective sense of belonging to a community and the commitment to respect differences—has become a prominent societal and policy concern. Cities characterized by intense social differences, however, need not be fragmented; the spatial clustering of like individuals in homogeneous neighbourhoods may not be a negative feature if it is based on choice rather than exclusion. Yet, for those with little choice about where to live or limited means of communicating with the wider urban society, separation can exacerbate feelings of alienation and reduce opportunities for economic improvement. How can we ensure that those lines of communication and avenues of improvement remain open and accessible?

One challenge to a community's sense of itself, and a factor that can undermine feelings of belonging and security, is the apparent increase in anti-social behaviour, notably crime and violence. Although the media tend to exaggerate the level of violence, painting images of cities as unsafe, threatening places, the simple concentration of crime in cities feeds the public perception. Moreover, the perception of crime does diminish the community's sense of control and comfort in its own space. Even if crime rates are exaggerated there is justifiable concern that rates are too high, that some spaces are frightening, and that some groups are especially vulnerable. It is also true that crime and physical violence tend to involve and impact on certain groups in society, often the most marginal. To the extent that crime rates are linked to social (e.g., income) inequalities and to feelings of alienation and isolation, they will only be reduced through co-ordinated actions by senior and local governments.

Public Goods, Services, and Infrastructure

Cities may be defined, accurately, as spatial collections of public goods and services. That is, cities only exist because the residents have agreed that certain needs must be provided collectively—typically by governments or public agencies. Examples of public goods include roads, transit, water supply, sewers, waste removal, police, schools, libraries, parks, and so forth. Cities also require governments to manage these systems and to set rules of behaviour. Generally, the levels of public goods and services in Canadian cities are high by international standards. But there is concern that the quality of social services and the basic physical infrastructure have deteriorated in recent years, due to the fiscal problems of local governments and to confusion about what level of government should do what. There is also the question of how we deal with public 'bads', such as waste dumps.

One of the debates that will shape the future of our cities invokes the question of which goods and services should be provided by the state or non-profit agencies and which (if any) should be privatized? This question goes to the heart of what we mean by government and by collective provision. Should some services be privatized, as has happened in a number of countries, for example, in water supply? Or should those services continue to be provided by governments or by arm's-length agencies? And if services do remain public, what level of government should provide that service? Either way, how should we pay for those services and who should pay? If services are to be privatized, who should regulate their provision? Who will be the losers? It should be remembered that the location, quality, and price of public goods and services have substantial effects on the quality of life in our cities. Think of the example of immense variations in the quality of schools in many American cities and the impact such variation has on social alienation and neighbourhood stability, not to mention the education of the next generation.

Governance and the Management of Growth and Change

The geographic scale, rate of growth, and increasing complexity of change in our cities, especially the larger metropolitan regions, raise fundamental questions about how we manage and plan those cities. The issue is not only one of designing appropriate government structures and agencies of service provision, but more broadly of redefining governance—that is, the links between civil society and the institutions that represent that society. Almost every society is struggling with the issue of governance in an urban world (Freire and Stren, 2001). What forms of institutions and governing structures are most appropriate, and how do these differ among cities and regions? The challenge here, of course, is closely related to issues raised above concerning enhanced urban economic efficiency, social equity, fiscal capacity, and service provision.

Clearly, the challenge differs from place to place. No single model of urban governance works everywhere. In those situations where urban growth has been rapid the structures of local government, and their revenue base, have been overwhelmed, most obviously by under-bounding, resulting in the physical expansion of the urban area into areas beyond the jurisdiction of the city or even the region. Here there is an obvious mismatch between the physical and social spaces that are the functioning urban region of daily living and the space that is managed by local and regional governments. Cities, as functional entities, are 'elastic' in that they change and spread quickly. Urban governments, on the other hand, tend to be 'inelastic' in that they change very slowly (if at all) and often painfully. In areas of slow growth or decline, municipalities find themselves not under-bounded but underfunded; their tax revenue bases are shrinking while the demands placed on their services have increased.

Numerous models for adapting local urban political structures to changing social and economic realities have been tried in Canada (see Chapter 17). These have varied from the imposition of three-tier (borough + local + regional) governments (e.g., Montreal), to two-tier special-purpose regional service districts (e.g., Greater Vancouver Regional District [GVRD] in Vancouver), to annexation of new suburban areas (e.g., Calgary), to the imposed amalgamation of cities and their surrounding suburbs (e.g., Ottawa, Hamilton, Winnipeg, Halifax), or the amalgamation of the central city and older suburbs (e.g., Metro Toronto). None of these has proven to be entirely satisfactory; indeed, some are seen as serious mistakes. The question still remains: what forms of government are best suited to the challenges we face today and in the future? The challenge is to find suitable structures that not only deliver the goods but contribute to social equity and to developing a broader sense of place and attachment to community.

The issue of government structures is most serious in those urban regions that are fragmented—i.e., that consist of several small local governments with no overarching regional authority. Perhaps the best (or worst) example in Canada is the greater Toronto region (Bourne, 2001b). As it now exists, this rapidly growing region of 5.2 million people is administered by some 25 local governments and four suburban regional governments. No regional authority, other than the province, has any clout. Political fragmentation, as is common in the larger US metropolises, can and often does lead to an uneven distribution of public goods and services, variable tax rates, and an uneven quality of life generally. One reason that Canadian cities have to date escaped severe concentrations of poverty is that services are more or less uniform across the entire metropolitan region. One of the benefits of regional governments is that, when supported by their provinces, they have been able to redistribute resources (e.g., revenues) from prosperous communities to weaker communities. However, given the fiscal problems faced by local governments and pressures for reductions in business and property tax levels, this regionally redistributive function and, thus, service equality are both under threat.

The Quality of the Built Environment

Often overlooked in discussions on the quality of life in cities is the quality of the built environment and public spaces—in short, the quality of urban design. It is now widely recognized that quality of life incorporates the design and maintenance of our buildings, institutions, and park space—both new and old. Design is no longer considered peripheral to the vision of what constitutes the livable city (Chapter 26); it is an important element that is attractive to residents, to investors, and to the mobile population of entrepreneurs and the creative

class generally. But design is not just for the elite: it can and does shape our sense of what cities are and how attached we are to those places. The challenge is how to improve overall levels of urban design without resorting to the construction of superficial monuments or leisure palaces (Hannigan, 1998), and without raising the costs of everyday needs.

Visions of the Future: The Good City

Public policies and planning legislation that have emerged as responses to the above challenges do not arise in a vacuum. As previous chapters have documented, the choices made among an infinite variety of policies and policy instruments reflect political realities, economic circumstances, networks of power and privilege, and the perceptions held by institutions, governments, businesses, professionals, and the media about what the real problems are and how they should be addressed. These perceptions in turn give rise to, or mirror, images or visions of the kind (e.g., the form) of urban area that would best address these problems (Bourne, 1996b; Downs, 1994; Lynch, 1981). These visions ultimately translate into selective policy responses. Of course, there are almost as many visions of the future city as there are participants in the urban debate, and the array of policy responses that have been proposed is immense.

To make sense of this complexity, and as a stepping stone to a discussion of urban futures, Table 27.1 summarizes several different visions of the good/new city. The left-hand column identifies major policy challenges (or problems) that flow from the previous discussion, and from earlier chapters. For each problem set there is a corresponding vision of the kind of city that, for those who rank that problem as a priority area, serves as a long-term goal (the middle column in the table). The right-hand column then offers examples of the types of policies that have been introduced or suggested as part of that vision. These visions include the entrepreneurial and culturally creative city, the physically compact city, the equitable and efficient city, the

Table 27.1   **The New City: Problems, Visions, and Policy Responses**

Definition of the Problem	The Vision	Examples of Policies
Economic growth and competitiveness	Creative city	Investment in infrastructure Skills training/productivity Innovation networks/clusters Reducing institutional bottlenecks Reducing commercial taxes
Sprawl and inner-city decline	Compact city	Growth management Intensification/reurbanization Multinucleated urban forms New Urbanism communities Variable development charges
Low income, poverty, and social polarization	Equitable city	Improving community services New social housing Rent controls/security of tenure Encouraging social mix
Congestion and access	Energy-efficient/transit-friendly city Wired city	Travel demand management Encouraging transit use Mixed uses, transit nodes User pricing, toll roads HOV (high occupancy vehicle) lanes Information technology innovations
Adapting to social change and diversity	Inclusive city	Supporting cultural services Encouraging community building Community empowerment Anti-discrimination measures Immigrant assistance services
Rising housing costs and homelessness	Affordable city	Rent supplements/allowances Transitional housing Legalizing accessory apartments Building affordable housing Shortening approval process
Environmental degradation	Sustainable city Green city	Bioregional/ecosystem planning Sustainable building practices

Table 27.1   **(continued)**

Definition of the Problem	The Vision	Examples of Policies
		Tighter pollution controls
		Agricultural land preservation
		Green space strategies
Crime and violence	Safe city	Community policing
		Improved youth services
		Law-and-order legislation
		Improved street lighting
		Gun controls
Public goods, services, and infrastructure	Healthy city	Improving local services
		Restoring fiscal imbalance
		Inter-agency co-operation
		Citizen participation
		Privatizing public services
Governance/managing growth and change	Efficient city/ Empowered city	New forms of governance
		City-regional co-ordination
		Revising municipal act
		Revising planning act
		Full-cost pricing for infrastructure
		Empowering local communities
Ugliness of the built environment	City beautiful	Enhanced urban design guidelines
		Design bonuses
		Improved maintenance
		Anti-litter campaigns
		New parks/green space

socially inclusive and affordable city, the sustainable/ green city, and the safe and beautiful city. These images shape our policy and political agendas.

There is insufficient space here to go through all of these visions and policies in detail, nor is it necessary or useful to do so at this stage. Most readers will already have digested the detailed analyses and arguments of previous chapters; in fact, for each of the problem areas identified here there is at least one chapter on the subject earlier in the text. Instead, the lesson here is that there is not a single urban future, even for one city; rather, there are multiple perceptions—for which 'vision' is a code word—of possible futures. In some instances the visions are mutually re-enforcing, such as in the need to jointly address social inequalities and affordable housing; in others the visions may be in conflict and the policies contradictory, or at least appear to be. Nonetheless, all of these visions represent laudable future urban conditions and reflect widely accepted objectives. The challenge for politicians is to sort out the conflicting goals and policies, and to minimize their negative effects, while taking advantage of those that are mutually supportive.

To illustrate these points consider the ongoing debate on the question of urban sprawl and the initiatives for more compact cities. For those who see the spread of urban development into adjacent rural and agricultural areas as a major problem, the ideal solution is more compact cities. For those, in contrast, who see suburban expansion as reflecting the aspirations of consumers for new housing and living space, and of firms for more land and highway-accessible locations, sprawl is not a major issue. It is possible to argue that if low-density suburban expansion becomes extreme the market will compensate and encourage infill and intensification efforts, as it has done in Los Angeles (Richardson and Bae, 2004). The jury is still out on the issue.

Compact cities do have obvious advantages. They are, by definition, easier and cheaper to service since the new infrastructure required is reduced and more use can be made of existing infrastructure. They may also make transit and service provision easier. This assumption, in turn, leads to proposals for a range of regional planning and associated policy initiatives, including tighter controls on suburban growth (e.g., growth boundaries and growth management schemes), higher development charges for new suburban areas, multi-nucleated urban forms linked to transit (transit-oriented developments), improved co-ordination of land use and transportation facilities, New Urbanism (higher-density) communities, and so forth. At the same time, efforts are being made to encourage infill and redevelopment within existing built-up areas through such instruments as density bonuses and tax deferrals. In

this context, the Vancouver story is probably the best example and the most carefully documented (Hutton, 1998; Punter, 2003). All (or at least most) of these initiatives may be appropriate under certain circumstances. The questions, however, are several. Whose vision do they represent? What are the contradictions in policies? And to the extent real costs are involved, who pays those costs?

The diversity of trends outlined above suggests that our cities can take on very different forms and characteristics. To illustrate the point, Table 27.2 summarizes a number of these characteristics through two contrasting scenarios for our urban future. Scenario 1, for example, indicates a future urban form that is decentralized, low density, socially segregated, auto-dependent, politically fragmented, and polluted, with increasing income inequalities and a deteriorating built environment. To some observers this scenario might represent a "more-of-the-same" future. Scenario 2 suggests a rather different future: a city that is more compact, higher density, socially mixed and inclusive, and transit-oriented, with regional level government, decreasing inequalities, reduced pollution and an enhanced built environment. These characteristics parallel the visions of the good city outlined in Table 27.1. Most cities will fall somewhere in between these two extremes. It should also be stressed that these scenarios represent tendencies, or directions of change, not end states as such. And, individual cities will show very different combinations of these tendencies. Thus, to a considerable degree, the future form of our cities is a work in progress.

Conclusion: Alternative Urban Futures

What will Canadian cities be like in the future? The argument here is that there is no predetermined future; rather, there are varied paths of growth and change, and thus multiple futures, for urban Canada and for individual cities. The urban future is a work in progress, combining what is here now, what we know will likely happen, and the largely

Table 27.2   **Future Urban Forms: Alternative Scenarios**

Characteristics	Scenario 1	Scenario 2
Spatial organization	Decentralized, dispersed city	Compact city, reurbanized, multi-nodal
Population densities	Low and declining (sprawl)	Stable (increasing in selected locations)
Land-use mix	Highly segmented, homogeneous zones	Mixed uses, heterogeneous zones
Social spaces	Increasingly segregated, homogeneous social and ethnic areas	Increasingly diverse, mixed communities
Income inequalities	Increasing: areas of extreme wealth and deep poverty	Stable or decreasing: mixed-income areas
Production spaces	Dispersed throughout urban areas	Decentralized, but re-concentrating in new suburban clusters
Local labour markets	De-integrating, dispersed	Re-integrating, balanced and diverse
Public goods and infrastructure	Uneven, unequal, largely privatized	Uniform, equitable, largely state-provided
Transportation mix	Exclusively auto-oriented and expressway-based	Auto/transit balanced
Governance	Fragmented, numerous local governments, highly competitive	Regionally co-operative, with local empowerment
Sense of place and community	Strong, but locally focused and exclusionary	Strong, but with a broader region-wide commitment
Environmental quality, green space	Decreasing: increased pollution, loss of greenery	Increasing: decreased pollution, greener
Built environment	Deteriorating: loss of heritage, banal design	Upgrading: strong heritage movement, enhanced design

unexpected. The purpose of this chapter has been to provide information and ideas that might help us anticipate those futures, not, for example, to provide a set of concrete forecasts of population or employment. Nonetheless, in conclusion, this section offers a perspective on the urban future, which ideally will stimulate further discussion as we chart our route through the early decades of the twenty-first century.

It is generally agreed that future population and economic growth will be at least as volatile as in the past. Any projections are subject to the uncertainties of the global market, trade disputes, technological change, immigration policy, and capital mobility. With slower national population growth, the processes acting to redistribute population, wealth, and economic activity (i.e., the geography of growth and change) will assume even greater importance. Lower fertility rates mean that the population will gradually age, at least through the next two decades. The elderly population will increase dramatically and the labour force will shrink. Also, domestic migration and immigration—assuming present immigration levels are maintained—will become strategically important as the dominant factors determining which cities and regions grow in population and which do not. The effects of all of the above changes will work their way through the urban system and within cities over the next few decades in ways that are difficult to predict.

Nevertheless, we can cautiously assume that most of the trends outlined in previous chapters will continue. Overall rates of population growth will decline but the concentration of population, jobs, wealth, and power in a few metropolitan regions will likely increase. The Toronto–Hamilton–Oshawa–Kitchener region, as well as greater Vancouver and Calgary, will become even more dominant as national centres, followed by Ottawa, Edmonton, Quebec City, and Winnipeg at a regional scale. Most smaller cities and towns outside these regions will not grow, and many will decline. The shift in economic growth to high-order sectors, and the net effects of information technologies, will continue to favour the larger metropolitan areas and their suburbs. As a result, the contrasts between the cities that are winners and those that are losers in the growth sweepstakes will become more pronounced and more visible. We may be creating two distinct urban Canadas.

It is informative, as Bunting and Filion (2001) have done, to paint contrasting scenarios of the daily life experiences of households in a growing city versus those in a stagnating city, set at some future date (2026). Those trapped in declining cities and towns are likely to face increasing hardships in finding jobs and necessary services (e.g., medical) as their populations age, with one compensation being less expensive housing. It is worth remembering, however, that differences in living conditions will continue to be greater within cities than between them.

Because of the effects of uneven growth and the impacts of immigration from increasingly diverse sources, cities will also become more sharply differentiated in social, ethnic, and cultural terms. Some cities, notably Toronto and Vancouver and their suburbs, will have a majority non-European population by the census of 2021 (or earlier), with a mix of many different language and religious groupings. This diversity is a bonus—the world-in-the-city concept of enhanced human capital—but it is also a challenge of accommodation and adaptation. The difficulty will be to avoid any direct link between diversity and poverty, social inequalities and spatial polarization. In parallel, those cities that receive few immigrants—especially smaller, slow-growth cities, and those in the north and to the east of Montreal—will remain relatively homogeneous. How these differences will influence social cohesion and urban politics remains to be seen.

Within metropolitan areas the processes of suburbanization, exurbanization, and employment dispersal will be difficult or impossible to reverse (Sewell, 1993). We have built immense suburban landscapes around the automobile, the truck, and the highway, and such landscapes are difficult to retrofit. Employment in the country's downtown areas is stagnant, and is declining in the older suburbs, while it booms in the new suburban fringe and in surrounding smaller communities. This decentralization trend is likely to continue, but perhaps at a somewhat reduced rate. Our outdated tax system still tends to favour new construction rather than rehabilitation and rebuilding, and development on greenfield sites over brownfield renewal. Other factors, notably higher servicing costs, zoning restrictions, and the severe fiscal problems of most city governments, add to the relative disadvantages for businesses of locating in the downtown and the inner suburbs.

Nonetheless, it is possible that a combination of higher land and housing prices, increased traffic congestion (at least in growing regions), an aging population, perhaps revisions to tax policies, and higher energy prices could force development into more compact, higher-density urban forms. In most growing cities inner-city populations have already increased significantly, in large part due to condominium construction. In parallel, gentrification has raised average incomes and house prices in many older neighbourhoods. In smaller and more slowly growing cities, however, attracting new populations and businesses to older central areas will remain very difficult unless there is a fundamental shift in the practices and policies of governments and in the perceptions of investors, employers, and residents.

This scenario of our urban future is varied and complex. On the one hand, we are observing the creation of immense and decentralized mega-city regions—the Greater Golden Horseshoe around Toronto, Vancouver and Lower Mainland, the Calgary–Edmonton corridor, Ottawa–Gatineau, and the Montreal region. These growing city regions will have expanding populations in their cores, extended urban fringes, satellite communities, and decaying older suburbs. On the other hand, we will see more slow-growing, stagnating, and declining places, some large and some small, typically with declining cores and slowly expanding suburban fringes. The most difficult challenge will be dealing with decline in small, rural, and remote communities in the resource-based periphery. There will be islands of growth in this broad landscape of decline, but they will be few and far between.

Governments will have to become more involved in shaping these development patterns in the next decade or so. Indeed, cities are now back on the political agenda, in most provinces and at the federal level. In Ontario, for example, the provincial government has returned to the arena of proactive regional planning after several decades of indifference or even hostility. The province has recently established a Smart Growth Secretariat and has introduced a new planning framework, *Places to Grow* (Ontario, 2005d), that outlines one vision of where growth should take place in the central Ontario urban region around Toronto. This plan, for a huge region of 7.4 million people extending from Oshawa to Barrie, Kitchener, and Niagara Falls, a region expected to add over 2.5 million more people by 2031, offers guidelines for local governments and land developers as to where growth should occur. In parallel, the Ontario government has introduced greenbelt legislation to protect an immense area of environmentally sensitive land along the Oak Ridges Moraine from suburban development. In effect, this area also serves as a growth boundary for the urbanized core of the region. The federal government has also re-entered the picture with the promise of a new deal for cities (Chapter 17; Bradford, 2005; Conference Board of Canada, 2005), including financial assistance for infrastructure, transit, and environmental improvements, and through the creation of a new Minister of State for Infrastructure and Communities.

Such initiatives seem to reflect a renewed willingness on the part of senior government to participate in the urban process and to develop 'place-based' policies that reflect the very distinctive needs of the cities and city regions that now house 80 per cent of the country's population. These initiatives also suggest an increasing awareness of and sensitivity to the importance of cities to Canada's future prosperity and social well-being, not to mention an awareness of the scale of decline in small towns and rural areas. What is unclear is how long these policies will last, given the experience of the 1970s (when the Ministry of State for Urban Affairs lasted but a decade), and how substantial their contributions will be. What is now obvious is that how well we, as a society, address the challenges outlined in this and earlier chapters will determine whether Canadian cities retain their existing strengths as living environments and whether they are able to improve the overall quality of life offered to their most disadvantaged citizens.

Appendix A

Sources of Information on Canadian Cities
Paul Langlois

This book addresses the notion of transition, and just as Canadian cities have been in transition in recent years, so, too, have the ways in which students and academics carry out research on cities. The primary transition has been the shift away from the use of isolated and static data, such as CD-ROMS and printed matter housed in libraries and archives, towards digital, networked data that can be explored and investigated interactively. This digital paradigm has been promised for a number of years but is only nearing reality at present, when many forms of digital data are being produced by both the public and private sectors.

While a significant portion of digital data are not available due to prohibitive cost, restrictive licensing agreements, or extremely conservative data-sharing policies, there is nonetheless a great deal of digital information freely available. This is especially true for students and academics at Canadian universities and colleges, which usually have data-sharing agreements with other institutions and which purchase access to commercial data from many vendors. The available data can be broadly categorized as either spatial or numeric. Spatial data include political, economic, and environmental boundary files, street network files, land-use maps, aerial photography, and satellite imagery. Numeric data typically take the form of census or survey data compiled by public organizations such as Statistics Canada and municipal, regional, and provincial government agencies.

For anyone studying Canadian cities, Statistics Canada (www.statcan.ca) is an invaluable resource. The United States Census Bureau (www.census.gov)

is the American counterpart. Statistics Canada makes a wealth of information available in digital form, from raw census data and summary tables to time series and boundary files for all census administrative units. A great deal of other information that is not made available publicly can be accessed through Statistics Canada by special order, though often it is very costly to purchase. Statistics Canada data sets are most reliably used to investigate phenomena for a particular census year, but caution must be used when comparing data from two or more different censuses. Because the collection of census data is prone to precisely the same problems as all statistical enterprises, and because the methods of collection and analysis change frequently, even the most fundamental of statistics from different censuses, such as population counts, may not be fully comparable. Researchers should, if at all possible, attempt to verify census data by cross-referencing them with data from other sources or from different tables within the same census. Another source of frustration in using Statistics Canada data is the limited range of information made available at no cost in public information files. By comparison the US Census Bureau provides much more data on its publicly accessible Web site.

Over the last decade, a wealth of information has been mounted for public consumption on municipal Web sites. This includes official plans, major planning reports, and often even minutes of key meetings. This information is of great assistance to people researching municipal policy-making and planning issues. It is worth remembering, however, that municipally based materials can be put together with political messages in mind and that municipal Web sites are often designed to 'showcase' a city for purposes of economic development.

For spatial data, there is no single source comparable to Statistics Canada. Instead, data come from a variety of public and private sources. Some are provided by special agreement to universities and colleges free of charge, some are purchased institutionally, some can be purchased relatively inexpensively, and some are free. Most universities and colleges publish a Web site listing their spatial data holdings and availability, along with well-known sources of free or inexpensive spatial data such as Natural Resources Canada (www.nrcan.gc.ca), GeoGratis (http://geogratis.cgdi.gc.ca/), and the US Geological Survey (www.usgs.gov). Special mention must also be made of Google maps (http://maps.google.com) and the Google Earth software, both of which provide free access to high-resolution satellite imagery of most major urban areas on the planet. While the imagery cannot be used for analysis, it can be a very useful aid to many forms of urban research.

As with numeric data, spatial data have their drawbacks, usually related to coverage, availability, and expense: particularly in the case of remotely sensed imagery, what you are looking for may not exist, may not be available due to licensing restrictions, or may be prohibitively expensive. Spatial data that are created rather than remotely sensed, such as land-use maps, parcel data, and street network files, are particularly prone to profound human error and must be cleaned and verified before use. This is especially true of commercial products; spatial data provided by public-sector organizations are usually of much higher quality.

The relatively widespread availability of spatial and numeric data has transformed how we formulate and carry out research. It is now, for example, a work of literally a few minutes to map out demographic or economic data that would have represented days or weeks of labour only a few years ago. The corollary, which we would do well to remember, is that with the widespread availability of spatial and numeric data, we also now have the ability to make more mistakes more quickly than ever before.

Appenidx B: **Selected Data on Canada's Census Metropolitan Areas**

Rank	CMA	Population (000s)		Foreign-Born (% of population)		Recent Immigrants* (% of population)		Single-Person Households (%)		Population Age 65 and Over (%)		Unemployment Rate (%)		Average Personal Income ($)		Average Household Income ($)		Incidence of Low Income (%)		University Degree (% of Population 20 years and above)	
		2001	1991–2001 Δ(%)	2001	1991–2001 Δ(%)	2001	1991–2001 Δ(%)	2001	1991–2001 Δ(%)	2001	1991–2001 Δ(%)	2001	1991–2001 Δ(%)	2001*	1991–2001 Δ(%)	2001	1991–2001 Δ(%)	2001	1991–2001 Δ(%)	2001	1991–2001 Δ(%)
1	Toronto	**4,683**	20.1	**45.0**	18.7	**16.9**	35.0	22.1	**1.5**	11.3	9.2	5.9	−30.6	35,618	4.6	**76,454**	8.8	16.7	14.4	24.9	37.7
2	Montreal	3,426	6.8	19.4	16.2	6.3	13.2	30.9	13.6	12.9	14.5	7.5	−35.9	29,199	3.2	53,725	4.7	**22.2**	0.9	19.1	43.8
3	Vancouver	1,987	24.0	39.0	30.3	16.3	64.6	28.0	4.4	12.2	0.1	7.2	−21.7	31,421	1.4	63,003	5.4	20.8	**19.5**	22.5	56.6
4	Ottawa–Hull	1,064	12.9	18.4	26.0	6.6	34.2	26.0	8.5	10.8	12.4	5.6	−23.3	**36,608**	9.1	70,886	10.3	15.0	3.4	**28.1**	39.6
5	Calgary	951	26.2	21.7	7.6	7.2	7.3	23.0	2.9	**9.0**	15.9	**4.9**	−38.8	35,693	11.6	74,042	19.0	14.1	**−18.0**	23.1	41.4
6	Edmonton	938	11.5	18.5	0.8	4.8	−15.9	25.1	8.8	10.6	24.7	5.5	−33.7	30,468	5.0	61,819	10.4	16.2	−13.8	17.8	35.0
7	Quebec City	683	5.8	3.2	**53.6**	1.2	42.9	32.3	21.8	13.1	22.6	6.9	−24.2	27,939	1.7	50,230	0.8	18.9	2.2	18.9	36.6
8	Winnipeg	671	1.6	17.0	−2.1	3.9	−22.3	30.1	10.7	13.7	6.6	5.6	−34.9	28,560	6.6	54,225	7.6	19.2	−5.4	18.0	38.5
9	Hamilton	662	10.4	24.5	4.5	5.4	24.8	25.2	12.4	14.3	11.2	5.7	−36.0	32,379	6.9	64,080	7.6	16.7	10.6	16.2	46.1
10	London	432	13.3	19.6	4.6	4.5	−8.1	27.9	11.5	13.2	8.8	6.7	−21.2	31,050	4.6	58,713	4.2	15.1	11.0	17.6	30.0
11	Kitchener	414	16.2	22.6	5.6	6.3	6.4	22.4	9.3	11.2	9.5	5.5	−38.9	32,457	9.9	65,737	11.3	11.3	−3.4	17.0	42.1
12	St Catharines–Niagara	377	3.4	18.3	−2.9	2.6	12.4	27.5	24.4	17.4	16.2	6.0	−36.8	28,693	4.9	55,167	3.9	13.2	2.3	12.1	46.5
13	Halifax	359	12.1	7.4	13.8	2.1	20.9	26.0	21.2	11.0	16.1	7.2	−21.7	29,586	3.2	56,361	1.9	15.5	9.9	22.9	36.1
14	Victoria	312	8.3	19.5	0.2	3.2	16.0	32.4	11.8	17.8	−4.2	6.6	−14.3	30,361	3.8	55,529	3.1	14.4	5.9	21.4	46.2
15	Windsor	308	17.5	22.9	10.7	7.9	63.9	25.5	5.7	12.6	−1.5	6.3	−46.6	33,938	16.6	66,066	**19.5**	13.2	−10.2	16.6	**60.5**
16	Oshawa	296	23.4	15.9	−6.8	2.3	**−22.5**	**18.8**	12.4	10.4	15.9	6.0	−29.4	33,682	3.9	69,770	6.5	**9.4**	1.1	12.1	45.1

17	Saskatoon	226	7.1	8.2	1.1	2.3	19.6	27.5	6.1	11.8	14.1	6.7	-23.0	28,045	5.0	53,025	7.4	18.0	-4.8	19.4	36.1
18	Regina	193	0.6	7.8	-5.6	1.7	-10.7	28.0	11.0	12.6	15.1	6.0	-17.8	29,780	3.3	56,609	4.3	15.5	-1.9	17.2	32.7
19	St John's	173	0.6	3.1	11.5	0.8	-1.0	20.9	**42.4**	10.7	14.6	11.3	-29.8	27,061	2.4	54,940	-2.5	17.4	7.4	18.3	54.4
20	Greater Sudbury	156	-1.3	7.1	-13.2	0.7	-0.6	26.5	24.0	13.8	32.5	9.2	**7.0**	29,000	-1.8	54,624	**-4.2**	14.9	10.4	12.0	33.6
21	Chicoutimi–Jonquière	155	**-3.7**	**1.0**	39.1	**0.5**	**79.5**	26.1	40.5	12.9	**41.5**	**12.4**	-6.1	25,908	**-4.9**	47,872	-1.8	16.4	1.9	11.9	43.0
22	Sherbrooke	154	9.3	5.1	38.2	2.3	45.7	**33.7**	19.8	13.2	14.9	6.9	-36.7	25,493	3.5	44,689	3.3	18.5	-8.0	16.7	39.1
23	Abbotsford	147	**29.8**	22.4	21.5	7.0	—	21.5	—	13.1	-3.7	8.2	—	27,011	—	56,348	—	13.5	—	**10.7**	—
24	Kingston	147	7.7	12.9	-3.7	2.3	-1.6	26.6	11.5	14.2	15.8	6.9	-8.0	30,374	3.9	57,652	3.6	15.2	16.0	20.3	**27.2**
25	Trois-Rivières	138	0.9	1.7	41.4	0.5	40.4	32.9	22.9	15.3	30.5	9.2	-30.8	**25,185**	0.1	**44,348**	0.6	19.8	-2.9	13.2	45.3
26	Saint John	123	-2.5	4.1	-9.9	0.6	-18.8	24.8	14.6	13.2	6.6	9.2	-19.3	26,932	2.5	51,460	3.7	17.8	5.3	14.0	57.9
27	Thunder Bay	**122**	-2.4	11.2	**-15.4**	1.1	-20.0	28.8	17.6	15.1	13.2	8.8	-7.4	29,728	1.5	56,147	-1.4	14.1	14.6	13.9	46.7
	Mean	715	9.6	15.5	10.6	4.3	15.6	26.7	15.0	12.9	13.8	7.2	-25.4	30,080	4.3	58,279	5.3	16.0	2.6	17.6	42.2
	Weighted Mean	—	13.8	25.9	15.7	8.9	23.2	26.3	9.3	12.2	11.6	6.5	-29.5	31,958	4.7	63,609	7.1	17.6	5.2	20.8	41.8
	Median	311.9	8.3	17.0	5.6	2.6	12.8	26.5	12.1	12.9	14.5	6.7	-26.8	29,728	3.8	56,348	4.2	15.5	2.2	17.6	41.8
	Std. Deviation	1061.4	9.4	18.0	28.7	4.2	28.7	3.8	10.1	2.0	10.5	1.8	12.4	3,118	4.2	8,262	5.7	2.9	9.4	4.4	8.4

Notes: Minimum and maximum values in bold.

*Arrived in Canada 1991–2001.

**Weighted using 2001 population.

Sources: 2001 data obtained from 2001 CMA profiles; 1991 data obtained from 1996 CMA profiles, 1991 EA profiles by region (long form), 1991 2B profile (detailed questionnaire), 1991 BST CT short form. (Compiled by Paul Langlois)

Bibliography

Abu-Laban, Y., and J.A. Garber. 2005. 'The construction of the geography of immigration as a policy problem: The United States and Canada compared', *Urban Affairs Review* 40: 520–61.

Acheson, W. 1972. 'The National Policy and industrialization of the Maritimes, 1880–1910', *Acadiensis* 1: 2–34.

Adams, J.S. 1970. 'Residential structure of midwestern cities', *Annals, Association of American Geographers* 60: 37–62.

Adams, M. 2003. *Fire and Ice: The United States, Canada and the Myth of Converging Values*. Toronto: Penguin Canada.

Adams, T. 1974 [1934]. *The Design of Residential Areas: Basic Considerations, Principles, and Methods*. New York: Arno Press.

Adkin, L. 2003. 'Ecology, political economy, and social transformation', in Clement and Vosko (2003).

Agricultural Land Reserve, Protection and Enhancement Committee (ALR-PEC). 2005. *Protecting the Agricultural Land Reserve: Our Foodlands Under Threat*. Vancouver: ALR-PEC.

Aibar, E., and W. Bijker. 1997. 'Constructing a city: The Cerda plan for the extension of Barcelona', *Science, Technology and Human Values* 22: 3–30.

Alcaly, R. 2003. *The New Economy: What It Is, How It Happened, and Why It Is Likely To Last*. New York: Farrar, Straus, Giroux.

Alexander, C. 1979. *The Timeless Way of Building*. New York: Oxford University Press.

———, S. Ishikawa, and M. Silverstein. 1977. *A Pattern Language: Towns, Buildings, Construction*. New York: Oxford University Press.

———, H. Neis, A. Anninou, and I. King. 1987. *A New Theory of Urban Design*. New York: Oxford University Press.

Alexander, D., and R. Tomalty, 2002. 'Smart growth and sustainable development: Challenges, solutions and policy directions', *Local Environment* 7: 397–409.

Allen, C., and S. Blandy. 2004. 'Fables of the reconstruction: Inner-urban regeneration, city centre living and the reinvention of urban space', paper presented at the international conference of the International Sociological Association, Research Committee 43 Housing and the Built Environment, 'Adequate and Affordable Housing for All', Toronto, 24–8 June. Available at: <www.urbancentre. utoronto.ca/pdfs/housingconference/Day_Three_ Program.pdf>.

Alliance to End Homelessness (ATEH). 2005. *Experiencing Homelessness: The First Report Card on Homelessness in Ottawa, 2005*. Ottawa: Alliance to End Homelessness/United Way of Ottawa.

Alonso, W. 1964. *Location and Land Use*. Cambridge, Mass.: Harvard University Press.

American Planning Association (APA). 1982. *Designing Effective Pedestrian Improvements in Urban Districts*. Chicago: APA (Planning Advisory Series Report 368).

American Public Transportation Association (APTA). 2005. *Public Transportation Fact Book*. Washington: APTA.

Ames, H. 1972 [1897]. *The City Below the Hill*. Toronto: University of Toronto Press.

Amin, A., ed. 1994. *Post-Fordism: A Reader*. Oxford: Blackwell.

——— and S. Graham. 1997. 'The ordinary city', *Transactions of the Institute of British Geographers* 22: 411–29.

Anderson, B.C., W.E. Watt, and J. Marsalek. 2002. 'Critical issues for stormwater ponds: Learning from a decade of research', *Water Science and Technology* 45, 9: 277–83.

Anderson, J.E. 1985. 'The changing structure of a city: Temporal changes in cubic spline urban density patterns', *Journal of Regional Science* 25: 413–25.

Anderson, K. 1991. *Vancouver's Chinatown: Racial Discourse in Canada, 1875–1980*. Montreal and Kingston: McGill-Queen's University Press.

Anderson, L. 1984. 'Hard choices: Supplying water to New England towns', *Journal of Interdisciplinary History* 15: 211–34.

———. 1988. 'Water-supply', in Ball (1988).

Andreae, C. 1988. 'Railways', in Ball (1988).

Andrew, C. 2003. 'Municipal restructuring: Urban services and the potential for the creation of transformative political spaces', in Clement and Vosko (2003).

———, ed. 2004. *Our Diverse Cities,* vol. 1. Ottawa: Metropolis Project.

———, C. Graham, and S.D. Phillips, eds. 2002. *Urban Affairs: Back on the Policy Agenda*. Montreal and Kingston: McGill-Queen's University Press.

——— and J. Morrison. 2002. 'Infrastructure', in E. Fowler and D. Siegel, eds, *Urban Policy Issues*. Toronto: Oxford University Press.

Anisef, P., and M. Lanphier, eds. 2003. *The World in a City*. Toronto: University of Toronto Press.

Applebaum, R., M. Dolny, P. Dreier, and J. Gilderbloom. 1991. 'Scapegoating rent control: Masking the causes of homelessness', *Journal of the American Planning Association* 57, 1: 153–64.

Applebaum, W. 1968. *A Guide to Store Location Research*. Reading, Mass.: Addison-Wesley.

Appleton, L. 1995. 'The gender regimes of American cities', in J. Garber and R. Turner, eds, *Gender in Urban Research*. Thousand Oaks, Calif.: Sage.

Applications Management Consulting Limited (AMCL). 1995. *Transportation Master Plan Household Travel Survey Project Report,* prepared for the City of Edmonton Transportation Department. Edmonton: Applications Management Consulting Ltd.

Arentze, T., and H. Timmermans. 2005. *ALBATROSS Version 2.0: A Learning Based Transportation Oriented Simulation System*. Eindhoven: EIRASS.

Armstrong, A. 1959. 'Thomas Adams and the Commission of Conservation', *Plan Canada* 1, 1: 14–32.

Armstrong, C., and H.V. Nelles. 1986. 'Suburban street railway strategies in Montreal, Toronto and Vancouver, 1896–1930', in G.A. Stelter and A.F.J. Artibise, eds, *Power and Place: Canadian Urban Development in North American Context*. Vancouver: University of British Columbia Press.

Armstrong, P., and H. Armstrong. 1994. *The Double Ghetto,* 3rd edn. Toronto: McClelland & Stewart.

Arnott, R.J., and F. Lewis. 1979. 'The transition of land to urban use', *Journal of Political Economy* 87, 4: 161–9.

Arthurs, H. 2000. 'The hollowing out of corporate Canada?', in J. Jenson and B. De Sousa Santos, eds, *Globalizing Institutions: Case Studies in Regulation and Innovation*. Ashgate: Aldershot.

Artibise, A.F.J. 1981. *Prairie Urban Development, 1870–1930*. Ottawa: Canadian Historical Association, Historical Booklet No. 34.

——— and J. Hill. 1993. *Governance and Sustainability in the Georgia Basin*. Victoria: British Columbia Roundtable on the Environment and the Economy.

Atwood, T.C., H.P. Weeks, and T.M. Gehring. 2004. 'Spatial ecology of coyotes along a suburban-to-rural gradient', *Journal of Wildlife Management* 68: 1000–9.

Aubin, H. 1977. *City for Sale: International Financiers Take a North American City by Storm*. Montreal: L'Étincelle.

Aubry, T., F. Klodawsky, E. Hay, and S. Birnie. 2003. *Panel Study on Persons Who Are Homeless in Ottawa: Phase 1 Results*. Ottawa: City of Ottawa and University of Ottawa. At: <www.socialsciences. uottawa.ca/crcs/pdf/FinalreportPaneStudy.pdf>. Accessed May 2005.

Austin. 1986. *Final Report: Task Force on the Homeless*. Austin, Tex.: City of Austin.

———. 2001. *Homeless Needs, Services and Characteristics: Based on Information from the 2001 Homeless Services Survey Data*. Austin, Tex.: City of Austin.

Bacher, J. 1993. *Keeping to the Marketplace: The Evolution of Canadian Housing Policy*. Montreal and Kingston: McGill-Queen's University Press.

Badoe, D.A., and E.J. Miller. 1997. *The Transportation–Land-Use Interaction: Empirical Findings and Implications for Modelling*. Toronto: University of Toronto Joint Program in Transportation (Technical Memorandum No. 2, Transit Cooperative Research Project H-12 'Integrated Urban Models for Simulation of Transit and Land-Use Policies').

Baerwaldt, W., and B. Reid. 1986. 'Re-reading suburbia', *City Magazine* 8, 1: 17–29.

Bailey, S. 1994. 'User charges for urban services', *Urban Studies* 31: 745–65.

Bain, A. 2003. 'Constructing contemporary artistic identities in Toronto neighbourhoods', *Canadian Geographer* 47: 303–17.

Balakrishnan, T.R., and S. Gyimah. 2003. 'Spatial residential patterns of selected ethnic groups: Significance and implications', *Canadian Ethnic Studies Journal* 35: 113–34.

Baldassare, M. 1986. *Trouble in Paradise: The Suburban Transformation in America*. New York: Columbia University Press.

Baldwin, D. 1988. 'Sewerage', in N. Ball, ed., *Building Canada: A History of Public Works*. Toronto: University of Toronto Press.

Baldwin, J. 1985. *Environmental Planning and Management*. Boulder, Colo.: Westview Press.

Baldwin, J., M. Brown, and T. Vinodrai. 2001. *Dynamics of the Canadian Manufacturing Sector in Metropolitan and Rural Regions*. Ottawa: Statistics Canada (Analytical Studies Branch Research Paper Series No. 169).

Ball, N., ed. 1988. *Building Canada: A History of Public Works*. Toronto: University of Toronto Press.

Barcelo, M. 1988. 'Urban development policies in Montreal, 1960–1978', *Quebec Studies* 6, 2: 26–40.

Basavarajappa, K.G., and F. Jones. 1999. 'Visible minority income differences', in S. Halli and L. Driedger, eds, *Immigrant Canada: Demographic, Economic, and Social Challenges*. Toronto: University of Toronto Press.

Batey, W.L., and P.J. Smith. 1981. 'The role of territory in political conflict in metropolitan fringe areas', in K.B. Beesley and L.H. Russwurm, eds, *The Rural-Urban Fringe: Canadian Perspectives*. Downsview, Ont.: York University-Atkinson College, Geographical Monographs No. 10.

Bauder, H. 2003. '"Brain abuse" or the devaluation of immigrant labour in Canada', *Antipode* 35: 699–717.

——— and B. Sharpe. 2002. 'Residential segregation of visible minorities in Canada's gateway cities', *Canadian Geographer* 46: 204–22.

Beasley, L. 2000. *'Living First' in Downtown Vancouver*. Vancouver: City of Vancouver. At: <www.city.vancouver.bc.ca/commsvcs/currentplanning/living.htm>. Accessed 2 May 2005.

———. 2003. 'Laws and processes behind the urban designer's pencil: Thoughts from the Vancouver experience', *Plan Canada* 43, 3: 41–4.

Beattie, L., and D. Ley. 2003. 'The German immigrant church in Vancouver: Service provision and identity formation', *Die Erde* 134: 3–22.

Beauchesne, A., and C.R. Bryant. 1999. 'Agriculture and innovation in the urban fringe: The case of organic farming in Quebec, Canada', *Tijdschrift voor Economische en Sociale Geografie* 90: 320–8.

Beaudet, P. 1987. 'Historical Spatial Dimensions of the Upper Status Population of Halifax, Hamilton, Winnipeg and Calgary'. Buffalo, NY: Department of Geography and Planning, State University College at Buffalo (unpublished report).

———. 1988. 'Elite residential areas in Toronto and Buffalo: Comparative examples from United States and Canadian Cities', in T. Bunting and P. Filion, eds, *The Changing Canadian Inner City*. Waterloo: University of Waterloo Department of Geography Publication Series No. 31.

Beaujot, R. 2000. *Earning and Caring in Canadian Families*. Peterborough, Ont.: Broadview Press.

———. 2004. *Delayed Life Transitions: Trends and Implications*. (Contemporary Family Trends). Ottawa: Vanier Institute of the Family. Available at: <www.vifamily.ca/library/cft/delayed_life.pdf>; accessed 11 May 2005.

Beaupré, P., and C. Le Bourdais. 2001. 'Le départ des enfants du foyer parental au Canada', *Cahiers québécois de démographie* 30, 1: 29–62.

Beauregard, L. 1972. 'Le centre-ville/the city centre', in Beauregard, ed., *Montréal: Guided Excursions/*

Field Guide. Montreal: Les Presses de l'Université Laval.

———. 1981. *La Rue Saint-Jacques à Montréal: une géographie de bureaux.* Montreal: Université de Montréal.

Beauregard, R.A. 2003. *Voices of Decline: The Postwar Fate of US Cities,* 2nd edn. New York: Routledge.

Beaverstock, J., P.J. Taylor, and R.G. Smith.1999. 'A roster of world cities', *Cities* 16: 445–58.

Beck, M.B. 2005. 'Vulnerability of water quality in intensively developing urban watersheds', *Environmental Modeling and Software* 20: 381–400.

Bedford, P. 1997. 'When they were Kings: Planning for reinvestment', *Plan Canada* 37, 4: 18–23.

Beesley, K.B. 1999. 'Agricultural land preservation in North America: A review and survey of expert opinion', in O.J. Furuseth and M.B. Lapping, eds, *Contested Countryside: The Rural Urban Fringe in North America.* Brookfield, Vt: Ashgate.

Begg, I. 1999. 'Cities and competitiveness', *Urban Studies* 36: 795–809.

Begin, P. 1994. *Homelessness in Canada.* Ottawa: Ministry of Supply and Services.

Bélanger, A., and É. Caron Malenfant. 2005. *Population Projections of Visible Minority Groups, Canada, Provinces and Regions, 2001–2017.* Ottawa: Statistics Canada (Demography Division).

Belec, J. 1997. 'The Dominion Housing Act', *Urban History Review* 25, 2: 53–62.

———, J. Holmes, and T. Rutherford. 1987. 'The rise of Fordism and the transformation of consumption norms: Mass consumption and housing in Canada, 1930–1945', in R. Harris and G. Pratt, eds, *Social Class and Housing Tenure.* Gavle, Sweden: National Swedish Institute for Building Research.

Belk, R. 1988. 'Possessions and the extended self', *Journal of Consumer Research* 15: 139–68.

Bellah, R.N., R. Madsen, W.M. Sullivan, A. Swindler, and S.M. Tipton. 1985. *Habits of the Heart: Individualism and Commitment in American Life.* New York: Harper and Row.

Ben-Akiva, M.E., and S.R. Lerman. 1985. *Discrete Choice Analysis: Theory and Application to Travel Demand.* Cambridge, Mass.: MIT Press.

Berelowitz, L. 2005. *Dream City: Vancouver and the Global Imagination.* Vancouver: Douglas & McIntyre.

Berger, J. 1972. *Ways of Seeing.* Harmondsworth: Penguin.

Berke, P.R., J. MacDonald, N. White, M. Holmes, D. Line, K. Oury, and R. Ryznar. 2003. 'Greening development to protect watersheds—Does new urbanism make a difference?', *Journal of the American Planning Association* 69: 397–413.

Berry, A.E. 1940. 'Developments in Canadian water works practice', *Water and Sewage* (Dec.): 9–19, 42–5.

Berry, B.J.L. 1963. *Commercial Structure and Commercial Blight: Retail Patterns and Process.* Chicago: University of Chicago, Department of Geography Research Paper No. 85.

———. 1976. 'The counterurbanization process: Urban America since 1970', in Berry, ed., *Urbanization and Counterurbanization.* London: Sage.

Bessey, K.M. 2002. 'Structure and dynamics in an urban landscape: Toward a multiscale view', *Ecosystems* 5: 360–75.

Bilson, G. 1980. *A Darkened House: Cholera in Nineteenth-Century Canada.* Toronto: University of Toronto Press.

Binford, H.C. 1985. *The First Suburbs: Residential Communities on the Boston Periphery, 1815–1860.* Chicago: University of Chicago Press.

Birch, D. 1971. 'Toward a stage model of urban growth', *Journal of the American Institute of Planners* 37: 78–87.

Birch, E.L. 2002. 'Having a longer view on downtown living', *Journal of the American Planning Association* 68: 5–21.

Bird, R., and E. Slack. 1993. *Urban Public Finance in Canada,* 2nd edn. Toronto: John Wiley and Sons.

Blair, T. 2004. 'The bicycle compatibility of streets in downtown Calgary', *Plan Canada* 44, 3: 41–4.

Blais, P. 1996. 'The economics of urban form', in GTA Task Force, *Report.* Toronto: Queen's Printer.

Blomley, N. 2004. *Unsettling the City: Urban Land and the Politics of Property.* New York: Routledge.

Bloomfield, E. 1985. 'Ubiquitous town planning missionary: The careers of Horace Seymour, 1892–1940', *Environments* 17, 2: 29–42.

Bluestone, B., and B. Harrison. 1982. *The Deindustrialization of America: Plant Closings,*

Community Abandonment and the Dismantling of Basic Industry. New York: Basic Books.

Blumenfeld, H. 1967. *The Modern Metropolis*. Cambridge, Mass.: MIT Press.

———. 1979. *Metropolis and Beyond: Selected Essays of Hans Blumenfeld*. New York: Wiley.

Boddy, T. 2005. '"Downtown" a fool's paradise? Council policy has encouraged the construction of new condos but not new office towers', *Vancouver Sun,* 10 Aug., 3.

Bolbier, D. 1998. *How Smart Growth Can Stop Sprawl*. Washington: Essential Books.

Bondi, L. 1992. 'Gender symbols and urban landscapes', *Progress in Human Geography* 16: 157–70.

——— and H. Christie. 2000. 'Working out the urban: Gender relations and the city', in G. Bridge and S. Watson, eds, *A Companion to the City*. Malden, Mass.: Blackwell.

——— and D. Rose. 2003. 'Constructing gender, constructing the urban: A review of Anglo-American feminist urban geography', *Gender, Place and Culture* 10: 229–45.

Booth, P. 1996. *Controlling Development: Certainty and Discretion in Europe, the USA and Hong Kong*. London: UCL Press.

Borins, S. 1997. Decision of Ontario Court of Justice (Motions Court), July re municipal amalgamation in Toronto.

Boschken, H. 2003. 'Global cities, systemic power, and upper-middle-class influence', *Urban Affairs* 38: 808–30.

Bottles, S. 1987. *Los Angeles and the Automobile: The Making of a Modern City*. Berkeley: University of California Press.

Boudreau, J. 2000. *The Mega-City Saga: Democracy and Citizenship in this Global Age*. Montreal: Black Rose.

Bourdieu, P. 1984. *Distinction. A Social Critique of the Judgement of Taste*. London: Routledge & Kegan Paul.

Bourne, L.S. 1967. *Private Redevelopment of the Central City: Spatial Processes of Structural Change in the City of Toronto*. Chicago: University of Chicago, Department of Geography Research Paper No. 112.

———. 1981. *The Geography of Housing*. London: Edward Arnold.

———. 1982. 'The inner city', in C. Christian and R. Harper, eds, *Modern Metropolitan Systems*. Columbus, Ohio: Charles Merrill.

———. 1987. 'Evaluating the aggregate spatial structure of Canadian metropolitan areas', *Canadian Geographer* 31: 194–208.

———. 1989. 'Are new urban forms emerging? Empirical tests for Canadian urban areas', *Canadian Geographer* 33: 312–28.

———. 1992. 'Population turnaround in the Canadian inner-city: Contextual factors and social consequences', *Canadian Journal of Urban Research* 1: 66–89.

———. 1993a. 'Close together and worlds apart: An analysis of changes in the ecology of income in Canadian cities', *Urban Studies* 30: 1293–317.

———. 1993b. 'The changing settlement environment of housing', in Miron (1993a).

———. 1996a. 'Reinventing the suburbs: Old myths and new realities', *Progress in Planning* 46, 3: 163–84.

———. 1996b. 'Reurbanization, uneven urban development and the debate on new urban forms', *Urban Geography* 17: 690–713.

———. 1997. 'Social inequalities, polarization and the redistribution of income within cities: A Canadian example', in B. Badcock and M. Browett, eds, *Developing Small Area Indicators for Policy Research in Canada*. Adelaide, Australia: University of Adelaide Key Centre for Social Applications of GIS (Monograph Series 2).

———. 2000. 'Urban Canada in transition to the twenty-first century: Trends, issues and visions', in Bunting and Filion (2000).

———. 2001a. 'The urban sprawl debate: Myths, realities and hidden agendas', *Plan Canada* 41, 4: 26–8.

———. 2001b. 'Designing an urban region: The lessons and lost opportunities of the Toronto experience', in Freire and Stren (2001).

———. 2004. *Beyond the New Deal for Cities: Confronting the Challenges of Uneven Urban Growth*. Toronto: Centre for Urban and Community Studies (Research Bulletin #21).

———. 2005. 'Neighbourhood change and social polarization: The scales and components of income inequalities', in Y. Murayama and G. Du, eds, *Cities in Global Perspective: Diversity and Transition*. Tokyo: Rikkyo University and IGU Urban Commission.

———, M. Bunce, L. Taylor, N. Luka, and J. Maurer. 2003. 'Contested ground: The dynamics of peri-urban growth in the Toronto region', *Canadian Journal of Regional Science* 26: 251–70.

——— and T. Bunting. 1993. 'Housing provision, residential development and neighbourhood dynamics', in Bourne and Ley (1993).

——— and D.E. Ley, eds. 1993. *The Changing Social Geography of Canadian Cities*. Montreal and Kingston: McGill-Queen's University Press.

——— and A. Lorius. 1999. 'How similar are urban neighbourhoods in Canada? A classification based on external environments', *Canadian Journal of Urban Research* 8: 143–71.

——— and D. Rose. 2001. 'The changing face of Canada: The uneven geographies of population and social change', *Canadian Geographer* 45: 105–19.

——— and J. Simmons. 2003. 'New fault lines? Recent trends in the Canadian urban system and their implications for planning and public policy', *Canadian Journal of Urban Research* 12: 22–47.

——— and ———. 2004. 'The conceptualization and analysis of urban systems: A North American perspective', in T. Champion and G. Hugo, eds, *New Forms of Urbanization: Beyond the Urban-Rural Dichotomy*. Aldershot, UK: Ashgate.

Bowman, J.L., and M.E. Ben-Akiva. 2001. 'Activity-based disaggregate travel demand model system with activity schedules', *Transportation Research Part A* 35A: 1–28.

Boyd, M. 2000. 'Ethnic variations in young adults living at home', *Canadian Studies in Population* 27: 135–58.

Boyer, M.C. 1983. *Dreaming the Rational City: The Myth of American City Planning*. Cambridge, Mass.: MIT Press.

———. *The City of Collective Memory: Its Historical Imagery and Architectural Entertainments*. Cambridge, Mass.: MIT Press.

Boyle, M., R. Gibson, and D. Curran. 2004. 'If not here, then perhaps not anywhere: Urban growth management as a tool for urban sustainability planning in British Columbia's capital regional district', *Local Environment* 9, 1: 21–43.

Bradbury, B. 1993. *Working Families: Age, Gender, and Daily Survival in Industrializing Montreal*. Toronto: McClelland & Stewart.

Bradbury, J. 1984. 'Industrial cycles and the mining sector in Canada', *International Journal of Urban and Regional Research* 8: 311–31.

Bradford, N. 2002. *Why Cities Matter: Policy Research Perspectives for Canada*. Ottawa: Canadian Policy Research Networks. At: <www.cprn.org>.

———. 2005. *Place-based Public Policy: Towards a New Urban and Community Agenda for Canada*. Ottawa: Canadian Policy Research Networks (Research Report F/51). At: <www.cprn.org>.

Bramadat, P. 2005. 'Beyond the Trojan horse: Religion, immigration and Canadian public discourse', *Canadian Issues/Thème Canadiens* (Spring): 78–81.

Brampton. 2000. *Proposed Revisions to Policies Regarding Places of Worship: Report to Planning and Building Committee*. Brampton, Ont.: Planning Policy and Research, City of Brampton.

Brander, K.E., K.E. Owen, and K.W. Potter. 2004. 'Modeled impacts of development type on runoff volume and infiltration performance', *Journal of the American Water Resources Association* 40: 961–9.

Braudel, F. 1984. *Civilization and Capitalism, 15th–18th Century*, vol. 3, *The Perspective of the World*. New York: Harper and Row.

Bread Not Circuses Coalition. 2000. *Real Guide to Toronto 2008 Olympic Bid*. Toronto: Bread Not Circuses Coalition.

Brenner, R. 2001. 'The world economy at the turn of the millennium toward boom or crisis?', *Review of International Political Economy* 8: 16–44.

Bresnan, A., and J. Bresnan. 1990. 'Parks and recreation', in G. Reiner, ed., *Understanding Infrastructure*. New York: John Wiley & Sons.

British Columbia Ministry of Social Development and Economic Security (BCMSDES). 2001. *Homelessness—Causes and Effects*, 4 vols. Victoria: BCMSDES and British Columbia Housing Management Commission.

British Columbia Round Table on the Environment and the Economy. 1994. *State of Sustainability: Urban Sustainability Reporting and Containment*. Victoria: Crown Publications.

Britton, J., ed. 1996. *Canada and the Global Economy: The Geography of Structural and Technological Change.* Montreal and Kingston: McGill-Queen's University Press.

Broadfoot, J.D., R.C. Rosatte, and D.T. O'Leary. 2001. 'Raccoon and skunk population models for urban disease control planning in Ontario, Canada', *Ecological Applications* 11: 295–303.

Broadway, M. 1989. 'A comparison of patterns of urban deprivation between Canadian and U.S. cities', *Social Indicators Research* 21: 531–51.

———. 1992. 'Differences in inner-city deprivation: An analysis of seven Canadian cities', *Canadian Geographer* 36: 189–96.

Brook, J.R., C.D. Lillyman, M.F. Shepherd, and A. Mamedov. 2002. 'Regional transport and urban contributions to fine particle concentrations in southeastern Canada', *Journal of the Air and Waste Management Association* 52: 855–66.

Brotchie, J., et al., eds. 1995. *Cities in Competition: Productive and Sustainable Cities for the 21st century.* Melbourne: Longman.

Brotman, S. 1999. 'Incidence of poverty among seniors in Canada: Exploring the impact of gender, ethnicity and race', *Canadian Journal on Aging* 17: 166–85.

Brown, D.D. 1999. 'Learning from First Nations', *Plan Canada* 39, 5: 22–3.

Brown, E.C. 1991. 'A history of Calgary's uni-city form of government', *Alberta and Northwest Territories Journal of Planning Practice* 11: 45–52.

———, R.M. Miller, and B.D. Simpkins. 1989. 'The City of Calgary's comprehensive annexation', *Alberta and Northwest Territories Journal of Planning Practice* 8: 39–78.

Brown, J.H., R.S. Phillips, and N. Roberts. 1981. 'Land markets at the urban fringe: New insights for policy makers', *Journal of the American Planning Association* 47: 131–44.

Brown, L.A., and E.G. Moore. 1970. 'The intra-urban migration process: A perspective', *Geografiska Annaler* 28: 1–13.

Brown, S. 1992. *Retail Location: A Micro-Scale Perspective.* Aldershot: Ashgate.

Brownstone, M., and T.J. Plunkett. 1983. *Metropolitan Winnipeg: Politics and Reform of Local Government.* Berkeley: University of California Press.

Bruce, D., A. Taillon, and J. Orser. 1999. *Population Change in Atlantic Canada.* Sackville, NB: Rural and Small Town Research and Studies Programme, Department of Geography, Mount Allison University.

Brunet, Y. 1980. 'L'exode urbain, essai de classification de la population exurbaine des cantons de l'est', *Canadian Geographer* 24: 386–405.

Bryant, C.R. 1984. 'The recent evolution of farming landscapes in urban-centred regions', *Landscape Planning* 11: 307–26.

———. 1986. 'L'évolution de la ville régionale en Amérique du nord: le cas de Toronto', *Annales de Géographie* 527: 69–85.

———. 1995. 'The role of local actors in transforming the urban fringe', *Journal of Rural Studies* 11: 255–67.

———. 1999. 'Community change in context', in J. Pierce and A. Dale, eds, *Communities, Development, and Sustainability Across Canada.* Vancouver: University of British Columbia Press.

———, P.M. Coppack, and C.J.A. Mitchell. 2000. 'The city's countryside', in Bunting and Filion (2000).

———, S. Desroches, and P. Juneau. 1996. 'Community mobilisation and power structures: Potentially contradictory forces for sustainable rural development', in I.R. Bowler, C.R. Bryant, and P.P.P. Huigen, eds, *Dimensions of Sustainable Rural Systems.* Utrecht/Groningen: Netherlands Geographical Studies (No. 244).

——— and D. Granjon. 2005. 'Agricultural land protection in Quebec: From provincial framework to local initiatives', in W. Caldwell, S. Hilts, and B. Wilton, eds, *Farmland Preservation: Challenges and Opportunities.* Guelph, Ont.: Farmland Preservation Trust.

——— and T.R. Johnston. 1992. *Agriculture in the City's Countryside.* London: Pinter.

———, L.H. Russwurm, and A.G. McLellan. 1982. *The City's Countryside: Land and its Management in the Rural-Urban Fringe.* London: Longman.

Buchanan, C. 1963. *Traffic in Towns: A Study of the Long Term Problems of Traffic in Urban Areas.* London: Her Majesty's Stationery Office.

Buck-Morss, S. 1991. *The Dialectics of Seeing: Walter Benjamin and the Arcades Project.* Cambridge, Mass.: MIT Press.

Bunting, T. 1987. 'Invisible upgrading in inner cities: Homeowners' reinvestment behaviour in central Kitchener', *Canadian Geographer* 31: 209–22.

———— and P. Filion, eds. 1988. *The Changing Canadian Inner City*. Waterloo, Ont.: University of Waterloo, Department of Geography (Publication Series No. 31).

———— and ————, eds. 1991. *Canadian Cities in Transition*. Toronto: Oxford University Press.

———— and ————. 1999. 'Dispersed city form in Canada: A Kitchener CMA case study', *Canadian Geographer* 43: 268–84.

———— and ————, eds. 2000. *Canadian Cities in Transition: The Twenty-First Century*. Toronto: Oxford University Press.

———— and ————. 2001. 'Uneven cities: Addressing rising inequality in the twenty-first century', *Canadian Geographer* 45: 126–31.

————, ————, S. Frenette, D. Curry, and R. Mattice. 2000. 'Housing strategies for downtown revitalization in mid-size cities: A City of Kitchener profile', *Canadian Journal of Urban Studies* 9: 145–76.

————, ————, and H. Priston. 2002. 'Density gradients in Canadian metropolitan regions, 1971–1996: Different patterns of central area and suburban growth and change', *Urban Studies* 39: 2531–52.

———— and H. Millward. 1999. 'A tale of two cities 1: Comparative analysis of retailing in downtown Halifax and Kitchener', *Canadian Journal of Urban Research* 7: 139–66.

————, R.A. Walks, and P. Filion. 2004. 'The uneven geography of housing affordability stress in Canadian metropolitan areas', *Housing Studies* 19: 361–93.

Burchell, R., G. Lowenstein, W. Dolphin, and C. Galley. 2002. *The Costs of Sprawl—2000*. Washington: National Academy Press.

Burgess, E.W. 1925. 'The growth of the city', in R.E. Park, Burgess, and R.D. McKenzie, eds, *The City*. Chicago: University of Chicago Press.

Burrows, R. 1997. 'The social distribution of homelessness experiences', in R. Burrows, N. Pleace, and D. Quilgars, eds, *Homelessness and Social Policy*. London: Routledge.

Buzzelli, M. 2001. 'Firm size structure in North American housebuilding: Persistent deconcentra-tion, 1945–98', *Environment and Planning A* 33: 533–50.

Byers, J. 1998. 'The privatization of downtown public space: The emerging grade-separated city in North America', *Journal of Planning Education and Research* 17: 189–205.

Byun, P., and A.X. Esparza. 2005. 'A revisionist model of suburbanization and sprawl', *Journal of Planning Education and Research* 24: 252–64.

Calgary. 2002. *The 2002 Count of Homeless Persons—2002 May 15*. Calgary: City of Calgary Community Vitality and Protection, Community Strategies, Policy and Planning Division.

————. 2004. *Biennial Count of Homeless Persons in Calgary: Enumerated in Emergency and Transitional Facilities, by Service Agencies, and On the Streets—2004 May 12*. Calgary: City of Calgary, Policy and Planning, Community Strategies.

Calgary Homeless Foundation. 2002. *The 2002 Calgary Homeless Study*. Calgary: Calgary Homeless Foundation. At: <www.calgaryhomeless.com/images/chsreport2002.pdf>. Accessed May 2005.

Calthorpe, P. 1993. *The Next American Metropolis: Ecology, Community, and the American Dream*. New York: Princeton Architectural Press.

———— and W.B. Fulton. 2001. *The Regional City: Planning for the End of Sprawl*. Washington: Island Press.

Camagni, R. 2001. 'The economic role and spatial contradictions of global city regions', in Scott (2001).

Campbell, C. 1995. 'The sociology of consumption', in D. Miller, ed., *Acknowledging Consumption: A Review of New Studies*. London: Routledge.

Campbell, S. 1996. 'Green cities, growing cities, just cities? Urban planning and the contradictions of sustainable development', *Journal of the American Planning Association* 62: 296–312.

Canada, Energy, Mines and Resources, Surveys and Mapping Branch. n.d. *National Atlas of Canada*, 5th edn. Ottawa: Geographical Services Division.

————, Natural Resources Canada. 2002. *Climate Change Plan for Canada*. Ottawa: Natural Resources Canada. At: <www.climatechange.gc.ca>.

————. 2005. *Climate Change Impacts and Adaptation Program*. Ottawa: Natural Resources Canada. At: <www.adaptation.nrcan.gc.ca>.

Canada Mortgage and Housing Corporation (CMHC). Various years. *Canadian Housing Statistics.* Ottawa: CMHC.

———. 1984. *Social Housing Review.* Ottawa: CMHC.

———. 1991. *Core Housing Need in Canada.* Ottawa: CMHC.

———. 1995. *Infrastructure Costs Associated with Conventional and Alternative Development Patterns.* Ottawa: CMHC.

———. 1999. *Understanding Private Rental Housing Investment in Canada.* Ottawa: CMHC, Housing Affordability and Finance Series, Research Report.

———. 2000. *Greenhouse Gas Emissions from Urban Travel:Tool for Evaluating Neighbourhood Sustainability.* Socio-Economic Series, Issue 50, Revision II. Ottawa: CMHC. At: <http://dsp-psd. pwgsc.gc.ca/ Collection/NH18-23-50-2E.pdf>.

———. 2001. *Residualization of Rental Tenure: Attitudes of Private Landlords toward Low-Income Households.* Ottawa: CMHC Research Highlights, Socio-Economic Series issue 93.

———. 2003. *2001 Census Housing Series, Issue 1: Housing Affordability Improves.* Ottawa: CMHC, Socio-Economic Series 03–017.

———. 2004a. *Canadian Housing Observer 2004.* Ottawa.

———. 2004b. *2001 Census Housing Series Issue 6: Aboriginal Households. Research Highlight.* Socio-Economic Series 04–036. Ottawa: CMHC. At: <www.cmhc-schl.gc.ca:50104/b2c/b2c/ init.do?language=en>.

———. 2004c. *2001 Census Housing Series, Issue 5: Growth in Household Incomes and Shelter Costs, 1991–2001.* Ottawa: CMHC, Socio-Economic Series 04–027.

———. 2005. *Brownfield Redevelopment for Housing: Literature Review and Analysis.* Ottawa: CMHC (Research Highlight).

Canadian Council for Refugees. 1998. *Best Settlement Practices.* Montreal: Canadian Council for Refugees.

Canadian Home Builders' Association. 2003. *The Need for Action: Pre-Budget Submission.* Ottawa: CHBA.

———. 2004. *Welcome Home to R2000.* Ottawa: CHBA. At: <http://r2000.chba.ca/What_is_R2000/ brief_history.php>.

Canadian Tax Foundation. 1955. *Taxes and Traffic: A Study of Highway Financing.* Toronto: Canadian Tax Foundation.

Canadian Telework Association. 2004. *Canadian Studies on Telework Etc.* At: <www.ivc.ca/studies/ canadianstudies.htm>. Accessed 18 Nov. 2004.

Canadian Urban Institute (CUI). 2001. *Smart Growth.* Toronto: CUI.

———. 2005. *Business Competitiveness in the Greater Toronto Area: Why Toronto Is Losing Ground?* Toronto: CUI.

Capozza, D., and R. Helsley. 1989. 'The fundamentals of land prices and urban growth', *Journal of Urban Economics* 26: 295–306.

Careless, J.M.S. 1984. *Toronto to 1918: An Illustrated History.* Toronto: James Lorimer.

Carlson, J., J. Keating, C.M. Mbogo, S. Kahindi, and J.C. Beier. 2004. 'Ecological limitations on aquatic mosquito predator colonization in the urban environment', *Journal of Vector Ecology* 29: 331–9.

Carlyle, I.P. 1991. 'Ethnicity and social areas within Winnipeg', in G.M. Robinson, ed., *A Social Geography of Canada.* Toronto: Dundurn Press.

Carroll, B. 1989. 'Neoliberalism and the recomposition of finance capital in Canada', *Capital and Class* 38: 63–92.

Carroll, B.W. 2002. 'Housing policy in the new millennium: The uncompassionate landscape', in Fowler and Siegel (2002).

Carruthers, J.I. 2003. 'Urban sprawl and the cost of public services', *Environment and Planning B: Planning & Design* 30: 503–22.

——— and G. Ulfarsson. 2002. 'Fragmentation and sprawl: Evidence from interregional analysis', *Growth and Change* 33: 312–40.

Carter, T. 1997. 'Current practices for procuring affordable housing: The Canadian context', *Housing Policy Debate* 8: 593–631.

——— and C. Polevychoc. 2004. *Housing Is Good Social Policy.* Ottawa: Canadian Policy Research Networks (CPRN Research Report F/50).

Carvalho, M. 1974. *The Nature of Demand for Exurban Living: The Winnipeg City Region.* Winnipeg: Department of City Planning, University of Manitoba.

Carver, A.D., D.R. Unger, and C.L. Parks. 2004. 'Modeling energy savings from urban shade trees: An assessment of the CITYgreen® energy conservation module', *Environmental Management* 34: 650–5.

Carver, H. 1962. *Cities in the Suburbs*. Toronto: University of Toronto Press.

———. 1975. *Compassionate Landscape*. Toronto: University of Toronto Press.

———. 1978. 'Building the suburbs: A planner's reflections', *City Magazine* 3, 1: 40–5.

———. 1979. 'The private and the social habitat', *Contact: Journal of Urban and Environmental Affairs* 11, 3: 33–42.

Castells, M. 1977. *The Urban Question: A Marxist Approach*. London: Edward Arnold.

———. 1983. *The City and the Grass-roots: A Cross-cultural Theory of Urban Social Movements*. London: Edward Arnold.

———. 1996, 2000. *The Rise of the Network Society*. Oxford: Blackwell.

——— and P. Hall. 1994. *Technopoles of the World*. London: Routledge.

Caulfield, J. 1988. '"Reform" as chaotic concept: The case of Toronto', *Urban History Review* 17: 107–11.

———. 1989. 'Gentrification and desire', *Canadian Review of Sociology and Anthropology* 26: 617–32.

———. 1994. *City Form and Everyday Life: Toronto's Gentrification and Critical Social Practice*. Toronto: University of Toronto Press.

——— and L. Peake, eds. 1996. *City Lives and City Forms: Critical Research and Canadian Urbanism*. Toronto: University of Toronto Press.

CBC Radio. 1963. 'Suburban living: It's perfect', *Citizens' Forum*, 14 Apr., Reporter: Neil Harris, Guest(s): Mrs Boyd, Mrs Lord, Mrs Muddyman. Available at: <http://archives.cbc.ca/400d.asp?id=1-69-1464-9947>; accessed 27 June 2005.

Centre for the Study of Commercial Activity (CSCA). 1998. *Toronto Area: Strip Retail Survey Summary Tables—1997*. Toronto: Ryerson University, CSCA.

———. 2004. National Power Centre Database. Toronto: Ryerson University, CSCA.

Cervero, R. 1986. 'Urban transit in Canada: Integration and innovation at its best', *Transportation Quarterly* 40: 293–316.

———. 1989. *America's Suburban Centers: The Land-Use Transportation Link*. London: Unwin Hyman.

——— and J. Landis. 1997. 'Twenty years of the Bay Area Rapid Transit system: Land use and development impacts', *Transportation Research Part A: Policy and Practice* 31A: 309–33.

Chapin, S.F. 1965. *Urban Land Use Planning*. Urbana: University of Illinois Press.

Charbonneau, F., P. Hamel, and M. Barcelo. 1994. 'Urban sprawl in the Montreal area—policies and trends', in Frisken (1994a).

Charney, I. 2005. 'Two visions of suburbia: Mississauga City Centre and Heartland Business Community', *Canadian Geographer* 49: 214–20.

Charron, M. 2002. 'L'évolution de la ségrégation résidentielle à Montréal de 1951 à 1996' MA thesis, Université du Québec à Montréal. Available at: <www.vrm.ca/documents/mathieuuuucharron.pdf>.

Charvet, J.-P., and C.R. Bryant. 2003. 'La zone péri-urbaine: structure et dynamiques d'une composante stratégique des régions métropolitaines', *Canadian Journal of Regional Science* 26: 241–50.

Chaudhry, M.A. 1996. 'Planning Policies and the Development of Mosques in Toronto', MA thesis, Queen's University.

Cheal, D. 1996. *The New Poverty: Families in Postmodern Society*. London: Greenwood Press.

Chen, Y.W., N. Belzile, and J.M. Gunn. 2001. 'Antagonistic effect of selenium on mercury assimilation by fish populations near Sudbury metal smelters?', *Limnology and Oceanography* 46: 1814–18.

Chicago Continuum of Care (CCC). 2004. *Homeless in Chicago: Numbers and Demographics. Point-In-Time Analysis*. Chicago: CCC. At: <www.chicagocontinuum.org/outreachandengagement/2004_homelesscountrpt.htm>. Accessed May 2005.

Chipman, J.G. 2002. *A Law Unto Itself: How the Ontario Municipal Board Has Developed and Applied Land-Use Planning Policy*. Toronto: University of Toronto Press.

Chodos, R., R. Murphy, and E. Hamovitch. 1993. *Canada and the Global Economy: Alternatives to the Corporate Strategy for Globalization*. Toronto: Lorimer.

Choko, M., and R. Harris. 1990. 'The local culture of property: A comparative history of housing tenure in Montreal and Toronto', *Annals of the Association of American Geographers* 80: 73–95.

Citizenship and Immigration Canada. 2001. *Towards a More Balanced Geographic Distribution of Immigrants*. Ottawa: CIC, Research Unit Special Study

———. 2002. *Facts and Figures*. Ottawa: CIC.

Clapham, D. 2002. 'Housing pathways: A postmodern analytical framework', *Housing, Theory and Society* 19, 1: 57–68.

Clark, C. 1951. 'Urban population densities', *Journal of the Royal Statistical Society*, Series A 114: 490–6.

Clark, D.E., and J. Cosgrove. 1991. 'Amenities versus labour market opportunities: Choosing the optimal distance to move', *Journal of Regional Science* 31: 311–27.

Clark, S.D. 1966. *The Suburban Society*. Toronto: University of Toronto Press.

Clark, W. 2002. 'Time alone', *Canadian Social Trends* 66: 2–6 (Statistics Canada, Cat. no. 11–008).

Clark, W.A.V., and F.M. Dieleman. 1996. *Households and Housing: Choice and Outcomes in the Housing Market*. New Brunswick, NJ: Rutgers University, Center for Urban Policy Research.

Clarkson, S. 1972. *City Lib: Parties and Reform*. Toronto: Hakkert.

———. 2001. 'The multi-level state: Canada in the semi-periphery of both continentalism and globalization', *Review of International Political Economy* 8: 501–27.

Clayton Research Associates. 1988. *The Changing Housing Industry in Canada, 1946–2001*. Ottawa: CMHC.

Clement, W., and L. Vosko. eds. 2003. *Changing Canada: Political Economy as Transformation*. Montreal and Kingston: McGill-Queen's University Press.

Cleveland, G., and M. Krashinsky. 2003. *Fact and Fantasy: Eight Myths about Early Childhood Education and Care*. Toronto: University of Toronto, Centre for Urban and Community Studies, Childcare Resource and Research Unit. Available at: <www.childcarecanada.org/pubs/other/FF/Fact &FantasyBN.pdf>.

Climate Action Network. 2002. *Kyoto and Beyond: The Low Emission Path to Innovation and Efficiency*. Ottawa: Canadian Action Network. At: <www.climateactionnetwork.ca/torriepdf.pdf>.

Clutterbuck, P., and M. Novick. 2003. *Building Inclusive Communities: Cross Canada Perspectives and Strategies*. Toronto: Laidlaw Foundation

Coalition for the Homeless (CFTH). 2003. *A History of Modern Homelessness in New York City*. New York: CFTH. (Data from New York City Human Resources Administration Shelter Census Reports.) At: <www.coalitionforthehomeless.org/downloads/>. Accessed May 2005.

Code, W.R. 1983. 'The strength of the centre: Downtown offices and metropolitan decentralization in Toronto', *Environment and Planning A* 15: 1361–80.

Coffey, W.J. 1994. *The Evolution of Canada's Metropolitan Economies*. Montreal: Institute for Research on Public Policy.

———, with R.G. Shearmur. 1996. *Employment Growth and Change in the Canadian Urban System, 1971–94*. Ottawa: Canadian Policy Research Network.

———, R. Drolet, and M. Polèse. 1996. 'The intrametropolitan location of high order services: Patterns, factors and mobility in Montreal', *Papers in Regional Science* 75: 293–323.

———, C. Manzagol, and R.G. Shearmur. 2000. 'L'évolution spatiale de l'emploi dans la région métropolitaine de Montréal, 1981–1996', *Cahiers de géographie du Québec* 44 (123): 325–39.

———, M. Polèse, and R. Drolet. 1996. 'Examining the thesis of central business district decline: Evidence from the Montreal metropolitan area', *Environment and Planning A* 28: 1795–1814.

——— and R.G. Shearmur. 2001. 'Intrametropolitan employment distribution in Montreal, 1981–1996', *Urban Geography* 22: 106–29.

——— and ———. 2002. 'Agglomeration and dispersion of high-order service employment in the Montreal metropolitan region, 1981–1996', *Urban Studies* 39: 359–78.

——— and D. Trépannier. 2003. 'La répartition spatiale de l'emploi dans la grande région de Montréal, 1996–2001', *Canadian Journal of Regional Science* 26, 2/3: 319–36.

Colby, C. 1933. 'Centripetal and centrifugal forces in urban geography', *Annals, Association of American Geographers* 23: 1–20.

Collacott, M. 2002. *Canada's Immigration Policy: The Need for Major Reform*. Vancouver: Fraser Institute (Occasional Paper).

Collier, R.W. 1974. *Contemporary Cathedrals: Large-Scale Development in Canadian Cities*. Montreal: Harvest House.

Colombo, J.C., M. Cabello, and A.M. Arambarri. 1996. 'Biodegradation of aliphatic and aromatic hydrocarbons by natural soil microflora and pure cultures of imperfect and lignolitic fungi', *Environmental Pollution* 94: 355–62.

Committee on the Status of Endangered Wildlife in Canada (COSEWIC). 2005. *Canadian Species at Risk*. At: <www.cosewic.gc.ca/eng/sct0/rpt/rpt_csar_e.cfm>. Accessed August 2005.

Conference Board of Canada. 2005. *The Premier's Leaders Forum on Strategic Growth*. Ottawa: Conference Board of Canada.

Conrad, S. 1996. 'Recycled suburbs: The case of Kitchener in new suburban area', in Filion, Bunting, and Curtis (1996).

Conway, J. 2004. *Identity, Place, Knowledge: Social Movements Contesting Globalization*. Toronto: Fernwood.

Cooke-Reynolds, M., and N. Zukewich. 2004. 'The feminization of work', *Canadian Social Trends* 72: 24–9 (Statistics Canada, Cat. no. 11–008).

Cooper, R.G. 1975. 'Mount Pearl New Town', *Living Places* 11, 4: 2–9.

Copp, J.T. 1974. 'The condition of the working class in Montreal, 1897–1920', in M. Horn and R. Sabourin, eds, *Studies in Canadian Social History*. Toronto: McClelland & Stewart.

Coppack, P. 1988. 'The role of amenity in the evolution of the urban field', *Geografisher Annaler* 70B: 353–61.

———, L.H. Russwurm, and C.R. Bryant, eds. 1988. *Essays on Canadian Urban Process and Form III: The Urban Field*. Waterloo, Ont.: University of Waterloo, Department of Geography Publication Series No. 30.

Cormick, G., N. Dale, D. Edmond, S.G. Sigurdson, and B.D. Stuart. 1996. *Building Consensus for a Sustainable Future: Putting Principles into Practice*. Ottawa: National Round Table on the Environment and the Economy.

Côté, R. 2000. 'It's not waste until it's wasted', *Alternatives Journal* 26, 1: 32–7.

Courchene, T.J. 2001. 'Ontario as a North American region-state, Toronto as global city-region: Responding to the NAFTA challenge', in Scott (2001).

———. 2005. 'Citistates and the state of cities: Political-economy and fiscal-federalism dimensions', Montreal: Institute for Research on Public Policy (IRPP Working Paper Series no. 2005–03).

———, with C. Telmer. 1998. *From Heartland to North American Region State: The Social, Fiscal and Federal Evolution of Ontario*. Toronto: Centre for Public Management, University of Toronto.

Courcier, S. 2005. 'Vers une définition du projet urbain: la planification du Vieux-Port de Montréal', *Canadian Journal of Urban Research* 14: 57–80.

Cousins, J.R., D. Hope, C. Gries, and J.C. Stutz. 2003. 'Preliminary assessment of arbuscular mycorrhizal fungal diversity and community structure in an urban ecosystem', *Mycorrhiza* 13: 319–26.

Cowan, R. 1983. *More Work for Mother: The Ironies of Household Technology from the Open Hearth to the Microwave*. New York: Basic Books.

Cox, K. 1982. 'Housing tenure and neighborhood activism', *Urban Affairs Quarterly* 18: 107–29.

Crawford, K.G. 1954. *Canadian Municipal Government*. Toronto: University of Toronto Press.

Crawford, P. 1993. 'Preserving rural character in an urban region: Rural planning in the Township of Langley', *Plan Canada* 33, 2: 16–23.

Crompton, S. 2005. 'Always the bridesmaid: People who don't expect to marry', *Canadian Social Trends* 77: 2–8 (Statistics Canada, Cat. no. 11–008).

Cullingworth, J.B. 1987. *Urban and Regional Planning in Canada*. New Brunswick, NJ: Transaction Books.

Curtis, K.R. 1994. 'A Comparative Analysis of CBD Planning in Kitchener and London, Ontario 1961–1991', Ph.D. dissertation, University of Waterloo.

Czerniak, J. 2001. *Case: Downsview Park Toronto*. New York: Prestel Verlag.

Dahms, F.A. 1996. 'The greying of south Georgian Bay', *Canadian Geographer* 40: 148–63.

———— and J. McComb. 1999. 'Counterurbanization, interaction and functional change in a rural amenity are—a Canadian example', *Journal of Rural Studies* 15: 129–46.

Dale, A. 2001. *At the Edge: Sustainable Development in the 21st Century*. Vancouver: University of British Columbia Press.

Daniels, P.N., and J.R. Bryson. 2002. 'Manufacturing services and servicing manufacturing: Knowledge-based cities and changing forms of production', *Urban Studies* 39: 977–91.

Daniels, T. 1999. *When City and Country Collide: Managing Growth in the Metropolitan Fringe*. Washington: Island Press.

————. 2001. 'Smart growth: A new American approach to regional planning', *Planning Practice and Research* 16: 271–9.

———— and K. Daniels. 2003. *Environmental Planning Handbook*. Chicago: APA Planners Press.

Danielsen, K., T. Lang, and W. Fulton. 1999. 'Retracting suburbia: Smart growth and the future of housing', *Housing Policy Debate* 10: 513–40.

Dansereau, F. 1993. 'Neighbourhood differentiation and social change', in Miron (1993a).

Dantas, A. 1988. 'Overspill as an alternative style of gentrification: The case of Riverdale, Toronto', in Bunting and Filion (1988).

Davies, R.L., and D.S. Rogers, eds. 1984. *Store Location and Store Assessment Research*. Chichester: John Wiley & Son.

Davies, W.K.D. 1984. *Factorial Ecology*. Aldershot, UK: Gower.

————. 1997. 'Sustainable development and urban policy: Hijacking the term in Calgary', *GeoJournal* 43: 359–69.

———— and D.P. Donoghue. 1993. 'Economic diversification and group stability in an urban system: Canada, 1951–1986', *Urban Studies* 30: 1165–86.

———— and R.A. Murdie. 1991. 'Changes in the intraurban social dimensionality of Canadian CMAs: 1981–1986', *Canadian Journal of Regional Science* 14: 207–32.

———— and ————. 1993. 'Measuring the social ecology of cities', in Bourne and Ley (1993).

———— and ————. 1994. 'The social complexity of Canadian metropolitan areas in 1986: A multivariate analysis of census data', in Frisken (1994a).

Davis, C., and T. Hutton. 1991. 'Producer service exports from the Vancouver metropolitan region', *Canadian Journal of Regional Science* 14: 371–89.

Davis, J.T. 1996. 'Canada's public space economy', in J. Britton, ed., *Canada and the Global Economy: The Geography of Structural and Technological Change*. Montreal and Kingston: McGill-Queen's University Press.

Davydova, S. 2005. 'Heavy metals as toxicants in big cities', *Microchemical Journal* 79: 133–6.

Dawson, J., and J. Lord. 1985. *Shopping Centre Development: Policies and Prospects*. London: Croom Helm.

Dear, M., ed. 2002. *From Chicago to L.A.: Making Sense of Urban Theory*. Thousand Oaks, Calif.: Sage.

———— and S. Flusty, eds. 1998. *The Spaces of Postmodernity: Readings in Human Geography*. Oxford: Blackwell.

———— and J. Wolch. 1993. 'Homelessness', in Bourne and Ley (1993).

De Chiara, J., ed. 1994. *Time-Saver Standards for Housing and Residential Development*. New York: McGraw-Hill.

Delaney, J. 1991. 'The first garden suburb of Lindenlea, Ottawa: A model project for the first federal housing policy, 1918–24', *Urban History Review* 19: 151–65.

Del Barrio, E.P. 1998. 'Analysis of the green roofs cooling potential in buildings', *Energy and Buildings* 27: 179–93.

Delcan, G., and McCarthy Tétrault. 1996. *Removing the Barriers to the Redevelopment of Contaminated Sites for Housing*. Ottawa: CMHC.

Dennis, M., and S. Fish. 1972. *Programs in Search of a Policy*. Toronto: Hakkert.

Derudder, B., and F. Witlox. 2004. 'Assessing central places in a global age: On the networked localization strategies of advanced producer services', *Journal of Retailing and Consumer Services* 11: 171–80.

Desfor, G., and R. Keil. 1999. 'Contested and polluted terrain', *Local Environment* 4: 333–52.

De Sousa, C. 2000. 'Brownfield redevelopment versus greenfield development: A private sector perspective on the costs and risks associated with brownfield redevelopment in the Greater Toronto Area', *Journal of Environmental Planning and Management* 43: 831–53.

———. 2003. 'Turning brownfields into green space in the City of Toronto', *Landscape and Urban Planning* 62: 181–98.

Després, C., and S. Lord. 2002. 'Vieillir en banlieue', in A. Fortin, C. Després, and G. Vachon, eds, *La banlieue revisitée*. Québec: Éditions Nota bene.

Desroches, S., and C.R. Bryant. 2005. 'Rethinking the construction of the city's countryside from the bottom up', paper presented to the Annual Conference of the Canadian Association of Geographers, London, Ont.

Des Rosiers, F. 1992. 'Urban sprawl and the central city', *Plan Canada* 32, 6: 14–18.

———. 2003. 'Problématique du logement social et abordable et crise de logement au Québec', *Urbanité* 2, 1: 13–16.

Des Rosiers, N. 2002. 'Public space, democracy and the living law', *Plan Canada* 42, 2: 23–4.

Destination Winnipeg. 2003. *Get to Know Me: Destination Winnipeg Three-Year Rolling Business Plan*. Winnipeg: Destination Winnipeg.

DeVerteuil, G. 1993. 'Evolution and Impacts of Public Policy on the Canadian Inner City: Case Study of Southwest Montreal, 1960–1990'. MA thesis, University of British Columbia.

———. 2003. 'Homeless mobility, institutional settings, and the new poverty management', *Environment and Planning A* 35: 361–79.

———. 2004. 'The changing landscapes of Southwest Montreal: A visual account', *Canadian Geographer* 48: 76–82.

Devlin, A.S. 1994. 'Gender-role and housing preferences', *Journal of Environmental Psychology* 14: 225–35.

Diamond, E. 2000. *And I Will Dwell in Their Midst: Orthodox Jews in Suburbia*. Chapel Hill: University of North Carolina Press.

Dicken, P. 2003. *Global Shift: Transforming the World Economy*. London: Guilford.

———. 2004. 'Geographers and "globalization": (Yet) another missed boat?', *Transactions of the Institute of British Geographers* 29: 5–26.

———, J. Peck, and A. Tickell. 1997. 'Unpacking the global', in R. Lee and J. Wills, eds, *Geographies of Economies*. London: Routledge.

Dieleman, F.M. 2001. 'Modelling residential mobility: A review of recent trends in research', *Journal of Housing and the Built Environment* 16: 249–65.

Dobriner, W.M., ed. 1958. *The Suburban Community*. New York: Putnam's.

Dock, F., and C. Swenson, 2003. 'Transit-oriented urban design impacts on suburban land use and transportation planning', *Travel Demand and Land Use*: 184–92.

Donald, B. 2002. 'Spinning Toronto's golden age: The making of a "city that worked"', *Environment and Planning A* 34: 2127–54.

Donaldson, S. 1969. *The Suburban Myth*. New York: Columbia University Press.

Donohue, I., D. Styles, C. Coxon, and K. Irvine. 2005. 'Importance of spatial and temporal patterns for assessment of risk of diffuse nutrient emissions to surface waters', *Journal of Hydrology* 304: 183–92.

Doucet, M.J. 1982. 'Politics, space and trolleys: Mass transit in early twentieth-century Toronto', in G.A. Stelter and A.F.J. Artibise, eds, *Shaping the Urban Landscape: Aspects of the Canadian City-Building Process*. Ottawa: Carleton University Press.

———, A.H. Jacobs, and K.G. Jones. 1988. 'Megachains in the Canadian retail environment', *International Journal of Retailing* 3: 5–23.

——— and K.G. Jones. 1997. *Shopping Centre Dynamics in the Greater Toronto Area*. Toronto: Ryerson University, CSCA (RP1997–4).

——— and J. Weaver, 1991. *Housing the North American City*. Montreal and Kingston: McGill-Queen's University Press.

Dowler, R. 1983. *Housing-Related Tax Expenditures: An Overview and Evaluation*. Toronto: Centre for Urban and Community Studies, University of Toronto, Major Report No. 22.

Dowling, R. 1996. 'Symbolic constructions of place in suburban Surrey, British Columbia', *Canadian Geographer* 40: 75–80.

Downs, A. 1994. *New Visions for Metropolitan America*. Washington: Brookings Institution.

———. 1999. 'Some realities about sprawl and urban decline', *Housing Policy Debate* 10: 955–74.

Doyon, M., and S. Frej. 2003. 'Le récréotourisme et l'environnement naturel dans les aires protégées périurbaines: la région métropolitaine de Montréal', *Canadian Journal of Regional Science* 26: 419–30.

Drache, D., and M. Gertler, eds. 1991. *The New Era of Global Competition*. Montreal and Kingston: McGill-Queen's University Press.

Dreier, P., and D. Hulchanski. 1993. 'The role of non-profit housing in Canada and the United States', *Housing Policy Debate* 4: 43–81.

Duany, A., and E. Plater-Zyberk. 1992. 'The second coming of the American small town', *Plan Canada* 32, 3: 6–13.

———, ———, and J. Speck. 2000. *Suburban Nation: The Rise of Sprawl and the Decline of the American Dream*. New York: North Point Press.

Dumont, M., M. Jean, M. Lavigne, and J. Stoddart (The Clio Collective). 1987. *Quebec Women: A History*, trans. R. Gannon and R. Gill. Toronto: Women's Press.

Dumoulin, O., and C. Marois. 2003. 'L'émergence des stratégies de développement des espaces agricoles périurbains: le cas des municipalités de banlieue de la région métropolitaine de Montréal', *Canadian Journal of Regional Science* 26: 337–72.

Duncan, J. 1994. 'Shaughnessy Heights: The protection of privilege', in S. Hasson and D. Ley, eds, *Neighbourhood Organizations and the Welfare State*. Toronto: University of Toronto Press.

Dunning, J. 1993. *Multinational Enterprises and the Global Economy*. Boston: Addison-Wesley.

E&B Data. 2004. *Greater Toronto Information and Communications Technologies Industry Profile*. Outremont, Que.: E&B Data.

Early, D.W. 1999. 'A microeconomic analysis of homelessness: An empirical investigation using microdata', *Journal of Housing Economics* 8: 312–27.

——— and E.O. Olsen. 1998. 'Rent control and homelessness', *Regional Science and Urban Economics* 28: 797–816.

Ebaugh, H.R., J. O'Brien, and J.S. Chafetz. 2000. 'The social ecology of residential patterns and membership in immigrant churches', *Journal for the Scientific Study of Religion* 39: 107–16.

Economic Council of Canada. 1990. *Good Jobs, Bad Jobs: Employment in the Service Economy*. Ottawa: Minister of Supply and Services.

Edgington, D., and T. Hutton. 2002. *Multiculturalism and Local Government in Greater Vancouver*. Vancouver: Vancouver Centre of Excellence, Research on Immigration and Integration in the Metropolis.

Edmonton, Joint Planning Committee on Housing. 2002. *A Count of Homeless Persons in Edmonton*. Edmonton.

Edmonton Task Force on Homelessness (ETFH). 1999. *Homelessness in Edmonton: A Call to Action*. Edmonton: City of Edmonton.

EKOS Research Associates. 2001. *Canadians and Working from Home: Rethinking the Information Highway*. Ottawa: EKOS. At: <www.ekos.ca/ admin/press_releases/telework4.pdf>.

Ellin, N. 1997. *Architecture of Fear*. New York: Princeton Architectural Press.

Elliott, B.S. 1991. *The City Beyond: A History of Nepean, Birthplace of Canada's Capital 1792–1900*. Nepean, Ont.: City of Nepean.

Emeneau, J., ed. 1996. *A Practitioner's Guide to Urban Intensification*. Toronto: Canadian Urban Institute.

England, J., R. Lewis, and S. Ehrlich. 2005. *Evolving Housing Conditions in Canada's Census Metropolitan Areas, 1991–2001*. Ottawa: Statistics Canada, Cat. no. 89–613–MWE2004005.

Environment Canada. 2001. *Canada's National Smog (Ground-Level Ozone) Management Program: Regional Smog Episodes*. Ottawa: Environment Canada. At: <www.etcentre.org/NAPS/naps_smog_e.html#smog88>. Accessed May 2005.

———. 2003. *Canada's National Environmental Indicator Series*. Ottawa: Environment Canada. At: <www.ec.gc.ca/soer_ree/English/Indicator_series/default.cfm>. Accessed May 2005.

Erickson, R.A. 1986. 'Multinucleation in metropolitan economies', *Annals of the Association of American Geographers* 76: 331–46.

Essiambre-Phillips-Desjardins Associates Ltd, J.L. Richards and Associates Ltd, C.N. Watson Associates Ltd, and A. Nelessen Associates Inc. 1995. *Infrastructure Costs Associated with Conventional* and *Alternative Development Patterns: Final Report*, vol. 1. Ottawa: CMHC, Aug.

Evan, R.D., and C.J. Forsyth. 2004. 'Risk factors, endurance of victimization, and survival strategies: The impact of the structural location of men and women on their experiences within homeless milieus', *Sociological Spectrum* 24: 479–505.

Evans, A. 1991. 'Rabbit hutches on postage stamps: Planning, development and political economy', *Urban Studies* 28: 853–70.

Evans, W.W. 2004. *Economics, Real Estate and the Supply of Land*. Oxford: Blackwell.

Evenden, L.J. 1978. 'Shaping the Vancouver suburbs', in Evenden, ed., *Vancouver: Western Metropolis*. Victoria: University of Victoria, Western Geographical Series vol. 16.

———. 1991a. 'Fleetwood in Surrey: The making of a place', in P.M. Koroscil, ed., *British Columbia: Geographical Essays in Honour of A. MacPherson*. Burnaby, BC: Department of Geography, Simon Fraser University.

———. 1991b. 'The expansion of domestic space on Vancouver's north shore', in G.M. Robinson, ed., *A Social Geography of Canada*. Toronto: Dundurn Press.

———, ed. 1995. *The Suburb of Happy Homes: Burnaby, Centennial Themes*. Burnaby, BC: Simon Fraser University.

———. 1997. 'Wartime housing as cultural landscape: National creation and personal creativity', *Urban History Review* 25, 2: 41–52.

——— and G.E. Walker. 1993. 'From periphery to centre: The changing geography of the suburbs', in L.S. Bourne and D. Ley, eds, *The Changing Social Geography of Canadian Cities*. Montreal and Kingston: McGill-Queen's University Press.

Everett-Green, R. 1996. 'Winnipeg arts scene gets standing ovation', *Globe and Mail,* 27 Jan., C3.

Ewing, R. 1996. *Best Development Practices*. Chicago: APA Planners Press.

———. 1997. 'Is Los Angeles-style sprawl desirable?', *Journal of the American Planning Association* 63: 107–26.

Fainstein, S. 1997. 'The egalitarian city: The restructuring of Amsterdam', *International Planning Studies* 2: 295–314.

Fairbairn, K.J., and H. Khatun. 1989. 'Residential segregation and the intra-urban migration of South Asians in Edmonton', *Canadian Ethnic Studies* 21: 45–64.

Fallis, G. 1985. *Housing Economics*. Toronto: Butterworths.

———. 1993. 'Postwar changes in the supply-side of housing', in Miron (1993a).

Federation of Canadian Municipalities (FCM). 2000. *A National Affordable Housing Strategy*. Ottawa: FCM.

———. 2004. *Quality of Life in Canadian Communities: Incomes, Shelter and Necessities*. Theme Report No. 1. Ottawa. At: <www.fcm.ca/english/communications/nov172004.pdf>.

———. 2005. *Incomes, Shelter, and Necessities: Quality of Life in Canadian Communities, Theme Report #1*. Ottawa: FCM.

Felbinger, C. 1995. 'Conditions of confusion and conflict: Rethinking the infrastructure-economic development linkage', in D. Perry, ed., *Building the Public City: The Politics, Governance, Finance of Public Infrastructure*. London: Sage.

Ferrante, A., and G. Mihalakakou. 2001. 'The influence of water, green and selected passive techniques on the rehabilitation of historical industrial buildings in urban areas', *Solar Energy* 70: 245–53.

Ferrigan, J., and J. Ghent. 2005. 'Why the PPS is a big deal', *Ontario Planning* 20, 3: 30–4.

Filey, M. 1996. *Remember Sunnyside: The Rise and Fall of a Magical Era*. Toronto: Dundurn Press.

Filion, P. 1987. 'Concepts of the inner city and recent trends in Canada', *Canadian Geographer* 31: 223–32.

———. 1991. 'The gentrification-social structure dialectic: A Toronto case study', *International Journal of Urban and Regional Research* 15: 553–73.

———. 1998. 'Potential and limitations of community economic development: Individual initiative and collective action in a post-Fordist context', *Environment and Planning A* 30: 1101–23.

———. 2001. 'Suburban mixed-use centres and urban dispersion: What difference do they make?', *Environment and Planning A* 33: 141–60.

———. 2003. 'Towards smart growth? The difficult implementation of alternatives to urban dispersion', *Canadian Journal of Urban Research* 12: 48–70.

———— and M. Alexander. 1994. 'Restrictive covenants: Hidden obstacles', *Plan Canada* 35, 1: 33–7.

———— and T. Bunting. 1990. *Affordability of Housing.* Ottawa: Minister of Supply and Services, Statistics Canada Catalogue no. 93–130.

———— and ————. 1993. 'Local power and its limits: Three decades of attempts to revitalize Kitchener's CBD', *Urban History Review* 22: 4–16.

———— and ————. 1996. 'Space and place: The social geography of the dispersed city', in Filion, Bunting, and Curtis (1996).

————, ————, and K. Curtis. 1996. *The Dynamics of the Dispersed City: Geographic and Planning Perspectives on Waterloo Region.* Waterloo, Ont.: University of Waterloo, Department of Geography Publication Series No. 47.

————, ————, and K. Warriner. 1999. 'The entrenchment of urban dispersion: Residential preferences and location patterns in the dispersed city', *Urban Studies* 36: 1317–47.

————, H. Hoernig, T. Bunting, and G. Sands. 2004. 'The successful few: Healthy downtowns of small metropolitan regions', *Journal of the American Planning Association* 70: 328–43.

———— and T. Rutherford. 2000. 'Employment transitions in the city', in Bunting and Filion (2000).

Fincher, R. 1998. 'In the right place at the right time? Life stages and urban spaces', in Fincher and Jacobs (1998).

———— and L. Costello. 2005. 'Narratives of high-rise housing: Placing the ethnicized newcomer in inner Melbourne', *Social and Cultural Geography* 6: 201–18.

———— and J. M. Jacobs, eds. 1998. *Cities of Difference.* New York: Guilford.

Fischler, R., J. Meligrana, and J.M. Wolfe. 2004. 'Canadian experiences of local government boundary reform: A comparison of Quebec and Ontario', in Meligrana, ed., *Redrawing Local Government Boundaries.* Vancouver: University of British Columbia Press.

———— and J. Wolfe. 2000. 'Regional restructuring in Montreal', *Canadian Journal of Regional Science* 23: 89–114.

Fisher, I.D. 1986. *Frederick Law Olmsted and the City Planning Movement in the United States.* Ann Arbor, Mich.: UMI Research Press.

Fishman, R. 1987. *Bourgeois Utopias: The Rise and Fall of Suburbia.* New York: Basic Books.

Florida Department of Children and Families (FDCF). 2003. *Council on Homelessness: 2003 Report.* Tallahassee: FDCF.

Florida, R.L. 2002. *The Rise of the Creative Class: And How It's Transforming Work, Leisure, Community and Everyday Life.* New York: Basic Books.

————. 2005. *Cities and the Creative Class.* New York: Routledge.

———— and M.M. Feldman. 1988. 'Housing in US Fordism', *International Journal of Urban and Regional Research* 12: 187–210.

Fogelson, R.M. 2001. *Downtown: Its Rise and Fall, 1880–1950.* New Haven: Yale University Press.

Foggin, P., and M. Polèse. 1977. *The Social Geography of Montreal in 1971.* Toronto: University of Toronto, Centre for Urban and Community Studies (Research Paper 88).

Foot, D.K., and D. Stoffman. 1996. *Boom, Bust, and Echo: How to Profit from the Coming Demographic Shift.* Toronto: McFarlane Walter and Ross.

Fortin, A., C. Després, and G. Vachon. 2002. *La banlieue revisitée.* Québec: Editions Nota Bene.

Fortin, N.M., and M. Huberman. 2002. 'Occupational gender segregation and women's wages in Canada: An historical perspective', *Canadian Public Policy* 28: 11–39.

Forward, C.N., ed. 1973a. *Residential and Neighbourhood Studies in Victoria.* Victoria: University of Victoria (Western Geographical Series No. 5).

————. 1973b. 'The immortality of a fashionable residential district: The Uplands', in Forward (1973a).

Fournier, L. 1991. *Itinérance et santé mentale à Montréal, étude descriptive de la clientèle des missions et refuges.* Montréal: Unité de Recherché Psychosociale, Centre de Recherche de l'Hôpital Douglas, Verdun.

————, S. Chevalier, M. Ostoj, M. Caulet, R. Courtemanche, and N. Plante. 1998. *Dénombrement de la clientèle itinérante dans les centres d'hébergement, les soupes populaires et les centres de Jour des villes de Montréal et de Québec, 1996–97.* Québec: Santé Québec.

Fowler. E.P. 1992. *Building Cities That Work*. Montreal and Kingston: McGill-Queen's University Press.

——— and J. Layton. 2002. 'Transportation policy in Canadian cities', in Fowler and Siegel (2002).

——— and D. Siegel, eds. 2002. *Urban Policy Issues: Canadian Perspectives*. Toronto: Oxford University Press.

Francis, M. 1984. 'Mapping downtown activity', *Journal of Architectural and Planning Research* 1: 21–35.

Frederick, J.A., and J.E. Fast. 1999. 'Eldercare in Canada: Who does how much?', *Canadian Social Trends* 54: 26–30 (Statistics Canada, Cat. no. 11–008).

Freeman, R. 2004. 'The great doubling: globalization and labor markets', presentation given to the Department of Economics, Syracuse University, 17 Nov. 2004.

Freire, M., and R. Stren, eds. 2001. *The Challenge of Urban Government*. Washington: World Bank Institute.

Frej, S., D. Granjon, M. Doyon, and C.R. Bryant. 2001. 'The social construction of sustainable rural communities: Tourism development in the rural urban fringe', in K. Kim, I. Bowler, and C.R. Bryant, eds, *Developing Sustainable Rural Systems*, Proceedings of the IGU Commission on Sustainable Development and Rural Systems. Pusan, Korea: Pusan National University Press.

Frieden, B.J., and L. Sagalyn. 1989. *Downtown, Inc.: How America Rebuilds Cities*. Cambridge, Mass.: MIT Press.

Friedman, A. 2002. *Planning the New Suburbia: Flexibility by Design*. Vancouver: University of British Columbia Press.

Friedman, T.L. 2005. *The World Is Flat: A Brief History of the Twenty-first Century*. New York: Farrar, Straus and Giroux.

Friedmann, J. 1986. 'The world city hypothesis', *Development and Change* 17: 69–83.

———. 1995. 'Where we stand: A decade of world city research', in P.L. Knox and P.J. Taylor, eds, *World Cities in a World System*. Cambridge: Cambridge University Press.

——— and G. Wolff. 1982. 'World city formation: An agenda for research and action', *International Journal of Regional and Urban Research* 3: 309–44.

Frisken, F. 1982. 'Old problems, new priorities: Changing perspectives on governmental needs in an expanding region', in Frisken, ed., *Conflict or Cooperation? The Toronto-Centred Region in the 1980s*. Downsview, Ont.: Urban Studies Program, York University.

———. 1990. *Planning and Servicing the Greater Toronto Area: The Interplay of Provincial and Municipal Interests*. North York, Ont.: York University, Urban Studies Working Paper No.12.

———, ed. 1994a. *The Changing Canadian Metropolis: A Public Policy Perspective*. Toronto and Berkeley: Canadian Urban Institute and Institute of Governmental Studies Press.

———. 1994b. 'Provincial transit policymaking for the Toronto, Montreal and Vancouver regions', in Frisken (1994a).

———, L.S. Bourne, G. Gad, and R.A. Murdie. 2000. 'Governance and social sustainability: The Toronto Experience', in M. Polèse and R. Stren, eds, *The Social Sustainability of Cities: Diversity and the Management of Change*. Toronto: University of Toronto Press.

——— and M. Wallace. 2003. 'Governing the multicultural city-region', *Canadian Public Administration* 46: 153–77.

Frumkin, H., L. Frank, and R. Jackson. 2004. *Urban Sprawl and Public Health: Designing, Planning and Building for Healthy Communities*. Washington: Island Press.

Fry, E. 1995. 'North American municipalities and their involvement in the global economy', in Kresl and Gappert (1995).

Fujii, T., and T.A. Hartshorn. 1995. 'The changing metropolitan structure of Atlanta, Georgia: Location of functions and regional structure in a multinucleated urban area', *Urban Geography* 16: 680–707.

Gad, G. 1979. 'Face-to-face linkages and office decentralization potentials: A study of Toronto', in P.W. Daniels, ed., *Spatial Patterns of Office Growth and Location*. New York: John Wiley and Sons.

———. 1985. 'Office location dynamics in Toronto: Suburbanization and central district specialization', *Urban Geography* 6: 331–51.

———. 1991a. 'Office location', in Bunting and Filion (1991).

———. 1991b. 'Toronto's financial district', *Canadian Geographer* 35: 203–7.

————. 1999. 'Downtown Montreal and Toronto: Distinct places with much in common', *Canadian Journal of Regional Science* 22: 143–70.

———— and D. Holdsworth. 1984. 'Building for city, region and nation: Office development in Toronto, 1834–1984', in V.L. Russell, ed., *Forging a Consensus: Historical Essays on Toronto*. Toronto: University of Toronto Press.

———— and ————. 1987. 'Corporate capitalism and the emergence of the high-rise office building', *Urban Geography* 8: 212–31.

Gale, D. 1980. 'Neighborhood resettlement: Washington D.C.', in S. Laska and D. Spain, eds, *Back to the City*. New York: Pergamon.

Gans, H. 1962a. 'Urbanism and suburbanism as ways of life: A re-evaluation of definitions', in A. Rose, ed., *Human Behavior and Social Processes*. Boston: Houghton-Mifflin.

————. 1962b. *The Urban Villagers*. New York: Free Press.

Garber, J. 2000. '"Not named or identified": Politics and the search for anonymity in the city', in K.B. Miranne and A.H. Young, eds, *Gendering the City: Women, Boundaries and Visions of Urban Life*. Lanham, Md.: Rowman & Littlefield.

Garreau, J. 1991. *Edge City: Life on the New Frontier*. New York: Doubleday.

Garrett-Petts, W.F. 2005. *The Small Cities Book: On the Cultural Future of Small Cities*. Vancouver: New Star Books.

Garrish, C. 2002–3. 'Unscrambling the omelette: Understanding British Columbia's Agricultural Land Reserve', *BC Studies* 136 (Winter): 25–55.

Gerber, R.E., and K. Howard. 2002. 'Hydrogeology of the Oak Ridges Moraine aquifer system: Implications for protection and management from the Duffins Creek watershed', *Canadian Journal of Earth Sciences* 39: 1333–48.

Germain, A., F. Dansereau, C. Poirier, M. Alain, and J.E. Gagnon. 2003. *Les pratiques municipales de gestion de la diversité à Montréal*. Montréal: Institut National de la Recherche Scientifique Urbanisation, Culture et Société.

———— and J.E. Gagnon. 2003. 'Minority places of worship and zoning dilemmas in Montreal', *Planning Theory and Practice* 4: 295–318.

————, G. Moreau, M.-C. Dumas, R. Arteau, M. Pontbriand, and A. Benbouzid. 2000. *Urban Diversity: Managing Multicultural Cities*. Montreal: Metropolis.

———— and D. Rose. 2000. *Montreal: The Quest for a Metropolis*. Chichester, UK: Wiley.

Gershuny, J.I., and I. D. Miles. 1983. *The New Service Economy*. London: Frances Pinter.

Gertler, L., and R. Crowley. 1977. *Changing Canadian Cities: The Next 25 Years*. Toronto: McClelland & Stewart.

Gertler, M. 1999. 'Negotiated path or "business as usual"? Ontario's transition to a continental production regime', *Space and Polity* 3: 171–97.

————, R. Florida, G. Gates, and T. Vinodrai. 2002. *Competing on Creativity: Placing Ontario's Cities in North American Context,* Report prepared for the Ontario Ministry of Enterprise, Opportunity and Innovation and the Institute for Competitiveness and Prosperity.

Ghosh, R. 2004. 'Public education and multicultural policy in Canada', *International Review of Education* 50: 543–66.

Gillespie, A., and R. Richardson. 2000. 'Teleworking and the city: Myths of workplace transcendence and travel reduction', in J.O. Wheeler, Y. Aoyama, and B. Wharf, eds, *Cities in the Telecommunications Age*. New York: Routledge.

Gillette, H. 1985. 'The evolution of the planned shopping center in suburb and city', *Journal of the American Planning Association* 51: 449–60.

Ginsler and Associates. 2001. *Community Plan on Homelessness in London*. London, Ont.: City of London.

Glassman, J. 1999. 'State power beyond the "territorial trap": The internationalization of the national state', *Political Geography* 18: 669–96.

Glazebrook, G.P. de T. 1964. *A History of Transportation in Canada*. Toronto: University of Toronto Press.

Gober, P. 1990. 'The urban demographic landscape: A geographic perspective', in D. Myers, ed., *Housing Demography: Linking Demographic Structure and Housing Markets*. Madison: University of Wisconsin Press.

Goddard, J.B. 1973. *Office Linkages and Location: A Study of Communication and Spatial Patterns in Central London*. Oxford: Pergamon.

Go for Green. 2005. *The Economic Benefits of Trails.* Ottawa: Go for Green. At: <www.goforgreen.ca>.

Goheen, P. 1970. *Victorian Toronto, 1850 to 1900.* Chicago: University of Chicago, Department of Geography Research Paper No. 127.

Goldberg, M., and J. Mercer. 1986. *The Myth of the North American City.* Vancouver: University of British Columbia Press.

Goldrick, M. 1982. 'The anatomy of urban reform in Toronto', in D.I. Roussopoulos, ed., *The City and Radical Social Change.* Montreal: Black Rose Books.

Golledge, R.G. 1997. 'Dynamics and ITS: Behavioral responses to information available from ATIS', conference resource paper, Eighth Meeting of the International Association for Travel Behaviour Research, Austin, Texas, 21–5 Sept.

Goonewardena, K. 2005. 'The urban sensorium: Space, ideology and the aestheticization of politics', *Antipode* 37: 46–70.

Gordon, D., and K. Tamminga. 2002. 'Large-scale traditional neighborhood development and pre-emptive ecosystem planning: The Markham experience, 1989–2001', *Journal of Urban Design* 7: 321–40.

——— and S. Vipond. 2005. 'Gross density and New Urbanism: Comparing conventional and New Urbanist suburbs in Markham, Ontario', *Journal of the American Planning Association* 71: 41–54.

Gordon, P., and H. Richardson. 1996. 'Beyond polycentricity: The dispersed metropolis, Los Angeles, 1970–1990', *Journal of the American Planning Association* 62: 289–95.

——— and ———. 1997. 'Are compact cities a desirable planning goal?', *Journal of the American Planning Association* 63: 95–106.

Gottdeiner, M. 2002. 'Urban analysis as merchandising: The "LA School" and the understanding of metropolitan development', in J. Eade and C. Mele, eds, *Understanding the City: Contemporary and Future Perspectives.* Oxford: Blackwell.

Gottschalk, P., and T. Smeeding. 1997. 'Cross-national comparisons of earnings and income inequality', *Journal of Economic Literature* 35: 633–87.

Gouldner, A.W. 1979. *The Future of Intellectuals and the Rise of the New Class.* New York: Seabury Press.

Gournay, I. 1998. 'Gigantism in downtown Montreal', in Gournay and F. Vanlaethem, eds, *Montreal*

Metropolis, 1880–1930. Montreal: Canadian Centre for Architecture.

Grabb, E.G. 1996. *Theories of Social Inequality: Classical and Contemporary Perspectives.* Toronto: Harcourt Brace.

Graham, P., L. Maclean, D. Medina, A. Patwardhan, and G. Vasarhelyi. 2004. 'The role of water balance modelling in the transition to low impact development', *Water Quality Research Journal of Canada* 39: 331–42.

Graham, S., and S. Marvin. 1996. *Telecommunications and the City.* London: Routledge.

Granjon, D. 2004. 'La multifonctionnalité de l'espace métropolitain et le développement des activités agrotouristiques en zone périurbaine de Montréal', Ph.D. thesis, Université de Montréal.

Grant, J. 1988. 'They say "you can't legislate public participation": The Nova Scotia experience', *Plan Canada* 27, 10: 260–7.

———. 1994a. 'Rhetoric and response: Sustainable development in residential environments', *Environments: A Journal of Interdisciplinary Studies* 22, 3: 3–12.

———. 1994b. *The Drama of Democracy: Contention and Dispute in Community Planning.* Toronto: University of Toronto Press.

———. 1999. 'Can planning save the suburbs?', *Plan Canada* 39, 4: 16–18.

———. 2002. 'From "sugar cookies" to "gingerbread men": Conformity in suburban design', *Planners' Network Magazine* (Spring) (Special Issue on New Urbanism), available at: <www.plannersnetwork. org/htm/pub/archives/152/grant.htm>; accessed 27 June 2005.

———. 2003. 'Exploring the influence of New Urbanism in community planning practice', *Journal of Architectural and Planning Research* 20: 234–53.

———. 2004. 'Open society or gated enclaves? Urban form in the information age', *Plan Canada* 44, 2: 42–4.

———. 2005. 'Planning responses to gated communities in Canada', *Housing Studies* 20, 2: 273–85.

———, K. Greene, and D.K. Maxwell. 2004. 'The planning and policy implications of gated communities', *Canadian Journal of Urban Research* 13 (Supplement): 70–88.

Grayson, L. 1990. *Green Belts, Greenfields and the Urban Fringe: The Pressure on Land in the 1980s, a Guide to*

Sources. London: London Research Centre and British Library.

Greater Toronto Area Task Force. 1996. *Report*. Toronto: Queen's Printer.

Greater Vancouver Regional District (GVRD). 1975. *The Livable Region 1976/1986: Proposals to Manage the Growth of Greater Vancouver*. Vancouver: Greater Vancouver Regional District.

———. 1994. *Livable Region Strategic Plan*. Vancouver: GVRD.

———. 1998. *Money, Money, Money: Analyzing the Region's Family Income, Composition of Income and Incidence of Low Income*. Burnaby, BC: GVRD Strategic Planning Department (Item 5.1).

———. 1999. *Liveable Region Strategic Plan*. Burnaby, BC: GVRD.

———. 2002. *Homelessness in Greater Vancouver*. Vancouver: GVRD.

———. 2005. *Homeless Count 2005: Preliminary Results*. Vancouver. At: <www.gvrd.bc.ca/home-lessness/pdfs/HomelessnessCount2005.pdf>. Accessed 16 June 2005.

Gregory, P. 1995. 'A select bibliography on cities and globalization', in Kresl and Gappert (1995).

Grimm, N.B., J.M. Grove, S.T.A. Pickett, and C.L. Redman. 2000. 'Integrated approaches to long-term studies of urban ecological systems', *BioScience* 50: 571–84.

Guillet, E.G. 1966. *The Story of Canadian Roads*. Toronto: University of Toronto Press.

Gunn, J., W. Keller, J. Negusanti, R. Potvin, P. Beckett, and K. Winterhalder. 1995. 'Ecosystem recovery after emission reductions: Sudbury, Canada', *Water, Air and Soil Pollution* 85: 1783–8.

Gunton, T. 1981. 'The Evolution and Practice of Urban and Regional Planning in Canada', Ph.D. dissertation, University of British Columbia.

———. 1991. 'Origins of Canadian urban planning', in K. Gerecke, ed., *The Canadian City*. Montreal: Black Rose Books.

Gurin, D. 2003. *Understanding Sprawl: A Citizen's Guide*. Vancouver: David Suzuki Foundation. At: <www.davidsuzuki.org/files/Climate/Ontario/Understanding_Sprawl.pdf>.

Gurstein, P. 1995. *Planning for Telework and Home-based Employment: A Canadian Survey on Integrating Work into Residential Environments*. Ottawa and Vancouver: CMHC and Centre for Human Settlements, University of British Columbia.

———. 1996. 'Telework and its impact on urban form', in Emeneau (1996).

Gutowski, M., and T. Field. 1979. *The Graying of Suburbia*. Washington: Urban Institute.

Gutstein, D. 1975. *Vancouver Ltd*. Toronto: James Lorimer.

Guy, C. 1994. *The Retail Development Process: Location, Property and Planning*. London: Routledge.

Gyton, G. 1999. *A Place for Canadians: The Story of the National Capital Commission*. Ottawa: National Capital Commission.

Haig, R.M. 1926. 'Toward an understanding of the metropolis', *Quarterly Journal of Economics* 40: 179–208, 402–34.

Halifax Regional Municipality (HRM). 2004a. *Guidebook to HRM's Alternatives to Growth*. Halifax: HRM. At: <www.halifax.ca/regionalplanning/Publications/guidebook.pdf>. Accessed 22 July 2004.

———. 2004b. *Homelessness in HRM: A Portrait of Streets and Shelters*. Halifax: Planning and Development Services, HRM.

———. 2005. *Draft Regional Plan*. At: <www.halifax.ca/regionalplanning/index.html>. Accessed 26 Apr. 2005.

Hall, P. 1988. *Cities of Tomorrow*. Oxford: Blackwell.

———. 1999. *Cities in Civilization: Culture, Innovation, and Urban Order*. London: Phoenix.

———. 2001a. 'Global city regions in the twenty-first century', in Scott (2001).

———. 2001b. 'Sustainable cities or town cramming?', in A. Layard, S. Dovoudi, and S. Batty, eds, *Planning for a Sustainable Future*. London: Spon Press.

——— and A. Markusen. 1985. *Silicon Landscapes*. London: Allen & Unwin.

Hall, T., and P. Hubbard, eds. 1998. *The Entrepreneurial City: Geographies of Political Regime and Representation*. London: John Wiley and Sons.

Hallman, B.C. 1999. 'The transition into eldercare: An uncelebrated passage', in E. Teather, ed., *Embodied Geographies: Spaces, Bodies and Rites of Passage*. London: Routledge.

———. 1996. 'Mapping residential redevelopment in a Canadian suburb,' *Canadian Journal of Urban Research* 5: 137–46.

Halseth, G. 1999. '"We came for the work": Situating employment migration in B.C.'s small, resource-based communities', *Canadian Geographer* 43: 363–81.

———. 2003. 'Attracting growth "back" to an amenity rich fringe: Rural-urban fringe dynamics around metropolitan Vancouver, Canada', *Canadian Journal of Regional Science* 26: 297–318.

Hamel, P. 1993. 'Modernity and postmodernity: The crisis of urban planning', *Canadian Journal of Urban Research* 2: 16–29.

———. 2005. 'Municipal reform in Quebec: The trade-off between centralization and decentralization', in J. Garcea and E. Lesage, eds, *Municipal Reform in Canada: Reconfiguration, Re-empowerment, and Rebalancing*. Toronto: Oxford University Press.

Hamilton. 2004. *Keys to the Home: A Housing Strategy for Hamilton*. Hamilton. At: <www.city.hamilton.on.ca/housing/housing-supply-programs/pdf/Keys%20to%20the%20Home.pdf>.

Hamilton, L., C. Haedrich, L. Richard, and C.M. Duncan. 2004. 'Above and below the water: Social/ecological transformation in northwest Newfoundland', *Population and Environment* 25: 195–215.

Hamnett, C. 2003. *Unequal City: London in the Global Arena*. London: Routledge.

Hancock, M.L. 1961. 'Flemingdon Park, a new urban community', *Plan Canada* 2: 4–24.

———. 1994. 'Don Mills, a paradigm of community design', *Plan Canada* 34, 4: 87–90.

Hanlon, N., and G. Halseth. 2005. 'The greying of resource communities in northern British Columbia: Implications for health care delivery in already-underserviced communities', *Canadian Geographer* 49: 1–24.

Hanna, D.B. 1980. 'Creation of an early Victorian suburb in Montreal', *Urban History Review* 9, 2: 38–64.

———. 1986. *The Layered City: A Revolution in Housing in Mid-Nineteenth Century Montreal*. Montreal: McGill University, Department of Geography (Shared Spaces No. 6).

Hanna, K.S. 2005. 'Planning for sustainability: Two contrasting communities', *Journal of the American Planning Association* 71: 27–40.

——— and M. Walton-Roberts. 2004. 'Quality of place and the rescaling of urban governance: The case of Toronto', *Journal of Canadian Studies* 38, 3: 37–67.

Hannigan, J. 1998. *Fantasy City: Pleasure and Profit in the Modern Metropolis*. New York: Routledge.

Hanson, S., and G. Pratt. 1995. *Gender, Work, and Space*. New York: Routledge.

Harasym, D.G., and P.J. Smith. 1975. 'Planning for retail services in new residential areas since 1944', in B.M. Barr, ed., *Calgary: Metropolitan Structure and Influence*. Victoria: University of Victoria, Western Geographical Series vol. 11.

Harrington, J.W., and H. Campbell. 1997. 'The suburbanization of producer service employment', *Growth and Change* 28: 335–59.

Harris, C.D., and E.L. Ullman. 1945. 'The nature of cities', *Annals, American Academy of Political and Social Science* 242: 7–17.

Harris, R. 1992. '"Canada's all right": The lives and loyalties of immigrant families in a Toronto suburb, 1900–1945', *Canadian Geographer* 36: 13–30.

———. 1994. 'The flexible house: The housing backlog and the persistence of lodging, 1891–1951', *Social Science History* 18: 31–53.

———. 1996. *Unplanned Suburbs: Toronto's American Tragedy, 1900 to 1950*. Baltimore: Johns Hopkins University Press.

———. 2000. 'More American than the United States: Housing in urban Canada in the twentieth century', *Journal of Urban History* 26: 456–78.

———. 2003. 'The suburban worker in the history of labor', *International Labor and Working Class History* 64: 8–24.

———. 2004. *Creeping Conformity: How Canada Became Suburban, 1900–1960*. Toronto: University of Toronto Press.

——— and M. Buzzelli. 2003. 'Small is transient: Housebuilding firms in Ontario, Canada 1978–1998', *Housing Studies* 18: 369–86.

——— and ———. 2005. 'House building in the machine age, 1920s–1970s: Realities and perceptions of modernisation in North America and Australia', *Business History* 47: 59–85.

———— and G. Pratt. 1993. 'The home, home owner-ship and public policy', in Bourne and Ley (1993).

———— and M.P. Sendbuehler. 1992. 'Hamilton's East End: The early working-class suburb', *Canadian Geographer* 36: 381–6.

Harris, R.C. 1974. *Canada before Confederation: A Study in Historical Geography*. Toronto: Oxford University Press.

Hartshorn, T. 1992. *Interpreting the City*. New York: Wiley.

Harvey, D. 1973. *Social Justice and the City*. London: Edward Arnold.

————. 1987. 'Flexible accumulation through urban-ization: Reflections on "post-modernism" in the American city', *Antipode* 19: 260–86.

————. 1989a. *The Condition of Postmodernity*. Oxford: Blackwell.

————. 1989b. 'From managerialism to entrepre-neurialism: The transformation in urban gover-nance in late capitalism', *Geografiska Annaler Series B* 1: 3–18.

————. 1996. *Justice, Nature and the Geography of Difference*. Cambridge, Mass.: Blackwell.

Harvey, T., and M. Works. 2002. 'Urban sprawl and rural landscapes: Perceptions of landscape as amenity in Portland, Oregon', *Local Environment* 7: 381–96.

Hasse, J., and R. Lathrop. 2003. 'Land resource impact indicators of urban sprawl', *Applied Geography* 23: 159.

Hasson, S., and D. Ley. 1994. *Neighbourhood Organizations and the Welfare State*. Toronto: University of Toronto Press.

Hayden, D. 1981. *The Grand Domestic Revolution: A History of Feminist Design for American Homes, Neighbourhoods, and Cities*. Cambridge, Mass.: MIT Press.

————. 2002. *Redesigning the American Dream: Gender, Housing and Family Life*, 2nd edn. New York: Norton.

————. 2003. *Building Suburbia: Green Fields and Urban Growth, 1820–2000*. New York: Pantheon Books.

Healy, P. 1997. *Collaborative Planning: Shaping Places in Fragmented Societies*. Vancouver: University of British Columbia Press.

Heath, T. 2001. 'Revitalizing cities: Attitudes toward city-center living in the United Kingdom', *Journal of Planning Education and Research* 20: 464–75.

Heilbrun, J. 1992. 'Art and culture as central place functions', *Urban Studies* 29: 205–15.

Heim, C. 2001. 'Leapfrogging, urban sprawl, and growth management: Phoenix 1950–2000', *American Journal of Economics and Sociology* 60: 245–83.

Heisz, A., M. Bordt, S. Das, S. Sudip, and S. Larochelle-Côté. 2005. *Labour Markets, Business Activity and Population Growth and Mobility in Canadian CMAs*. Ottawa: Statistics Canada (Trends and conditions in census metropolitan areas), Cat. no. 89–613–MIE 2005006. Available at: <www.statcan.ca/english/research/89-613-MIE/89-613-MIE2005006.pdf>.

———— and L. McLeod. 2004. *Low-income in Census Metropolitan Areas, 1980–2000*. Ottawa: Statistics Canada (Business and Labour Market Analysis Division, Trends and Conditions in Canadian Metropolitan Areas No. 1).

Held, D., A. McGrew, D. Goldblatt, and J. Perraton. 1999. *Global Transformations: Politics, Economics and Culture*. Cambridge: Polity Press.

Helfield, J.M., and M.L. Diamond. 1997. 'Use of con-structed wetlands for urban stream restoration: A critical analysis', *Environmental Management* 21: 329–41.

Helleiner, E. 2003. 'Toward a North American com-mon currency', in Clement and Vosko (2003).

Hempel, L. 1999. 'Conceptual and analytical challenges in building sustainable communities', in D. Mazmanian and M. Kraft, eds, *Toward Sustainable Communities: Transition and Transformation in Environmental Policy*. Cambridge, Mass.: MIT Press.

Henripin, J. 1968. *Tendances et facteurs de la fécondité au Canada*. Ottawa: Bureau fédéral de la statistique, Monographie sur le recensement de 1961.

Henry, F., and C. Tator. 2002. *Discourses of Domination: Racial Bias in the Canadian English-Language Press*. Toronto: University of Toronto Press.

Herbert, D.T., and C.J. Thomas. 1997. *Cities in Space: City as Place*. New York: Wiley.

Herman, D.B., E.S. Susser, E.L. Struening, and B.L. Link. 1997. 'Adverse childhood experiences: Are they risk factors for adult homelessness?', *American Journal of Public Health* 87: 249–55.

Hernandez, T., M. Biasiotto, and K. Jones. 2003. *Power Retail: Growth in Canada and the GTA*. Toronto: Ryerson University, CSCA (RL2003–01).

———, K. Jones, and A. Maze. 2003. *US Retail Chains in Canada*. Toronto: Ryerson University, CSCA (RL2003–10).

———, M. Yeates, and T. Lea. 2003. *Residential Property Valuation: An Application of Geographically Weighted Regression (GWR)*. Toronto: Ryerson University, CSCA (RL2003–05).

Hiebert, D. 1992. 'Winnipeg's North End', *Canadian Geographer* 36: 92–7.

———. 1993a. 'Integrating production and consumption: Industry, class, ethnicity, and the Jews of Toronto', in Bourne and Ley (1993).

———. 1993b. 'Jewish immigrants and the garment industry of Toronto, 1901–1931: A study of ethnic and class relations', *Annals of the Association of American Geographers* 83: 243–71.

———. 1999. 'Immigration and the changing social geography of Greater Vancouver', *BC Studies* 121: 35–82.

———. 2000a. 'Immigration and the changing Canadian city', *Canadian Geographer* 44: 25–43.

———. 2000b. *The Social Geography of Immigration and Urbanization in Canada: A Review and Interpretation*. Vancouver: Research on Immigration and Integration in the Metropolis.

Higgins, D.J.H. 1986. *Local and Urban Politics in Canada*. Toronto: Gage.

Hirst, P., and G. Thompson. 1999. *Globalization in Question: The International Economy and the Possibilities of Governance*. Cambridge: Polity Press.

Hise, G. 1993. 'Home building and industrial decentralization in Los Angeles: The roots of the postwar urban region', *Journal of Urban History* 19: 95–125.

Hitchcock, J., and N. McMaster, eds. 1985. *The Metropolis: Proceedings in Honour of Hans Blumenfeld*. Toronto: University of Toronto, Department of Geography.

Hobden, D.W., G.E. Laughton, and K.E. Morgan. 2004. 'Green space borders—a tangible benefit? Evidence from four neighbourhoods in Surrey, British Columbia, 1980–2001', *Land Use Policy* 21: 129–38.

Hodge, G. 1991. *Planning Canadian Communities*. Scarborough, Ont.: Nelson Canada.

———. 1998. *Planning Canadian Communities: An Introduction to the Principles, Practice, and Participants*. Toronto: ITP Nelson.

———. 2003. *Planning Canadian Communities: An Introduction to the Principles, Practice, and Participants*, 4th edn. Toronto: Thomson Nelson.

——— and I.M. Robinson. 2001. *Planning Canadian Regions*. Vancouver: University of British Columbia Press.

Holdsworth, D. 1977. 'House and home in Vancouver: Images of West Coast urbanism, 1881–1929', in G.A. Stelter and A.F.J. Artibise, eds, *The Canadian City: Essays in Urban History*. Toronto: McClelland & Stewart.

———. 1985. *Reviving Main Street*. Toronto: University of Toronto Press.

——— and G. Laws. 1994. 'Landscapes of old age in coastal British Columbia', *Canadian Geographer* 38: 174–81.

Holmes, J. 1991. 'The globalization of production and the future of Canada's mature industries: The case of the automotive industry', in Drache and Gertler (1991).

Hoover, E.M., and R. Vernon. 1959. *Anatomy of a Metropolis: The Changing Distribution of People and Jobs within the New York Metropolitan Area*. Cambridge, Mass.: Harvard University Press.

——— and ———. 1962. *Anatomy of a Metropolis*. New York: Doubleday Anchor.

Horwood, E.A., and R.R. Boyce. 1959. *Studies of the Central Business District and Urban Freeway Development*. Seattle: University of Washington Press.

Hossé, H.A. 1978. 'The greenbelt and Ottawa's "urban containment"', in R. Wesche and M. Kugler-Gagnon, eds, *Ottawa–Hull: Spatial Perspectives and Planning*. Ottawa: University of Ottawa Press, Department of Geography and Regional Planning Occasional Papers 4.

Hotelling, H. 1931. 'The economics of exhaustible resources', *Journal of Political Economy* 39: 137–75.

Hough, M. 1990. *Out of Place: Restoring Identity to the Regional Landscape*. New Haven: Yale University Press.

———. 1995. *Cities and Natural Processes*. London: Routledge.

———. 2004. *Cities and Natural Process: A Basis for Sustainability*, 2nd edn. New York: Routledge.

Howard, E. 1985 [1898]. *Garden Cities of To-Morrow*. Powys, Wales: Attic Books.

Howard, R. 1995. 'Master plan provides destination, but no route', *Globe and Mail*, 22 Apr., A6.

Howe, D., and W. Rabiega. 1992. 'Beyond strips and centres: The ideal commercial form', *Journal of the American Planning Association* 58: 213–19.

Howell, L. 1986. 'The affordable housing crisis in Toronto', *City Magazine* 9, 1: 25–9.

Hoyle, B.S. 1995. *Redeveloping Waterfronts in Canadian Port Cities: Perspectives on Principles and Practice*. Le Havre: Association internationale villes et ports.

Hoyt, H. 1939. *The Structure and Growth of Residential Neighborhoods in American Cities*. Washington: Federal Housing Administration.

Hulchanski, J.D. 1984. *St. Lawrence and False Creek: A Review of the Planning and Development of Two New Inner City Neighbourhoods*. Vancouver: University of British Columbia, School of Community and Regional Planning.

———. 1986. 'General introduction to the issue' (Special issue on the history of Canadian housing policy), *Urban History Review* 15, 1: 1–2.

———. 1993. 'New Forms of Owning and Renting', in Miron (1993a).

———. 2004. 'A tale of two Canadas: Home owners getting richer, renters getting poorer', in Hulchanski and Shapcott (2004).

——— and M. Shapcott, eds. 2004. *Finding Room: Policy Options for a Canadian Rental Housing Strategy*. Toronto: University of Toronto, Centre for Urban and Community Studies.

Human Resources Development Canada. 2001. 'Recent immigrants have experienced unusual economic difficulties', *Applied Research Bulletin* 7.

Hurd, R. 1903. *Principles of City Land Values*. New York: Record and Guide.

Hutton, T. 1998. *The Transformation of Canada's Pacific Metropolis: A Study of Vancouver*. Montreal: IRPP.

———. 2004a. 'The new economy of the inner city', *Cities* 21: 89–108.

———. 2004b. 'Post-industrialism, post-modernism and the reproduction of Vancouver's central area: Re-theorising the 21st-century city', *Urban Studies* 41: 1953–82.

Huxley, A. 1960. 'The Desert', in *Collected Essays*. London: Chatto and Windus.

Ibbitson, J. 1997. *Promised Land: Inside the Mike Harris Revolution*. Toronto: Prentice-Hall.

IBI Group. 1990. *Greater Toronto Area Urban Structure Concepts Study: Background Report No. 1, Description of Urban Structure Concepts*. Toronto: IBI Group.

Illegems, V., and A. Verbeke. 2003. *Moving Towards the Virtual Workplace: Managerial and Societal Perspectives on Telework*. Cheltenham, UK: Edward Elgar.

Information Highway Advisory Council. 1997. *Preparing Canada for a Digital World*. Ottawa: Industry Canada.

Innes, J. 1995. 'Planning theory's emerging paradigm: Communicative action and interactive practice', *Journal of Planning Education and Research* 14: 183–90.

Institute for the Study of Homelessness and Poverty (ISHP). 2004. *Homelessness in Los Angeles: A Summary of Recent Research*. Los Angeles: Institute for the Study of Homelessness and Poverty.

International Council of Shopping Centers (ICSC). 1997. *The Scope of the Shopping Centre Industry in Canada: 1997*. New York: ICSC.

———. 2005a. *Scope of the Shopping Centre Industry in Canada: 2005*. New York: ICSC.

———. 2005b. *Shopping Centre Definitions*. New York: ICSC.

Irwin, E.G., and N.E. Bockstael. 2004. 'Land use externalities, open space preservation, and urban sprawl', *Regional Science and Urban Economics* 34, 6: 705–25.

Isard, W., and R.E. Coughlin. 1957. *Municipal Costs and Revenues Resulting from Growth*. Wellesley, Mass.: Chandler-Davis.

Isenberg, A. 2004. *Downtown America: A History of the Place and the People Who Made It*. Chicago: University of Chicago Press.

Isin, E.F. 1992. *Cities without Citizens: The Modernity of the City as a Corporation*. Montreal: Black Rose.

———. 2000. *Democracy, Citizenship and the Global City*. London: Routledge.

———— and M. Siemiatycki. 1999. *Fate and Faith: Claiming Urban Citizenship in Immigrant Toronto.* Toronto: Centre of Excellence for Research on Immigration and Settlement (Working Paper Series, Report No. 8).

Ito, K. 1995. 'Metrotown: A time and a place', in Evenden (1995).

Jackson, K.T. 1985. *Crabgrass Frontier: The Suburbanization of the United States.* New York: Oxford University Press.

Jackson, P. 1999. 'Commodity cultures: The traffic in things', *Transactions, Institute of British Geographers* 24: 95–108.

Jacobs, A.B. 1980. *Making City Planning Work.* Washington: American Planning Association.

———— and D. Appleyard. 1987. 'Toward an urban design manifesto', *Journal of the American Planning Association* 53: 112–20.

Jacobs, J. 1961. *The Death and Life of Great American Cities.* New York: Random House.

————. 1969. *The Economy of Cities.* New York: Random House.

————. 1971. *City Limits.* Ottawa: National Film Board.

————. 1984. *Cities and the Wealth of Nations.* New York: Random House.

————. 2000. *The Nature of Economies.* Toronto: Random House.

Jacobs, J.M., and R. Fincher. 1998. 'Introduction', in Fincher and Jacobs (1998).

JAPA. 1997. 'Symposium: Alternative views of sprawl' (P. Gordon and H.W. Richardson, 'Are compact cities a desirable planning goal?', and R. Ewing, 'Is Los Angeles-style sprawl desirable?'), *Journal of the American Planning Association* 63: 94–126.

Jarvis, H. 1999. 'Housing mobility as a function of household structure: Towards a deeper understanding of housing-related disadvantage', *Housing Studies* 14: 491–505.

————, A.C. Pratt, and P. Wu. 2001. *The Secret Life of Cities: The Social Reproduction of Everyday Life.* Harlow, UK: Prentice-Hall.

Jencks, C. 1994. *The Homeless.* Cambridge, Mass.: Harvard University Press.

Jenkins, B.M. 2001. *Protecting Public Surface Transportation against Terrorism and Serious Crime: Continuing Research on Best Security Practices.* San José, Calif.: Mineta Transportation Institute (Report 01–14).

Jenson, J. 1989. 'Different but not exceptional: Canada's permeable Fordism', *Canadian Review of Anthropology and Sociology* 26: 69–93.

———— and S. Phillips. 1996. 'Regime shift: New citizenship practices in Canada', *International Journal of Canadian Studies* 14: 111–35.

Jerrett, M., J. Eyles, and C. Dufournaud. 2002. 'Regional population size and the cost of municipal environmental protection services: Empirical evidence from Ontario', *Canadian Journal of Regional Science* 25: 279–300.

Jessop, B. 1994. 'Post-Fordism and the state', in A. Amin, ed., *Post-Fordism: A Reader.* Oxford: Blackwell.

————. 2002. *The Future of the Capitalist State.* Cambridge: Polity Press.

Jim, C.Y. 2004. 'Green-space preservation and allocation for sustainable greening of compact cities', *Cities* 21: 311–20.

Johnson, D.B. 1987. 'The West Edmonton Mall—From super-regional to mega-regional shopping centre', *International Journal of Retailing* 2: 53–69.

Johnson, M. 2001. 'Environmental impacts of urban sprawl: A survey of the literature and proposed research agenda', *Environment and Planning A* 33: 717–35.

Jones, C., L. Marsden, and L. Tepperman. 1990. *Lives of Their Own: The Individualization of Women's Lives.* Toronto: Oxford University Press.

Jones, D. 1985. *Urban Transit Policy: An Economic and Political History.* Englewood Cliffs, NJ: Prentice-Hall.

Jones, K. 1991. 'The urban retail landscape', in Bunting and Filion (1991).

———— and M. Doucet. 1999. *The Impact of Big-Box Development on Toronto's Retail Structure.* Toronto: Ryerson University, Centre for the Study of Commercial Activity.

———— and ————. 2000. 'Big-box retailing and the urban retail structure: The case of the Toronto area', *Journal of Retailing and Consumer Services* 7: 233–47.

————, W. Evans, and C. Smith. 1994 'New formats in the Canadian retail economy', *Journal of Shopping Centre Research* 1, 1: 161–208.

———— and J. Simmons. 1990. *The Retail Environment.* London: Routledge.

———— and ————. 1993 *Location, Location, Location: Analyzing the Retail Environment*, 2nd edn. Toronto: Nelson Canada.

Jones, P., D. Comfort, and D. Hillier. 2005. 'Regeneration through culture', *Geography Review* 18, 4: 21–3.

Joseph, A., and D. Cloutier. 1991. 'Elderly migration and its implications for service provision in rural communities: An Ontario perspective', *Journal of Rural Studies* 7: 433–44.

———— and B. Hall. 1985. 'The locational concentration of group homes in Toronto', *Professional Geographer* 37: 143–54.

———— and B.C. Hallmann. 1998. 'Over the hill and far away: Distance as a barrier to the provision of assistance to elderly relatives', *Social Science and Medicine* 46: 631–9.

————, P. Keddie, and B. Smit. 1988. 'Unraveling the population turnaround', *Canadian Geographer* 32: 17–31.

Judd, D. 2003. 'Building the tourist city', in Judd, ed., *The Infrastructure of Play: Building the Tourist City.* New York: M.E Sharpe.

Justis, M. 2004. 'Immigrants in Canada's cities', in C. Andrew, ed., *Our Diverse Cities* (Metropolis Project and Federation of Canadian Municipalities) 1: 41–7.

Kaplan, H. 1967. *Urban Political Systems: A Functional Analysis of Metro Toronto.* New York: Columbia University Press.

Kaplinsky, R. 1999. 'Is globalisation all it is cracked up to be?', *IDS Bulletin* 30: 106–16.

Kauppi, C. 2003. *Report on Homelessness in Sudbury: Comparison of Findings: July 2000 to January 2003.* Sudbury: City of Greater Sudbury and Social Planning Council of Sudbury.

Kaye, J.P., R.L. McCulley, and I.C. Burke. 2005. 'Carbon fluxes, nitrogen cycling, and soil microbial communities in adjacent urban, native and agricultural ecosystems', *Global Change Biology* 11: 575–87.

Kazemipur, A., and S. Halli. 2001. 'The changing colour of poverty in Canada', *Canadian Review of Sociology and Anthropology* 38: 217–38.

Keating, A.D. 1994. *Invisible Networks.* Melbourne, Fla: Krieger.

Keating, D. 1997. 'Cleveland: "Comeback city": The politics of redevelopment and sports stadiums amidst urban decline', in M. Lauria, ed., *Reconstructing Urban Regime Theory: Regulating Urban Politics in a Global Economy.* Thousand Oaks, Calif.: Sage.

Keller, W., P. Dillon, J. Heneberry, M. Malette, and J. Gunn. 2001. 'Sulphate in Sudbury, Ontario, Canada, lakes: Recent trends and status', *Water, Air and Soil Pollution* 130: 793–8, Part 2.

Kellet, P., and J. Moore. 2003. 'Routes to home: Homelessness and home-making in contrasting societies', *Habitat International* 27: 123–41.

Kemble, R. 1989. *The Canadian City, St. John's to Victoria: A Critical Commentary.* Montreal: Harvest House.

Kendall, J. 1971. 'The construction and maintenance of Coteau du Lac: The first lock canal in North America', *Journal of Transport History* 1: 39–50.

Kennedy, C.A., E.J. Miller, A.S. Shalaby, H. Maclean, and J. Coleman. 2005. 'The four pillars of sustainable urban transportation', *Transport Reviews* 25: 393–414.

Kennedy, G., and T. Mayer. 2002. 'Natural and constructed wetlands in Canada: An overview', *Water Quality Research Journal of Canada* 37: 295–25.

Kent, T., ed. 1997. *In Pursuit of the Public Good.* Montreal and Kingston: McGill-Queen's University Press.

Kenworthy, J., and F. Laube. 1999. *An International Sourcebook of Automobile Dependence in Cities 1960–1990.* Boulder: University Press of Colorado.

Kerr, D. 1977. 'Review of George A. Nader, *Cities of Canada* Vols. 1 and 2', *Annals, Association of American Geographers* 61: 163–5.

————. 1998. 'The emergence of the industrial heartland, c. 1760–1960', in L.D. McCann and A. Gunn, eds, *Heartland and Hinterland: A Geography of Canada*, 3rd edn. Scarborough, Ont.: Prentice-Hall Canada.

————, D. Holdsworth, and S. Laskin, eds. 1991. *Historical Atlas of Canada*, vol. 3, *Addressing the Twentieth Century.* Toronto: University of Toronto Press.

Kholer, B., and M. Wissen. 2003. 'Glocalizing protest: Urban conflicts and urban social movements', *International Journal of Urban and Regional Research* 27: 942–51.

Kidd, K. 1996. 'Where have all the shoppers gone?', *Globe and Mail Report on Business Magazine* (Dec.): 38–50.

Kim, K.G. 2004. 'The application of the biosphere reserve concept to urban areas—the case of green rooftops for habitat network in Seoul', *Urban Biosphere and Society: Partnership of Cities* 1023: 187–214.

Kincaid, J. 1995. 'Cities and citizens in flux: Global consumer integration and local civic fragmentation', in Kresl and Gappert (1995).

King, A. 1990. *Global Cities: Post-Imperialism and the Internationalisation of London*. London: Routledge.

King, A.D. 1997. 'Excavating the multicultural suburb: Hidden histories of the bungalow', in R. Silverstone, ed., *Visions of Suburbia*. London: Routledge.

King, R.S., M.E. Baker, D.F. Whigham, D.E. Weller, T.E. Jordan, P.F. Kazyak, and M.K. Hurd. 2005. 'Spatial considerations for linking watershed land cover to ecological indicators in streams', *Ecological Applications* 15: 137–53.

Kipfer, S.R., and R. Keil. 2002. 'Toronto Inc.? Planning the competitive city in the new Toronto', *Antipode* 34: 227–64.

Kitchen, H. 2002. *Municipal Revenue and Expenditure Issues in Canada* (Canadian Tax Paper No. 107). Toronto: Canadian Tax Foundation.

——— and D. Auld. 1995. *Financing Education and Training in Canada* (Canadian Tax Paper No. 99). Toronto: Canadian Tax Foundation.

——— and M. McMillan. 1985. 'Local government and Canadian federalism', in R. Simeon, ed., *Intergovernmental Relations*. Toronto: University of Toronto Press.

Kling, R., S. Olin, and M. Poster, eds. 1991. *Postsuburban California: The Transformation of Orange County Since World War II*. Berkeley: University of California Press.

Knaap, G. 1998. 'The determinants of residential property values: Implications for metropolitan planning', *Journal of Planning Literature* 12: 267–83.

Knack, R.E. 1998. 'Downtown is where the living is easy: From New York to Aiken, South Carolina, downtown housing is hot. But will it do all it's supposed to?', *Planning* 64, 1: 4–9.

Knox, P. 1994. *Urbanization: An Introduction to Urban Geography*. Englewood Cliffs, NJ: Prentice-Hall.

Kominkova, D., D. Stransky, G. St'astna, J. Caletkova, J. Nabelkova, and Z. Handova. 2005. 'Identification of ecological status of stream impacted by urban drainage', *Water Science and Technology* 51: 249–56.

Kousky, C., and S.H. Schneider. 2003. 'Global climate policy: will cities lead the way?', *Climate Policy* 3: 359–72.

Kozol, J. 1988. *Rachel and Her Children*. New York: Crown Press.

Kraehling, P. 2004. 'Secondary suites: Obstacles and opportunities demonstrated by a case study in Guelph, Ontario', *Plan Canada* 44, 4: 33–6.

Kresl, P. 1995. 'The determinants of urban competitiveness: A survey', in Kresl and Gappert (1995).

——— and G. Gappert, eds. 1995. *North American Cities and the Global Economy*. Thousand Oaks, Calif.: Sage.

Krohn, R.G., B. Fleming, and M. Manzer. 1977. *The Other Economy: The Internal Logic of Local Rental Housing*. Toronto: Peter Martin.

Krumholz, N., and J. Forester. 1990. *Making Equity Planning Work: Leadership in the Public Sector*. Philadelphia: Temple University Press.

Kuhn, R., and D.P. Culhane. 1998. 'Applying cluster analysis to test a typology of homelessness by pattern of shelter utilization: Results from the analysis of administrative data', *American Journal of Community Psychology* 26: 207–32.

Kumar, S. 2002. 'Canadian urban design practice: A review of urban design regulations', *Canadian Journal of Urban Research* 11: 239–63.

Kunstler, J.H. 1993. *The Geography of Nowhere: The Rise and Decline of America's Man-made Landscape*. New York: Simon & Schuster.

———. 1996. *Home from Nowhere: Remaking Our Everyday World for the Twenty-First Century*. New York: Simon & Shuster.

Ladner, P. 2004. 'Changing welfare rules is first step to eliminating homelessness', *Business in Vancouver*.

At: <www.peterladner.ca/news-col-041109-homelessness.html>. Accessed 18 Feb. 2005.

Laflamme, V. 2001. 'Familles et modes de résidence en milieu urbain québécois au début du 20ième siècle: l'exemple de la ville de Québec, 1901', *Cahiers québécois de démographie* 30, 2: 261–88.

Lake, R.W. 1999. 'Postmodern urbanism?', *Urban Geography* 20: 393–5.

Lang, J. 1994. *Urban Design: The American Experience.* New York: Van Nostrand Reinhold.

Lang, R. 1972. *Nova Scotia Municipal and Regional Planning in the 1970s.* Halifax: Nova Scotia Department of Municipal Affairs.

Lang, R.E. 2003. *Edgeless Cities: Exploring the Elusive Metropolis.* Washington: Brookings Institution Press.

Lapointe, A. 2003. *Croissance des villes et économie du savoir.* Sainte-Foy, Que.: Les Presses de l'Université Laval.

Lash, H. 1977. *Planning in a Human Way: Personal Reflections on the Regional Planning Experience in Greater Vancouver.* Ottawa: Ministry of State for Urban Affairs.

Lavigne, G. 1987. *Les ethniques et la ville: L'aventure urbaine des immigrants Portugais à Montréal.* Montréal: Le Préambule.

Laws, G. 1994. 'Community activism around the built form of Toronto's welfare state', *Canadian Journal of Urban Research* 3: 1–28.

Layton, J. 2000. *Homelessness: The Making and Unmaking of a Crisis.* Toronto: Penguin.

Lea, A.C. 1989. 'An overview of formal methods for retail site evaluation and sales forecasting', *Operational Geographer* 7, 2: 8–17

Lea, T., K. Jones, and G. Bylov. 2003. *Retail Sales Trends in Downtown Canada.* Toronto: Centre for the Study of Commercial Activity, Ryerson University.

Leach, C. 2005. 'First Nations land management capacity-building initiative', *Plan Canada* 45, 1: 4–5.

League for Social Reconstruction. 1935. *Social Planning for Canada.* Toronto: Thomas Nelson and Sons.

Le Bourdais, C., and M. Beaudry. 1988. 'The changing residential structure of Montreal: 1971–1981', *Canadian Geographer* 32: 98–113.

———, G. Neill, and P. Turcotte, with N. Vachon and J. Archambault. 2000. 'The changing face of

conjugal relationships', *Canadian Social Trends* 56: 14–17 (Statistics Canada, Cat. no. 11–008).

Lee, B.A., T. Price-Spratlen, and J.W. Kanan. 2003. 'Determinants of homelessness in metropolitan areas', *Journal of Urban Affairs* 25: 335–55.

Lee, D.B. 1973. 'Requiem for large scale models', *Journal of the American Institute of Planners* 39: 163–78.

Lee, J. 2002. 'Visioning Diversity: Planning Vancouver's Multicultural Communities', MA thesis, University of Waterloo.

Lees, L. 1987. 'Ageographia, heterotopia, and Vancouver's new public library', *Environment and Planning D* 15: 321–47.

———. 1998. 'Vancouver: A portfolio', *Urban Geography* 19: 283–86.

———. 1999. 'Urban renaissance and the streets: Spaces of control and contestation', in N. Fyfe, ed., *Images of the Streets: Representation, Experience and Control in Public Space.* London: Routledge.

Lefebvre, H. 1991. *The Production of Space.* Oxford: Blackwell.

———. 2003. *Henri Lefebvre: Key Writings.* London: Continuum.

———. 2004. *Rhythmanalysis: Space, Time and Everyday Life.* London: Continuum.

Lehrer, U., and R. Milgrom. 1996. 'New (sub) urbanism: Countersprawl or repackaging the product', *Capitalism, Nature, Socialism* 7, 26: 49–64.

Lemieux, D., and L. Mercier. 1992. *Les femmes au tournant du siècle, 1880–1940. Âges de la vie, maternité et quotidien.* Québec: Institut québécois de recherche sur la culture.

Lemon, J.T. 1985. *Toronto Since 1918: An Illustrated History.* Toronto: James Lorimer.

———. 1996. *Liberal Dreams and Nature's Limits: Great Cities of North America Since 1600.* Toronto: Oxford University Press.

Lennon, R., and C. Leo. 2001. 'Metropolitan growth and municipal boundaries: Problems and proposed solutions', *International Journal of Canadian Studies* 24: 77–104.

Leo, C. 1977. *The Politics of Urban Development: Canadian Urban Expressway Disputes.* Toronto: Institute of Public Administration of Canada, Monographs on Canadian Urban Government No. 3.

———. 1994. 'The urban economy and the power of the local state: The politics of planning in Edmonton and Vancouver', in Frisken (1994a).

———. 2002. 'Urban development: Planning aspirations and political realities', in Fowler and Siegel (2002).

——— and M. August. 2005. *The Federal Government and Homelessness: Community Initiation or Dictation from Above?* Winnipeg: Canadian Centre for Policy Alternatives.

——— and W. Brown. 2000. 'Slow growth and urban development policy', *Journal of Urban Affairs* 22: 193–213.

——— and L. Shaw, with K. Gibbons and C. Goff. 2002. 'What causes inner-city decay and what can be done about it?', in K. Graham and C. Andrew, eds, *Urban Affairs: Is It Back on the Policy Agenda?* Montreal and Kingston: McGill-Queen's University Press, 2002.

Leslie, D., and S. Reimer. 2003. 'Gender, modern design, and home consumption', *Environment and Planning D Society and Space* 21: 293–316.

Leung, H.-L. 1996. 'Designer suburbs', in Emeneau (1996).

Levin, I. 2004. 'Living apart together: A new family form', *Current Sociology* 52: 223–40.

Levine, M. 1995. 'Globalization and wage polarization in US and Canadian cities: Does public policy make a difference?', in Kresl and Gappert (1995).

———. 2003. 'Tourism infrastructure and urban redevelopment in Montreal', in D. Judd, ed., *The Infrastructure of Play: Building the Tourist City*. New York: M.E Sharpe.

Levy, J. 1985. *Urban and Metropolitan Economics*. New York: McGraw-Hill.

Lewinburg, F. 1996. 'Some thoughts about intensification', in Emeneau (1996).

Lewis, P. 1983. 'The galactic metropolis', in R. Platt and G. Macinko, eds, *Beyond the Urban Fringe*. Minneapolis: University of Minnesota Press.

Lewis, R.D. 1985. *The Segregated City: Class and Occupation in Montreal, 1861–1901*. Montreal: McGill University, Department of Geography (Shared Spaces No. 3).

———. 1991. 'The development of an early suburban industrial district: The Montreal ward of Saint-Ann, 1851–71', *Urban History Review* 19: 166–80.

———. 2000. *Manufacturing Montreal: The Making of an Industrial Landscape, 1850–1930*. Baltimore: Johns Hopkins University Press.

———. 2002. 'The industrial suburb is dead, long live the industrial slum: Suburbs and slums in Chicago and Montreal, 1850–1950', *Planning Perspectives* 17: 123–44.

———, ed. 2004. *Manufacturing Suburbs: Building Work and Home on the Metropolitan Fringe*. Philadelphia: Temple University Press.

Ley, D. 1974. *The Black Inner City as Frontier Outpost: Images and Behavior of a Philadelphia Neighborhood*. Washington: Association of American Geographers (Monograph Series No. 7).

———. 1987. 'Styles of the times: Liberal and neo-conservative landscapes in Inner Vancouver, 1968–1986', *Journal of Historical Geography* 13: 40–56.

———. 1988. 'Social upgrading in six Canadian inner cities', *Canadian Geographer* 32: 31–45.

———. 1993. 'Past elites and present gentry: Neighbourhoods of privilege in Canadian cities', in Bourne and Ley (1993).

———. 1994. 'The Downtown Eastside: "One Hundred Years of Struggle"', in Hasson and Ley (1994).

———. 1995. 'Between Europe and Asia: The case of the missing sequoias', *Ecumene* 2: 185–210.

———. 1996a. *The New Middle Class and the Remaking of the Central City*. Oxford: Oxford University Press.

———. 1996b. 'The new middle class in Canadian central cities', in Caulfield and Peake (1996).

———. 2000. 'Multicultural planning: Whose city? Whose identity?', in K. Dosen and I. Molina, eds, *Best Practices for the Social Inclusion of Ethnic Minorities in Local Communities*. Norrkoping: PfMI.

———. 2003a. 'Artists, aestheticisation and the field of gentrification', *Urban Studies* 40: 2527–44.

———. 2003b. 'Seeking homo economicus: The Canadian state and the strange story of Canada's business immigration program', *Annals of the Association of American Geographers* 93: 426–41.

———. 2004. 'Transnational space and everyday lives', *Transactions of the Institute of British Geographers* new series 29: 151–64.

——— and A. Germain. 2000. 'Immigration and the changing social geography of large Canadian cities', *Plan Canada* 40, 4: 29–32.

———— and D. Hiebert. 2001. 'Immigration policy as population policy', *Canadian Geographer* 45: 120–5.

————, ————, and G. Pratt. 1992. 'Time to grow up? From urban village to world city, 1966–91', in G. Wynne and T. Oakes, eds, *Vancouver and its Region*. Vancouver: University of British Columbia Press.

———— and P. Murphy. 2001. 'Immigration in gateway cities: Sydney and Vancouver in comparative perspective', *Progress in Planning* 55: 119–94.

———— and H. Smith. 1997. *Is There an Immigrant 'Underclass' in Canadian Cities?* Vancouver: Vancouver Centre of Excellence, Research on Immigration and Integration in the Metropolis (Working Paper Series #97–08).

———— and ————. 2000. 'Relations between deprivation and immigrant groups in large Canadian cities,' *Urban Studies* 37: 37–62.

———— and J. Tutchener. 2001. 'Immigration, globalisation and house prices in Canada's gateway cities', *Housing Studies* 16: 199–223.

————, ————, and G. Cunningham. 2002. 'Immigration, polarization, or gentrification? Accounting for changing house prices and dwelling values in gateway cities', *Urban Geography* 23: 703–27.

Li, F., R.S. Wang, J. Paulussen, and X.S. Liu. 2005. 'Comprehensive concept planning of urban greening based on ecological principles: A case study in Beijing, China', *Landscape and Urban Planning* 72: 325–36.

Li, P.S. 1992. 'Ethnic enterprise in transition: Chinese business in Richmond, BC, 1980–1990', *Canadian Ethnic Studies* 24: 120–38.

————. 1994. 'Unneighbourly houses or unwelcome Chinese: The social construction of race in the battle over "Monster Homes" in Vancouver, Canada', *International Journal of Comparative Race and Ethnic Studies* 1: 14–33.

————. 2003. *Destination Canada: Immigration Debates and Issues*. Toronto: Oxford University Press.

Li, W. 1998. 'Anatomy of a new ethnic settlement: The Chinese ethnoburb in Los Angeles', *Urban Studies* 35: 479–501.

Lidstone, D. 2004. *Assessment of the Municipal Acts of the Provinces and Territories*. Ottawa: Federation of Canadian Municipalities.

Lightman, E., and A. Irving. 1991. 'Restructuring Canada's welfare state', *Journal of Social Policy* 20: 65–86.

Linteau, P.-A. 1985. *The Promoter's City: Building the Industrial Town of Maisonneuve 1883–1918*. Toronto: James Lorimer.

————. 1987. 'Canadian suburbanization in a North American context—Does the border make a difference?', *Journal of Urban History* 13: 252–74.

————. 1988. 'Urban mass transit', in Ball (1988).

Livey, J. 1995. 'Urbanizing York region', *Plan Canada* 35, 2: 25–8.

Lloyd, P., and P. Dicken. 1990. *Location in Space: Theoretical Perspectives in Economic Geography*. London: Harper and Row.

Lo, L., and C. Teixeira. 1998. 'If Quebec goes . . . The "exodus" impact?', *Professional Geographer* 50: 481–98.

———— and S. Wang. 1997. 'Settlement patterns of Toronto's Chinese immigrants: Convergence or divergence?', *Canadian Journal of Regional Science* 20: 49–72.

Lochead, C., and C. Scott. 2000. *The Dynamics of Women's Poverty in Canada*. Ottawa: Canadian Council on Social Development.

Logan, J.R., and H.L. Molotch. 1987. *Urban Fortunes: The Political Economy of Place*. Berkeley: University of California Press.

London, M. 2003. 'Heritage preservation and the Lachine Canal project', *Plan Canada* 43, 2: 33–5.

Lorch, B.J., and M.J. Smith. 1993. 'Pedestrian movement and the downtown enclosed shopping center', *Journal of the American Planning Association* 59: 75–86.

Lorimer, J. 1978. *The Developers*. Toronto: James Lorimer.

———— and M. Phillips. 1971. *Working People: Life in a Downtown City Neighbourhood*. Toronto: James Lewis and Samuel.

Lortie, A. 2004a. *The 60s: Montreal Thinks Big*. Montreal: Canadian Centre for Architecture.

————. 2004b. 'Montreal 1960: The singularities of a metropolitan archetype', in Lortie (2004a).

Low, S. 2003. *Behind the Gates: Life, Security and the Pursuit of Happiness in Fortress America*. New York: Routledge.

Lucas, R. 1988. 'On the mechanics of economic development', *Journal of Monetary Economics* 22: 38–59.

Lucas, S. 2002. 'From Levittown to Luther Village: Retirement communities and the changing suburban dream', *Canadian Journal of Urban Research* 11: 323–41.

Lucy, W.H., and D.L. Phillips. 2000. *Confronting Suburban Decline: Strategic Planning for Metropolitan Renewal.* Washington: Island Press.

Lynch, K. 1960, 1964. *The Image of the City.* Cambridge, Mass.: MIT Press.

———. 1981, 1984. *Good City Form.* Cambridge, Mass.: MIT Press.

Lyons, T. 1998. 'The Parkdale rebellion: Local politicians called it "re-balancing", residents called it "social cleansing"—and the fight was on', *Eye Magazine* 29 (Oct.)

McAvoy, P.V., M.B. Driscoll, and B.J. Gramling. 2004. 'Integrating the environment, the economy, and community health: A community health center's initiative to link health benefits to smart growth', *American Journal of Public Health* 94: 525–7.

McCann, E. 2002. 'The cultural politics of local economic development: Meaning-making, place-making and the urban policy process', *Geoforum* 33: 385–98.

McCann, L. 1975. *Neighbourhoods in Transition.* Edmonton: University of Alberta, Department of Geography (Occasional Papers No. 2).

———. 1980. 'Canadian resource towns: A heartland-hinterland perspective', in R.E. Preston and L. Russwurm, eds, *Essays on Canadian Process and Form II.* Waterloo, Ont.: University of Waterloo, Department of Geography.

———. 1994. 'Shock waves in the old economy: Maritime cities and the great transformation, c. 1867–1939', in G. DeBenedetti and R. Lamarche, eds, *Shock Waves: The Maritime Urban System in the New Economy.* Moncton, NB: Canadian Institute for Research on Regional Development.

———. 1996. 'Planning and building the corporate suburb of Mount Royal, 1910–1925', *Planning Perspectives* 11: 259–301.

———. 1998. 'Interpreting Canada's heartland and hinterland', in McCann and Gunn (1998).

———. 1999. 'Suburbs of desire: Shaping the suburban landscape of Canadian cities, c. 1900–1950', in R. Harris and P. Larkham, eds, *Changing Suburbs: Foundation, Form, and Function.* London: E & FN Spon.

——— and A. Gunn, eds. 1998. *Heartland and Hinterland: A Geography of Canada,* 3rd edn. Scarborough, Ont.: Prentice-Hall Canada.

——— and P.J. Smith 1991. 'Canada becomes urban: Cities and urbanization in historical perspective', in T. Bunting and P. Filion, eds, *Canadian Cities in Transition.* Toronto: Oxford University Press.

Macaulay Shiomi Howson Ltd. 2002. *Town of Markham Places of Worship Study: Background Issues and Options Report.* Markham, Ont.: Town of Markham.

McClain, J. 1993. 'Housing as a human service: Accommodating special needs', in Miron (1993a).

McCormick, K. 1994. 'Llamas in the landscape: Permaculture landscape for the Nyland co-housing community in Lafayette, Colorado', *Landscape Architecture* 84, 5: 54–6.

McHarg, I. 1969. *Design with Nature.* Garden City, NY: Doubleday/Natural History Press.

McIlwraith, T. 1983. 'The influence of street railways upon street engineering: The Toronto experience, 1860–1890', in R.A. Jarrell and A.E. Ross, eds, *Critical Issues in the History of Canadian Science, Technology, and Medicine.* Thornhill, Ont.: HSTC Publications.

McIntosh, T., ed. 2000. *Federalism, Democracy, and Labour Market Policy in Canada.* Montreal and Kingston: McGill-Queen's University Press.

McKay, R. 2002. 'Groupthink in municipal infrastructure planning: Decision-making behind the proposed Red Hill expressway', *Environments* 29: 2–9.

McKellar, J. 1993. 'Building technology and the production process', in Miron (1993a).

McKenzie, E. 1996. *Privatopia: Homeowner Associations and the Rise of Residential Private Government.* New Haven: Yale University Press.

Mackenzie, S. 1988. 'Building women, building cities: Toward gender sensitive theory in the environmental disciplines', in C. Andrew and B. Moore-Milroy, eds, *Life Spaces: Gender, Household, Employment.* Vancouver: University of British Columbia Press.

————— and D. Rose. 1983. 'Industrial change, the domestic economy and home life', in J. Anderson et al., eds, *Redundant Spaces in Cities and Regions: Studies in Industrial Decline and Social Change*. London: Academic Press.

————— and M. Truelove. 1993. 'Access to public services: The case of day care', in Bourne and Ley (1993).

————— and G. Wekerle. 1985. 'Reshaping the neighbourhood of the future as we age in place', *Canadian Woman Studies* 6: 69–72.

MacLachlan, I. 1996. 'Organizational restructuring of U.S.-based manufacturing subsidiaries and plant closure', in J.N.H. Britton, ed., *Canada and the Global Economy: The Geography of Structural and Technological Change*. Montreal and Kingston: McGill-Queen's University Press.

—————. 2001. *Kill and Chill: Restructuring Canada's Beef Commodity Chain*. Toronto: University of Toronto Press.

Maclean-Hunter. 2005. *Canadian Directory of Shopping Centres 2005*. Toronto: Maclean-Hunter.

McLemore, R., C. Aass, and P. Keilhofer. 1975. *The Changing Canadian Inner City*. Ottawa: Ministry of State for Urban Affairs.

McRae, J.D. 1981. *The Influence of Exurbanite Settlement in Rural Areas: A Review of the Canadian Literature*. Ottawa: Environment Canada Lands Directorate (Paper No. 23).

Main, T.J. 1996. 'Analyzing evidence for the structural theory of homelessness', *Journal of Urban Affairs* 18: 449–57.

Majury, N. 1994. 'Signs of the times: Kerrisdale, a neighbourhood in transition', *Canadian Geographer* 38: 265–70.

Malmberg, A., and P. Maskell. 2002. 'The elusive concept of localization economies', *Environment and Planning A* 34: 429–49.

Manitoba. n.d. *Welcome to Manitoba's Capital Region*. At: <www.gov.mb.ca/ia/capreg/index.html>. Accessed 5 May 2005.

—————. 1976. *Committee of Review, City of Winnipeg Act, Report and Recommendations*. Winnipeg: Government of Manitoba.

Mann, W. 1970. 'The Lower Ward', in Mann, ed., *The Underside of Toronto*. Toronto: McClelland & Stewart.

Manuel, P.M. 2003. 'Cultural perceptions of small urban wetlands: Cases from the Halifax Regional Municipality, Nova Scotia, Canada', *Wetlands* 23: 921–40.

Marchak, P. 1995. *Logging the Globe*. Montreal and Kingston: McGill-Queen's University Press.

Marcuse, P., and R. van Kempen, eds. 2000. *Globalizing Cities: A New Spatial Order?* Oxford: Blackwell.

Markham. n.d. *Markham Centre*. Markham, Ont.: City of Markham. Available at: <www.markham.ca/markham/channels/markhamcentre/mc_home.htm>; accessed July 2005.

Markusen, A.R. 1984. 'Class and urban social expenditure: A Marxist theory of metropolitan government', in W.K. Tabb and L. Sawers, eds, *Marxism and the Metropolis*. New York: Oxford University Press.

Marsden, T., J. Murdoch, P. Lowe, R. Munton, and A. Flynn. 1993. *Constructing the Countryside*. Boulder, Colo.: Westview Press.

Marsh, W. 1998. *Landscape Planning: Environmental Applications*. New York: Wiley.

Martin, M.A. 1995. *Urban Policing in Canada: Anatomy of an Aging Craft*. Toronto: University of Toronto Press.

Martin, M.D. 2001. 'The landscapes of Winnipeg's Wildwood Park', *Urban History Review* 30, 1: 22–39.

Martin-Matthews, A. 2001. *The Ties That Bind Aging Families*. Ottawa: Vanier Institute of the Family (Contemporary Family Trends Series). Available at: <www.vifamily.ca/library/cft/aging.html>; accessed 12 May 2005.

Marx, K. 1962 [1887]. *Capital: A Critique of Political Economy*, vol. 3. Moscow: Foreign Languages Publication House, Reprint of the English translation of *Das Kapital* by Friedrich Engels.

Masi, A. 1991. 'Structural adjustment and technological change in the Canadian steel industry, 1970–1986', in Drache and Gertler (1991).

Massey, D., and R. Meegan. 1978. 'Industrial restructuring versus the cities', *Urban Studies* 15: 273–88.

Masson, J., and J.D. Anderson, eds. 1972. *Emerging Party Politics in Urban Canada*. Toronto: McClelland & Stewart.

Matthew, M.R. 1992. 'Office buildings in office parks and suburban downtowns', *Canadian Journal of Urban Research* 1: 39–57.

———. 1993. 'Towards a general theory of suburban office morphology in North America', *Progress in Human Geography* 17: 471–89.

———. 2001. 'Detroit suburban office centres', *Canadian Journal of Urban Research* 10: 47–68.

Matthews, R. 1976. *'There's No Better Place Than Here': Social Change in Three Newfoundland Communities.* Toronto: Peter Martin Associates.

Mayer, T., W.J. Snodgrass, and D. Morin. 1999. 'Spatial characterization of the occurrence of road salts and their environmental concentrations as chlorides in Canadian surface waters and benthic sediments', *Water Quality Research Journal of Canada* 34: 545–74.

Mazy, M.E., and D.R. Lee. 1983. *Her Space Her Place.* Washington: Association of American Geographers.

Medlock, J.M., K.R. Snow, and S. Leach. 2005. 'Potential transmission of West Nile virus in the British Isles: An ecological review of candidate mosquito bridge vectors', *Medical and Veterinary Entomology* 19: 2–21.

Meligrana, J., and A. Skaburskis. 2005. 'Extent, location and profiles of continuing gentrification in Canadian metropolitan areas, 1981–2001' *Urban Studies* 42: 1569–92.

Mensah, J. 1994. 'Gender, spatial constraints, and the employment activities of low-income people in a local labour market', *Canadian Journal of Urban Research* 3: 113–33.

———. 2002. *Black Canadians: History, Experiences, Social Conditions.* Halifax: Fernwood.

Mercer, J. 1995. 'Canadian cities and their immigrants: New realities', *Annals, American Academy of Political and Social Science* 538: 169–84.

——— and K. England. 2000. 'Canadian cities in continental context: Global and continental perspectives on Canadian urban development', in Bunting and Filion (2000).

——— and D. Phillips. 1981. 'Attitudes of homeowners and the decision to rehabilitate property', *Urban Geography* 2: 216–36.

Merriman, J.M. 1991. *The Margins of City Life: Explorations on the French Urban Frontier, 1815–1851.* New York: Oxford University Press.

Metropolitan Denver Homeless Initiative (MDHI). 2004. *Profile of Homelessness in Metropolitan Denver,*

Colorado: 2004 Homelessness Point-In-Time Study. Denver: MDHI.

Metro Toronto. 1980. *Official Plan for the Urban Structure.* Toronto: Municipality of Metropolitan Toronto.

Meyer, M.D., and E.J. Miller. 2001. *Urban Transportation Planning: A Decision-Oriented Approach*, 2nd edn. New York: McGraw-Hill.

Meyer, J.R., J.F. Kain, and M. Wohl. 1965. *The Urban Transportation Problem.* Cambridge, Mass.: Harvard University Press.

Michelson, W. 1977. *Environmental Choice: Human Behavior and Residential Satisfaction.* New York: Oxford University Press.

———. 1984. *From Sun to Sun: Daily Obligations and Community Structure in the Lives of Employed Mothers and Their Families.* Totowa, NJ: Rowman and Allanheld.

Milan, A., and A. Peters. 2003. 'Couples living apart', *Canadian Social Trends* 69: 2–6 (Statistics Canada, Cat. no. 11–008).

Milgrom, R. 2003. 'Sustaining Diversity: Participatory Design and the Production of Urban Space', Ph.D. dissertation, York University.

Miller, D. 1987. *Material Culture and Mass Consumption.* Oxford: Blackwell.

Miller, E.J. 2003a. 'Microsimulation', in K.G. Goulias, ed., *Transportation Systems Planning Methods and Applications.* Boca Raton, Fla: CRC Press.

———. 2003b. 'Land Use–Transportation Modelling', in K.G. Goulias, ed., *Transportation Systems Planning Methods and Applications.* Boca Raton, Fla: CRC Press.

——— and M.J. Roorda. 2003. 'A prototype model of household activity/travel scheduling', *Journal of Transportation Research Record* 1831: 114–21.

——— and A. Shalaby. 2003. 'Evolution of personal travel in the Toronto area and policy implication', *Journal of Urban Planning and Development* 129: 1–26.

Miller, M. 1978. *Straight Lines in Curved Space: Colonization Roads in Eastern Ontario.* Toronto: University of Toronto Press.

Miller, M. 1992. *Raymond Unwin: Garden Cities and Town Planning.* Leicester: Leicester University Press.

Mills, E.S. 1979. *Studies in the Structure of the Urban Economy.* Baltimore: Johns Hopkins University Press.

Millward, H. 1988. 'Classification of residential upgrading processes: A Halifax case study', in Bunting and Filion (1988).

———. 1996. 'Greater Halifax: Public policy issues in the post-1960 period', *Canadian Journal of Urban Research* 5: 1–17.

———. 2000. 'The spread of commuter development in the eastern shore zone of Halifax, Nova Scotia, 1920–1988', *Urban History Review* 29: 21–32.

———. 2002. 'Peri-urban residential development in the Halifax Region 1960–2000: Magnets, constraints, and planning policies', *Canadian Geographer* 46: 33–47.

———. 2005. 'Urban containment strategies: A case-study appraisal of plans and policies in Japanese, British, and Canadian cities', *Land Use Policy* (forthcoming).

——— and T. Bunting. 1999. 'A tale of two cities 2: Comparative analysis of retailing in downtown Halifax and Kitchener', *Canadian Journal of Urban Research* 8: 1–21.

——— and D. Davis. 1986. 'Housing renovation in Halifax: Gentrification or incumbent upgrading', *Plan Canada* 26: 148–55.

Miranne, K.B., and A.H. Young, eds. 2000. *Gendering the City: Women, Boundaries, and Visions of Urban Life.* Lanham, Md: Rowman & Littlefield.

Miron, J. 1988. *Housing in Postwar Canada: Demographic Change, Household Formation, and Housing Demand.* Montreal and Kingston: McGill-Queen's University Press.

———, ed. 1993a. *House, Home, and Community: Progress in Housing Canadians, 1945–1986.* Montreal and Kingston: McGill-Queen's University Press.

———. 1993b. 'Demographic and economic factors in housing demand', in Miron (1993a).

———. 1993c. 'Demographic change, household formation and housing demand: Canada's postwar experience', in Miron (1993a).

Mississauga. 1994. *Urban Design Vision: Mississauga City Centre.* Mississauga, Ont.: City of Mississauga.

———. 2000. *The Review of Parking Standards for Multi-use Places of Religious Assembly and Worship Areas in Schools.* Mississauga, Ont.: City of Mississauga.

———. 2002. *Response to Comments—the Review of Parking Standards for Multi-use Places of Religious Assembly—Supplementary Report.* Mississauga, Ont.: City of Mississauga.

———. 2003. *Mississauga Plan (Official Plan).* Mississauga, Ont. Available at: <www.mississauga.ca/portal/residents/mississaugaplan>; accessed July 2002.

Mitchell, B. 2005. 'Integrated water resource management, institutional arrangements, and land-use planning', *Environment and Planning A* 37: 1335–52.

Mitchell, B., and E.M. Gee. 1996. 'Young adults returning home: Implications for social policy', in B. Galaway and J. Hudson, eds, *Youth in Transition: Perspectives on Research and Policy.* Toronto: Thompson.

Mitchell, C.J.A. 1992. 'Economic impact of the arts: Theatre festivals in small Ontario communities', *Journal of Cultural Economics* 17: 55–65.

———. 1998. 'Entrepreneurialism, commodification and creative destruction: A model of post-modern community development', *Journal of Rural Studies* 14: 273–86.

———. 2004. 'Making Sense of Counter-urbanization', *Journal of Rural Studies* 20: 15–34.

———, G. Atkinson, and A. Clark. 2001. 'The creative destruction of Niagara-on-the-Lake', *Canadian Geographer* 42: 285–99.

———, T.E. Bunting, and M. Picionni. 2004. 'Visual artists: Counterurbanites at work in the Canadian countryside?', *Canadian Geographer* 48: 152–66.

——— and C. Coghill. 2000. 'Elora, Ontario, the creation of a Heritage Landscape', *Great Lakes Geographer* 7: 88–105.

Mitchell, K. 1997. 'Conflicting geographies of democracy and the public sphere in Vancouver, BC', *Transactions of the Institute of British Geographers* 22: 162–79.

———. 2004. *Crossing the Neoliberal Line: Pacific Rim Migration and the Metropolis.* Philadelphia: Temple University Press.

Mok, D. 2005a. 'The wealth of cities: How risky is our suburbanized residential built environment', *Urban Geography* (forthcoming).

———. 2005b. 'Young households' life stages and housing decisions: An insider perspective', *Environment and Planning A* (forthcoming).

———, B. Wellman, and R. Basu. 2005. 'Did distance matter: A pre-internet analysis', *Social Network* (forthcoming).

Moktarian, P.L. 2003. 'Telecommunications and travel: The case for complementarity', *Journal of Industrial Ecology* 6: 43–57.

——— and I. Salomon. 1997. 'Emerging travel patterns: Do telecommunications make a difference', conference resource paper, Eighth Meeting of the International Association for Travel Behaviour Research, Austin, Texas, 21–5 Sept.

Mongeau, J. 1999. 'The living conditions of families: Income and labour force activity', in Y. Péron, H. Desrosiers, H. Juby, É. Lapierre-Adamcyk, C. Le Bourdais, N. Marcil-Gratton, and Mongeau, *Canadian Families at the Approach of the Year 2000* (Census Monograph Series). Ottawa: Statistics Canada (Cat. no. 96–321–MPE no. 4), 235–71.

Monk, J., and C. Katz. 1993. 'When in the world are women?' in Katz and Monk, eds, *Full Circles: Geographies of Women over the Life Course*. London: Routledge.

Monterusso, M.A., D.B. Rowe, and C.L. Rugh. 2005. 'Establishment and persistence of *Sedum* spp. and native taxa for green roof applications', *Hortscience* 40: 391–6.

Montreal. n.d. 'The underground city in numbers'. Available at: <www2.ville.montreal.qc.ca/urb_demo/mtlbref/engl/underground.htm>; accessed Mar. 2005.

———. 2004. *Plan d' urbanisme*. Available at: <www2.ville.montreal.qc.ca/plan-urbanisme/>; accessed July 2005.

Montreal Metropolitan Community (MMC). 2005. *Cap sur la monde (Schéma d'aménagement)*. Montréal: Communauté métropolitaine de Montréal.

Moore, E.G., and M.W. Rosenberg. 2001. 'Canada's elderly population: The challenges of diversity', *Canadian Geographer* 45, 1: 145–50.

——— and ———, with D. McGuinness. 1997. *Growing Old in Canada: Demographic and Geographic Perspectives*. Ottawa and Toronto: Statistics Canada and ITP Nelson.

Moore, E., and A. Skaburskis. 2004. 'Canada's increasing housing affordability burdens', *Housing Studies* 19: 395–413.

Moore, P. 1979. 'Zoning and planning: The Toronto experience', in A. Artibise and G. Stelter, eds, *The Usable Urban Past*. Toronto: Macmillan of Canada.

——— and P. Smith. 1993. 'Cities as a social responsibility: Planning and urban form', in Bourne and Ley (1993).

Moore, P.S. 2004. 'Movie palaces on Canadian downtown main streets: Montreal, Toronto, and Vancouver', *Urban History Review* 32, 2: 3–20.

Moore Milroy, B., and M. Wallace. 2002. *Ethnoracial Diversity and Planning Practices in the Greater Toronto Area*. Toronto: Centre of Excellence for Research on Immigration and Settlement.

Morissette, R., and A. Johnson. 2004. *Earnings of Couples with High and Low Levels of Education, 1980–2000*. Ottawa: Statistics Canada, Analytical Studies Branch Research Paper Series, Cat. no.11F0019MIE2004230. Available at: <www.statcan.ca/english/research/11-621-MIE/11-621-MIE2004017.pdf>.

——— and G. Picot. 2005. *Low-paid Work and Economically Vulnerable Families over the Last Two Decades*. Ottawa: Statistics Canada, Business and Labour Market Analysis Division, Cat. no. 11F0019 No. 248. Available at: <www.statcan.ca/english/research/11F0019MIE/11F0019MIE2005248.pdf>.

Morris, A.E.J. 1972. *History of Urban Form: Prehistory to the Renaissance*. London: George Goodwin.

Morrow-Jones, H.A., and W. van Vliet. 1989. 'Homelessness in Colorado', in J.A. Momeni, ed., *Homelessness in the United States, Volume 1: State Surveys*. New York: Greenwood Press.

Mortberg, U.M. 2001. 'Resident bird species in urban forest remnants: Landscape and habitat perspectives', *Landscape Ecology* 16: 193–203.

Moscovitch, A., and G. Drover. 1987. 'Social expenditures and the welfare state: The Canadian experience in historical perspective', in Moscovitch and J. Albert, eds, *The Benevolent State: The Growth of Welfare in Canada*. Toronto: Garamond.

Moss, B. 2003. *A Walking Tour of the Downtown Eastside: Footprints Community Art Project*. Vancouver: Carnegie Community Centre Association and Western Economic Diversification Canada Program.

Muise, D., et al. 1993. *Urban and Community Development in Atlantic Canada, 1867–1991*. Ottawa: Canadian Museum of Civilization, Mercury Series Paper No. 44.

Muller, P.O. 1976. *The Outer City: Geographical Consequences of the Urbanization of the Suburbs*. Washington: Association of American Geographers, Resource Paper No. 75–2.

————. 1981. *Contemporary Suburban America*. Englewood Cliffs, NJ: Prentice-Hall.

Mumford, L. 1938. *The Culture of Cities*. New York: Harcourt, Brace and Company.

————. 1961. *The City in History: Its Origins, Its Transformations, Its Prospects*. New York: Harcourt, Brace and World.

————. 1968. *The Urban Prospect*. New York: Harcourt, Brace and World.

Murdie, R.A. 1969. *Factorial Ecology of Metropolitan Toronto, 1951–1961*. Chicago: University of Chicago (Research Paper No. 116).

————. 1991. 'Local strategies in resale home financing in the Toronto housing market', *Urban Studies* 28: 465–83.

————. 1994a. 'Social polarisation and public housing in Canada: A case study of the Metropolitan Toronto Housing Authority', in Frisken (1994a).

————. 1994b. 'Blacks in near-ghettoes? Black visible minority population in Metropolitan Toronto Housing Authority public housing units', *Housing Studies* 9: 435–58.

————. 1996. 'Economic restructuring and social polarization in Toronto', in J. O'Loughlin and J. Friedrichs, eds, *Social Polarization in Post-Industrial Metropolises*. Berlin and New York: Walter de Gruyter.

————. 1998. 'The welfare state, economic restructuring and immigrant flows: Impacts on sociospatial segregation in Greater Toronto', in S. Musterd and W. Ostendorf, eds, *Urban Segregation and the Welfare State: Inequality and Exclusion in Western Cities*. London: Routledge.

———— and C. Teixeira. 2003. 'Towards a comfortable neighbourhood and appropriate housing: Immigrant experiences in Toronto', in Anisef and Lanphier (2003).

Murphy, P. 1973. 'Apartment location: The balance between developer and community', in Forward (1973a).

Murphy, R.E. 1972. *The Central Business District*. Chicago: Aldine-Atherton.

———— and J.E. Vance. 1954a. 'Delimiting the CBD', *Economic Geography* 30: 189–222.

———— and ————. 1954b. 'A comparative study of nine central business districts', *Economic Geography* 30: 301–36.

————, ————, and B.J. Epstein. 1955. 'Internal structure of the CBD', *Economic Geography* 31: 21–46.

Murphy, S.D. 2004. 'A more sustainable urban environment: Beyond idealism and cynicism', *Ontario Planning Journal* 19, 1: 28–9.

———— and L.R.G. Martin. 2001. 'Urban ecology in Ontario, Canada: Moving beyond the limits of city and ideology', *Environments* 29: 67–83.

Murray, A. 1990. 'Homelessness: The people', in G. Fallis and A. Murray, eds, *Housing the Homeless and Poor: New Partnerships among the Private, Public and Third Sectors*. Toronto: University of Toronto Press.

Muth, R.F. 1969. *Cities and Housing*. Chicago: University of Chicago Press.

————. 1975. *Urban Economic Problems*. New York: Harper and Row.

Mwarigha, M.S. 2002. *Towards a Framework for Local Responsibility: Taking Action to End the Current Limbo in Immigrant Settlement—Toronto*. Toronto: Maytree Foundation.

Myles, J., and F. Hou. 2004. 'Changing colours: Spatial assimilation and new racial minority immigrants', *Canadian Journal of Sociology* 29: 29–59.

———— and P. Pierson. 1997. 'Friedman's revenge: The reform of "liberal" welfare states in Canada and the United States', *Politics and Society* 25: 443–72.

Nader, G.A. 1976. *Cities of Canada, Volume Two: Profiles of Fifteen Metropolitan Centres*. Toronto: Macmillan of Canada.

National Broadband Task Force. 2001. *Networking the Nation for Broadband Access*. Ottawa: Industry Canada.

National Housing and Homeless Network (NHHN). 2001. *State of the Crisis: A Report on Housing and Homelessness in Canada*. Toronto: NHHN and the Toronto Disaster Relief Committee. At: <www.tdrc.net/Report-01-11-NHHN.htm>. Accessed May 2005.

National Round Table on the Environment and the Economy (NRTEE). 1997. *The Road to Sustainable Transportation in Canada*. Ottawa: NRTEE.

———. 1998. *Greening Canada's Brownfield Sites*. Ottawa: NRTEE.

———. 2001. *The Sustainable Cities Initiative: Putting the City at the Centre of Public-Private Infrastructure Investment*. Ottawa: NRTEE.

———. 2003. *The State of the Debate on the Environment and the Economy. Environmental Quality in Canadian Cities: The Federal Role*. Ottawa: NRTEE. At: <www.nrtee-trnee.ca>.

Naveh, Z. 2005. 'Epilogue: Toward a transdisciplinary science of ecological and cultural landscape restoration', *Restoration Ecology* 13: 228–34.

Neef, D., ed. 1998. *The Knowledge Economy*. Boston: Butterworth-Heinemenn.

Nelson, A., and K. Dueker. 1994. 'The new burbs: The exurbs and their implications for planning policy', *Journal of the American Planning Association* 45: 459–71.

———, J. Duncan, C. Mullen, and K. Bishop. 1995. *Growth Management Principles and Practices*. Chicago: APA Planners Press.

Nelson, K. 1986. 'Labor demand, labor supply and the suburbanization of low wage office work', in A. Scott and M. Storper, eds, *Production, Work and Territory*. Winchester, Mass.: Allen and Unwin.

Neutze, M. 1997. *Funding Urban Services: Options for Physical Infrastructure*. St Leonards, Australia: Allen & Unwin.

Newling, B.E. 1969. 'The spatial variation of urban population densities', *Geographical Review* 59: 242–52.

Niachou, A., K. Papakonstantinou, M. Santamouris, A. Tsangrassoulis, and G. Mihalakakou. 2001. 'Analysis of the green roof thermal properties and investigation of its energy performance', *Energy and Buildings* 33: 719–29.

Nicholson, T.G., and M.H. Yeates. 1969. 'The ecological and spatial structure of the socio-economic characteristics of Winnipeg, 1961', *Canadian Review of Sociology and Anthropology* 6: 162–78.

Niemala, J. 1999. 'Ecology and urban planning', *Biodiversity and Conservation* 8: 119–31.

Noland, R.B. 2000. 'Relationship between highway capacity and induced vehicle travel', *Transportation Research Part A, Policy and Practice* 35: 47–72.

Norcliffe, G. 2001. 'Canada in a global economy', *Canadian Geographer* 45: 14–30.

North, R.N., and W.G. Hardwick. 1992. 'Vancouver since the Second World War: An economic geography', in G. Wynn and T. Oke, eds, *Vancouver and Its Region*. Vancouver: University of British Columbia Press.

Northwest Environment Watch. 2002. *Sprawl and Smart Growth in Greater Vancouver: A Comparison of Vancouver, British Columbia, with Seattle, Washington*. Seattle and Vancouver: Northwest Environment Watch/Smart Growth BC.

Nova Scotia, Department of Development. 1973. *Halifax–Dartmouth Metro Area: Natural Land Capability*. Halifax: Government of Nova Scotia, Department of Development.

Nowlan, D., and N. Nowlan. 1970. *The Bad Trip: The Untold Story of Spadina Highway*. Toronto: Anansi Press.

——— and G. Steuart. 1991. 'Downtown population growth and commuting trips: Recent experience in Toronto', *Journal of the American Planning Association* 57: 165–82.

Office for the Greater Toronto Area (OGTA). n.d. *Urban Form: Bringing the Vision into Focus*. Toronto: OGTA.

O'Flaherty, B. 2003. 'Wrong person and wrong place: For homelessness, the conjunction is what matters', *Journal of Housing Economics* 13: 1–15.

Ogden, P.E., and R. Hall. 2004. 'The second demographic transition, new household forms and the urban population of France during the 1990s', *Transactions of the Institute of British Geographers* new series 29: 88–105.

Ohmae, K. 1990. *The Borderless World: Power and Strategy in the Interlinked Economy*. New York: Harper Business.

Olds, K. 1995. 'Globalization and the production of new urban spaces: Pacific Rim mega-projects in the late 20th century', *Environment and Planning A* 27: 1713–43.

———. 1998. 'Globalization and urban change: Tales from Vancouver via Hong Kong', *Urban Geography* 19: 360–85.

———. 2001. *Globalization and Urban Change: Capital, Culture, and Pacific Rim Mega-projects.* Oxford: Oxford University Press.

Olsen, D.J. 1976. *The Growth of Victorian London.* London: Batsford.

Olson, S.H., and A.L. Kobayashi. 1993. 'The emerging ethnocultural mosaic', in Bourne and Ley (1993)

Olson, S., P. Thornton, and Q. Thach. 1987. *A Geography of Little Children in Nineteenth-Century Montreal.* Montreal: McGill University, Department of Geography (Shared Spaces No. 10).

Omidvar, R., and T. Richmond. 2003. *Immigrant Settlement and Social Inclusion in Canada.* Toronto: Laidlaw Foundation.

Ontario. 1996. *Greater Toronto: Report of the GTA Task Force.* Toronto: Publications Ontario.

———, Municipal Affairs and Housing. 2002. *Oak Ridges Moraine Conservation Plan.* Toronto: Government of Ontario, Ministry of Municipal Affairs and Housing. At: <www.mah.gov.on.ca/userfiles/HTML/nts_1_6846_1.html>. Accessed 5 May 2005.

———. 2004a. *Toward a Golden Horseshoe Greenbelt.* Toronto: Ministry of Municipal Affairs and Housing.

———. 2004b. *Places to Grow: A Growth Plan for the Greater Golden Horseshoe.* Toronto: Ministry of Public Infrastructure Renewal and Ministry of Municipal Affairs and Housing.

———. 2005a. Bill 136, An Act Respecting the Establishment of Growth Plan Areas and Growth Plans (royal assent 13 June 2005).

———. 2005b. *Places to Grow: Draft Growth Plan for the Greater Golden Horseshoe.* Toronto: Public Infrastructure Renewal. At: <www.pir.gov.on.ca/userfiles/HTML/cma_4_40948_1.html>. Accessed 13 Apr. 2005.

———, Municipal Affairs. 2005c. *Greenbelt Plan 2005.* Toronto: Government of Ontario, Ministry of Municipal Affairs. At: <www.mah.gov.on.ca/userfiles/HTML/nts_1_22087_1.html>. Accessed 13 Apr. 2005.

———, Ministry of Public Infrastructure Renewal. 2005d. *Places to Grow.* Toronto: Ontario Smart Growth Secretariat.

Ontario Municipal Board. 2001. *Malin v. Town of Richmond Hill Committee of Adjustment.* Toronto: Ontario Municipal Board (Report No. PL010210).

———. 2002. *Smith v. City of Toronto Committee of Adjustment.* Toronto: Ontario Municipal Board (Report No. PL020652).

Onyschuk, B.S., M.G. Kovacevic, and P. Nikolakakos. 2001. *Smart Growth in North America: New Ways to Create Liveable Communities.* Toronto: Canadian Urban Institute.

Orfield, M. 2002. *American Metropolitics.* Washington: Brookings Institution Press.

Ornstein, M. 2002. *Ethno-racial Inequality in the City of Toronto: An Analysis of the 1996 Census.* Toronto: City of Toronto and Centre of Excellence for Research on Immigration and Settlement.

Ortuzar, J.D., and L.G. Willumsen. 2001. *Modelling Transport,* 3rd edn. New York: John Wiley and Sons.

Osborne, D., and T. Gaebler. 1992. *Reinventing Government: How the Entrepreneurial Spirit is Transforming the Public Sector.* New York: Addison-Wesley.

O'Toole, T.P., A. Conde-Martel, J.L. Gibbon, B.H. Hanusa, P.J. Freyder, and M.J. Fine. 2004. 'Substance-abusing urban homeless in the late 1990s: How do they differ from non-substance abusing homeless persons?', *Journal of Urban Health, Bulletin of the New York Academy of Medicine* 81: 606–17.

Ottawa, Planning, Environment, Infrastructure and Policy Branch. 2003. *A Window on Ottawa 20/20: Ottawa's Growth Management Strategy.* Ottawa: City of Ottawa.

Owen, D. 2004. 'Green Manhattan: Why New York is the greenest city in the U.S.', *New Yorker* (18 Oct. 2004): 111–23.

Owen, W. 1966. *The Metropolitan Transportation Problem.* Washington: Brookings Institution.

———. 1972. *The Accessible City.* Washington: Brookings Institution.

Owusu, T. 1999. 'Residential patterns and housing choices of new immigrants in Canada: The case of the Ghanaians in Toronto', *Housing Studies* 14: 77–97.

———. 2000. 'The role of Ghanaian immigrant associations in Toronto, Canada', *International Migration Review* 34: 1155–81.

Pacey, M.A. 2002. *Living Alone and Living with Children: The Living Arrangements of Canadian and Chinese-Canadian Seniors* (Social and Economic Dimensions of an Aging Population, Research Paper No. 74). Hamilton, Ont.: McMaster University. Available at: <http://socserv.socsci.mcmaster.ca/sedap/p/sedap74.pdf>.

Park, R. 1969 [1925]. 'The city: Suggestions for the investigation of human behavior in the urban environment', in R. Park and E.W. Burgess, eds, *The City*. Chicago: University of Chicago Press.

Parthasarathi, P., D.M. Levinson, and R. Karamalaputi. 2003. 'Induced demand: A microscopic perspective', *Urban Studies* 40: 1335–51.

Pas, E.I. 1990. 'Is travel demand analysis and modelling in the doldrums?', in P. Jones, ed., *Developments in Dynamic and Activity-Based Approaches to Travel Analysis*. Aldershot, UK: Gower.

Paterson, R. 1984. 'The development of an interwar suburb: Kingsway Park, Etobicoke', *Urban History Review* 13: 225–35.

———. 1991. 'Housing finance in early 20th century suburban Toronto', *Urban History Review* 20: 63–71.

Patterson, J. 1993. 'Housing and community development policies', in Miron (1993a).

Paul, D.E. 2004. 'World cities as hegemonic projects: The politics of global imagineering in Montreal', *Political Geography* 23: 571–96.

Paul, T. 2000. *Innovations in Practice: Keys to Alternative Development Standards*. Ottawa: CMHC.

Paumier, C.B. 1988. *Designing Successful Downtowns*. Washington: Urban Land Institute.

Pearson, N. 1961. 'Conurbation Canada', *Canadian Geographer* 5: 10–17.

Peck, J. 2002. *Workfare States*. London: Guilford Press.

Peel, Region of. 2002. *Second Annual Report Card on Housing and Homelessness Initiatives: A Strategy for Breaking the Cycles of Homelessness* (Appendix I and II, Region of Peel Emergency Shelters and New Shelter Initiatives Annual Report). Brampton: Region of Peel.

Peiser, R.B. 1989. 'Density and urban sprawl', *Land Economics* 65: 194–204.

Perkins, R. 1993. 'What's happening in the suburbs of Greater Vancouver?', *City Magazine* 14, 3: 19–24.

Perks, W.T., and W. Jamieson. 1991. 'Planning and development in Canadian cities', in Bunting and Filion (1991).

Perl, A., and J. Pucher. 1995. 'Transit in trouble? The policy challenge posed by Canada's changing urban mobility', *Canadian Public Policy* 21: 261–83.

Péron, Y. 1999. 'Households and families', in Péron, H. Desrosiers, H. Juby, É. Lapierre-Adamcyk, C. Le Bourdais, N. Marcil-Gratton, and J. Mongeau. 1999. *Canadian Families at the Approach of the Year 2000*. (Census Monograph Series). Ottawa: Statistics Canada (Cat. no. 96–321–MPE no. 4), 1–45.

Perras, F., and J. Huyder. 2003. *Interagency Shelter Use Count for 2002: A Collaboration with the Interagency Committee*. Calgary: Mustard Seed Street Ministry and City of Calgary. At: <www.theseed.ca/about/researchreports/interagencyShelterCount2002.pdf>.

Perraton, J. 2001. 'The global economy: Myths and realities', *Cambridge Journal of Economics* 25: 669–84.

Perry, C. 1929. 'The neighborhood unit', in *Neighborhood and Community Planning*. New York: Regional Survey of New York and Environs, vol. VII.

Perry, D. 1995. 'Building the public city', in Perry, ed., *Building the Public City: The Politics, Governance, Finance of Public Infrastructure*. London: Sage.

Peters, E. 1996. 'Aboriginal people in urban areas', in D. Long and O.P. Dickason, eds, *Visions of the Heart: Canadian Aboriginal Issues*. Toronto: Harcourt Brace.

———. 2002. '"Our city Indians": Negotiating the meaning of First Nations urbanization in Canada, 1945–1975', *Journal of Historical Geography* 30: 75–92.

——— and R. Walker. 2005. 'Indigeneity and marginalization: Planning for and with urban aboriginal communities in Canada', *Progress in Planning* 63: 327–404.

Peterson, P.E. 1981. *City Limits*. Chicago: University of Chicago Press.

Phipps, A. 1983. 'Housing renovation by recent movers into the core neighbourhoods of Saskatoon', *Canadian Geographer* 27: 240–62.

———— and J.J. Cimer. 1994. 'Late-1980s voluntary residential mobility in Windsor and Niagara Falls, Ontario', *Canadian Journal of Urban Research* 3: 148–65.

Pickett, S.T.A., M.L. Cadenasso, and J.M. Grove. 2004. 'Resilient cities: Meaning, models, and metaphor for integrating the ecological, socio-economic, and planning realms', *Landscape and Urban Planning* 69: 369–84.

————, ————, ————, C.H. Nilon, R.V. Pouyat, W.C. Zipperer, and R. Costanza. 2001. 'Urban ecological systems: Linking terrestrial ecological, physical, and socioeconomic components of metropolitan areas', *Annual Review of Ecology and Systematics* 32: 127–57.

Pickvance, C. 2003. 'From urban social movements to urban movements', *International Journal of Urban and Regional Research* 27: 102–9.

Pierce, J.T. 1981a. 'The B.C. Agricultural Land Commission: A review and evaluation', *Plan Canada* 21: 48–56.

————. 1981b. 'Conversion of rural land to urban: A Canadian profile', *Professional Geographer* 21: 163–73.

Pigou, A.C. 1948. *The Economics of Welfare*, 4th edn. London: Macmillan.

Pim, L., and J. Ornoy. 1996. *A Smart Growth Future for Ontario*. Toronto: Federation of Ontario Naturalists. At: <www.ontarionature.org/enviroandcons/issues/sprawl.html>. Accessed 8 Mar. 2005.

Platt, R.H. 2004. 'Regreening the metropolis: Pathways to more ecological cities', *Urban Biosphere and Society: Partnership of Cities* 1023: 49–61.

Plunkett, T.J., and G.E. Betts. 1978. *The Management of Canadian Urban Government*. Kingston: Queen's University Institute of Local Government.

Poapst, J.V. 1993. 'Financing of postwar housing', in Miron (1993a).

Pocock, D., and R. Hudson. 1978. *Images of the Urban Environment*. London: Macmillan.

Polèse, M., and R. Shearmur. 2002. *The Periphery in the Knowledge Economy: The Spatial Dynamics of the Canadian Economy and the Future of Non-Metropolitan Regions in Quebec and the Atlantic Provinces*. Montreal and Moncton: INRS-Urbanisation, Culture et Société, and Canadian Institute for Research on Regional Development.

Pomeroy, S.P. 2004. 'Toward a comprehensive affordable housing strategy for Canada', in Hulchanski and Shapcott (2004).

Pomfret, R. 1981. *The Economic Development of Canada*. Agincourt, Ont.: Methuen.

Popenoe, D. 1977. *The Suburban Environment*. Chicago: University of Chicago Press.

Porat, M. 1977. *The Information Economy: Definition and Measurement*. Office of Telecommunications Special Publication 77–12(1). Washington: US Department of Commerce.

Porteous, D., and S. Smith. 2001. *Domicide: The Global Destruction of Home*. Montreal and Kingston: McGill-Queen's University Press.

Porter, C. 2005. 'To eat, homeless steal, trade sex: Desperation fuels unorthodox ways of finding food: study', *Toronto Star*, 27 Apr., B5.

Porter, J. 1965. *The Vertical Mosaic*. Toronto: University of Toronto Press.

Poulton, M. 1995. 'Affordable homes at an affordable [social] price', in G. Fallis et al., eds, *Home Remedies: Rethinking Canadian Housing Policy*. Toronto: C.D. Howe Institute.

Pratt, G., in collaboration with the Philippine Women Centre. 1999. 'Is this really Canada? Domestic workers' experiences in Vancouver, B.C.', in J. Momsen, ed., *Gender, Migration and Domestic Service*. London: Routledge.

————. 2000. 'Suburb', in R.J. Johnston, D. Gregory, Pratt, and M. Watts, eds, *Dictionary of Human Geography*, 4th edn. Oxford: Blackwell.

Pratt, L., and J. Richards. 1979. *Prairie Capitalism: Power and Influence in the New West*. Toronto: McClelland & Stewart.

Preston, R.E., and D.W. Griffin. 1966. 'A restatement of the zone of transition concept', *Annals, Association of American Geographers* 56: 339–50.

Preston, V., D. Rose, G. Norcliffe, and J. Holmes. 2000. 'Shift work and the divisions of labour in childcare and domestic work in Canadian paper mill communities', *Gender, Place & Culture* 7: 5–29.

———— and L. Lo. 2000. '"Asian theme" malls in suburban Toronto: Land use conflict in Richmond Hill', *Canadian Geographer* 44: 182–90.

Price, G. 2002. 'The view from '56: Thoughts on the short term future of transportation planning', *Plan Canada* 42, 3: 21–2.

Price Waterhouse. 1990. *City of Winnipeg: Economic Development Strategy*. Winnipeg: Price Waterhouse.

Proudfoot, M.J. 1937. 'City retail structure', *Economic Geography* 13: 425–8.

Prus, S. 2003. *A Life-course Perspective on the Relationship between Socio-economic Status and Health: Testing the Divergence Hypothesis* (Social and Economic Dimensions of an Aging Population, Working Paper No. 91). Hamilton, Ont.: McMaster University. Available at: <http://socserv.socsci.mcmaster.ca/sedap/p/sedap91.pdf>; accessed 13 May 2005.

Pucher, J.R., and C. Lefèvre. 1996. *The Urban Transport Crisis in Europe and North America*. London: Macmillan.

Pulido, L. 2000. 'Rethinking environmental racism: White privilege and urban development in Southern California', *Annals of the Association of American Geographers* 90: 12–40.

Punter, J. 2003. *The Vancouver Achievement: Urban Planning and Design*. Vancouver: University of British Columbia Press.

Purdy, S. 1997. 'Industrial efficiency, social order and moral purity: Housing reform thought in English Canada, 1900–1950', *Urban History Review* 25, 2: 30–40.

————. 2003. '"Ripped off" by the system: Housing policy, poverty, and territorial stigmatization in Regent Park housing project, 1951–1991', *Labour/Le Travail* 50: 45–108.

————. 2004. 'By the people, for the people: Tenant organizing in Toronto's Regent Park housing project in the 1960s and 1970s', *Journal of Urban History* 30: 519–48.

Pushkarev, B.S., and J.M. Zupan. 1977. *Public Transport and Land Use Policy*. Bloomington: Indiana University Press.

Qadeer, M. 1997. 'Pluralistic planning for multicultural cities: The Canadian practice', *Journal of the American Planning Association* 63: 481–94.

————. 2001. 'Urban planning and multiculturalism: Beyond sensitivity', *Plan Canada* 40: 16–18.

————. 2003. *Ethnic Segregation in a Multicultural City: The Case of Toronto, Canada*. Toronto: CERIS Working Paper No. 28.

———— and M. Chaudhry. 2000. 'The planning system and the development of mosques in the Greater Toronto Area', *Plan Canada* 40: 17–21.

Québec, Ministère des affaires municipales. 2001. *Cadre d'aménagement et orientations gouvernementales: Région métropolitaine de Montréal 2001–2021*. Québec: Ministère des affaires municipales.

————, Commission de protection du territoire agricole du Québec. 2002a. *Commission de protection du territoire agricole du Québec: Rapport annuel de gestion 2001–2002*. Québec: CPTA.

————. 2002. *La prise de décision en urbanisme*. Québec: Ministère des affaires municipales.

Quesnel, L. 1994. 'Party politics in the metropolis: Montreal 1960–1990', in F. Frisken, ed., *The Changing Canadian Metropolis: A Public Policy Perspective*. Berkeley, Calif.: Institute of Governmental Studies Press.

Quigley, J., S. Raphael, and E. Smolensky. 2001. 'Homeless in America, homeless in California', *Review of Economics and Statistics* 83, 1: 37–51.

Quon, S.P., L.R.G. Martin, and S.D. Murphy. 1999. 'Ecological rehabilitation: A new challenge for planners', *Plan Canada* 39, 4:18–21.

————, S.D. Murphy, and L.R.G. Martin. 2001. 'Effective planning and implementation of ecological rehabilitation projects: A case study of Regional Municipality of Waterloo (Ontario, Canada)', *Environmental Management* 27: 421–33.

Rae, D. 2003. *City: Urbanism and Its End*. New Haven: Yale University Press.

Rainham, D.G.C. 2005. 'Ecological complexity and West Nile Virus—Perspectives on improving public health response', *Canadian Journal of Public Health* 96: 37–40.

Ratcliffe, R.U. 1949. *Urban Land Economics*. New York: McGraw-Hill.

————. 1955. 'The dynamics of efficiency in the location distribution of urban activities', in R.M. Fischer, ed., *The Metropolis in Modern Life*. New York: Doubleday.

Ray, B.K., G. Halseth, and B. Johnson. 1997. 'The changing "face" of the suburbs: Issues of ethnicity and residential change in suburban Vancouver', *International Journal of Urban and Regional Research* 21: 75–99.

———— and E. Moore. 1991. 'Access to homeownership among immigrants in Canada', *Canadian Review of Sociology and Anthropology* 28: 1–27.

———— and D. Rose. 2000. 'Cities of the everyday: Socio-spatial perspectives on gender, difference and diversity', in T. Bunting and P. Filion, eds, *Canadian Cities in Transition: The Twenty-First Century*, 2nd edn. Toronto: Oxford University Press.

Razin, E., and M. Rosentraub. 2000. 'Are fragmentation and sprawl interlinked? North American evidence', *Urban Affairs Review* 35: 821–36.

Real Estate Research Corporation. 1974. *The Cost of Sprawl: Environmental and Economic Costs of Alternative Residential Development Patterns at the Urban Fringe*. Washington: Real Estate Research Corporation.

Redstone, L. 1976. *The New Downtowns: Rebuilding Business Districts*. New York: McGraw-Hill.

Reed, P. 2003. 'Fault lines and enclaves: The rise of city regions in Canada', *Ideas That Matter* 3, 1: 3–8.

Reeder, A.L., M.O. Ruiz, A. Pessier, L.E. Brown, J.M. Levengood, C.A. Phillips, M.B. Wheeler, R.E. Warner, and V.R. Beasley. 2005. 'Intersexuality and the cricket frog decline: Historic and geographic trends', *Environmental Health Perspectives* 113: 261–5.

Rees, W.E., and M. Roseland. 1991. 'Sustainable communities: Planning for the 21st century', *Plan Canada* 31, 3: 15–26.

———— and M. Wackernagel. 1994. 'Ecological footprints and appropriate carrying capacity: Measuring the natural capital requirements of the human economy', in A.-M. Jansson, M. Hammer, C. Folke, and R. Constanza, eds, *Investing in Natural Capital: Ecological Economics Approach to Sustainability*. Washington: Island Press.

———— and ————. 1996. 'Urban ecological footprints: Why cities cannot be sustainable; and why they are key to sustainability', *Environmental Impact Assessment Review* 16: 223–48.

Regional Municipality of Ottawa–Carleton (RMOC). 1999. *Homelessness in Ottawa–Carleton*. Ottawa: RMOC.

Reich, R. 1992. *The Work of Nations*. New York: Vintage Books.

————. 2002. *The Future of Success: Working and Living in the New Economy*. New York: Vintage Books.

Reid, B. 1990. 'Suburbs in transition: The urbanization and greening of Surrey', *City Magazine* 11, 4: 38–41.

————. 1991. 'Primer on the corporate city', in K. Gerecke, ed., *The Canadian City*. Montreal: Black Rose Books.

Reisman, D. 1958. 'The suburban sadness', in Dobriner (1958).

Reitz, J. 2001. 'Immigrant skill utilization in the Canadian labour market: Implications of human capital research', *Journal of International Migration and Integration* 2: 347–78.

Relph, E. 1976. *Place and Placelessness*. London: Pion.

————. 1987. *The Modern Urban Landscape*. Baltimore: Johns Hopkins University Press.

————. 1991. 'Suburban downtowns of the Greater Toronto Area', *Canadian Geographer* 35: 421–5.

Ricardo, D. 1969 [1817]. *The Principles of Political Economy and Taxation*. London: Everyman's Library, J.M. Dent & Sons.

Richardson, H.1988. 'Monocentric vs polycentric models: The future of urban economics in regional science', *Annals of Regional Science* 22, 2: 1–12.

———— and C. Bae, eds. 2004. *Urban Sprawl in Western Europe and the United States*. Aldershot: Ashgate.

Richmond, T., and J. Shields. 2004. *Third Sector Restructuring and the New Contracting Regime: The Case of Immigrant Serving Agencies in Ontario*. Toronto: Centre of Excellence for Research on Immigration and Settlement, Report No. 3.

Ricketts, E., and I. Sawhill. 1988. 'Defining and measuring the "underclass"', *Journal of Policy Analysis and Management* 7: 316–25.

Rifkin, J. 1995. *The End of Work*. New York: Putnam.

Ringheim, K. 1990. *At Risk of Homelessness: The Roles of Income and Rent*. New York: Praeger

Robbins, L. 1989. 'Les sorties au restaurant', *Tendances sociales canadiennes* 13: 7–9 (Statistics Canada, Cat. no. 11–008).

Robertson, K.A. 1993a. 'Pedestrianization strategies for downtown planners: Skywalks versus pedestrian malls', *Journal of the American Planning Association* 59: 361–70.

———. 1993b. 'Pedestrians and the American downtown', *Town Planning Review* 64: 273–86.

———. 1995. 'Downtown redevelopment strategies in the United States: An end-of-the-century assessment', *Journal of the American Planning Association* 61: 429–37.

———. 1999. 'Can small-city downtowns remain viable? A national study of development issues and strategies', *Journal of the American Planning Association* 65: 270–83.

———. 2001. 'Downtown development principles for small cities', in M. Burayidi, ed., *Downtowns: Revitalizing the Centers of Small Communities.* New York: Routledge.

Robertson, R. 1973. 'Anatomy of a renewal scheme', in Forward (1973a).

———. 1992. *Globalisation.* London: Sage.

Robinson, J., G. Francis, F. Legge, and S. Lerner. 1990. 'Defining a sustainable society: Values, principles and definitions', *Alternatives* 17: 36–46.

Robinson, L., J.P. Newell, and J.A. Marzluff. 2005. 'Twenty-five years of sprawl in the Seattle region: Growth management responses and implications for conservation', *Landscape and Urban Planning* 71: 51–72.

Robinson, P.A. 1995. 'Protecting the environment in a rapidly urbanizing community', *Plan Canada* 35, 6: 22–5.

Robinson, P.J., and C.D. Gore. 2005. 'Barriers to Canadian municipal response to climate change', *Canadian Journal of Urban Research* 14:102–20.

Rodriguez-Pose, A., and N. Gill. 2004. 'Is there a global link between regional disparities and devolution?', *Environment and Planning A* 36: 12–28.

Rose, A. 1958. *Regent Park: A Study in Slum Clearance.* Toronto: University of Toronto Press.

———. 1972. *Governing Metropolitan Toronto: A Social and Political Analysis, 1953–1971.* Berkeley: University of California Press.

Rose, D. 1989. 'A feminist perspective on employment restructuring and gentrification: The case of Montreal', in J. Wolch and M. Dear, eds, *The Power of Geography: How Territory Shapes Social Life.* Boston: Unwin Hyman.

———. 1996. 'Economic restructuring and the diversification of gentrification in the 1980s: The view from a marginal metropolis', in Caulfield and Peake (1996).

———. 2004. '"Gentrifiers" or "affordable housing" consumers? Living alone and owning one's home in the inner city: The case of Montreal, Canada', paper presented at the international conference of the International Sociological Association, Research Committee 43 Housing and the Built Environment, 'Adequate and Affordable Housing for All', Toronto, 24–8 June. Available at: <www.urbancentre.utoronto.ca/pdfs/housingconference/Rose_Conf-Presentation-2004.pdf>.

——— and C. Le Bourdais. 1986. 'The changing conditions of female single parenthood in Montreal's inner city and suburban neighborhoods', *Urban Resources* 3: 45–52.

———, J. Mongeau, and N. Chicoine. 1999. *Housing Canada's Youth* (Distinct Housing Needs Series). Ottawa: CMHC.

——— and P. Villeneuve. 1993. 'Work, labour markets and households in transition', in Bourne and Ley (1993).

——— and ———. 1998. 'Engendering class in the metropolitan city: Occupational pairings and income disparities among two-earner couples', *Urban Geography* 19: 123–59.

——— and M. Wexler. 1993. 'Post-war social and economic changes and housing adequacy', in Miron (1993a).

Rose, J. 1999. *Immigration, Neighbourhood Change and Racism: Immigrant Reception in Richmond, BC.* Vancouver: Research on Immigration and Integration in the Metropolis (Working Paper No. 99–15).

———. 2001. 'Contexts of interpretation: Assessing immigrant reception in Richmond, Canada', *Canadian Geographer* 45: 474–93.

Rosenberg, M., E. Moore, and S. Ball. 1989. 'Components of change in the spatial distribution of the elderly population of Ontario, 1976–1986', *Canadian Geographer* 33: 218–19.

Roseneil, S., and S. Budgeon. 2004. 'Cultures of intimacy and care. Beyond "the family": Personal life and social change in the early 21st century', *Current Sociology* 52: 135–59.

Rosenzweig, M.L. 2003. 'Reconciliation ecology and the future of species diversity', *Oryx* 37: 194–205.

Ross, N., C. Houle, J. Dunn, and M. Aye. 2004. 'Dimensions and dynamics of residential segregation by income in urban Canada, 1991–1996', *Canadian Geographer* 48: 433–45.

Rossi, P.H., J.D. Wright, G.A. Fisher, and G. Willis. 1987. 'The urban homeless: Estimating composition and size', *Science* 235 (1749): 1336–41.

Rothblatt, D.N. 1998. *North American Metropolitan Planning Re-examined*. Berkeley: Institute of Government Studies, University of California, Working Paper 99–2.

Rowe, A. 1989. 'Self-help housing provision: Production, consumption, accumulation and policy in Atlantic Canada', *Housing Studies* 4: 75–91.

Rowe, P.G. 1991. *Making a Middle Landscape*. Cambridge, Mass.: MIT Press.

Rowe, S., and J. Wolch. 1990. 'Social networks in time and space: Homeless women in skid row, Los Angeles', *Annals of the Association of American Geographers* 80: 184–204.

Rowe, W.M. 2004. 'Background on the neighbourhood of Regent Park, Toronto', *Ideas That Matter* 3, 2: 20–2.

Rowley, G. 1978. 'Plus ça change . . . a Canadian skid row', *Canadian Geographer* 22: 211–24.

Royal Commission on Price Spreads. 1935. *Report*. Ottawa: King's Printer.

Royal LePage. 2005. *Office Statistics*. Toronto: Royal LePage.

Rudd, H., J. Vala, and V. Schaefer. 2002. 'Importance of backyard habitat in a comprehensive biodiversity conservation strategy: A connectivity analysis of urban green spaces', *Restoration Ecology* 10: 368–75.

Rural Development Institute. 2005. *Manitoba Rural Immigration Community Case Studies: Steinbach*. Brandon, Man.: RDI working paper, Apr.

Russwurm, L.H. 1977. *The Surroundings of Our Cities*. Ottawa: Community Planning Press.

Rutherford, P. 1984. 'Tomorrow's metropolis revisited: A critical assessment of urban reform in Canada, 1890–1920', in G.A. Stelter and A.F.J. Artibise, eds, *The Canadian City: Essays in Urban and Social History*. Ottawa: Carleton University Press.

Rutherford, T. 1996. 'The socio-spatial restructuring of Canadian labour markets', in J. Britton, ed., *Canada and the Global Economy: The Geography of Structural and Technological Change Space Economy*. Montreal and Kingston: McGill-Queen's University Press.

Ryan, W. 1976. *Blaming the Victim*, 2nd edn. New York: Vintage.

Rypkema, D.D. 2003. 'The importance of downtown in the 21st century', *Journal of the American Planning Association* 69: 9–15.

Sadella, E.K., B. Verschure, and J. Burroughs. 1987. 'Identity symbolism in housing', *Environment and Behavior* 19: 569–87.

Sadiq, K. 2004. *The Two Tier Settlement System: A Review of Newcomer Services in Canada*. Toronto: CERIS Working Paper 34, Nov.

Safdie, M. 1970. *Beyond Habitat*. Cambridge, Mass.: MIT Press.

Salomon, I. 1986. 'Technological change and social forecasting: The case of telecommuting as a travel substitute', *Transportation Research A* 6: 17–45.

Sancton, A. 1985. *Governing the Island of Montreal: Language Differences and Metropolitan Politics*. Berkeley: University of California Press.

———. 1994. *Governing Canada's City-Regions: Adapting Form to Function*. Montreal: Institute for Research on Public Policy.

———. 2000. *Merger Mania: The Assault on Local Government*. Montreal and Kingston: McGill-Queen's University Press.

——— and B. Montgomery. 1994. 'Municipal government and residential land development: A comparative study of London, Ontario, in the 1920s and 1980s', in Frisken (1994a).

Sandercock, L. 1998. *Towards Cosmopolis: Planning for Multicultural Cities*. New York: John Wiley and Sons.

———. 2003. *Cosmopolis II: Mongrel Cities in the 21st Century*. London: Continuum.

Sanford, B. 1987. 'The political economy of land development in nineteenth century Toronto', *Urban History Review* 16: 17–33.

Santink, J.L. 1990. *Timothy Eaton and the Rise of His Department Store*. Toronto: University of Toronto Press.

Sartori, F., and S. Assini. 2001. 'Vegetation evolution in a reclaimed area contaminated with dioxin', *Chemosphere* 43: 525–35.

Sassen, S. 1991. *The Global City: New York, London, Tokyo.* Princeton, NJ: Princeton University Press.

———. 1994. *Cities in a World Economy.* Thousand Oaks, Calif.: Pine Forge Press.

———. 2001a. 'Global cities and global city-regions: A comparison', in Scott (2001).

———. 2001b. *The Global City,* 2nd edn. Princeton, NJ: Princeton University Press.

Saul, J.R. 2005. *The Collapse of Globalism and the Reinvention of the World.* Toronto: Viking Canada.

Sauvé, R., People Patterns Consulting. 2005. *The Current State of Canadian Family Finances—2004 Report* (Contemporary Family Trends). Ottawa: Vanier Institute of the Family. Available at: <www.vifamily.ca/library/cft/state04.html>; accessed 11 May 2005.

Savitch, H.V., and P. Kantor. 2002. *Cities in the International Marketplace: The Political Economy of Urban Development in North America and Europe.* Princeton, NJ: Princeton University Press.

Savoie, D. 1992. *Regional Economic Development: Canada's Search for Solutions.* Toronto: University of Toronto Press.

Schellenberg, G. 2004. *Immigrants in Canada's Census Metropolitan Areas.* Ottawa: Statistics Canada. At: <www.statcan.ca:80/english/research/89-613-MIE/2004003/89-613-MIE2004003.pdf>.

Schultze, C.L. 1977. *The Public Use of Private Interest.* Washington: Brookings Institution.

Scott, A.J. 1982. 'Industrial patterns and dynamics of industrial activity in the modern metropolis', *Urban Studies* 19: 111–42.

———, ed. 2001. *Global City-Regions.* Oxford: Oxford University Press.

———, J. Agnew, E. Soja, and M. Storper. 2001. 'Global city-regions', in Scott (2001).

Seelig, M.Y. 1995. 'Vancouver's CityPlan: Citizen participation as a political cop-out', *Globe and Mail,* 27 Feb., A15.

Séguin, A.-M. 1989. 'Madame Ford et l'espace: lecture féministe de la suburbanisation', *Recherches féministes* 2, 1: 51–68.

———. 1997. 'Poverty and social exclusion in the Montreal metropolitan area', paper presented to the conference of the Canadian Association of Geographers, St John's.

——— and P. Apparicio. 2004. 'Évolution de la distribution spatiale de la population âgée dans la région métropolitaine montréalaise: constat et enjeux', *Canadian Journal of Regional Science/Revue canadienne des sciences régionales* 27: 79–98.

——— and G. Divay. 2002. *Urban Poverty: Fostering Sustainable and Supportive Communities.* Ottawa: Canadian Policy Research Networks.

——— and A. Germain. 2000. 'The social sustainability of Montreal: A local or a state matter?', in M. Polèse and R. Stren, eds, *The Social Sustainability of Cities: Diversity and the Management of Change.* Toronto: University of Toronto Press.

——— and P. Villeneuve. 1993. 'The Saint-Jean-Baptiste neighbourhood in Québec City: A microcosm of the relations between the state and civil society', *Canadian Geographer* 37: 167–73.

Semple, R.K. 1996. 'Quaternary places in Canada', in J. Britton, ed., *Canada and the Global Economy: The Geography of Structural and Technological Change.* Montreal and Kingston: McGill-Queen's University Press.

Sénécal, G. 1995. 'Le quartier Hochelaga-Maisonneuve à Montréal', *Canadian Geographer* 39: 353–62.

———, R. Haf, P.J. Hamel, C. Poitras, and N. Vachon. 2002. 'La forme de l'agglomération montréalaise et la réduction des gaz à effet de serre: la polycentricité est-elle durable?', *Canadian Journal of Regional Science* 25: 259–78.

——— and D. Saint-Laurent. 2000. *Les espaces dégradés: contraintes et conquêtes.* Sainte-Foy, Que.: Presses de l'Université du Québec.

Serageldin, I. 1995. *Sustainability and the Wealth of Nations: First Steps in an Ongoing Journey.* Washington: World Bank (Environmentally Sustainable Development Studies and Monographs Series).

Sewell, J. 1977. 'The suburbs', *City Magazine* 2, 6: 19–55.

———. 1984. 'Old and new city', *City Magazine* 6, 4: 11–14.

————. 1993. *The Shape of the City: Toronto Struggles with Modern Planning*. Toronto: University of Toronto Press.

————. 1994. *Houses and Homes: Housing for Canadians*. Toronto: James Lorimer.

————. 2005. *Local Government Bulletin* 58 (July). At: <www.localgovernment.ca>.

Shapcott, M. 2004. 'Where are we going? Recent federal and provincial housing policy', in Hulchanski and Shapcott (2004).

Sharma, M., and E.A. McBean. 2002. 'Atmospheric PAH deposition: Deposition velocities and washout ratios', *Journal of Environmental Engineering-ASCE* 128: 186–95.

Sharpe, L.J. 1981. 'The failure of local government modernization in Britain: A critique of functionalism', in L.D. Feldman, ed., *Politics and Government of Urban Canada*. Toronto: Methuen.

Shearman, R. 1990. 'The meaning and ethics of sustainability', *Environmental Management* 14: 1–8.

Shearmur, R.G., and C. Alvergne. 2002. 'Intra-metropolitan patterns of high-order business service location: A comparative study of seventeen sectors in Ile-de-France', *Urban Studies* 39: 1143–64.

———— and M. Charron. 2004. 'From Chicago to L.A. and back again: A Chicago-inspired quantitative analysis of income distribution in Montreal', *Professional Geographer* 56:109–26.

———— and W.J. Coffey. 2002. 'A tale of four cities: Intrametropolitan employment distribution in Toronto, Montreal, Vancouver and Ottawa–Hull, 1981–1996', *Environment and Planning A* 34: 575–98.

Sheffi, Y. 1985. *Urban Transportation Networks: Equilibrium Analysis with Mathematical Programming Methods*. Englewood Cliffs, NJ: Prentice-Hall.

Sherwood, D.H. 1994. 'Canadian Institute of Planners', *Plan Canada* (special issue) 34 (July): 20–1.

Shevky, E., and W. Bell. 1955. *Social Area Analysis*. Stanford, Calif.: Stanford University Press.

Shibley, R., and L. Schneekloth. 1995. *Place Making: The Art and Practice of Building Communities*. New York: Wiley.

Short, J., and Y.-H. Kim. 1999. *Globalization and the City*. Harlow, UK: Prentice-Hall.

————, Y. Kim, M. Kuus, and H. Wells. 1996. 'The dirty little secret of world city research', *International Journal of Regional and Urban Research* 20: 697–717.

Shoup, D. 1970. 'The optimal timing of urban land development', *Papers of the Regional Science Association* 75: 33–44.

Siegel, D. 2005. 'Municipal reform in Ontario: Revolutionary evolution', in J. Garcea and E. Lesage, eds, *Municipal Reform in Canada: Reconfiguration, Re-empowerment, and Rebalancing*. Toronto: Oxford University Press.

Siemiatycki, M., T. Rees, R. Ng, and K. Rahi. 2001. *Integrating Community Diversity in Toronto: On Whose Terms?* Toronto: CERIS Working Paper No. 14.

Sierra Club. 1998. *The Dark Side of the American Dream: The Costs and Consequences of Suburban Sprawl*. College Park, Md: Sierra Club. At: <www.sierraclub.org/sprawl/report98>.

————. 2004. *The National Sewage Report Card (Number Three): Grading the Sewage Treatment of 22 Canadian Cities*. Vancouver: Sierra Club.

Silver, J. 1996. *Thin Ice: Money, Politics and the Demise of an NHL Franchise*. Halifax: Fernwood.

Simmel, G. 1950 [1903]. 'The metropolis and mental life', in K.H. Wolff, ed., *The Sociology of Georg Simmel*. New York: Free Press.

Simmons, A. 1999 'Immigration policy: Imagined futures', in S. Halli and L. Driedger, eds, *Immigrant Canada: Demographic, Economic and Social Challenges*. Toronto: University of Toronto Press.

Simmons, J.W. 1966. *Toronto's Changing Retail Complex*. Chicago: University of Chicago, Department of Geography (Research Paper No. 104).

————. 1974. *Patterns of Residential Movement in Metropolitan Toronto*. Toronto: University of Toronto Press.

————. 1984. 'Government and the Canadian urban system: Income tax, transfer payments, and employment', *Canadian Geographer* 28: 18–45.

————. 1986. 'The impact of the public sector on the Canadian urban system', in G.A. Stelter and A.F.J. Artibise, eds, *Power and Place: Canadian Urban Development in North American Context*. Vancouver: University of British Columbia Press.

———, M. Biasiotto, D. Montgomery, M. Robinson, and S. Simmons. 1996. *Commercial Structure of the Greater Toronto Area: 1996*. Toronto: Ryerson University, CSCA (RP1996–4).

——— and L.S. Bourne. 2003. *The Canadian Urban System, 1971–2001: Responses to a Changing World*. Toronto: University of Toronto, Centre for Urban and Community Studies, Research Paper No. 200.

——— and ———. 2004. *Urban Growth in Canada, 1971–2001: Explanations and Interpretations*. Toronto: University of Toronto, Centre for Urban and Community Studies, Research Paper No. 201.

———, ———, and J. Cantos. 2004. *How Cities Grow: A Study of Time Series Data for Canadian Cities*. Toronto: Centre for Urban and Community Studies, University of Toronto (Research Paper 202).

——— and T. Hernandez. 2004a. *Power Retail: Close to Saturation*. Toronto: Ryerson University, CSCA (RP2004–08).

——— and ———. 2004b. *Power Retail within Canada's Major Metropolitan Markets*. Toronto: Ryerson University, CSCA (RP2004–09).

Simon, J., and D. Holdsworth. 1993. 'Housing Form and Use of Domestic Space', in Miron (1993a).

Simpson, M. 1985. *Thomas Adams and the Modern Planning Movement: Britain, Canada and the United States, 1900–1940*. London: Alexandrine Press Book.

Simpson, J.R. 2002. 'Improved estimates of tree-shade effects on residential energy use', *Energy and Buildings* 34: 1067–76.

Simpson, R. 1996. 'Residential intensification: The wrong planning debate', in Emeneau (1996).

Sinclair, P.R., and K. Westhues. 1974. *Village in Crisis*. Toronto: Holt, Rinehart and Winston of Canada.

Singer, A. 2004. *The Rise of New Immigrant Gateways*. Washington: Center on Urban and Metropolitan Policy, Brookings Institution.

Skaburskis, A. 1988. 'The nature of Canadian condominium submarkets and their effect on the evolution of the urban spatial structure', *Urban Studies* 25: 109–23.

———. 1989. 'Inversions in urban density gradients: A brief look at the Vancouver metropolitan area's density profile', *Urban Studies* 26: 397–401.

———. 1995. 'The consequences of land-value taxation', *Journal of Planning Literature* 10: 3–21.

———. 1997. 'Gender differences in housing demand', *Urban Studies* 34: 275–320.

———. 1999. 'Modelling the choice of tenure and building type', *Urban Studies* 36: 2199–215.

———. 2000. 'Housing prices and housing density: Do higher prices make more compact cities?', *Canadian Journal of Regional Science* 23: 455–80.

———. 2004. 'Decomposing Canada's growing housing affordability problem: Do city differences matter?', *Urban Studies* 41: 117–49.

———. 2005. 'New urbanism and density: The housing decisions of Toronto Cornell residents', *Journal of Planning Education and Research* (forthcoming).

——— and D. Geros. 1997. 'The changing suburb: Burnaby, B.C. revisited', *Plan Canada* 37, 2: 37–45.

——— and R. Tomalty. 2001. 'How property taxes and development charges can be used to shape cities', *Plan Canada* 41, 4: 24–40.

Skelton, I. 1994. 'The geographic distribution of social housing in Ontario, Canada: Comparing public housing and locally sponsored, third sector housing', *Housing Studies* 11: 189–206.

Slater, T. 2004. 'Municipally managed gentrification in South Parkdale, Toronto', *Canadian Geographer* 48: 303–25.

———. 2005. 'Gentrification in Canada's cities', in R. Atkinson and G. Bridge, eds, *Gentrification in a Global Context*. London: Routledge.

Slingenbergh, J., M. Gilbert, K. de Balogh, and W. Wint. 2004. 'Ecological sources of zoonotic diseases', *Revue Scientifique et Technique de L'Office International des Epizooties* 23: 467–84.

Smart, A., and J. Smart. 1996. 'Monster homes: Hong Kong immigration to Canada, urban conflicts, and contested representations of space', in Caulfield and Peake (1996).

Smart Growth BC. 2003. *Smart Growth BC's Position on the Provincial Agricultural Land Reserve (ALR)*. Vancouver: Smart Growth BC.

———. 2005. *Smart Growth BC: Creating More Liveable Communities*. At: <www.smartgrowth.bc.ca/index.cfm>.

Smith, A. 1970 [1776]. *The Wealth of Nations*. London: Everyman's Library, J.M. Dent & Sons.

Smith, D. 1989. 'Local area conservation: How one suburban municipality utilizes environmental planning to conserve its natural heritage', *Plan Canada* 29, 5: 39–42.

Smith, H.A. 2002. 'Planning, policy and polarisation in Vancouver's Downtown Eastside', *Tijdschrift voor Economishe en Social Geografie* 94: 496–509.

————. 2004. *The Evolving Relationship between Immigrant Settlement and Neighbourhood Disadvantage in Canadian Cities, 1991–2001*. Vancouver: Vancouver Centre of Excellence, Research on Immigration and Integration in the Metropolis (Working Paper Series 04–20).

Smith, N. 1990. *Uneven Development: Nature, Capital and the Production of Space*. Oxford: Blackwell.

————. 1996a. *The New Urban Frontier: Gentrification and the Revanchist City*. London: Routledge.

————. 1996b. 'New globalism, new urbanism: Gentrification as global urban strategy', *Antipode* 34: 427–50.

Smith, P.J. 1962. 'Fort Saskatchewan: An industrial satellite of Edmonton', *Plan Canada* 3: 4–16.

————. 1991. 'Community aspirations, territorial justice and the metropolitan form of Edmonton and Calgary', in G.M. Robinson, ed., *A Social Geography of Canada*. Toronto: Dundurn Press.

————. 1995. 'Planning for residential growth since the 1940s', in B. Hesketh and F. Swyripa, eds, *Edmonton: The Life of a City*. Edmonton: NeWest Publishers.

———— and P.E. Bayne. 1994. 'The issue of local autonomy in Edmonton's regional plan process: Metropolitan planning in a changing political climate', in Frisken (1994a).

———— and T. Cohn. 1994. 'International cities and municipal paradiplomacy: A typology for assessing the changing Vancouver metropolis', in Frisken (1994a).

———— and H.L. Diemer. 1978. 'Equity and the annexation process: Edmonton's bid for the Strathcona industrial corridor', in Smith, ed., *Edmonton: The Emerging Metropolitan Pattern*. Victoria: University of Victoria, Western Geographical Series vol. 15.

———— and P.W. Moore. 1993. 'Cities as a social responsibility: Planning and urban form', in Bourne and Ley (1993).

———— and D. Johnston. 1978. *The Edmonton–Calgary Corridor*. Edmonton: University of Alberta Press.

Smith, W. 1964. *Filtering and Neighborhood Change*. Berkeley: University of California, Center for Real Estate and Urban Economics, Report No. 24.

Social Planning and Research Council of Hamilton (SPRC). 2003. *Progress Report on Homelessness in Hamilton 2003*. Hamilton: SPRC.

Soja, E.W. 2000. *Postmetropolis: Critical Studies of Cities and Regions*. Oxford: Blackwell.

Sokoloff, B., and V. Ahtik. 1992. 'Centralité urbaine et aménagement du centre-ville de Montréal', *Cahiers de géographie du Québec* 36, 99: 463–82.

Song, Y. 2005. 'Smart growth and urban development pattern: A comparative study', *International Regional Science Review* 28: 239–65.

Sosin, M.R., M. Bruni, and M. Reidy. 1995. 'Paths and impacts in the progressive independence model: A homelessness and substance abuse intervention in Chicago', *Journal of Addictive Diseases* 14: 1–20.

Southworth, M. 1997. 'Walkable suburbs? An evaluation of neotraditional communities at the urban edge', *Journal of the American Planning Association* 63: 28–44.

Spear, B. 1994. *New Approaches to Travel Forecasting Models: A Synthesis of Four Research Proposals*. Washington: US Department of Transportation (DOT–T–94–15).

Spectorsky, A.C. 1955. *The Exurbanites*. Philadelphia: Lippincott.

Speir, C., and K. Stephenson. 2002. 'Does sprawl cost us all?', *Journal of the American Planning Association* 68: 56–70.

Springer, J., J. Mars, and M. Dennison. 1998. *A Profile of the Toronto Homeless Population*. Report prepared for the Homelessness Action Task Force, City of Toronto.

Spurr, P. 1976. *Land and Urban Development: A Preliminary Study*. Toronto: James Lorimer.

Stabler, J., and R. Olfert. 2002. *Saskatchewan's Communities in the 21st Century: From Places to*

Regions. Regina: Canadian Plains Research Centre, University of Regina.

Stanback, T.M. 1991. *The New Suburbanization: Challenge to the Central City.* Boulder, Colo.: Westview Press.

Stanford, J. 1999. 'It's time to loosen the purse strings', *Canadian Business Economics* (Feb.): 6–7.

Statistics Canada. Various years. *Census of Canada.* Ottawa: Statistics Canada.

———. 2001a. *Census of the Population: Labour Force Dimension.* Ottawa: Minister of Industry.

———. 2001b. *Small Area Retail Trade Estimates.* Ottawa: Statistics Canada.

———. 2001c. *Community Profiles.* At: <www12. statcan.ca/english/profil01/PlaceSearchForm1. cfm>. Accessed 25 Jan. 2005.

———, Housing, Family and Social Statistics Division. 2002a. *Family History. General Social Survey—Cycle 15.* Ottawa, Cat. no. 89–575–XIE. Available at: <www.statcan.ca/english/freepub/ 89-575-XIE/89-575-XIE2001001.pdf>; accessed 11 May 2005.

———. 2002b. *Household Living Arrangements (10), Age Groups (17A) and Sex (3) for Population in Private Households, for Canada, Provinces, Territories, Census Metropolitan Areas and Census Agglomerations. 2001 Census—20% Sample Data* (Canadian Overview Tables, Table 97F005XCB01004). Ottawa.

———. 2002c. *Profile of Canadian Families and Households: Diversification Continues* (Analysis series, 2001 Census, Cat. no. 96F0030XIE2001003). Available at: <www12.statcan.ca/english/census01/ products/analytic/companion/fam/pdf/96F0030 XIE2001003.pdf>; accessed 11 May 2005.

———. 2003a. *Where Canadians Work and How They Get There.* Ottawa: Industry Canada, Census of Canada, Cat. no. 96F0030XIE2001010.

———. 2003b. 'Census of population: Labour force activity, occupation, industry, class of worker, place of work, mode of transportation, language of work and unpaid work', *The Daily,* 11 Feb. 2003. At: <www.statcan.ca/Daily/English/030211/d030211 a.htm>. Accessed May 2005.

———. 2003c. *Longitudinal Survey of Immigration to Canada.* Ottawa: Statistics Canada.

———. 2004a. CANSIM, Table 111–0009: Family Characteristics, Summary, Annual (2000–2002). Available at: <http://estat.statcan.ca>; accessed 14 June 2005.

———. 2004b. *Profile of Census Tracts.* Ottawa: Industry Canada. 2001 census, Cat. no. 95–244–XPB.

———. 2005a. *The Ice Storm 1998.* Ottawa: Statistics Canada.

———. 2005b. *Road motor vehicle, trailer, and snowmobile registration (Table 405–0001).* Ottawa: Statistics Canada. At: <http:IICansim2.statsCan.ca>.

———. 2005c. *Population and Dwelling Counts, for Canada, Provinces and Territories, Census Metropolitan Areas and Census Agglomerations, 2001 and 1996 Censuses—100 Per Cent Data.* Ottawa: Statistics Canada.

———. 2005d. *Gross Domestic Product.* Ottawa: Minister of Industry, Cat. no. 13–001–XIB.

———. 2005e. *Canadian Statistics.* At: <www40. statcan.ca/l01/cst01/demo05b.htm>. Accessed 3 May 2005.

Steele, M. 1993. 'Incomes, prices and tenure choice', in Miron (1993a).

Stein, D.L. 1972. *Toronto for Sale: The Destruction of a City.* Toronto: New Press.

———. 1994a. 'Thomas Adams, 1871–1940', *Plan Canada* (special issue) 34 (July): 14–15.

———. 1994b. 'The Commission of Conservation', *Plan Canada* (special issue) 34 (July): 55.

Stelter, G. 1990. *Cities and Urbanization.* Toronto: Copp Clark Pitman.

Stephenson, G. 1957. *A Redevelopment Study of Halifax, Nova Scotia.* Halifax: City of Halifax.

Stewart, D. 2002. 'Habitat and ecology: The co-housing experiment in the United States', *Revue française d'études américaines* 94: 113–27.

Stiglitz, J. 2000. *Economics of the Public Sector,* 3rd edn. New York: W.W. Norton.

Stoffman, D. 2002. *Who Gets In: What's Wrong with Canada's Immigration Program, and How to Fix It.* Toronto: Macfarlane Walter & Ross.

———. 2003. 'The mystery of Canada's high immigration levels', *Canadian Issues* (Apr.): 23–5.

Stojanovic, D., B.C. Weitzman, M. Shinn, L.E. Labay, and N.P. Williams. 1999. 'Tracing the path out of homelessness: The housing patterns of families after exiting shelter', *Journal of Community Psychology* 27: 199–208.

Stone, B. 2003. 'Air quality by design: Harnessing the Clean Air Act to manage metropolitan growth', *Journal of Planning Education and Research* 23: 177–90.

Stone, L.O. 1967. *Urban Development in Canada. An Introduction to the Demographic Aspects*. Ottawa: Dominion Bureau of Statistics, 1961 Census Monograph.

Stone, M.E. 1993. *Shelter Poverty: New Ideas on Housing Affordability*. Philadelphia: Temple University Press.

Storper, M. 1997. *The Regional World: Territorial Development in a Global Economy*. New York: Guilford.

Strom, E. 2002. 'Converting pork into porcelain: Cultural institutions and downtown development', *Urban Affairs Review* 38: 3–21.

Strong-Boag, V. 1988. *The New Day Recalled: Lives of Girls and Women in English Canada, 1919–1939*. Markham, Ont.: Penguin.

———. 1991. 'Home dreams: Women and the suburban experiment in Canada, 1945–60', *Canadian Historical Review* 72: 471–504.

———, I. Dyck, K. England, and L. Johnson. 1999. 'What women's spaces?: Women in Australian, British, Canadian and US suburbs', in R. Harris and P.J. Larkham, eds, *Changing Suburbs: Foundation, Form, and Function*. London: Chapman and Hall.

Susser, E.S, S.P. Lin, and S.A. Conover. 1991. 'Risk factors for homelessness among patients admitted to a state mental hospital', *American Journal of Psychiatry* 148: 1659–64.

Suttles, G. 1968. *The Social Order of the Slum*. Chicago: University of Chicago Press.

Tabb, W., and L. Sawyer. 1978. *Marxism and the Metropolis*. New York: Oxford University Press.

Takahashi, L.M., J. McElroy, and S. Rowe. 2002. 'The sociospatial stigmatization of homeless women and children', *Urban Geography* 23: 301–22.

Tamminga, K. 1996. 'Restoring biodiversity in the urbanizing region: Towards pre-emptive ecosystems planning', *Plan Canada* 36, 4: 10–15.

Tassonyi, A. 1997. 'Financing municipal infrastructure in Canada's city regions', in P. Hobson and F. St-Hilaire, eds, *Urban Governance and Finance: A Question of Who Does What*. Ottawa: IRPP.

Taylor, J., C. Paine, and J. FitzGibbon. 1995. 'From greenbelt to greenways: Four Canadian case studies', *Landscape and Urban Planning* 33: 47–64.

Taylor, P.J. 2001. 'Urban hinterworlds: Geographies of corporate service provision under conditions of contemporary globalization', *Geography* 86: 51–60.

———. 2004. *World City Network: A Global Urban Analysis*. London: Routledge.

———, G. Catalano, and D.R.F. Walker. 2002. 'Exploratory analysis of the world city network', *Urban Studies* 39: 2377–94.

Taylor, S.M. 1987. 'Social change in Hamilton 1961–1981', in M.J. Dear, J.J. Drake, and L.G. Reeds, eds, *Steel City: Hamilton and Region*. Toronto: University of Toronto Press.

Teixeira, C. 1996. 'The suburbanization of Portuguese communities in Toronto and Montreal: From isolation to residential integration?', in A. Laperrièrre, V. Lindstrom, and T.P. Seiler, eds, *Immigration and Ethnicity in Canada*. Montreal: Association for Canadian Studies.

——— and R.A. Murdie. 1997. 'The role of ethnic real estate agents in the residential relocation process: A case study of the Portuguese homebuyers in suburban Toronto', *Urban Geography* 18: 497–520.

Terral, L., and R. Shearmur. 2005. 'Structures et logiques du redéploiement de l'emploi métropolitain', paper presented at the conference of the Institut Fédératif de Recherche sur les Économies et les Sociétés Industrielles, Lille, June.

Theobald, D.M., J.R. Miller, and N.T. Hobbs. 1997. 'Estimating the cumulative effects of development on wildlife habitat', *Landscape and Urban Planning* 39: 25–36.

Thissen, W., and P. Herder. 2003. 'Critical infrastructures: A new and challenging research field', in Thissen and Herder, eds, *Critical Infrastructures: State of the Art in Research and Application*. Boston: Kluwer.

Thomas, R. 2002. *Site Planning and Design Handbook*. New York: McGraw-Hill

Thompson, S.J., D.E. Pollio, K. Eyrich, E. Bradbury, and C.S. North. 2004. 'Successfully exiting homelessness: Experiences of formerly homeless mentally ill individuals', *Evaluation and Program Planning* 27: 423–31.

Thompson, W.R. 1995. 'Introduction: Urban economics in a global age', in Kresl and Gappert (1995).

Thompson-Fawcett, M., and S. Bond. 2003. 'Urbanist intentions for the built landscape: Examples of concept and practice in England, Canada and New Zealand', *Progress in Planning* 60: 147–234.

Thomson, J.M. 1977. *Great Cities and Their Traffic.* London: Gollancz.

Timmer, D.A., D.S. Eitzen, and K.D. Talley. 1994. *Paths to Homelessness: Extreme Poverty and the Urban Housing Crisis.* Boulder, Colo.: Westview Press.

Timusk, C. 1976. 'Kanata: A new community approaches its tenth year', *Contact: Journal of Urban and Environmental Affairs* 8, 3: 222–32.

Tindal, C.R., and S.N. Tindal. 2004. *Local Government in Canada*, 6th edn. Toronto: Nelson.

Todd, G. 1995. 'Going global in the semi-periphery: World cities as political projects: The case of Toronto', in P. Knox and P. Taylor, eds, *World Cities in a World System.* Cambridge: Cambridge University Press.

Todd, J., E.J.G. Brown, and E. Wells. 2003. 'Ecological design applied', *Ecological Engineering* 20: 421–40.

Toderian, B. 2004. 'Integrated communities by design: The Calgary approach', *Plan Canada* 44, 4: 37–40.

Todhunter, R. 1983. 'Vancouver and the City Beautiful Movement', *Habitat* 26, 3: 8–13.

Toffler, A. 1980. *The Third Wave.* New York: Morrow.

Tomalty, R. 1994. 'An ecosystem approach to growth management', *Environments: A Journal of Interdisciplinary Studies* 22, 3: 13–25.

———. 1997. *The Compact Metropolis: Intensification in Vancouver, Toronto and Montreal.* Toronto: ICURR Publications.

———. 2002. 'Growth management in the Vancouver region', *Local Environment* 7: 431–45.

——— and A. Skaburskis. 2003. 'Development charges and city planning objectives: The Ontario disconnect', *Canadian Journal of Urban Research* 12: 142–61.

Topalov, C. 1989. 'A history of urban research: The French experience since 1965', *International Journal of Urban and Regional Research* 13: 625–51.

Toronto, n.d. *Attraction Highlights.* At: <www.Toronto. ca/attractions/attraction-highlights.htm>.

———, Core Area Task Force. 1974. *Report and Recommendations and Technical Appendix.* Toronto: City of Toronto.

———, City Planning Board. 1975. *Proposals. Central Area Plan Review Part 1: General Plan.* Toronto: City of Toronto Planning Board.

———, Planning and Development Department. 1986. *Trends in Housing Occupancy.* Toronto: City of Toronto, Research Bulletin No. 26.

———. 2002. *Official Plan.* Toronto: City of Toronto.

———. 2003a. *Plan of Action for the Elimination of Racism and Discrimination.* Toronto: City of Toronto.

———. 2003b. *The Toronto Report Card on Housing and Homelessness.* Toronto: City of Toronto.

———. 2005a. *Facts about Toronto Trash: Fact Sheet.* Toronto: City of Toronto, Solid Waste Management Services.

———. 2005b. Custom tabulations provided by the City of Toronto Department of Social and Housing Services.

Toronto City Summit Alliance. 2003. 'Enough talk: An action plan for the Toronto Region'. At: <www. torontoalliance.ca/docs/TCSA_report.pdf>.

Toronto Community Housing. n.d. *Regent Park Revitalization.* At: <www.regentparkplan.ca>. Accessed Oct. 2005.

Train, K. 2003. *Discrete Choice Methods with Simulation.* Cambridge: Cambridge University Press.

Trancik, R. 1986. *Finding Lost Space: Theories of Urban Design.* New York: Van Nostrand Reinhold.

Transportation Development Agency. 1976. *Highway Systems in Canada.* Montreal: Transportation Development Agency.

Transportation Tomorrow Survey. 1991, 2001. Carried out by the Joint Program in Transportation, University of Toronto. At: <www.jpint.utoronto. ca>.

Transport Canada. 2004. *Road Safety in Canada: An Overview.* Ottawa: Transport Canada. Available at: <www.tc.gc.ca/roadsafety/stats/overview/2004/ menu/htm>.

Transport 2021. 1993a. *A Long-Range Transportation Plan for Greater Vancouver.* Vancouver: Transport 2021.

———. 1993b. *A Medium-Range Transportation Plan for Greater Vancouver.* Vancouver: Transport 2021.

TTNCCP. 1998. *Foundation Paper on Climate Change—Transportation Sector*. Ottawa: Transportation Table National Climate Change Process.

Tuan, Y. 1973. 'Visual blight: Exercises in interpretation', in P.F. Lewis, D. Lowenthal, and Y. Tuan, eds, *Visual Blight in America*. Washington: Association of American Geographers (Commision on College Geography, Resource Paper No. 23).

———. 1974. 'Space and place: A humanistic perspective', *Progress in Geography* 6: 233–46.

———. 1979. *Landscapes of Fear*. Oxford: Blackwell.

———. 1990. 'Space and context', in R. Schechner and W. Appel, eds, *By Means of Performance: Intercultural Studies of Theatre and Ritual*. Cambridge: Cambridge University Press.

Tunbridge, J. 1986. *Of Heritage and Many Other Things: Merchants' Location Decisions in Ottawa's Lower Town West*. Ottawa: Carleton University, Department of Geography (Discussion Papers No. 5).

———. 2001. 'Ottawa's Byward Market: A festive bone of contention?', *Canadian Geographer* 45: 356–70.

Turner, R.S. 2002. 'The politics of design and development in the post-modern downtown', *Journal of Urban Affairs* 24: 533–48.

Union internationale des architectes/American Institute of Architects (UIA/AIA). 1993. *Declaration of Interdependence for a Sustainable Future* (World Congress of Architects, June 1993). Chicago: UIA/AIA.

United Nations Human Development Report. 2004. *Cultural Liberty in Today's Diverse World*. At: <http://hdr.undp.org/reports/global/2004/pdf/hdr04_complete.pdf>. Accessed May 2005.

United States Census Bureau. 2001. *Ranking Tables for Metropolitan Areas: Population in 2000 and Population Change from 1990 to 2000 (PHC-T-3)*. At: <www.census.gov/population/www/cen2000/phc-t3.html>. Accessed 3 May 2005.

———. 2002. *Demographic Characteristics, Miami City, Florida*. At: <http://quickfacts.census.gov/qfd/states/12/1245000.html>. Accessed June 2005.

United States Conference of Mayors (USCOM). 2002. *A Status Report on Hunger and Homelessness in America's Cities: A 25-City Survey*. Washington: USCOM.

United Way of Greater Toronto. 2004. *Poverty by Postal Code: The Geography of Neighbourhood Poverty, City of Toronto, 1981–2001*. Toronto: United Way of Greater Toronto and Canadian Council on Social Development.

Untermann, R.K. 1984. *Accommodating the Pedestrian: Adapting Towns and Neighborhoods for Walking and Bicycling*. New York: Van Nostrand and Reinhold.

Urquhart, M.C., K.A.H. Buckley, and F.H. Leacy. 1983. *Historical Statistics of Canada*. Ottawa: Statistics Canada and Social Science Federation of Canada.

Usher, P.J. 2003. 'Environment, race and nation reconsidered: Reflections on aboriginal land claims in Canada', *Canadian Geographer* 47: 365–82.

Valverde, M., and R. Levi. 2005. *Still the Creatures of the Provinces? Canadian Cities' Quest for Governmental Status*. Toronto: University of Toronto, Centre of Criminology (Report submitted to the Law Commission of Canada under the LCC/SSHRC joint initiative on 'Freedom of choice').

Vance, J. 1995. *The North American Railroad*. Baltimore: Johns Hopkins University Press.

Vancouver. 1990. *False Creek North Official Development Plan*. Vancouver: City of Vancouver.

———. 1991. *Central Area Plan: Goals and Land Use Policy*. Vancouver: City Planning Department.

———. 1992. *Urban Landscape Ideas Paper*. Vancouver: City of Vancouver Urban Landscape Task Force.

———. 1995. *City Plan: Directions for Vancouver*. Vancouver: City Planning Department.

———. 2004a. *Greenways Program*. Vancouver: City of Vancouver. At: <http://vancouver.ca/engsvcs/streets/greenways/index.htm>. Accessed 25 Oct. 2004.

———. 2004b. *Multiculturalism and Diversity. Community Services: Social Planning*. At: <www.city.vancouver.bc.ca/commsvcs/socialplanning/initiatives/multcult/civicpolicy.htm>. Accessed June 2005.

———. 2005. *City Plan: Community Visions*. Vancouver: City of Vancouver. At: <www.city.vancouver.bc.ca/commsvcs/planning/cityplan/Visions/index.htm>. Accessed 3 May 2005.

Vancouver Economic Development Commission. 2001. *Defining Vancouver's Competitive Advantage*.

Vancouver: VEDC. At: <www.boardoftrade.com/policy/reports/CompetitiveAnalysis_nov01.pdf>. Accessed 18 Feb. 2005.

Van der Ryn, S., and P. Calthorpe. 1986. *Sustainable Communities: A New Design Synthesis for Cities, Suburbs, and Towns*. San Francisco: Sierra Club.

Van Nus, W. 1984a. 'The role of suburban government in the city-building process: The case of Notre Dame de Grâces, Quebec, 1876–1910', *Urban History Review* 13: 91–103.

———. 1984b. 'The fate of City Beautiful thought in Canada, 1893–1930', in G.A. Stelter and A.F.J. Artibise, eds, *The Canadian City: Essays in Urban and Social History*. Ottawa: Carleton University Press.

Vayda, E., and R. Deber. 1992. 'The Canadian health care system', in D. Naylor, ed., *Canadian Health Care and the State*. Montreal and Kingston: McGill-Queen's University Press.

Venn, S.J., and J.K. Niemela. 2004. 'Ecology in a multi-disciplinary study of urban green space: The URGE project', *Boreal Environment Research* 9: 479–89.

Vineberg, R. 2005. 'Regional immigration strategies: A policy-research perspective', presentation at the Rural Development Institute 'Rural Think Tank Meeting', Brandon, Man., 28 Apr. 2005.

Virilio, P. 1996. *Cybermonde, la Politique du Pire*. Paris: Textuel.

Vischer, J.C. 1987. 'The changing Canadian suburb', *Plan Canada* 27: 130–40.

Voinov, A., and C. Smith. 1998. *Dimensions of Sustainability*. Solomons, Md: International Institute of Ecological Economics (Discussion Paper).

Voisey, P. 1975. 'The urbanization of the Canadian prairies, 1871–1916', *Histoire Sociale/Social History* 15: 77–101.

Vojnovic, I. 1998. 'Municipal consolidation in the 1990s: An analysis of British Columbia, New Brunswick, and Nova Scotia', *Canadian Public Administration* 41: 239–83.

———. 1999a. 'The environmental costs of modernism: An assessment of Canadian cities', *Cities* 16: 301–13.

———. 1999b. 'The fiscal distribution of the provincial-municipal service exchange in Nova Scotia', *Canadian Public Administration* 42: 512–41.

———. 2000a. 'Shaping Metropolitan Toronto: A study of linear infrastructure subsidies', *Environment and Planning B* 27: 197–230.

———. 2000b. 'The transitional impacts of municipal consolidations', *Journal of Urban Affairs* 22: 385–417.

———. 2000c. 'Municipal restructuring, regional planning, and fiscal accountability', *Canadian Journal of Regional Science* 23: 49–72.

———. 2003a. 'Laissez-faire governance and the archetype laissez-faire city in the USA: Exploring Houston', *Geografiska Annaler Series B* 85: 19–38.

———. 2003b. 'Governance in Houston: Growth theories and urban pressures', *Journal of Urban Affairs* 25: 589–624.

von Hausen, M. 2002. 'Alternative development standards: Practical tools for sustainable land development', *Plan Canada* 42, 3: 26–8.

Von Thünen, J.H. 1966 [1826]. *Von Thünen's Isolated State*, ed. P. Hall, trans. C.M. Wartenberg. Oxford: Pergamon.

Vovsha, P., E. Petersen, and R. Donnelly. 2002. 'Microsimulation in travel demand modelling: Lessons learned from the New York Best Practice Model', *Journal of the Transportation Research Record* 1805: 68–77.

Wackernagel, M., and W. Rees. 1996. *Our Ecological Footprint: Reducing Human Impact on the Earth*. Gabriola Island, BC: New Society Publishers.

Wade, R.C. 1959. *The Urban Frontier: The Rise of Western Cities, 1790–1830*. Cambridge, Mass.: Harvard University Press.

Walker, G. 2003. 'Stabilizing the new residential frontier in the countryside', in K. Beesley, ed, *The New Countryside: Geographic Perspectives on Rural Change*. Brandon, Man.: Brandon University, Rural Development Institute.

Walks, R.A. 2001. 'The social ecology of the post-Fordist/global city? Economic restructuring and socio-spatial polarisation in the Toronto urban region', *Urban Studies* 38: 407–47.

———. 2004a. 'Place of residence, party preferences, and political attitudes in Canadian cities and suburbs', *Journal of Urban Affairs* 26: 269–95.

———. 2004b. 'Suburbanization, the vote, and changes in federal and provincial political representation and influence between inner cities and suburbs in large Canadian urban regions, 1945 to 1999', *Urban Affairs Review* 3: 411–40.

Wallace, M., and F. Frisken. 2000. *City-Suburban Differences in Government Responses to Immigration in the Greater Toronto Area*. Toronto: Centre for Urban and Community Studies, University of Toronto.

——— and B. Moore Milroy. 2001. 'Ethno-racial diversity and planning practices in the Greater Toronto Area', *Plan Canada* 41, 3: 31–3.

Walmsley, A. 1995. 'Greenways and the making of urban form', *Landscape and Urban Planning* 33: 81–127.

Walton-Roberts, M. 2005. 'Regional immigration and dispersal: Lessons from small and medium-sized urban centres in British Columbia', *Canadian Ethnic Studies* 37 (forthcoming).

——— and D. Hiebert. 1997. 'Immigration, entrepreneurship, and the family: Indo-Canadian entrepreneurship in the construction industry of Greater Vancouver', *Canadian Journal of Regional Science* 20: 119–40.

——— and W. Smith. 2005. 'Reaping what you sow: Immigration to rural and small town Canada, 1980–2000', Backgrounder, Rural Development Institute 'Rural Think Tank Meeting', Brandon, Man., 28 Apr. 2005.

Wang, S. 1996. *New Development Patterns of Chinese Commercial Activity in the Toronto CMA*. Toronto: Ryerson University, CSCA (RP1996–8).

——— and L. Lo. 2000. 'Economic impacts of immigrants in the Toronto CMA: A tax-benefit analysis', *Journal of International Migration and Integration* 1: 273–303.

——— and P.J. Smith. 1997. 'In quest of "forgiving" environment: Residential planning and pedestrian safety in Edmonton, Canada', *Planning Perspectives* 12: 225–50.

———. 1999. 'Chinese commercial activity in the Toronto CMA: New development patterns and impacts', *Canadian Geographer* 43: 19–35.

Ward, K. 2000. 'From rentiers to rantiers: "Active entrepreneurs", "structural spectators", and the politics of marketing the city', *Urban Studies* 37: 1093–1107.

——— and A. Jonas. 2004. 'Competitive city-regionalism as a politics of space: A critical inter-

pretation of the new regionalism', *Environment and Planning A* 36: 12–27.

Ward, S.V. 1998. *Selling Places: The Marketing and Promotion of Towns and Cities 1850–2000*. London: E & FN Spon.

Warner, B.J. 1962. *Streetcar Suburbs: The Process of Growth in Boston*. Cambridge, Mass.: Harvard University Press.

Waterloo Region. 2003. *Planning Our Future: Regional Growth Management Strategy*. Waterloo, Ont.: Waterloo Region. At: <www.region.waterloo.on.ca/web/region.nsf/DocID/71DC3804F65AFA94-85256B1A0062B956?OpenDocument>. Accessed 20 July 2004.

Watson, S. 1986. *Housing and Homelessness: A Feminist Perspective*. London: Routledge & Kegan Paul.

Weaver, J. 1971. 'From land assembly to social maturity: The suburban life of Westdale (Hamilton), Ontario, 1911–1951', *Histoire Sociale/Social History* 11: 411–40.

———. 1976. 'Reconstruction of the Richmond District in Halifax: A Canadian episode in public housing and town planning', *Plan Canada* 16, 1: 36–47.

Webb, J.K., and R. Shine. 2000. 'Paving the way for habitat restoration: Can artificial rocks restore degraded habitats of endangered reptiles?', *Biological Conservation* 92: 93–9.

Webber, M., and M. Rigby. 1996. *The Golden Age Illusion*. New York: Guilford.

Weber, A. 1929 [1909]. *Theory of the Location of Industries*. Chicago: University of Chicago Press.

Wekerle, G.R. 1995. *Safe Cities: Guidelines for Planning, Design, and Management*. New York: Van Nostrand Reinhold.

Wheaton, W.L., and M.J. Schussheim. 1955. *The Cost of Municipal Services in Residential Areas*. Washington: US Department of Commerce.

Wheeler, J.O., Y. Aoyama, and B. Warf. 2000. 'Introduction: City space, industrial space, and cyberspace', in Wheeler, Aoyama, and Warf, eds, *Cities in the Telecommunications Age: The Fracturing of Geographies*. New York: Routledge.

White, M., and P. Allmendinger. 2003. 'Land-use planning and the housing market: A comparative review of the UK and the USA', *Urban Studies* 40: 953–72.

White, R. 1996. 'Designing more sustainable suburban communities: Calgary's approach', *Plan Canada* 36, 4: 16–19.

Wicksell, K. 1935. *Lectures on Political Economy*. London: Routledge.

Williams, A. 2001. 'Home care restructuring at work: The impact of policy transformations on women's labour', in I. Dyck, N.D. Lewis, and S. McLafferty, eds, *Geographies of Women's Health*. London: Routledge.

Williams, C. 2004. 'The sandwich generation', *Perspectives on Labour and Income* (Sept.): 5–12 (Statistics Canada, Cat. no. 75–001–XIE).

Williams, G. 1994. *Not for Export: The International Competitiveness of Canadian Manufacturing*, 3rd edn. Toronto: McClelland & Stewart.

Williamson, T., A. Radford, and H. Bennetts. 2003. *Understanding Sustainable Architecture*. Abingdon, UK: Spon Press.

Wilson, W.J. 1987. *The Truly Disadvantaged: The Inner City, the Underclass and Public Policy*. Chicago: University of Chicago Press.

Wingo, L. 1961. *Transportation and Urban Land*. Washington: Resources for the Future.

Winnipeg. 1998. *Strategic Infrastructure Reinvestment Policy: Report and Recommendations*. Winnipeg: City of Winnipeg.

———. 2001. *A Homegrown Economic Development Strategy for Winnipeg*. Winnipeg: City of Winnipeg.

———, City Council, Hansard. 2004. Debate on first reading of Plan Winnipeg Amendment—Waverley West; Item No. 2—Plan Winnipeg Amendment—Waverley West. March 24, File EP–1.1 (PW 2/2003). Winnipeg: City of Winnipeg.

———, Planning, Property and Development. 2004. *City of Winnipeg Residential Land Supply Study*. Winnipeg: City of Winnipeg.

Wolch, J.R., A. Rahimian, and P. Koegel. 1993. 'Daily and periodic mobility patterns of the urban homeless', *Professional Geographer* 45: 159–69.

Wolfe, D., ed. 2003. *Clusters Old and New: The Transition to a Knowledge Economy in Canada's Regions*. Montreal and Kingston: McGill-Queen's University Press.

Wolfe, J.M. 1994. 'Our common past: An interpretation of Canadian planning history', *Plan Canada* (special issue) 34 (July): 12–34.

———. 1998. 'Canadian housing policy in the 1990s', *Housing Studies* 13: 121–34.

———. 2002. 'Reinventing planning: Canada', *Progress in Planning* 57: 207–35.

———. 2003. 'A national urban policy for Canada? Prospects and challenges', *Canadian Journal of Urban Research* 12: 1–7.

——— and J.M. Glenn. 1992. 'The effects of regional county municipal plans and agricultural zoning in the region of Montreal', *Plan Canada* 32, 6: 9–13.

Woodsworth, J.S. 1972 [1911]. *My Neighbour*. Toronto: University of Toronto Press.

World Commission on Environment and Development (WCED). 1987. *Our Common Future*. Oxford: Oxford University Press.

Wright, G. 1983. *Building the Dream: A Social History of Housing in America*. Cambridge, Mass.: MIT Press.

Wright, J.D., and J. Lam. 1987. 'Homelessness and the low income housing supply', *Social Policy* 17 (Spring): 48–53.

Wright, J.M. 1978. 'The Regional Municipality of Ottawa-Carleton: Planning objectives, concepts and principal policies', in R. Wesche and M. Kugler-Gagnon, eds, *Ottawa–Hull: Spatial Perspectives and Planning*. Ottawa: University of Ottawa Press, Department of Geography and Regional Planning Occasional Paper 4.

Wright, R. 2001. *Clara Callan*. Toronto: HarperCollins Canada.

Wyly, E.K., and D.J. Hammel. 2004. 'Gentrification, segregation, and discrimination in the American urban system', *Environment and Planning A* 36: 1215–41.

Wynn, G. 1998. 'Places at the margin: The Atlantic provinces', in McCann and Gunn (1998).

Wynne, D. 1992. *The Culture Industry: The Arts in Regeneration*. Ashgate: Avebury Press.

Yakabuski, K. 2004. 'Bob the builder', *Report on Business* (Oct.): 84–92, 94, 96.

Yauk, C.L., G.A. Fox, B.E. McCarry, and J.S. Quinn. 2000. 'Induced minisatellite germline mutations in herring gulls (*Larus argentatus*) living near steel mills', *Mutation Research—Fundamental and Molecular Mechanisms of Mutagenesis* 452: 211–18.

Yeates, M. 1998a. 'The heartland today: Its changing role and internal structure', in McCann and Gunn (1998).

———, ed. 1998b. 'Metropolitan commercial structure and the globalization of consumer services', *Progress in Planning* 50, 4.

——— and B. Garner. 1980. *The North American City*, 3rd edn. New York: Harper and Row.

———, J. Piazza, D. Montgomery, M. Robinson, G. Hardman, and S. Simmons. 1996. *The Retail Structure of Non-Metropolitan Urban Centres: Sault Ste. Marie, Sturgeon Falls, Collingwood, Cobourg and Port Hope*. Toronto: Centre for the Study of Commercial Activity, Ryerson Polytechnic University.

Yip, S. 1994. 'Applying sustainable development principles to residential community planning', *Plan Canada* 34, 2: 31–4.

York, Regional Municipality of. 2004. *Report No. 3 of the Planning and Economic Development Committee: Official Plan Amendment No. 115. Places of Worship. Town of Markham.* Newmarket, Ont.: Regional Municipality of York.

Zhou, Q.X., and T. Hua. 2004. 'Bioremediation: A review of applications and problems to be resolved', *Progress in Natural Science* 14: 937–44.

Zhuang, Z.X.C. 2003. 'Ethnic commercial landscape and the planning response', unpublished report.

Zimmerman, J. 2001. 'The "nature" of urbanism on the new urbanist frontier: Sustainable development, or defense of the suburban dream?', *Urban Geography* 22: 249–67.

Zmyslony, J., and D. Gagnon. 2000. 'Path analysis of spatial predictors of front-yard landscape in an anthropogenic environment', *Landscape Ecology* 15: 357–71.

Zolnik, E.J. 2004. 'The North American city revisited: Urban quality of life in Canada and the United States', *Urban Geography* 25: 217–40.

Zugazaga, C. 2004. 'Stressful life event experiences of homeless adults: A comparison of single men, single women and women with children', *Journal of Community Psychology* 32: 643–54.

Zukin, S. 1982. *Loft Living: Culture and Capital in Urban Change*. Baltimore: Johns Hopkins University Press.

———. 1991. *Landscapes of Power: From Detroit to Disney World*. Berkeley: University of California Press.

———. 1995. *The Culture of Cities*. Oxford: Blackwell.

———. 1998. 'Urban lifestyles: Diversity and standardization in spheres of consumption', *Urban Studies* 35: 825–39.

Index